Public Women, Public Words

VOLUME III: 1960 TO THE PRESENT

PUBLIC WOMEN, PUBLIC WORDS

A Documentary History of American Feminism

Edited by Dawn Keetley & John Pettegrew

A MADISON HOUSE BOOK
ROWMAN & LITTLEFIELD PUBLISHERS, INC.
Lanham • Boulder • New York • Oxford

ROWMAN & LITTLEFIELD PUBLISHERS, INC.

Published in the United States of America
by Rowman & Littlefield Publishers, Inc.
An Imprint of the Rowman & Littlefield Publishing Group
4720 Boston Way, Lanham, Maryland 20706
www.rowmanlittlefield.com

12 Hid's Copse Road, Cumnor Hill, Oxford OX2 9JJ, England

British Library Cataloguing in Publication Information Available

Library of Congress Cataloging-in-Publication Data

Keetley, Dawn Elizabeth, 1965–
  Public women, public words : a documentary history of American feminism / edited by Dawn
Elizabeth Keetley and John Charles Pettegrew
     p. cm.
  Includes bibliographical references and index.
  ISBN 0-7425-2235-0 (alk. paper)
  1. Feminism—United States—History—18th century—sources. 2. Feminism—United
States—History—19th century—sources. I. Pettegrew, John Charles, 1959– .
HQ1410 .K444 2002
305.42'0973—dc21   97-3580

Printed in the United States of America

Contents

PART II

Of Continuity and Discontent:
Late-Twentieth-Century Feminism

Preface and Acknowledgments

VOLUMES II AND III OF *Public Women, Public Words,* released five years after volume I, are different in form and intent. The greater number of documents for much shorter periods of time offer material proof of the proliferation of U.S. feminism during the twentieth century. And because of the diffusion of feminist thought and activism over the last one hundred years, volumes II and III make no real claims to comprehensiveness: a great many canonical feminist texts can be found in the pages that follow, but others are missing—due to copyright law, permissions costs, their accessibility in other volumes, and the fact that we decided early on that it would be impossible to include all the period's major works in two volumes.

In continuing our focus on the relationship between feminist thought and action, volumes II and III present documents that locate different institutions through which women's movements for equality and liberation occurred. While public writing and speech-making remain paramount, we also looked into newer media such as Hollywood, television, and the Internet. The result is a somewhat impressionistic account of U.S. feminism, with some important topics such as pornography, women's health and medicine, abortion, and women in law and religion given relatively little attention. Late-twentieth and early-twenty-first-century American feminism has been a dispersed and uncertain undertaking: volume III contributes an early effort toward its historicization.

A note on the text: obvious typographical errors in the original documents have been corrected, as in a misspelled word or name; for some of the older documents, footnotes have been omitted when their content was deemed unnecessary to understanding or appreciating the document.

The better part of this project's work was done at the University of Wisconsin, Madison, and we therefore want to thank the staffs at the University of Wisconsin Memorial Library and especially at the State Historical Society of Wisconsin Library and Special Collections. Also helpful were the librarians at Stanford University's Green Library. The speedy work of Pat Ward and others in Lehigh University's Inter Library Loan office proved invaluable to the completion of volumes II and III.

The latter volumes also benefited from the work of a number of Lehigh research assistants: Jonathan Hagel, Robert Nill, and Suzanne Shriver—thanks to all. Janet Walters of Lehigh's history department also helped considerably in handling these volumes' seemingly endless printing and correspondence. And John Lennon, Chris Robe, and Lisa Vetere contributed timely proofreading for volume II.

Mary Fiorenza's copyediting and intelligently close reading made significant improvements to the section introductions to volumes II and III.

Over the past nine years of work on *Public Women, Public Words,* several friends, colleagues, and teachers have offered help, advice, and inspiration. Thank you Paul Boyer, Ellen DuBois, Susan Stanford Friedman, Linda Gordon, Daniel Horowitz, William Shade, and Landon Storrs.

We are indebted to Gregory Britton, John Kaminski, and Madison House Publishers for picking up this project when it was little more than an outline on a napkin; after Rowman & Littlefield took over production of the last two volumes, Mary Carpenter, Janice Braunstein, and Laura Roberts have seen it through with great patience, efficiency, and consideration.

We have made a good faith effort to contact those who have rights to the documents printed here. We would like to thank everyone who responded and who granted permission.

INTRODUCTION

Splitting Differences: Conceiving of American Feminism

THIS COLLECTION OF DOCUMENTS traces the development of feminist thought from colonial North America through U.S. political and popular culture of the late twentieth century. A primary goal of the book is to offer an intellectual history of American feminism: that is, to examine not only the *conceptual* composition of the subject, but also to study how women have used ideas *practically* to gain power within specific historical circumstances. We understand feminism as a process, an activity, a social movement that has flourished through the polypragmatic expression of women's needs in public-political discourses and institutions. Feminism describes *enactments* of thought meant to improve social-sexual relations.

Overview

Many of the following documents reflect our interest in revealing the confluence between thought and action in American feminism. For example, Frances Wright—a founding figure of the early-nineteenth-century women's rights movement—not only wrote and lectured throughout the 1820s but also established the utopian community of Nashoba in Tennessee. Maintaining that "mankind must reasonably hesitate to receive as truths, theories, however ingenious, if unsupported by experiment," Wright instituted greater freedom for women at Nashoba than any other American community of its time, nullifying all marriage laws and further declaring that no woman entering the community would "forfeit individual rights and her independent existence." Insisting on "liberty" and "equality" for every individual, Wright infused immediate substance into these ideals by founding Nashoba.

A second principal goal of this collection is to represent the diversity of American feminism. Rather than rendering feminism as the battle of a homogeneous group of women in the name of a single cause such as suffrage or equal rights with men, we discuss feminism specific to various races, ethnicities, classes, regions, and sexualities and seek to illuminate the distinct interests that have sprung from these social groups. We document, in other words, a history that has been varied, multiple, and far from unified. But even while concentrating on the contested nature of American feminism, we do not want to rule out the possibility of locating shared concerns and common actions among women of different orientations. Our selection of texts attempts to establish a middle ground between arguments for, on one side, the dispersion of an infinite number of feminisms and, on the other side, the overarching unanimity of American feminism.

This effort to represent both the diversity and the common purposes of feminism is reinforced by our use of an eclectic mix of published documents, including speeches and manifestos, fiction and poetry, articles in radical, popular, and middle-brow magazines, underground newspapers, professional and academic journals, and courtroom transcripts and records of other official proceedings. Such published texts may be used historically to connect ideas and actions to specific groups of people. Attention to the author of a feminist tract, for example, places that woman and her thoughts within a certain time and place and suggests further the identities and mind-sets and circumstances of the women for whom she wrote. Close examination of a document, then, may reveal not only textual meaning regarding specific principles of feminist thought but also crucial information about the context of its production. We have tried to include documents—the 1794 commencement oration to the Young Ladies Academy of Philadelphia, for instance, or the 1971 preamble to *Asian Women*, a feminist newspaper published at the University of California–Berkeley—that help locate and detail women's institutional organization and political activism.

It should be emphasized that this collection is meant to chronicle the activism of different groups of American women. We are concerned with the interrelationship between ideas and the circumstances of social change, between words and political action. We have a bias for documents that place women in specific public contexts. Some texts provide official record of feminist activism, as in the trial transcript of the U.S. government's case against Susan B. Anthony for voting in the congressional election of 1872. This account of Anthony's willful defiance of federal law, along with her impassioned and insistent courtroom defense of the "fundamental privilege" of female citizenship, offer dramatic evidence of how feminists have publicly opposed state-sanctioned subordination of women.

Feminist activism, of course, has not been limited to legal proceedings; public opposition to women's subordination can be found in every one of the texts in this collection. In fact, we see literature itself as a form of activism. Even though writing and reading are often understood as acts of private or personal dimension, literature should also be seen, ideally, as something that happens between people. We hope readers of this book will consider the following documents as types of public speech. American feminism has developed in the form of argument; it has been produced with the self-conscious intention of persuasion. This includes feminist fiction, autobiography, and poetry—work, which, in its own way, has been written to change minds.

In contrast to the battle for legal rights, undertaken in more formal arenas such as the courtroom or the political convention, "creative" writing demonstrates how feminism has also been concerned with the subjective development of diverse women. These forms of feminist literature attempt to displace fixed ideas of the female self, conceptions that support women's subordinate position in the workplace, the family, and, more generally, in relationships with men and male-dominated structures of power. Finally, feminist fiction, autobiography, and poetry are historically valuable because they allow the reader to compare subjectivities among different racial, ethnic, and class-based groups of American women, reminding one that a woman's identity is determined through a number of factors, not just sexuality and gender.

Competing Definitions of Feminism

Despite the fact that no common identity exists among American women, there is philosophical support for the idea that in some ways women have been united by historical circumstance. There has been a type of "synchronicity" involved in the female experience of living in cultures and societies similarly influenced by masculine interests: social institutions, relations, and practices have, as the theorist Iris Marion Young describes, situated women "serially," placing them within sexually determined "limits and restraints"; "enforced heterosexuality," for instance, and the "sexual division of labor," work to "collectivize" women's conceptions of how they have been individually constrained by male-based systems of power. Young is quick to point out that this shared history of women is not the same thing as *feminism*, which she defines as an explicit attempt to improve women's conditions. Feminism is "a particularly reflexive impulse of women grouping," Young emphasizes, "women grouping in order to change or eliminate the structures that serialize them."[1] This distinction is crucial to understanding the specific scope and purpose of this book. It explains the difference between the history of American women and the history of American feminism. Feminist thought and activism—the organizing theme of the following collection of documents—are only a small (albeit crucial) part of the history of women in colonial North America and the United States. Both women's history and feminism depend on female subjectivity: the felt experience of being a woman. But another, essential, element of feminism is the deliberate creation of solidarity among women: it is a self-conscious effort to connect with others for the express purpose of more effectively challenging sexual inequality.

One problem, though, with defining feminism through the idea of solidarity is that the history of feminism, at least among women in the United States, is anything but one of unity. In both its theory and practice, American feminism has embraced exclusion, in some ways matching the social divisiveness found in U.S. history at large. African American female thinkers have made clear how racial bias has been written into nonblack feminist politics. White feminist thought, as bell hooks explains, is often produced "from a standpoint that ignores black women's experiences and thus reinforces white supremacist thinking by viewing white women's experiences as the universal standard for evaluating gender status and identity."[2] By concentrating purely on issues of sexism, many white feminists extend the prejudices of a dominant race, failing to realize their own implication in and to some extent responsibility for the subjugation of other women.

Consider Charlotte Perkins Gilman, who—as author of "The Yellow Wallpaper" (1892); *Women and Economics* (1898); her own monthly journal, *The Forerunner* (1909–1916); and voluminous other writings of social science, literary criticism, utopian fiction, autobiography, and poetry—is rightfully considered to be one of the most intellectually productive feminists in U.S. history. Gilman also adopted, however, some of the most conservative racial views of her day—prejudices that necessarily "color" the value of her feminist thought. Gilman openly described blacks as an "inferior" race, adding that their current "degenerative" status caused a drag on "human evolution," inevitably slowing the social progress of white America. In typical fashion, Gilman offered a comprehensive answer to the "negro problem," suggesting that the least evolved blacks be separated out of society and placed in a compulsory state-run corps until they could pass out of that group. This class of black internees would include, of course, a large number of "women," the same group Gilman insisted, in other contexts, needed to "set ourselves free" and whose independence determined overall "human development."[3] This contradiction in Gilman's thought is an extreme example of racism within feminism—of course not all white feminists have believed these things—but the point should by now be clear: if feminism involves the coming together of women (a process of "grouping"), then it needs to be realized that the social dynamics of that process have brought diversity as well as consensus, exclusion as well as solidarity, and opposition as well as unity.

The intellectual history of feminism—how the movement developed conceptually and theoretically, as a body of political thought, as an "ism"—is also largely a story of conflict and schism. Consider, for instance, the origins of the word "feminism" in the United States. As Nancy Cott has explained, "feminism" did not appear regularly in print or public speech until the 1910s, with common usage beginning in 1913.[4] And yet by 1914 one could read in the popular magazine *Current Opinion* that, in addition to the immediate rise of antifeminist thought, "[n]ow it appears that there are two emergent forces in the feminist movement itself." The article goes on to cite Charlotte Perkins Gilman in *The Forerunner*, who distinguished between "female feminists"—those who believe fundamental differences exist between the sexes and that women need the opportunity for full expression of their distinct attributes—and "human feminists"—those who minimize sexual difference and emphasize that women should be allowed to develop themselves as people, free from preexistent notions of proper feminine identity and behavior.

Notice how these two strands of feminism are, as *Current Opinion* recognized, "not only distinct but opposed."[5] The prefixes "human" and "female" do not signify variations of a common definition of feminism; they are, rather, set against each other as opposites, involving wholly different formulations of female self-identity and suggesting competing agendas for political mobilization. American feminism—before and after the word entered the national lexicon—has had no true "essence," except perhaps this one of opposition and duality. This point, as paradoxical as it is, needs to be considered in any intellectual history of American feminism: American feminist thought has developed through the creation of a series of mutually exclusive categories, usually organized in a series of either–or choices, or what some theorists would call "binary oppositions."

Keep this point in mind while studying the documents. To recognize the binate nature of feminist thought is to gain critical distance on the intellectual limitations of American feminism. This distancing is not necessarily in order to transcend these dualisms, or even to try always to move past them. If we return to Gilman's delineation of "female" and "human" feminists we can see how this binary (and its many variations) is ingrained in generations of American feminist discourse. In 1855, for instance, we find Elizabeth Cady Stanton debating Antoinette Brown in the women's journal *The Una* about the existence of "natural" differences between the sexes. And this same core issue— whether women should deem themselves not only equal to but also fundamentally the same as men—still constitutes the most basic division in late-twentieth-century feminist theory. What Gilman called "human" feminism is commonly known today as "equality" feminism: it urges the full integration of women into society, demanding women's equal rights, equal work, equal pay, and, generally, equal status and treatment in private and public relations; equality feminism bases itself on an ideal of the autonomous human individual, aiming ultimately to erase most if not all distinctions based on sex. And what Gilman labeled "female" feminism is now known as "difference" feminism: it values women's unique perspective and envisions a society in which women are not subject to male-dominated institutions, values, and individualist-based standards of self-identity; instead of pushing for a sexually integrated society, difference feminism envisions an autonomous female world, one that ultimately separates the concepts of femininity and masculinity.

Attention to this and other categories within feminist thought, then, is crucial to understanding the intellectual history of American feminism: dualisms help us reconstruct ideas as they were thought at the time under study; they also help locate continuities in feminism, giving it a visible and "usable past." We can see something of a tradition, for instance, running from Anne Hutchinsons's battle to realize equal status of men within the Puritan church, through Mary Gove Nichols's strong, wide-ranging assertions in the 1850s of women's sexual freedom, up to Naomi Wolf's problematic lifestyle feminism or "power feminism," in which individualist-minded women succeed in corporate America and simply have "fun." We can also recognize a countertradition, from Catharine Beecher's mid-nineteenth-century insistence that women's power to effect social reform, including abolition of slavery, lay exclusively in her private feminine influence, to Camille Paglia's assertion of absolute differences between active male sexuality and a passive female sex principle.

We want to urge readers here, though, to guard against accepting the equality-difference split as a complete accounting of American feminism. Dualisms, while historically edifying, have always been far too schematic. The categorization of feminism into sets of either–or decisions obscures the full range of ways women have formulated their opposition to male-based systems of power. To draw mutually exclusive lines of feminist thought is to overlook how individual feminists have mixed and matched categories, refusing the confines of neatly delineated binaries.

Once again, the expansive thought of Charlotte Perkins Gilman provides a good example. Even though she recognized (and thereby promoted) the equality-difference split—and even though she identified with the equality or "human" side of the equation—much of her thought advanced the difference or "female" tradition of feminism. Gilman recognized distinctive female characteristics, as in her utopian novel *Herland* (1915), which presents a separate society of women who have a strong commitment to mothering and who have banished "masculine" values of competition.

In general terms, dualisms work against appreciation of the multiplicity of feminist perspectives. To assert an either–or vision of feminism not only lessens the ability to recognize those women who choose both (or neither) poles, but it can finally narrow that vision until only one side of the equation is illuminated. Most dualistic accounts of feminism privilege one viewpoint or the other as the essence of feminism, representing it as the most productive for contemporary feminism and, in less than objective hindsight, the one that has predominated historically. This is a pivotal point at which unnecessary exclusion begins in feminist theorizing. The act of defining "true feminism" involves subordinating those outside of the fold. While categorical systems of thought have made it easier to tell who is a feminist, they have also made it easier to identify who is *not* a feminist—a concern, in some feminist discourses, that eclipses attention to the different ways women subvert male power. Indeed, this is another problem of dualist thinking: one's politics are determined by and, ultimately, confined to what one opposes; one is defined, in other words, in the negative—by what one is not rather than what one is.

In light of the dangers of essentializing feminism, some women's historians and other scholars have fashioned an explicitly inclusive and self-consciously antitheoretical formulation of the movement. This effort begins with finding an "unrestrictive definition of feminism" itself, as Nancy Cott has written, one that "dispense[s] with totalizing, either/or questions (was she a feminist or not?)." One definition that Cott favors is offered by Linda Gordon: "Feminism is a critique of male supremacy, formed and offered in the light of a will to change it, which in turn assumes a conviction that it is changeable."[6] Gordon's definition has been central to our project, as it values action over essence, circumventing rigid, dualistic tests of true feminism. Moreover, this conception of feminism not only eliminates the need to choose one side or another of a binary opposition, it goes one step further in suggesting the benefit of holding equality-difference, individualism-community, and other dualisms in creative and productive tension. The conceptual umbrella of feminism is broad enough to contain diverse and even contradictory elements, allowing women to choose the ideas that best apply to the political exigencies of the time; they are thus not always constrained by an overarching and predetermined agenda that dictates choices without regard to context and consequences.

"Feminism" or "Feminisms"?

This broad-based, nonexclusive conceptualization of feminism is pluralist in nature: it is most concerned with practical details of activism, focusing on specific strategies of political organization and local sites of resistance.

But does feminism comprise nothing more or less than a sequence of local acts of resistance? As suggested above, some feminists (Iris Marion Young and Nancy Cott, for example) believe that a necessary part of the movement has been the recognition of "women acting as women"—that is, a self-consciousness of womanhood and of one's connection to that community. Who, though, are the "women" who have self-consciously acted as women? With what women have they tried to connect? And in the name of which "women" has the feminist movement acted? Historically, mainstream feminist thought has too often relied uncritically on the concept of "women" as a legitimating and cohesive category, while in practice including only a few social groups and racial types within its rubric. The utopian female intersubjectivity—women acting as, with, and for women—that has undergirded so much feminist discourse has in fact been imperfect, excluding and omitting large numbers of American women.

As articulated by middle-class white women, feminism has more often that not served the needs and interests of those women alone, women who have often been unable to recognize that the "sisterhood" of women extended also to women of color. For instance, both before and after the Civil War some women's rights activists debated whether or not they should work for the abolition of slavery and for the rights of black women during the Reconstruction—about whether or not, in other words, the rights of African American women were "woman's rights." A century later, Betty Friedan's *The Feminine Mystique* centered its analysis on the plight of upper-middle-class housewives, women confined to the home and a life of mindless leisure. Clearly not accounting for variables of race and class, Friedan omitted the majority of women who had neither the money nor the ideological impetus to leave the paid workforce and stay at home. To the extent that African American women—to name just one marginalized group—have been less than supportive of mainstream or white American feminism, it is because, as Pauline Terrelonge Stone has argued, "[r]acism . . . is so entrenched among many white women, that black females have been reluctant to admit that anything affecting the white female could also affect them."[7] Women of all races have both perceived and construed the category of "women" as a bar to collective action as much as they have seen it as the foundation of feminist collectivity.

In addition to disagreeing over the identity of feminist subjects, marginalized groups of women have also pointed out the propensity of the movement to fix exclusively on issues of sexual inequality. Deborah King describes this single-minded agenda as "monist": it illuminates only one form of domination, insisting that "social relations can be reduced to one factor" of gender.[8] For an illustrative case of monism in practice, consider how the debate over the extension of suffrage after the Civil War routinely asserted that either black men or white women could gain the vote—but not both. Black women found themselves torn between former antislavery organizations, which sought to extend the franchise to blacks (i.e., black men), and the woman's rights movement, which sought the vote for women (i.e., white women). In such an either–or situation, black women fell into a middle ground of nonidentity; neither black men nor white women, they were asked to support causes that did not include them.

The liminal situation of African American women reveals how the subjugation of most women has arisen not simply from an ingrained sexism but also from intersecting forms of oppression such as racism, heterosexism, and class inequality. Women who are oppressed by other systems as well as the sex/gender system are necessarily oppressed *differently* by sexism: a poor, black woman does not experience sexual inequality in the same way that a wealthy white woman does. As a consequence, women who are not white, middle class, and heterosexual, while not denying the importance of fighting sexism, have refused to grant that it is paramount. Many black feminists, for instance, will not make a choice between race or gender as the predominant category that structures their resistance, insisting on the need to hold both within the same worldview.

The phenomenon of monism among American feminists results from a failure to conceptualize adequately the relation between sexism and forms of oppression based on categories other than gender. When they have theorized the relation between race and feminism at all, white feminists have traditionally done so mostly through analogy, claiming that oppression on the grounds of race is structurally equal to oppression on the grounds of sex and is experienced in the same way. When

Mary Gove Nichols argued in 1857 that white women are "enslaved" by marriage laws as inexorably as the African American is by slavery, she implied not only that institutionalized racism and sexism are analogous but also that racism is secondary, serving merely to illuminate the horrors of sexism. In fact, Nichols adds, slavery is only "*nearly* parallel in its evils" to marriage. This method of integrating race into theories of feminism works to subsume race into gender—making race invisible at the very moment it is ostensibly being rendered visible.

Recently, feminist theorists of color have moved beyond the confines of the race-sex analogy, employing first the concept of the "double jeopardy" of race and sex oppression and then of the "triple jeopardy" of racism, sexism, and classism. Deborah King has called for a move even beyond the "triple jeopardy" model, which, while it does recognize the different kinds of discrimination women of color face, does so in an additive way: the effects of race and class are simply appended to the effects of sex. The model of triple jeopardy presupposes that each variable—race, sex, and class—has a "single, direct, and independent effect on status." King, on the other hand, thinks that the effects are not independent of each other, proposing an "interactive model," which she calls "multiple jeopardy." The term "multiple" incorporates "not only . . . several, simultaneous oppressions" but also the "multiplicative relationships among them as well. In other words," she continues, "the equivalent formulation is racism multiplied by sexism multiplied by classism."[9] This model recognizes the multiple linkages between different forms of structural inequality and also the "multiplicative"—as opposed to additive—oppressive effect that such linkages bring to bear on an individual.

Our collection—our historical vision of American feminism, as it were—is fundamentally shaped by the theorizing of women of color in terms of the multiple ways in which women have been oppressed and by the similarly multiple and contextualized positions from which women have acted to challenge their oppression. These positions are always gendered somehow—or they could not be considered "feminism"—but gender is not the only or even always the principal point of critique or site of resistance. For women of all races—including white—those disempowering systems that support male privilege often also support class privilege, heterosexual privilege, or white privilege. When one subverts a certain racist practice, then, one may also be subverting sexism at the same time. For instance, when Harriet Jacobs exposed in her autobiography the evils of slavery, she also exposed the sexual and economic power that white men had over both white and black women.

In light of the wholesale critique of the category "women" as it has historically been employed by the mainstream feminist movement, the word has lost its status as a unified concept fixed in a simple binary opposition to "men." It can best be understood, instead, as a dispersed, fluid, and contested category. This is not to say, however, that a woman's self-conscious belief that she is a part of the collective group "women" is no longer important to a definition of feminism. Philosopher Judith Butler has argued that it is precisely "the rifts among women over the content of the term ["women"] that ought to be affirmed as the ungrounded ground of feminist theory."[10] While continuing to act for "women," feminists should constantly question their own internal preconceptions and biases about what that entails.

This collection of documents demonstrates that there has indeed been a history of such self-questioning; it reveals both a lack of and a struggle toward consensus about who the "women" are in whose name feminism has spoken, written, and acted. These rifts need not be wholly divisive but can be, rather, the basis of a self-aware, flexible, and contingent community of feminist interests.

Women and the Public

Our conception of the public nature of American feminism is influenced by two key points. The first is the imbrication of public spheres of feminist activism with the private realm of women's lives. "The personal is political"—a stock phrase of mid- to late-twentieth-century feminism—still provides an important reminder that, in contrast to the traditionally masculine world of electoral politics, feminist politics has always concerned itself with so-called private issues of domestic labor, sexuality, family, and the like. Feminists have strived continually to transform personal power relations between men and women into the stuff of politics, taking what often occurs "behind closed doors" and exposing it to the vicissitudes of public analysis and opinion making. Integral to this understanding of a feminist public, as Sara Evans has pointed out, is the history of American women's voluntary associations.[11] Organizations such as moral reform and temperance societies have provided an essential link between the lived daily experience of women and opportunities for political change, collapsing the border between public and private worlds.

A second critical idea concerning women's public sphere involves the political value of those feminist institutions, discourses, and strategies that are separate from and opposed to dominant social and cultural forces. Women's integration into masculine sources of power and prestige—from labor unions to elite social clubs, from schools and colleges to the U.S. Congress—is certainly a central component of American feminism; but we also mean to emphasize the "contestatory function" of what Nancy Fraser calls "subaltern counterpublics"—"parallel discursive arenas where members of subordinated social groups invent and circulate counterdiscourses, which in turn permit them to formulate oppositional interpretations of their identities, interests, and needs." Counterpublics, as Fraser points out, have a dual purpose: they provide "spaces of withdrawal and regroupment" for those already located outside of the fold of power; at the same time, though, they "function as bases and training ground for agitational activities directed towards wider publics."[12] In as much as feminist counterpublics are separate enclaves, then, they also foster communication for the purpose of disseminating their oppositional message. Many of the feminist words and deeds represented in this collection originated from such public associations of activism and subversion—counterpublics of women created both to provide a separate source of strength and purity of feminist purpose but also meant to connect with and change the institutional powers that be.

This documentary history does not pretend to provide the impossible—a coherent, comprehensive narrative of integrative and "counterpublic" American feminism; but we do, however, want to close by tracing the various key institutions, both separatist and integrated, into which women have entered at specific historical periods.

Women's voices were first heard within the church, as they intermittently challenged traditional religious practices in the colonies. In particular, women questioned their place within the Puritan establishment, drawing for their dissent on more marginal religions, such as Quakerism, or on their own material experiences as women.

In the post-Revolutionary period, some women not only had available, for the first time, some kind of systematic formal education, but they also started to found separate female academies. The subsequent rise in women's literacy rates led at the end of the eighteenth century to the creation of a distinctly feminine literary culture, which included the first women's magazines and the first popular women's fiction—novels of seduction and sentiment.

Beginning in the late 1830s and 1840s, American women became active in a variety of reform movements, notably antislavery, from which the nineteenth-century women's rights movement grew. Central to this key development were woman's rights conventions, which proliferated in the middle of the century; while not formal institutions, the conventions established networks and communities of activist women and inculcated strategies of organization building—not the least of which was the art of public speaking. Drawing on organizational skills acquired in the early years of the women's rights movement, feminists in the second half of the nineteenth century created a number of women's institutions—from middle-class women's clubs to trade unions and suffrage associations.

While women had first gained entry into the medical profession, as physicians, in the 1840s, it was not until the 1870s and 1880s that women's encroachment into the previously male bastions of the elite professions such as the law and higher education became discernable.

With the dramatic increase in immigration and the rapid growth of an urban industrial social environment at the turn of the twentieth century, American feminism became markedly more diverse and complex. Along with mass immigration to the United States, a more regionally, racially, and ethnically diverse group of American women started to challenge forms of masculine dominance. This variegated feminist consciousness shaped itself during and in conjunction with the rise of modern mass culture and media, including widely circulated popular magazines and newspapers, many of which represented the interests of specific populations such as Chinese Americans in California or Jews in New York. White middle-class women made still greater inroads within the university, gaining a foothold in both white-collar professions and academia itself, hence adding to the burgeoning intellectual class in New York and other large cities.

While many historians continue to characterize the period between the passage of the Nineteenth Amendment (which, in 1920, gave all women the vote) and the 1960s as a time in which feminism remained dormant, we trace the continued activity of women within already established institutions such as trade unions, voluntary clubs, and professional associations. These four decades were a particularly active period for those women interested in women's labor rights, in part because of women's massive entry into the paid labor force during two world wars. The period is also marked by heightened socialist consciousness, and some feminists even attempted a union between feminist activism and communism.

The late 1960s saw what has been called the "second wave" of American feminism, a reemergent, broad-based, and coherent movement for women's "liberation" akin to that of the 1850s. Just as the "first wave" of American feminism had grown from the antislavery movement, the "second wave" was historically interwoven with African Americans' struggle for civil rights. Along with the founding of mainstream organizations such as the National Organization for Women (NOW), the 1960s and 1970s also saw the large-scale emergence of women's small groups and collectives, each centered on experiences of oppression and communal responses including radical plans for liberation.

In the late twentieth and early twenty-first centuries, during a time of a "backlash" against feminism and a retrenchment of the movement, women continued to assert themselves in public life, attaining increasingly influential positions in business, the university, and in the government. Perhaps in part as a result of the success of some highly visible women, some heralded a "postfeminist" age, claiming that feminism is obsolete and should be either abandoned or radically revised. Feminism has thus become still more fragmented and contentious, producing internally conflicted and opposing views of itself and its potential role in women's lives. While the rhetoric of the 1990s put feminism in an unprecedented state of crisis, our book aims to show that such contention has not only always been present but is, perhaps, feminism's grounding premise. In other words, American feminism continues.

Notes

1. Iris Marion Young, "Gender as Seriality: Thinking about Women as a Social Collective," *Signs* 19 (Spring 1994), 728, 736.

2. bell hooks, "Black Students Who Reject Feminism," *The Chronicle of Higher Education*, July 13, 1994, A44.

3. Charlotte Perkins Gilman, "A Suggestion on the Negro Problem," originally published in *The American Journal of Sociology* 14 (July 1908), 78–85, reprinted in *Charlotte Perkins Gilman: A Nonfiction Reader*, ed. Larry Ceplair (New York: Columbia University Press, 1991), 176–83; Charlotte Perkins Gilman, "Our Androcentric Culture; or the Man-Made World," *The Forerunner* 1 (June 1910), 20.

4. Nancy F. Cott, *The Grounding of Modern Feminism* (New Haven: Yale University Press, 1987), 13.

5. "The Conflict between 'Human' and 'Female' Feminism," *Current Opinion* 56 (1914), 9.

6. Nancy F. Cott, "What's in a Name? The Limits of 'Social Feminism': or, Expanding the Vocabulary of Women's History," *Journal of American History* 76 (1989), 826; Linda Gordon, "What's New in Women's History," in *Feminist Studies/Critical Studies*, ed. Teresa De Lauretis (Bloomington: Indiana University Press, 1986), 29.

7. Pauline Terrelonge Stone, "Feminist Consciousness and Black Women," in *Women: A Feminist Perspective*, ed. Jo Freeman (Palo Alto: Mayfield, 1979), 583.

8. Deborah K. King, "Multiple Jeopardy, Multiple Consciousness: The Context of a Black Feminist Ideology," *Signs* 14 (1988), 51.

9. King, "Multiple Jeopardy," 46–47.

10. Judith Butler, "Contingent Foundations: Feminism and the Question of 'Postmodernism,'" in *Feminists Theorize the Political*, ed. Judith Butler and Joan Scott (New York: Routledge, 1992), 16.

11. Sara M. Evans, "Women's History and Political Theory: Toward a Feminist Approach to Public Life," in *Visible Women: New Essays On American Activism*, ed. Nancy A. Hewitt and Suzanne Lebstock (Urbana: University of Illinois Press, 1993), 119–39; also important is Mary P. Ryan, *Women in Public: Between Banners and Ballots, 1825–1880* (Baltimore: Johns Hopkins University Press, 1990).

12. Nancy Fraser, "Rethinking the Public Sphere: A Contribution to the Critique of Actually Existing Democracy," in *Between Borders: Pedagogy and the Politics of Cultural Studies*, ed. Henry A. Giroux and Peter McLaren (New York: Routledge, 1994), 84–85.

PART I

The Second Wave

I. Liberal Feminism, Women's Liberation, and the Emergence of Radical Feminism

THE LABEL "SECOND WAVE" HAS BEEN USED to identify a specific historical phase of American feminism, with the "first wave" stretching from the woman's rights conventions of the mid-nineteenth century to the federal guarantee of universal women's suffrage in 1920, and the second wave marking a new beginning of activism in the late 1960s and early 1970s—activism characterized by decidedly militant feminist politics and grassroots organization.

This taxonomy of feminist waves does have its limitations. As the documents in part II demonstrate, feminism did not cease to exist in the mid-twentieth century: many women kept pushing for equality through voluntary associations, in the workplace, and on other public fronts. Nor is it clear how distinct the ideas of second-wave feminism are when compared to the thought of earlier periods of the women's movement—one finds striking similarities between the liberationist discourse of the 1960s and 1970s and, say, the cultural radicalism of early-twentieth-century New York City feminists. But the term *second wave* is valuable in that it approximates the meaning this era of feminism had for the participants themselves. In the most general terms, feminism of this time was animated by the idea and experiences of beginning anew and found a good part of its energy generationally, as women self-consciously worked to free themselves from the past.

Although this period of feminist activism is known for its militancy, it would be a mistake to characterize it as singular in its political goals, ideology, or orientation. In fact, most historians recognize a distinctly moderate, bourgeois beginning to the second wave with the publication of *The Feminine Mystique,* Betty Friedan's exposé of the bored and busy life of American housewives and the psychological box in which they find themselves trapped. In describing the feminine mystique as an ideology "not easily seen and not easily shaken off," the introductory chapter, "A Problem That Has No Name"(1963), anticipates the study of gender in coming decades. Despite providing useful insights into the interplay between culture and the formation of feminine identities, the book has been justifiably criticized for its fixedness in the peculiar, less-than-material problems of white middle-class suburban women. Such criticism is compounded by Friedan's role in founding (1966) and providing a relatively conservative early leadership for the National Organization for Women (NOW), the first nationwide organization of the second wave.

As can be seen in NOW's "Statement of Purpose" (1967), the fledgling group dedicated itself to achieving equality between the sexes. Founded in part in the image of black civil rights organizations, NOW adopted legalistic policy and strategies. Early goals included enforcement of Title VII of the 1964 Civil Rights Act in regard to sexual discrimination against women, ratification of the Equal Rights Amendment, and the "repeal of all abortion laws." NOW strived toward a pure ideal of sexual equality, a society in which women could assume "all the privileges and responsibilities thereof in truly equal partnership with men."

NOW's goal of raising women to the level of men stood in clear contrast to the goals of the many women, organizations, and journals, magazines, and newspapers that came to identify with "women's liberation," "radical feminism," or both. Rather than working for women's "full participation in the mainstream of American society," as NOW would have it, some second-wave feminists wanted complete freedom *from* that system, thereby gaining the necessary power and position to oppose and change its very structure. This oppositionalism lies at the root of the strategies and self-understanding of radical feminists: it explains, for instance, the penchant for targeting and attacking cultural icons of femininity like motherhood and the Miss America Beauty Pageant; oppositionalism also sheds light on the studied impatience with and rejection of liberal feminism and the politics of reform; and, finally, it supports the critical position of separatism and opposition to masculine institutions and structures of power.

Women's liberation, for radical feminists, would be achieved only after completely eliminating male supremacy. This is, perhaps, the most important theoretical contribution of second-wave thought. Today the idea that feminism involves the critique of men may sound commonplace, but to feminists of the late 1960s it marked a dramatic step. Many of these women had been deeply involved in the black civil rights and student movements of the time and were committed to eradicating racism and the economic and social inequities of American capitalism. Within this context, the decision to leave "the movement" and focus attack on sexism was revolutionary, as described in "To the Women of the Left" (1969), which appeared in a weekly published by Students for a Democratic Society; and Anne Koedt's "Women and the Radical Movement" (1968), which appeared in *Notes from the First Year,* a journal produced by New York Radical Women, a group of mostly middle-class white women who believed in addressing women's oppression by organizing separately from men. Koedt was one of the journal's editors and helped to found the radical feminist movement in New York (among other things, she worked with New York Radical Women, The Feminists, and New York Radical Feminists).

The emergence of radical feminism was marked by the publication of numerous founding statements and manifestos—documents declaring a group's revolutionary intention and offering comprehensive or systematic accounts of the social subjugation of women. Theories varied among feminists, but the heightened political discourse of the time seemed to demand ideological explanation of one's position. Many radical feminists displayed their roots in the socialist-oriented politics of the New Left by depending on the concept of class to explain how men as a group gained and held power over women. The "Redstockings Manifesto" (1969), for example, draws clear lines between woman "the oppressed" and man "the oppressor." Another New York City group, The Feminists, defined itself as "A Political Organization to Annihilate Sex Roles" (1969). It also uses the language of oppressed and oppressor, declaring, "The class separation between men and women is a political division." The New York Radical Feminists, in "Politics of the Ego: A Manifesto" (1969), argue that men as a class subjugate women to serve their ego, while the Westchester Radical Feminists—a group of suburban New York women—discuss the coercive power of sex roles in its "Statement of Purpose" (1972).

More than any previous period of American feminism, the second wave was communicated through the written word. Several leading feminist intellectuals gained national attention after publishing major interpretive books examining sexual inequality. Three appeared in 1970 alone: Kate Millet's *Sexual Politics,* Shulamith Firestone's *The Dialectic of Sex: The Case for Feminist Revolution,* and Robin Morgan's anthology *Sisterhood is Powerful.* Perhaps even more important, feminist thought reached the public through an unprecedented number of periodicals; between the years 1968 and 1973, American feminists founded more than five hundred of them. Why this literary eruption? Surely, part of the explanation is that many women of the second wave were acutely aware of the power of the mass media and its conservative influence, and they were determined to counter that power. Self-consciously radical, issue-oriented, and developed specifically to mobilize women, feminist journals led the way. With varied emphases, all were committed to letting women's voices be heard. *Aphra* ("named in honor of Aphra Behn . . . the first woman known to have earned her living by writing") devotes itself to "art, not ideology," according to the "Preamble" (1969) in its first issue. *Asian Women* provides a place for women of Asian descent to share their thoughts and ideas. In "This Isn't One of Those Blonds That Anyone Can Pick Up in a Supermarket" (1971), the editors describe the process of putting their journal together in a way that honors a diversity of voices from the Asian community. The "Founding Editorial" (1969) of *Women: A Journal of Liberation* specifically states, "We want everyone to have her say." Likewise, the wide-ranging "Founding Editorial" (1970) of *Up from Under* invites "all women" to join in the women's movement.

This same combination of radical politics and inclusiveness is found in the countless underground feminist newspapers of the late 1960s and early 1970s. Many of these publications arose from the underground press of the male-dominated New Left. As female staff became more and more dissatisfied with the content of the papers—which included sex ads, pornography, and total disregard of women's issues—some insisted on editorial control of their own papers. The most acclaimed example of this type of move happened in 1970, when a coalition of women seized the well-known New York underground newspaper *Rat: Subterranean News.* Robin Morgan's angry and eloquent article "Goodbye to All That" (1970), which appeared in the takeover issue, describes how women are exploited by male "revolutionaries" and why women need to claim their own power.

Some of the most seditious thought of the second wave appeared in the underground feminist press of the early 1970s. For example, "Who We Are" (1970) and "What the Counter-Culture Isn't Just" (1970), both from *A Journal of Anarcho-Feminism,* put forth the notion that women must "question all authoritarian structure." Everything—every ideology, every theorist, every institution—should be questioned and all hierarchies abolished. The opening statement for *Battle Acts,* "Specific Characteristics of Women's Liberation" (1970), by the group Women of Youth Against War and Racism, calls for a "strike at the very root of women's oppression" and envisions "a total transformation of the subservient, secondary status of women in all phases of life." It became common to call for a total revolution not only in large social institutions but in every aspect of personal life—including (or especially) the nuclear family. In "A Statement about Female Liberation" (1971) the publishers of the magazine *Second Wave* reiterate that "we must question every aspect of our lives" and point out that sexism "is so deeply ingrained in every person's consciousness that most of it is not noticed or is accepted as normal." Feminist newspapers, underground or otherwise, also served a valuable local purpose: because of low printing costs, small locally organized groups of women could afford to publish a weekly or monthly that could form connections among women (relieving isolation), keep them informed about women's news and events, and even mobilize them to effect change within their communities. "About Us" (1970) describes this kind of purpose; it's from the first issue of a paper called *Goodbye to All That,* published by a San Diego County, California, women's collective. "Who We Are" (1972) describes the more specific motivation for a group of working women in San Francisco to publish the paper they called *Change.*

The locally distributed feminist newsletters and underground magazines of the late 1960s and early 1970s appealed mainly to women already a part of the women's liberation movement. *Ms.* magazine—founded in 1972 by a group of women that included Patricia Carbine, Joanne Edgar, Nina Finkelstein, Mary Peacock, Letty Cottin Pogrebin, and Gloria Steinem—intended from the start not only to contribute to an already politicized feminist base, but also to reach out to readers not yet touched by the movement. In "A Personal Report from *Ms.*" (1972), the editors of the new magazine describe the challenges they faced trying to find financial backing for a national-circulation woman-owned and -controlled magazine, especially when its editor wanted to share some of its profits with certain causes of the women's movement. Clay Felker, editor of *New York* magazine, finally agreed to finance a preview issue of *Ms.* to be published in January 1972. That first issue sold over 300,000 copies in less than eight days, demonstrating the broad appeal of a feminist magazine and inspiring Warner Communications to underwrite the publication, while leaving control with the staff. *Ms.* magazine was on its way, able to guarantee advertisers a circulation of at least 500,000 by the end of the 1970s. Like so many smaller-circulation feminist publications, *Ms.* was committed to shaping "a world in which no one is born into a subordinate role" and encouraged women to speak up about their lives as well as about "their" magazine. In 1990 *Ms.* editors made the unusual decision for a commercial publication of no longer taking advertising, because they wanted to make certain that the magazine's content would in no way be beholden to commercial interests.

1

BETTY FRIEDAN

The Problem That Has No Name (1963)

The problem lay buried, unspoken, for many years in the minds of American women. It was a strange stirring, a sense of dissatisfaction, a yearning that women suffered in the middle of the twentieth century in the United States. Each suburban wife struggled with it alone. As she made the beds, shopped for groceries, matched slipcover material, ate peanut butter sandwiches with her children, chauffeured Cub Scouts and Brownies, lay beside her husband at night—she was afraid to ask even of herself the silent question—"Is this all?"

For over fifteen years there was no word of this yearning in the millions of words written about women, for women, in all the columns, books and articles by experts telling women their role was to seek fulfillment as wives and mothers. Over and over women heard in voices of tradition and of Freudian sophistication that they could desire no greater destiny than to glory in their own femininity. Experts told them how to catch a man and keep him, how to breastfeed children and handle their toilet training, how to cope with sibling rivalry and adolescent rebellion; how to buy a dishwasher, bake bread, cook gourmet snails, and build a swimming pool with their own hands; how to dress, look, and act more feminine and make marriage more exciting; how to keep their husbands from dying young and their sons from growing into delinquents. They were taught to pity the neurotic, unfeminine, unhappy women who wanted to be poets or physicists or presidents. They learned that truly feminine women do not want careers, higher education, political

rights—the independence and the opportunities that the old-fashioned feminists fought for. Some women, in their forties and fifties, still remembered painfully giving up those dreams, but most of the younger women no longer even thought about them. A thousand expert voices applauded their femininity, their adjustment, their new maturity. All they had to do was devote their lives from earliest girlhood to finding a husband and bearing children.

By the end of the nineteen-fifties, the average marriage age of women in America dropped to 20, and was still dropping, into the teens. Fourteen million girls were engaged by 17. The proportion of women attending college in comparison with men dropped from 47 per cent in 1920 to 35 per cent in 1958. A century earlier, women had fought for higher education; now girls went to college to get a husband. By the mid-fifties, 60 per cent dropped out of college to marry, or because they were afraid too much education would be a marriage bar. Colleges built dormitories for "married students," but the students were almost always the husbands. A new degree was instituted for the wives—"Ph.T." (Putting Husband Through).

Then American girls began getting married in high school. And the women's magazines, deploring the unhappy statistics about these young marriages, urged that courses on marriage, and marriage counselors, be installed in the high schools. Girls started going steady at twelve and thirteen, in junior high. Manufacturers put out brassieres with false bosoms of foam rubber for little girls of ten. And an advertisement for a child's dress, sizes 3–6x, in the *New York Times* in the fall of 1960, said: "She Too Can Join the Man-Trap Set."

By the end of the fifties, the United States birthrate was overtaking India's. The birth-control movement, renamed Planned Parenthood, was asked to find a method whereby women who had been advised that a third or fourth baby would be born dead or defective might have it anyhow. Statisticians were especially astounded at the fantastic increase in the

From Betty Friedan, *The Feminine Mystique* (New York: Dell, 1963), 15–32. Reprinted from *The Feminine Mystique* by Betty Friedan, by permission of W.W. Norton & Company, Inc. Copyright 1963 by Betty Friedan. Copyright renewed 1991 by Betty Friedan.

number of babies among college women. Where once they had two children, now they had four, five, six. Women who had once wanted careers were now making careers out of having babies. So rejoiced *Life* magazine in a 1956 paean to the movement of American women back to the home.

In a New York hospital, a woman had a nervous breakdown when she found she could not breastfeed her baby. In other hospitals, women dying of cancer refused a drug which research had proved might save their lives: its side effects were said to be unfeminine. "If I have only one life, let me live it as a blonde," a larger-than-life-sized picture of a pretty, vacuous woman proclaimed from newspaper, magazine, and drugstore ads. And across America, three out of every ten women dyed their hair blonde. They ate a chalk called Metrecal, instead of food, to shrink to the size of thin young models. Department-store buyers reported that American women, since 1939, had become three and four sizes smaller. "Women are out to fit the clothes, instead of vice-versa," one buyer said.

Interior decorators were designing kitchens with mosaic murals and original paintings, for kitchens were once again the center of women's lives. Home sewing became a million-dollar industry. Many women no longer left their homes, except to shop, chauffeur their children, or attend a social engagement with their husbands. Girls were growing up in America without ever having jobs outside the home. In the late fifties, a sociological phenomenon was suddenly remarked: a third of American women now worked, but most were no longer young and very few were pursuing careers. They were married women who held part-time jobs, selling or secretarial, to put their husbands through school, their sons through college, or to help pay the mortgage. Or they were widows supporting families. Fewer and fewer women were entering professional work. The shortages in the nursing, social work, and teaching professions caused crises in almost every American city. Con-

cerned over the Soviet Union's lead in the space race, scientists noted that America's greatest source of unused brainpower was women. But girls would not study physics: it was "unfeminine." A girl refused a science fellowship at Johns Hopkins to take a job in a real-estate office. All she wanted, she said, was what every other American girl wanted—to get married, have four children and live in a nice house in a nice suburb.

The suburban housewife—she was the dream image of the young American women and the envy, it was said, of women all over the world. The American housewife—freed by science and labor-saving appliances from the drudgery, the dangers of childbirth and the illnesses of her grandmother. She was healthy, beautiful, educated, concerned only about her husband, her children, her home. She had found true feminine fulfillment. As a housewife and mother, she was respected as a full and equal partner to man in his world. She was free to choose automobiles, clothes, appliances, supermarkets; she had everything that women ever dreamed of.

In the fifteen years after World War II, this mystique of feminine fulfillment became the cherished and self-perpetuating core of contemporary American culture. Millions of women lived their lives in the image of those pretty pictures of the American suburban housewife, kissing their husbands goodbye in front of the picture window, depositing their stationwagonsful of children at school, and smiling as they ran the new electric waxer over the spotless kitchen floor. They baked their own bread, sewed their own and their children's clothes, kept their new washing machines and dryers running all day. They changed the sheets on the beds twice a week instead of once, took the rug-hooking class in adult education, and pitied their poor frustrated mothers, who had dreamed of having a career. Their only dream was to be perfect wives and mothers; their highest ambition to have five children and a beautiful house, their only fight to get and keep their husbands. They had no thought for the unfeminine problems of the world outside the home; they wanted the men to make the major decisions. They gloried in their role as women, and wrote proudly on the census blank: "Occupation: housewife."

For over fifteen years, the words written for women, and the words women used when they talked to each other, while their husbands sat on the other side of the room and talked shop or politics or septic tanks, were about problems with their children, or how to keep their husbands happy, or improve their children's school, or cook chicken or make slipcovers. Nobody argued whether women were inferior or superior to men; they were simply different. Words like "emancipation" and "career" sounded strange and embarrassing; no one had used them for years. When a Frenchwoman named Simone de Beauvoir wrote a book called *The Second Sex,* an American critic commented that she obviously "didn't know what life was all about," and besides, she was talking about French women. The "woman problem" in America no longer existed.

If a woman had a problem in the 1950's and 1960's, she knew that something must be wrong with her marriage, or with herself. Other women were satisfied with their lives, she thought. What kind of woman was she if she did not feel this mysterious fulfillment waxing the kitchen floor? She was so ashamed to admit her dissatisfaction that she never knew how many other women shared it. If she tried to tell her husband, he didn't understand what she was talking about. She did not really understand it herself. For over fifteen years women in America found it harder to talk about this problem than about sex. Even the psychoanalysts had no name for it. When a woman went to a psychiatrist for help, as many women did, she would say, "I'm so ashamed," or "I must be hopelessly neurotic." "I don't know what's wrong with women today," a suburban psychiatrist said uneasily. "I only know something is wrong because most of my patients happen to be women. And their problem isn't sexual." Most women with this problem did not go to

see a psychoanalyst, however. "There's nothing wrong really," they kept telling themselves. "There isn't any problem."

But on an April morning in 1959, I heard a mother of four, having coffee with four other mothers in a suburban development fifteen miles from New York, say in a tone of quiet desperation, "the problem." And the others knew, without words, that she was not talking about a problem with her husband, or her children, or her home. Suddenly they realized they all shared the same problem, the problem that has no name. They began, hesitantly, to talk about it. Later, after they had picked up their children at nursery school and taken them home to nap, two of the women cried, in sheer relief, just to know they were not alone.

Gradually I came to realize that the problem that has no name was shared by countless women in America. As a magazine writer I often interviewed women about problems with their children, or their marriages, or their houses, or their communities. But after a while I began to recognize the telltale signs of this other problem. I saw the same signs in suburban ranch houses and split-levels on Long Island and in New Jersey and Westchester County; in colonial houses in a small Massachusetts town; on patios in Memphis; in suburban and city apartments; in living rooms in the Midwest. Sometimes I sensed the problem, not as a reporter, but as a suburban housewife, for during this time I was also bringing up my own three children in Rockland County, New York. I heard echoes of the problem in college dormitories and semi-private maternity wards, at PTA meetings and luncheons of the League of Women Voters, at suburban cocktail parties, in station wagons waiting for trains, and in snatches of conversation overheard at Schrafft's. The groping words I heard from other women, on quiet afternoons when children were at school or on quiet evenings when husbands worked late, I think I understood first as a woman long before I understood their larger social and psychological implications.

Just what was this problem that has no name? What were the words women used when they tried to express it? Sometimes a woman would say "I feel empty somehow . . . incomplete." Or she would say, "I feel as if I don't exist." Sometimes she blotted out the feeling with a tranquilizer. Sometimes she thought the problem was with her husband, or her children, or that what she really needed was to redecorate her house, or move to a better neighborhood, or have an affair, or another baby. Sometimes, she went to a doctor with symptoms she could hardly describe: "A tired feeling . . . I get so angry with the children it scares me . . . I feel like crying without any reason." (A Cleveland doctor called it "the housewife's syndrome.") A number of women told me about great bleeding blisters that break out on their hands and arms. "I call it the housewife's blight," said a family doctor in Pennsylvania. "I see it so often lately in these young women with four, five and six children who bury themselves in their dishpans. But it isn't caused by detergent and it isn't cured by cortisone."

Sometimes a woman would tell me that the feeling gets so strong she runs out of the house and walks through the streets. Or she stays inside her house and cries. Or her children tell her a joke, and she doesn't laugh because she doesn't hear it. I talked to women who had spent years on the analyst's couch, working out their "adjustment to the feminine role," their blocks to "fulfillment as a wife and mother." But the desperate tone in these women's voices, and the look in their eyes, was the same as the tone and the look of other women, who were sure they had no problem, even though they did have a strange feeling of desperation.

A mother of four who left college at nineteen to get married told me:

"I've tried everything women are supposed to do—hobbies, gardening, pickling, canning, being very social with my neighbors, joining committees, running PTA teas. I can do it all, and I like it, but it doesn't leave you anything to think about—any feeling of who you are. I never had any career ambitions. All I wanted was to get married and have four children. I

love the kids and Bob and my home. There's no problem you can even put a name to. But I'm desperate. I begin to feel I have no personality. I'm a server of food and a putter-on of pants and a bedmaker, somebody who can be called on when you want something. But who am I?"

A twenty-three-year-old mother in blue jeans said:

"I ask myself why I'm so dissatisfied. I've got my health, fine children, a lovely new home, enough money. My husband has a real future as an electronics engineer. He doesn't have any of these feelings. He says maybe I need a vacation, let's go to New York for a weekend. But that isn't it. I always had this idea we should do everything together. I can't sit down and read a book alone. If the children are napping and I have one hour to myself I just walk through the house waiting for them to wake up. I don't make a move until I know where the rest of the crowd is going. It's as if ever since you were a little girl, there's always been somebody or something that will take care of your life: your parents, or college, or falling in love, or having a child, or moving to a new house. Then you wake up one morning and there's nothing to look forward to."

A young wife in a Long Island development said:

"I seem to sleep so much. I don't know why I should be so tired. This house isn't nearly so hard to clean as the cold-water flat we had when I was working. The children are at school all day. It's not the work. I just don't feel alive."

In 1960, the problem that has no name burst like a boil through the image of the happy American housewife. In the television commercials the pretty housewives still beamed over their foaming dishpans and *Time*'s cover story on "The Suburban Wife, an American Phenomenon" protested: "Having too good a time . . . to believe that they should be unhappy." But the actual unhappiness of the American housewife was suddenly being reported— from the *New York Times* and *Newsweek* to *Good Housekeeping* and CBS Television ("The Trapped Housewife"), although almost everybody who talked about it found some superficial reason to dismiss it. It was attributed to incompetent appliance repairmen (*New York Times*), or the distances children must be chauffeured in the suburbs (*Time*), or too much PTA (*Redbook*). Some said it was the old problem—education: more and more women had education, which naturally made them unhappy in their role as housewives. "The road from Freud to Frigidaire, from Sophocles to Spock, has turned out to be a bumpy one," reported the *New York Times* (June 28, 1960). "Many young women—certainly not all—whose education plunged them into a world of ideas feel stifled in their homes. They find their routine lives out of joint with their training. Like shut-ins, they feel left out. In the last year, the problem of the educated housewife had provided the meat of dozens of speeches made by troubled presidents of women's colleges who maintain, in the face of complaints, that sixteen years of academic training is realistic preparation for wifehood and motherhood."

There was much sympathy for the educated housewife. ("Like a two-headed schizophrenic . . . once she wrote a paper on the Graveyard poets; now she writes notes to the milkman. Once she determined the boiling point of sulphuric acid; now she determines her boiling point with the overdue repairman. . . . The housewife often is reduced to screams and tears. . . . No one, it seems, is appreciative, least of all herself, of the kind of person she becomes in the process of turning from poetess into shrew.")

Home economists suggested more realistic preparation for housewives, such as high-school workshops in home appliances. College educators suggested more discussion groups on home management and the family, to prepare women for the adjustment to domestic life. A spate of articles appeared in the mass magazines offering "Fifty-eight Ways to Make Your Marriage More Exciting." No month went by without a new book by a psychiatrist or sexologist offering technical advice on finding greater fulfillment through sex.

A male humorist joked in *Harper's Bazaar* (July, 1960) that the problem could be solved by taking away woman's right to vote. ("In the pre–19th Amendment era, the American woman was placid, sheltered and sure of her role in American society. She left all the political decisions to her husband and he, in turn, left all the family decisions to her. Today a woman has to make both the family *and* the political decisions, and it's too much for her.")

A number of educators suggested seriously that women no longer be admitted to the four-year colleges and universities; in the growing college crisis, the education which girls could not use as housewives was more urgently needed than ever by boys to do the work of the atomic age.

The problem was also dismissed with drastic solutions no one could take seriously. (A woman writer proposed in *Harper's* that women be drafted for compulsory service as nurses' aides and baby-sitters.) And it was smoothed over with the age-old panaceas: "love is their answer," "the only answer is inner help," "the secret of completeness—children," "a private means of intellectual fulfillment," "to cure this toothache of the spirit—the simple formula of handing one's self and one's will over to God."

The problem was dismissed by telling the housewife she doesn't realize how lucky she is—her own boss, no time clock, no junior executive gunning for her job. What if she isn't happy—does she think men are happy in this world? Does she really, secretly, still want to be a man? Doesn't she know yet how lucky she is to be a woman?

The problem was also, and finally, dismissed by shrugging that there are no solutions: this is what being a woman means, and what is wrong with American women that they can't accept their role gracefully? As *Newsweek* put it (March 7, 1960):

"She is dissatisfied with a lot that women of other lands can only dream of. Her discontent is deep, pervasive, and impervious to the superficial remedies which are offered at every hand. . . . An army of professional explorers have already charted the major sources of trouble. . . . From the beginning of time, the female cycle has defined and confined woman's role. As Freud was credited with saying: "Anatomy is destiny." Though no group of women has ever pushed these natural restrictions as far as the American wife, it seems that she still cannot accept them with good grace. . . . A young mother with a beautiful family, charm, talent and brains is apt to dismiss her role apologetically. "What do I do?" you hear her say. "Why nothing. I'm just a housewife." A good education, it seems, has given this paragon among women an understanding of the value of everything except her own worth." . . .

And so she must accept the fact that "American women's unhappiness is merely the most recently won of women's rights," and adjust and say with the happy housewife found by *Newsweek:* "We ought to salute the wonderful freedom we all have and be proud of our lives today. I have had college and I've worked, but being a housewife is the most rewarding and satisfying role. . . . My mother was never included in my father's business affairs . . . she couldn't get out of the house and away from us children. But I am an equal to my husband; I can go along with him on business trips and to social business affairs."

The alternative offered was a choice that few women would contemplate. In the sympathetic words of the *New York Times:* "All admit to being deeply frustrated at times by the lack of privacy, the physical burden, the routine of family life, the confinement of it. However, none would give up her home and family if she had the choice to make again." *Redbook* commented: "Few women would want to thumb their noses at husbands, children and community and go off on their own. Those who do may be talented individuals, but they rarely are successful women."

The year American women's discontent boiled over, it was also reported (*Look*) that the more than 21,000,000 American women who are single, widowed, or divorced do not cease even after fifty their frenzied, desperate search for a man. And the search begins early—for seventy per cent of all American women now marry before they are twenty-four. A pretty twenty-five-year-old secretary took thirty-five different jobs in six months in the futile hope of finding a husband. Women were moving from one political club to another, taking evening courses in accounting or sailing, learning to play golf or ski, joining a number of churches in succession, going to bars alone, in their ceaseless search for a man.

Of the growing thousands of women currently getting private psychiatric help in the United States, the married ones were reported dissatisfied with their marriages, the unmarried ones suffering from anxiety and, finally, depression. Strangely, a number of psychiatrists stated that, in their experience, unmarried women patients were happier than married ones. So the door of all those pretty suburban houses opened a crack to permit a glimpse of uncounted thousands of American housewives who suffered alone from a problem that suddenly everyone was talking about, and beginning to take for granted, as one of those unreal problems in American life that can never be solved—like the hydrogen bomb. By 1962 the plight of the trapped American housewife had become a national parlor game. Whole issues of magazines, newspaper columns, books learned and frivolous, educational conferences and television panels were devoted to the problem.

Even so, most men, and some women, still did not know that this problem was real. But those who had faced it honestly knew that all the superficial remedies, the sympathetic advice, the scolding words and the cheering words were somehow drowning the problem in unreality. A bitter laugh was beginning to be heard from American women. They were admired, envied, pitied, theorized over until they were sick of it, offered drastic solutions or silly choices that no one could take seriously. They got all kinds of advice from the growing armies of marriage and child-guidance counselors, psychotherapists, and armchair psychologists, on how to adjust to their role as housewives. No other road to fulfillment was offered to American women in the middle of the twentieth century. Most adjusted to their role and suffered or ignored the problem that has no name. It can be less painful, for a woman, not to hear the strange, dissatisfied voice stirring within her.

It is no longer possible to ignore that voice, to dismiss the desperation of so many American women. This is not what being a woman means, no matter what the experts say. For human suffering there is a reason; perhaps the reason has not been found because the right questions have not been asked, or pressed far enough. I do not accept the answer that there is no problem because American women have luxuries that women in other times and lands never dreamed of; part of the strange newness of the problem is that it cannot be understood in terms of the age-old material problems of man: poverty, sickness, hunger, cold. The women who suffer this problem have a hunger that food cannot fill. It persists in women whose husbands are struggling interns and law clerks, or prosperous doctors and lawyers; in wives of workers and executives who make $5,000 a year or $50,000. It is not caused by lack of material advantages; it may not even be felt by women preoccupied with desperate problems of hunger, poverty or illness. And women who think it will be solved by more money, a bigger house, a second car, moving to a better suburb, often discover it gets worse.

It is no longer possible today to blame the problem on loss of femininity: to say that education and independence and equality with men have made American women unfeminine. I have heard so many women try to deny this dissatisfied voice within themselves because it does not fit the pretty picture of femininity the experts have given them. I think, in fact, that this is the first clue to the mystery: the problem cannot be understood in the generally accepted terms by which scientists have studied women, doctors have treated them, counselors have advised them, and writers have written about them. Women who suffer this problem, in whom this voice is stirring, have lived their whole lives in the pursuit of feminine fulfillment. They are not career women (although career women may

have other problems); they are women whose greatest ambition has been marriage and children. For the oldest of these women, these daughters of the American middle class, no other dream was possible. The ones in their forties and fifties who once had other dreams gave them up and threw themselves joyously into life as housewives. For the youngest, the new wives and mothers, this was the only dream. They are the ones who quit high school and college to marry, or marked time in some job in which they had no real interest until they married. These women are very "feminine" in the usual sense, and yet they still suffer the problem.

Are the women who finished college, the women who once had dreams beyond housewifery, the ones who suffer the most? According to the experts they are, but listen to these four women:

"My days are all busy, and dull, too. All I ever do is mess around. I get up at eight—I make breakfast, so I do the dishes, have lunch, do some more dishes and some laundry and cleaning in the afternoon. Then it's supper dishes and I get to sit down a few minutes before the children have to be sent to bed. . . . That's all there is to my day. It's just like any other wife's day. Humdrum. The biggest time, I am chasing kids."

"Ye Gods, what do I do with my time? Well, I get up at six. I get my son dressed and then give him breakfast. After that I wash dishes and bathe and feed the baby. Then I get lunch and while the children nap, I sew or mend or iron and do all the other things I can't get done before noon. Then I cook supper for the family and my husband watches TV while I do the dishes. After I get the children to bed, I set my hair and then I go to bed."

"The problem is always being the children's mommy, or the minister's wife and never being myself."

"A film made of any typical morning in my house would look like an old Marx Brothers' comedy. I wash the dishes, rush the older children off to school, dash out in the yard to cultivate the chrysanthemums, run back in to make a phone call about a committee meeting, help the youngest child build a blockhouse, spend fifteen minutes skimming the newspapers so I can be well-informed, then scamper down to the washing machines where my thrice-weekly laundry includes enough clothes to keep a primitive village going for an entire year. By noon I'm ready for a padded cell. Very little of what I've done has been really necessary or important. Outside pressures lash me through the day. Yet I look upon myself as one of the more relaxed housewives in the neighborhood. Many of my friends are even more frantic. In the past sixty years we have come full circle and the American housewife is once again trapped in a squirrel cage. If the cage is now a modern plate-glass-and-broadloom ranch house or a convenient modern apartment, the situation is no less painful than when her grandmother sat over an embroidery hoop in her gilt-and-plush parlor and muttered angrily about women's rights."

The first two women never went to college. They live in developments in Levittown, New Jersey, and Taxoma, Washington, and were interviewed by a team of sociologists studying workingmen's wives. The third, a minister's wife, wrote on the fifteenth reunion questionnaire of her college that she never had any career ambitions, but wishes now she had. The fourth, who has a Ph.D. in anthropology, is today a Nebraska housewife with three children. Their words seem to indicate that housewives of all educational levels suffer the same feeling of desperation.

The fact is that no one today is muttering angrily about "women's rights," even though more and more women have gone to college. In a recent study of all the classes that have graduated from Barnard College, a significant minority of earlier graduates blamed their education for making them want "rights," later classes blamed their education for giving them career dreams, but recent graduates blamed the college for making them feel it was not enough simply to be a housewife and mother; they did not want to feel guilty if they did not read books or take part in community activities. But if education is not the cause of the problem, the fact that education somehow festers in these women may be a clue.

If the secret of feminine fulfillment is having children, never have so many women, with the freedom to choose, had so many children, in so few years, so willingly. If the answer is love, never have women searched for love with such determination. And yet there is a growing suspicion that the problem may not be sexual, though it must somehow be related to sex. I have heard from many doctors evidence of new sexual problems between man and wife—sexual hunger in wives so great their husbands cannot satisfy it. "We have made woman a sex creature," said a psychiatrist at the Margaret Sanger marriage counseling clinic. "She has no identity except as a wife and mother. She does not know who she is herself. She waits all day for her husband to come home at night to make her feel alive. And now it is the husband who is not interested. It is terrible for the women, to lie there, night after night, waiting for her husband to make her feel alive." Why is there such a market for books and articles offering sexual advice? The kind of sexual orgasm which Kinsey found in statistical plenitude in the recent generations of American women does not seem to make this problem go away.

On the contrary, new neuroses are being seen among women—and problems as yet unnamed as neuroses—which Freud and his followers did not predict, with physical symptoms, anxieties, and defense mechanisms equal to those caused by sexual repression. And strange new problems are being reported in the growing generations of children whose mothers were always there, driving them around, helping them with their homework—an inability to endure pain or discipline or pursue any self-sustained goal of any sort, a devastating boredom with life. Educators are increasingly uneasy about the dependence, the lack of self-reliance, of the boys and girls who are entering college today. "We fight a continual battle to make our students assume manhood," said a Columbia dean.

A White House conference was held on the physical and muscular deterioration of American children: were they being overnurtured? Sociologists noted the astounding organization of suburban children's lives: the lessons, parties, entertainments, play and study groups organized for them. A suburban housewife in Portland, Oregon, wondered why the children "need" Brownies and Boy Scouts out here. "This is not the slums. The kids out here have the great outdoors. I think people are so bored, they organize the children, and then try to hook everyone else on it. And the poor kids have no time left just to lie on their beds and daydream."

Can the problem that has no name be somehow related to the domestic routine of the housewife? When a woman tries to put the problem into words, she often merely describes the daily life she leads. What is there in this recital of comfortable domestic detail that could possibly cause such a feeling of desperation? Is she trapped simply by the enormous demands of her role as modern housewife: wife, mistress, mother, nurse, consumer, cook, chauffeur; expert on interior decoration, child care, appliance repair, furniture refinishing, nutrition, and education? Her day is fragmented as she rushes from dishwasher to washing machine to telephone to dryer to station wagon to supermarket, and delivers Johnny to the Little League field, takes Janey to dancing class, gets the lawnmower fixed and meets the 6:45. She can never spend more than 15 minutes on any one thing; she has no time to read books, only magazines; even if she had time, she has lost the power to concentrate. At the end of the day, she is so terribly tired that sometimes her husband has to take over and put the children to bed.

This terrible tiredness took so many women to doctors in the 1950's that one decided to investigate it. He found, surprisingly, that his patients suffering from "housewife's fatigue" slept more than an adult needed to sleep—as much as ten hours a day—and that the actual energy they expended on housework did not tax their capacity. The real problem must be something else, he decided—perhaps boredom. Some doctors told their women patients they must get out of the house for a day, treat themselves to a movie in town. Others prescribed tranquilizers. Many suburban housewives were taking tranquilizers like cough drops. "You wake up in the morning, and you feel as if there's no point in going on another day like this. So you take a tranquilizer because it makes you not care so much that it's pointless."

It is easy to see the concrete details that trap the suburban housewife, the continual demands on her time. But the chains that bind her in her trap are chains in her own mind and spirit. They are chains made up of mistaken ideas and misinterpreted facts, of incomplete truths and unreal choices. They are not easily seen and not easily shaken off.

How can any woman see the whole truth within the bounds of her own life? How can she believe that voice inside herself, when it denies the conventional, accepted truths by which she has been living? And yet the women I have talked to, who are finally listening to that inner voice, seem in some incredible way to be groping through to a truth that has defied the experts.

I think the experts in a great many fields have been holding pieces of that truth under their microscopes for a long time without realizing it. I found pieces of it in certain new research and theoretical developments in psychological, social and biological science whose implications for women seem never to have been examined. I found many cues by talking to suburban doctors, gynecologists, obstetricians, child-guidance clinicians, pediatricians, high-school guidance counselors, college professors, marriage counselors, psychiatrists and ministers—questioning them not on their theories, but on their actual experience in treating American women. I became aware of a growing body of evidence, much of which has not been reported publicly because it does not fit current modes of thought about women—evidence which throws into question the standards of feminine normality, feminine adjustment, feminine fulfillment, and feminine maturity by which most women are still trying to live.

I began to see in a strange new light the American return to early marriage and the large families that are causing the population explosion; the recent movement to natural childbirth and breastfeeding; suburban conformity, and the new neuroses, character pathologies and sexual problems being reported by the doctors. I began to see new dimensions to old problems that have long been taken for granted among women: menstrual difficulties, sexual frigidity, promiscuity, pregnancy fears, childbirth depression, the high incidence of emotional breakdown and suicide among women in their twenties and thirties, the menopause crises, the so-called passivity and immaturity of American men, the discrepancy between women's tested intellectual abilities in childhood and their adult achievement, the changing incidence of adult sexual orgasm in American women, and persistent problems in psychotherapy and in women's education.

If I am right, the problem that has no name stirring in the minds of so many American women today is not a matter of loss of femininity or too much education, or the demands of domesticity. It is far more important than anyone recognizes. It is the key to these other new and old problems which have been torturing women and their husbands and children, and puzzling their doctors and educators for years. It may well be the key to our future as a nation and a culture. We can no longer ignore that voice within women that says: "I want something more than my husband and my children and my home."

2

NATIONAL ORGANIZATION FOR WOMEN
Statement of Purpose (1967)

We, men and women who hereby constitute ourselves as The National Organization for Women, believe that the time has come for a new movement toward true equality for all

From Aileen C. Hernandez, *The First Five Years, 1966–1971* (Chicago: National Organization for Women, [1971]), 5.

women in America, and toward a fully equal partnership of the sexes, as part of the worldwide revolution of human rights now taking place within and beyond our national borders.

The purpose of NOW is to take action to bring women into full participation in the mainstream of American society now, exercising all the privileges and responsibilities thereof in truly equal partnership with men.

. . . NOW is dedicated to the proposition that women, first and foremost, are human beings, who, like all other people in our society, must have the chance to develop their fullest potential. We believe that women can achieve such equality only by accepting to the full the challenges and responsibilities they share with all other people in our society, as part of the decision-making mainstream of American political, economic and social life.

. . . We realize that women's problems are linked to many broader questions of social justice; their solution will require concerted action by many groups. Therefore, convinced that human rights for all are indivisible, we expect to give active support to the common cause of equal rights for all those who suffer discrimination and deprivation, and we call upon other organizations committed to such goals to support our efforts toward equality for women.

3
To the Women of the Left (1967)

Below is a Preliminary Statement of Principles used as a working paper by a group of Chicago women. Most of us, tho not all, are of the Movement.

A few, very few, are in SDS.

We have been meeting weekly for the last two months to discuss our colonial status in this society and to propound strategy and methods of attacking it. Our political awareness of our op-

From *New Left Notes*, November 13, 1967.

pression has developed thru the last couple years as we sought to apply the principles of justice, equality, mutual respect and dignity which we learned from the Movement to the lives we lived as part of the Movement; only to come up against the solid wall of male chauvinism.

Realizing that this is a social problem of national significance not at all confined to our struggle for personal liberation, within the Movement we must approach it in a political manner. Therefore it is incumbent on us, as women, to organize a movement for woman's liberation.

Women must not make the same mistake the blacks did at first of allowing others (whites in their case, men in ours) to define our issues, methods and goals. Only we can and must define the terms of our struggle.

The time has come for us to take the initiative in organizing ourselves for our own liberation. It is for that purpose that this group came together and this Statement was written.

While we welcome inquiries and assistance from all concerned persons this organization and its sister chapter now forming in New York are open only to women. Any woman who would like to join us or who would like help in organizing a local group should write or call. The liberation of women cannot be divorced from the larger revolutionary struggle.

STATEMENT OF RADICAL WOMEN

We recognize that radical change is necessary in the structure and institutions of this society before women will be able to function and fulfill themselves in every way as human beings. We call for concerted effort in the development of programs which will free women from their traditional roles in order that we may participate in meaningful and creative activities.

Specifically, it is imperative that we unite behind the following points as a beginning step towards full and equal participation of women in our society.

1. As women are 51% of the population of this country, they must be proportionally rep-resented on all levels of society rather than relegated to trivial functions that have been predetermined for them. Particularly they must be allowed to assume full participation in the decision-making processes and positions of our political, economic and social institutions.

2. We condemn the mass media for perpetuating the stereotype of women as always in an auxiliary position to men, being no more than mothers, wives or sexual objects. We specifically condemn the advertising concerns for creating the myths about women solely to profit from them as consumers. Furthermore, we call for a boycott of the thriving women's magazines, such as *McCalls, Good Housekeeping, Mademoiselle, Seventeen, Vogue, Glamour, Ladies' Home Journal* and *Cosmopolitan,* for romanticizing drudgery and promoting a false mystique of emancipation.

3. There must be total equality of opportunity for education, at all levels and in all fields. Women should be fully educated to their individual potential instead of being subtly persuaded that education is of little value to their long-range interests.

4. Equal employment opportunities must be enforced. This includes equal pay for equal work, no discrimination on the basis of women's childbearing functions, and open access to all jobs, particularly managerial and policy making positions.

5. The labor movement and all labor organizations, unions and groups must admit women on an equal basis to all executive and policy levels while encouraging women to assume leadership roles in their organizations. There must be a concerted effort to organize and unionize those low-paying, servile occupations in which women are primarily employed.

6. Women must have complete control of their own bodies. This means (a) the dissemination of birth control information and devices, free of charge by the state, to all women regardless of age and marital status; (b) the availability of a competent, inexpensive medical abortion for all women who so desire.

7. The structure of the family unit in our society must be reconsidered and the following

institutional changes must be incorporated: (a) a fundamental revamping of marriage, divorce and property laws and customs which cause an injustice to or a subjection of either sex; (b) the equal sharing by husbands and wives of the responsibility for maintaining the home and raising the children; (c) the creation of communal child care centers which would be staffed by women and men assuming equal responsibility and controlled by the adults and children involved in the center; (d) the creation of non-profit-making food preparation centers conveniently located in all communities.

8. We must fight against male domination in all aspects of society and correct the entrenched assumption of superiority on which it thrives, recognizing that the right to define is the most powerful characteristic of any ruling group. In particular, we must be on guard against paternalism, the potent weapon which through condescension and ridicule can reduce women's most legitimate demands to the level of domestic squabbles.

We recognize that women are often their own worst enemies because they have been trained to be prejudiced against themselves. Women must become conscious of the fact that they represent the largest "minority" group in this country and as such are subject to the same segregation, discrimination and dehumanizing influences as other dominated peoples. We know that to become truly free, we must abdicate the superficial privilege which has been purposely substituted for equality and replace it with an equal share of responsibility for taking power in our society.

We believe these minimal demands for equality and full participation in a society that is based on one group victimizing another cannot be met without a restructuring of that society.

We also realize that men are similarly subjected to this victimization. Our criticism of men as a group is based on the fact that historically men have controlled and continue to control the institutions that shape this society. Not just women, but most people feel powerless in the face of these institutions but do not under-

stand their roots. Cries for full inclusion in this corrupt society are a first response of groups coming to awareness of their impotence and sensing their potential strength.

We are conscious that reform may not be the most direct route towards that social restructuring. However, women are a widely dispersed group with little recognition of their common oppression. We hope our words and actions will help make women more aware and organized in their own movement through which a concept of free womanhood will emerge.

Towards this end, we identify with those groups now in revolutionary struggle within our country and abroad. Until the movement recognizes the necessity that women be free and women recognize the necessity for all struggles of liberation, there can be no revolution.

4

ANNE KOEDT

Women and the Radical Movement (1968)

Within the last year many radical women's groups have sprung up throughout the country. This was caused by the fact that movement women found themselves playing secondary roles on every level . . . be it in terms of leadership, or simply in terms of being listened to. They found themselves (and others) afraid to speak up because of self-doubts when in the presence of men. Their roles ended up concentrating on food-making, typing, mimeographing, general assistance work, and as a sexual supply for their male comrades after hours.

As these problems began being discussed, it became clear that what had at first been assumed to be a personal problem was in fact a social and political one. We found strong parallels between the liberation of women and the black power struggle, being oppressed by similar

From *Notes from the First Year*, June 1968.

psychological/economic dynamics. And the deeper we analyzed the problem, and realized that all women suffer from this kind of oppression, the more we realized that the problem was not just isolated to movement women.

It became necessary to go to the root of the problem, rather than to become engaged in solving secondary problems arising *out* of that condition. Thus, rather than storming the Pentagon as women, or protest the Democratic Convention as women, we must begin to expose and eliminate the causes of our oppression as women. Our job is not *only* to improve the conditions of the movement any more than it is to only improve the condition of professional working women. Both are reformist if thought of only as ends in themselves; and it ignores the broader concept that one cannot achieve equality for some members of one's group while the rest are not free.

In choosing to fight for women's liberation it is not enough, either, to explain it only in general terms of "the system." For the system oppresses many groups in many ways. Women must learn that the *specific methods* used to keep her oppressed are to convince her that she is at all times secondary to men, and that her life is defined in terms of him. We cannot speak of liberating ourselves until we free ourselves from this myth and accept ourselves as primary.

In our role as radical women we are confronted with the problem of assuring a female revolution within the general revolution. And we must begin to distinguish the real from the apparent freedom.

Radical men may advocate certain freedoms for women when they overlap with their own interest, but these are not true freedoms unless they spring out of the concept of male and female equality and confront the issue of male supremacy.

For example, men may want women to fight in the revolution because they need every able bodied person they can get. And they may need women to join the work force under a socialist economic system because they cannot afford, like capitalism, to have an unemployed

(surplus) labor force not contributing work, being supported by the state. And man may therefore advocate state nurseries so that mothers are not kept from work.

But has the fundamental concept of women changed? Do these changes mean that men have renounced the old supremacy relationship, wherein women must always be defined in terms of her man? Has the basic domination changed?

It is important to analyze the history of revolutions in terms of special interest groups. The American Revolution was a white male bourgeois revolution. The issue was being able to freely make a profit without England's interference: the Declaration of Independence was specifically written to justify independence from England. It was a document which guaranteed rights neither to the blacks or to women. Crispus Attucks, one of the first black men to lose his life for the revolution, was fighting in a vicarious revolution—the white revolution. Betsy Ross sewing the flag was participating vicariously in a male revolution. The rights gained were not for her.

It is always true of an oppressed group that the mere fact of their existence means that to a certain extent they have accepted their inferior-colonial-secondary status. Taught self-hatred, they identify instead with the oppressor. Thus such phenomena as blacks bleaching their skin and straightening their hair, and women responding with horror at the thought of a woman president.

The economic revolution—i.e. change from capitalism to socialism—can also be viewed in terms of male interest. Under capitalism, the majority of men were exploited and controlled by a few men who held the wealth and power over their lives. By changing the economic structure to socialism, this particular economic exploitation was eradicated.

Women in the Soviet Union fought for and supported such a revolution. But whether out of genuine hope that non-domination and non-exploitation would be applied as liberally to them, or worse, out of a lack of even a minimum awareness that they themselves were important, the Soviet revolution remained a male power revolution, although many new benefits fell to women. The Soviet Union is still primarily male governed; women's integration into the labor force meant simply that she transferred her auxiliary, service relationship with men into the area of work. Soviet women are teachers, doctors, assistants, food handlers. And when they come home from work they are expected to continue the submission role to men and do the housework, cooking and assume primary responsibility for the child-rearing.

It is important for radical women to learn from these events. The dominant/submissive relationship between men and women was not challenged. Not confronted. We were asked by them instead to equate our liberation with theirs . . . to blame our inferior conditions on the economic structure rather than confront the obvious male interest in keeping women "in their place." We never insisted upon as *explicit* a program for freeing women as the man had demanded for freeing himself from economic exploitation. We never confronted men and demanded that unless they give up their domination over us, we would not fight for their revolution, work in their revolution. We never fought the primary cause, hoping instead that changing the secondary characteristics would win us freedom. And we ended up with a revolution that simply transferred male supremacy, paternalism and male power onto the new economy. A reformist revolution that only improved upon our privileges but did not change the basic structure causing our oppression.

A black revolutionary today would not be satisfied knowing only that the economic structure went from private to collective control; he would want to know about racism. And you would have to show him how white power and supremacy would be eliminated in that revolution before he would join you.

Until we make such similar demands, revolution will pass us by.

5
REDSTOCKINGS
Redstockings Manifesto (1969)

I. After centuries of individual and preliminary political struggle, women are uniting to achieve their final liberation from male supremacy. Redstockings is dedicated to building this unity and winning our freedom.

II. Women are an oppressed class. Our oppression is total, affecting every facet of our lives. We are exploited as sex objects, breeders, domestic servants, and cheap labor. We are considered inferior beings, whose only purpose is to enhance men's lives. Our humanity is denied. Our prescribed behavior is enforced by the threat of physical violence.

Because we have lived so intimately with our oppressors, in isolation from each other, we have been kept from seeing our personal suffering as a political condition. This creates the illusion that a woman's relationship with her man is a matter of interplay between two unique personalities, and can be worked out individually. In reality, every such relationship is a *class* relationship, and the conflicts between individual men and women are *political* conflicts that can only be solved collectively.

III. We identify the agents of our oppression as men. Male supremacy is the oldest, most basic form of domination. All other forms of exploitation and oppression (racism, capitalism, imperialism, etc.) are extensions of male supremacy: men dominate women, a few men dominate the rest. All power structures throughout history have been male-dominated and male-oriented. Men have controlled all

From *Redstockings Manifesto*, July 7, 1969. Reprinted with permission of the Redstockings Women's Liberation Archives. The "Redstockings Manifesto" was launched by Redstockings of the Women's Liberation Movement on July 7, 1969. A catalog containing ordering information for this and other documents from the 1960s rebirth years of feminism, is available from the Redstockings Women's Liberation Archives Distribution Project, P.O. Box 2625, Gainesville, FL 32602-2625.

political, economic and cultural institutions and backed up this control with physical force. They have used their power to keep women in an inferior position. *All men* receive economic, sexual, and psychological benefits from male supremacy. *All men* have oppressed women.

IV. Attempts have been made to shift the burden of responsibility from men to institutions or to women themselves. We condemn these arguments as evasions. Institutions alone do not oppress; they are merely tools of the oppressor. To blame institutions implies that men and women are equally victimized, obscures the fact that men benefit from the subordination of women, and gives men the excuse that they are forced to be oppressors. On the contrary, any man is free to renounce his superior position provided that he is willing to be treated like a woman by other men.

We also reject the idea that women consent to or are to blame for their own oppression. Women's submission is not the result of brainwashing, stupidity, or mental illness but of continual, daily pressure from men. We do not need to change ourselves, but to change men.

The most slanderous evasion of all is that women can oppress men. The basis for this illusion is the isolation of individual relationships from their political context and the tendency of men to see any legitimate challenge to their privileges as persecution.

V. We regard our personal experience, and our feelings about that experience, as the basis for an analysis of our common situation. We cannot rely on existing ideologies as they are all products of male supremacist culture. We question every generalization and accept none that are not confirmed by our experience.

Our chief task at present is to develop female class consciousness through sharing experience and publicly exposing the sexist foundation of all our institutions. Consciousness-raising is not "therapy," which implies the existence of individual solutions and falsely assumes that the male-female relationship is purely personal, but the only method by which we can ensure that our program for liberation is based on the concrete realities of our lives.

The first requirement for raising class consciousness is honesty, in private and in public, with ourselves and other women.

VI. We identify with all women. We define our best interest as that of the poorest, most brutally exploited woman.

We repudiate all economic, racial, educational or status privileges that divide us from other women. We are determined to recognize and eliminate any prejudices we may hold against other women.

We are committed to achieving internal democracy. We will do whatever is necessary to ensure that every woman in our movement has an equal chance to participate, assume responsibility, and develop her political potential.

VII. We call on all our sisters to unite with us in struggle.

We call on all men to give up their male privileges and support women's liberation in the interest of our humanity and their own.

In fighting for our liberation we will always take the side of women against their oppressors. We will not ask what is "revolutionary" or "reformist," only what is good for women.

The time for individual skirmishes has passed. This time we are going all the way.

6

THE FEMINISTS

A Political Organization to Annihilate Sex Roles (1969)

HISTORY

On October 17, 1968, in New York City, a group of feminists decided to begin a new kind of feminist movement: radical feminism. Most of us

From *Notes from the Second Year*, 1970.

had been crossing organizational lines during the past year in the attempt to formulate an adequate solution to the persecution of women. But it had finally become evident that what we were groping for was not the sum of current ideas on women, but an approach altogether new not only to feminism but to political theory as well.

We decided to operate under the transitional name of the day of our beginning, *October 17th,* until we were prepared to outline our analysis of the class condition of women and its implications and to present our program for the elimination of that class condition. We are now ready to present our analysis and plan and, therefore, announce the formation of our organization: THE FEMINISTS.   *June 13, 1969*

I. CONCEPTUAL ANALYSIS

The class separation between men and women is a political division. It is in the interests of those individuals who assume the powerful role and against the interests of those assigned the powerless role. The role (or class) system must be destroyed.

The role system is neither necessary to nor in the interests of society. It distorts the humanity of the Oppressor and denies the humanity of the Oppressed. The members of the powerful class substitute the appropriation of others to extend the significance of their own existence as an alternative to individual self-creativity. The members of the powerless class are thereby prevented from individual self-creativity. The role system is an attempt to justify living for those who believe there is no possible justification for life in and of itself.

Women, or "females," were the first class to be separated out from humanity and thus denied their humanity. While men performed this expulsion, it is the male role or the role of the Oppressor that must be annihilated—not necessarily those individuals who presently claim the role. Men, as the only possible embodiment of the male role and as the first embodiment of the Oppressor role, are the enemies and the Oppressors of women. The female role is the product of the male role: it is the female's self-defense against the external coercions imposed by the male role. But because the female role is the internal adjustment of the female to the male role, the female role stabilizes the role system. Both the male role and the female role must be annihilated.

It is clear that, in addition to the role system, all those institutions which reinforce these humanly restrictive definitions must be eliminated. But we are not sure yet how many forms in human culture are patterned on the role system. Certainly all those institutions which were designed on the assumption and for the reinforcement of the male and female role system such as the family (and its sub-institution, marriage), sex, and love must be destroyed. In order to annihilate these institutions, we must clearly understand the dynamics *within* them. Until we fully understand these dynamics, we cannot know everything that must be eliminated nor the desirable form of our alternative.

All political classes grew out of the male-female role system, were modeled on it, and are rationalized by it and its premises. Once a new class system is established on the basis of this initial one, the new class is then used to reinforce the male-female system. It is necessary for the members of all classes to understand and root out of our value system those principles and justifications for classifying any individual out of humanity.

The pathology of oppression can only be fully comprehended in its primary development: the male-female division. Because the male-female system is primary, the freedom of every oppressed individual depends upon the freeing of every individual from every aspect of the male-female system. The sex roles themselves must be destroyed. If any part of these role definitions is left, the disease of oppression remains and will reassert itself again in new, or the same old, variations throughout society.

In addition, we must propose a moral alternative for the self-justification of life to our present system of the appropriation and denial of other individuals' humanity. We need a new premise for society: that the most basic right of every individual is to create the terms of its own definition.   *July 15, 1969*

II. ORGANIZATIONAL PRINCIPLES AND STRUCTURE

THE FEMINISTS is a group of radical feminists committed to intense study of the persecution of women and direct action to eradicate this persecution.

The group is open only to women who accept our principles as recorded in these FEMINISTS papers. Membership must be a primary commitment and responsibility; no other activity may supersede work for the group.

THE FEMINISTS is an action group. The theoretical work we do is aimed directly at studying the means by which women are oppressed so that we may effectively plan positions and actions to fight our oppression. Outside study, participation in discussions, completion of individual assignments *and* attendance at actions are all equally important and compulsory.

In order to achieve the goal of freeing women, the group must maintain discipline. Any member who consistently disrupts or interferes with our discussions or activities may be expelled. A single action which goes against the will of the group, constitutes an exploitation of the group, or seriously endangers its work or survival, is grounds for expulsion. Expulsion of a member requires a two-thirds majority decision of all members present at a meeting about which notification has been sent to all members at least ten days in advance.

Since infiltration of the group is not unlikely, if a member suspects another of being an infiltrator, that member should confront her before a meeting of the group. When the act of infiltration is established to the satisfaction of the group, the agent(s) will be expelled immediately.

THE FEMINISTS is an organization without officers which divides work according to the principle of participation by lot. Our goal is a just society all of whose members are equal. Therefore, we aim to develop knowledge and skills in all members and prevent any one member or small group from hoarding information or abilities.

Traditionally official posts such as the chair of the meeting and the secretary are determined by lot and change with each meeting. The treasurer is chosen by lot to function for one month.

Assignments may be menial or beyond the experience of a member. To assign a member work she is not experienced in may involve an initial loss of efficiency but fosters equality and allows all members to acquire the skills necessary for revolutionary work. When a member draws a task beyond her experience she may call on the knowledge of other members, but her own input and development are of primary importance. The group has the responsibility to support a member's efforts, as long as the group believes that member to be working in good faith. A member has the duty to submit her work for the group—such as articles and speeches—to the group for correction and approval.

In order to make efficient use of all opportunities for writing and speaking, in order to develop members without experience in these areas, members who are experienced in them are urged to withdraw their names from a lot assigning those tasks. Also those members, experienced or inexperienced, who have once drawn a lot to write or speak must withdraw their names until all members have had a turn.

The system of the lot encourages growth by maximizing the sharing of tasks, but the responsibility for contributions rests ultimately with the individual. One's growth develops in proportion to one's contributions.   *August 22, 1969*

7

NEW YORK RADICAL FEMINISTS

Politics of the Ego: A Manifesto (1969)

Radical feminism recognizes the oppression of women as a fundamental political oppression

From *Notes from the Second Year*, 1970.

wherein women are categorized as an inferior class based upon their sex. It is the aim of radical feminism to organize politically to destroy this sex class system.

As radical feminists we recognize that we are engaged in a power struggle with men, and that the agent of our oppression is man insofar as he identifies with and carries out the supremacy privileges of the male role. For while we realize that the liberation of women will ultimately mean the liberation of men from their destructive role as oppressor, we have no illusion that men will welcome this liberation without a struggle.

Radical feminism is political because it recognizes that a group of individuals (men) have organized together for power over women, and that they have set up institutions throughout society to maintain this power.

A political power institution is set up for a purpose. We believe that the purpose of male chauvinism is primarily to obtain psychological ego satisfaction, and that only secondarily does this manifest itself in economic relationships. For this reason we do not believe that capitalism, or any other economic system, is the cause of female oppression, nor do we believe that female oppression will disappear as a result of a purely economic revolution. The political oppression of women has its own class dynamic; and that dynamic must be understood in terms previously called "non-political"—namely the politics of the ego.

Thus the purpose of the male power group is to fulfill a need. That need is psychological, and derives from the supremacist assumptions of the male identity—namely that the male identity be sustained through its ability to have power over the female ego. Man establishes his "manhood" in direct proportion to his ability to have his ego override woman's, and derives his strength and self-esteem through this process. This male need, though destructive, is in that sense impersonal. It is not out of a desire to hurt the woman that man dominates and destroys her; it is out of a need for a sense of power that he necessarily must destroy her ego and make it subservient to his. Hostility

to women is a secondary effect; to the degree that a man is not fulfilling his own assumptions of male power he hates women. Similarly, a man's failure to establish himself supreme among other males (as for example a poor white male) may make him channel his hostility into his relationship with women, since they are one of the few political groups over which he can still exercise power.

As women we are living in a male power structure, and our roles become necessarily a function of men. The services we supply are services to the male ego. We are rewarded according to how well we perform these services. Our skill—our profession—is our ability to be feminine—that is, dainty, sweet, passive, helpless, ever-giving and sexy. In other words, everything to help reassure man that he is primary. If we perform successfully, our skills are rewarded. We "marry well"; we are treated with benevolent paternalism; we are deemed successful women, and may even make the "women's pages."

If we do not choose to perform these ego services, but instead assert ourselves as primary to ourselves, we are denied the necessary access to alternatives to express our self-assertion. Decision-making positions in the various job fields are closed to us; politics (left, right or liberal) are barred in other than auxiliary roles; our creative efforts are *a priori* judged not serious because we are females; our day-to-day lives are judged failures because we have not become "real women."

Rejection is economic in that women's work is underpaid. It is emotional in that we are cut off from human relationships because we choose to reject the submissive female role. We are trapped in an alien system, just as the worker under capitalism is forced to sell his economic services in a system which is set up against his self-interest.

SEXUAL INSTITUTIONS

The oppression of women is manifested in particular institutions, constructed and maintained to keep women in their place. Among these are the institutions of marriage, motherhood, love, and sexual intercourse (the family unit is incorporated by the above). Through these institutions the woman is taught to confuse her biological sexual differences with her total human potential. Biology is destiny, she is told. Because she has childbearing capacity, she is told that motherhood and child rearing is her function, not her option. Because she has childbearing capacity she is told that it is her function to marry and have the man economically maintain her and "make the decisions." Because she has the physical capacity for sexual intercourse, she is told that sexual intercourse too is her function, rather than just a voluntary act which she may engage in as an expression of her general humanity.

In each case *her* sexual difference is rationalized to trap her within it, while the male sexual difference is rationalized to imply an access to all areas of human activity.

Love, in the context of an oppressive male-female relationship, becomes an emotional cement to justify the dominant-submissive relationship. The man "loves" the woman who fulfills her submissive ego-boosting role. The woman "loves" the man she is submitting to—that is, after all, why she "lives for him." LOVE, magical and systematically unanalyzed, becomes the emotional rationale for the submission of one ego to the other. And it is deemed every woman's natural function to love.

Radical feminism believes that the popularized version of love has thus been used politically to cloud and justify an oppressive relationship between men and women, and that in reality there can be no genuine love until the need to *control* the growth of another is replaced by love *for* the growth of another.

LEARNING TO BECOME FEMININE

The process of training women for their female role begins as far back as birth, when a boy child is preferred over a girl child. In her early years, when the basic patterns of her identity are being established, it is reinforced in her that her female role is not a choice but a fact. Her future will be spent performing the same basic func-

tions as her mother and women before her. Her life is already determined. She is not given the choice of exploring activity toys. Her brothers play astronaut, doctor, scientist, race-car driver. She plays little homemaker, future mother (dolls), and nurse (doctor's helper). Her brothers are given activity toys; the world is their future. She is given service toys. She is already learning that her future will be in the maintenance of others. Her ego is repressed at all times to prepare her for this future submissiveness. She must dress prettily and be clean; speak politely; seek approval; please. Her brothers are allowed to fight, get dirty, be aggressive and be self-assertive.

As she goes through school she learns that subjects which teach mastery and control over the world, such as science and math, are male subjects; while subjects which teach appearance, maintenance, or sentiment, such as home economics or literature, are female subjects. School counselors will recommend nursing for girls, while they will encourage boys to be doctors. Most of the best colleges will accept only a token sprinkling of women (quota system), regardless of academic abilities.

By the time she is of marrying age she has been prepared on two levels. One, she will realize that alternatives to the traditional female role are both prohibitive and prohibited; two, she will herself have accepted on some levels the assumptions about her female role.

INTERNALIZATION

It is not only through denying women human alternatives that men are able to maintain their positions of power. It is politically necessary for any oppressive group to convince the oppressed that they are in fact inferior, and therefore deserve their situation. For it is precisely through the destruction of women's egos that they are robbed of their ability to resist.

For the sake of our own liberation, we must learn to overcome this damage to ourselves through internalization. We must begin to destroy the notion that we are indeed only servants to the male ego, and must begin to reverse the systematic crushing of women's egos by constructing alternate selves that are healthy, independent and self-assertive. We must, in short, help each other to transfer the ultimate power of judgment about the value of our lives from men to ourselves.

It remains for us as women to fully develop a new dialectic of sex class—an analysis of the way in which sexual identity and institutions reinforce one another.   *A. K. / December, 1969*

8
WESTCHESTER RADICAL FEMINISTS
Statement of Purpose (1972)

Suburban women, in common with all women, have lived in intimacy with and dependence on our oppressor. In isolation and tightly bound to our families, we have viewed the world and our condition from the level of patriarchal ideas of money and power. We now recognize that these patriarchal concepts have and still do dominate and control our lives, but our thinking, hopes and aspirations are changing. We are analyzing our past, present and future according to new feminist concepts and are beginning to discover that there can be new ways of dealing with our problems and our lives.

As suburban women, we recognize that many of us live in more economic and material comfort than our urban sisters, but we have come to realize through the woman's movement, feminist ideas and consciousness raising, that this comfort only hides our essential powerlessness and oppression. We live in comfort only to the extent that our homes, clothing and the services we receive feed and prop the status and egos of the men who support us. Like dogs on a leash, our own status and power will reach as far as our husbands and their income and prestige will allow. As human beings, as individuals, we, in fact,

From Anne Koedt, Ellen Levine, and Anita Rapone, eds., *Radical Feminism* (New York: Quadrangle Books, 1973), 384–87.

own very little and should our husbands leave us or us them, we will find ourselves with the care and responsibility of children and without money, jobs, credit or power. For this questionable condition, we have paid the price of isolation and exploitation by the institutions of marriage, motherhood, psychiatry and consumerism. Although our life styles may appear materially better, we are, as all women, dominated by men at home, in bed and on the job; emotionally, sexually, domestically and financially.

Traditionally, as women and suburban women, we have put the cause of others before our own and are now determined to uphold our rights as top priority. Because we are convinced that all oppression stems from the fundamental oppression of women by men, it will follow that men will benefit from our liberation even though they may fight, resist and not welcome the change. We want to be identified as female liberationists and not as human liberators. Those men who agree with our cause will find a way to support us and we will welcome them, but it is not our job to convince, care for or teach men what we know to be right.

Although we are, as women, united on the basis of our common feelings and experiences, we are also individuals with varied ideas, preferences and goals. These differences are not antagonistic but are an indication of the richness and variety of our ideas and contributions. We, therefore, hope to remain loosely organized to allow individual expression and freedom to work and struggle through thoughts, feelings and ideas. Total agreement is not our goal but self realization, self initiative, mutual respect and a large variety of alternatives and choices are essentially what we hope to achieve.

We believe that:

1. The notion of fixed sex roles is arbitrary and unjust.

2. That suburbia is a wasteland; a human ghetto for women minimizing their opportunity for growth.

3. That diverse forms of sexual relationships based on mutual consent are a matter of individual choice and right.

4. The institution of marriage presumes and establishes the life-long servitude of women.

5. All economic institutions subject and deprive the suburban women, as well as all women, of economic power; even her power as a consumer is a myth since she spends and buys no more than her husband will allow.

6. Women are no more inherently suited to child rearing than men and men must be held responsible also for the emotional, educational and physical development of children.

7. The mutual dependence of mothers and children is in essence an act of tyranny which serves to thwart, retard and immobilize both mother and children.

8. The adjustment theories adhered to by most psychologists and psychiatrists and their institutions perpetuate destructive attitudes towards women, undermine their self value and self esteem and are generally harmful to the wholesome development and welfare of women.

9. The fact that we live with and even support some of these institutions which are sexist does not in any way alter our basic beliefs. We presently live the way we do because there are no good alternatives.

10. Women's liberation is not human liberation and we place the cause of women above all other causes.

11. We are committed to the understanding of our condition as women so that we may create and invent new ways to live and to find both collective and individual realization and strength.

A group of 15 Westchester women

May, 1972

The WESTCHESTER RADICAL FEMINISTS is currently involved in:

1. Consciousness raising.

2. Analyzing our condition in the institutions of psychiatry, marriage, motherhood.

3. Writing about the problems of suburban women.

4. Actively supporting abortion legislation.

5. Engaging in self-help supportive counseling.

6. Attacking sexist practices in local institutions such as schools, town clubs, local governments.

7. Each woman is encouraged to find or organize an action which interests her.

9

APHRA

Preamble (1969)

Tired of Bellowing and Rothing, Mailering and Malamuding, we looked around at the current literary scene and decided that, for whatever reasons of history and economics, it is still, or perhaps more than ever, dominated by the Judeo-Christian patriarchal ethos. Women have more to give the world than babies. Whole areas of life, of consciousness and feeling are crying for recording and interpretation from within. Too long have women been seen from outside and from afar. Too long have we been brainwashed with male stereotypes of what they are like and what we are like. The view from the bottom may not be wide, but it is deep and upward, and for centuries women have had unique opportunities for practicing observation.

Works of art are bigger than theses, subject to multiple planes of interpretation. We propose a magazine that will give outlet to the feminine consciousness, a magazine free of ulterior motives, interested only in giving women a chance to express themselves and to see themselves. In these days of artistic confusion when the words avant-garde and arriere-garde have lost meaning, leaving fashion as the dominator, we shall seek work that will speak to women on an esthetic level. We submit that one reason for the form of the current upsurge in feminism—the rap session, the group meeting with individuals bearing witness, the opportunity for community and

From *Aphra*, Fall 1969.

identification—is that the mass media provide such biased and commercially oriented material. The literary and entertainment scene are dominated by male stereotypes, male fantasies, male wish fulfillment, a male power structure. In consequence women have begun spontaneously to band together and create their own consciousness. Groups have been springing up all over the country, multiplying by division. This is all well and good, but there is a need for a less evanescent form of expression. We shall meet on paper, offering work in which women can see themselves, offering them the identification and shock of recognition which art traditionally gives, but which is clearly underexpressed in the current scene—be it book publishing, television, theatre, magazine or film.

The idea then is to encourage women as women, not in terms of male syndromes nor with preconceptions imposed from outside, whether by Freud or Madison Avenue market researchers. If we have a special bias for women it is because they need it: they have been getting a raw deal for centuries, and the reform movement of the nineteenth and early twentieth centuries has suffered from the backlash of the forties and fifties. The emphasis will be on art, not ideology. We shall publish what we like and what we respond to, with the idea that we shall be speaking directly to women so that they can say "There am I" and feel stronger and more doing.

10

ASIAN WOMEN

This Isn't One of Those Blonds That Anyone Can Pick Up in a Supermarket (1971)

During this last year a group of us in Berkeley began to meet to critically examine and discuss our roles as Asian women. Significantly, our efforts have been met with enthusiasm, hostility,

From *Asian Women*, July 1971.

curiosity, understanding, caution, relief, anger, joy and always—controversy.

We discovered other Asian women were meeting, too, so we decided that we should begin to share our thoughts, ideas, and experiences. As a vehicle for this communication, we would attempt to publish a journal in April on and by Asian women.

We contacted Asian women in all parts of the country, of many political beliefs, of all ages and backgrounds. We invited all women in the Asian community to submit articles, whether historical, analytical, or personal, art work, photos, poetry, and short stories. We hoped that this journal would give more Asian sisters an opportunity to express their opinions.

In the process of creating the journal, we discovered that we were ill-prepared. Most of us met in Asian Studies 170, a Proseminar on Asian Women given by Asian Studies at UC Berkeley. We came to the course seeking knowledge and relief to the uneasiness in being Asian women. We faced a dilemma. We were not satisfied with the traditional Asian roles, the white middle-class standards, or the typical Asian women stereotypes in America. We wanted our own identity.

Beginning with this course we saw the roles of women in history were ignored even though women had played a large part in making history. In addition, we saw that we faced a double oppression not only as being women but also as Asians. The white middle-class woman's liberation movement was not totally relevant to our lives. We had to create our own roles as Asian women.

WE BEGAN ENTHUSIASTICALLY because we were not alone anymore in our struggle for womanhood. At first we expected the journal to be published in April, but as you can see the journal was not completed until July. Articles were late, and the deadline was pushed back again and again because the writers and our group had so many other commitments—school, jobs, families—and significantly, because we were reluctant to write. There seems to be a mysticism about putting ideas and experiences onto paper. We would talk to women about writing articles about some aspect of their work or lives and they answered: "Oh, not me. I can't write."

We constantly struggled with this problem in our sisters and within the group. In fact, the articles from the group were the very last to be completed for the journal.

For a while in the beginning, we worried if anyone would submit articles, but they did eventually trickle in. When we had the articles, we were unsure as to how much or what kind of editing we should do. Some of us in editing found that we differed with what articles said, and if we ourselves had written them, we would have written them differently. We questioned ourselves. Were we trying to make the articles represent our thoughts and not the author's? We finally resolved this by printing the articles essentially as the authors meant them to be except for grammatical corrections. The articles vary in topics and vary in quality in terms of writing style. Some are well-documented research papers and others are intensely personal essays. The Journal is a wide assortment of articles, photos, poems, graphics, and sundry papers.

This journal has no hierarchy. We feel that every woman has something to say, and each is valuable. Though we did not always agree with the articles, we feel each article has something to offer.

Another delay in the completion is that we as a group in the course of the last six months found other projects that needed attention—Chinese New Year's Dinner in S.F. Chinatown, working with new students in the Asian women's course, Asian political organization, organizing Bay Area Third World women for the Indochina Women's Conference in Vancouver. It is not to say that these projects were not worthwhile, but that there is so much for us to do as women, as Asians, and as Asian women.

Within our group there were so many problems for us to deal with. Most of our meetings were involved with the mechanics of printing the Journal—when could we all meet (minor you think, but it was major fitting our 12 odd schedules together), division of responsibilities, finding a place to work, what format and type to use, which printer would give us the best price, what should be the price of the journal, and how to finance the cost. Not only did we have technical problems but we had policy questions like—editing and whether we would accept article contributions from men or white women. We decided that our first priority were Asian women. We felt women must learn to work collectively and to be self-reliant. It is more of a unique building experience for women to create something by themselves, and to know they did it together without men helping or directing. There are only three incidents of this policy breaking down—1) the printers, 2) use of historical photos, and 3) the annotated bibliography which white sisters from the Asian women's course worked on.

WE HAD MANY PROBLEMS WITH OUR brothers, they would say:

"Oh, one of the women's group . . ." with all-knowing smiles. They would classify and lump us into a women's liberation stereotype without knowing very much about it, except for images from the mass media or images conjured up by their own prejudices. They somehow assumed to know everything about the women's liberation movement, without ever bothering to do serious reading or bothering to have serious discussion about the multiplicity of perspectives and politics in the movement. So we became the target of joking and ignorance. Individuals became so identified with the group that it inhibited our participation in other activities. . . . [O]ur suggestions and questions were written off by calling us "one of the women's group." Even our most progressive brothers were guilty of this! In fact it was even more discouraging to hear lip service from supposedly "together, radical" brothers. As for ourselves we were often guilty of not confronting our brothers and sisters on the problems of sexism out of weariness, fear of destroying our relationships or inability to deal with the situation in a constructive manner.

The most crucial problem that we realized happened while we were writing our position paper. We discovered that in putting out the journal we neglected the personal development of the group. We failed to explore ideologies and analyses of other women's groups. We failed to discuss our personal problems in being women. As a result, we have yet to raise our consciousness as fully as we hoped. In reflection many problems about the direction of the journal came from the need of discussion sessions.

IN SPITE OF all the problems in putting out this journal, we feel it has a lot to offer to our sisters and brothers and would appreciate hearing your feelings.

As a result of this journal, we would like to work on another with more definite positions on institutions which affect women. If there is anything that we have learned in the last year, it is that personal experiences are not private but common to all women. Out of common experiences political struggle is created.

SISTERHOOD IS POWERFUL

11

Women: A Journal of Liberation
Founding Editorial (1969)

This Journal is intended to be of use to women engaged in struggle: struggle for greater awareness and struggle to change conditions. The Journal will serve as a forum of opinion and expression vital to a growing Women's Liberation Movement. Each issue will be built around a theme in an attempt to push beneath the generalizations concerning women and the rhetoric which cramps the movement.

It is clear that a mass movement of women is surging across the country. In every historical period of social upheaval, the woman question has emerged. This is so because women have always been oppressed. This time, the consciousness of women is extending beyond being a special constituency within the struggle. Now women realize that because of their special oppression and experience, they have creative insight and ability to contribute leadership to the total shaping of history.

All over the country women are talking and moving in new and diverse ways to combat their oppression. The potential creativity within the masses of women who are beginning to question their roles and identity is great and should not be destroyed by insistence upon rigid positions at this stage of our movement. To insist upon hard lines is not only a simple way out, but very dangerous. Women who refuse to listen to other women, who reject other women and their ideas, are detrimental to our movement. Each woman must come to a deep understanding of her own oppression through her own struggle; we cannot be told what we are supposed to think. We must go through the process ourselves in order for our commitment to be complete. At this time we do not believe any one person or group can speak for the diversity of women in this country. We are confident of the approach which says: Let dialogue take place; let action occur; the truth will be learned in the struggle.

We are a national magazine only in the sense that we wish to communicate the ideas and activities of women around the country. There are many different types of articles in this magazine. Some articles will appeal to women who are just starting to realize their oppression. Other articles will appeal to those who have already begun to struggle to change conditions. It is important that women who are isolated in pockets all over the country have an understanding of the vast complexity of what is going on and of the range and possibility of what we face at this moment in history.

We want everyone to have her say. That is what the whole upheaval today is about: people have not had their say about what is happening to them. We are dedicated to that end.

Our magazine is divided into four sections. In the theme section, articles were cho-

From *Women: A Journal of Liberation*, Fall 1969.

sen not necessarily for quality, in an academic or journalistic sense, but because of interest to a wider range of people, without overlapping topics. We realize that there are gaps in the theme section. We did not receive articles about women's home and work experiences. However, these topics fit into the theme of the next issue.

In the "Excerpts and Ideas" section we have printed something from almost every paper we received because every woman has a right to express her opinion and to be listened to. Women need to write. For too long, we have been afraid to have ideas and even more afraid to express them. We believe in this section because people can grow and change and develop by expressing their ideas.

The movement section is divided into news items and perspectives. In this issue the news covers a long time period since we've been receiving communications for the Journal for over a year. We hope that all groups will send us information about current activities so that this section will be up-to-date. In our perspective section, we are interested in specific strategies and analysis for our movement.

The next issue is "Liberation: Abortion, Childcare, Jobs, Self- Defense?" This idea is difficult to express in a title. These are topics which have been considered important in women's liberation struggles. We want to explore them more fully, to see what liberation really *means,* not only for women, but for men, children, and the whole society. We want to examine how the liberation of women is impossible under capitalism. We do not want vague rhetoric. We want details, specific experiences, studies of existing conditions, and models for structural change. The deadline for the next issue is December 1st. We encourage everyone to send articles, short stories, and art work.

We desperately need your support and money. This issue is going to press only 50% paid for. We need your contributions and subscriptions. We need your help in spreading the word about our magazine to your friends, your groups, and your local bookstore. This magazine is for *all* of us; it will succeed or fail depending on a *collective* effort.

12

Up from Under
Founding Editorial (1970)

When was the last time you heard someone say, "Mary just gave birth to her first baby, a little girl." Perhaps your response was, "Oh, that's nice, but didn't she want a boy?" Why don't we feel as lucky to have a girl? Why, right from the start, is a girl's life somehow less valuable than a boy's?

How often do we find little to speak about with pride but the accomplishments of our husbands, boyfriends, or children?

We *want* to like ourselves and each other. We know we can be creative and productive. But what happens to us? Are we the goddess-like creatures that supposedly represent us in the almost religious cliches about Home & Hearth? Certainly we don't feel like goddesses at the end of the day after we have removed our outrageously priced makeup, our new clothes already becoming obsolete, our padded bras, our girdles, and crawled into bed with stomachs grumbling because of some new diet. Hair too straight? Make it curly! Too curly? Make it straight! Too fat? Skinny? Whatever we are in our natural state is *no good,* and billions of dollars spent on advertising ("Blondes have more fun") each year won't let us forget it!

Seventy-five percent of all consumer purchases are made by women, but we have little economic power. We are the lowest paid workers. And what kind of jobs do we get? Never mind our educational achievements—can we type? Take shorthand? Make coffee? Sleep with the boss? Don't be "unfeminine" by showing how bright you really are.

Why should we work for low salaries all our lives, doing the work nobody wants to do?

From *Up from Under,* May/June 1970.

Why should we do more than half the boss's job at less than half his pay? Even the rare woman who manages to climb to the "top" still earns less than a man in the same position and she is often considered less of a woman. Marriage as a career begins to seem a desirable alternative. A great fear overtakes us; what will happen if we do not find a man? Our families pressure us. Nobody thinks that some of us might prefer to remain unmarried. To live without a man is to be subject to ridicule and ostracism.

And once we find husbands, what then? Full and loving relationships become difficult to realize as our lives and ambitions become secondary to our husbands'. After all, we were raised and educated to be helpmates and comforters, weren't we? Our heroes, all the important and exciting people, have always been men. We learned early that the boys would be firemen and we would be "mommies." They would be the doctors, we the nurses. They would grow up to be kings and presidents, and we—with the deepest sense of gratitude for being chosen—would be their faithful wives.

Then the shock to find ourselves in the dull, unending routine of housework. The movies never showed it that way! Chase Manhattan Bank estimates the average American woman works 99.6 hours a week. Much of this is in the home, work for which we receive no pay. And while having a baby is a wonderful experience, many of the pleasures of bringing up a child are negated as motherhood is made our only outlet for self-expression. We love our children, but we become disappointed and frustrated when they cannot fill all our needs. Moreover, most of us have finished raising our children by the age of thirty-five and are left with nothing meaningful to do. Loneliness and a sense of isolation set in, along with the fear that we are becoming uninteresting and dull.

Those of us who want to work outside our homes are made to feel guilty for not having the proper "instincts" to be full-time wives and mothers. This guilt has kept many women from entering the labor market—a situation not accidental, but which keeps most women as a sur-plus labor force to be called upon in times of crisis, such as during wartime. Nowadays, most women who do work are those that have to. (In 1964, 70 percent of working women supported themselves or others, or had husbands who earned less than $5,000.) Coming home, late at night, exhausted, these women still must shop, cook, and clean.

Our lives are said to be the most privileged, the most free of any women in the world. But what about the 10,000 of us who die each year from illegal abortions, the thousands of women in mental institutions, the quiet suicides in lovely suburban homes, the one in three marriages that ends in divorce, and the millions of women who turn in desperation to alcohol, tranquilizers, and barbiturates?

And what about those of us who get down on our hands and knees to clean the floors of empty offices when everybody else has gone home? Caring for a family—always left to the woman—is made extra difficult for low-income women who cannot afford modern conveniences. And when the children get sick—which happens often because of inadequate diets and cold and crowded slum dwellings—it is their mothers who must wait with them for hours in understaffed, poorly serviced health clinics. Many of these women must face the compounded burden of being non-white in a racist society.

We feel strongly that the ways women are exploited in this society are *not the result of inherent differences between women and men*. We think the inferior roles women play, and the limited options available, are perpetuated by our society, a society which finds it profitable to keep us "in our place." We are determined to redefine what it means to be a woman.

We do not believe that role-reversal is the answer, that men should spend their time thinking of ways to appear sexy and planning elaborate meals for us, or that we should be in their places. We feel sadness for those men who are stunted in their stereotyped and strong-but-silent roles, emotional outlets denied them, alienated from their work and families, their manliness equated with the size of their paychecks. Like us, they have been channeled by their education and economic needs into routinized jobs over which they have little control.

This magazine will examine all aspects of the "American way of life" to see what it does to us and what must be done to change it. We are not looking for more women in Congress, lady judges, or even female astronauts—tokenism will make no essential difference to our lives. We must learn that the problems we thought were our own are shared by all women, that only by understanding the *social* basis for our predicament and joining with other women in struggle can we make the basic structural changes that are necessary. We demand a society which will not divide and condemn people because of their sex, color, or class, a society which will be responsive to the real needs of all its people.

Thousands of women in this country have been discovering that their lives are of profound importance; that being a woman can be a cause for celebration; that even the smallest changes in our self-images can bring about new relationships with other women, with men, and with our children. Women everywhere are getting together. Small discussion and action groups are springing up across the country. We are finding new hope and strength in discovering that our experiences, our secret thoughts, our anger are shared by many, many other women.

Up From Under is designed, written, and produced by such a group of women. We are working women, students, and mothers who have been active in radical politics and have come to feel women's issues are crucial. We want to explore with all women the new insights, understanding, and enthusiasm that are growing out of the women's movement. Women deserve a magazine that will speak honestly and directly to their situation, a magazine that is not designed to push useless products, or to re-enforce the convenient stereotypes.

Women are 51 percent of this nation. Together we have enormous strength! Join us!

13

ROBIN MORGAN

Goodbye to All That (1970)

So, *Rat* has been liberated, for this week, at least. Next week? If the men return to reinstate the porny photos, the sexist comic strips, the "nude-chickie" covers (along with their patronizing rhetoric about being in favor of Women's Liberation)—if this happens, our alternatives are clear. *Rat* must be taken over permanently by women—or *Rat* must be destroyed.

Why *Rat*? Why not EVO or even the obvious new pornzines (Mafia-distributed alongside the human pornography of prostitution)? First, they'll get theirs—but it won't be a takeover, which is reserved for something at least *worth* taking over. Nor should they be censored. They should just be helped not to exist—by any means necessary. But *Rat*, which has always tried to be a really radical *cum* lifestyle paper—that's another matter. It's the liberal co-optative masks on the face of sexist hate and fear, worn by real nice guys we all know and like, right? We have met the enemy and he's our friend. And dangerous. "What the hell, let the chicks do an issue; maybe it'll satisfy 'em for a while, it's a good controversy, and it'll maybe sell papers"—runs an unheard conversation that I'm sure took place at some point last week.

And that's what I wanted to write about—the friends, brothers, lovers in the counterfeit male-dominated Left. The good guys who think they know what "Women's Lib," as they so chummily call it, is all

From *Rat: Subterranean News*, February 6, 1970. Reprinted in Robin Morgan, *The Word of a Woman: Feminist Dispatches 1968–1992,* 2d ed. (New York: W. W. Norton & Company, Inc., 1994). Copyright 1994 by Robin Morgan. Reprinted by permission of Edite Kroll Literary Agency, Inc.

about—and who then proceed to degrade and destroy women by almost everything they say and do: The cover on the last issue of *Rat* (front *and* back). The token "pussy power" or "clit militancy" articles. The snide descriptions of women staffers on the masthead. The little jokes, the personal ads, the smile, the snarl. NO more, brothers. No more well-meaning ignorance, no more co-optation, no more assuming that this thing we're all fighting for is the same: one revolution under *man*, with liberty and justice for all. No more.

Let's run it on down. White males are most responsible for the destruction of human life and environment on the planet today. Yet who is controlling the supposed revolution to change all that? White males (yes, yes, even with their pasty fingers back in black and brown pies again). It just could make one a bit uneasy. It seems obvious that a legitimate revolution must be led by, *made* by those who have been most oppressed: black, brown, and white *women*—with men relating to that the best they can. A genuine Left doesn't consider anyone's suffering irrelevant or titillating; nor does it function as a microcosm of capitalist economy, with men competing for power and status at the top, and women doing all the work at the bottom (and functioning as objectified prizes or "coin" as well). Goodbye to all that.

Run it all the way down.

Goodbye to the male-dominated peace movement, where sweet old Uncle Dave can say with impunity to a woman on the staff of *Liberation*, "The trouble with you is you're an aggressive woman."

Goodbye to the "straight" male-dominated Left: to PL who will allow that some workers are women, but won't see all women (say, housewives) as workers (just like the System itself); to all the old Leftover parties who offer their "Women's Liberation caucuses" to us as if that were not a contradiction in terms; to the individual anti-leadership leaders who handpick certain women to be leaders and then relate only to them, either in the male Left or in Women's Liberation—bringing their hang-ups

about power-dominance and manipulation to everything they touch.

Goodbye to the WeatherVain, with the Stanley Kowalski image and theory of free sexuality but practice of sex on demand for males. "Left Out!"—not Right On—to the Weather Sisters who, and they know better—they know—reject their own radical feminism for that last desperate grab at male approval that we all know so well, for claiming that the *machismo* style and the gratuitous violence is their own style by "free choice" and for believing that this is the way for a woman to make her revolution . . . all the while, oh my sister, not meeting my eyes because WeatherMen chose Manson as their—and your—Hero. (Honest, at least . . . since Manson is only the logical extreme of the normal American male's fantasy (whether he is Dick Nixon or Mark Rudd): master of a harem, women to do all the shitwork, from raising babies and cooking and hustling to killing people on order.) Goodbye to all that shit that sets women apart from women; shit that covers the face of any Weatherwoman which is the face of any Manson Slave which is the face of Sharon Tate which is the face of Mary Jo Kopechne which is the face of Beulah Saunders which is the face of me which is the face of Pat Nixon which is the face of Pat Swinton. *In the dark we are all the same*—and you better believe it: we're in the dark, baby. (Remember the old joke: Know what they call a black man with a Ph.D.? A nigger. Variation: Know what they call a Weatherwoman? A heavy cunt. Know what they call a Hip Revolutionary Woman? A groovy cunt. Know what they call a radical militant feminist? A crazy cunt. Amerika is a land of free choice—take your pick of titles. Left Out, my Sister—don't you see? Goodbye to the illusion of strength when you run hand in hand with your oppressors; goodbye to the dream that being in the leadership collective will get you anything but gonorrhea.

Goodbye to RYM II, as well, and all the other RYMs—not that the Sisters there didn't pull a cool number by seizing control, but because they let the men back in after only *a day or so* of self-criticism on male chauvinism. (And goodbye to the inaccurate blanket use of that phrase, for that matter: male chauvinism is an *attitude*—male supremacy is the *objective reality, the fact*.) Goodbye to the Conspiracy who, when lunching with fellow sexist bastards, Norman Mailer and Terry Southern in a bunny-type club in Chicago, found Judge Hoffman at the neighboring table no surprise: *in the light they are all the same.*

Goodbye to the Hip Culture and the so-called Sexual Revolution, which has functioned toward women's freedom as did the Reconstruction toward former slaves—reinstituted oppression by another name. Goodbye to the assumption that Hugh Romney is safe in his "cultural revolution," safe enough to refer to "our women, who make all our clothes" without somebody not forgiving that. Goodbye to the arrogance of power indeed that lets Czar Stan Freeman of the Electric Circus sleep without fear at night, or permits Tomi Ungerer to walk unafraid in the street after executing the drawing for the Circus advertising campaign against women. Goodbye to the idea that Hugh Hefner is groovy 'cause he lets Conspirators come to parties at the Mansion—goodbye to Hefner's dream of a ripe old age. Goodbye to Tuli and the Fugs and all the boys in the front room— who always knew they hated the women they loved. Goodbye to the notion that good ol' Abbie is any different from any other up and coming movie star (like, say Cliff Robertson) who ditches the first wife and kids, good enough for the old days but awkward once you're Making It. Goodbye to his hypocritical double standard that reeks through all the tattered charm. Goodbye to lovely pro-Women's-Liberation Paul Krassner, with all his astonished anger that women have lost their sense of humor "on this issue" and don't laugh anymore at little funnies that degrade and hurt them; farewell to the memory of his "Instant Pussy" aerosol-can poster, to his column for *Cavalier*, to his dream of a Rape-In against legislators' wives, to his Scapegoats

and Realist Nuns and cute anecdotes about the little daughter he sees as often as any proper divorced Scarsdale middle-aged (38) father; goodbye forever to the notion that he is my brother who, like Paul, buys a prostitute for the night as a birthday gift for a male friend, or who, like Paul, reels off the names in alphabetical order of people in the Women's Movement he has fucked, reels off names in the best locker room tradition—as proof that *he's* no sexist oppressor.

Let it all hang out. Let it seem bitchy, catty, dykey, frustrated, crazy, Solanisesque, nutty, frigid, ridiculous, bitter, embarrassing, man-hating, libelous, pure, unfair, envious, intuitive, low-down, stupid, petty, liberating. We are the women that men have warned us about.

And let's put one lie to rest for all time: the lie that men are oppressed, too, by sexism—the lie that there can be such a thing as "men's liberation groups." Oppression is something that one group of people commits against another group specifically because of a "threatening" characteristic shared by the latter group—skin color or sex or age, etc. The oppressors are indeed *fucked up* by being masters (racism hurts whites, sexual stereotypes are harmful to men) but those masters are not *oppressed*. Any master has the alternative of divesting himself of sexism or racism—the oppressed have no alternative—for they have no power— but to fight. In the long run, Women's Liberation will of course free men—but in the short run it's going to *cost* men a lot of privilege, which no one gives up willingly or easily. Sexism is *not* the fault of women—kill your fathers, not your mothers.

Run it on down. Goodbye to a beautiful new ecology movement that could fight to save us all if it would stop tripping off women as earth-mother types or frontier chicks, if it would *right now* cede leadership to those who have *not* polluted the planet because that action implies power and women haven't had any power in about 5,000 years, cede leadership to those whose brains are as tough and clear as any man's but whose bodies are also unavoidably aware of the locked-in relationship between humans and their biosphere—the earth, the tides, the atmosphere, the moon. Ecology is not big *schtick* if you're a woman—it's always been there.

Goodbye to the complicity inherent in the Berkeley Tribesmen being part publishers of the Trashman Comics; goodbye, for that matter, to the reasoning that finds whoremaster Trashman a fitting model, however comic-strip far out, for a revolutionary man—somehow related to the same Supermale reasoning that permits the first statement on Women's Liberation and male chauvinism that came out of the Black Panther Party to be made *by a man*, talkin' a whole lot 'bout how the Sisters should speak up for themselves. Such ignorance and arrogance ill befits a revolutionary.

We know how racism is worked deep into the unconscious by our System—the same way sexism is, as it appears in the very name of The Young Lords. What are you if you're a "macho woman"—a female Lord? Or god forbid, a Young Lady? Change it, change it to The Young Gentry if you must, or never assume that the name itself is innocent of pain, of oppression.

Theory and practice—and the light-years between them. "Do it!" says Jerry Rubin in *Rat's* last issue—but he doesn't, or every *Rat* reader would have known the pictured face next to his article as well as they know his own much-photographed face: it was Nancy Kurshan, the power behind the clown.

Goodbye to the New Nation and Earth People's Park, for that matter, conceived by men, announced by men, led by men—doomed before its birth by the rotting seeds of male supremacy which are to be transplanted in fresh soil. Was it my brother who listed human beings among the *objects* which would be easily available after the Revolution: "Free grass, free food, free women, free acid, free clothes, etc."? Was it my brother who wrote "Fuck your women till they can't stand up" and said that groupies were liberated chicks 'cause they dug a "tit-shake instead of a handshake"? The epitome of female exclusionism—"men

will make the Revolution and their chicks." Not my brother, no. Not my revolution. Not one breath of my support for the new counterleft Christ John Sinclair. Just one less to worry about for ten years. I do not choose my enemy for my brother.

Goodbye, goodbye. The hell with the simplistic notion that automatic freedom for women—or non-white peoples—will come about ZAP! with the advent of a socialist revolution. Bullshit. Two evils pre-date capitalism and have been clearly able to survive and post-date socialism: sexism and racism. Women were the first property when the Primary Contradiction occurred: when one half of the human species decided to subjugate the other half, because it was "different," alien, the Other. From there it was an easy enough step to extend the Other to someone of different skin shade, different height or weight or language—or strength to resist. Goodbye to those simple-minded optimistic dreams of socialist equality all our good socialist brothers want us to believe. How liberal a politics that is! How much further we will have to go to create those profound changes that would give birth to a genderless society. *Profound*, Sister. Beyond what is male or female. Beyond standards we all adhere to now without daring to examine them as male-created, male-dominated, male-fucked-up, and in male self-interest. *Beyond all known standards*, especially those easily articulated revolutionary ones we all rhetorically invoke. Beyond, to a species with a new name, that would not dare define itself as Man.

I once said, "I'm a revolutionary, not just a woman," and knew my own lie even as I said the words. The pity of that statement's eagerness to be acceptable to those whose revolutionary zeal no one would question, i.e., any male supremacist in the counterleft. But to become a true revolutionary one must first become one of the oppressed (not organize or educate or manipulate them, but become one of them) or realize that you *are* one of them already. No woman wants that. Because that realization is humiliating, it hurts. It hurts to understand that at Woodstock or Altamont a woman could be declared uptight or a poor sport if she didn't want to be raped. It hurts to learn that the Sisters still in male-Left captivity are putting down the crazy feminists to make themselves look okay and unthreatening to our mutual oppressors. It hurts to be pawns in those games. It hurts to try and change *each day of your life right now*—not in talk, not "in your head," and not only conveniently "out there" in the Third World (half of which is women) or the black and brown communities (half of which are women) but in your own home, kitchen, bed. No getting away, no matter how else you are oppressed, from the primary oppression of being female in a patriarchal world. It hurts to hear that the Sisters in the Gay Liberation Front, too, have to struggle continually against the male chauvinism of their gay brothers. It hurts that Jane Alpert was cheered when rapping about imperialism, racism, the Third World, and All Those Safe Topics but hissed and booed by a Movement crowd of men who wanted none of it when she began to talk about Women's Liberation. The backlash is upon us.

They tell us the alternative is to hang in there and "struggle," to confront male domination in the counterleft, to fight beside or behind or beneath our brothers—to show 'em we're just as tough, just as revolushunerry, just as whatever-image-they-now-want-of-us-as once-they-wanted-us-to-be-feminine-and-keep-the-home-fire-burning. They will bestow titular leadership on our grateful shoulders, whether it's being a token woman on the Movement Speakers Bureau Advisory Board, or being a Conspiracy groupie or one of the "respectable" chain-swinging Motor City Nine. Sisters all, with only one real alternative: to seize our own power into our own hands, all women, separate and together, and make the Revolution the way it must be made—no priorities this time, no suffering group told to wait until after.

It is the job of revolutionary feminists to build an ever stronger independent Women's Liberation Movement, so that the Sisters in counterleft captivity will have somewhere to turn, to use their power and rage and beauty and coolness in their own behalf for once, on their own terms, on their own issues, in their own style—whatever that may be. Not for us in Women's Liberation to hassle them and confront them the way their men do, nor to blame them—or ourselves—for what any of us are: an oppressed people, but a people raising our consciousness toward something that is the other side of anger, something bright and smooth and cool, like action unlike anything yet contemplated or carried out. It is for us to survive (something the white male radical has the luxury of never really worrying about, what with all his options), to talk, to plan, to be patient, to welcome new fugitives from the counterfeit Left with no arrogance but only humility and delight, to plan, to push—to strike.

There is something every woman wears around her neck on a thin chain of fear—an amulet of madness. For each of us, there exists somewhere a moment of insult so intense that she will reach up and rip the amulet off, even if the chain tears at the flesh of her neck. And the last protection from seeing the truth will be gone. Do you think, tugging furtively every day at the chain and going nicely insane as I am, that I can be concerned with the puerile squabbles of a counterfeit Left that laughs at my pain? Do you think such a concern is noticeable when set alongside the suffering of more than half the human species for the past 5,000 years—due to a whim of the other half? No, no, no, goodbye to all that.

Women are Something Else. This time, we're going to kick out all the jams, and the boys will just have to hustle to keep up, or else drop out and openly join the power structure of which they are already the illegitimate sons. Any man who claims he is serious about wanting to divest himself of cock privilege should trip on this: all male leadership out of the Left is the only way; and it's going to happen, whether through men stepping down or through women seizing the helm. It's up to the "brothers"—after all, sexism is their concern, not ours; we're too busy getting ourselves together to have to deal with their bigotry. So they'll have to make up their own minds as to whether they will be divested of just cock privilege or—what the hell, why not say it, *say it?*—divested of cocks. How deep the fear of that loss must be, that it can be suppressed only by the building of empires and the waging of genocidal wars!

Goodbye, goodbye forever, counterfeit Left, counterleft, male-dominated cracked-glass-mirror reflection of the Amerikan Nightmare. Women are the real Left. We are rising, powerful in our unclean bodies; bright glowing mad in our inferior brains; wild hair flying, wild eyes staring, wild voices keening; undaunted by blood we who hemorrhage every twenty-eight days; laughing at our own beauty we who have lost our sense of human; mourning for all each precious one of us might have been in this one living time-place had she not been born a woman; stuffing fingers into our mouths to stop the screams of fear and hate and pity for men we have loved and love still; tears in our eyes and bitterness in our mouths for children we couldn't have, or couldn't *not* have, or didn't want, or didn't want *yet*, or wanted and had in this place and this time of horror. We are rising with a fury older and potentially greater than any force in history, and this time we will be free or no one will survive. **Power to all the people or to none.** All the way down, this time.

Free Kathleen Cleaver!
Free Anita Hoffman!
Free Bernadine Dohrn!
Free Donna Malone!
Free Ruth Ann Miller!
Free Leni Sinclair!
Free Jane Alpert!
Free Gumbo!
Free Bonnie Cohen!
Free Judy Lampe!
Free Kim Agnew!
Free Holly Krassner!
Free Lois Hart!

Free Alice Embree!
Free Nancy Kurshan!
Free Lynn Phyillips!
Free Dinky Forman!
Free Sharon Krebs!
Free Iris Luciano!
Free Robin Morgan!
Free Valerie Solanis!
FREE OUR SISTERS!   FREE OURSELVES!

14

SIREN: A JOURNAL OF ANARCHO-FEMINISM

Who We Are (1970)

We are dedicated to extremism in the cause of liberty.

We consider Anarcho-Feminism to be the ultimate and necessary radical stance at this time in world history, far more radical than any form of Marxism.

We believe that a Woman's Revolutionary Movement must not mimic but destroy all vestiges of the male-dominated power structure up to and including the apex of that power structure, the State itself—with its whole ancient and dismal apparatus of jails, armies, and armed robbery (taxation); with all of its murder; with all of its grotesque and repressive legislative and military attempts, internal and external, to interfere with people's private lives and freely-chosen co-operative enterprises.

The world obviously cannot survive many more decades of rule by gangs of armed males calling themselves governments. The situation is insane, ridiculous, and even suicidal. Whatever its varying forms or justifications, the armed State is what is threatening all of our lives at present. The State, by its inherent nature, is really incapable of reform. True Socialism, peace and plenty for all, can be achieved only by people themselves, not by "representatives," especially "representatives" ready and

From *Siren: A Journal of Anarcho-Feminism*, 1970.

able to turn guns on all who do not comply with State directives. As to how we proceed against the pathological State structure, perhaps the best word is outgrow rather than overthrow. This process entails, among other things, a tremendous thrust of education and communication among all peoples. The intelligence of womankind has at last been brought to bear on such oppressive male inventions as the Church and the Legal Family; it must now be brought to re-evaluate the ultimate stronghold of male domination, the State.

While we recognize important differences in the rival systems, our analysis of the evils of the State must extend to both its communist and its capitalist versions.

We intend to put to the test the concept of freedom of expression, which we trust will be incorporated in the ideology of the coming Socialist Sisterhood which is destined to play a determining role in the future of the race, if there really is to be a future.

We are all Socialists. We refuse to give up this pre-Marxist term which has been used as a synonym by many Anarchist thinkers. Another synonym for Anarchism is Libertarian Socialism, as opposed to statist and authoritarian varieties. Anarchism (from the Greek anarchos—without a ruler) is the affirmation of human freedom and dignity expressed in a negative, cautionary term signifying that no person should rule or dominate another person by force or threat of force. Anarchism indicates what people should not do to one another. Socialism, on the other hand, means all the groovy things people can do and build together, once they are able to combine efforts and resources on the basis of common interest, rationality, and creativity.

We love our Marxist sisters and all our sisters everywhere, and have no interest in disassociating ourselves from their constructive struggles. However, we reserve the right to criticize their politics when we feel that they are obsolete or irrelevant or inimical to the welfare of womankind.

As Anarcho-Feminists we aspire to have the courage to question and challenge ab-

solutely everything—including, when it proves necessary, our own assumptions.

15

SIREN: A JOURNAL OF ANARCHO-FEMINISM

What the Counter-Culture Isn't Just (1970)

Most people believe that the Counter Culture both begins and ends with rock music, dope, and fucking. In truth, it is compounded of religious and political philosophies taken from both East and West. The renaissance began well before this decade, was nourished in the early Bohemian cultures, flowered in Beatnik writings, and grew in earnest around the world as young people began exploring the thoughts of revolutionary sociologists, prophets, poets, junkies. Music was an energizing force; pot and acid opened our heads to new mystical, sensual, religious, and often whimsical experiences.

At the same time, a growing sense of social injustice was the motivating force which awakened us to the horrors of war, racism, and our own oppression as women. The emptiness, hypocrisy, and corruption of Twentieth Century industrialized, mechanized, plasticized Amerika made us search deeper for real values and meaning in our own lives.

As women, we have a special stake in criticizing not only capitalist society and government, but also male social theorists who, however well-meaning, have created different forms of bondage for women, even in some revolutionary societies. As women, we must question all authoritarian structure. People are beginning to realize that women will create the most revolutionary social change of all.

We begin to perceive our strength. Hope is a golden word.

From *Siren: A Journal of Anarcho-Feminism*, 1970.

16

WOMEN OF YOUTH AGAINST WAR AND RACISM

Specific Characteristics of Women's Liberation (1970)

The Women's Liberation Movement of today differs profoundly from all previous ones. Even the name suggests a fundamental change in the character of the movement. The very word "liberation" introduces a qualitatively different concept of the struggle than did words like "suffrage" and "equal rights."

No longer is it just another phase in the slow, gradual evolutionary process to merely enlarge the rights of women. No longer does it aim only to gain partial political, economic or social rights in one area or another.

The Women's Liberation Movement today seeks to strike at the very root of women's oppression. It calls for a total transformation of the subservient, secondary status of women in all phases of life.

This does not mean that many of the great women who waged such a stupendous battle in the last century for women's suffrage, as well as other political rights, didn't think in terms of changing the fundamental character of our entire role, status and position in society. Some actively fought for it all their lives, all the way back to the period of the French Revolution, when Mary Wollstonecraft wrote "A Vindication of the Rights of Woman," which was not one iota less eloquent than Tom Paine's "Rights of Man."

But the historical context of these early struggles was entirely different than that of today. It was no accident that the struggle for women's suffrage took place in this country concomitantly with the rise and development of the capitalist system itself. It was also the period of struggle against chattel slavery. It was a period when it seemed to many that new laws could provide justice and solve all inequities.

From *Battle Acts*, November 1970.

Women fought passionately and energetically for a variety of laws to improve our condition in a great many areas. Full equality, they hoped, would flow from that.

But many "feminine" traits and "masculine" traits, rooted in social prejudice and male privilege, were accepted even by some leaders as nothing more than norms of proper behavior and were not seriously challenged by and large. Education and the vote appeared to be, in the minds of most women active in the struggle, the basic remedy which would ultimately abolish female servitude.

In sharp contrast today, every concept that perpetuates inequality of the sexes is exposed and resolutely fought as part of the overall struggle. Each passing day brings new evidence that the struggle is conducted on the broadest front and covers the most varied forms of all the institutionalized, built-in forms of male domination on every level of capitalist society.

The earlier struggles of the women's movement were viewed within the framework of the establishment. Countless women waged a heroic, uphill fight in the face of monumental opposition. They valiantly faced ridicule, intimidation, isolation, harassment, physical violence and jail. But difficult as it was, the solution appeared to be within the confines of the existing system—in the struggle for equal laws.

How vastly different today! It is undoubtedly true that the moderate current in the movement, as exemplified by NOW (National Organization of Women) and similar groupings, is still the predominant one. But that is not what has special significance. Virtually all the great movements since the dawn of capitalist society, like this one, have been led in the initial stage by the middle class.

What is particularly significant and extremely encouraging is that there is also another current—a genuine revolutionary tendency among women. We only need look at some of the prolific literature in this movement to verify this. Much of it comes from the young militant women.

Today there are few who really believe that mere legislation under the present system will really change the basic status of women. On many levels, women are groping, seeking a way to hammer out a sound theoretical foundation as well as a strategic and tactical approach for the struggle.

As soon as the question is opened theoretically, the entire subject of the origin and development of the patriarchy is unavoidably and inevitably brought to the fore. This makes it necessary to open the books of Marx and Engels. Many women who have grappled with the question theoretically, beginning in 1945 with Simone de Beauvoir up to the present with Kate Millett, have been unable to avoid giving extensive attention to Frederick Engels' book, "Origin of the Family, Private Property and the State." This book, although written over 85 years ago, remains the bedrock for any historical materialist understanding of the family, the patriarchy and women's oppression.

Like today, the nineteenth-century women's movement had its origins in the white middle class, but over a period of decades, it gradually moved further and further to the right. By 1920, when the amendment granting women the right to vote was finally passed, the women's movement virtually disintegrated.

The contemporary movement also has its origins in the middle class, but in contradistinction to the earlier movement, it has considerable and growing revolutionary currents moving to the left. These currents not only identify with working, poor and oppressed women, but see themselves as a world force, and many within it are allied with all the anti-imperialist forces of the world.

In still another way the present movement is profoundly different in character from the earlier movement in that it carries on a *simultaneous struggle* on *all levels* and against all forms of male domination.

There is scarcely a city of any size these days in which we do not have *at least one* of more than a hundred possible activities of the women's movement—be it a consciousness-raising session in Croton Falls, a women's karate class in Champaign, Illinois, the seizing of the *Ladies Home Journal,* interruption of a CBS meeting in Los Angeles, innumerable picket liners, demonstrations and protests against restaurants, clubs, bars, newspapers, magazines, supermarkets, business institutions of every variety, as well as struggles and experiments on day care, welfare, liberation schools, abortion and contraception, etc., ad infinitum, and this is happening not only in every part of the country, but within differing class stratifications.

This broad-based, wide-front participation is not the way it used to be in the older movement. True, the actual level of struggle is still in a very early stage, but the *potential* is enormous.

There are some in the progressive movement today who say, or imply, that the struggle for women's liberation, vital as it is, should be a second priority; that the struggle for a revolutionary transformation of society, the elimination of capitalism, is the first priority.

The fundamental error in this view is that such a transformation of society is impossible if our struggle is second priority. The women's struggle is an indispensable element in the very prosecution of every struggle for the transformation to socialism.

Not only must we ceaselessly conduct a struggle on the specific issues of women's oppression, and against male chauvinism, but we must apply it in the general struggle against capitalism and imperialism. Whether it be in the opposition to the wars, the struggle against racism, for self-determination, or in struggles for national liberation, for higher wages or union representation, wherever there is any kind of progressive struggle, there must be the struggle for women's liberation. One segment or another of the revolutionary current of women's liberation must struggle actively, energetically and deliberately intervene, making its presence felt. And woe unto any progressive movement that fails to take this into account!

Superficially, or initially, it seems that the movement for Women's Liberation disregards or denies the validity of the class struggle. But already, there is a class differentiation going on within the movement. We believe that the struggle for Women's Liberation must be deepened and developed as a necessary requisite for any successful transformation of society to socialism.

17
FEMALE LIBERATION
A Statement About Female Liberation (1971)

Social attitudes toward women exist as the overt expression of centuries of female subjugation. The subordination of women is a real phenomenon which can be pointed out in every institution and structure in society. These institutions and structures through which women are oppressed constitute a system we define as sexism which is so deeply ingrained in every person's consciousness that most of it is not noticed or is accepted as normal. This system of sexism has also created a category of oppressed people comprising 53 percent of the human population.

Women have begun to voice their discontent with society. We have begun to talk about new alternatives. We are demanding complete control over our own lives and are beginning to act on these ideas and decisions. It is in this period of general awakening that women have come out wholly in favor of the basic rights long denied them. This insistence on the rights of women goes beyond simple legislative corrections (although we support and work for any legislation that improves our conditions here and now) and poses the question of woman's control of her life.

The nature of female oppression is such that we must question every aspect of our lives. There is nothing that we do or experience that can be separated from the fact that we are female. When we go out on the street, apply for a job, engage in any kind of social exchange or relations, society dictates that we are female

From *The Second Wave*, Spring 1971.

first and human beings second (if at all). All women are subject to this degradation and this is the source of our unity.

We are beginning to question every basic institution of society, including the nuclear family, because of the roles these institutions play in perpetuating our oppression.

We realize that we know nothing of female potential since all the energy, genius, strength and dignity of woman is refracted through the prism of sexism which distorts and limits our possibilities in every conceivable way.

In this emerging period of feminism we have come to understand the legitimacy of our grievances. We have insisted on the right to determine the character of our movement, and will not be turned back by those who feel that the oppression of females is of minor consequence. We are independent of and not a subcategory of other groups and movements.

Female Liberation is an organization which encompasses all aspects of the feminist struggle, including education, consciousness-raising activities, and action around such basic demands of the movement as childcare, abortion and equal pay. No woman is excluded from **Female Liberation** who is interested in the development of a strong, autonomous women's movement capable of bringing about change on every level.

It is becoming clear that this movement is reaching into every layer of the female population. We want to help mobilize the energies and power of these masses of women to fight for nothing less than our total liberation.

18
A SAN DIEGO WOMEN'S COLLECTIVE
About Us (1970)

Goodbye to All That was started by women from all over San Diego County. Our number includes students, artists, working women,

From *Goodbye to All That*, September 15, 1970.

mothers, housewives, and refugees from male-dominated groups in the San Diego Movement.

We have seen the systematic and pervasive oppression of women: economic, educational, psychological. For women to become liberated we feel we must work together *as women*. To liberate one we must end the oppression of all women.

We view Women's Liberation as part of the struggle of other oppressed people; true liberation can be achieved only when workers, blacks, Chicanos and homosexuals are free to fully develop their capacities as human beings. We believe that this presupposes a radical restructuring of society, including the creation of alternatives to the nuclear family and an end to the exploitation of human labor for profit.

GTAT is published by women working together in a truly collective way—no editors, hierarchy or big-wig "non-leaders."

Although we realize that our radical perspective is not at this time representative of the whole movement, we are open to ALL San Diego women who are interested in change. One great strength of the women's movement is that it cuts across all economic strata and applies to women of every race.

We cover relevant news in San Diego and elsewhere. In addition, we shall carry poetry, creative writing, letters, reviews and what-have-you. In short, we're here for you. We need your comments and contributions, literary and financial. We may also solicit your opinion on specific issues from time to time.

19

CHANGE
Who We Are (1972)

Change is written, published, and lived by a group of women who work in San Francisco. Our backgrounds are varied, but nearly all of us work in offices because that's what is open to

From *Change*, May 1972.

us. We don't have a common political party, but we have a common political experience.

Years ago working women fought for better conditions in the factories where they had to work for minimal wages while the factory owners made huge profits. We who work in offices now are the "factory workers" of San Francisco, in that it is the banks, insurance companies, etc., which form the basis of the economy here and now. And so we suffer inhuman conditions of our own age.

The basis for *Change* is our common realization that it is we working people whose daily production provides the means by which a very few other people make profit and derive power. Women in particular are a cheap labor force, with no control over our work places; in various ways we are kept in a position of having to sell ourselves to maintain this unbalanced system.

Among the common experiences which brought us together are anger/resentment/depression over things like these:

too little pay: constant hassle to meet basic expenses (rent, food, medical expenses, etc.); having to spend money on clothes, hair, makeup, etc., to maintain a "jobworthy" appearance;

having to work at jobs with no dignity: the job seems unnecessary or trivial, or you can't see its relation to anything, especially to your own life;

belittling job situation: you can't contribute your own ideas, or if you do, you don't get credit for them; you're always doing someone else's work (e.g., typing someone else's letters); you feel like a machine (an extension of the typewriter, keypunch, or whatever);

personally degrading circumstances: having to take abuse from your boss; doing humiliating slave labor like fetching coffee; not being able to fight back when you're put down by the boss; being referred to as "honey" or one of "the girls" (which through a false consciousness we often mistake for flattery) when we're mature and responsible adults;

sexist/racist discrimination: being fired or refused a raise or promotion for no apparent reason; getting less pay than someone else who is doing identical work; doing a kind of work you hate because that's all you *can* do or were trained to do (because of tracking systems in school, for instance); wanting to get into a different type of work but being prevented from it (for no apparent reason, but you know it's because you're a woman, a Chicana, a Black, or . . .);

inability to work or go to school because of being tied down to the children—you can't find or afford a babysitter;

being too tired from spending all day at work to do a lot of things you *want* to do (including trying to change things);

having two jobs at once—one 8-hour job for pay, one continual job keeping house for nothing.

As we've talked about these experiences and others, we've come to realize they aren't isolated instances of a nasty boss, an unfortunate home life, or our own neurotic intolerance, but they are interrelated, being tools of those few in power for maintaining a labor force for their own ends.

One of these tools, sexism, makes our particular experience as working women something we are especially aware of and something we feel especially committed to changing. Sexism, like racism or religious intolerance, is just one concept which divides the majority into minorities—to prevent the majority from gaining control over our own lives. It is therefore in the interests of the minority in power to turn male against female, white against black, Protestant against Catholic, etc., and to maintain those divisions.

As women we are beginning to recognize the particular ways in which we suffer *because* we're women (getting lower wages, feeling inferior, feeling guilty for not staying home with the children, being prevented from doing certain types of work because they are "men's" jobs, feeling we're worthless if we don't keep ourselves physically attractive, etc., etc.) and to recognize the ways in which we and others participate in and contribute to

our particular oppression. We're also becoming aware of the ways in which other groups of people suffer, and beginning to see the ways in which all of our oppression has the same origin—our lives are controlled by others who have their own interests—not ours—at heart.

As *working* women we feel a sense of our potential power to change these situations. One of the most important experiences for us has been that of discovering and feeling that each of us is not alone in our individual reaction (anger/resentment/apathy) to the inhumanities of our job situation and our lives. We have given each other support and understanding and shared ideas about how to change these conditions.

Our particular strength—as yet largely untapped—lies in discovering the nature of our common problems and their common origins, and it lies in our numbers. We are the very basis of a system which works against our own interests; as individuals we have little influence, but, as that basis, we can be very powerful *together*. Unionization is the first step in this consolidation—the means to greater control.

We see *Change* as a way of exchanging and communicating our own experiences and ideas and information to other working women in the hope that it will help us grow and bring us together—to enlarge our numbers so that control of our work places and our lives will someday rest in our own hands.

In this issue we have articles about two efforts of women to unionize at work. Our "employee advisor" series is intended to allow us to deal with the job market knowledgeably. In previous issues we have printed articles about abortion, child care, bladder infections, auto care, and other areas of general interest where we feel more knowledge can give us greater self-sufficiency and control.

All of these articles are the product of our own effort and the contributions of other working women. We welcome your ideas, comments, and news of your struggles.

20
Ms.

A Personal Report from *Ms.*
(1972)

First, there were some women writers and editors who started asking questions. Why was our work so unconnected to our lives? Why were the media, including women's magazines, so rarely or so superficially interested in the big changes happening to women? Why were we always playing the game by somebody else's (the publisher's, the advertiser's) rules?

Then, there were questions from activists; women who were trying to raise money for an information service and self-help projects particularly for poor or isolated women, and having very little luck. Mightn't a publication—say, a newsletter—serve to link up women, and to generate income as well?

The two groups met several times early in 1971, and agreed that we all wanted a publication that was owned by and honest about women. Then we did some hard financial figuring. Newsletters that made decent profits seem confined to giving stock-market tips, or servicing big corporations. Some small but valuable ones for women were already struggling along. Besides, newsletters were a fine service for people already interested, but weren't really meant to reach out in a populist way.

So the idea of a full-fledged national magazine came up; a publication created and controlled by women that could be as serious, outrageous, satisfying, sad, funky, intimate, global, compassionate, and full of change as women's lives really are.

Of course, we knew that many national magazines were folding, or doing poorly. Rocketing production and mailing costs, plus competition from television for both advertising and subject matter, had discouraged some of the people who loved magazines most. Even

From *Ms.*, July 1972. Reprinted by permission of *Ms.* Magazine, copyright 1972.

those magazines still flourishing were unresponsive to the silenced majority. Women just weren't getting serious or honest coverage, and we doubted that we were the only people who felt the need for change. Besides, the Women's Movement had raised our hopes; it had given us courage.

So we had many more meetings, and we made big plans: long lists of article ideas, a mock-up of illustration and design, proposed budgets; everything. Then we spent many months making appointments, looking for backing from groups that invest in new ventures—and just as many months getting turned down. Flat.

Why? Well, we usually heard one or several reasons like these from potential investors:

. . . all around us, magazines are failing; why spend money to buck the tide?

. . . even though local or "special interest" magazines are making money (curiously, anything directed at the female 53 percent of the population is regarded as "special interest"), they are bad investments compared to, say, apartment buildings, computer hardware, and the like;

. . . the more we insisted on retaining at least 51 percent of the stock, the more everyone told us that investors don't give money without getting control; who ever heard of a national magazine controlled by its staff?

. . . setting aside some of the profits (supposing there were any) to go back to the Women's Movement is so unbusinesslike as to be downright crazy—even black magazines or other publications attached to movements haven't managed that;

. . . and, finally, the investors said, there are probably only ten or twenty thousand women in the country interested in changing women's status anyway; certainly not enough to support a nationwide magazine.

We got discouraged. Some of us thought we would either have to jettison a requirement or two, or give up. But there was support: friendly magazine people who thought we should try to find "public-spirited" money;

women in advertising who were themselves trying to create ads that were a service to women; feminist speakers who had been traveling around the country and knew that a mass audience was there.

Most of all, there were the several women writers and editors, one businesswoman, and some all-purpose feminist volunteers who were willing to contribute their talents and time in return for very little except hope. "It's very simple," said one of the writers. "We all want to work for a magazine we read."

Then, two concrete things happened to bolster our hopes. First, Katherine Graham, one of the few women publishers in the country, was willing to pretend that a few shares of stock in a nonexistent magazine were worth buying; a fiction that allowed us some money for out-of-pocket expenses. (She preferred to be generous in anonymity, but her help—a matter of corporate record anyway—was noted in a newspaper report, so we include her name here as an inadequate way of saying thank you for helping women in hard times.) Second and even more unusual was an offer from Clay Felker, editor and publisher of *New York,* a weekly metropolitan magazine. He had thought up an ingenious way of helping *Ms.* produce the thing it needed most: a nationwide test; a sample issue to prove that we could create a new kind of magazine, and that women would buy it.

The plan was this. *New York* needed something special for its year-end double issue, and also wanted practice in producing national "one-shot" magazines (single issues devoted to a particular area or subject). *Ms.* needed the money and editorial freedom to produce a sample issue. Therefore, *New York* offered to bear the full risk of the $125,000 necessary to pay printers, binders, engravers, paper mills, distributors, writers, artists, and all the other elements vital to turning out 300,000 copies of our Preview Issue. (Plus supplying the great asset of *New York*'s production staff, without which the expenses would have been much higher.) In return, some of the *Ms.* articles and features would appear first as an insert in that year-end issue of *New York,* half of the newsstand profits (if any) of our own Preview Issue would go to *New York,* and so would all of the advertsing proceeds. (We had editorial autonomy but no say about advertising: all but two of the ads were the same as those in *New York*'s issue anyway.)

It was an odd way of introducing a magazine, but a generous and unusual offer—the first time, as far as we knew, that one magazine would give birth to another without the *quid pro quo* of editorial control, or some permanent financial interest. Clay Felker made a few gruff noises about how it was strictly a business deal. After all, didn't *New York* stand to make a profit if *Ms.* did very well? (This last was generally said in earshot of his Board of Directors, who might otherwise think he was as crazy as we were.)

Several of us were regular writers for *New York,* however, and we had a different idea. Over the years, we must have convinced him, or at least worn him down: Clay had begun to believe, like us, that something deep, irresistible, and possibly historic was happening to women.

THE PREVIEW ISSUE

In a small office, with four people working full time and the rest of us helping when we could get away from our jobs, the Spring Preview Issue was put together, start to finish, in two months. There were a lot of close calls and emergencies: cherished article ideas that didn't get finished on time, authors whose other commitments made them drop out at the last minute, indecision about the cover which resulted in doing four of them, and an eleventh-hour discovery that we had one week and eight pages less than we thought.

But the work got done, and the decisions got made. They happened communally. We never had time to sit down and discuss our intellectual aversion to the hierarchy of most offices, where decisions and orders float down from above. We just chose not to do anything with which one of us strongly disagreed. And we didn't expect our more junior members to get coffee, or order lunch, or do all the typing, or hold some subordinate title. We each did as much of our own phone-answering and manuscript typing as deadlines and common sense would allow. On the masthead, we listed ourselves alphabetically, divided only by area of expertise and full- or part-time work.

Feminist philosophies often point out that a hierarchy, military or otherwise, is an imitation of patriarchy, and that there are many other ways of getting work done. We didn't approach the idea so intellectually, but we did arrive at the same conclusion from gut experience. As women, we had been on the bottom of hierarchies for too long. We knew how wasteful they really were.

The crowded *Ms.* office had an atmosphere of camaraderie; of people doing what they cared about. But there was apprehension, too. Could there possibly be even 100,000 women in the country who wanted this unconventional magazine? We had been listening to doomsayers for so long that we ourselves began to doubt it.

When the insert from our Preview Issue appeared as part of *New York* in December, the issue set a newsstand sales record; more than *New York* had ever sold. Of course, said the doomsayers, women in a metropolitan area might be interested. But would we appeal to the women of Ohio or Arizona?

When the full-length Spring Preview Issue of *Ms.* was distributed nationally in January, we packed off all available authors and staff to talk to women's groups around the country, and to appear on any radio or television shows that reached women. (Thus changing the lives of several of us, who had never spoken in public before.)

The preview Issue was designed to stay on the newsstands for at least two months (which is why it was dated "Spring"), and we wanted to make sure women knew about it. But we got to our various assigned towns only to be met with phone calls: "Where is *Ms.?*" "We can't find a copy." "What newsstands are selling it?"

Worriedly, we called the distributor, and the truth finally dawned on us. The 300,000 copies supposed to last for at least eight weeks had virtually disappeared in eight days. *Ms. had sold out.*

We celebrated. We breathed sighs of relief. And only in that moment did we realize how worried we had been—worried that we would make the Women's Movement seem less far-reaching and strong than it was by creating a feminist magazine that did poorly; worried about *New York* Magazine's risk, and all the friends who had helped us; worried about letting down ourselves, and other women.

But the most gratifying experience was still to come. Letters came pouring into our crowded office: more than 20,000 long, literate, simple, disparate, funny, tragic and very personal letters from women all over the country, including Ohio and Arizona. They wrote about their experiences and problems. They supported or criticized, told us what they needed, what they thought should be included or excluded, and generally spoke of *Ms.* as "our" magazine. (We've reprinted a few of them in this issue, and we will continue to make more use of readers' letters than most magazines do. After all, using only women who happen to be writers is itself a kind of discrimination, and misrepresents the lives that women lead.)

We were feeling inundated by all the mail, but didn't realize how unusual it was until we asked the editor of another women's magazine—with a circulation of 7 million, compared to our 300,000—how much editorial response each issue got. "About 2,000 letters," she said, "and a lot of them not very worthwhile. Four thousand letters of any kind would be considered quite extraordinary."

Obviously, the need for and interest in a non-establishment magazine were greater and deeper than even we had thought. More out of instinct than skill, the women of *Ms.* had tapped an emerging and deep cultural change that was happening to us, and happening to our sisters.

When all the returns were in, *New York* breathed a sigh of relief, too. Their share of the newsstand sales was $20,000. And so was ours. We felt very rich indeed, until we figured out that our check wouldn't pay even half the postage for one national mailing of a letter inviting people to subscribe. In fact, if we had paid ourselves salaries, we would have just about broken even. We were learning the terrible truth of how much it costs to start a magazine, even one that readers want.

So we set off again to look for financial backers, but this time we had that magic thing known as a track record. And we also had more than 50,000 subscription orders; each one a potential asset, but each one a promise to keep.

REGRETS AND NEW PLANS . . .

During this interim time, we assessed our mistakes. And we had made some.

New York's price of $1.50 for the Preview Issue was necessary because of the risk involved, of course, but we should have arranged a reduced price for women's groups, and some free distribution for women who simply couldn't pay. (We had intended to use returned issues for both purposes, but now there were none left.) After all, *Ms.* and the social change that gave birth to it is for all women, regardless of the family incomes or jobs or men we happen to be dependent on. Because of job discrimination and responsibility for children, some of us became poor precisely because we happened to be born female.

Each monthly issue is $1, and a year's subscription is $9: still a healthy price, but one that is imperative if we are to be less dependent on advertising than conventional magazines have been. (Most newsstand and subscription costs, especially of women's publications, are heavily subsidized by ad revenues. Only by paying a little more will we buy our freedom from magazines that are top-heavy with commercial messages.) But to offset that cost, we have figured out a group deduction: women's groups that sell 25 or more subscriptions need only send us $6 per sub, along with the name and address of each new subscriber. In other words, if your

group sells subs at the charter $9 price, you keep $3 for your own fund-raising, or to save money for individual members.

We will also do our best to provide some free issues to women who can't be expected to pay at all: women on welfare, in prisons, or who are just plain having a hard time. A few of our subscribers included extra money for just that purpose, without even being asked. If more of you would like to help, there are gift subscription cards in this issue. We will match up your gift with a woman who needs it. Or just send us a check, and indicate how you would like your contribution used.

There was a second problem created by our disappearing first issue. We had promised it, free, to people who had heard of our existence only through a letter or an ad. We wanted them to know what we were all about before subscribing, and we intended to send out the Preview Issue as a sample. So, if you are one of these people, that's why you have received *this* issue instead.

Of course, proud as we were of that Preview Issue, we still had some editorial regrets. Not enough air and illustration made it type-heavy and difficult to read. We had just tried to cram in too much.

Furthermore there were no articles directed explicitly at teen-age or over-fifty women, and blue-collar women were included in a marginal way. We want future issues to make up that balance.

Oddly, questions about the kinds of women we wanted to reach focused not on our content, but on the fact that we were "slick." In fact, slick paper can cost less, and take illustration better, than most dull-finish stock. (The exception is newsprint, but that would make us something other than a magazine.)

Though we had some funny and satirical articles, there were people—especially, but not only, men—who accused us of having no sense of humor. We're not sure what they meant by that, but we'll see to it in the future that there's as much laughter in the magazine as there is in the office. And that's a lot.

Finally, there was the advertising. Now that we are responsible for our own advertising, we will do our best to emphasize ads that are a service to women, and reflect the real balance of our lives. We don't spend half our money on makeup, for instance, and the other half on food, as traditional women's magazines would make it appear. We also buy cars, books, airline tickets, cameras, records, stereos, sporting equipment, liquor, gasoline, insurance, and the many products that aren't usually directed to women at all.

Obviously, *Ms.* won't solicit or accept ads, whatever the product they're presenting, that are downright insulting to women. (Nor will we accept product categories that might be harmful. Feminine-hygiene deodorants for instance, are definitely out until doctors are sure of their safety, and until the ads themselves are less guilt-producing and more like the deodorant ads directed at men.) But there may be some borderline cases with which we need your help. We've already summarized the nearly 8,000 of your letters that discussed the Preview Issue's ads, pro and con, and asked advertisers to look at the results. Those letters have gone a long way toward rewarding advertisers who portrayed women as people, and encouraging some change in those who did not. So keep the letters coming, and we promise to forward each of them to the advertising agency or manufacturer concerned. Tell us about the ads you like or don't like; about the products you want to see advertised, but don't find. The people who make both the ads and the products know that women's self-image and consumer needs are changing. They need your advice.

Meanwhile, the *Ms.* staff will use our own sensibilities to provide improvement, if not perfection, in return for your newsstand and subscription support that gives us this freedom.

One thing is clear. *Ms.* readers take its advertisements very seriously. You give them almost as much importance as the editorial pages, and that's the attention advertisers dream about. We'll do our best to make *Ms.* a laboratory that is useful to the advertiser and to you.

WHERE WE ARE NOW . . .

After the Preview Issue, we spent another three months looking for investors who believed in the magazine, and who would therefore give us the backing we needed without taking financial and editorial control.

In spite of all the looking, we can't take credit for finding Warner Communications. They found us. We are grateful to them for exploring many kinds of new media. And we are especially impressed that they took the unusual position of becoming the major investor, but minority stockholder, in *Ms.* It's a step forward for free women, and free journalism.

We still must reach the break-even point with a third of the money, and in a third of the time, that most magazines require. (The average seems to be $3 million and three years before a national publication begins to show profit.) But, thanks to the head start from *New York* and our subscribers, plus the opportunity given us by Warner Communications, we have a fighting chance.

If we do make it, we will own ourselves. We will also be able to give a healthy percentage of our profits back to the Women's Movement; to programs and projects that can help change women's lives.

In addition to financial struggles, the past few months have been spent gathering a staff. Our full-time members now number twenty instead of four, and a few more of us are helping part-time. Soon, there will be more names added to the masthead, mostly in advertising and circulation.

At the moment, we vary in age from 17 to 45, from no college at all to a Ph.D., and from experience as the editor of one of the country's biggest magazines to experience as a taxi driver. We are white Southerners, black Midwesterners, Latin American–born New Yorkers, homesick country-lovers and urbanites who never miss fresh air. One of us, an assistant art director, is male. (Since he was already working for our woman art director, he feels right at home. And so do we.) One of us is a radical Catholic, several are Jewish, and many are garden-variety WASP. We got more or less educated at Malcolm X College, Darien High School, Vassar, Smith, the University of Delhi, Millsaps College, Columbia, Radcliffe, Willamette University, the Sorbonne, the University of Wisconsin, and VISTA. We are married, never-been-married, and divorced. Some of us have children; some don't. Some of us have turned our friends into family, and some have done just the reverse.

All together, we're not a bad composite of the changing American woman.

If you asked us our philosophy for ourselves and for the magazine, each of us would give an individual answer. But we agree on one thing. We want a world in which no one is born into a subordinate role because of visible difference, whether that difference is of race or of sex. That's an assumption we make personally and editorially, with all the social changes it implies. After that, we cherish our differences. We want *Ms.* to be a forum for many views.

Most of all, we are joyfully discovering ourselves, and a world set free from old patterns, old thoughts. We hope *Ms.* will help you—and us—to explore this new world. There are few guidelines in history, or our own past. We must learn from each other.

So keep writing. *Ms.* belongs to us all.

II. Black Feminism

THE CIVIL RIGHTS MOVEMENT AND WOMEN'S LIBERATION were the two movements within which—and more important *against* which—an emergent Black feminism defined itself. The common refrain of Black feminist writers and activists declares both of these crucial liberation movements inadequate, by themselves, to explain or rectify the oppression of Black women. These Black feminists all, in one way or another, call for an analysis of discrimination that moves beyond the singular categories of either race or sex: phrases like "interlocking categories," "double jeopardy," and the "simultaneous action of different forms of oppression" emerge in their sophisticated analyses of how one is never subjugated on the basis of a lone aspect of identity.

Still, despite the shortcomings of the civil rights movement, it was deemed important by most Black women, the majority of whom experienced oppression on a daily basis primarily as a result of *race*. A shared history crystallizes this affiliation between men and women on the basis of race, and so almost all of the essays in this section contain a historical explanation for the solidarity of Black women and Black men based on slavery, segregation, and racially motivated violence—a solidarity broken only at great cost. Nevertheless, many have broken ranks in order to critique the prevailing sexism on the part not only of white men but also of Black men. In the late 1960s there were increasing signs of women's discontent in the civil rights movement. As Black nationalism, Black Power, and the Black Muslim organization took greater hold with their cult of masculinity and corollary sanctioning of violence, sexism became more virulent. Consequently, even some of the earliest documents in this section, which are written by women first and foremost committed to racial equality, criticize women's exclusion from leadership roles in the movement and disagree with the new calls for women to stay at home and cultivate the kind of feminine submissiveness that will best accentuate and affirm Black manhood.

The divisions between activist men and women came to a head over the presidential campaign of New York congresswoman Shirley Chisholm in 1972. Chisholm was the first Black woman elected to Congress. Having been an effective legislator for Black interests and also an early member of the National Organization for Women (NOW) and the National Women's Political Caucus, she looked to both Black and women constituents for support. But while feminists finally did endorse her presidential bid, Black men, it was felt, let her down egregiously. Most Black leaders refused to support her.

In "The Negro Woman in the Quest for Equality" (1964), Pauli Murray became one of the first voices to question whether Black women should be solely devoted to ending racial discrimination. Murray recognized that the civil rights movement was itself becoming increasingly representative of the paternalism (even sexism) of the larger society. Women, she argues, must fight oppression on the grounds of race and sex *simultaneously*. A poet, lawyer, and professor, Murray was both a cofounder of NOW and a member of the National Association for the Advancement of Colored People. Even as Murray shines a light on sexism in the civil rights movement—pointing out, for instance, that no women were invited to speak at the historic 1963 March on Washington—she does not seem able to imagine as yet a coalition between white and Black women. Indeed, the primary reason Murray gives for Black women's having to organize to fight for their rights as women is that there is a severe shortfall of Black men, and it is—in her analysis—American society's innate hostility to the Black male that ensures their short-livedness and thus necessitates Black women's self-determination. Clearly, for Murray, racism remains the core problem for Black Americans.

Frances M. Beal's "Double Jeopardy: To Be Black and Female" (1970) is an influential essay originally written in 1968 as a staff position paper for the by-then all-black civil rights group SNCC, the Student Nonviolent Coordinating Committee. Significantly, it was also reprinted in several anthologies of (mostly white) radical feminist writings—notably *The New Women,* drawn largely from the radical journal *MOTIVE,* and *Sisterhood is Powerful,* edited by Robin Morgan. Given her association with radical feminists, it is interesting that Beal is even stronger in her critique of women's liberation than Murray, claiming that a movement that is antimale and that sees "chauvinism" as the mainspring of oppression can never help or even interest Black women. Beal accuses women's liberation activists of naivete for believing that men exploit them, when in fact oppression stems from the twin systems of capitalism and racism: "[T]he main emphasis of black women," she writes, "must be to combat the capitalist, racist exploitation of black people." For Beal, capitalism is the originating system of oppression, with racism as its inevitable "after birth." Like Murray, she addresses the "turmoil" in Black family structure—primarily female-headed households—but whereas Murray writes vaguely of American society as the culprit, Beal specifically identifies a capitalist economy as the enemy of Black men and women for having made it impossible for African American men to find meaningful employment.

Although Beal notes, as do almost all Black feminists, the rising sexism in the civil rights movement (mostly the Black Power movement), she is clearly sympathetic with groups that primarily target racism and is even somewhat sympathetic with the Black Power position on the highly controversial issue of birth control. The Black movement was concerned that the birth control pill (a technology approved by the Food and Drug Administration in 1960) was potentially a tool of genocide, on a continuum with the forced sterilization of Third World women and women of color in the United States. Beal does insist that Black women should decide for themselves when to have and when not to have children and to what extent their childbearing is relevant to the race struggle, but she agrees that the effort to distribute technologies of birth control in underdeveloped nonwhite areas of the world and in the United States was "nothing but a method of surgical genocide."

In contrast, Patricia Robinson, author of the short pamphlet "Poor Black Women" (1968), unequivocally defends the right of poor Black women to take the pill. Robinson, concerned about the rise of Black single mothers, had been a "volunteer visitor" for Planned Parenthood, distributing information about contraception in poor neighborhoods. Rather than declaring birth control a potential instrument of race control, as Beal does, Robinson takes the more conventional line of class analysis which asserts that women's childbearing is *encouraged* in the service of capitalism. In fact, Robinson uses the same label as Beal (genocide) but regards the truly genocidal impulse of U.S. society to be that which refuses the poor Black woman birth control and takes "the surplus product of her body, the child, to use and exploit." Robinson was part of a radical group of mostly lower working-class and welfare women who called themselves the Mount Vernon/New Rochelle group. While much of the Black movement was turning toward Black Power and nationalism, the Mount Vernon women kept their eyes on the sexism of this movement and insisted on the importance of women's issues, as well as issues related to race and class. Like Beal, Robinson insists on the centrality of capitalism as an oppressive system, but whereas Beal sees sexism as a relatively superfluous by-product of capitalism, Robinson claims that capitalism and sexism work in tandem against Black women. In a capitalist society, she writes, "all power is imagined in male symbols and, in fact, all power in a capitalist society is in male hands." An inseparable male power and capitalist economy are served by women remaining at home to breed workers and fighters—whether those children fight and work for white men or Black men.

As the civil rights movement waned and the women's movement gained momentum, more Black women began examining their persistently tenuous and fraught relationship with both radical and mainstream feminism. In her article for *The New York Times,* "Many Blacks Wary of 'Women's Liberation' Movement" (1970), Charlayne Hunter contrasts the views of those few Black women working within organizations like NOW—Aileen Hernandez had just replaced Betty Friedan as NOW president—and those of Black women choosing to work primarily within Black groups. An incident described by Frances Beal epitomizes the relationship between Black and white feminists at that time. In 1970 feminist leaders planned a women's "Liberation Day" parade to commemorate the fiftieth anniversary of the Nineteenth Amendment. It was a day on which the second wave of feminism was going to reveal its strength for the first time to the American public, but it was also to be marred by an incident that marked the alienation of Black women from the women's movement. Led by Beal, the Third World Women's Alliance (the only SNCC project still functioning) participated in the parade after first holding out; its members originally felt they should not take part in an event that did not adequately represent the interests of Black women. The alliance marched while brandishing placards reading "Hands off Angela Davis," in support of Davis, who had recently been fired from her teaching position at the University of California and charged with murder, kidnapping, and conspiracy as a result of her participation in the disruption of the trial of a Black prisoner. Beal recalls how one of the leaders of NOW came running up to the alliance and said, "Angela Davis has nothing to do with women's liberation." Beal retorted, "It has nothing to do with the kind of liberation you're talking about, but it has everything to do with the kind of liberation we're talking about."

The prominent Black women Hunter interviewed for her *Times* article all voice two stances that demarcate the ideology of Black feminist thinkers from that of white feminists. First, they reiterate their unshakable sense of solidarity with Black men—no matter how sexist they may be. For these activists, Black women's freedom is inextricably bound to the freedom of Black men, even if, as civil rights worker Shirley Lacy puts it, "today I walk behind the black man." The second source of the divide between Black and white feminists is simply Black women's deep suspicion of white women, who often ignore the privilege of their skin color while at the same time relying on it. Frances Beal, for instance, questions white women's demands for equality, suggesting that they are actually demanding the same right as white men to exploit the prerogatives of whiteness.

A year after Toni Morrison published her first novel, *The Bluest Eye,* the future Nobel prize winner elaborated a still more complex set of reasons for Black women's misgivings about the mainstream women's liberation movement. In "What the Black Woman Thinks about Women's Lib" (1971), also published in *The New York Times,* Morrison adds an important qualification to black women's plain distrust of white women apparently pursuing only their own privilege and narrow interests. Says Morrison, Black women find it impossible to respect white women because all those problems faced by middle-class suburban women (a large part of NOW's constituency) and diagnosed in Betty Friedan's *The Feminine Mystique* are problems incurred at least partially by choice. The "oppressions" of economic and emotional dependence on men, moreover, are merely an evasion of responsibility which Black women have never been allowed, and which they would never allow themselves. Black women, Morrison argues, feel *superior* to white women "in terms of their ability to function healthily in the world." Morrison does end optimistically, however, suggesting that Women's Liberation is outgrowing its status as a "family quarrel" between white men and women: she points to a recent meeting of the National Women's Political Caucus—attended by Shirley Chisholm, Fannie Lou Hamer, and Beulah Sanders, among others—and expresses the hope that women are beginning to talk about "human rights rather than sexual rights."

Several specifically Black feminist organizations arose out of Black women's dissatisfaction with both civil rights and women's liberation groups. One of the most influential of these groups was the Combahee River Collective (CRC), formed in Boston. The CRC began meeting in 1974 immediately after the first eastern meeting of the National Black Feminist Organization (NBFO), a group begun in 1973 by mostly New York women. "A Black Feminist Statement" (1977), written by Barbara Smith, Beverly Smith, and Demita Frazier, makes it clear that the CRC was dissatisfied with the

NBFO's "bourgeois feminist stance" and "lack of a clear feminist focus." The "Black Feminist Statement" was first published in 1978 in the groundbreaking collection *Capitalist Patriarchy and the Case for Socialist Feminism,* edited by Zillah Eisenstein, which originated at the first organized conference of socialist feminists (held in Yellow Springs, Ohio, in 1975). Like Frances Beal, the CRC considered capitalism central to Black women's oppression, although the CRC did not label itself as explicitly socialist. Instead, it described its relation to all liberation movements—including socialism, civil rights, Black nationalism, and women's liberation—as purposefully peripheral, locating itself both inside and outside. The CRC drew ideas and strategies from these movements and yet remained relentlessly critical of the monolithic vision of each, of their inability to recognize and fight more than a single source of oppression. How does one explain, for instance, the long-standing problem of white men's rape of Black women with the sole explanatory concept of *either* gender *or* race?

The "Black Feminist Statement" is a sophisticated analysis of how systems of oppression (racism, sexism, heterosexism, class oppression) are interlocking and thus must be addressed simultaneously. Although the CRC is clearly interested in understanding these systems analytically, they also see them as embodied in people, specifically in Black lesbian women: "The synthesis of these oppressions creates the conditions of our lives." The "Statement" is one of the first documents to use the phrase *identity politics,* which became a term central to late-twentieth-century feminism: identity politics refers to the conviction that a person's politics emerges from his or her identity, from his or her own experience and distinct location in time and place, and in relation to the oppressive systems that structure that location. Although the CRC augured the notion of identity politics, it eschewed the "essentialism" of which this kind of liberationist ideology would be accused in the late 1980s. Identity politics, the argument would go, was based on a false biological determinism, which mandated that a person's sex or race, for instance, would inevitably shape his or her actions and beliefs. The CRC avoids this essentialist pitfall by stressing the determinative power of social systems to create identities. Society, in other words, *not* biology, precedes and determines identity. Hence, the CRC argues that white men are not inevitably and "essentially" the enemy. Their biological maleness and whiteness do not enforce their oppression of others; the systems that give power to maleness and whiteness do. "As black women," they write, "we find any type of biological determinism a particularly dangerous and reactionary basis upon which to build a politic." Destroying oppressive systems will radically change white men's identity—their position in terms of power and privilege—as much as it will radically change the lives and experiences of Black women.

Despite the role some prominent Black women played in mainstream women's liberation organizations like NOW and, more important, despite the formation of Black feminist organizations throughout the 1970s, Michele Wallace lamented in 1979 that "the black woman has no legitimate way of coming together with other black women, no means of self-affirmation—in other words, no Women's Movement." That charge came from her *Ms.* article "Black Macho and the Myth of the Superwoman" (1979), an excerpt from her book of the same name. Wallace focuses on the subject almost all the Black writers in this section have mentioned, albeit more tangentially. From Pauli Murray and Frances Beal, who wrote of sexism in the civil rights and Black Power movements, to Toni Morrison, who argued that the opposition of Black men was one of the reasons Black women remained suspicious of the white women's movement, all the writers in this section name the obstacles that Black men put in the way of a viable Black feminism. Whereas most of these women trace a history that explains the mutual allegiance of Black men and Black women—on matters of race, at least—Wallace traces and debunks a mythological history that has been used to justify sexism.

According to Wallace it was the Moynihan Report, published in 1965, that crystallized "a growing distrust, even hatred, between black men and black women." Named after its author, Daniel Patrick Moynihan, the Moynihan Report contributed to Lyndon B. Johnson's "War on Poverty," identifying "the deterioration of the Negro family" as the root cause of the "deterioration of the fabric of Negro society." The reason the Moynihan report caused so much controversy was, first, that it separated external structures of racism from the internal dynamic of the Black family, and second, that it located the dominance of Black women within the family as the primary symptom of the damaged family. Thus it perpetuated the misconception that the success and strength of Black women, not racism, were responsible for the problems of Blacks (notably Black men), and it cast Black women's success and strength as a flaw and a failure. Other Black writers, including both Murray and Beal, had pointed out the dearth of Black men and the increasing number of female-headed houses in the Black community, but they located blame more accurately in racism and capitalism, and they emphasized Black women's effectiveness in stanching the ills created by a society that was particularly hostile to Black men and that denied them meaningful and adequately compensated work. Moynihan's report, as much as it was vilified, was nonetheless taken seriously by many. As Wallace sardonically puts it: "[H]e did have a point after all. The black woman had gotten out of hand. She got all the jobs, all the everything. The black man had never had a chance. No wonder he wanted a white woman. The black woman should keep her big, black mouth shut." So many Black men *and* Black women thought, says Wallace, thus giving rise to a particularly virulent form of what she calls "Black Macho."

In the bulk of her essay, Wallace elaborates the false version of history that led to the mistaken notion that the Black "superwoman" somehow had it all and was able to evade the ill-effects of racism, while the Black man was more oppressed and thus needed to assert his authority. The myth has been, she writes, that Black men suffered more under slavery and Jim Crow; they were metaphorically if not literally castrated, while Black women, often coerced into sexual relationships with white men, seemed (as a result) more free, more powerful, even complicit in the emasculation of Black men. In truth, the Black man's grievance, Wallace acerbically notes, is that the Black woman has been the white man's slave—while all the time the Black man wanted her to be his own.

As Wallace asserts at the end of her essay, "History has been written without us"—and her essay is an attempt to rewrite the history of Black women, revealing their suffering from racism and sexism as well as their strength. In fact, a crucial word in all the documents in this section, from Murray to Wallace, is *history*. All of the political essays that define a contemporary Black feminism depend on a reconstruction of the history of Black women's struggle in the United States. They all implicitly or explicitly acknowledge the historical invisibility of Black women who have been represented, if at all, perversely mutated into contradictory stereotypes—the mammy, the slave, the matriarch, the mule, the castrating bitch, the lascivious temptress. A viable feminism in the late twentieth century requires the debunking of these stereotypes.

In a document that is less obviously political than the others, "In Search of Our Mothers' Gardens" (1974), novelist and poet Alice Walker constructs part of the foundation for Black feminism by brilliantly reenvisioning the history of Black women. Specifically, she writes of the violently suppressed but nonetheless triumphant flowering of Black women's creativity in the face of incredibly adverse circumstances. In part, Walker's essay weaves itself around Virginia Woolf's famous 1929 feminist essay *A Room of One's Own,* which is a sustained exploration of why there have been virtually no (white) women artists: women have had, Woolf argues, neither an independent income nor an independent space. Imagine, then, Walker suggests, the miracle of Phillis Wheatley, an African-born American slave who became a poet while bereft of income, a room, *and her freedom.* Walker's main purpose, though, is not to celebrate the published writer. She urges her readers to look "low," not "high," for signs of Black women's abiding creative power—to their quilts, their gardens, and the fabric of their everyday lives. If the Combahee River Collective set out to redefine meaningful political action from the standpoint of the most marginal group—poor Black lesbian women—Walker redefines art from the perspective of one of the most historically marginalized groups in America. Her essay makes it clear, though, that any separation between art and politics is arbitrary, for Black women's art was sustaining the spirit and the pride that flourished in the 1970s as political Black feminism.

A forum in *Ms.*, "Other Voices, Other Moods" (1979) by Alice Walker, Sandra Flowers, Christine Bond, and Audre Lorde, stresses Black women's solidarity across both time and continents as well as in the here and now—and it joins Walker's essay to end this section with the movement of Black feminists away from their vexed relations with Black men and white women and toward their (still sometimes vexed) relations with each other. Lorde's piece looks to African cowives and Dahomey warriors as precedents for the power Black women can wield when they band together and when they identify with and love other women. Walker's contribution stresses the need for Black women to celebrate each other, but not at the cost of ignoring either moments of defeat or Black women who fall victim to despair and violence. Walker describes delivering "In Search of Our Mothers' Gardens" to a group of two hundred educated Black women at a symposium at Radcliffe College. During the course of the conference she slowly realized that when her audience applauded her speech, they were applauding the invincibility of Black women and ignoring the implicit message that some women had struggled and failed—gone crazy, died. As Walker finds the women around her unwilling to see her own tears of pain, she also realizes that "there was no sympathy for the struggle that ended in defeat." Laughter *and* tears, Walker warns, have been and will be integral to Black women's struggle.

21

Pauli Murray

The Negro Woman in the Quest for Equality (1964)

Negro women, historically, have carried the dual burden of Jim Crow and Jane Crow. They have not always carried it graciously, but they have carried it effectively. They have shared with their men a partnership in a pioneer life on spiritual and psychological frontiers not inhabited by any other group in the United States. For Negroes have had to hack their way through the wilderness of racism produced by the accumulated growth of nearly four centuries of a barbarous international slave trade, two centuries of chattel slavery and a century of illusive citizenship in a desperate effort to make a place of dignity for themselves and their children.

In this bitter struggle, into which has been poured most of the resources and much of the genius of successive generations of American Negroes, these women have often carried disproportionate burdens in the Negro family as they strove to keep its integrity intact against the constant onslaught of indignities to which it was subjected. Not only have they stood shoulder to shoulder with Negro men in every phase of the battle, but they have also continued to stand when their men were destroyed by it. Who among us is not familiar with that heroic, if formidable, figure exhorting her children to overcome every disappointment, humiliation and obstacle. This woman's lullaby was very often "Be something!" "Be somebody!" . . .

Langston Hughes' poem "Mother to Son" has great meaning for a generation which still recalls the washtub and the steaming wooden stove as the source of hard earned dollars which sent it to school. It reveals the great gift of the Negro woman for mothering, consoling, encouraging:

From *The Acorn*, June 1964. Reprinted in Gerda Lerner, ed. *Black Women in White America: A Documentary History*. New York: Pantheon, 1972.

Well, son, I'll tell you:
Life for me ain't been no crystal stair.
It's had tacks in it,
And splinters,
And boards torn up,
And places with no carpets on the floor—
Bare.
But all the time
I's been a-climbin' on,
And reachin' landin's,
And turnin' corners,
And sometimes goin' in the dark
Where there ain't been no light,
So boy, don't you turn back,
Don't you set down on the steps
Cause you finds it kinder hard.
Don't you fall now—
For I'se still goin', honey,
I's still climbin'
And life for me ain't been no crystal stair.

In the course of their climb, Negro women have had to fight against the stereotypes of "female dominance" on the one hand and loose morals on the other hand, both growing out of the roles forced upon them during the slavery experience and its aftermath. But out of their struggle for human dignity, they also developed a tradition of independence and self-reliance. This characteristic, said the late Dr. E. Franklin Frazier, sociologist, "has provided generally a pattern of equalitarian relationship between men and women in America." Like the Western pioneer settlements, the embattled Negro society needed the strength of all of its members in order to survive. The economic necessity for the Negro woman to earn a living to help support her family—if indeed she was not the sole support—fostered her independence and equalitarian position. . . .

Not only have women whose names are well known given this great human effort [the human rights battle] its peculiar vitality but women in many communities whose names will never be known have revealed the courage and strength of the Negro woman. These are the mothers who have stood in school yards with their children, many times alone. These are the images which have touched America's heart. Painful as these experiences have been, one cannot help asking: would the Negro struggle have come this far without the indomitable determination of its women?

In the larger society, Negro and white women share a common burden because of traditional discriminations based upon sex. Dr. Gunnar Myrdal pointed out the similarities between the Negro problem and the women's problem in *An American Dilemma*. What he saw is common knowledge among Negro women, but it is interesting to see the United States through the eyes of a foreign observer. He said:

"As in the Negro problem, most men have accepted as self-evident, until recently, the doctrine that women had inferior endowments in most of those respects which carry prestige, power, and advantages in society. . . . The arguments that were used have been about the same: smaller brains, scarcity of geniuses and so on. . . . As in the case of the Negro, women themselves have often been brought to believe in their inferiority of endowment. As the Negro was awarded his 'place' in society, so there was a 'woman's place.' . . . The myth of the 'contented women' who did not want to have suffrage or other civil rights and equal opportunities, had the same social function as the myth of the 'contented Negro.' . . ."

Despite the common interests of Negro and white women, however, the dichotomy of the segregated society has prevented them from cementing a natural alliance. Communication and cooperation between them have been hesitant, limited and formal. Negro women have tended to identify all discrimination against them as racial in origin and to accord high priority to the civil rights struggle. They have had little time or energy for consideration of women's rights. But as the civil rights struggle gathers momentum, they began to recognize the similarities between paternalism and racial arrogance. They also begin to sense that the struggle into which they have poured their energies may not afford them rights they assumed would be theirs when the civil rights cause has triumphed.

Recent disquieting events have made imperative an assessment of the role of the Negro woman in the quest for equality. The civil rights revolt, like many social upheavals, has released powerful pentup emotions, cross currents, rivalries, and hostilities. . . . There is much jockeying for position as ambitious men push and elbow their way to leadership roles. Part of this upsurge reflects the Negro male's normal desire to achieve a sense of personal worth and recognition of his manhood by a society which has so long denied it. One aspect is the wresting of the initiative of the civil rights movement from white liberals. Another is the backlash of a new male aggressiveness against Negro women.

What emerges most clearly from events of the past several months is the tendency to assign women to a secondary, ornamental or "honoree" role instead of the partnership role in the civil rights movement which they have earned by their courage, intelligence and dedication. It was bitterly humiliating for Negro women on August 28 to see themselves accorded little more than token recognition in the historic March on Washington. Not a single woman was invited to make one of the major speeches or to be part of the delegation of leaders who went to the White House. This omission was deliberate. Representations for recognition of women were made to the policy-making body sufficiently in advance of the August 28 arrangements to have permitted the necessary adjustments of the program. What the Negro women leaders were told is revealing: that no representation was given to them because they would not be able to agree on a delegate. How familiar was this excuse! It is a typical response from an entrenched power group. . . .

It is also pointedly significant that in the great mass of magazine and newsprint expended upon the civil rights crisis, national editors have selected Negro men almost exclusively to articulate the aspirations of the Negro community. There has been little or no public discussion of the problems, aspirations and role of Negro women. Moreover, the undertone of news stories of recent efforts to create career opportunities for Negroes in government and industry seems to be that what is being talked about is jobs for Negro men only. The fact that Negro women might be available and, as we shall see, are qualified and in need of employment, is ignored. While this is in keeping with the tenor of a male-dominated society, it has grave consequences for Negro women. . . .

At the very moment in history when there is an international movement to raise the status of women and a recognition that women generally are underemployed, are Negro women to be passed over in the social arrangements which are to create new job opportunities for Negroes? Moreover, when American women are seeking partnership in our society, are Negro women to take a backward step and sacrifice their equalitarian tradition? . . .

A fact of enormous importance to the whole discussion of Negro family life and one which has received little analysis up to now is the startling 1960 census figure showing an excess of 648,000 Negro females over Negro males. More than a half million of these were 14 years and over. In the past century, the ratio of Negro males to females has decreased steadily. In 1960 there were only 93.3 Negro males to every 100 females.

The statistical profile of a Negro woman which emerges from the latest census reports is that she has a harder time finding a mate, remains single more often, bears more children, is in the labor market longer, has less education, earns less, is widowed earlier and carries a heavier economic burden as a family head than her white sister.

Moreover, while it is now generally known that women are constitutionally stronger than men, that male babies are more fragile than female babies, that boys are harder to rear than girls, that the male death rate is slightly higher and life expectancy for males is shorter than that of females, the numerical imbalance between the sexes in the Negro group is more dramatic than in any group in the United States. Within the white population the excess of women shows up in the middle and later years. In the Negro population, the excess is present in every age group over 14 and is greatest in the 15–44 age group which covers the college years and the age when most marriages occur. Consider, for example, the fact that in the 15–24 age group, there are only 96.7 nonwhite males for every 100 females. This ratio drops to 88.4 in the 25–44 age group. Compare this with the white population in which the ratios for these two age groups are 102.2 and 98.1 respectively.

The explosive social implications of an excess of more than half a million Negro girls and women over 14 years of age are obvious. . . . The problem of an excess female population is a familiar one in European countries which have experienced heavy male casualties during wars, but an excess female ethnic minority as an enclave within a larger population raises important social issues. What is there in the American environment which is hostile to both the birth and survival of Negro males? How much of the tensions and conflicts traditionally associated with the matriarchal frame-work of Negro society are in reality due to this imbalance and the pressure it generates? Does this excess explain the active competition between Negro professional men and women seeking employment in markets which have limited or excluded Negroes? And does this competition intensify the stereotype of the matriarchal society and female dominance? . . .

I have stressed the foregoing figures, however, because it seems to me that the Negro woman's fate in the United States, while inextricably bound with that of the Negro male in one sense, transcends the issue of civil rights. Equality for the Negro woman must mean equal opportunity to compete for jobs and to find a mate in the total society. For as long as she is confined to an area in which she must compete fiercely for a mate, she will remain the object of sexual exploitation and the victim of all of the social evils which such exploitation involves.

In short, many of the 645,000 excess Negro women will never marry at all unless they marry outside of the Negro community. And many others will marry men whose educational and cultural standards may not be the same as their own. Add to the large reservoir of unmarried white women (22.3%), a higher proportion of widowed, separated and divorced nonwhite women than of white women, and you have factors which have combined to make the Negro woman the responsible family head in more than one fifth of all nonwhite families.

The point I am trying to make here is that the Negro woman cannot assume with any degree of confidence that she will be able to look to marriage for either economic or emotional support. She must prepare to be self-supporting and to support others, perhaps, for a considerable period or for life. . . . Bearing in mind that everything possible must be done to encourage Negro males to develop their highest educational potential and to accept their family responsibilities and feel secure in their marital relationships, Negro women have no alternative but to insist upon equal opportunities without regard to sex in training, education and employment at every level. This may be a matter of sheer survival. And these special needs must be articulated by the civil rights movement so that they are not overlooked. . . .

One thing is crystal clear. The Negro woman can no longer postpone or subordinate the fight against discrimination because of sex to the civil rights struggle but must carry on both fights simultaneously. She must insist upon a partnership role in the integration movement. . . .

22

Frances M. Beal

Double Jeopardy: To Be Black and Female (1970)

In attempting to analyze the situation of the black woman in America, one crashes abruptly

From Joanne Cooke, Charlotte Bunch-Weeks, and Robin Morgan, eds., *The New Women: A MOTIVE Anthology on Women's Liberation* (New York: Bobbs-Merrill, 1970), 44–57.

into a solid wall of grave misconceptions, outright distortions of fact and defensive attitudes on the part of many. The system of capitalism (and its afterbirth—racism) under which we all live has attempted by many devious ways and means to destroy the humanity of all people, and particularly the humanity of black people. This has meant an outrageous assault on every black man, woman and child who resides in the United States.

In keeping with its goal of destroying the black race's will to resist its subjugation, capitalism found it necessary to create a situation where it was impossible for the black man to find meaningful or productive employment. More often than not, he couldn't find work of any kind. The black woman likewise was manipulated by the system, economically exploited and physically assaulted. She could often find work in the white man's kitchen, however, and sometimes became the sole breadwinner of the family. This predicament has led to many psychological problems on the part of both man and woman and has contributed to the turmoil found in the black family structure.

Unfortunately, neither the black man nor the black woman understood the true nature of the forces working upon them. Many black women accepted the capitalist evaluation of manhood and womanhood and believed, in fact that black men were shiftless and lazy, that otherwise they would get a job and support their families as they ought to. Personal relationships between black men and women were torn asunder, and one result has been the separation of husband from wife, mother from child, etc.

America has defined the roles to which each individual should subscribe. It has defined "manhood" in terms of its own interests and "femininity" likewise. An individual who has a good job, makes a lot of money and drives a Cadillac is a real "man," and conversely, an individual who is lacking these "qualities" is less of a man. The advertisement media in this country continuously inform the American male of his need for indispensable signs of his virility—the brand of cigarettes that cowboys prefer, the whiskey that has a masculine tang or the label of the jock strap that athletes wear.

The ideal model that is projected for a woman is to be surrounded by hypocritical homage and estranged from real work, spending idle hours primping and preening, obsessed with conspicuous consumption, and limited in function to simply a sex role. We unqualitatively reject these models. A woman who stays at home caring for the children and the house often leads an extremely sterile existence. She must lead her entire life as a satellite to her mate. He goes into society and brings back a little piece of the world for her. His interests and his understanding of the world become her own and she cannot develop herself as an individual, having been reduced to a biological function. This kind of woman leads to a parasitic existence that can aptly be described as "legalized prostitution."

Furthermore, it is idle dreaming to think of black women simply caring for their homes and children like the middle-class white model. Most black women have to work to help house, feed and clothe their families. Black women make up a substantial percentage of the black working force from the poorest black family to the so-called "middle class" family.

Black women were never afforded such phony luxuries. Though we have been browbeaten with this white image, the reality of the degrading and dehumanizing jobs that were relegated to us quickly dissipated this mirage of womanhood. The following excerpt from a speech that Sojourner Truth made at Women's Rights Convention in the 19th century shows us how misleading and incomplete a life this model represents for us:

". . . Well, chilern, whar dar is so much racket dar must be something out o'kilter. I tink dat 'twixt de niggers of de Souf and de women at de Norf all a talkin' bout rights, de white men will be in a fix pretty soon. But what's all dis here talkin' 'bout? Dat man ober dar say dat women needs to be helped into carriages, and lifted ober ditches, and to have de

best place every whar. Nobody ever help me into carriages, or ober mud puddles, or gives me any best places, . . . and ar'nt I a woman? Look at me! Look at my arm! . . . I have plowed, and planted, and gathered into barns, and no man could head me—and ar'nt I a woman? I could work as much as a man (when I could get it), and bear de lash as well—and ar'nt I a woma? I have borne five chilern and I seen 'em mos' all sold off into slavery, and when I cried out with a mother's grief, none but Jesus heard—and ar'nt I a woman?"

Unfortunately, there seems to be some confusion in the Movement today as to who has been oppressing whom. Since the advent of black power, the black male has exerted a more prominent leadership role in our struggle for justice in this country. He sees the system for what it really is for the most part, but where he rejects its values and mores on many issues, when it comes to women, he seems to take his guidelines from the pages of the *Ladies' Home Journal*. Certain black men are maintaining that they have been castrated by society but that black women somehow escaped this persecution and even contributed to this emasculation.

The black woman in America can justly be described as a "slave of a slave." Since the black man in America was reduced to such abject oppression, the black woman had no protector and was used and is still being used in some cases, as the scapegoat for the evils that this horrendous system has perpetrated on black men. Her physical image has been maliciously maligned; she has been sexually molested and abused by the white colonizer; she has suffered the worst kind of economic exploitation, having been forced to serve as the white woman's maid and as wet nurse for white offspring while her own children were, more often than not, starving and neglected. It is the depth of degradation to be socially manipulated, physically raped, used to undermine your own household, and to be powerless to reverse the situation.

It is true that our husbands, fathers, brothers and sons have been emasculated, lynched and brutalized. They have suffered from the cruelest assault on mankind that the world has ever known. However, it is a gross distortion of fact to state that black women have oppressed black men. The capitalist system found it expedient to enslave and oppress them and proceeded to do so without consultation or the signing of any agreements with black women.

It must also be pointed out at this time that black women are not resentful of the rise to power of black men. We welcome it. We see in it the eventual liberation of all black people from this corrupt system of capitalism. However, it is fallacious to think that in order for the black man to be strong, the black woman must be weak.

Those who are exerting their "manhood" by telling black women to step back into a domestic, submissive role are assuming a counterrevolutionary position. Black women, likewise, have been abused by the system, and we must begin talking about the elimination of all kinds of oppression. If we are talking about building a strong nation, capable of throwing off the yoke of capitalist oppression, then we are talking about the total involvement of every man woman, and child, each with a highly developed political consciousness. We need our whole army out there dealing with the enemy, not half the army.

There are also some black women who feel that there is no more productive role in life than having and raising children. This attitude often reflects the conditioning of the society in which we all live and is adopted from a bourgeois white model. Some young sisters who have never had to maintain a household or to accept the confinement which this entails, tend to romanticize (along with the help of a few brothers) the role of housewife and mother. Black women who have had to endure this function are less apt to have such utopian visions.

Those who portray in an intellectual manner how great and rewarding this role will be, and who feel the most important thing that they can contribute to the black nation is children, are doing themselves a great injustice. This reasoning completely negates the contributions that black women such as Sojourner

Truth, Harriet Tubman, Mary McLeod Bethune, and Fannie Lou Hamer have historically made to our struggle for liberation.

We live in a highly industrialized society, and every member of the black nation must be as academically and technologically developed as possible. To wage a revolution, we need competent teachers, doctors, nurses, electronics experts, chemists, biologists, physicists, political scientists, and so on. Black women sitting at home reading bedtime stories to their children are just not going to make it.

ECONOMIC EXPLOITATION OF BLACK WOMEN

Capitalism finds it expedient to reduce women to a state of enslavement. They often serve as a scapegoat for the evilness of this system. Much in the same way that the poor white cracker of the South, who is equally victimized, looks down upon blacks and contributes to the oppression of blacks, so, by giving to men a false feeling of superiority (at least in their own homes or in their relationships with women), the oppression of women acts as an escape valve for capitalism. Men may be cruelly exploited and subjected to all sorts of dehumanizing tactics on the part of the ruling class but at least they're not women.

Women also represent a surplus labor supply, the control of which is absolutely necessary to the profitable functioning of capitalism. Women are systematically exploited by the system. They are paid less for the same work that men do, and the jobs that are specifically relegated to women are low-paying and without the possibility of advancement. Statistics from the Woman's Bureau of the U.S. Department of Labor show that in 1967, the wage scale for non-white women was the lowest of all:

White Males	$6,704
Non-White Males	$4,277
White Females	$3,991
Non-White Females	$2,861

Those industries which employ mainly black women are the most exploitative. Domestic and hospital workers are good examples of this oppression, as are the garment workers in New York City. The International Ladies Garment Workers Union (ILGWU) whose overwhelming membership consists of black and Puerto Rican women had a leadership that is nearly all lily white and male. This leadership has been working in collusion with the ruling class and has completely sold its soul to the corporate structure.

To add insult to injury, the ILGWU has invested heavily in business enterprises in racist, apartheid South Africa—with union funds. Not only does this bought-off leadership contribute to our continued exploitation in this country by not truly representing the best interests of its membership, but it audaciously uses funds that black and Puerto Rican women have provided to support the economy of a vicious government that is engaged in the economic rape and murder of our black brothers and sisters in our Motherland, Africa.

The entire labor movement in the United States has suffered as a result of the super-exploitation of black workers and women. The unions have historically been racist and chauvinist. They have upheld racism in this country and have failed to fight the white skin privileges of white workers. They have failed to fight or even make an issue against the inequities in the hiring and pay of women workers. There has been virtually no struggle against either the racism of the white worker or the economic exploitation of the working woman, two factors which have consistently impeded the advancement of the real struggle against the ruling class.

The racist, chauvinist and manipulative use of black workers and women, especially black women, has been a severe cancer on the American labor scene. It therefore becomes essential for those who understand the workings of capitalism and imperialism to realize that the exploitation of black people and women works to everyone's disadvantage and that the liberation of these two groups is a stepping stone to the liberation of all oppressed people in this country and around the world.

BEDROOM POLITICS

I have briefly discussed the economic and psychological manipulation of black women, but perhaps the most outlandish act of oppression in modern times is the current campaign to promote sterilization of non-white women in an attempt to maintain the population and power imbalance between the white haves and the non-white have nots.

These tactics are but another example of the many devious schemes that the ruling class elite attempts to perpetrate on the black population in order to keep itself in control. A massive campaign for so-called "birth control" is presently being promoted not only in the underdeveloped non-white areas of the world, but also in black communities here in the United States. However, what the authorities in charge of these programs refer to as "birth control" is in fact nothing but a method of surgical genocide.

The United States has been sponsoring sterilization clinics in non-white countries, especially in India, where already some 3 million young men and boys in and around New Delhi have been sterilized in makeshift operating rooms set up by American Peace Corps workers. Under these circumstances, it is understandable why certain countries view the Peace Corps not as a benevolent project, not as evidence of America's concern for underdeveloped areas, but rather as a threat to their very existence. This program could more aptly be named "The Death Corps."

The vasectomy, which is performed on males and takes only six or seven minutes, is a relatively simple operation. The sterilization of a woman, on the other hand, is admittedly major surgery. This operation (salpingectomy) must be performed in a hospital under general anesthesia. This method of "birth control" is a common procedure in Puerto Rico. Puerto Rico has long been used by the colonialist exploiter, the United States, as an experimental laboratory for medical research before allowing certain practices to be imported and used here. When the birth control pill was first being perfected, it was tried out on Puerto Rican women and selected black women (poor), using them like guinea pigs to evaluate its effects and its efficiency.

The salpingectomy has now become the most common operation in Puerto Rico, more common than an appendectomy or tonsillectomy. It is so widespread that it is referred to simply as "la operacion." *On the Island, 20 percent of the women between the ages of 15 and 45 have already been sterilized.*

Now, as previously occurred with the pill, this method has been imported into the United States. Sterilization clinics are now cropping up around the country in the black and Puerto Rican communities. These so-called "Maternity Clinics," specifically outfitted to purge black women and men of their reproductive possibilities, are appearing more and more in hospitals and clinics across the country.

A number of organizations have been formed to popularize the idea of sterilization, such as the Association for Voluntary Sterilization and The Human Betterment [!!!?] Association for Voluntary Sterilization, Inc., which has its headquarters in New York City. Front Royal, Virginia, has one such "Maternity Clinic" in Warren Memorial Hospital. The tactics used in the clinic in Fauquier County, Virginia, where poor and helpless black mothers and young girls are pressured into undergoing sterilization are certainly not confined to that clinic alone.

Threatened with the cut-off of relief funds, some black welfare women have been forced to accept this sterilization procedure in exchange for a continuation of welfare benefits. Mt. Sinai Hospital in New York City performs these operations on many of its ward patients whenever it can convince the women to undergo this surgery. Mississippi and some of the other Southern States are notorious for this act. Black women are often afraid to permit any kind of necessary surgery because they know from bitter experience that they are more likely than not to come out of the hospital

without their insides. Both salpingectomies and hysterectomies are performed.

We condemn this use of the black woman as a medical testing ground for the white middle class. Reports of ill effects, including deaths, from the use of the birth control pill only started to come to light when the white-privileged class began to be affected. These outrageous Nazi-like procedures on the part of the medical researchers are but another manifestation of the totally amoral and dehumanizing brutality that the capitalist system perpetrates on black women. The sterilization experiments carried on in concentration camps some twenty-five years ago have been denounced the world over, but no one seems to get upset by the repetition of these same racist tactics today in the United States of America—land of the free and home of the brave. This campaign is as nefarious a program as Germany's gas chambers and, in a long term sense, as effective and with the same objective.

The rigid laws concerning abortions in this country are another vicious means of subjugation and, indirectly, of outright murder. Rich white women somehow manage to obtain these operations with little or no difficulty. It is the poor black and Puerto Rican woman who is at the mercy of the local butcher. Statistics show that the non-white death rate at the hands of unqualified abortionists is substantially higher than for white women. Nearly half of the child-bearing deaths in New York City are attributed to abortion alone, and out of these 79 percent are among non-white and Puerto Rican women.

We are not saying that black women should not practice birth control. Black women have the right and the responsibility to determine when it is *in the interest of the struggle to have children or not to have them and this right must not be relinquished to anyone*. It is also the black woman's right and responsibility to determine when it is in her own best interest to have children, how many she will have, and how far apart. Forced sterilization practices, abortion laws, and the unavailability of safe birth control methods are all symptoms of a decadent society that jeopardizes the health of black women (and thereby the entire black race) in its attempts to control the very life processes of human beings. These are symptoms of a society that believes it has the right to bring political factors into the privacy of the bedchamber. The elimination of these horrendous conditions will free black women for full participation in the revolution and, thereafter, in the building of the new society.

RELATIONSHIP TO WHITE MOVEMENT

Much has been written recently about the white women's liberation movement in the United States, and the question arises whether there are any parallels between this struggle and the movement on the part of black women for total emancipation. While there are certain comparisons that one can make, simply because we both live under the same exploitative system, there are certain differences, some of which are quite basic.

The white women's movement is far from being monolithic. Any white group that does not have an anti-imperialist and anti-racist ideology has nothing in common with the black woman's struggle. In fact, some groups come to the incorrect conclusion that their oppression is due simply to male chauvinism. They therefore have an extremely anti-male tone. Black people are engaged in a life and death struggle and the main emphasis of black women must be to combat the capitalist, racist exploitation of black people. While it is true that male chauvinism has become institutionalized in American society, one must always look for the main enemy—the fundamental cause of the condition of females.

Another major differentiation is that the white women's liberation movement is basically middle class. Very few of these women suffer the extreme economic exploitation that most black women are subjected to day by day. This is the factor that is most crucial for us. It is not an intellectual persecution alone, it is not an intellectual outburst for us; it is quite real. We as black women have got to deal with the problems that the black masses deal with, for our problems in reality are one and the same.

If the white groups do not realize that they are in fact fighting capitalism and racism, we do not have common bonds. If they do not realize that the reasons for their condition lie in the system and not simply that men get a vicarious pleasure out of "consuming their bodies for exploitative reasons" (this reasoning seems to be quite prevalent in certain white women's groups), then we cannot unite with them around common grievances or even discuss these groups in a serious manner because they're completely irrelevant to the black struggle.

THE NEW WORLD

The black community and black women especially must begin raising questions about the kind of society we wish to see established. We must note the ways in which capitalism oppresses us and then move to create institutions that will eliminate these destructive influences.

The new world that we are attempting to create must destroy oppression of every type. The value of this new system will be determined by the status of the person who was lowest on the totem pole. Unless women in any enslaved nation are completely liberated, the change cannot really be called a revolution. If the black woman has to retreat to the position she occupied before the armed struggle, the whole movement and the whole struggle will have retreated in terms of truly freeing the colonized population.

A people's revolution that engages the participation of every member of the community, including man, woman, and children, brings about a certain transformation in the participants as a result of this participation. Once we have caught a glimpse of freedom or experienced a bit of self-determination, we can't go back to old routines that were established under a racist, capitalist regime. We must begin to understand that a revolution entails not only the willingness to lay our lives on the firing line and get killed. In some ways, this is an easy commitment to make. To die for the revolution is a one-shot deal; to live for the revolution means taking on the more difficult commitment of changing our day-to-day life patterns.

This will mean changing the traditional routines that we have established as a result of living in a totally corrupting society. It means changing how one relates to one's wife, husband, parents and co-workers. If we are going to liberate ourselves as people, it must be recognized that black women have very specific problems that have to be spoken to. We cannot wait to start working on those problems until that great day in the future when the revolution somehow, miraculously, is accomplished.

To assign women the role of housekeeper and mother while men go forth into battle is a highly questionable doctrine for a revolutionary to maintain. Each individual must develop a high political consciousness in order to understand how this system enslaves us all and what actions we must take to bring about its total destruction. Those who consider themselves to be revolutionary must begin to deal with other revolutionaries as equals. So far as I know, revolutionaries are not determined by sex.

Old people, young people, men and women must take part in the struggle. To relegate women to purely supportive roles or to purely cultural considerations is dangerous. Unless black men who are preparing themselves for armed struggle understand that the society which we are trying to create is one in which the oppression of *all members* of that society is eliminated, then the revolution will have failed in its avowed purpose.

Given the mutual commitment of black men and black women alike to the liberation of our people and other oppressed peoples around the world, the total involvement of each individual is necessary. A revolutionary has the responsibility not only to topple those who are now in a position of power, but to create new institutions that will eliminate all forms of oppression. We must begin to rewrite our understanding of traditional personal relationships between man and woman. All the resources that the black community can muster must be channeled into the struggle. Black women must take an active part in bringing about the kind of society where our children, our loved ones, and each citizen can grow up and live as decent human beings, free from the pressures of racism and capitalist exploitation.

23

BLACK SISTERS

Birth Control Pills and Black Children (1968)

BIRTH CONTROL PILLS AND BLACK CHILDREN: A STATEMENT BY THE BLACK UNITY PARTY (PEEKSKILL, NEW YORK)

The Brothers are calling on the Sisters to not take the pill. It is this system's method of exterminating Black people here and abroad. To take the pill means that we are contributing to our own *GENOCIDE*.

However, in not taking the pill, we must have a new sense of value. When we produce children, we are aiding the REVOLUTION in the form of NATION building. Our children must have pride in their history, in their heritage, in their beauty. Our children must not be brainwashed as we were.

PROCREATION is beautiful, especially if we are devoted to the Revolution which

From Patricia Robinson, *Poor Black Women* (Boston: New England Free Press, 1968), 1–2.

means that our value system be altered to include the Revolution as the responsibility. A good deal of the *Supremacist* (White) efforts to sterilize the world's (Non-whites) out of existence is turning toward the black people of America. New trends in Race Control have led the architects of *GENOCIDE* to believe that Sterilization projects aimed at the black man in the United States can cure American internal troubles.

Under the cover of an alleged campaign to "alleviate poverty," white supremacist Americans and their dupes are pushing an all-out drive to put rigid birth control measures into every black home. No such drive exists within the White American world. In some cities, Peekskill, Harlem, Mississippi and Alabama, welfare boards are doing their best to force black women receiving aid to submit to *Sterilization*. This disguised attack on black future generations is rapidly picking up popularity among determined genocide engineers. This country is prepared to exterminate people by the pill or by the bomb; therefore, we must draw strength from ourselves.

The Sisters Reply

Dear Brothers:

Poor black sisters decide for themselves whether to have a baby or not to have a baby. If we take the pills or practise [*sic*] birth control in other ways, it's because of poor black men.

Now here's how it is. Poor black men won't support their families, won't stick by their women—all they think about is the street, dope and liquor, women, a piece of ass, and their cars. That's all that counts. Poor black women would be fools to sit up in the house with a whole lot of children and eventually go crazy, sick, heartbroken, no place to go, no signs of affection—nothing. Middle class white men have always done this to their women—only more sophisticated like.

So when whitey put out the pill and poor black sisters spread the word, we saw how simple it was not to be a fool for men any more (politically we would say men could no longer exploit us sexually or for money and leave the babies with us to bring up). That was the first step in our waking up!

Black women have always been told by black men that we were black, ugly, evil, bitches and whores—in other words, we were the real niggers in this society—oppressed by whites, male and female, and the black man, too. Now a lot of the black brothers are into a new bag. Black women are being asked by militant black brothers not to practise birth control because it is a form of whitey committing genocide on black people. Well, true enough, but it takes two to practise genocide and black women are able to decide for themselves, just like poor people all over the world, whether they will submit to genocide. For us, birth control is freedom to fight genocide of black women and children.

Like the Vietnamese have decided to fight genocide, the South American poor are beginning to fight back, and the African poor will fight back, too. Poor black women in the U.S. have to fight back out of our own experience of oppression. Having too many babies stops us from supporting our children, teaching them the truth or stopping the brainwashing as you say, and fighting black men who still want to use and exploit us.

But we don't think you are going to understand us because you are a bunch of little middle class people and we are poor black women. The middle class never understands the poor because they always need to use them as you want to use poor black women's children to gain power for yourself. You'll run the black community with your kind of black power—you on top!   *Mount Vernon, New York*

Patricia Haden—welfare recipient
Sue Rudolph—housewife
Joyce Hoyt—domestic
Rita Van Lew—welfare recipient
Catherine Hoyt—grandmother
Patricia Robinson—housewife and
   psychotherapist

24

PATRICIA ROBINSON

Poor Black Women (1968)

It is time to speak to the whole question of the position of poor black women in this society and in this historical period of revolution and counterrevolution. We have the foregoing analysis of their own perspective and it offers all of us some very concrete points.

First, that the class hierarchy as seen from the poor black woman's position is one of white male in power, followed by white female, then the black male and lastly the black female.

Historically, the myth in the black world is that there are only two free people in the United States, the white man and the black woman. The myth was established by the black man in the long period of his frustration when he longed to be free to have the material and social advantages of his oppressor, the white man. On examination of the myth, this so-called freedom was based on the sexual prerogatives taken by the white man on the black female. It was fantasied by the black man that she enjoyed it.

The black woman was needed and valued by the white female as a domestic. The black female diluted much of the actual oppression of the white female by the white male. With the help of the black woman, the white woman had free time from mother and housewife responsibilities and could escape her domestic prison overseered by the white male.

The poor black woman still occupies the position of a domestic in this society, rising no higher than public welfare, when the frustrated male deserts her and the children. (Public welfare was instituted primarily for poor whites during the depression of the thirties to stave off their rising revolutionary violence. It was considered as a temporary stopgap only.)

From Patricia Robinson, *Poor Black Women* (Boston: New England Free Press, 1968), 3–4.

The poor black male deserted the poor black female and fled to the cities where he made his living by his wits—hustling. The black male did not question the kind of society he lived in other than on the basis of racism: "The white man won't let me up 'cause I'm black!" Other rationalizations included blaming the black woman, which has been a much described phenomenon. The black man wanted to take the master's place and all that went with it.

Simultaneously, the poor black woman did not question the social and economic system. She saw her main problem as . . . social, economic and psychological oppression by the black man. But awareness in this case has moved to a second phase and exposes an important fact in the whole process of oppression. It takes two to oppress, a proper dialectical perspective to examine at this point in our movement.

An examination of the process of oppression in any or all of its forms shows simply that at least two parties are involved. The need for the white man, particularly, to oppress others reveals his own anxiety and inadequacy about his own maleness and humanity. Many black male writers have eloquently analyzed this social and psychological fact. Generally a feeling of inadequacy can be traced to all those who desperately need power and authority over others throughout history.

In other words, one's concept of oneself becomes based on one's class or power position in a hierarchy. Any endangering of this power position brings on a state of madness and irrationality within the individual which exposes the basic fear and insecurity beneath—politically speaking, the imperialists are paper tigers.

But the oppressor must have the cooperation of the oppressed, of those he must feel better than. The oppressed and the damned are placed in an inferior position by force of arms, physical strength, and later, by threats of such force. But the long-time maintenance of power over others is secured by psychological manipulation and education. The oppressed must begin to believe in the divine right and position of kings, the inherent right of an elite to rule, the supremacy of a class or an ethnic group, the power of such condensed wealth as money and private property to give its owners high social status. So a gigantic and complex myth has been woven by those who have power in this society of the inevitability of classes and the superiority and inferiority of certain groups. The oppressed begin to believe in their own inferiority and are left in their lifetime with two general choices: to identify with the oppressor (imitate him) or to rebel against him. Rebellion does not take place as long as the oppressed are certain of their inferiority and the innate superiority of the powerful, in essence a neurotic illusion. The oppressed appear to be in love with their chains.

In a capitalist society, all power to rule is imagined in male symbols and, in fact, all power in a capitalist society is in male hands. Capitalism is a male supremacist society. Western religious gods are all male. The city, basis of 'civilization,' is male as opposed to the country which is female. The city is a revolt against earlier female principles of nature and man's dependence on them. All domestic and international political and economic decisions are made by men and enforced by males and their symbolic extension—guns. Women have become the largest oppressed group in a dominant, male, aggressive, capitalistic culture. The next largest oppressed group is the product of their wombs, the children, who are ever pressed into service and labor for the maintenance of a male-dominated class society.

If it is granted that it takes two to oppress, those who neurotically need to oppress and those who neurotically need to be oppressed, then what happens when the female in a capitalist society awakens to the reality? She can either identify with the male and opportunistically imitate him, appearing to share his power and giving him the surplus product of her body, the child, to use and exploit. Or she can rebel and remove the children from exploitative and oppressive male authority.

Rebellion by poor black women, the bottom of a class hierarchy heretofore not discussed, places the question of what kind of society will the poor black woman demand and struggle for. Already she demands the right to have birth control, like middle class black and white women. She is aware that it takes two to oppress and that she and other poor people no longer are submitting to oppression, in this case genocide. She allies herself with the have-nots in the wider world and their revolutionary struggles. She has been forced by historical conditions to withdraw the children from male dominance and to educate and support them herself. In this very process, male authority and exploitation are seriously weakened. Further, she realizes that the children will be used as all poor children have been used through history—as poorly paid mercenaries fighting to keep or put an elite group in power. Through these steps . . . she has begun to question aggressive male domination and the class society which enforces it, capitalism. This question, in time, will be posed to the entire black movement in this country.

25

CHARLAYNE HUNTER

Many Blacks Wary of "Women's Liberation" Movement (1970)

Despite the fact that a black woman, Aileen Hernandez, heads one of the largest "women's liberation" groups in the country (the National Organization for Women), black women have been conspicuously absent from such groups. And while liberation is being discussed by black women—in workshops, liberation groups and privately—it is usually in a context different from that of white women.

The kind of liberation that black women are talking about raises some of the same questions being posed by the white groups.

They include such issues as a guaranteed adequate income, day-care centers controlled and administered by the community they serve, and the role of the woman in relation to her man.

The differences are rooted in historical traditions that have placed black women—in terms of work, family life, education and men—in a relationship quite apart from that of white women. To militant black women—such as Frances Beal, a member of the newly formed Third World Women's Alliance—the white women's liberation charge of "sexism" is irrelevant; blackness is more important than maleness

THE HOSTILE MALE

"Often, as a way of escape," she said in an interview, "black men have turned their hostility toward their women. But this is what we have to understand about him. It is a long, slow and sometimes painful process for the black man who has been so oppressed. But as black women, we have to have a conciliatory attitude. Firm, but creating together."

Such different perspectives make it all but impossible for some black women to relate to the white "women's lib" movement.

Mrs. Hernandez, as head of the National Organization for Women, which has a membership of roughly 10,000, said she was dismayed that "people are making a lot of generalizations about the movement and not getting an accurate portrayal."

"It is a predominantly white and middle-class movement—which all movements are," she asserted in a telephone interview from her San Francisco office. "But we feel an identity with all women."

AN ALTERNATIVE BECKONS

Mrs. Hernandez, former Commissioner of the Federal Equal Employment Opportunity Commission, said she felt that "many more young women and many more black and Chicano women" are becoming active in NOW, "particularly in the Southern chapters."

"I find it strange that people are having to make a decision about which to be involved in," she said.

Miss Dorothy I. Height, president of the National Council of Negro Women—a coalition of more than 25 black women's groups, representing about four million black women—said that she hoped eventually to have a "dialogue with women's liberation groups." But even though she participated as a speaker in the Women's Liberation Day Program last August, she felt the presence of a wide gulf between them.

"Fifty years ago all women got suffrage," Miss Height said she reminded the group, "but it took lynching, bombing, the civil-rights movement and then the Voting Rights Act of 1965 to get it for black women and black people."

"SPECIAL ATTENTION" ASKED

Miss Height said she felt it absolutely essential that "special attention be paid" to black women.

"With all the advances that black women have made—and we are in every field occupied by women—it is still true that we are in predominantly household and related services, with a median income of $1,523," she said.

Eleanor Holmes Norton, chairman of New York City's Commission on Human Rights, supplied another economic statistic concerning the black female labor force. Almost 70 percent of black women with children between the ages of 6 and 18 work, she said.

"Black women feel resentful that white women are raising issues of oppression even, because black women do not see white women in any kind of classic oppressed position," Mrs. Norton said.

Miss Beal recalled, for example, that the Third World Women's Alliance had been against marching in the women's "Liberation Day" parade last August. But "at the last minute," she said, they decided that marching might be a way of letting other minority-group women who might be standing on the sidelines know of their organization.

"We had signs reading 'Hands Off Angela Davis'—that was before her capture—and one of the leaders of NOW ran up to us and said angrily, 'Angela Davis has nothing to do with women's liberation.' And that's really the difference right there.

"'It has nothing to do with the kind of liberation you're talking about,'" Miss Beal said she told the woman, "'but it has everything to do with the kind of liberation we're talking about.'"

The Third World group, which has a New York City membership of about 200, and is establishing chapters in other states, includes young women who were formerly in the Black Women's Alliance of the Student National Coordinating Committee as well as a wide range of non-affiliated women. They see themselves as "part of the national liberation struggle" and, as such, believe that "the struggle against racism and imperialism must be waged simultaneously with the struggle for women's liberation."

Miss Beal, who is the mother of two daughters, said: "When white women demand from men an equal part of the pie, we say, 'Equal to what? What makes us think that white women, given the positions of white men in the system, would not turn around and use their white skin for the same white privileges? This is an economy that favors whites. And white women would have the privilege of their class.'"

While class and sex distinction undoubtedly exist in the black community, there are those like Mrs. Norton who declare that the distinctions are minimized by the experience of slavery and of discrimination.

"The black woman already has a rough equality which came into existence out of necessity and is now ingrained in the black life style," said Mrs. Norton, a Yale law school graduate, and mother of a 3-month-old child. "Black women had to work with or beside their men, because work was necessary to survival. As a result, that give the black fam-

ily very much of a head start on egalitarian family life."

What about black women's attitudes toward black men?

According to Mrs. Norton: "Black men are the one group accustomed to women who are able and assertive, because their mothers and sisters were that way. And I don't think they reject their mothers and sisters and wives. I don't think they want wives to be like the white suburban chocolate eaters who live in Larchmont."

Mrs. Shirley Lacy, director of training for the Scholarship Education and Defense Fund for Racial Equality—an integrated civil rights leadership training organization—has been called in by some black women's groups to hold workshops that include discussions on the black woman's role in the feminist movement.

Mrs. Lacy said that it was terribly important for black women to look at where they are in this time and say: "Given what I've got, how can I best use that in the context of the black struggle?"

"And if it means that today I walk behind the black man," she said, "that's what I do today, but that may not be true tomorrow. It may be that tomorrow he's going to fall, and I'm going to have to jump in there and be the leader. And the black man is going to have to understand that kind of juxtaposition, too."

26

Toni Morrison

What the Black Woman Thinks About Women's Lib (1971)

They were always there. Whenever you wanted to do something simple, natural and inoffensive. Like drink water, sit down, go to the bathroom or buy a bus ticket to Charlotte, N.C. Those classifying signs that told you who you were, what to do. More than those abrupt and discourteous signs one gets used to in this

From *The New York Times Magazine*, August 22, 1971.

country—the door that says "Push," the towel dispenser that says "Press," the traffic light that says "No"—these signs were not just arrogant, they were malevolent: "White Only," "Colored Only," or perhaps just "Colored," permanently carved into the granite over a drinking fountain. But there was one set of signs that was not malevolent; it was, in fact, rather reassuring in its accuracy and fine distinctions: the pair that said "White Ladies" and "Colored Women."

The difference between white and black females seemed to me an eminently satisfactory one. White females were *ladies*, said the sign maker, worthy of respect. And the quality that made ladyhood worthy? Softness, helplessness and modesty—which I interpreted as a willingness to let others do their labor and their thinking. Colored females, on the other hand, were *women*—unworthy of respect because they were tough, capable, independent and immodest. Now, it appears, there is a consensus that those anonymous sign makers were right all along, for there is no such thing as Ladies' Liberation. Even the word "lady" is anathema to feminists. They insist upon the "woman" label as a declaration of their rejection of all that softness, helplessness and modesty, for they see them as characteristics which served only to secure their bondage to men.

Significant as that shift in semantics is, obvious as its relationship to the black-woman concept is, it has not been followed by any immediate comradery between black and white women, nor has it precipitated any rush of black women into the various chapters of NOW. It is the *Weltanschauung* of black women that is responsible for their apparent indifference to Women's Lib, and in order to discover the nature of this view of oneself in the world, one must look very closely at the black woman herself—a difficult, inevitably doomed proposition, for if anything is true of black women, it is how consistently they have (deliberately, I suspect) defied classification.

It may not even be possible to look at those militant young girls with lids lowered in dreams of guns, those middle-class socialites with 150 pairs of shoes, those wispy girl junkies who have always been older than water, those beautiful Muslim women with their bound hair and flawless skin, those television personalities who think chic is virtue and happiness a good coiffure, those sly old women in the country with their ancient love of Jesus—and still talk about The Black Woman. It is a dangerous misconception, for it encourages lump thinking. And we are so accustomed to that in our laboratories that it seems only natural to confront all human situations, direct all human discourse, in the same way. Those who adhere to the scientific method and draw general conclusions from "representative" sampling are chagrined by the suggestion that there is any other way to arrive at truth, for they like their truth in tidy sentences that begin with "all."

In the initial confrontation with a stranger, it is never "Who are you?" but "Take me to your leader." And it is this mode of thought which has made black-white relationships in this country so hopeless. There is a horror of dealing with people one by one, each as he appears. There is safety and manageability in dealing with the leader—no matter how large or diverse the leader's constituency may be. Such generalizing may be all right for plant analysis, superb for locating carcinogens in mice, and it used to be all right as a method for dealing with schools and politics. But no one would deny that it is rapidly losing effectiveness in both those areas—precisely because it involves classifying human beings and anticipating their behavior. So it is with some trepidation that anyone should undertake to generalize about still another group. Yet something in that order is legitimate, not only because unity among minorities is a political necessity, but because, at some point, one wants to get on with the differences.

What do black women feel about Women's Lib? Distrust. It is white, therefore, suspect. In spite of the fact that liberating movements in the black world have been catalysts for white feminism, too many movements and organizations have made deliberate overtures to enroll blacks and have ended up by rolling them. They don't want to be used again to help somebody gain power—a power that is carefully kept out of their hands. They look at white women and see them as the enemy—for they know that racism is not confined to white men, and that there are more white women than men in this country, and that 53 percent of the population sustained an eloquent silence during times of greatest stress. The faces of those white women hovering behind that black girl at the Little Rock school in 1957 do not soon leave the retina of the mind.

When she was interviewed by Nikki Giovanni last May in *Essence* magazine, Ida Lewis, the former editor-in-chief of *Essence,* was asked why black women were not more involved in Women's Lib, and she replied: "The Women's Liberation Movement is basically a family quarrel between white women and white men. And on general principles, it's not good to get involved in family disputes. Outsiders always get shafted when the dust settles. On the other hand, I must support some of the goals [equal pay, child-care centers, etc.]. . . . But if we speak of a liberation movement, as a black woman I view my role from a black perspective—the role of black women is to continue the struggle in concert with black men for the liberation and self-determination of blacks. White power was not created to protect and preserve us as women. Nor can we view ourselves as simply American women. We are black women, and as such we must deal effectively in the black community."

To which Miss Giovanni sighed: "Well, I'm glad you didn't come out of that Women's Lib or black-man bag as if they were the alternatives." . . .

Miss Lewis: "Suppose the Lib movement succeeds. It will follow, since white power is the order of the day, that white women will be the first hired, which will still leave black men and women outside." . . .

It is an interesting exchange, Miss Lewis expressing suspicion and identifying closely with black men, Miss Giovanni suggesting that the two are not necessarily mutually exclusive.

But there is not only the question of color, there is the question of the color of experience. Black women are not convinced that Women's Lib serves their best interest or that it can cope with the uniqueness of their experience, which is itself an alienating factor. The early image of Women's Lib was of an élitist organization made up of upper-middle-class women with the concerns of that class (the percentage of women in professional fields, etc.) and not paying much attention to the problems of most black women, which are not in getting into the labor force but in being upgraded in it, not in getting into medical school but in getting adult education, not in how to exercise freedom from the "head of the house" but in how to *be* head of the household.

Black women are different from white women because they view themselves differently and lead a different kind of life. Describing this difference is the objective of several black women writers and scholars. But even without this newly surfacing analysis, we can gain some understanding of the black woman's world by examining archetypes. The archetypes created by women about themselves are rare, and even those few that do exist may be the result of a female mind completely controlled by male-type thinking. No matter. The most unflattering stereotypes that male minds have concocted about black women contain, under the stupidity and the hostility, the sweet smell of truth.

Look, for example, at Geraldine and Sapphire—Geraldine, that campy character in Flip Wilson's comic repertory, and Sapphire, the wife of Kingfish in the Amos and Andy radio and TV series. Unlike Nefertiti, an archetype that black women have appropriated for themselves, Geraldine and Sapphire are the comic creations of men. Nefertiti, the romantic black queen with the enviable neck, is particularly appealing to young black women, mainly because she existed (and there are few admirable heroines in our culture), was a great beauty and is remote enough to be worshiped. There is a lot of talk about Sojourner Truth, the freed slave who preached emancipation and women's rights, but there is a desperate love for Nefertiti, simply because she was so pretty.

I suppose at bottom we are all beautiful queens, but for the moment it is perhaps just as well to remain useful women. One wonders if Nefertiti could have lasted 10 minutes in a welfare office, in a Mississippi gas station, at a Parent Association meeting or on the church congregation's Stewardess Board No. 2. And since black women have to endure, that romanticism seems a needless *cul de sac*, an opiate that appears to make life livable if not serene but eventually must separate us from reality. I maintain that black women are already O.K. O.K. with our short necks, O.K. with our callused hands. O.K. with our tired feet and paper bags on the Long Island Rail Road. O.K. O.K. O.K.

As for Geraldine, her particular horror lies in her essential accuracy. Like any stereotype she is a gross distortion of reality and as such highly offensive to many black women and endearing to many whites. A single set of characteristics provokes both hatred and affection. Geraldine is defensive, cunning, sexy, egocentric and transvestite. But that's not all she is. A shift in semantics and we find the accuracy: for defensive read survivalist; for cunning read clever; for sexy read a natural unembarrassed acceptance of her sexuality; for egocentric read keen awareness of individuality; for transvestite (man in woman's dress) read a masculine strength beneath the accouterments of glamour.

Geraldine is offensive to many blacks precisely because the virtues of black women are construed in her portrait as vices. The strengths are portrayed as weaknesses—hilarious weaknesses. Yet one senses even in the laughter some awe and respect. Interestingly enough, Geraldine is absolutely faithful to one man, Killer, whom one day we may also see as caricature.

Sapphire, a name of opprobrium black men use for the nagging black wife, is also important, for in that marriage, disastrous as it was, Sapphire worked, fussed, worked and fussed, but (and this is crucial) Kingfish did whatever he pleased. Whatever. Whether he was free or irresponsible, anarchist or victim depends on your point of view. Contrary to the black-woman-as-emasculator theory, we see, even in these unflattering caricatures, the very opposite of a henpecked husband and emasculating wife— a wife who never did, and never could, manipulate her man. Which brings us to the third reason for the suspicion black women have of Women's Lib: the serious one of the relationship between black women and black men.

There are strong similarities in the way black and white men treat women, and strong similarities in the way women of both races react. But the relationship is different in a very special way.

For years in this country there was no one for black men to vent their rage on except for black women. And for years black women accepted that rage—even regarded that acceptance as their unpleasant duty. But in doing so, they frequently kicked back, and they seem never to have become the "true slave" that white women see in their own history. True, the black woman did the housework, the drudgery; true, she reared the children, often alone, but she did all of that while occupying a place on the job market, a place her mate could not get or which his pride would not let him accept. And she had nothing to fall back on: not maleness, not whiteness, not ladyhood, not anything. And out of the profound desolation of her reality she may very well have invented herself.

If she was a sexual object in the eyes of the men, that was their doing. Sex was *one* of her dimensions. It had to be just one, for life required many other things of her, and it is difficult to be regarded solely as a sex object when the burden of field and fire is on your shoulders. She could cultivate her sexuality but dared not be obsessed by it. Other people may have been obsessed by it, but the circumstances of her life did not permit her to dwell on it or survive by means of its exploitation.

So she combined being a responsible person with being a female—and as a person she felt free to confront not only the world at large (the rent man, the doctor and the rest of the marketplace) but her man as well. She fought him and nagged him—but know that you don't fight what you don't respect. (If you don't respect your man, you manipulate him, the way some parents treat children and the way white women treat their men—if they can get away with it or if they do not acquiesce entirely.) And even so, the black man was calling most of the shots—in the home or out of it. The black woman's "bad" relationships with him were often the result of his inability to deal with a competent and complete personality and her refusal to be anything less than that. The saving of the relationship lay in her unwillingness to feel free when her man was not free.

In a way black women have known something of the freedom white women are now beginning to crave. But oddly, freedom is only sweet when it is won. When it is forced, it is called responsibility. The black woman's needs shrank to the level of her responsibility; her man's expanded in proportion to the obstacles that prevented him from assuming his. White women, on the other hand, have had too little responsibility, white men too much. It's a wonder the sexes of either race even speak to each other.

As if that were not enough, there is also the growing rage of black women over unions of black men and white women. At one time, such unions were rare enough to be amusing or tolerated. The white woman moved with the black man into a black neighborhood, and everybody tried to deal with it. Chances are the white woman who married a black man liked it that way, for she had already made some statement about her relationship with her own race by marrying him. So there were no frictions. If a white woman had a child out of wedlock by a black man, the child was deposited with the black community, or grouped with the black orphans, which is certainly one of the reasons why lists of black foundling children are so long. (Another reason is the willingness of black women to have their children instead of aborting and to keep them, whatever the inconvenience.)

But now, with all the declarations of independence, one of the black man's ways of defining it is to broaden his spectrum of female choices, and one consequence of his new pride is the increased attraction white women feel for him. Clearly there are more and more of these unions, for there is clearly more anger about it (talking black and sleeping white is a cliché) among black women. The explanations for this anger are frequently the easy ones: there are too few eligible men, for wars continue to shoot them up; the black woman who complains is one who would be eliminated from a contest with any good-looking woman—the complaint simply reveals her inadequacy to get a man; it is a simple case of tribal sour grapes with a dash of politics thrown in.

But no one seems to have examined this anger in the light of what black women understand about themselves. These easy explanations are obviously male. They overlook the fact that the hostility comes from both popular beauties and happily married black women. There is something else in this anger, and I think it lies in the fact that black women have always considered themselves superior to white women. Not racially superior, just superior in terms of their ability to function healthily in the world.

Black women have been able to envy white women (their looks, their easy life, the attention they seem to get from their men); they could fear them (for the economic control they have had over black women's lives) and even love them (as mammies and domestic workers can); but black women have found it impossible to respect white women. I mean they never had what black men have had for white men—a feeling of awe at their accomplishments. Black women have no abiding admiration of white women as competent, complete people. Whether vying with them for the few professional slots available to women in general, or moving their dirt from one place to another, they regarded them as willful children, pretty children, mean children, ugly children, but never as real adults capable of handling the real problems of the world.

White women were ignorant of the facts of life—perhaps by choice, perhaps with the assistance of men, but ignorant anyway. They were totally dependent on marriage or male support (emotionally or economically). They confronted their sexuality with furtiveness, complete abandon or repression. Those who could afford it, gave over the management of the house and the rearing of children to others. (It is a source of amusement even now to black women to listen to feminists talk of liberation while somebody's nice black grandmother shoulders the daily responsibility of child rearing and floor mopping and the liberated one comes home to examine the housekeeping, correct it, and be entertained by the children. If Women's Lib needs those grandmothers to thrive, it has a serious flaw.) The one great disservice black women are guilty of (albeit not by choice) is that they are the means by which white women can escape the responsibilities of womanhood and remain children all the way to the grave.

It is this view of themselves and of white women that makes the preference of a black man for a white woman quite a crawful. The black women regard his choice as an inferior one. Over and over again one hears one question from them: "But why, when they marry white women, do they pick the raggletail ones, the silly, the giddy, the stupid, the flat nobodies of the race? Why no real women?" The answer, of course, is obvious. What would such a man who preferred white women do with a real woman? And would a white woman who is looking for black exotica ever be a complete woman?

Obviously there are black and white couples who love each other as people, and marry each other that way. (I can think of two such.) But there is so often a note of apology (if the woman is black) or bravado (if the man is) in such unions, which would hardly be necessary if the union was something other than a political effort to integrate one's emotions and therefore, symbolically, the world. And if all the black partner has to be is black and exotic, why not?

This feeling of superiority contributes to the reluctance of black women to embrace Women's Lib. That and the very important fact that black men are formidably opposed to their involvement in it—and for the most part the women understand their fears. In The Amsterdam News, an editor, while deploring the conditions of black political organizations, warns his readers of the consequences: "White politicians have already organized. And their organizers are even attempting to co-opt Black women into their organizational structure, which may well place Black women against Black men, that is, if the struggle for women's liberation is viewed by Black women as being above the struggle for Black liberation."

The consensus among blacks is that their first liberation has not been realized; unspoken is the conviction of black men that any more aggressiveness and "freedom" for black women would be intolerable, not to say counterevolutionary.

There is also a contention among some black women that Women's Lib is nothing more than an attempt on the part of whites to become black without the responsibilities of being black. Certainly some of the demands of liberationists seem to rack up as our thing: common-law marriage (shacking); children out of wedlock, which is even fashionable now if you are a member of the Jet Set (if you are poor and black it is still a crime); families without men; right to work; sexual freedom, and an assumption that a woman is equal to a man.

Now we have come full circle: the morality of the welfare mother has become the avant-garde morality of the land. There is a good deal of irony in all of this. About a year ago in the *Village Voice* there was a very interesting exchange of letters. Cecil Brown was explaining to a young black woman the "reasons" for the black man's interest in white girls: a good deal about image, psychic needs and what not. The young girl answered in a rather poignant way to this effect: yes, she said, I suppose, again, we black women have to wait, wait for the brother to get himself together—be enduring, understanding, and, yes, she thought they could do it again . . . but, in the meantime, what do we tell the children?

This woman who spoke so gently in those letters of the fate of the children may soon discover that the waiting period is over. The softness, the "she knows how to treat me" (meaning she knows how to be a cooperative slave) that black men may be looking for in white women is fading from view. If Women's Lib *is* about breaking the habit of genuflection, if it *is* about controlling one's own destiny, *is* about female independence in economic, personal and political ways, if it is indeed about working hard to become a person, knowing that one has to work hard at becoming anything, *Man* or *Woman*—and it succeeds—then we may have a nation of white Geraldines and white Sapphires, and what on earth is Kingfish gonna do then?

The winds are changing, and when they blow, new things move. The liberation movement has moved from shrieks to shape. It is focusing itself, becoming a hard-headed power base, as the National Women's Political Caucus in Washington attested last month. Representative Shirley Chisholm was radiant: "Collectively we've come together, not as a Women's Lib group, but as a women's political movement." Fannie Lou Hamer, the Mississippi civil-rights leader, was there. Beulah Sanders, chairman of New York's Citywide Coordinating Committee of Welfare Groups, was there. They see, perhaps, something real: women talking about human rights rather than sexual rights—something other than a family quarrel, and the air is shivery with possibilities.

27
COMBAHEE RIVER COLLECTIVE
A Black Feminist Statement (1977)

We are a collective of Black feminists who have been meeting together since 1974. During that time we have been involved in the process of defining and clarifying our politics, while at the

From Cherríe Moraga and Gloria Anzaldúa, eds., *This Bridge Called My Back: Writings by Radical Women of Color*, 2d ed. (New York: Kitchen Table, Women of Color Press, 1983), 210–18. Reprinted by permission of Barbara Smith and Kitchen Table: Women of Color Press.

same time doing political work within our own group and in coalition with other progressive organizations and movements. The most general statement of our politics at the present time would be that we are actively committed to struggling against racial, sexual, heterosexual, and class oppression and see as our particular task the development of integrated analysis and practice based upon the fact that the major systems of oppression are interlocking. The synthesis of these oppressions creates the conditions of our lives. As Black women we see Black feminism as the logical political movement to combat the manifold and simultaneous oppressions that all women of color face.

We will discuss four major topics in the paper that follow: (1) the genesis of contemporary black feminism; (2) what we believe, i.e., the specific province of our politics; (3) the problems in organizing Black feminists, including a brief herstory of our collective; and (4) Black feminist issues and projects.

1. THE GENESIS OF CONTEMPORARY BLACK FEMINISM

Before looking at the recent development of Black feminism we would like to affirm that we find our origins in the historical reality of Afro-American women's continuous life-and-death struggle for survival and liberation. Black women's extremely negative relationship to the American political system (a system of white male rule) has always been determined by our membership in two oppressed racial and sexual castes. As Angela Davis points out in "Reflections on the Black Woman's Role in the Community of Slaves," Black women have always embodied, if only in their physical manifestation, an adversary stance to white male rule and have actively resisted its inroads upon them and their communities in both dramatic and subtle ways. There have always been Black women activists—some known, like Sojourner Truth, Harriet Tubman, Frances E. W. Harper, Ida B. Wells Barnett, and Mary Church Terrell, and thousands upon thousands unknown—who had a shared awareness of how their sexual identity combined with their racial identity to make their whole life situation and the focus of their political struggles unique. Contemporary Black feminism is the outgrowth of countless generations of personal sacrifice, militancy, and work by our mothers and sisters.

A Black feminist presence has evolved most obviously in connection with the second wave of the American women's movement beginning in the late 1960s. Black, other Third World, and working women have been involved in the feminist movement from its start, but both outside reactionary forces and racism and elitism within the movement itself have served to obscure our participation. In 1973 Black feminists, primarily located in New York, felt the necessity of forming a separate Black feminist group. This became the National Black Feminist Organization (NBFO).

Black feminist politics also have an obvious connection to movements for Black liberation, particularly those of the 1960s and 1970s. Many of us were active in those movements (civil rights, Black nationalism, the Black Panthers), and all of our lives were greatly affected and changed by their ideology, their goals, and the tactics used to achieve their goals. It was our experience and disillusionment within these liberation movements, as well as experience on the periphery of the white male left, that led to the need to develop a politics that was antiracist, unlike those of white women, and antisexist, unlike those of Black and white men.

There is also undeniably a personal genesis for Black feminism, that is, the political realization that comes from the seemingly personal experiences of individual Black women's lives. Black feminists and many more Black women who do not define themselves as feminists have all experienced sexual oppression as a constant factor in our day-to-day existence. As children we realized that we were different from boys and that we were treated differently. For example, we were told in the same breath to be quiet both for the sake of being "ladylike" and to make us less objectionable in the eyes of white people. As we grew older we became aware of the threat of physical and sexual abuse by men. However, we had no way of conceptualizing what was so apparent to us, what we *knew* was really happening.

Black feminists often talk about their feelings of craziness before becoming conscious of the concepts of sexual politics, patriarchal rule, and most importantly, feminism, the political analysis and practice that we women use to struggle against our oppression. The fact that racial politics and indeed racism are pervasive factors in our lives did not allow us, and still does not allow most Black women, to look more deeply into our own experiences and, from that sharing and growing consciousness, to build a politics that will change our lives and inevitably end our oppression. Our development must also be tied to the contemporary economic and political position of Black people. The post World War II generation of Black youth was the first to be able to minimally partake of certain educational and employment options, previously closed completely to Black people. Although our economic position is still at the very bottom of the American capitalistic economy, a handful of us have been able to gain certain tools as a result of tokenism in education and employment which potentially enable us to more effectively fight our oppression.

A combined antiracist and antisexist position drew us together initially, and as we developed politically we addressed ourselves to hetero-sexism and economic oppression under capitalism.

2. WHAT WE BELIEVE

Above all else, our politics initially sprang from the shared belief that Black women are inherently valuable, that our liberation is a necessity not as an adjunct to somebody else's but because of our need as human persons for autonomy. This may seem so obvious as to sound simplistic, but it is apparent that no other ostensibly progressive movement has ever considered our specific oppression as a priority or worked seriously for the ending of that oppression. Merely naming the perjorative stereotypes attributed to Black women (e.g., mammy, matriarch, Sapphire, whore, bulldagger), let alone cataloguing the cruel, often murderous, treatment we receive, indicates how little value has been placed upon our lives during four centuries of bondage in the Western hemisphere. We realize that the only people who care enough about us to work consistently for our liberation is us. Our politics evolve from a healthy love for ourselves, our sisters and our community which allows us to continue our struggle and work.

This focusing upon our own oppression is embodied in the concept of identity politics. We believe that the most profound and potentially the most radical politics come directly out of our own identity, as opposed to working to end somebody else's oppression. In the case of Black women this is a particularly repugnant, dangerous, threatening, and therefore revolutionary concept because it is obvious from looking at all the political movements that have preceded us that anyone is more worthy of liberation than ourselves. We reject pedestals, queenhood, and walking ten paces behind. To be recognized as human, levelly human, is enough.

We believe that sexual politics under patriarchy is as pervasive in Black women's lives as are the politics of class and race. We also often find it difficult to separate race from class from sex oppression because in our lives they are most often experienced simultaneously. We know that there is such a thing as racial-sexual oppression which is neither solely racial nor solely sexual, e.g., the history of rape of Black women by white men as a weapon of political repression.

Although we are feminists and lesbians, we feel solidarity with progressive Black men and do not advocate the fractionalization that white women who are separatists demand. Our situation as Black people necessitates that we have solidarity around the fact of race, which white women of course do not need to have with white men, unless it is their negative solidarity as racial oppressors. We struggle together with Black men against racism, while we also struggle with Black men about sexism.

We realize that the liberation of all oppressed peoples necessitates the destruction of the political-economic systems of capitalism and imperialism as well as patriarchy. We are socialists because we believe the work must be organized for the collective benefit of those who do the work and create the products, and not for the profit of the bosses. Material resources must be equally distributed among those who create these resources. We are not convinced, however, that a socialist revolution that is not also a feminist and antiracist revolution will guarantee our liberation. We have arrived at the necessity for developing an understanding of class relationships that takes into account the specific class position of Black women who are generally marginal in the labor force, while at this particular time some of us are temporarily viewed as doubly desirable tokens at white-collar and professional levels. We need to articulate the real class situation of peons who are not merely raceless, sexless workers, but for whom racial and sexual oppression are significant determinants in their working/economic lives. Although we are in essential agreement with Marx's theory as it applied to the very specific economic relationships he analyzed, we know that his analysis must be extended further in order for us to understand our specific economic situation as Black women.

A political contribution which we feel we have already made is the expansion of the feminist principle that the personal is political. In our consciousness-raising sessions, for example, we have in many ways gone beyond white women's revelations because we are dealing with the implications of race and class as well as sex. Even our Black women's style of talking/testifying in Black language about what we have experienced has a resonance that is both cultural and political. We have spent a great deal of energy delving into the cultural and experiential nature of our oppression out of necessity because none of these matters has ever been looked at before. No one before has ever examined the multilayered texture of Black women's lives. An example of this kind of revelation/conceptualization occurred at a meeting as we discussed the ways in which our early intellectual interests had been attacked by our peers, particularly Black males. We discovered that all of us, because we were "smart" had also been considered "ugly", *i.e.,* "smart-ugly." "Smart-ugly" crystallized the way in which most of us had been forced to develop our intellects at great cost to our "social" lives. The sanctions in the Black and white communities against Black women thinkers is comparatively much higher than for white women, particularly ones from the educated middle and upper classes.

As we have already stated, we reject the stance of lesbian separatism because it is not a viable political analysis or strategy for us. It leaves out far too much and far too many people, particularly Black men, women, and children. We have a great deal of criticism and loathing for what men have been socialized to be in this society: what they support, how they act, and how they oppress. But we do not have the misguided notion that it is their maleness, per se—i.e., their biological maleness—that makes them what they are. As Black women we find any type of biological determinism a particularly dangerous and reactionary basis upon which to build a politic. We must also question whether lesbian separatism is an adequate and progressive political analysis and strategy, even for those who practice it, since it so completely denies any but the sexual sources of women's oppression, negating the facts of class and race.

3. PROBLEMS IN ORGANIZING BLACK FEMINISTS

During our years together as a Black feminist collective we have experienced success and defeat, joy and pain, victory and failure. We have found that it is very difficult to organize around Black feminist issues, difficult even to

announce in certain contexts that we *are* Black feminists. We have tried to think about the reasons for our difficulties, particularly since the white women's movement continues to be strong and to grow in many directions. In this section we will discuss some of the general reasons for the organizing problems we face and also talk specifically about the stages in organizing our own collective.

The major source of difficulty in our political work is that we are not just trying to fight oppression on one front or even two, but instead to address a whole range of oppressions. We do not have racial, sexual, heterosexual, or class privilege to rely upon, nor do we have even the minimal access to resources and power that groups who possess any one of these types of privilege have.

The psychological toll of being a Black woman and the difficulties this presents in reaching political consciousness and doing political work can never be underestimated. There is a very low value placed upon Black women's psyches in this society, which is both racist and sexist. As an early group member once said, "We are all damaged people merely by virtue of being Black women." We are dispossessed psychologically and on every other level, and yet we feel the necessity to struggle to change the condition of all Black women. In "A Black Feminist's Search for Sisterhood," Michele Wallace arrives at this conclusion:

"We exist as women who are Black who are feminists, each stranded for the moment, working independently because there is not yet an environment in this society remotely congenial to our struggle—because, being on the bottom, we would have to do what no one else has done: we would have to fight the world."

Wallace is pessimistic but realistic in her assessment of Black feminists' position, particularly in her allusion to the nearly classic isolation most of us face. We might use our position at the bottom, however, to make a clear leap into revolutionary action. If Black women were free, it would mean that everyone else would have to be free since our freedom would necessitate the destruction of all the systems of oppression.

Feminism is, nevertheless, very threatening to the majority of Black people because it calls into question some of the most basic assumptions about our existence, i.e., that sex should be a determinant of power relationships. Here is the way male and female voices were defined in a Black nationalist pamphlet from the early 1970's.

"We understand that it is and has been traditional that the man is the head of the house. He is the leader of the house/nation because his knowledge of the world is broader, his awareness is greater, his understanding is fuller and his application of this information is wiser. . . . After all, it is only reasonable that the man be the head of the house because he is able to defend and protect the development of his home. . . . Women cannot do the same things as men—they are made by nature to function differently. Equality of men and women is something that cannot happen even in the abstract world. Men are not equal to other men, i.e., ability, experience or even understanding. The value of men and women can be seen as in the value of gold and silver—they are not equal but both have great value. We must realize that men and women are a complement to each other because there is no house/family without a man and his wife. Both are essential to the development of any life."[1]

The material conditions of most Black women would hardly lead them to upset both economic and sexual arrangements that seem to represent some stability in their lives. Many Black women have a good understanding of both sexism and racism, but because of the everyday constrictions of their lives cannot risk struggling against them both.

The reaction of Black men to feminism has been notoriously negative. They are, of course, even more threatened than Black women by the possibility that Black feminists might or-

ganize around our own needs. They realize that they might not only lose valuable and hardworking allies in their struggles but that they might also be forced to change their habitually sexist ways of interacting with and oppressing Black women. Accusations that Black feminism divides the Black struggle are powerful deterrents to the growth of an autonomous Black women's movement.

Still, hundreds of women have been active at different times during the three-year existence of our group. And every Black woman who came, came out of a strongly-felt need for some level of possibility that did not previously exist in her life.

When we first started meeting early in 1974 after the NBFO first eastern regional conference, we did not have a strategy for organizing, or even a focus. We just wanted to see what we had. After a period of months of not meeting, we began to meet again late in the year and started doing an intense variety of consciousness-raising. The overwhelming feeling that we had is that after years and years we had finally found each other. Although we were not doing political work as a group, individuals continued their involvement in Lesbian politics, sterilization abuse and abortion rights work, Third World Women's International Women's Day activities, and support activity for the trials of Dr. Kenneth Edelin, Joan Little, and Inéz García. During our first summer, when membership had dropped off considerably, those of us remaining devoted serious discussion to the possibility of opening a refuge for battered women in a Black community. (There was no refuge in Boston at that time.) We also decided around that time to become an independent collective since we had serious disagreements with NBFO's bourgeois-feminist stance and their lack of a clear political focus.

We also were contacted at that time by socialist feminists, with whom we had worked on abortion rights activities, who wanted to encourage us to attend the National Socialist

1. Mumininas of Committee for Unified Newark, *Mwanamke Mwananchi* (The Nationalist Woman), Newark, N.J., © 1971, pp. 4–5.

Feminist Conference in Yellow Springs. One of our members did attend and despite the narrowness of the ideology that was promoted at that particular conference, we became more aware of the need for us to understand our own economic situation and to make our own economic analysis.

In the fall, when some members returned, we experienced several months of comparative inactivity and internal disagreements which were first conceptualized as a Lesbian-straight split but which were also the result of class and political differences. During the summer those of us who were still meeting had determined the need to do political work and to move beyond consciousness-raising and serving exclusively as an emotional support group. At the beginning of 1976, when some of the women who had not wanted to do political work and who also had voiced disagreements stopped attending of their own accord, we again looked for a focus. We decided at that time, with the addition of new members, to become a study group. We had always shared our reading with each other, and some of us had written papers on Black feminism for group discussion a few months before this decision was made. We began functioning as a study group and also began discussing the possibility of starting a Black feminist publication. We had a retreat in the late spring which provided a time for both political discussion and working out interpersonal issues. Currently we are planning to gather together a collection of Black feminist writing. We feel that it is absolutely essential to demonstrate the reality of our politics to other Black women and believe that we can do this through writing and distributing our work. The fact that individual Black feminists are living in isolation all over the country, that our own numbers are small, and that we have some skills in writing, printing, and publishing makes us want to carry out these kinds of projects as a means of organizing Black feminists as we continue to do political work in coalition with other groups.

4. BLACK FEMINIST ISSUES AND PROJECTS

During our time together we have identified and worked on many issues of particular relevance to Black women. The inclusiveness of our politics makes us concerned with any situation that impinges upon the lives of women, Third World and working people. We are of course particularly committed to working on those struggles in which race, sex and class are simultaneous factors in oppression. We might, for example, become involved in workplace organizing at a factory that employs Third World women, or picket a hospital that is cutting back on already inadequate health care to a Third World community, or set up a rape crisis center in a Black neighborhood. Organizing around welfare and daycare concerns might also be a focus. The work to be done and the countless issues that this work represents merely reflect the pervasiveness of our oppression.

Issues and projects that collective members have actually worked on are sterilization abuse, abortion rights, battered women, rape and health care. We have also done many workshops and eduationals on Black feminism on college campuses, at women's conferences, and most recently for high school women.

One issue that is of major concern to us and that we have begun to publicly address is racism in the white women's movement. As Black feminists we are made constantly and painfully aware of how little effort white women have made to understand and combat their racism, which requires among other things that they have a more than superficial comprehension of race, color, and black history and culture. Eliminating racism in the white women's movement is by definition work for white women to do, but we will continue to speak to and demand accountability on this issue.

In the practice of our politics we do not believe that the end always justifies the means. Many reactionary and destructive acts have been done in the name of achieving "correct" political goals. As feminists we do not want to mess over people in the name of politics. We believe in a collective process and a nonhierarchical distribution of power within our own group and in our vision of a revolutionary society. We are committed to a continual examination of our politics as they develop through criticism and self-criticism as an essential aspect of our practice. In her introduction to *Sisterhood is Powerful* Robin Morgan writes:

"I haven't the faintest notion what possible revolutionary role white heterosexual men could fulfill, since they are the very embodiment of reactionary-vested-interest-power."

As Black feminists and lesbians we know that we have a very definite revolutionary task to perform and we are ready for the lifetime of work and struggle before us.

28

MICHELE WALLACE

Black Macho and the Myth of the Superwoman (1979)

Sapphire. Mammy. Tragic mulatto wench. Workhorse, can swing ax. Lift a load, pick cotton with any man. A wonderful housekeeper. Excellent with children. Very clean. Very religious. A terrific mother. A great little singer and dancer and a devoted teacher and social worker. She's always had more opportunities than the black man because she was no threat to the white man so he made it easy for her. Curiously enough, she frequently ends up on welfare. Not beautiful, rather hard-looking unless she has white blood, but then very beautiful. The black ones are exotic though, great in bed, tigers. And very fertile. If she is middle-class, she tends to be uptight about sex, prudish. She is unsupportive of black men, domineering, castrating. Very strong. Sorrow tolls right off her brow like so

From *Ms.*, January 1979. Adapted from Michele Wallace, *Black Macho and the Myth of the Superwoman* (New York: The Dial Press, 1978). Reprinted by permission of the author.

much rain. Tough, unfeminine. Opposed to women's rights movements, considers herself already liberated.

From the intricate web of mythology that surrounds the black woman a fundamental image emerges. It is of a woman of inordinate strength, who does not have the same fears, weaknesses, and insecurities as other women, but believes herself to be and is, in fact, stronger emotionally than most men. In other words, she is a superwoman

Through the years this image has remained basically intact. Right now, I can imagine my reader thinking, *Of course she's stronger. Look what she's been through.* Even for me, it continues to be difficult to let the myth go.

I remember once I was watching a news show with a black male friend of mine who had a Ph.D. in psychology. We were looking at some footage of a black woman who seemed barely able to speak English, though at least six generations of her family before her had certainly claimed it as their first language. She was in bed wrapped in blankets, her numerous small poorly clothed children huddled around her. Her apartment looked rat-infested, cramped, and dirty. She had not, she said, had heat and hot water for days. My friend, a solid member of the middle class now but surely no stranger to poverty in his childhood, felt obliged to comment—in order to assuage his guilt, I can think of no other reason—"That's a *strong* sister," as he bowed his head in reverence.

By the time I was 15 there was nothing I dreaded more than being like the women in my family. Their sharp tongues were able to disassemble any human ego in five minutes flat. Nearly all had been divorced at least once. They all worked. Never as domestics and none had ever been on welfare.

"Too proud," they said.

When I brought a young man to the house, I watched nervously, pleading silently with them not to submit him to the family Xray. As soon as the door was closed behind him, they would begin to make pronouncements. "He's cheap," or "He's very immature." They were always right, and that disturbed me. They told me that they were only trying to help me, that it was ever so difficult growing up to be a whole black woman. But I didn't want to hear that.

I can't remember when I first learned that my family expected me to work, but it had been drilled into me that the best and only sure support was self-support.

The fact that my family expected me to have a career should have made the things I wanted different from what little white girls wanted according to the popular sociological view. But I don't believe any sociologist took into account a man like my stepfather. My stepfather gave me "housewife lessons." It was he who taught me how to clean house and how I should act around men. "Don't be like your mother," he told me. "She's a nice lady but she's a bad wife. She was just lucky with me. I want you to get a *good* husband."

Although he never managed to fully domesticate me, it was him I finally listened to because he was saying essentially the same things I read in the magazines, saw in the movies, gaped at on television. Growing up in Harlem, I listened to these messages no less intently than the little white girls who grew up on Park Avenue, in Scarsdale, or on Long Island. In a way I needed to hear them even more than they did. Their alternative was not eternal Aunt Jemimahood, Porgy-'n'-Besshood. Mine was.

Then in 1968, the year I turned 16, blackness came to Harlem. Black artists, musicians, writers, poets, many of them fresh from the East Village, began to gather in response to the cries of "black power" and "kill whitey" that had echoed in the streets during the recent riots. And Harlemites, who had always been divided into two distinct categories—the black bourgeoisie, and the poor—now began to split into more factions.

The black bourgeoisie became the "knee-grows" and the poor became the "lumpen" or the "grass roots." The two new factions were the "militants" and the "nationalists." The militants had no patience with the singing, dancing, incense, and poetry-reading of the black nationalists; with the black bourgeoisie's appeals for restraint; or the inertia of the poor. The nationalists could not abide the militant's insistence that everyone "hit the streets" or their Marxist rhetoric; the black bourgeoisie's loyalty to European culture; and the frequent cultural obtuseness of the poor about everything but rock, blues, and gospel. The black bourgeoisie was temporarily, but thoroughly, intimidated by everyone. And the poor thought they were *all* crazy. But all parties managed to agree on at least one issue: the black woman's act needed intensive cleaning up. She was one of the main reasons the black man had never been properly able to take hold of his situation in this country.

I was fascinated by all of this. Not by the political implications of a black movement in a white America. I quickly realized that was a male responsibility. But by how it would affect my narrow universe. To me and many other black women the Black Movement seemed to guarantee that our secret dreams of being male-dominated and supported women were that much more attainable. If black men had power, as in black power, then we would become the women of the powerful.

But first we had a hell of a history to live down. We had been rolling around in bed with the slave master while the black man was having his penis cut off; we had never been able to close our legs to a white man nor deny our breast to a white child; we had been too eagerly loyal to our white male employer, taking the job he offered when he would give none to our man, cleaning his house with love and attention while our man was being lynched by white men in white hoods. We had not allowed the black man to be a man in his own house. We had driven him to alcohol, to drugs, to crime, to every bad thing he had ever done to harm himself or his family because our eyes had not reflected his manhood.

I felt shocked by this history. My mother had done her best to keep all of it from me. I did know that the men in my family had seemed to be very sweet, very intelligent, but a bit ineffectual and spineless. And the women had seemed to be relentless achievers, often providers. At 16 I had no use for paradoxes. The women in my family could not be both strong and weak, both victimizers and victimized. It was much easier just to believe these women were the bloodless monsters the Black Movement said they were, and to reckon with my share in that sin. What must I do, I wondered, to atone for my errors and make myself more palatable? I must be, black men told me, more feminine, more attractive, and above all more submissive, in other words a "natural woman."

Never realizing how imaginary my "strength" really was, I swore never to use it. But that didn't seem to be enough. I was not terribly convincing as a passive woman. The men seemed to go right through my fingers. I was overeager, too impatient, and somehow I could not stop getting angry from time to time.

It must be a difficult thing to be the mother of a teenage daughter in a black community. The nice little old men who used to pat her on the head when she was a child begin to want to pat her on the ass when she is 13. The neighborhood pimps and hustlers begin to proposition her. They know that she is tired of the rules and regulations of family life, that her head is filled with escapist fantasies. Adolescence is also the point at which peer pressure begins to take over.

Now I can understand my mother's fears. No one else thought it would be particularly horrible if I got pregnant or got married before I had grown up, if I never completed college. I was a black girl; I had done as well as could be expected under the circumstances. My mother wanted to compel me to think for myself because she knew, whatever else she didn't know, that I would never be able to survive if I didn't. Little black girls who had a predilection for moving in with anyone who had a handsome face and a king-size bed tended to end up dead, or with needles in their arms or on welfare.

In 1967, the streets of New York had witnessed the grand coming out of all time of black male/white female couples. Frankly, I found this confusing. I was enough of a slave to white liberal fashions around me to believe that two people who wanted each other had a right to each other, but was that what this was about? It all seemed strangely inappropriate, poorly timed. Black was angry, anywhere from vaguely to militantly antiwhite; black was sexy and had unlimited potential. What did the black man want with a white woman now?

What convinced me that this situation had a broader meaning was the amazing way people were taking it. Educated middle-class white liberals seemed to feel it was their duty to condone relationships between white women and black men because that would mean they weren't racist. Black men often could not separate their interest in white women from their hostility toward black women: "I can't stand that black bitch." Some black men argued that white women gave them money, didn't put them down, made them feel like men. And black women made no attempt to disguise their anger and disgust, to the point of verbal, if not physical, assaults in the streets—on the white woman or the black man or both.

Meanwhile Dr. Martin Luther King, in a move that was definitely ahead of his time, was beginning to shift his emphasis from civil rights to economic issues and was planning a Poor People's March on Washington. On March 28, 1968, Dr. King marched with a band of striking sanitation workers in Memphis. The garbage men wore signs that read I AM A MAN. On April 4, King was shot and the rioting began again, worse than ever. Suddenly praying, waiting, singing, and anything white was out. Rioting was viewed as urban guerrilla warfare, the first step toward the complete overthrow of the honkie, racist government. On the cultural level everything had to be rehauled. Brothers, with softly beating drums in the background, were talking about beautiful black Queens of the Nile and beautiful full lips and black skin and big asses. Yet the "problem" with the white sisters downtown persisted.

Some of the more militant sisters uptown would tell you that the "problem" was that white women were *throwing* themselves at black men and that if they would just let the man be, he'd come home. And, furthermore, there was this matter of a black matriarchy. Everybody wanted to cut Daniel Moynihan's heart out and feed it to the dogs, but he did have a point after all. The black woman had gotten out of hand. She got all the jobs, all the everything. The black man had never had a chance. No wonder he wanted a white woman. The black woman should keep her big, black mouth shut.

And the black woman started to do just that. The Women's Movement came along, and she went right on trimming her fro, having her babies for the revolution. Admirably thorough about not allowing a word of feminist rhetoric to penetrate their minds, some black women even attacked the Women's Movement out of their feelings of inadequacy, shame, and hatred for white women. Others cleaned house and fried chicken. They just knew that their man, the black man, would not stand for no back talk from no white girl. He was on his way home for sure. But they were wrong.

There was between the black man and the black woman a misunderstanding as old as slavery. The push toward black liberation caused this accumulation of rage to explode upon the heads of black women. The black woman did not, could not, effectively fight back. It was a man's world.

Now that freedom, equality, rights, wealth, power were assumed to be on their way, she had to understand that manhood was essential to revolution. Could you imagine Che Guevara with breasts? Mao with a vagina? She had had her day. Womanhood was not essential to revolution. Or so everyone thought by the beginning of the 1970s.

I am saying, among other things, that for perhaps the last 50 years there has been a growing distrust, even hatred, between black men and black women. It has been nursed along not only by racism on the part of whites, but also by an almost deliberate ignorance on the part of blacks about the sexual politics of their experience in this country. It is from this perspective that the black man and woman faced the challenge of the Black Revolution—a revolution subsequently dissipated and distorted by their inability to see each other clearly through the fog of sexual myths and fallacies. This has cost us unity for one thing.

Though I am a black feminist, and that label rightly suggests that I feel black men could stand substantial improvement, I still find it difficult to blame them alone. Black men have had no greater part than black women in perpetuating the ignorance with which they view one another. The black man, however, particularly since the Black Movement, has been in the position to define the black woman. He is the one who tells her whether or not she is a woman and what it is to be a woman. And therefore, whether he wishes to or not, he determines her destiny as well as his own.

Though originally it was the white man who was responsible for the black woman's grief, a multiplicity of forces act upon her life now and the black man is one of the most important. The white man is downtown. The black man lives with her. He's the head of her church and may be the principal of her local school or even the mayor of the city in which she lives.

She is the workhorse that keeps his house functioning, she is the foundation of his community, she raises his children, and she faithfully votes for him in elections, goes to his movies, reads his books, watches him on television, buys in his stores, solicits his services as doctor, lawyer, accountant.

The black man has not really kept his part of the bargain they made in the sixties. When she stood by silently as he became a "man," she assumed that he would finally glorify and dignify black womanhood just as the white man had done for the white woman. But he did not. He refused her. His involvement with white women was only the most dramatic form that refusal took. He refused her because the assertion of his manhood required something quite different of him. He refused her because it was too late to carbon-copy the male/female relationships of the Victorian era. And he refused her because he felt justified in his anger that she had betrayed him. She believed that, even as she denied it. She too was angry, but paralyzed by the feeling that she had no right to be.

Therefore her strange numbness, her determination, spoken or unspoken, to remain basically unquestioning of the black man's authority and thereby supportive of all he has done, even that which has been abusive of her. She is in the grip of Black macho and it has created within her inestimable emotional devastation.

The black woman's silence is a new silence. She knows that. There has been from slavery until the civil rights movement a thin but continuous line of black women who have prodded their sisters to self-improvement, to education, to an industrious and active position in the affairs of their communities. In their time a woman's interest in herself was not automatically interpreted as hostile to men and their progress, at least not by black people. Day by day these women, like most women, devoted their energies to their husbands and children. When they found time, they worked on reforms in education, medicine, housing, and their communities through their organizations and churches. Besides their other pursuits they took particular interest in the problems of their fellow beings, black women. Little did they know that one day their activities would be used as proof that the black woman has never known her place and has mightily battled the black man for his male prerogative as head of household.

The American black woman is haunted by the mythology that surrounds the American black man. It is a mythology based upon the real persecution of black men: castrated black men hanging by their necks from trees; black men shining shoes; black men behind bars, whipped raw by prison guards and police; black men with needles in their arms, with wine bottles in their hip pockets; jobless black men on street corners; black men being pushed out in front to catch the enemy's bullets in every American war since the Revolution of 1776—these ghosts, rendered all the more gruesome by their increasing absence of detail, are crouched in the black woman's brain. Every time she starts to wonder about her own misery, to think about reconstructing her life, the ghosts pounce. "*You* crippled the black man. *You* worked against him. *You* betrayed him. *You* laughed at him. *You* scorned him. *You* and the white man."

Not only does the black woman continue to see the black man historically as a cripple; she refuses to take seriously the various ways he's been able to assert his manhood and capabilities in recent years. Granted that many of his gains of the past decade have been temporary and illusory, he is, nevertheless, no longer a pathetic, beaten-down slave (if indeed he ever was only that). But whether he is cast as America's latest sex object, king of virility and violence, master of the ghetto art of cool, or a Mickey Mouse copy of a white capitalist, the black woman pities him. She sees only the masses of unemployed black men, junkies, winos, prison inmates. She does not really see the masses of impoverished, unemployed black women, their numerous children pulling at their skirts; or if she does, she sees these women and children only as a further humiliation and burden to that poor, downtrodden black man.

She sees only the myth. In fact what most people see when they look at the black man is the myth.

American slavery was a dehumanizing experience for everyone involved. Yet somehow the story goes that the black man suffered a special denigration as the constant victim of an unholy alliance between his woman and the enemy, the white man. The facts are a good deal more complicated and ambiguous.

The slave family was constantly subject to disruption by sales of children, of father, and mother. Many black women did have sex with and bear children for their white masters. Many slave fathers did lack traditional authority over their family. But to accept these features of slavery as the entire picture is to accept that the character of life in the black slave community was solely a product of white oppression.

Despite the obstacles, the slave family was often a stable entity. Most black families were headed by a stable male/female partnership, by a husband and a wife. Slaves were not usually required by their masters to form such permanent unions, but these unions did, nevertheless, exist in great quantities. That fact suggests that blacks, both males and females, took traditional marriage and all it entailed, including male authority, quite seriously.

That so many slave narratives show evidence of attachment for fathers would indicate that the father/child relationship was not taken lightly.

Yes, black men were called boys. Black women were also called girls. But the slaves thought of themselves as "mens and womens." There were cases of black women who were raped as their husbands looked on, powerless. There were also cases of men who fought to the death to prevent such things. Most of the women engaged in interracial unions were probably single; many were unwilling, some were not. There was also some sexual contact between black male slaves and white women. White men did not seem to become obsessed with preventing such relations until much later. In fact, before the American Revolution free blacks in the colonies were usually the products of unions between black male slaves and indentured white women.

A slave woman really had four ways in which to distinguish herself. The first way was by excelling at physical labor. Whereas women who were delicate suffered a great deal in slavery (and there were a great many such women), women who were physically robust were highly valued.

Second, there were women who rose by becoming the sex partners of their masters. Sometimes their white owners lived with them openly as their wives. More often they and their children were given their freedom upon the master's death. But such women were sometimes the victims of special abuse, were sold away to avoid scandal in the larger white community and embarrassment to the master's wife.

The third way a black woman slave might achieve some status was as a mammy. The mammy is a hated figure in black history and perhaps with good reason. Legend has it that she often controlled the household, its white members as well, that she was sometimes over-loyal to her master and guarded his wealth and position with great vigor. But she also served a useful function to the slave community. She might intercede in behalf of a slave and prevent his being punished, and she often provided much of the information from the big house.

The fourth way for a black woman to be set apart from the ordinary slaves was as a house servant with a special skill. She might be a laundress, a weaver, a spinner, and, as a good worker she might come to be greatly valued by the master. But here again the record also shows that she was often the victim of special abuse and suffered under the constant eye of her mistress.

The distinctions available to black male slaves were actually somewhat more impressive and more varied. First, men might become artisans, craftsmen, mechanics. These men were among the most respected members of the slave community and were frequently allowed to take some percentage of wages when they were hired out. Second, black men might become "drivers" or even *de facto* overseers. The black driver, another hated figure in black history, had the job of seeing that the slaves performed well in the fields. Sometimes he was vicious. On occasion he might force some of the slave women to have sex with him. But sometimes he was lenient. Clearly he was an important tool of the master class, but he also benefited the slave community in that he was a living example of a black man in a position of authority, and he helped to counter the notion of the black man as a boy.

A black male slave might also become the body servant, butler, or coachman of his master. As such, he might over the years win a great deal of trust and subsequent authority. And of course it was often the black male, not the female, who won prestige through his achievements in field labor. In addition, black men won influence in the slave community by fighting in the American Revolution and then in the War of 1812. Many slaves reported proudly that some male ancestor had fought for his country.

Lastly, it was the men, in virtually all cases, who planned and/or led the slave revolts. Although women participated, it seems that every known slave plot or actual rebellion was the result of male initiative.

Viewing American slavery with any kind of objectivity is extremely difficult, mostly because the record was unevenly and inconsistently kept. Nevertheless, to suggest that the black man was emasculated by slavery is to suggest that the black man and the black woman were creatures without will, as well as that a black woman could not be equally humiliated. Slave men and women formed a coherent and, as much as possible, a beneficial code of behavior and values, based upon the amalgamation of their African past and the forced realities of their American experience—in other words, an African-American culture.

Yet the myth of the black man's castration in slavery has been nurtured over a century. The presumed dominance of the black female during slavery would not be quite enough to explain the full extent of black male anger, especially since it was more untrue than not, and at some point the black man must have known that. Rather his actual gripe must be that the black woman, his woman, was not *his* slave, that his right to expect her complete service and devotion was usurped. She *was*, after all, the white man's slave.

Nevertheless, the record shows that black men and black women emerged from slavery in twos, husbands and wives. It was mostly after slavery that the fear white men had of black men began to take some of its more lascivious forms. It was then that the myth of the black man's sexuality as a threat to pure white womanhood began to gain force.

Sacred white womanhood had been an economically necessary assumption under the slavery system. It had also been necessary to assume that black women were promiscuous and fickle and gave no more thought to their offspring than pigs did to their litter. Therefore whites might sell black children with impunity and do with them what they pleased. But the white woman would be the mother of the little man who would inherit the white man's fortune. One had to be certain of the child's origin. Thus the white woman's purity, like the black female's promiscuity, was based upon her status as property. After the ill-fated Reconstruction period came the rise of the Ku Klux Klan, the thousands of lynchings and the group effort on the part of white men to sever the black man's penis from his body and render him economically unable to provide for his family, despite his legal freedom.

How did the black family respond to this pressure? For the most part it continued the tradition of adaptation that had marked the evolution of the Afro-American family from slavery. There was the pressure of the American white standard but there was also the standard that black Americans had set for themselves. Slave rule provided for trial marriage, for pregnancy followed by marriage, for some degree of sexual experimentation prior to settling down. All of which had precedents in African societies, as well as in most precapitalist agrarian societies. After marriage, however, adultery was considered intolerable. If possible, the man worked and provided for all. If not, the woman also worked. But at no point in American history have more black women been employed than black men.

Only as American blacks began to accept the standards of family life, as well as manhood and womanhood, embraced by American whites, did black men and women begin to resent one another.

Americanization for the black man in particular meant more than coming to view the deviation of his woman from the American ideal as an affront to his manhood. It also meant that the inaccessibility of the white woman represented a severe limitation of that manhood. Furthermore, the experience of the civil rights movement would teach him that nonviolence did not work, nor did restraint, cleverness, wittiness, or patience. America, he thought, respected bravado, violence, and macho.

Around the time that Shirley Chisholm was running for President in 1972, a black comedian and television star made an infamous joke about her. He said that he would prefer Raquel Welch to Shirley Chisholm any day. That joke was widely publicized, particularly in the black community, and thought quite funny. It expressed the comparisons black men were making between black women and white women: responsibility, always tiresome, versus the illusion of liberation and freedom. But this joke had yet another level of meaning as well. We black men, the comedian's joke seemed to say, are more interested in going to bed with Raquel Welch than we are in having a black President.

Shirley Chisholm was the first black woman to run for President of the United States, and be taken seriously. However, almost none of the black political forces in existence at the time—in other words, the black male political forces—supported her. In fact, they actively opposed her nomination. The black man in the street seemed either outraged that she dared to run or simply indifferent. The campaign was composed largely of black and white women.

Ever since then it has really baffled me to hear black men say that black women have no time for feminism because black comes first. For them, when it came to Shirley Chisholm, being black no longer came first at all. It turned out that what they really meant all along was that the black man came before the black woman.

The reaction of black men to Chisholm's campaign marked the point at which the Black Movement breathed its last as a viable entity. Black male hostility to Chisholm exploded any illusion that blacks might actually be able to sustain a notion of themselves apart from America's racist, sexist influence, a notion essential to their autonomy and inner direction. Misogyny was an integral part of Black Macho.

Meanwhile, the Women's Movement was redefining womanhood for white women in a manner that allowed them to work, to be manless, but still women. White women replaced some of their traditional activities with new ones—consciousness-raising, feminist meetings and demonstrations, political campaigns, anti-discrimination suits against employers, and the pursuit of an entirely new range of careers. And some white women dragged their men right along with them, not to mention a good many black men.

But the black woman, who had pooh-poohed the Women's Movement, was left with only one activity that was not considered suspect: motherhood. A baby could counteract the damaging effect a career might have upon her feminine image. A baby clarified a woman's course for at least the next five years. No need for her to bother with difficult decisions about whether or not she ought to pursue promotion or return to school for an advanced degree, both of which might attract even more hostility from black men. If she didn't find a man, she might just decide to have a baby anyway.

Although black women have been having babies outside of marriage since slavery, there are several unusual things about the current trend. Whereas unmarried black women with babies have usually lived with extended families, these women tend to brave it alone. Whereas black women of previous generations generally married soon after the baby was born, these women may not and often say they do not wish to marry. Whereas the practice of having babies out of wedlock was generally confined to the poorer classes, it is now not uncommon among middle-class, moderately successful black women. While I don't believe that anything like a majority of black women are going for this, it is worth finding out why so many of us have.

I am inclined to believe it is because the black woman has no legitimate way of coming together with other black women, no means of self-affirmation—in other words, no Women's Movement, and therefore no collective ideology. Career and success are still the social and emotional disadvantages to her that they were to white women in the fifties. There is little in the black community to reinforce a young black woman who does not have a man or a child and who wishes to pursue a career. She is still considered against nature.

Some young black women are beginning to be honest about seeing themselves as victims rather than superwomen. An alarming number go one disastrous step further. They become angry with black men, black people, blackness; it is simply a new way of blaming someone else for their underdevelopment.

When I was a newborn infant, my mother used to wonder why I was always scratching. It wasn't long before the cause became evident: I had eczema, a then incurable skin condition which causes peeling, flaking, and scabs. As I got older, it got worse. Other children were afraid to touch me. I greeted new schoolmates with "Don't worry, it isn't contagious."

As I approached puberty, it spread to my face. I was the only kid in the seventh grade who didn't have eyebrows. Because I was always chip dry, I had to put a lot of creams on my skin, couldn't go swimming or tumble around in the dirt. There wasn't a single moment of my life that I wasn't acutely aware of my skin. It was my excuse for everything—even for why I didn't do homework.

When I was 13, I was sent to a famous dermatologist who cured me completely in three weeks. My skin was not only clear; it seemed perfect. I remember people used to stop me on the street to ask me what I used on my skin. Suddenly I was beautiful, but my inner feelings never adjusted to the change in my appearance.

The sense of being handicapped of having a right to special considerations, never left me. When people complained about my lateness or my seeming lack of a sense of responsibility, I was baffled and hurt. Didn't they understand I couldn't be expected to perform as if I were healthy?

I believe that the black woman thinks of her history and conditions as a wound that makes her different and therefore special and therefore exempt from human responsibility. The impartial observer may look at her and see a beautiful, healthy, glowing, vigorous woman, but none of that matters. What matters is that inside she feels powerless to do anything about her condition or anyone else's. Her solution is to simply not participate, or to participate on her own limited basis.

Yes, it is very important that we never forget the tragedy of our history or how racist white people have been or how the black man has let us down. But all of that must be set in its proper perspective. It belongs to the past and we must belong to the future. The future is something we can control.

Lately I've noticed the appearance of a number of black women's organizations and conferences. The organizations break up quickly and yet they keep forming. Every now and then, someone still mentions that white women are going to rip them off if they join the Women's Movement—that is, white women will use their support to make gains and then not share with the black women. Unfortunately, this is probably true. It would be true of any movement the black woman joined in her present condition, that is, without some clear understanding of her own priorities.

In February, 1978, there was a series of articles in the *New York Times* on the changes in the black community since 1968. It covered the civil rights movement, the Black Movement, the economic and social situation for blacks today. Never once did it mention the contribution black women made to the civil rights movement. The articles spoke of three Americas: one white, one middle-class black, one poor black. No particular notice was given to the fact that poor black America consists largely of black women and children. It was as if these women and children did not exist.

History has been written without us. The imperative is clear: either we will make history or remain the victims of it.

29
ALICE WALKER

In Search of Our Mothers' Gardens (1974)

"I described her own nature and temperament. Told how they needed a larger life for their expression. . . . I pointed out that in lieu of proper channels, her emotions had overflowed into paths that dissipated them. I talked, beautifully I thought, about an art that would be born, an art that would open the way for women the likes of her. I asked her to hope, and build up an inner life against the coming of that day. . . . I sang, with a strange quiver in my voice, a promise song."

—"Avey," Jean Toomer, *Cane*
(The poet speaking to a prostitute who falls asleep while he's talking)

When the poet Jean Toomer walked through the South in the early twenties, he discovered a curious thing: black women whose spirituality was so intense, so deep, so *unconscious,* that they were themselves unaware of the richness they held. They stumbled blindly through their lives: creatures so abused and mutilated in body, so dimmed and confused by pain, that they considered themselves unworthy even of hope. In the selfless abstractions their bodies became to the men who used them, they became more than "sexual objects," more even than mere women: they became "Saints." Instead of being perceived as whole

From *Ms.*, May 1974. Reprinted by permission of *Ms.* Magazine, copyright 1974.

persons, their bodies became shrines: what was thought to be their minds became temples suitable for worship. These crazy Saints stared out at the world, wildly, like lunatics—or quietly, like suicides; and the "God" that was in their gaze was as mute as a great stone.

Who were these Saints? These crazy, loony, pitiful women?

Some of them, without a doubt, were our mothers and grandmothers.

In the still heat of the post-reconstruction South, this is how they seemed to Jean Toomer: exquisite butterflies trapped in an evil honey, toiling away their lives in an era, a century, that did not acknowledge them, except as "the *mule* of the world." They dreamed dreams that no one knew—not even themselves, in any coherent fashion—and saw visions no one could understand. They wandered or sat about the countryside crooning lullabies to ghosts, and drawing the mother of Christ in charcoal on courthouse walls.

They forced their minds to desert their bodies and their thriving spirits sought to rise, like frail whirlwinds from the hard red clay. And when those frail whirlwinds fell, in scattered particles, upon the ground, no one mourned. Instead, men lit candles to celebrate the emptiness that remained, as people do who enter a beautiful but vacant space to resurrect a God.

Our mothers and grandmothers, some of them: moving to music not yet written. And they waited.

They waited for a day when the unknown thing that was in them would be made known; but guessed, somehow in their darkness, that on the day of their revelation they would be long dead. Therefore to Toomer they walked, and even ran, in slow motion. For they were going nowhere immediate, and the future was not yet within their grasp. And men took our mothers and grandmothers, "but got no pleasure from it." So complex was their passion and their calm.

To Toomer, they lay vacant and fallow as autumn fields, with harvest time never in sight: and he saw them enter loveless marriages, without joy; and become prostitutes, without resistance; and become mothers of children, without fulfillment.

For these grandmothers and mothers of ours were not Saints, but Artists; driven to a numb and bleeding madness by the springs of creativity in them for which there was no release. They were Creators, who lived lives of spiritual waste, because they were so rich in spirituality—which is the basis of Art—that the strain of enduring their unused and unwanted talent drove them insane. Throwing away this spirituality was their pathetic attempt to lighten the soul to a weight their workworn, sexually abused bodies could bear.

What did it mean for a black woman to be an artist in our grandmothers' time? In our great-grandmothers' day? It is a question with an answer cruel enough to stop the blood.

Did you have a genius of a great-great-grandmother who died under some ignorant and depraved white overseer's lash? Or was she required to bake biscuits for a lazy backwater tramp, when she cried out in her soul to paint watercolors of sunsets, or the rain falling on the green and peaceful pasturelands? Or was her body broken and forced to bear children (who were more often than not sold away from her)—eight, ten, fifteen, twenty children—when her one joy was the thought of modeling heroic figures of rebellion, in stone or clay?

How was the creativity of the black woman kept alive, year after year and century after century, when for most of the years black people have been in America, it was a punishable crime for a black person to read or write? And the freedom to paint, to sculpt, to expand the mind with action did not exist. Consider, if you can bear to imagine it, what might have been the result if singing, too, had been forbidden by law. Listen to the voices of Bessie Smith, Billie Holiday, Nina Simone, Roberta Flack, and Aretha Franklin, among others, and imagine those voices muzzled for life. Then you may begin to comprehend the lives of our "crazy," "Sainted" mothers and grandmothers. The agony of the lives of women who might have been Poets, Novelists, Essayists, and Short-

Story Writers (over a period of centuries), who died with their real gifts stifled within them.

And, if this were the end of the story we would have cause to cry out in my paraphrase of Okot p'Bitek's great poem:

O, my clanswomen
Let us all cry together!
Come,
Let us mourn the death of our mother,
The death of a Queen
The ash that was produced
By a great fire,
O, this homestead is utterly dead
Close the gates
With *lacari* thorns,
For our mother
The creator of the
Stool is lost!
And all the young women
Have perished in the wilderness!

But this is not the end of the story, for all the young women—our mothers and grandmothers, *ourselves*—have not perished in the wilderness. And if we ask ourselves why, and search for and find the answer, we will know beyond all efforts to erase it from our minds, just exactly who, and of what, we black American women are.

One example, perhaps the most pathetic, most misunderstood one, can provide a backdrop for our mothers' work: Phillis Wheatley, a slave in the 1700s.

Virginia Woolf, in her book *A Room of One's Own,* wrote that in order for a woman to write fiction she must have two things, certainly: a room of her own (with key and lock) and enough money to support herself.

What then are we to make of Phillis Wheatley, a slave, who owned not even herself? This sickly, frail black girl who required a servant of her own at times—her health was so precarious—and who, had she been white, would have been easily considered the intellectual superior of all the women and most of the men in the society of her day.

Virginia Woolf wrote further, speaking of course not of our Phillis, that "any woman born with a great gift in the sixteenth century [insert "eighteenth century," insert "black woman," insert "born or made a slave"] would certainly have gone crazed, shot herself, or ended her days in some lonely cottage outside the village, half witch, half wizard [insert "Saint"], feared and mocked at. For it needs little skill and psychology to be sure that a highly gifted girl who had tried to use her gift for poetry would have been so thwarted and hindered by contrary instincts [add "chains, guns, the lash, the ownership of one's body by someone else, submission to an alien religion"], that she must have lost her health and sanity to a certainty."

The key words, as they relate to Phillis, are "contrary instincts." For when we read the poetry of Phillis Wheatley—as when we read the novels of Nella Larsen or the oddly false-sounding autobiography of that freest of all black women writers, Zora Hurston—evidence of "contrary instincts" is everywhere. Her loyalties were completely divided, as was, without question, her mind.

But how could this be otherwise? Captured at seven, a slave of wealthy, doting whites who instilled in her the "savagery" of the Africa they "rescued" her from . . . one wonders if she was even able to remember her homeland as she had known it, or as it really was.

Yet, because she did try to use her gift for poetry in a world that made her a slave, she was "so thwarted and hindered by . . . contrary instincts, that she . . . lost her health. . . ." In the last years of her brief life, burdened not only with the need to express her gift but also with a penniless, friendless "freedom" and several small children for whom she was forced to do strenuous work to feed, she lost her health, certainly. Suffering from malnutrition and neglect and who knows what mental agonies, Phillis Wheatley died.

So torn by "contrary instincts" was black, kidnapped, enslaved Phillis that her description of "the Goddess"—as she poetically called the liberty she did not have—is ironically, cruelly

humorous. And, in fact, has held Phillis up to ridicule for more than a century. It is usually read prior to hanging Phillis's memory as that of a fool. She wrote:

The Goddess comes, she moves divinely fair,
Olive and laurel binds her *golden* hair.
Wherever shines this native of the skies,
Unnumber'd charms and recent graces rise.
[My italics]

It is obvious that Phillis, the slave, combed the "Goddess's" hair every morning; prior, perhaps, to bringing in the milk, or fixing her mistress's lunch. She took her imagery from the one thing she saw elevated above all others.

With the benefit of hindsight we ask, "How could she?"

But at last, Phillis, we understand. No more snickering when your stiff, struggling, ambivalent lines are forced on us. We know now that you were not an idiot or a traitor; only a sickly little black girl, snatched from your home and country and made a slave; a woman who still struggled to sing the song that was your gift, although in a land of barbarians who praised you for your bewildered tongue. It is not so much what you sang, as that you kept alive, in so many of our ancestors, *the notion of song.*

Black women are called, in the folklore that so aptly identifies one's status in society, "the *mule* of the world," because we have been handed the burdens that everyone else—*everyone* else—refused to carry. We have also been called "Matriarchs," "Superwomen," and "Mean and Evil Bitches." Not to mention "Castraters" and "Sapphire's Mama." When we have pleaded for understanding, our character has been distorted; when we have asked for simple caring, we have been handed empty inspirational appellations, then stuck in the farthest corner. When we have asked for love, we have been given children. In short, even our plainer gifts, our labors of fidelity and love, have been knocked down our throats. To be an artist and a black woman, even today, lowers our status in many respects, rather than raises it: and yet, artists we will be.

Therefore we must fearlessly pull out of ourselves and look at and identify with our lives the living creativity some of our great-grandmothers were not allowed to know. I stress *some* of them because it is well known that the majority of our great-grandmothers knew, even without "knowing" it, the reality of their spirituality, even if they didn't recognize it beyond what happened in the singing at church—and they never had any intention of giving it up.

How they did it—those millions of black women who were not Phillis Wheatley, or Lucy Terry or Frances Harper or Zora Hurston or Nella Larsen or Bessie Smith; or Elizabeth Catlett, or Katherine Dunham, either—brings me to the title of this essay, "In Search of Our Mothers' Gardens," which is a personal account that is yet shared, in its theme and its meaning, by all of us. I found, while thinking about the far-reaching world of the creative black woman, that often the truest answer to a question that really matters can be found very close.

In the late 1920s my mother ran away from home to marry my father. Marriage, if not running away, was expected of seventeen-year-old girls. By the time she was twenty, she had two children and was pregnant with a third. Five children later, I was born. And this is how I came to know my mother: she seemed a large, soft, loving-eyed woman who was rarely impatient in our home. Her quick, violent temper was on view only a few times a year, when she battled with the white landlord who had the misfortune to suggest to her that her children did not need to go to school.

She made all the clothes we wore, even my brothers' overalls. She made all the towels and sheets we used. She spent the summers canning vegetables and fruits. She spent the winter evenings making quilts enough to cover all our beds.

During the "working" day, she labored beside—not behind—my father in the fields.

Her day began before sunup, and did not end until late at night. There was never a moment for her to sit down, undisturbed, to unravel her own private thoughts; never a time free from interruption—by work or the noisy inquiries of her many children. And yet, it is to my mother—and all our mothers who were not famous—that I went in search of the secret of what has fed that muzzled and often mutilated, but vibrant, creative spirit that the black woman has inherited, and that pops out in wild and unlikely places to this day.

But when, you will ask, did my over-worked mother have time to know or care about feeding the creative spirit?

The answer is so simple that many of us have spent years discovering it. We have constantly looked high, when we should have looked high—and low.

For example: in the Smithsonian Institution in Washington, D.C., there hangs a quilt unlike any other in the world. In fanciful, inspired, and yet simple and identifiable figures, it portrays the story of the Crucifixion. It is considered rare, beyond price. Though it follows no known pattern of quilt-making, and though it is made of bits and pieces of worthless rags, it is obviously the work of a person of powerful imagination and deep spiritual feeling. Below this quilt I saw a note that says it was made by "an anonymous Black woman in Alabama, a hundred years ago."

If we could locate this "anonymous" black woman from Alabama, she would turn out to be one of our grandmothers—an artist who left her mark in the only materials she could afford, and in the only medium her position in society allowed her to use.

As Virginia Woolf wrote further, in *A Room of One's Own*:

"Yet genius of a sort must have existed among women as it must have existed among the working class. [Change this to "slaves" and "the wives and daughters of sharecroppers."] Now and again an Emily Brontë or a Robert Burns [change this to "a Zora Hurston or a Richard Wright"] blazes out and proves its presence. But certainly it never got itself on to paper. When, however, one reads of a witch being ducked, of a woman possessed by devils [or "Sainthood"], of a wise woman selling herbs [our root workers], or even a very remarkable man who had a mother, then I think we are on the track of a lost novelist, a suppressed poet, of some mute and inglorious Jane Austen. . . . Indeed, I would venture to guess that Anon, who wrote so many poems without signing them, was often a woman. . . ."

And so our mothers and grandmothers have, more often than not anonymously, handed on the creative spark, the seed of the flower they themselves never hoped to see: or like a sealed letter they could not plainly read.

And so it is, certainly, with my own mother. Unlike "Ma" Rainey's songs, which retained their creator's name even while blasting forth from Bessie Smith's mouth, no song or poem will bear my mother's name. Yet so many of the stories that I write, that we all write, are my mother's stories. Only recently did I fully realize this: that through years of listening to my mother's stories of her life, I have absorbed not only the stories themselves, but something of the manner in which she spoke, something of the urgency that involves the knowledge that her stories—like her life—must be recorded. It is probably for this reason that so much of what I have written is about characters whose counterparts in real life are so much older than I am.

But the telling of these stories, which came from my mother's lips as naturally as breathing, was not the only way my mother showed herself as an artist. For stories, too, were subject to being distracted, to dying without conclusion. Dinners must be started, and cotton must be gathered before the big rains. The artist that was and is my mother showed itself to me only after many years. This is what I finally noticed:

Like Mem, a character in *The Third Life of Grange Copeland,* my mother adorned with flowers whatever shabby house we were forced to live in. And not just your typical straggly country stand of zinnias, either. She planted ambitious gardens—and still does—with over fifty different varieties of plants that bloom profusely from early March until late November. Before she left home for the fields, she watered her flowers, chopped up the grass, and laid out new beds. When she returned from the fields she might divide clumps of bulbs, dig a cold pit, uproot and replant roses, or prune branches from her taller bushes or trees—until night came and it was too dark to see.

Whatever she planted grew as if by magic, and her fame as a grower of flowers spread over three counties. Because of her creativity with her flowers, even my memories of poverty are seen through a screen of blooms—sunflowers, petunias, roses, dahlias, forsythia, spirea, delphiniums, verbena . . . and on and on.

And I remember people coming to my mother's yard to be given cuttings from her flowers; I hear again the praise showered on her because whatever rocky soil she landed on, she turned into a garden. A garden so brilliant with colors, so original in its design, so magnificent with life and creativity, that to this day people drive by our house in Georgia—perfect strangers and imperfect strangers—and ask to stand or walk among my mother's art.

I notice that it is only when my mother is working in her flowers that she is radiant, almost to the point of being invisible—except as Creator: hand and eye. She is involved in work her soul must have. Ordering the universe in the image of her personal conception of Beauty.

Her face, as she prepares the Art that is her gift, is a legacy of respect she leaves to me, for all that illuminates and cherishes life. She has handed down respect for the possibilities—and the will to grasp them.

For her, so hindered and intruded upon in so many ways, being an artist has still been a daily part of her life. This ability to hold on, even in very simple ways, is work black women have done for a very long time.

This poem is not enough, but it is something, for the woman who literally covered the holes in our walls with sunflowers:

> They were women then
> My mama's generation
> Husky of voice—Stout of Step
> With fists as well as
> Hands
> How they battered down
> Doors
> And ironed
> Starched white
> Shirts
> How they led
> Armies
> Headragged Generals
> Across mined
> Fields
> Booby-trapped
> Ditches
> To discover books
> Desks
> A place for us
> How they knew what we
> *Must* know
> Without knowing a page
> Of it
> Themselves.

Guided by my heritage of a love of beauty and a respect for strength—in search of my mother's garden, I found my own.

And perhaps in Africa over two hundred years ago, there was just such a mother; perhaps she painted vivid and daring decorations in oranges and yellows and greens on the walls of her hut; perhaps she sang—in a voice like Roberta Flack's—*sweetly* over the compounds of her village; perhaps she wove the most stunning mats or told the most ingenious stories of all the village storytellers. Perhaps she was herself a poet—though only her daughter's name is signed to the poems that we know.

Perhaps Phillis Wheatley's mother was also an artist.

Perhaps in more than Phillis Wheatley's biological life is her mother's signature made clear.

30
ALICE WALKER, SANDRA FLOWERS, CHRISTINE BOND, AND AUDRE LORDE
Other Voices, Other Moods (1979)

It's a familiar truth that the black community is weakened each time its members are kept from using their talents and celebrating strength. But what happens when black women try to do exactly that?

ALICE WALKER

Alice Walker is living in San Francisco and working on her third novel. Her third book of poetry, Good Night Willie Lee, I'll See You in the Morning *(Dial), will be published in the spring.*

From the time I was two years old, until I was six, one of my closest friends was a little girl exactly my age, whose name was Cassie. We looked like sisters: with gleaming brown skin and bright dark eyes—with plenty of shining, springy hair which our mothers decorated with large satin bows. . . . Cassie and I used to spend the night at each other's house, and we would giggle half the night away.

When I was six, Cassie and her family moved to Michigan, and I suffered my first separation trauma. I tried to encourage my father to move to Michigan, but he wouldn't. For a long time I held him responsible, poor man, for my loss of Cassie—whom I was not to see again for 20 years. And whom I didn't forget for a single year.

Throughout grade school, high school, and college, I had close friends like Cassie. I loved them deeply and loyally—always with the fear that they'd be taken away. And in so many cases, they were. When next I saw Cassie, for example, she had been married for years to a man who literally kept her from eating. When her family

From *Ms.*, February 1979. Reprinted by permission of *Ms.* Magazine, copyright 1979.

finally went to rescue her, she was so weak and malnourished they had to carry her off in their arms. She was in this condition when I saw her again. Gone the gleaming skin and bright dark eyes. Gone the spring from her plentiful hair—in fact, gone a good bit of the plentiful hair.

One reason I had loved her was that I love, simply *love*, to giggle, and love to *hear* giggling. And Cassie, at five and six, was an incomparable giggler. Her giggle was one of the best sounds I ever heard in the world. How could anyone, for any reason, wish to stop it?

And yet, for years, her giggling was stopped.

On my desk there is a picture of me when I was six—dauntless eyes, springy hair, optimistic satin bow and all—and I look at it often; I realize I am always trying to keep faith with the child I was. The child I was thought the women in our local church held together the world. Often kind beyond understanding. Sometimes shrewish, stubborn, wilfully obtuse, but always *there*, with their dimes and quarters, their spotless children and beloved husbands, building up the church first, and the local school second, for the benefit of the community. The child that I was rarely saw individualistic behavior, and when I did see it, for a long time I could only understand it as rejection of community, rather than the self-affirmation it very often was.

The men in my community seemed to love and appreciate their wives; and if the wife had more initiative and energy than the husband, this was not held against her. My father loved my mother's spunk and her inability to lie when asked a direct question. He was himself innately easygoing and disinclined to waste any part of life in argument, and with a mind that easily turned any question asked of him into a "story."

This is what I remember; but surely this memory is too good to be entirely true.

In 1973 I was keynote speaker at a symposium at Radcliffe College called "The Black Woman: Myths and Realities." It was to that gathering of some 200 black educated women that I delivered a speech I'd written especially for black women, "In Search of Our Mothers' Gardens." [See *Ms.*, May, 1974.] It is largely about the tenacity of the artistic spirit among us, from a historical perspective. Many women wept, they later told me, as I read it. But I was looking forward to an exchange among all of us that would be more than a sharing of history and survivalist emotion.

Later, June Jordan and I were sitting together in the audience. A panel of four or five women was onstage. One was a psychologist, one a well-known actress, one a civil rights lawyer. Every one was *some*thing. I was so excited!

June and I had often talked between ourselves about the plight of young black women who were killing themselves at an alarming (to us) rate. We thought *this* should be brought before our sisters. In fact, the week before I had been told of one young woman, a Sarah Lawrence student. She had been ridiculed by the black men on campus because she dated white guys (meanwhile these black guys dated white women and each other). She couldn't take it. She killed herself. That *same* week, a young Oriental woman had jumped to her death from a window at Radcliffe. And from all sides I had been hearing how impossible it was becoming to be a young woman of color. It appeared that any kind of nonconformity was not permitted.

When June and I brought all this up, there was *no* response whatsoever. Instead, we were treated to a lecture on the black woman's responsibilities to the black man. I will never forget my sense of horror and betrayal when one of the panelists said to me (and to the rest of that august body of black women): "The responsibility of the black women is to support the black man; *whatever* he does."

It occurred to me that my neck could be at that minute under some man's heel, and this woman would stroll by and say, "Right on."

I burst into tears. And though I soon dried my face, I didn't stop crying inside for . . . maybe I haven't stopped yet.

But a really fascinating thing happened around my crying: many of the women blamed me for crying! They came over to me, one or two at a time, and said:

"I understand what you are trying to say. . . ." (I wasn't *trying,* I muttered through clenched teeth. I *said* it; you just didn't listen.) But don't let it *get* to you!"

Or: "Why would you let *anyone* make you cry?"

Not *one* of them *ever* said a word about why young women of color were killing themselves. They could take the black woman as invincible, as she was portrayed to some extent, in my speech (what they applauded was, apparently, the invincible part), but there was no sympathy for struggle that ended in defeat. Which meant there was no sympathy for struggle itself— only for "winning."

I was reminded of something that had puzzled me about the response of black people to Movement people in the South. During the seven years I lived in Mississippi, I never knew a Movement person (and I include myself) who wasn't damaged in some way from having to put her or his life, principles, children on the line over long, stressful periods. And this is only natural but there was a way in which the black community could not look at this.

I knew a young girl who "desegregated" the local white high school in her small town. No one, except her teachers, spoke to her *for four years.* There was one white guy—whom she spoke of with contempt—who left love notes in her locker. This girl suffered acute anxiety; so that when she dragged herself home from school every day, she went to bed, and stayed there until the next morning, when she walked off, ramrod straight, to school. Even her parents talked only about the bravery, never about the cost.

It was at the Radcliffe symposium that I saw that many black women are more loyal to black men than they are to themselves, a dangerous state of affairs that has its logical end in self-destructive behavior.

But I also learned something else:

The same panelist who would not address the suicide rate of young women of color also took the opportunity to tell me what she thought my "problem" was. Since I spoke so much of my mother, she said my problem was that I was "trying to 'carry' my mother, and the weight is too heavy."

June, who was sitting beside me, and who was angry but not embarrassed by my tears, put her arms around my shoulders and said:

"But why shouldn't you carry your mother, she carried *you,* didn't she?"

I had to giggle. And the giggle and the tears and the holding and the sanctioning of responsibility to those we love and those who have loved us, is what I know will see us through.

SANDRA FLOWERS

Sandra Flowers was a coordinator of the Atlanta chapter of the National Black Feminist Organization in 1974 and 1975, and a consultant to women's groups on antirape programs. She is now a student in a creative writing program at the University of Arizona.

I accept the premise that black women inherently are feminists. Our struggle makes this so, regardless of how we feel about the label. Yet, those of us who live as feminists and collaborate with the Women's Movement do so at the expense of a particular place in the black community. Let's face it—a whole lot of black women are satisfied with the male dominance of our culture. This makes feminism a risky business for black women because the options it inevitably generates tend to alienate black men as well as those black women who read feminism as antimale, hence antiblack (even black feminism, which is considered by some a white idea in blackface).

It's impossible to encapsulate the ways black women relate to each other. We might shut each other out for long periods, but when it hits the fan, we turn to a black woman, the only person who can feel what we're feeling when the feeling is inexpressible.

I think the answers lie more in the nature of an understanding about what black womanness entails, a very private, esoteric understanding that varies among classes of black women. Even then, the variations are no greater than the shades of meaning between "adequate" and "enough." Black women relate to each other, shall we say, by filling needs *no one else* has been able to fill from Africa to now.

CHRISTINE BOND

Christine Bond is a sex educator, family-planning supervisor, and team member of the adolescent clinic at the Harvard Street Neighborhood Health Center in Dorchester, Massachusetts. Bond, who is 27, is trying to encourage a more feminist approach to counseling in the health center—being more in touch with what the woman client might be feeling and asking questions that encourage her to define her own sexuality.

What's interesting about my situation—and I'm very proud of it—is that two of the counselors I supervise are black women who are in their fifties. They're very much from the old school, and we have talked about their attitudes about sex issues. At first, they were uncomfortable about people's sexual liberation. But after seven or eight years of family-planning counseling, they're very much in touch—and no one ever pushed them. I asked them to prepare in-service presentations on topics they were interested in, and one woman prepared "Why Men Aren't Good Lovers." Just the fact that she was involved in this got her family to talking in a way they hadn't before.

I've thought a lot about my definition of feminism. What I say in classes with women is just to be pro-self, to be proud of the fact that you're a woman and not to look negatively on yourself. If you're into your reproductivity, that's a function you can direct, and it's very beautiful. But no one should say, "If I don't have a man, I'm not a woman." Unfortunately, that's still the feeling of a lot of black women I run into.

Then I also explain what other people's feelings and definitions of feminism are. I think it's important for women to support women's issues, to go out and research them. What affects one woman, regardless of her race, affects us all.

The only distinction between women's issues and black women's issues is the racism, and the negative image that black people have about themselves, which is compounded by the negative image that we have about ourselves as women.

I often say that just because I was born packing a vagina doesn't mean that I want to be identified by that small space. I don't want people to be identified by that small space. I want people to deal with the whole of me and what I am about.

I'd like to start a battered women's shelter in this community. My other dream is to start a black feminist health center. I feel that we can't do it all at once. We have to keep hacking away; we have to begin to be comfortable to say certain things, and to say them. I'm only doing a small part. I have what I call "heavy-duty feminist" friends who sometimes speak in angry exclamations that prevent people from hearing what they have to say. But especially because I'm a sex educator, I try to give the women I talk with real situations and ask them for their response. "A woman performed an abortion on herself and was really messed up and came into our clinic. What do you think about that?" I say. Or, "What would you do in a situation where a friend was getting beat up? How would you handle that?" We talk and get a chance to think. Feminism is about women sharing.

AUDRE LORDE

Audre Lorde is a poet and scholar. Her most recent volume of poetry is The Black Unicorn *(Norton). She is an associate professor of English at the John Jay College of Criminal Justice of the City University of New York.*

With increasing regularity, the red herring of homophobia and lesbian-baiting is being used in the black community to obscure the true double face of racism/sexism. But black women sharing close ties with each other, politically or emotionally, are not the enemies of black men. Only to those black men who are unclear as to the paths of their own self-definition can the self-actualization and bonding together of black women be seen as a threatening development. After all, in the black community today, it is certainly not the black lesbian who is battering and raping our underage girl children, out of displaced and sickening frustration and anger.

Women-identified women—those who sought our own destinies and attempted to execute them in the absence of male support—have been around in all black communities for a long time. But their presence goes largely unrecorded, except by word of mouth; for in those periods women-identified black women were doing what all black people were doing—confronting daily issues of survival. In this context the research being done by young black feminist critics such as Lorraine Bethel and Barbara Smith assumes an important perspective. More recently, as Yvonne Flowers has pointed out, the unmarried aunt, childless or otherwise, whose home and resources were often a welcome haven for different members of the family, was a familiar figure in many of our childhoods.

Yet within this country, for so long, we as black women have been encouraged to view each other with suspicion and distrust; as eternal competitors for the scarce male; or as the visible face of our own self-rejection. Nevertheless, black women have always bonded together in support of each other, however uneasily and in the face of whatever other allegiances militated against that bonding. In the African tradition, we have banded together with each other for wisdom and strength and support, even when it was merely in relationship to one man. We need only look at the close—although highly complex and involved—relationship between African co-wives; or at the

Amazon warriors of ancient Dahomey, who fought side by side as the kings' main and ferocious bodyguard. We need only look at the more promising power wielded by today's West African market women's associations which have been so influential, for example, in the changing political scene in Ghana.

African women have banded together and moved in their own self-interests, also. In her essay from the collection *Women in Africa*, Judith Van Allen discusses how tens of thousands of women from two provinces in Nigeria in 1929 marched upon native administration centers in protest against new taxes on goods they controlled. In British history, these events are known as the "Aba Riots," but the Igbo People call them the "Women's War."

On a more personal level, love between women was no cause for guilt. In a verbatim retelling of her life to Iris Andreski, in *Old Wives' Tales*, a 90-year-old Efik-Ibibio woman of Nigeria recalls her love for another woman:

I had a woman friend to whom I revealed my secrets. She was very fond of keeping secrets to herself. We acted as husband and wife. We always moved hand in glove and my husband and hers knew about our relationship. The villagers nicknamed us twin sisters. When I [was] out of gear with my husband, she would be the person to restore peace. . . . I often sent my children to go and work for her in return for her kindness to me. My husband, being very fortunate to get more pieces of land than her husband, allowed some to her even though she was not my co-wife.

The Fon people of Dahomey still have 13 different kinds of marriage. One of these is known as "giving-the-goat-to-the-buck," where a woman of independent means marries another woman, who then may or may not bear children, all of whom will belong to the bloodline of the other woman. As Melville Herskovits tells us in his book *Dahomey*, some marriages of this kind are arranged to provide heirs for women of means who wish to remain "free"—*i.e.*, unencumbered by male expectations upon their time, attention, or financial resources. Some of these marriages are homosexual relationships. Nor was this practice confined to Dahomey; according to Herskovits, marriages between women occur among different peoples in eastern and southern Africa as well.

In all these cases, the women involved are evaluated not by their sexuality, but by their respective place within the community.

The lesbian presents to the black community today the *imagined* menace of a self-motivated, self-defined black woman who will not fear some terrible retribution from the gods merely because she does not seek her face within a man's eyes, even if he has fathered her children. For that matter, the racist/sexist bias of much current sociological research tends to hide the fact that female-headed households in the black community, regardless of economic status, are not always formed by default.

Just as for the racist, black people seem so powerful that the presence of one can contaminate a whole lineage, for the homophobe, lesbians seem so powerful that the presence of one can contaminate the whole sex. The all-too-common fear that the existence of black lesbians threatens the existence of the black race implies that if we do not eradicate lesbians, all black women will become lesbians. It also implies that lesbians do not have children. Both implications are patently false.

As black women, we must all deal with the realities of our lives which place us at risk as black women, homosexual or heterosexual. In a Detroit suburb, a young black actress named Patricia Cowan was invited to audition for a play called *Hammer* and was then bludgeoned to death by the young black male self-described playwright. Patricia Cowan was not killed because she was **black. She** was killed because she was a black **woman, and** her cause belongs to us all.

Black women have the lowest average wage of the four groups: black women and white women, black men and white men. This is a true concern for us all, no matter whom we sleep with.

As black women we have the right and responsibility to define ourselves, and to seek allies in common cause with black men against racism, and with each other and white women against sexism. But most of all, as black women we have the right and responsibility to recognize each other without fear and to love where we choose. Both homosexual and heterosexual black women today share a history of bonding and strength to which our particular differences must not blind us.

III. Lesbian Identities and Critiques of Heterosexuality

AS PART OF THE RIOTS, REBELLIONS, AND rights consciousness of the late 1960s and 1970s, unprecedented numbers of gay men and lesbians organized. The first known lesbian organization in America, the Daughters of Bilitis—founded in the 1950s as a private social group to give middle-class lesbians an alternative to the gay bar scene—came to be viewed as hopelessly conservative after the post-1969 explosion of lesbian-feminist militancy. The Stonewall Rebellion, a landmark in the history of gay and lesbian rights, made 1969 a pivotal year. On June 28, 1969, police raided the Stonewall Inn, a gay bar in New York City's Greenwich Village. The raid itself was a common occurrence, but on that night the gay men and few lesbians in attendance did not leave peacefully as usual. Instead, they decided to fight back, triggering riots through that night and the following. The rallying cry "support gay power" was scrawled on buildings; the gay liberation movement had begun. Within a year of Stonewall, hundreds of gay publications and organizations had sprung up, many of them lesbian.

The most visible and influential lesbian activists in the early 1970s were the new self-identified "lesbian feminists." Lillian Faderman, author of *Odd Girls and Twilight Lovers: A History of Lesbian Life in Twentieth-Century America* (1991), distinguishes the new lesbian feminists, who were primarily young—coming of political age in the radicalism of the 1960s—from those women who identified as "gay." While older women tended to believe they were born gay, she says, and thus traced their oppression solely to society's attitudes toward homosexuality, young lesbian feminists typically believed that they *chose* to be lesbians and identified their problems as rooted primarily in societal attitudes toward *women,* not homosexuality. Lesbianism, or woman-identification, was part of the *solution* to this problem—not the source. There were very strong ties between lesbian feminists and the rest of the women's liberation movement, though at least at first the support seemed unidirectional. Lesbian feminists often emerged from and wanted to further the goals of women's lib, but some of the more mainstream leaders in the feminist movement did not want to be associated with the still pejorative label *lesbian*. Before too long, however, many heterosexual feminists in the women's movement realized they could shy away neither from lesbians nor from the label *lesbian,* and to a certain degree they recuperated the term as a badge of persistent female resistance and as a sign that lesbians, precisely because they were so vilified, posed perhaps the most powerful threat to the patriarchal system that all feminists were trying to undermine or destroy.

In some ways, lesbian feminism in the 1970s came to be regarded as the epitome of feminism, and many lesbians saw their "sexual preference" as a political *choice,* often the only choice they could make in a culture in which heterosexual relationships seemed irrevocably grounded in constraining and degrading notions of womanhood. "Lesbian" became associated with the idea of the "third sex," as lesbians saw themselves not only breaking free of the oppressive role-playing of the heterosexual hegemony but also breaking down the artificial and destructive binary of "masculine" and "feminine." As Peggy Kornegger writes in "What Is a Lesbian?" (1977), the "woman who chooses herself, who chooses other women, is denying the necessity to choose opposites—is, in fact, denying the necessity *of* opposites." By intervening in the ostensible inevitability of heterosexuality and the dichotomy of masculine and feminine identities, lesbian feminism was a truly radical movement, both politically and theoretically. It did not strive to integrate women into a society organized by traditional (masculine) values, and it did not seek equality on the basis of those values; it sought a restructuring of society. Although feminism had been challenging social definitions of womanhood since its inception, the lesbian feminists of the 1970s were the first to identify how essential heterosexuality was to oppressive standards of femininity. Many lesbians viewed lesbianism as the *only* means to develop a woman's whole self, beyond gendered binaries, and thus the only means to attain true freedom.

One of the earliest lesbian-feminist documents is "The Woman-Identified Woman" (1970), written by the New York feminist group Radicalesbians (the first East Coast lesbian group since Daughters of Bilitis). This statement incorporates all the main strands of lesbian-feminist thought, including the paramount assertion that women can only become free by "facing the basic heterosexual structure that binds us in one-to-one relationship with our oppressors." Confronting and bringing down this edifice is a necessary precondition to redefining the concept of woman in any meaningful way. Interestingly, though, the document expresses a tremendous amount of ambivalence about the term *lesbian,* as do many other lesbian-feminist documents. On the one hand, Radicalesbians claims that *lesbian* is an "inauthentic" term generated by a sexist society, only necessary in a world of rigidly binarized sex roles and male dominance; were sex oppression to disappear, so too would the labels of lesbianism and homosexuality. At the same time, however, Radicalesbians embraces the term *lesbian,* intended as an opprobrium, as the marker of a woman who has dared to be the equal of man.

In yet another turn in this ambiguous adopting of the label *lesbian,* Radicalesbians expresses its unease with the primarily sexual connotations of the term because, it argues, to define oneself in terms of sexuality is "divisive and sexist." Many lesbian-feminist thinkers questioned the term *lesbian* precisely because it was hypersexualized, denoting a sexual practice rather than a way of being. An emphasis on genital sex, the argument went, veered too close to exploitative aspects of heterosexuality; instead, expanded definitions of sex, including mutual sensuality, hugging, touching, loving, and even political activism became more important than genital sex (as one writer put it succinctly, "Nobody Needs to Get Fucked"). The Radicalesbians' skepticism about the primarily sexual connotation of *lesbian* illustrates how lesbian feminists went a long way toward breaking down the pathologizing of lesbianism that had emerged with the new sexual sciences (notably Freud and Havelock Ellis) at the turn of the twentieth century. They unsettled what they saw as the widespread association of lesbianism not just with deviant sexuality but with sexuality. The group used the phrase "woman-identified woman" instead to express the conviction that lesbians' devotion to other women is not purely or even mostly sexual: it is about emotion, love, energy, and political commitment.

An interview conducted by Anne Koedt, "Loving Another Woman" (1971), reveals the importance of ideological feminism to 1970s lesbianism. This interview, like the statement by Radicalesbians, appeared in the journal, *Notes from the Third Year*—a continuation of the journal launched in 1968 as *Notes from the First Year,* which was produced by New York Radical Women. As can be seen from other documents in part I, this interview is only one of Koedt's many contributions to early 1970s radical feminism. The interview is with an anonymous subject who had recently become the lover of a good friend; both had previously considered themselves heterosexual. Although the subject of the interview says that they did not sleep together "to put our ideological beliefs into reality," she does make it clear how important feminist consciousness-raising was to her ability to think about the possibility of loving another woman. Like many lesbian feminists, the interviewee suggests that the only thing that mandates heterosexuality is male-dominated society, and that once women are freed (by women's lib) to love whom they will, they are just as likely (more likely, given the way men are socialized) to fall in love with a woman. In a refrain that runs through virtually all lesbian feminist writing, the subject claims that the most distinctive part of being a lesbian is that she and her lover engage in no role-playing; her new relationship, she hopes, harbingers the breakdown of debilitating notions of femininity.

If becoming a lesbian was a choice any woman *could* make, some lesbian feminists went so far as to declare that every woman *should* make it, not only for reasons of personal liberation and happiness but for the purpose of ending universal male power and privilege. Emerging second-wave feminism had recently begun, after all, to point out that after two hundred years American men *still* oppressed women—legally, economically, politically, psychologically, and sexually. The forces of those opposed to patriarchy could be still more powerful, lesbian feminists argued, if they could stop fighting a consistently losing battle, that is, if women devoted *all* their energies to *each other* and did not go home to "sleep in the enemy camp"—if they did not go home, in other words, and expend their energies replenishing the resources of men. In a sense, this *separatist ideal* developed by lesbian feminists emerged from earlier female-centered—although not explicitly lesbian—reform movements and institutions, such as women's academies and colleges, women's clubs, and most notably, settlement houses (out of which developed many lifelong companionate female relationships).

In "The Shape of Things to Come" (1972), novelist Rita Mae Brown, a prominent activist in the lesbian-feminist movement and in Radicalesbians in particular, articulates the separatist impulse. "Did the Chinese love and support the capitalists?" she asks. "Do the Viet Cong cook supper for the Yankees? Are Blacks supposed to disperse their communities and each live in a white home?" The answer is obvious, she says, yet women have fought to end male oppression and then with too few exceptions gone home to a man ("polishing your chains," as Brown puts it). Brown here makes a move that is common for feminist separatists: she conflates patriarchy and male domination with individual men, implicitly denying the possibility that an individual man could be relatively free of male supremacist impulses or could even fight against patriarchy in the same way, for instance, that some whites fought for abolition and, later, civil rights. But Brown's main target is women. Women who cannot "find it in themselves to love another woman, and that includes physical love," cannot say they truly care about women's liberation, she writes. Suspicion of heterosexual women was, indeed, a part of radical lesbian feminism in the early 1970s—and it was a logical stance given the premise that heterosexuality was a determinative system that trapped both men and women into an inescapable posture of domination and subordination. Even lesbian role-playing (butch-femme couples) was frowned upon as not having sufficiently exorcized the disempowering patterns of the heterosexual system. Brown and other Radicalesbians put their ideals into practice in the mid-1970s when they left New York City to live in communes in rural Vermont.

Some of the principles that fostered a lesbian separatist ideal—that lesbianism was the most effective tool against male oppression, that it was a choice every woman could make, that lesbianism was less a biological than a political imperative—could also lead to a very inclusive notion of lesbianism. In the forum, "What Is a Lesbian?" (1977) Judy Antonelli elucidates lesbian separatism—giving one's energy to other women, as she explains it—but then she immediately goes on to assert that "[t]here is a lesbian (strong, woman-identified woman) in every woman, which has been suppressed by patriarchy." Far from being exclusionary Antonelli implies that *all* women are essentially lesbians, coerced into "forgetting" or repressing their natural love of other women by a male-dominated culture. Activist, essayist, and poet Adrienne Rich also articulates such an inclusive definition of lesbianism in her celebrated essay "Compulsory Heterosexuality and Lesbian Existence" (1980/1986). In an excerpt from this essay, Rich elaborates what she calls the "lesbian continuum," arguing that patriarchy inaccurately holds lesbianism to solely "clinical associations." In truth, says Rich, lesbian existence covers the entire range of women's experiences in which relationships between females are primary—from a mother breastfeeding her infant daughter, to the intense friendships of girls, to women who resist marriage, and various other groups of women throughout history and in all cultures who have banded together, lived together, and refused to devote themselves to men. Rich even brings under the umbrella of the lesbian continuum women who lead lives *apparently* acquiescent to patriarchy, women who lead what she calls "double lives" and who may seem convinced of their heterosexuality or of the predominance of men in their lives. As an illustration, Rich gives two examples from fiction of such women whose heterosexual convictions are belied by the people who are truly important to them—other women: in Meridel Le Sueur's *The Girl* and Toni Morrison's *Sula,* main characters act on their attraction to men but are finally sustained by their female friends. The doubleness of women's lives—the ways in which they often fail to realize or even actively repress their bonds with other women—is a result and a symptom of "compulsory heterosexuality." As Rich adeptly describes, women have been daily persuaded and even forced to form sexual relationships with men by every major institution, from medicine to economics; adopting heterosexuality has thus frequently been a matter of sheer survival, as throughout history women have often had few other economic options.

During the course of the 1980s, as ideals of integration superseded separatism, the more inclusive conceptions of lesbian feminism won increasing support. Separatism was perhaps a necessary stage in the movement as a whole, with lesbians defining themselves fervently *against* a U.S. culture that rendered them invisible from its very beginnings. Increasingly, though, lesbians brought their presence and values to the broader community, becoming involved in more diverse causes. As historian Lillian Faderman puts it, "most of the lesbian community felt by the end of the decade [the 1970s] that while separatism may be effective for a specific struggle at a certain time, as a lifestyle it attests to a 'failure of global vision.'" In "Speaking Out, Reaching Out" (1977–1985), Charlotte Bunch collects excerpts from speeches she delivered over a period of a dozen years, all of which articulate an interconnectedness between ways in which lesbians are oppressed and other oppressive systems. Bunch was, along with Rita Mae Brown, one of the foremost spokeswomen for separatism in the early 1970s and had heeded Brown's call for all women (and certainly all feminists) to identify as lesbians if they wanted to overthrow patriarchy. By the late 1970s, however, Bunch is arguing that isolated groups are more easily defeated and urging the creation of coalitions among the numerous groups seeking to broaden the scope of human rights. Bunch claims that the forces that promote pornographic culture and militarism, among other injustices, are the same as those that victimize lesbians. Her speech presented at the National AIDS Forum in 1982 illustrates how central the AIDS epidemic has been in coalescing the interests and activism of gay men and lesbians, certainly a change from the early 1970s when lesbian feminists emphasized how gay men partook of patriarchy and had themselves rendered lesbians invisible within gay organizations.

The 1970s was a decade when sexuality became not only "liberated" but also scrutinized— debunked as a "natural" or "personal" choice and reconceived as an enforced system with powerful interests invested in women's continued heterosexual behavior. And it was not only explicitly lesbian theorizing that proffered a powerful critique of the system that Adrienne Rich called compulsory heterosexuality. In the groundbreaking essay "The Myth of the Vaginal Orgasm" (1970), radical feminist Anne Koedt unmasked the most seemingly physiological of women's experiences as infused with gendered power relations. Koedt's thesis, drawing on the revolutionary sex research of both Kinsey and Masters and Johnson, is that the vagina has been actively promoted by doctors as the source of women's sexual pleasure when in fact there are virtually no nerve endings in the vagina and the actual source of women's orgasms is the clitoris. Male interests have enforced this so-called truth about women's sexuality for various obvious reasons: penetration and vaginal stimulation give *men* pleasure, and the clitoris is often too far away from the vagina to receive any stimulation during penetration. In the interests of men, says Koedt, heterosexual intercourse has thus become all about the vagina and very little about the clitoris. One clear implication of Koedt's undermining of the vaginal orgasm by labeling it a myth is that heterosexuality (and even men) can suddenly be seen as irrelevant to women's sexual pleasure: "[T]he establishment of clitoral orgasm," Koedt writes, "would threaten the heterosexual *institution*. For it would indicate that sexual pleasure was obtainable from either men *or* women, thus making heterosexuality not an absolute, but an option." Aside from other reasons that a woman might seek another woman as a lover, Koedt suggests anatomy seems to favor that arrangement—which is exactly why sexual theorists from Freud onward have insisted, against all empirical evidence, that women have only vaginal orgasms.

Black lesbian feminist and poet Audre Lorde offers a still more sweeping revision of traditional views of (hetero)sexuality in "Uses of the Erotic: The Erotic as Power" (1978). Lorde argues that the "euro-american male tradition" has insistently compartmentalized sexuality from other arenas of life—notably work, politics, and spirituality. Lorde uses the concept of the erotic to join all these arenas: the erotic is "the sharing of joy, whether physical, emotional, psychic." The erotic is, moreover, a source of power for women—their "lifeforce" and creative energy—but only if women can wrest the erotic away from debilitating racist, patriarchal visions of sexuality as confined to the bedroom and structured by domination, all of which Lorde calls pornographic and which contradicts the genuinely erotic. The erotic is intrinsically political in that once women begin to "feel deeply all the aspects of our lives, we begin to demand from ourselves and from our life-pursuits that they feel in accordance with that joy which we know ourselves to be capable of." A woman whose life is infused with the erotic, in other words, will not be satisfied with shallow and degrading relationships, with demeaning, meaningless work, and with the absence of spirituality from both relationships and work.

An essential and enduring aspect of the wholesale feminist critique of heterosexuality in the 1970s was the recognition of rape as a national and international problem. In Susan Brownmiller's encyclopedic survey *Against Our Will: Men, Women and Rape* (1975), Brownmiller describes how rape became an imperative issue for her and other feminists in 1971. One evening someone in her New York Radical Feminists (NYRF) group brought in a newspaper with a first-person account of a rape. The group started talking, and it turned out two of the women present had themselves been raped. By the end of the evening there was a proposal for a speakout. Gradually other consciousness-raising groups began to talk about rape, and the pervasiveness of the problem became apparent. The NYRF held a conference on rape as well as speakouts in 1971, and as women began realizing how incredibly biased the law was, outrage and activism spread. The laws in New York were particularly offensive: before a rapist could be convicted in that state, the prosecution had to corroborate *independently* (i.e., by some other source than the testimony of the victim herself) three points: that penetration had occurred, that the woman did not consent, and the identity of the rapist; in other words, there had to be a witness, a standard held for no other violent crime. Also, although a defendant's record could not be raised in court, the victim's past sexual history could be. No wonder less than 1 percent of complaints of rape in the early 1970s ended in conviction! The fact that these laws are now obsolete suggests how efficacious 1970s feminists were in changing cultural attitudes about rape. During these years feminists in various cities began to set up rape crisis centers, and by 1976 there were fifteen hundred antirape projects in the United States. Furthermore, almost all states rewrote their rape laws under pressure from feminist groups. In the space of merely five years or so, feminists spurred a revolution in the way rape was treated (under the law and in the media), and for the first time there was institutional support for victims. The fight has been ongoing, of course, as recognition of marital rape and date rape, for instance, has taken longer to achieve (even as late as 1991, four states allowed a man to rape his wife with impunity).

Although Brownmiller's 1975 book *Against Our Will* is considered the classic text on rape, two essays written four years earlier, at the very inception of the feminist campaign against rape, anticipate her arguments. Both lay out the theoretical underpinning of feminist action against the cultural sanction of rape. In an essay published in *Ramparts Magazine,* "Rape: The All-American Crime" (1971), Susan Griffin proffers a multitude of arguments to support the basic claim that rapists are not anomalies in the United States and rape is not an aberrant practice; rather, rape is a product of deeply held cultural beliefs about male and female sexuality and is an integral part of our patriarchal culture. Rape is taught in America, Griffin claims, and it is, moreover, not far removed from ostensibly consensual heterosexual practices. As she succinctly puts it, "the basic elements of rape are involved in all heterosexual relationships"; the difference is quantitative, not qualitative. In this comprehensive essay, which Griffin later expanded into a book (1979), this poet and writer surveys the numerous cultural values that support rape as an inevitable and even acceptable practice: male sexuality is considered "naturally" aggressive and uncontrollable, for instance, while female sexuality is deemed "passive," and women are alleged to have fantasies of being "ravished" (a fancy term for rape); men are taught not only to desire power and supremacy but to achieve it by violence if necessary, and rape springs not only from their desire to dominate women but also to prove their prowess and courage to other men (hence group rapes are more vicious, as males spur each other on to extremes of violence); the code of chivalry depends for its very existence on rape as the threat from which men protect women; finally, rape has its roots in the very concept of the family, in which women are considered essentially property—that which is exchanged between men. Rape, says Griffin, is "the symbolic expression of the white male hierarchy" and will only end with patriarchy itself.

In "Rape: An Act of Terror" (1971), Barbara Mehrhof and Pamela Kearon take Griffin's argument one step further and conceive of rape not just as a *product* of patriarchy but as a *self-conscious act of terrorism* by men to sustain the ideology of sexism that underwrites patriarchy. They give a degree of intentionality to an act that Griffin presents as a more or less accidental (although inevitable) part of a pernicious system; for Mehrhof and Kearon, rape is actively being "used" by men "as a terror tactic," and it is "supported by a consensus in the male class." Mehrhof and Kearon argue that rape is punishment for nothing more than a woman's femaleness, as it serves to reinforce her preexistent subordinate place in the male-female hierarchy. While their argument may seem radical now, at a time when rape laws have been dramatically improved, Mehrhof and Kearon drew support from the fact that rape laws in 1971 made rape virtually unpunishable and therefore seemed to imply not just tacit institutional consent to the act but even support. The more persistently compelling argument offered by Griffin and Mehrhof and Kearon is that rape lies on a continuum with the continuing legal, political, economic, psychological, and sexual oppression of women. To the extent that the conception of rape as an act of terror logically follows from such a society, things have not changed so much as has the cosmetic surface of rape laws.

In "Rape, Racism and the Myth of the Black Rapist" (1981) from the book *Women, Race and Class,* Angela Y. Davis gives a historical account of how rape has been inseparable from racism and criticizes the failure of white feminist activists in the antirape crusade to mention this centuries-long entanglement. Rape, Davis argues, has served as a tool to justify violence against Black men—who are falsely viewed as chronic rapists—and at the same time has been systematically perpetrated by white men on Black women. In light of Davis's textured consideration of gender, race, and class, Griffin's analysis of the origins of rape—framed around the dualism of gender—seems disarmingly simple.

31

RADICALESBIANS

The Woman-Identified Woman (1970)

What is a lesbian? A lesbian is the rage of all women condensed to the point of explosion. She is the woman who, often beginning at an extremely early age, acts in accordance with her inner compulsion to be a more complete and freer human being than her society— perhaps then, but certainly later—cares to allow her. These needs and actions, over a period of years, bring her into painful conflict with people, situations, the accepted ways of thinking, feeling and behaving, until she is in a state of continual war with everything around her, and usually with her self. She may not be fully conscious of the political implications of what for her began as personal necessity, but on some level she has not been able to accept the limitations and oppression laid on her by the most basic role of her society—the female role. The turmoil she experiences tends to induce guilt proportional to the degree to which she feels she is not meeting social expectations, and/or eventually drives her to question and analyze what the rest of her society more or less accepts. She is forced to evolve her own life pattern, often living much of her life alone, learning usually much earlier than her "straight" (heterosexual) sisters about the essential aloneness of life (which the myth of marriage obscures) and about the reality of illusions. To the extent that she cannot expel the heavy socialization that goes with being female, she can never truly find peace with herself. For she is caught somewhere between accepting society's view of her—in which case she cannot accept herself—and coming to understand what this sexist society has done to her and why it is functional and necessary for it to do so. Those of us who work that through find ourselves on the other side of a tortuous journey

From *Notes from the Third Year*, 1970.

through a night that may have been decades long. The perspective gained from that journey, the liberation of self, the inner peace, the real love of self and of all women, is something to be shared with all women—because we are all women.

It should first be understood that lesbianism, like male homosexuality, is a category of behavior possible only in a sexist society characterized by rigid sex roles and dominated by male supremacy. Those sex roles dehumanize women by defining us as a supportive/serving caste *in relation to* the master caste of men, and emotionally cripple men by demanding that they be alienated from their own bodies and emotions in order to perform their economic/political/military functions effectively. Homosexuality is a by-product of a particular way of setting up roles (or approved patterns of behavior) on the basis of sex; as such it is an inauthentic (not consonant with "reality") category. In a society in which men do not oppress women, and sexual expression is allowed to follow feelings, the categories of homosexuality and heterosexuality would disappear.

But lesbianism is also different from male homosexuality, and serves a different function in the society. "Dyke" is a different kind of putdown from "faggot," although both imply you are not playing your socially assigned sex role . . . are not therefore a "real woman" or a "real man." The grudging admiration felt for the tomboy, and the queasiness felt around a sissy boy point to the same thing: the contempt in which women—or those who play a female role—are held. And the investment in keeping women in that contemptuous role is very great. Lesbian is the word, the label, the condition that holds women in line. When a woman hears this word tossed her way, she knows she is stepping out of line. She knows that she has crossed the terrible boundary of her sex role. She recoils, she protests, she reshapes her actions to gain approval. Lesbian is a label invented by the Man to throw at any woman who dares to be his equal, who dares to challenge his prerogatives (including that of all women as part of the exchange medium among men), who dares to assert the primacy of her own needs. To have the label applied to people active in women's liberation is just the most recent instance of a long history; older women will recall that not so long ago, any woman who was successful, independent, not orienting her whole life about a man, would hear this word. For in this sexist society, for a woman to be independent means she *can't be* a woman—she must be a dyke. That in itself should tell us where women are at. It says as clearly as can be said: women and person are contradictory terms. For a lesbian is not considered a "real woman." And yet, in popular thinking, there is really only one essential difference between a lesbian and other women: that of sexual orientation—which is to say, when you strip off all the packaging, you must finally realize that the essence of being a "woman" is to get fucked by men.

"Lesbian" is one of the sexual categories by which men have divided up humanity. While all women are dehumanized as sex objects, as the objects of men they are given certain compensations: identification with his power, his ego, his status, his protection (from other males), feeling like a "real woman," finding social acceptance by adhering to her role, etc. Should a woman confront herself by confronting another woman, there are fewer rationalizations, fewer buffers by which to avoid the stark horror of her dehumanized condition. Herein we find the overriding fear of many women toward being used as a sexual object by a woman, which not only will bring her no male-connected compensations, but also will reveal the void which is woman's real situation. This dehumanization is expressed when a straight woman learns that a sister is a lesbian; she begins to relate to her lesbian sister as her potential sex object, laying a surrogate male role on the lesbian. This reveals her heterosexual conditioning to make herself into an object when sex is potentially involved in a relationship, and it denies the lesbian her full humanity. For women, especially those in the movement, to perceive their lesbian sisters through this male

grid of role definitions is to accept this male cultural conditioning and to oppress their sisters much as they themselves have been oppressed by men. Are we going to continue the male classification system of defining all females in sexual relation to some other category of people? Affixing the label lesbian not only to a woman who aspires to be a person, but also to any situation of real love, real solidarity, real primacy among women, is a primary form of divisiveness among women: it is the condition which keeps women within the confines of the feminine role, and it is the debunking/scare term that keeps women from forming any primary attachments, groups, or associations among ourselves.

Women in the movement have in most cases gone to great lengths to avoid discussion and confrontation with the issue of lesbianism. It puts people up-tight. They are hostile, evasive, or try to incorporate it into some "broader issue." They would rather not talk about it. If they have to, they try to dismiss it as a "lavender herring." But it is no side issue. It is absolutely essential to the success and fulfillment of the women's liberation movement that this issue be dealt with. As long as the label "dyke" can be used to frighten a woman into a less militant stand, keep her separate from her sisters, keep her from giving primacy to anything other than men and family—then to that extent she is controlled by the male culture. Until women see in each other the possibility of a primal commitment which includes sexual love, they will be denying themselves the love and value they readily accord to men, thus affirming their second-class status. As long as male acceptability is primary—both to individual women and to the movement as a whole—the term "lesbian" will be used effectively against women. Insofar as women want only more privileges within the system, they do not want to antagonize male power. They instead seek acceptability for women's liberation, and the most crucial aspect of the acceptability is to deny lesbianism—i.e., to deny any fundamental challenge to the basis of the female. It should also be said that some younger, more radical women have honestly begun to discuss lesbianism, but so far it has been primarily as a sexual "alternative" to men. This, however, is still giving primacy to men, both because the idea of relating more completely to women occurs as a negative reaction to men, and because the lesbian relationship is being characterized simply by sex, which is divisive and sexist. On one level, which is both personal and political, women may withdraw emotional and sexual energies from men, and work out various alternatives for those energies in their own lives. On a different political/psychological level, it must be understood that what is crucial is that women begin disengaging from male-defined response patterns. In the privacy of our own psyches, we must cut those cords to the core. For irrespective of where our love and sexual energies flow, if we are male-identified in our heads, we cannot realize our autonomy as human beings.

But why is it that women have related to and through men? By virtue of having been brought up in a male society, we have internalized the male culture's definition of ourselves. That definition consigns us to sexual and family functions, and excludes us from defining and shaping the terms of our lives. In exchange for our psychic servicing and for performing society's non-profitmaking functions, the man confers on us just one thing: the slave status which makes us legitimate in the eyes of the society in which we live. This is called "femininity" or "being a real woman" in our cultural lingo. We are authentic, legitimate, real to the extent that we are the property of some man whose name we bear. To be a woman who belongs to no man is to be invisible, pathetic, inauthentic, unreal. He confirms his image of us—of what we have to be in order to be acceptable by him—but not our real selves; he confirms our womanhood—as he defines it, in relation to him—but cannot confirm our personhood, our own selves as absolutes. As long as we are dependent on the male culture for this definition, for this approval, we cannot be free.

The consequence of internalizing this role is an enormous reservoir of self-hate. This is not to say the self-hate is recognized or accepted as such; indeed most women would deny it. It may be experienced as discomfort with her role, as feeling empty, as numbness, as restlessness, as a paralyzing anxiety at the center. Alternatively, it may be expressed in shrill defensiveness of the glory and destiny of her role. But it does exist, often beneath the edge of her consciousness, poisoning her existence, keeping her alienated from herself, her own needs, and rendering her a stranger to other women. They try to escape by identifying with the oppressor, living through him, gaining status and identity from his ego, his power, his accomplishments. And by not identifying with other "empty vessels" like themselves. Women resist relating on all levels to other women who will reflect their own oppression, their own secondary status, their own self-hate. For to confront another woman is finally to confront one's self—the self we have gone to such lengths to avoid. And in that mirror we know we cannot really respect and love that which we have been made to be.

As the source of self-hate and the lack of real self are rooted in our male-given identity, we must create a new sense of self. As long as we cling to the idea of "being a woman" we will sense some conflict with that incipient self, that sense of I, that sense of a whole person. It is very difficult to realize and accept that being "feminine" and being a whole person are irreconcilable. Only women can give to each other a new sense of self. That identity we have to develop with reference to ourselves, and not in relation to men. This consciousness is the revolutionary force from which all else will follow, for ours is an organic revolution. For this we must be available and supportive to one another, give our commitment and our love, give the emotional support necessary to sustain this movement. Our energies must flow toward our sisters, not backward toward our oppressors. As long as woman's liberation tries to free women without facing the basic heterosexual structure that binds us in one-to-one relationship with our oppressors, tremendous energies will continue to flow into trying to straighten up each particular relationship with a man, into finding how to get better sex, how to turn his head around—into trying to make the "new man" out of him, in the delusion that this will allow us to be the "new woman." This obviously splits our energies and commitments, leaving us unable to be committed to the construction of the new patterns which will liberate us.

It is the primacy of women relating to women, of women creating a new consciousness of and with each other, which is at the heart of women's liberation, and the basis for the cultural revolution. Together we must find, reinforce, and validate our authentic selves. As we do this, we confirm in each other that struggling, incipient sense of pride and strength, the divisive barriers begin to melt, we feel this growing solidarity with our sisters. We see ourselves as prime, find our centers inside of ourselves. We find receding the sense of alienation, of being cut off, of being behind a locked window, of being unable to get out what we know is inside. We feel a real-ness, feel at last we are coinciding with ourselves. With that real self, with that consciousness, we begin a revolution to end the imposition of all coercive identifications, and to achieve maximum autonomy in human expression.

32

ANNE KOEDT

Interview: Loving Another Woman (1971)

The following is from a taped interview with a woman who talked about her love relationship with another woman. Both of these women, who requested anonymity, had previously had only heterosexual relationships; both are feminists. The interview was conducted by Anne Koedt.

QUESTION: *You said you had been friends for a while before you realized you were attracted to each other. How did you become aware of it?*

From *Notes from the Third Year*, 1971.

ANSWER: I wasn't conscious of it until one evening when we were together and it all just sort of exploded. But, looking back, there are always signs, only one represses seeing them.

For example, I remember one evening— we are in the same feminist group together— and we were all talking very abstractly about love. All of a sudden, even though the group was carrying on the conversation in a theoretical way, we were having a personal conversation. We were starting to tell each other that we liked each other. Of course one of the things we discussed was: What is the thin line between friendship and love?

Or, there were times when we were very aware of having "accidentally" touched each other. And Jennie told me later that when we first met she remembered thinking, "abstractly" again, that if she were ever to get involved with a woman, she'd like to get involved with someone like me.

The mind-blowing thing is that you aren't at all conscious of what you are feeling; rather, you subconsciously, and systematically, refuse to deal with the implications of what's coming out. You just let it hang there because you're too scared to let it continue and see what it means.

Q: *What did you do when you became aware of your mutual attraction?*

A: We'd been seeing a lot of each other, and I was at her house for dinner. During the evening—we were having a nice time, but I remember also feeling uncomfortable—I became very aware of her as we were sitting together looking at something. There was an unusual kind of tension throughout the whole evening.

It was quite late by the time we broke up, so she asked me whether I wanted to stay over and sleep on her couch. And I remember really being very uptight—something I certainly wouldn't have felt in any other situation with a friend. Yet, even when I was uptight and felt that in some way by staying I would get myself into something, I wasn't quite sure what— something new and dangerous—I decided to stay anyway.

It wasn't really until I tried to fall asleep, and couldn't, that all of a sudden I became very, very aware. I was flooded with a tremendous attraction for her. And I wanted to tell her, I wanted to sleep with her, I wanted to let her know what I was feeling. At the same time I was totally bewildered, because here I was—not only did I want to tell her, but I was having a hard time just facing up to what was coming out in myself. My mind was working overtime trying to deal with this new thing.

She was awake too, and so we sat and talked. It took me about two hours to build up the courage to even bring up the subject. I think it is probably one of the most difficult things I ever had to do. To say—to in any way whatsoever open up the subject—to say anything was just so hard.

When I did bring it up in an oblique way and told her that I was attracted to her, she replied somewhat generally that she felt the same way. You see, she was as scared as I was, but I didn't know it. I thought she seemed very cool, so I wasn't even sure if she was interested. Although I think subconsciously I knew, because otherwise I wouldn't have asked her—I think I would have been too scared of rejection.

But when I finally did bring it up, and she said she felt the same way, well, at that point there was really no space left for anything in your mind. So we agreed to just drop it and let things happen as they would at a later time. My main, immediate worry was that maybe I had blown a good friendship which I really valued. Also, even if she did feel the same way, would we know what to do with it?

Q: *When you first realized that you were possibly getting involved with a woman were you afraid or upset?*

A: No. The strange thing is that the next morning, after I left, I felt a fantastic high. I was bouncing down the street and the sun was shining and I felt tremendously good. My mind was on a super high.

When I got home I couldn't do any kind of work. My mind kept operating on this emergency speed, trying to deal with my new feel-

ings for her. So I sat down and wrote a letter to myself. Just wrote it free association—didn't try to work it out in any kind of theory—and as I was writing I was learning from myself what I was feeling. Unexpectedly I wasn't feeling guilty or worried. I felt great.

Q: *When did you start sleeping with each other?*

A: The next time we were together. Again, we really wanted each other, but to finally make the move, the same move that with a man would have been automatic, was tremendously difficult . . . and exhilarating. Although we did sleep together, it wasn't sexual; just affectionate and very sensual. After that evening we started sleeping together sexually as well.

I guess it was also a surprise to find that you weren't struck down by God in a final shaft of lightning. That once you fight through that initial wall of undefined fears (built to protect those taboos), they wither rapidly, and leave you to operate freely in a new self-defined circle of what's natural. You have a new sense of boldness, of daring, about yourself.

Q: *Was it different from what you had thought a relationship with a woman would be like?*

A: Generally, no. Most of the things that I had thought intellectually in fact turned out to be true in my experience. One thing, however, was different. Like, I'd really felt that very possibly a relationship with a woman might not be terribly physical. That it would be for the most part warm and affectionate. I think I probably thought this because with men sex is so frequently confused with conquest. Men have applied a symbolic value to sex, where the penis equals dominance and the vagina equals submission. Since sensuality has no specific sex and is rather a general expression of mutual affection, its symbolic value, power-wise, is nil. So sex with a man is usually genitally oriented.

Perhaps I wasn't quite sure what would happen to sexuality once it was removed from its conventional context. But one of the things I discovered was that when you really like somebody, there's a perfectly natural connection between affection and love and sensuality and sexuality. That sexuality is a natural part of sensuality.

Q: *How is sex different with a woman?*

A: One of the really mind-blowing things about all this has been that it added a whole new dimension to my own sexuality. You can have good sex, technically, with a woman or a man. But at this point in time I think women have a much broader sense of sensuality. Since she and I both brought our experiences as women to sexuality, it was quite something.

Another aspect of sexuality is your feelings. Again, this is of course an area that has been delegated to women; we are supposed to provide the love and affection. It is one of our duties in a male-female relationship. Though it has been very oppressive in the context that we've been allowed it, the *ability* to show affection and love for someone else is, I think, a fine thing—which men should develop more in themselves, as a matter of fact. Love and affection are a necessary aspect of full sexuality. And one of the things I really enjoy with Jennie is this uninhibited ability to show our feelings.

Q: *Is the physical aspect of loving women really as satisfying as sex with a man?*

A: Yes.

Q: *You've been together a while now. What's your relationship like?*

A: Once we got over the initial week or so of just getting used to this entirely new thing, it very quickly became natural—natural is really the word I'd use for it. It was like adding another dimension to what we'd already been feeling for each other. It is quite a combination to fall in love with your friend.

We don't have any plans, any desire, to live together, although we do see a great deal of each other. We both like our own apartments, our own space.

I think one of the good things we did in the beginning was to say: Let's just see where it will go. We didn't say that we loved each other, just that we liked each other. We didn't immediately proclaim it a "relationship," as one is accustomed to do with a man—you know, making mental plans for the next ten years. So each

new feeling was often surprising, and very intensely experienced.

Q: *What would you say is the difference between this relationship and those you have had with men?*

A: Well, one of the biggest differences is that for the first time I haven't felt those knots-in-the-stomach undercurrents of trying to figure out what's *really* happening under what you *think* is happening.

I think it all boils down to an absence of role-playing; I haven't felt with Jen that we've fallen into that. Both of us are equally strong persons. I mean, you can ask yourself the question, if there were going to be roles, who'd play what? Well, I certainly won't play "the female," and I won't play "the male," and it's just as absurd to imagine her in either one of them. So in fact what we have is much more like what one gets in a friendship, which is more equalized. It's a more above-board feeling.

I don't find the traditional contradictions. If I do something strong and self-assertive, she doesn't find that a conflict with her having a relationship with me. I don't get reminded that I might be making myself "less womanly." And along with that there's less *self*-censorship, too. There's a mutual, unqualified, support for daring to try new things that I have never quite known before.

As a result, my old sense of limits is changing. For example, for the first time in my life I'm beginning to feel that I don't have a weak body, that my body isn't some kind of passive baggage. The other day I gritted my teeth and slid down a fireman's pole at a park playground. It may sound ordinary, but it was something I had never dared before, and I felt a very private victory.

Q: *Given the social disapproval and legal restrictions against lesbianism, what are some of the external problems you have faced?*

A: One thing is that I hesitate to show my affection for her in public. If you're walking down the street and you want to put your arm around someone or give them a kiss—the kind of thing you do without thinking if it is a man—well, that's hardly considered romantic by most people if it's done with someone of your own sex. I know that if I were to express my feelings in public with Jennie, there would be a lot of social intrusion that I would have to deal with. Somehow, people would assume a license to intrude upon your privacy in public; their hostile comments, hostile attitudes, would ruin the whole experience. So you're sort of caught in a bind. But we have in fact begun to do it more and more, because it bothers me that I can't express my feeling as I see fit, without hostile interference.

Q: *What made you fall in love with a woman?*

A: Well, that's a hard question. I think maybe it's even a bit misleading the way you phrased it. Because I didn't fall in love with "a woman," I fell in love with Jen—which is not exactly the same thing. A better way to ask the question is: How were you able to *overcome* the fact that it was a woman? In other words, how was I able to overcome my heterosexual training and allow my feelings for her to come out?

Certainly in my case it would never have happened without the existence of the women's movement. My own awareness of "maleness" and "femaleness" had become acute, and I was really probing what it meant. You see, I think in a sense I never wanted to be either male *or* female. Even when I was quite little and in many ways seemed feminine and "passive"—deep down, I never felt at home with the kinds of things women were supposed to be. On the other hand, I didn't particularly want to be a man either, so I didn't develop a male identity. Before I even got involved with the women's movement, I was already wanting something new. But the movement brought it out into the open for me.

Another thing the movement helped me with was shedding the notion that, however independent my life was, I must have a man: that somehow, no matter what I did myself, there was something that needed that magical element of male approval. Without confronting this I could never have allowed myself to fall in love with Jennie. In a way, I am like an addict who has kicked the habit.

But most important of all, I like her. In fact I think she's the healthiest person I have ever been involved with. See, I think we were lucky, because it happened spontaneously and unexpectedly from both sides. We didn't do it because we felt compelled to put our ideological beliefs into reality.

Many feminists are now beginning to at least theoretically consider the fact that there's no reason why one shouldn't love a woman. But I think that a certain kind of experimentation going on now with lesbianism can be really bad. Because even if you do ideologically think that it is perfectly fine—well, that's a *political* position; but being able to love somebody is a very personal and private thing as well, and even if you remove political barriers, well, then you are left with finding an individual who particularly fits *you*.

So I guess I'm saying that I don't think women who are beginning to think about lesbianism should get involved with anyone until they are really attracted to somebody. And that includes refusing to be seduced by lesbians who play the male seduction game and tell you, "you don't love women," and "you are oppressing us" if you don't jump into bed with them. It's terrible to try to seduce someone on ideological grounds.

Q: *Do you now look at women in a more sexual way?*

A: You mean, do I now eye all women as potential bed partners? No. Nor did I ever see men that way. As a matter of fact, I've never found myself being attracted to a man just because, for example, he had a good physique. I had a sexual relationship with whatever boy friend I had, but I related to most other men pretty asexually. It's no different with women. My female friends—well, I still see them as friends, because that's what they are. I don't sit around and have secret fantasies of being in bed with them.

But there's a real question here: What is the source, the impetus, for one's sexuality? Is it affection and love, or is it essentially conquest in bed? If it's sex as conquest in bed, then the question you just asked is relevant, for adding the category of women to those you sleep with would mean that every woman—who's attractive enough to be a prize worth conquering, of course—could arouse your sexuality. But if the sexual source lies in affection and love, then the question becomes absurd. For one obviously does not immediately fall in love with every woman one meets simply because one is *able* to sleep with women.

Also, one thing that really turns me off about this whole business of viewing women as potential bedmates is the implied possessiveness of it. It has taken me this long just to figure out how men are treating women sexually; now when I see some lesbians doing precisely the same kinds of things, I'm supposed to have instant amnesia in the name of sisterhood. I have heard some lesbians say things like, "I see all men as my rivals," or have heard them proudly discuss how they intimidated a heterosexual couple publicly to "teach the woman a political lesson." This brings out in me the same kind of intense rage that I get when, for example, I hear white men discussing how black men are "taking their women" (or vice versa). Who the hell says we belong to anyone?

Q: *Do you think that you would have difficulty relating to a man again if this relationship broke up? That is, can you "go back" to men after having had a relationship with a woman?*

A: It's an interesting thing that when people ask that question, most often what they're really asking is, are you "lost" to the world of what's "natural"? Sometimes I find myself not wanting to answer the question at all just because they're starting out by assuming that something's wrong with having a relationship with a woman. That's usually what's meant by "go back to men"—like you've been off someplace wild and crazy and, most of all, unsafe, and can you find your way home to papa, or something. So first of all it wouldn't be "going back."

And since I didn't become involved with a woman in order to make a political statement, by the same token I wouldn't make the converse statement. So, sure I could have a relationship with a man if he were the right kind of person and if he had rejected playing "the man" with me—that leaves out a lot of men here, I must add. But if a man had the right combination of qualities, I see no reason why I shouldn't be able to love him as much as I now love her.

At a certain point, I think, you realize that the final qualification is not being male or female, but whether they've joined the middle. That is—whether they have started from the male or the female side—they've gone toward the center where they are working toward combining the healthy aspects of so-called male and female characteristics. That's where I want to go and that's what I'm beginning to realize I respond to in other people.

Q: *Now that you've gotten involved with a woman, what is your attitude toward gay and lesbian groups?*

A: I have really mixed feelings about them. To some extent, for example, there has been a healthy interplay between the gay movement and the feminist movement. Feminists have had a very good influence on the gay movement because women's liberation challenges the very nature of the sex role system, not just whether one may be allowed to make transfers within it. On the other hand, the gay movement has helped open up the question of women loving other women. Though some of this was beginning to happen by itself, lesbians made a point of pressing the issue and therefore speeded up the process.

But there is a problem to me with focusing on sexual choice, as the gay movement does. Sleeping with another woman is not *necessarily* a healthy thing by itself. It does not mean—or prove, for that matter—that you therefore love women. It doesn't mean that you have avoided bad "male" or "female" behavior. It doesn't guarantee you anything. If you think about it, it can be the same game with new partners: On the one hand, male roles are learned, not genetic; women can ape them too. On the other, the feminine role can be comfortably carried into lesbianism, except now instead of a woman being passive with a man, she's passive with another woman. Which is all very familiar and is all going nowhere.

The confusing of sexual *partners* with sexual *roles* has also led to a really bizarre situation where some lesbians insist that you aren't really a radical feminist if you are not in bed with a woman. Which is wrong politically and outrageous personally.

Q: *Did the fact that lesbians pushed the issue in the women's movement have a major effect upon your own decision to have a relationship with a woman?*

A: It's hard to know. I think that the lesbian movement has escalated the thinking in the women's movement and to that extent it probably escalated mine.

But at the same time I know I was slowly getting there myself anyway. I'd been thinking about it for a long time. Because it is a natural question; if you want to remove sexual roles, and if you say that men and women are equal human beings, well, the next question is: Why should you only love men? I remember asking myself that question, and I remember it being discussed in many workshops I was in—what is it that make us assume that you can only receive and give love to a man?

33

RITA MAE BROWN

The Shape of Things to Come (1972)

If you love women then you are in revolt against male supremacy. The world which men have built hates women. Women, according to male supremacy, exist to serve the male. A woman who loves women then defies the basic building block of male supremacy: woman hatred. Women who love women are Lesbians.

From *Women: A Journal of Liberation*, June 1972. Also in Nancy Myron and Charlotte Bunch, eds., *Lesbianism and the Women's Movement* (Baltimore: Diana Press, 1975). Reprinted by permission of the author.

Men, because they can only think of women in sexual terms, define Lesbian as sex between women. However, Lesbians know that it is far more than that, it is a different way of life. It is a life determined by a woman for her own benefit and the benefit of other women. It is a life that draws its strength, support and direction from women. About two years ago this concept was given the name woman-identified woman. That's not a bad name, it is just a fancy way of saying that you love yourself and other women. You refuse to limit yourself by the male definitions of women. You free yourself from male concepts of "feminine" behavior.

Lesbianism, politically organized, is the greatest threat that exists to male supremacy. How can men remain supreme, how can they oppress women if women reject them and fight the entire world men have built to contain us? The beginning rejection is to put women first in your life, put yourself first. If you do that then you begin to understand that the only way you can lead the life you would like to lead is by smashing male supremacy—and its offshoot oppressions, class and race supremacy.

Any oppressed person who gives in to her oppression insures that others will remain oppressed and she exposes her sisters who are fighting that oppression. The emerging political Lesbians, or women-identified women, realize the scope of male supremacy and are changing their lives to fight it. Women who remain silent leave these outspoken women to face the common oppressor. Committing yourself to women is the first concrete step toward ending that common oppression. If you cannot find it in yourself to love another woman, and that includes physical love, then how can you truly say you care about women's liberation? If you don't feel other women are worthy of your total commitment—love, energy, sex, all of it—then aren't you saying that women aren't worth fighting for? If you reserve those "special" commitments for men then you are telling other women they aren't worth those commitments, they aren't important. You also don't understand or else avoid recognizing that individual relationships—your "personal" life—are political. Relationships between men and women involve power, dominance, role play, and oppression. A man has the entire system of male privilege to back him up. Another woman has nothing but her own self. Which relationship is better for you? It's obvious.

If women still give primary commitment and energy to the oppressors how can we build a strong movement to free ourselves? Did the Chinese love and support the capitalists? Do the Viet Cong cook supper for the Yankees? Are Blacks supposed to disperse their communities and each live in a white home? The answer, again, is obvious. Only if women give their time to women, to a women's movement, will they be free. You do not free yourself by polishing your chains, yet that is what heterosexual women do.

Lesbians who have tried to pull women into a supportive women's community are often attacked by these heterosexual women who hang onto the privileges they get from their men. These Lesbian-haters are not always vicious women. Most of them don't understand how heterosexuality maintains male supremacy. They also don't want to understand because if they did then they would have to change their lives and lose the scant privileges men have given them. The facts are simple: Heterosexuality keeps women separated from each other. Heterosexuality ties each woman to a man. Heterosexuality exhausts women because they struggle with their man—to get him to stop oppressing them—leaving them little energy for anything else. For this destruction of women's communities, for this betrayal of other women, women indeed get privileges from men: legitimacy (you are a real woman if you are with a man—a sexual definition again), prestige, money, social acceptance, and in some token cases political acceptance.

If you are a Lesbian who has come out then you cut yourself off from these privileges. You have ended your stake in maintaining the heterosexual world. You are in total revolt against male supremacy. How can women liberate themselves if they are still tied to that male supremacist world? How can a woman tied to men through heterosexuality keep from betraying her sisters? When push comes to shove, she will choose her man over other women; heterosexuality demands that she make that choice. How can you build a serious political movement when women do this to each other? You can't. Lesbianism is a necessary step in the struggle for liberation.

Why would any heterosexual woman give up the privileges men grant her for being heterosexual? Most often she will only give them up if she sees there is something better than the crumbs thrown to her from men. What can Lesbianism offer? It offers double oppression. It offers the threat of getting fired from your job, estranged from your family and old straight friends, it offers getting your throat slit by straight women in the service of men, it offers constant struggle against an inhumane and diseased world where violence is the key to power and love is a word found in poetry but not on the streets. Why take on those burdens?

Because Lesbianism also offers you the freedom to be yourself. It offers you potential equal relationships with your sisters. It offers escape from the silly, stupid, harmful games that men and women play, having the nerve to call them "relationships." It offers change. You will change yourself by discovering your woman-identified self, by discovering other women. No one, not even another Lesbian, can tell you who that self is. It is your individual challenge, your life. You will be on unfamiliar ground with no old patterns to guide you. As you change yourself, you begin to change your society also. A free, strong self cannot live in the muck that men have made. You will make mistakes and suffer from them. You will hurt and be hurt trying to find new ways. But you will learn and push on. You will discover the thousand subtle ways that heterosexuality destroyed your true power; you will discover how male supremacy destroys all women and eventually the creators of it, men. You will find once your consciousness is raised it cannot be unraised. Once you have a vision of the new world you can no longer accept the old one. You will become a fighter. You will find love and that you are beautiful, strong and that you care. You will build communities with other women from all classes and races, those communities will change the material parts of our lives. You will share what you have with others and they with you. You will revolt against this whole filthy world that tried to cover you and your beauty under a ton of male supremacist slime. That is what Lesbianism offers you.

Those of us who have found those new lives, that hope and courage, find ourselves in the position of being attacked and undermined by women in the women's liberation movement to say nothing of forces outside that movement. We cannot allow ourselves to be oppressed by men; how then can we turn around and allow ourselves to be oppressed and harrassed by women clinging to heterosexual privilege? We can't. Therefore, large portions of the political Lesbian population in women's liberation and gay liberation have split from those movements in order to survive. Does that mean we hate straight women? No. But would you volunteer your neck for someone to step on? Does this mean we can never again work with straight women or with gay men? No. But we aren't going to work with anyone until they begin to change their behavior. Some changes are: they can no longer push us around, hide us under rugs or try to seduce us when everyone else has gone home only to deny us in the morning.

Straight women by virtue of being tied to men don't understand Lesbians or the political meaning of Lesbianism. Straight women don't know what our lives are like. They can't think like we do. We understand their lives because we were all raised to be straight. It is one-way communication. Straight women are confused by men, don't put women first, they betray Lesbians and in its deepest form, they betray their own selves. You can't build a strong movement if your sisters are out there fucking with the oppressor. . . .

34
PEGGY KORNEGGER, JUDY ANTONELLI, AND MARIANNE RUBENSTEIN
What Is a Lesbian? (1977)

PEGGY KORNEGGER

There are things about women
That draw me to women.
There are things about women
That draw me to myself.
                    —Fran Winant

I am lesbian because I love women—and because I love myself as a woman. When I became a feminist, I was already moving toward recognition of myself as a lesbian (the "self-chosen woman"—Adrienne Rich). The woman who chooses herself, who chooses other women, is denying the necessity to choose opposites, is, in fact, denying the necessity *of* opposites. We live in a hetero, mono-istic society which gives us narrow, either/or options. By refusing polarities and one-at-the-expense-of-another dynamics (self-abnegation, subject/object relationships)—in short, by choosing to love oneself and other women (subject-to-subject)—we transform the present in revolutionary ways.

When I became a lesbian, all the many parts of myself came together; I made a "leap of consciousness" (Mary Daly) that opened me up to womanvision—a vision of the future that is expansive, connective, and everchanging. The choice of lesbianism (and the opening to womanvision) is a wholistic, integrated choice: the blending of a politics, poetics, sexuality, spirituality, philosophy, psychology, etc. that transcends opposites, heals schisms, and affirms a multi-dimensional reality. To move in the direction of this multi-dimensionality is to choose revolution in the deepest, most transforming sense of the word—(for me) lesbian-feminist-anarchist revolution.

From *Sinister Wisdom*, Fall 1977.

JUDY ANTONELLI

A lesbian is a woman whose primary physical, sexual, emotional, political and social interests are directed towards other women (whether she had ever acted upon that by sleeping with a woman or not). In short, she is a woman-identified woman. Lesbianism is not just a personal choice of who to sleep with; it is a political stand. The lesbian is a woman in total revolt against patriarchy; she does not give primary energy to men on *any* level. Lesbianism is a primary strategy in restoring female bonding as the basic social unit of a matriarchal society (as opposed to the patriarchal unit of the heterosexual couple). I don't identify with the term "homosexual" at all; to me that implies male. A separatist is a lesbian who gives as little energy to men as is realistically possible. Separatist politics come from placing a high value on our energy and power, realizing that without our nurturance men cannot survive. Separatism does NOT (as Adrienne Rich says) "proceed first out of hatred and rejection of others" [*Sinister Wisdom,* Issue 3, Spring '77]. Our motive is love of women. Nor does separatism imply hatred of straight women; it is withdrawal from MEN. Emotional withdrawal from men does not deny the necessity of political confrontation of men, either. While our *primary* motive is not hatred of men, I do feel it is healthy to feel hostility towards those who are daily killing and mutilating us. There is a lesbian (strong, woman-identified woman) in *every* woman, which has been suppressed by the patriarchy.

Feminism is NOT humanism. I cannot emphasize this point enough! Humanism is a "love everybody" liberal philosophy which does not identify an enemy; i.e., everyone is oppressed by "society." Feminism says that women are oppressed by men (who built the structures of society to reinforce their dominance); it therefore identifies an enemy. Humanism is responsible for the "men are oppressed by sexism, too" garbage.

Lesbians are an "emerging species" in the sense that we are Amazons and witches; women with a new strength and sense of power. We are building a new society, reclaiming what is rightfully ours. It is Lesbians who will save Life on this planet, not just for ourselves, but for animals and vegetation also. As I see Lesbians growing stronger, becoming more psychic, taking more power—women who are on TV, models, Playboy bunnies, etc., look more and more like plastic dolls, man-made caricatures. We look and act *so* differently that it amazes me at times. Lesbians have gotten rid of the "drag" by which patriarchy defines women. We are discovering the true meaning and potential of womanhood. . . .

MARIANNE RUBENSTEIN

A Lesbian is utmost an individual—especially under patriarchy. I define a Lesbian as a woman motivated by our *love* for other women. We are not reactionary beings. This love extends through all levels—be they known or unknown. I use the word "motivated" intentionally. Lesbians know, for survival in all senses, we must move. To fall into stagnation, the deathbed of the patriarchy, is to fall into oblivion. To name ourselves Lesbian is to assert our most primary desire: to live. We are explorers, creators, indeed spacemakers. For to wield the name Lesbian is to pull out of time a space. Womanspace.

We are very special. Artists, all of us, so capable of perceiving our own beauty, we seek communion with it. The spirit of the wild burns through our soul like an uncontrollable brush fire. Yes. We are in revolt. Like Phoenixes we rise from our mothers' ashes. And with the integration of ancient and newly discovered wisdom we will spread what has been misconstrued as the most deadly disease: Compassion.

35

ADRIENNE RICH

Compulsory Heterosexuality and Lesbian Existence (1980/1986)

. . . I have chosen to use the terms *lesbian existence* and *lesbian continuum* because the word *lesbianism* has a clinical and limiting ring. *Lesbian existence* suggests both the fact of the historical presence of lesbians and our continuing creation of the meaning of that existence. I mean the term *lesbian continuum* to include a range—through each woman's life and throughout history—of woman-identified experience, not simply the fact that a woman has had or consciously desired genital sexual experience with another woman. If we expand it to embrace many more forms of primary intensity between and among women, including the sharing of a rich inner life, the bonding against male tyranny, the giving and receiving of practical and political support, if we can also hear it in such associations as *marriage resistance* and the "haggard" behavior identified by Mary Daly (obsolete meanings: "intractable," "willful," "wanton," and "unchaste," "a woman reluctant to yield to wooing"),[1] we begin to grasp breadths of female history and psychology which have lain out of reach as a consequence of limited, mostly clinical, definitions of *lesbianism*.

Lesbian existence comprises both the breaking of a taboo and the rejection of a compulsory way of life. It is also a direct or indirect attack on male right of access to women. But it is more than these, although we may first begin to perceive it as a form of naysaying to patriarchy, an act of resistance. It has, of course, included isolation, self-hatred, breakdown, alcoholism, suicide, and intrawoman violence; we romanticize at our peril what it means to love and act against the grain, and under heavy penalties; and lesbian existence has been lived (unlike, say, Jewish or Catholic existence) without access to any knowledge of a tradition, a continuity, a social underpinning. The destruction of records and memorabilia and letters documenting the realities of lesbian existence must be taken very seriously as a means of keeping heterosexuality compulsory for women, since what has been kept from our knowledge is joy, sensuality, courage, and community, as well as guilt, self-betrayal, and pain.[2]

Lesbians have historically been deprived of a political existence through "inclusion" as female versions of male homosexuality. To equate lesbian existence with male homosexuality because each is stigmatized is to erase female reality once again. Part of the history of lesbian existence is, obviously, to be found where lesbians, lacking a coherent female community, have shared a kind of social life and common cause with homosexual men. But there are differences: women's lack of economic and cultural privilege relative to men; qualitative differences in female and male relationships—for example, the patterns of anonymous sex among

From Adrienne Rich, *Blood, Bread, and Poetry: Selected Prose 1979–1985* (New York: W. W. Norton & Co., 1986). Also in *Signs: Journal of Women in Culture and Society* (Sexuality), Summer 1980. Originally written in 1978 for *Signs*, this essay was also reprinted by Antelope Publications in 1982 as a pamphlet. Copyright 1986 by Adrienne Rich. Reprinted by permission of the author and W. W. Norton & Company, Inc.

1. Daly, *Gyn/Ecology*, p. 15.

2. "In a hostile world in which women are not supposed to survive except in relation with and in service to men, entire communities of women were simply erased. History tends to bury what it seeks to reject" (Blanche W. Cook, "'Women Alone Stir My Imagination': Lesbianism and the Cultural Tradition," *Signs: Journal of Women in Culture and Society* 4, no. 4 [Summer 1979]: 719–720). The Lesbian Herstory Archives in New York City is one attempt to preserve contemporary documents on lesbian existence—a project of enormous value and meaning, working against the continuing censorship and obliteration of relationships, networks, communities in other archives and elsewhere in the culture.

male homosexuals, and the pronounced ageism in male homosexual standards of sexual attractiveness. I perceive the lesbian experience as being, like motherhood, a profoundly *female* experience, with particular oppressions, meanings, and potentialities we cannot comprehend as long as we simply bracket it with other sexually stigmatized existences. Just as the term *parenting* serves to conceal the particular and significant reality of being a parent who is actually a mother, the term *gay* may serve the purpose of blurring the very outlines we need to discern, which are of crucial value for feminism and for the freedom of women as a group.[3]

As the term *lesbian* has been held to limiting, clinical associations in its patriarchal definition, female friendship and comradeship have been set apart from the erotic, thus limiting the erotic itself. But as we deepen and broaden the range of what we define as lesbian existence, as we delineate a lesbian continuum, we begin to discover the erotic in female terms: as that which is unconfined to any single part of the body or solely to the body itself; as an energy not only diffuse but, as Audre Lorde has described it, omnipresent in "the sharing of joy, whether physical, emotional, psychic," and in the sharing of work; as the empowering joy which "makes us less willing to accept powerlessness, or those other supplied states of being which are not native to me, such as resignation, despair, self-effacement, depression, self-denial."[4] In another context, writing of women and work, I quoted the autobiographical passage in which the poet H.D. described how her friend Bryher supported her in persisting with the visionary experience which was to shape her mature work.

"I knew that this experience, this writing-on-the-wall before me, could not be shared with anyone except the girl who stood so bravely there beside me. This girl said without hesitation, "Go on." It was she really who had the detachment and integrity of the Pythoness of Delphi. But it was I, battered and dissociated . . . who was seeing the pictures, and who was reading the writing or granted the inner vision. Or perhaps, in some sense, we were "seeing" it together, for without her, admittedly, I could not have gone on."[5]

If we consider the possibility that all women—from the infant suckling at her mother's breast, to the grown woman experiencing orgasmic sensations while suckling her own child, perhaps recalling her mother's milk smell in her own, to two women, like Virginia Woolf's Chloe and Olivia, who share a laboratory,[6] to the woman dying at ninety, touched and handled by women—exist on a lesbian continuum, we can see ourselves as moving in and out of this continuum, whether we identify ourselves as lesbian or not.

We can then connect aspects of woman identification as diverse as the impudent, intimate girl friendships of eight or nine year olds and the banding together of those women of the twelfth and fifteenth centuries known as Beguines who "shared houses, rented to one another, bequeathed houses to their roommates . . . in cheap subdivided houses in the artisans' area of town," who "practiced Christian virtue on their own, dressing and living simply and not associating with men," who earned their livings as spinsters, bakers, nurses, or ran schools for young girls, and who managed—until the Church forced them to disperse—to live independent both of marriage and of conventual restrictions.[7] It allows

3. [A.R., 1986: The shared historical and spiritual "crossover" functions of lesbians and gay men in cultures past and present are traced by Judy Grahn in *Another Mother Tongue: Gay Words, Gay Worlds* (Boston: Beacon, 1984). I now think we have much to learn both from the uniquely female aspects of lesbian existence and from the complex "gay" identity we share with gay men.]

4. Audre Lorde, "Uses of the Erotic: The Erotic as Power," in *Sister Outsider* (Trumansburg, N.Y.: Crossing Press, 1984).

5. Adrienne Rich, "Conditions for Work: The Common World of Women," in *On Lies, Secrets, and Silence*, p. 209; H.D., *Tribute to Freud* (Oxford: Carcanet, 1971), pp. 50–54.

6. Woolf, *A Room of One's Own*, p. 126.

us to connect these women with the more celebrated "Lesbians" of the women's school around Sappho of the seventh century B.C., with the secret sororities and economic networks reported among African women, and with the Chinese marriage-resistance sisterhoods—communities of women who refused marriage or who, if married, often refused to consummate their marriages and soon left their husbands, the only women in China who were not footbound and who, Agnes Smedley tells us, welcomed the births of daughters and organized successful women's strikes in the silk mills.[8] It allows us to connect and compare disparate individual instances of marriage resistance: for example, the strategies available to Emily Dickinson, a nineteenth-century white woman genius, with the strategies available to Zora Neale Hurston, a twentieth-century Black woman genius. Dickinson never married, had tenuous intellectual friendships with men, lived self-convented in her genteel father's house in Amherst, and wrote a lifetime of passionate letters to her sister-in-law Sue Gilbert and a smaller group of such letters to her friend Kate Scott Anthon. Hurston married twice but soon left each husband, scrambled her way from Florida to Harlem to Columbia University to Haiti and finally back to Florida, moved in and out of white patron-

age and poverty, professional success, and failure; her survival relationships were all with women, beginning with her mother. Both of these women in their vastly different circumstances were marriage resisters, committed to their own work and selfhood, and were later characterized as "apolitical." Both were drawn to men of intellectual quality; for both of them women provided the ongoing fascination and sustenance of life.

If we think of heterosexuality as *the* natural emotional and sensual inclination for women, lives such as these are seen as deviant, as pathological, or as emotionally and sensually deprived. Or, in more recent and permissive jargon, they are banalized as "life styles." And the work of such women, whether merely the daily work of individual or collective survival and resistance or the work of the writer, the activist, the reformer, the anthropologist, or the artist—the work of self-creation—is undervalued, or seen as the bitter fruit of "penis envy" or the sublimation of repressed eroticism or the meaningless rant of a "man-hater." But when we turn the lens of vision and consider the degree to which and the methods whereby heterosexual "preference" has actually been imposed on women, not only can we understand differently the meaning of individual lives and work, but we can begin to recognize a central fact of women's history: that women have always resisted male tyranny. A feminism of action, often though not always without a theory, has constantly re-emerged in every culture and in every period. We can then begin to study women's struggle against powerlessness, women's radical rebellion, not just in male-defined "concrete revolutionary situations"[9] but in all the situations male ideologies have not perceived as revolutionary—for example, the refusal of some women to produce children, aided at great risk by other women;[10] the

7. Gracia Clark, "The Beguines: A Mediaeval Women's Community," *Quest: A Feminist Quarterly* 1, no. 4 (1975): 73–80.

8. See Denise Paulmé, ed., *Women of Tropical Africa* (Berkeley: University of California Press, 1963), pp. 7, 266–267. Some of these sororities are described as "a kind of defensive syndicate against the male element," their aims being "to offer concerted resistance to an oppressive patriarchate," "independence in relation to one's husband and with regard to motherhood, mutual aid, satisfaction of personal revenge." See also Audre Lorde, "Scratching the Surface: Some Notes on Barriers to Women and Loving," in *Sister Outsider*, pp. 45–52; Marjorie Topley, "Marriage Resistance in Rural Kwangtung," in *Women in Chinese Society*, ed. M. Wolf and R. Witke (Stanford, Calif.: Stanford University Press, 1978), pp. 67–89; Agnes Smedley, *Portraits of Chinese Women in Revolution*, ed. J. MacKinnon and S. MacKinnon (Old Westbury, N.Y.: Feminist Press, 1976), pp. 103–110.

9. See Rosalind Petchesky, "Dissolving the Hyphen: A Report on Marxist-Feminist Groups 1–5," in *Capitalist Patriarchy and the Case for Socialist Feminism*, ed. Zillah Eisenstein (New York: Monthly Review Press, 1979), p. 387.

refusal to produce a higher standard of living and leisure for men (Leghorn and Parker show how both are part of women's unacknowledged, unpaid, and ununionized economic contribution). We can no longer have patience with Dinnerstein's view that women have simply collaborated with men in the "sexual arrangements" of history. We begin to observe behavior, both in history and in individual biography, that has hitherto been invisible or misnamed, behavior which often constitutes, given the limits of the counterforce exerted in a given time and place, radical rebellion. And we can connect these rebellions and the necessity for them with the physical passion of woman for woman which is central to lesbian existence: the erotic sensuality which has been, precisely, the most violently erased fact of female experience.

Heterosexuality has been both forcibly and subliminally imposed on women. Yet everywhere women have resisted it, often at the cost of physical torture, imprisonment, psychosurgery, social ostracism, and extreme poverty. "Compulsory heterosexuality" was named as one of the "crimes against women" by the Brussels International Tribunal on Crimes against Women in 1976. Two pieces of testimony from two very different cultures reflect the degree to which persecution of lesbians is a global practice here and now. A report from Norway relates:

"A lesbian in Oslo was in a heterosexual marriage that didn't work, so she started taking tranquilizers and ended up at the health sanatorium for treatment and rehabilitation. . . . The moment she said in family group therapy that she believed she was a lesbian, the doctor told her she was not. He knew from "looking into her eyes," he said. She had the eyes of a woman who wanted sexual intercourse with her husband. So she was subjected to so-called "couch

therapy." She was put into a comfortably heated room, naked, on a bed, and for an hour her husband was to . . . try to excite her sexually. . . . The idea was that the touching was always to end with sexual intercourse. She felt stronger and stronger aversion. She threw up and sometimes ran out of the room to avoid this "treatment." The more strongly she asserted that she was a lesbian, the more violent the forced heterosexual intercourse became. This treatment went on for about six months. She escaped from the hospital, but she was brought back. Again she escaped. She has not been there since. In the end she realized that she had been subjected to forcible rape for six months."

And from Mozambique:

"I am condemned to a life of exile because I will not deny that I am a lesbian, that my primary commitments are, and will always be to other women. In the new Mozambique, lesbianism is considered a left-over from colonialism and decadent Western civilization. Lesbians are sent to rehabilitation camps to learn through self-criticism the correct line about themselves. . . . If I am forced to denounce my own love for women, if I therefore denounce myself, I could go back to Mozambique and join forces in the exciting and hard struggle of rebuilding a nation, including the struggle for the emancipation of Mozambiquan women. As it is, I either risk the rehabilitation camps, or remain in exile."[11]

Nor can it be assumed that women like those in Carroll Smith-Rosenberg's study, who married, stayed married, yet dwelt in a profoundly female emotional and passional world, "preferred" or "chose" heterosexuality. Women have married because it was necessary, in order to survive economically, in order to have children who would not suffer economic deprivation or social ostracism, in order to remain respectable, in order to do what was expected of women, because coming out of "abnormal" childhoods they wanted to feel "normal" and because heterosexual romance has been repre-

10. [A.R., 1986: See Angela Davis, *Women, Race and Class* (New York: Random House, 1981), p. 102; Orlando Patterson, *Slavery and Social Death: A Comparative Study* (Cambridge: Harvard University Press, 1982), p. 133.]

11. Russell and van de Ven, pp. 42–43, 56–57.

sented as the great female adventure, duty, and fulfillment. We may faithfully or ambivalently have obeyed the institution, but our feelings—and our sensuality—have not been tamed or contained within it. There is no statistical documentation of the numbers of lesbians who have remained in heterosexual marriages for most of their lives. But in a letter to the early lesbian publication *The Ladder,* the playwright Lorraine Hansberry had this to say:

"I suspect that the problem of the married woman who would prefer emotional-physical relationships with other women is proportionally much higher than a similar statistic for men. (A statistic surely no one will ever really have.) This because the estate of woman being what it is, how could we ever begin to guess the numbers of women who are not prepared to risk a life alien to what they have been taught all their lives to believe was their 'natural' destiny—AND—their only expectation for ECONOMIC security. It seems to be that this is why the question has an immensity that it does not have for male homosexuals. . . . A woman of strength and honesty may, if she chooses, sever her marriage and marry a new male mate and society will be upset that the divorce rate is rising so—but there are few places in the United States, in any event, where she will be anything remotely akin to an 'outcast.' Obviously this is not true for a woman who would end her marriage to take up life with another woman."[12]

This *double life*—this apparent acquiescence to an institution founded on male interest and prerogative—has been characteristic of female experience: in motherhood and in many kinds of heterosexual behavior, including the

rituals of courtship; the pretense of asexuality by the nineteenth-century wife; the simulation of orgasm by the prostitute, the courtesan, the twentieth-century "sexually liberated" woman.

Meridel Le Sueur's documentary novel of the depression, *The Girl,* is arresting as a study of female double life. The protagonist, a waitress in a St. Paul working-class speakeasy, feels herself passionately attracted to the young man Butch, but her survival relationships are with Clara, an older waitress and prostitute, with Belle, whose husband owns the bar, and with Amelia, a union activist. For Clara and Belle and the unnamed protagonist, sex with men is in one sense an escape from the bedrock misery of daily life, a flare of intensity in the gray, relentless, often brutal web of day-to-day existence:

"It was like he was a magnet pulling me. It was exciting and powerful and frightening. He was after me too and when he found me I would run, or be petrified, just standing in front of him like a zany. And he told me not to be wandering with Clara to the Marigold where we danced with strangers. He said he would knock the shit out of me. Which made me shake and tremble, but it was better than being a husk full of suffering and not knowing why."[13]

Throughout the novel the theme of double life emerges; Belle reminisces about her marriage to the bootlegger Hoinck:

"You know, when I had that black eye and said I hit it on the cupboard, well he did it the bastard, and then he says don't tell anybody. . . . He's nuts, that's what he is, nuts, and I don't see why I live with him, why I put up with him a minute on this earth. But listen kid, she said, I'm telling you something. She looked at me and her face was wonderful. She said, Jesus Christ, Goddam him I love him that's why

---

12. I am indebted to Jonathan Katz's *Gay American History* (op. cit.) for bringing to my attention Hansberry's letters to *The Ladder* and to Barbara Grier for supplying me with copies of relevant pages from *The Ladder,* quoted here by permission of Barbara Grier. See also the reprinted series of *The Ladder,* ed. Jonathan Katz et al. (New York: Arno, 1975), and Deirdre Carmody, "Letters by Eleanor Roosevelt Detail Friendship with Lorena Hickok," *New York Times* (October 21, 1979).

13. Meridel Le Sueur, *The Girl* (Cambridge, Mass.: West End Press, 1978), pp. 10–11. Le Sueur describes, in an afterword, how this book was drawn from the writings and oral narrations of women in the Workers Alliance who met as a writers' group during the depression.

I'm hooked like this all my life, Goddam him I love him."[14]

After the protagonist has her first sex with Butch, her women friends care for her bleeding, give her whiskey, and compare notes.

"My luck, the first time and I got into trouble. He gave me a little money and I come to St. Paul where for ten bucks they'd stick a huge vet's needle into you and you start it and then you were on your own. . . . I never had no child. I've just had Hoinck to mother, and a hell of a child he is."[15]

"Later they made me go back to Clara's room to lie down. . . . Clara lay down beside me and put her arms around me and wanted me to tell her about it but she wanted to tell about herself. She said she started it when she was twelve with a bunch of boys in an old shed. She said nobody had paid any attention to her before and she became very popular. . . . They like it so much, she said, why shouldn't you give it to them and get presents and attention? I never cared anything for it and neither did my mama. But it's the only thing you got that's valuable."[16]

Sex is thus equated with attention from the male, who is charismatic though brutal, infantile, or unreliable. Yet it is the women who make life endurable for each other, give physical affection without causing pain, share, advise, and stick by each other. (*I am trying to find my strength through women—without my friends, I could not survive.*) Le Sueur's *The Girl* parallels Toni Morrison's remarkable *Sula,* another revelation of female double life:

"Nel was the one person who had wanted nothing from her, who had accepted all aspects of her. . . . Nel was one of the reasons Sula had drifted back to Medallion. . . . The men . . . had merged into one large personality: the same language of love, the same entertainments of love, the same cooling of love. Whenever she introduced her private thoughts into their rubbings and goings, they hooded their eyes. They taught her nothing but love tricks, shared nothing but worry, gave nothing but money. She had been looking all along for a friend, and it took her a while to discover that a lover was not a comrade and never could be—for a woman."

But Sula's last thought at the second of her death is "Wait'll I tell Nel." And after Sula's death, Nel looks back on her own life:

"'All that time, all that time, I thought I was missing Jude.' And the loss pressed down on her chest and came up into her throat. 'We was girls together,' she said as though explaining something. 'O Lord, Sula,' she cried, 'Girl, girl, girlgirlgirl!' It was a fine cry—loud and long—but it had no bottom and it had no top, just circles and circles of sorrow."[17]

The Girl and *Sula* are both novels which examine what I am calling the lesbian continuum, in contrast to the shallow or sensational "lesbian scenes" in recent commercial fiction.[18] Each shows us woman identification untarnished (till the end of Le Sueur's novel) by romanticism; each depicts the competition of heterosexual compulsion for women's attention, the diffusion and frustration of female bonding that might, in a more conscious form, reintegrate love and power. . . .

---

14. Ibid., p. 20.
15. Ibid., pp. 53–54.
16. Ibid., p. 55.

17. Toni Morrison, *Sula* (New York: Bantam, 1973), pp. 103–104, 149. I am indebted to Lorraine Bethel's essay "'This Infinity of Conscious Pain': Zora Neale Hurston and the Black Female Literary Tradition," in *All the Women Are White, All the Blacks Are Men, but Some of Us Are Brave: Black Women's Studies,* ed. Gloria T. Hull, Patricia Bell Scott, and Barbara Smith (Old Westbury, N.Y.: Feminist Press, 1982).

18. See Maureen Brady and Judith McDaniel, "Lesbians in the Mainstream: The Image of Lesbians in Recent Commercial Fiction," *Conditions* 6 (1979): 82–105.

36

CHARLOTTE BUNCH

Speaking Out, Reaching Out (1977–1985)

After 1977, I stopped writing about lesbianism as a separate issue and worked instead to incorporate an understanding of lesbian feminism into other areas. The following is a medley of excerpts taken from speeches where I discussed lesbian/gay rights in relation to other topics in a variety of contexts between 1977 and 1985.

GAY RIGHTS/HUMAN RIGHTS AND TRADITION IN AMERICA

[This is taken from my presentation at a "Speak Out For Human Rights" in Washington, D.C., on September 23, 1977, sponsored by a coalition of organizations called the Dialog for Human Rights.]

I decided to speak about patriotism tonight after watching a spoof on a TV talk show where the "human rights" expert discussed the solution to the "problem" of gays. He suggested that people in the United States might be willing to grant rights to homosexuals if we formed our own country, outside of North America or in a desert that not too many people were using, with a fence around it. It was meant to be funny, but it sounded all too familiar: Indian reservations for the Native American problem; Japanese detention camps during World War II; sending Negroes "back" to Liberia when their labor was no longer needed here, and so on.

One tendency in this country is indeed to deal with "problem populations" by trying to get them out of sight. A territory, a ghetto, a closet, a jail or mental hospital—anywhere, so long as it is not necessary to look at and treat

"them" as human beings. Our struggle for gay rights today is one of the present stages of a civil war that has been going on within the U.S. for centuries. That war is the conflict between the tradition of human rights and tolerance for diversity versus the tradition of bigotry and intolerance.

Both sides in this war have seen themselves as battling for what they thought was good versus evil. But recently, we have seen the right wing using more of that language and claiming to be "saving America" through everything from "right to life" and "save our children" slogans to the waving of the flag by Ku Klux Klansmen. But I believe that it is the people represented here from civil rights, feminist, gay rights, and community-activist groups who are upholding the better traditions of our country. We should claim to be saving the possibility of a humane society in America. We must resurrect some of the spiritual conviction that freedom and justice are on our side that sustained the civil rights movement of the '60s.

We have talked a lot about unity among our groups tonight, but we also need to see that unity as part of a long-term tradition of struggle in this country. Radicals often lack a sense of connection to the past, seeing ourselves as breaking away from the old rather than as continuing the best ideals of certain traditions. I think that we can gain strength from recognizing ourselves as carrying on a tradition we inherited from the abolitionists and trade unionists as well as the women's and peace movements of the past century.

In thinking about our claim to traditions in this country, I was reminded of that bumper sticker, "America, love it or leave it." I don't know how many of you have felt uncertainty about responding to this, but I, for one, feel ambiguous about being an American. I feel shame over the injustices perpetrated in my name, but I also have hope that we can move toward the promises for justice and freedom of this country. So, since I do not intend to leave it, I am trying to learn what it means to love a sinner like America.

From Charlotte Bunch, *Passionate Politics: Essays 1968–1986* (New York: St. Martin's Press, 1987). Copyright 1987 by Charlotte Bunch. Reprinted by permission of St. Martin's Press.

I have thought about the Vietnamese making a distinction between hating the U.S. government waging a war against them and the people here whom they always tried to reach as human beings. I remember the focus on love in the early civil rights movement as well as among women and gays who have sought to counter the self-hatred taught to us by society with love for ourselves. America is like an unfaithful lover who promised us more than we got. Yet, if we do not choose to leave, we must find ways to love what is best in her traditions and fight against the transgressions. Now I say to "love it or leave it," that we are going to "love it and change it."

In order to realize our hopes for change in this country, we must find more ways to unite and not allow any of our groups to be isolated and defeated. At the moment, the attack on gay rights is like the tip of the iceberg of reactionary efforts. If other progressives allow gays to be persecuted, all of us will suffer. Our society has tried to keep us divided and fighting each other for small privileges. But if we realize how little those privileges mean in terms of power, we can see that we have more in common as those seeking to broaden human rights and tolerance for diversity and choice, than we do in identifying with the status quo.

I have been encouraged by the state and national coalitions that diverse groups of women—including lesbians and women of color—have built around the International Women's Year National Conference to be held later this year. At the California state conference where this coalition passed a progressive feminist plan of action, we also saw the intensity of our opposition. One of the right-wing delegates gave a raving speech about how she was going to appeal the proceedings "all the way to the Supreme Court until they finally rule on what a woman really is." I see her as a symbol of those forces in America who want some authority—church or state—to straighten out the issues of sex and sex roles and enforce their views on all of us. To counter them, we must unite in defending our vision of a diverse America that does not draw lines limiting what a woman or any other person is, and what he or she can be in life.

If those of us fighting against oppression in this country see that human rights are indivisible and that our battles are connected, then we can further all of our concerns and avoid becoming isolated in our struggles. For this, we must work together and understand better what each of us needs to survive and flourish. In so doing, we continue the tradition that has sought justice, tolerance, and the advance of human rights in America. Indeed, we will not leave her, but we will love her and change her. For we are your children, America, we are your sisters and brothers, your teachers and students; we are your future and we are here to stay.

LESBIANISM AND EROTICA IN PORNOGRAPHIC AMERICA

[This is taken from a speech delivered at the first March on Times Square [New York City], organized by Women Against Pornography, on October 20, 1979.]

We are here to demand and organize an end to violence against women in pornography. But we are also here to ask some questions of America: What kind of society is it that calls love and affection between two women perverse, while male brutality to women is made profitable? What kind of society is it that takes a child away from a loving mother simply because she is a lesbian, while another child can be used by her parents to produce child pornography? What kind of society is it where the lifelong partnership of two women has no standing in court, while a husband can batter and rape his wife without interference?

It is a pornographic society; America is a pornographic patriarchy. We are here to say that it is not the kind of society we want and that it is going to change. We are here to demand better of America. Last week at the National Gay Rights Rally in Washington, over a hundred thousand people demanded the right to control our bodies, including our sexuality, and called for an end to social degradation and violence against lesbians and gay men. Today many lesbians are marching again to demand that same right as women—to control our bodies and to protect ourselves from the violence of pornography. Both of these marches are about the right of all people to the dignity of our sexuality, to the control of our own bodies, and to an end to all forms of violence and degradation against us.

Lesbians are tired of having our love labeled "pornographic," while the real pornographers make money off of women's bodies. Lesbians know about love, sex, and eroticism of the female body: we know it and we love it. And we know that it has nothing to do with woman-hating pornography. Indeed, it is only in such pornography where men exploit lesbianism to their own ends, that the portrayal of lesbianism becomes okay to patriarchy. Lesbian love is for women, and it is abused precisely because it is outside of male control.

Lesbians are tired of having our love, our culture, and our publications threatened with censorship by labels of "perversion." We will continue fighting for our right to proclaim and portray our love and our sexuality openly. But we will not be intimidated into silence about woman-hating and violent pornography out of fear that we will then be labeled and censored as "pornographic." We will not be pushed into a closet of blindness toward pornography and the culture it thrives on. Lesbian oppression is perpetrated by the same forces that promote pornographic culture; bringing lesbian love out of the closet goes hand in hand with exposing the woman-hating bias of most pornography.

We have seen the exploitation of lesbian love in pornography. We can tell how phony are the lesbian scenes in which our reality is distorted to fit male fantasies and feed male consumption of female bodies. As lovers of our sex, if we had a small portion of the money that goes into pornography, we could produce genuine erotica about lesbian love, portraying the real beauty of women and of women loving women, for ourselves, not for male consumption. I am sure that our productions would be different from woman-hating pornography.

Finally, I must add that pornography is not just symbolic violence against women. It is part of an international slave traffic in women that operates as a multinational effort, where our bodies are the product, often procured unwillingly and usually abused. Our fight against violence in pornography in its widest implications is therefore a global struggle. It extends from local street actions to the United Nations. It includes exposing the cover-up of reports on slave trade in women that has gone on at all levels for decades.

We begin this international struggle in our own streets and nowhere is that more appropriate than here on Forty-second Street—Times Square—the pornography capital of America. We begin by reclaiming our bodies and our sexuality for ourselves. We begin by demanding that a society that punishes us for loving ourselves and each other, and then demeans our bodies for the profit of others, must change. We begin by no longer tolerating a pornographic and heterosexist patriarchy in any of its aspects. We begin by calling on America to do better—to take violence and degradation out of the category of sexuality in order to discover fully and celebrate the joy and eroticism of female sexuality.

JUNE 12th DISARMAMENT RALLY

[This speech was given at the National Disarmament and Nuclear Freeze Rally held in Central Park, New York City, June 12, 1982.]

I am especially proud to be here today for all the lesbians and gay men of all races, classes, and nations who have been present in movements for equality, justice, peace, and liberation for many years. We have always been here, but until we began a movement for our own liberation as gay people, we were present in those movements as second-class citizens, hiding ourselves and hiding those whom we loved. And you can be sure that fighting for change from behind closet doors cost us a lot; it cost us in terms of our personal dignity and it diminished the energy that we had to give to those movements.

Today that is changing. Today, we are a proud and open part of this struggle. Some of us are wearing lavender armbands at this rally to make our presence among you more visible. Today, we bring the energies released by our movement of love for ourselves to join in this demand for an end to the nuclear arms race.

We know that the forces of bigotry, fear, and violence that threaten to destroy our lives simply because of who we love are linked to the forces of militarism, prejudice, and greed that threaten to destroy this planet—denying all love, all justice, all freedom, indeed all life on earth.

We understand that the demand by some for control over our intimate lives—denying each person's right to control and express her or his own sexuality and denying women the right to control over the reproductive process in our bodies—creates an atmosphere in which domination over others and militarism are seen as acceptable. For society to continue accepting the idea that certain groups have the right to control and violate others can only end in our day with nuclear holocaust.

Something is amiss in our world.

We know that priorities are amiss in the world when there is enough food to feed the hungry but political and economic policies prevent that and allow food to rot.

We know that priorities are amiss in the world when a man gets a military medal of honor for killing another man and a dishonorable discharge for loving one.

We know that priorities are amiss in the world when children are not protected from parents who abuse them sexually while a lesbian mother is denied custody of her child and labeled immoral simply because she loves women.

We know that priorities are amiss when the military budgets of all nations combined for one day equal enough money to feed, clothe, and house all the people in the world for one year.

The list is endless and each of you can add examples. But we are not here to lament. We are here to act. We are here to turn those priorities around—to value love in its many forms and to bring an end to the violence of militarism and the arms race.

As we join together, there is great strength in our diversity. Too many of us have come too far—out of closets, kitchens, ghettos, and out of our isolated fears about the nuclear age—to allow this madness to destroy us now. We cannot go back. We can and must go forward to stop the arms race so that we can address the tasks of meeting human needs and expanding human capabilities for life and love. The possibilities are endless if we stop this nuclear madness in time. Let us go forward and be proud of what we do with the future that is in our hands.

AIDS AND THE GAY / LESBIAN COMMUNITY AS FAMILY

[This is an edited version of a presentation given at the National AIDS Forum held as part of the National Gay Leadership Conference in Dallas, Texas, August 14, 1982.]

Several people have asked "why me?" speaking on this panel, since I am not directly affected by this disease and am not a medical expert. Even I asked this question at first, but then I realized how important it is that we be clear that lesbians are affected by AIDS, and that we not simply treat it as a medical matter. As a community, lesbians and gay men must respond to this crisis together. How we approach issues that affect only some of us most seriously—whether those some are men, women, racial minorities, or another group—reflects the nature and future of our movement.

This crisis challenges us to demonstrate to ourselves and to the world that our community has the capacity to be a caring, intelligent, and effective unit in society. Gay pride rallies have asserted that "we are family." Now we can show the substance behind that slogan. Families are not always about agreeing with each other, but they *are* about uniting in a crisis. Families must respond to matters of sickness, fear, and death as well as to joy, sex, and food. Much of the right wing's "profamily" rhetoric against us has assumed that our sexual activity is antithetical to such family concerns. This is a time to counter that stereotype of us. For while we are not units of Mom, Pop, and two kids, our community is an extended family that can take care of its own in matters of life and death.

Understanding ourselves as family can help in organizing both short- and long-term responses to AIDS. Other speakers have outlined the organizing needed: to give personal assistance to those in immediate need and pressure to get social-service resources for them from government. To educate our community about this problem and to educate the heterosexual world in order to prevent antigay use of this issue. To mobilize support for medical research and demand more government assistance in this effort.

We must also deal with the fears that have been generated within our own community. This requires looking at a whole range of issues brought into focus by this crisis: questions of disease and death; of aging, security, and love; of stress, drugs, and life-style; and of lingering guilt and self-hatred that is exacerbated by hostility from the society toward gays.

These issues are not causes of AIDS nor are they unique to lesbians and gay men. Rather, most of our concerns are the problems of environmental health in industrialized urban society. But since the life-styles of lesbians and gay men in the twentieth century are generally entering into uncharted territory, we face such issues with particular intensity. Our efforts to create new forms of family and community that respond to stress, aging, and death may also be useful to other groups dealing with these concerns in today's world.

In addition, we face the particular problem of homophobia in the society as well as within our own psyches. We tend to react to discussions of health and life-style either moralistically, as issues of right and wrong, or defensively, asserting our right to do what we please.

But neither of these attitudes is very helpful in dealing with AIDS. We need to discuss these questions honestly and nonjudgmentally. We must understand them as matters of survival for our people, just as ethnic groups understand survival of the race as the responsibility of all its members. Or, to use another example, if your family has a history of heart attacks, you pay attention to the factors that contribute to that disease—because it is wise to do so, not in order to be morally correct; and you do not conclude that your family is to blame for having "bad blood" because of it.

In looking at our fears about illness and aging, we face questions of who will care for us and will we be desirable as we age. In considering drugs and alcohol, we need to look at how they affect our health and also to remember that they are often used politically to defuse movements. I am haunted, for example, by reports of the FBI promoting heroin in Harlem in the '50s as part of a plan to divert political energy. In relation to life-style, we need to discuss not only sexuality but also stress and how our community can help us to reduce tension in our lives. These are only some of the discussions we need to have, but we must do so without adding to the guilt and self-hatred felt by so many homosexuals. We must reaffirm that gayness is positive and our examination of our health is part of the process of improving, not judging, our lives. It is a way to value ourselves and express love for each other, not to deny or punish us for being gay.

In facing homophobic reactions to AIDS, we can remember that we are not the only oppressed group that has had health problems used against it. The fact that blacks are the only ones to get sickle-cell anemia has kept it a low medical priority and been used to justify prejudice against blacks as "inferior." Women who get toxic shock from tampons or diseases from faulty birth-control devices face the insinuation that this is the price of control over reproduction or of wanting more sex. But has anyone suggested that the American Legion should stop having conventions because of Legionnaire's disease?

We need all the intelligence, care, and co-operation of the lesbian and gay community to respond to this crisis in its broadest implications. We have the opportunity to set a model for how a community can cope with such a difficult and deadly problem as AIDS, and we can demonstrate to the world what we can be as a community. Perhaps most important, we can expand our capacities as a community in crisis and show ourselves that we are indeed a family that cares for its own.

LESBIAN LIVES:
A BLUEPRINT FOR ACTION

[These excerpts are from my keynote speech at a National Lesbian Agenda Conference in New York City, sponsored by the National Gay and Lesbian Task Force, November 23, 1985.]

The agenda for this conference, calling for a lesbian blueprint for action, is very ambitious. But I am glad to see that ambition because addressing such a task is long overdue in the lesbian movement. One of the problems that lesbians have is that while we are everywhere—in all kinds of groups making many things happen—we have few lesbian political groups nationally or locally. We seem to organize others well and certainly thrive in our own culture, but a lesbian political action agenda is not always clearly stated. And that agenda should serve as a linkage between our woman-selves as part of the feminist movement, our participation in the gay movement, and our actions around other issues of concern.

Over the past few years, a number of us have sought to expand concern about gay rights and homophobia into other arenas besides the gay movement. This has often been difficult. There is a tendency for others to feel that it is okay for us to be open about sexual preference if we work on gay/lesbian issues; but if we work in other areas, we are asked to be in the closet publicly or at least not to keep bringing up "that issue." Unfortunately, we do have to keep bringing up homophobia because if we do not, no one else will. It is still an issue that most nongay people wish would go away. Yet, many of us do not want to work on lesbian/gay issues in isolation from feminism or from other concerns such as racism or militarism. So each of us devises her own balance of how to keep our various interests and needs alive.

What I miss since I left the women's caucus of the National Gay Task Force is a place where lesbians talk together about that balance and share strategies for personal survival and political work. We need more lesbian spaces—whether caucuses in national organizations or locally based groups—that make plans for how each of us can affect issues and how we can support each other's efforts.

In 1971, when I was part of The Furies, a lesbian-feminist collective, I wrote a twenty-five-year plan with a five-year timeline for how we would change the world. I really believed in such planning, but no one would discuss it, so I put it away. I think that it is now time for us to talk in terms of five-year plans. When we state what our goals and strategies are, as is proposed for your working groups in this conference, we gain greater clarity on where to move politically. With such a framework, we can evaluate each opportunity and tactic more productively.

A lesbian agenda or blueprint can serve also as a useful way to show nongay supporters what it means to deal with homophobia concretely. For example, in the women's agenda coalitions that exist in about ten states, we can tell them our specific lesbian demands in relation to such areas as employment and child custody so that inclusion of our perspectives is not just an abstraction to them. The lesbian caucus for the National Women's Conference in Houston in 1977 did this by first deciding on three specific points on lesbian feminism that we wanted to have included in the Plan of Action; this then enabled us to show concretely how we are oppressed and to establish a way that others could support us.

We have to keep pushing on this issue because it is still unpopular, often even with our friends. While we have made progress, the backlash we see today over the AIDS crisis demonstrates that our work on homophobia has just begun. In fighting that backlash, we can gain strength and insights from the growth of the feminist and gay movements globally. For as feminism has developed, not only in the West but also in Third World countries, there is greater possibility for discussion of lesbianism.

We saw this growth at the NGO Forum held as part of the UN World Conference on Women in Nairobi, Kenya, in July 1985. Every day there was a lesbian caucus with several hundred women on the lawn, and many African women came there eager to talk. There was visible leadership from women of color and Third World women in the lesbian workshops, including one press conference on lesbianism. The topic has also gained greater acceptance among women in Latin America, where at the regional feminist conferences held every two years since 1981, significant lesbian sessions have been held. There are several lesbian-feminist groups in the region, and some have started publications. There is also now a newsletter for South Asian lesbians.

We can draw inspiration from lesbian-organizing around the world as an indication that we can have a more diverse movement in the future. We can also draw inspiration from the lesbians in our past whose survival against all odds shows that we are a strong and determined people. We are learning more about that past all the time and we have just begun to see the breadth of possibilities for our future. All of this should help to sustain us for we have a lot of work to do today.

37

ANNE KOEDT

The Myth of the Vaginal Orgasm (1970)

Whenever female orgasm and frigidity is discussed, a false distinction is made between the

From *Notes from the Second Year*, 1970.

vaginal and the clitoral orgasm. Frigidity has generally been defined by men as the failure of women to have vaginal orgasms. Actually the vagina is not a highly sensitive area and is not constructed to achieve orgasm. It is the clitoris which is the center of sexual sensitivity and which is the female equivalent of the penis.

I think this explains a great many things: First of all, the fact that the so-called frigidity rate among women is phenomenally high. Rather than tracing female frigidity to the false assumptions about female anatomy, our "experts" have declared frigidity a psychological problem of women. Those women who complained about it were recommended psychiatrists, so that they might discover their "problem"—diagnosed generally as a failure to adjust to their role as women.

The facts of female anatomy and sexual response tell a different story. There is only one area for sexual climax, although there are many areas for sexual arousal; that area is the clitoris. All orgasms are extensions of sensation from this area. Since the clitoris is not necessarily stimulated sufficiently in the conventional sexual positions, we are left "frigid."

Aside from physical stimulation, which is the common cause of orgasm for most people, there is also stimulation through primarily mental processes. Some women, for example, may achieve orgasm through sexual fantasies, or through fetishes. However, while the stimulation may be psychological, the orgasm manifests itself physically. Thus, while the cause is psychological, the *effect* is still physical, and the orgasm necessarily takes place in the sexual organ equipped for sexual climax—the clitoris. The orgasm experience may also differ in degree of intensity—some more localized, and some more diffuse and sensitive. But they are all clitoral orgasms.

All this leads to some interesting questions about conventional sex and our role in it. Men have orgasms essentially by friction with the vagina, not the clitoral area, which is external and not able to cause friction the way penetration does. Women have thus been defined sexually in terms of what pleases men; our own biology has not been properly analyzed. Instead, we are fed the myth of the liberated woman and her vaginal orgasm—an orgasm which in fact does not exist.

What we must do is redefine our sexuality. We must discard the "normal" concepts of sex and create new guidelines which take into account mutual sexual enjoyment. While the idea of mutual enjoyment is liberally applauded in marriage manuals, it is not followed to its logical conclusion. We must begin to demand that if certain sexual positions now defined as "standard" are not mutually conducive to orgasm, they [can] no longer be defined as standard. New techniques must be used or devised which transform this particular aspect of our current sexual exploitation.

FREUD—A FATHER OF THE VAGINAL ORGASM

Freud contended that the clitoral orgasm was adolescent, and that upon puberty, when women began having intercourse with men, women should transfer the center of orgasm to the vagina. The vagina, it was assumed, was able to produce a parallel, but more mature, orgasm than the clitoris. Much work was done to elaborate on this theory, but little was done to challenge the basic assumptions.

To fully appreciate this incredible invention, perhaps Freud's general attitude about women should first be recalled. Mary Ellman, in *Thinking About Women*, summed it up this way:

"Everything in Freud's patronizing and fearful attitude toward women follows from their lack of a penis, but it is only in his essay *The Psychology of Women* that Freud makes explicit . . . the deprecations of women which are implicit in his work. He then prescribes for them the abandonment of the life of the mind, which will interfere with their sexual function. When the psychoanalyzed patient is male, the analyst sets himself the task of developing the man's capacities; but with women patients, the job is to resign them to the limits of their sex-

uality. As Mr. Rieff puts it: For Freud, 'Analysis cannot encourage in women new energies for success and achievement, but only teach them the lesson of rational resignation.'"

It was Freud's feelings about women's secondary and inferior relationship to men that formed the basis for his theories on female sexuality.

Once having laid down the law about the nature of our sexuality, Freud not so strangely discovered a tremendous problem of frigidity in women. His recommended cure for a woman who was frigid was psychiatric care. She was suffering from failure to mentally adjust to her "natural" role as a woman. Frank S. Caprio, a contemporary follower of these ideas, states:

". . . whenever a woman is incapable of achieving an orgasm via coitus, provided her husband is an adequate partner, and prefers clitoral stimulation to any other form of sexual activity, she can be regarded as suffering from frigidity and requires psychiatric assistance" (*The Sexually Adequate Female*, p. 64).

The explanation given was that women were envious of men—"renunciation of womanhood." Thus it was diagnosed as an anti-male phenomenon.

It is important to emphasize that Freud did not base his theory upon a study of woman's anatomy, but rather upon his assumptions of woman as an inferior appendage to man, and her consequent social and psychological role. In their attempts to deal with the ensuing problem of mass frigidity, Freudians created elaborate mental gymnastics. Marie Bonaparte, in *Female Sexuality*, goes so far as to suggest surgery to help women back on their rightful path. Having discovered a strange connection between the non-frigid woman and the location of the clitoris near the vagina, "it then occurred to me that where, in certain women, this gap was excessive, and clitoridal fixation obdurate, a clitoridal-vaginal reconciliation might be effected by surgical means, which would then benefit the normal erotic function. Professor Halban, of Vienna, as much a biologist as surgeon, became interested in the problem and worked out a simple operative technique. In this, the suspensory ligament of the clitoris was severed and the clitoris secured to the underlying structures, thus fixing it in a lower position, with eventual reduction of the labia minora" (p. 148).

But the severest damage was not in the area of surgery, where Freudians ran around absurdly trying to change female anatomy to fit their basic assumptions. The worst damage was done to the mental health of women, who either suffered silently with self-blame, or flocked to the psychiatrists looking desperately for the hidden and terrible repression that kept them from their vaginal destiny.

LACK OF EVIDENCE?

One may perhaps at first claim that these are unknown and unexplored areas, but upon closer examination this is certainly not true today, nor was it true even in the past. For example, men have known that women suffered from frigidity often during intercourse. So the problem was there. Also, there is much specific evidence. Men knew that the clitoris was and is the essential organ for masturbation, whether in children or adult women. So obviously women made it clear where *they* thought their sexuality was located. Men also seem suspiciously aware of the clitoral powers during "foreplay," when they want to arouse women and produce the necessary lubrication for penetration. Foreplay is a concept created for male purposes, but works to the disadvantage of many women, since as soon as the woman is aroused the man changes to vaginal stimulation, leaving her both aroused and unsatisfied.

It has also been known that women need no anesthesia inside the vagina during surgery, thus pointing to the fact that the vagina is in fact not a highly sensitive area.

Today, with extensive knowledge of anatomy, with Kinsey, and Masters and Johnson, to mention just a few sources, there is no ignorance on the subject. There are, however, social reasons why this knowledge has not been popularized. We are living in a male society which has not sought change in women's role.

ANATOMICAL EVIDENCE

Rather than starting with what women *ought* to feel, it would seem logical to start out with the anatomical facts regarding the clitoris and vagina.

The Clitoris is a small equivalent of the penis, except for the fact that the urethra does not go through it as in the man's penis. Its erection is similar to the male erection, and the head of the clitoris has the same type of structure and function as the head of the penis. G. Lombard Kelly, in *Sexual Feeling in Married Men and Women*, says:

"The head of the clitoris is also composed of erectile tissue, and it possesses a very sensitive epithelium or surface covering, supplied with special nerve endings called genital corpuscles, which are peculiarly adapted for sensory stimulation that under proper mental conditions terminates in the sexual orgasm. No other part of the female generative tract has such corpuscles" (Pocketbooks, p. 35).

The clitoris has no other function than that of sexual pleasure.

The Vagina—Its functions are related to the reproductive function. Principally, 1) menstruation, 2) receive penis, 3) hold semen, and 4) birth passage. The interior of the vagina, which according to the defenders of the vaginally caused orgasm is the center and producer of the orgasm is:

"like nearly all other internal body structures, poorly supplied with end organs of touch. The internal entodermal origin of the lining of the vagina makes it similar in this respect to the rectum and other parts of the digestive tract" (Kinsey, *Sexual Behavior in the Human Female*, p. 580).

The degree of insensitivity inside the vagina is so high that "Among the women who were tested in our gynecologic sample, less than 14% were at all conscious that they had been touched" (Kinsey, p. 580).

Even the importance of the vagina as an *erotic* center (as opposed to an orgasmic center) has been found to be minor.

Other Areas—Labia minora and the vestibule of the vagina. These two sensitive areas may trigger off a clitoral orgasm. Because they can be effectively stimulated during "normal" coitus, though infrequent, this kind of stimulation is incorrectly thought to be vaginal orgasm. However, it is important to distinguish between areas which can stimulate the clitoris, incapable of producing the orgasm themselves, and the clitoris:

"Regardless of what means of excitation is used to bring the individual to the state of sexual climax, the sensation is perceived by the genital corpuscles and is localized where they are situated: in the head of the clitoris or penis" (Kelly, p. 49).

Psychologically Stimulated Orgasm—Aside from the above mentioned direct and indirect stimulations of the clitoris, there is a third way an orgasm may be triggered. This is through mental (cortical) stimulation, where the imagination stimulates the brain, which in turn stimulates the genital corpuscles of the glans to set off an orgasm.

WOMEN WHO SAY THEY HAVE VAGINAL ORGASMS

Confusion—Because of the lack of knowledge of their own anatomy, some women accept the idea that an orgasm felt during "normal" intercourse was vaginally caused. This confusion is caused by a combination of factors. One, failing to locate the center of the orgasm, and two, by a desire to fit her experience to the male-defined idea of sexual normalcy. Considering that women know little about their anatomy, it is easy to be confused.

Deception—The vast majority of women who pretend vaginal orgasms to their men are faking it to, as Ti-Grace Atkinson says, "get the job." In a new best-selling Danish book, *I Accuse* (my own translation), Mette Ejlersen specifically deals with this common problem, which she calls the "sex comedy." This comedy has many causes. First of all, the man brings a great deal of pressure to bear on the woman, because he considers his ability as a lover at stake. So as not to offend his ego, the woman will comply with the prescribed role and go through simulated ecstasy. In some of the other Danish women mentioned, women who were left frigid were turned off to sex, and pretended vaginal orgasm to hurry up the sex act. Others admitted that they had faked vaginal orgasm to catch a man. In one case, the woman pretended vaginal orgasm to get him to leave his first wife, who admitted being vaginally frigid. Later she was forced to continue the deception, since obviously she couldn't tell him to stimulate her clitorally.

Many more women were simply afraid to establish their right to equal enjoyment, seeing the sexual act as being primarily for the man's benefit, and any pleasure that the woman got as an added extra.

Other women, with just enough ego to reject the man's idea that they needed psychiatric care, refused to admit their frigidity. They wouldn't accept self-blame, but they didn't know how to solve the problem, not knowing the physiological facts about themselves. So they were left in a peculiar limbo.

Again, perhaps one of the most infuriating and damaging results of this whole charade has been that women who were perfectly healthy sexually were taught that they were not. So in addition to being sexually deprived, these women were told to blame themselves when they deserved no blame. Looking for a cure to a problem that has none can lead a woman on an endless path of self-hatred and insecurity. For she is told by her analyst that not even in her one role allowed in a male society—the role of a woman—is she successful. She is put on the defensive, with phony data as evidence that she better try to be even more feminine, think more feminine, and reject her envy of men. That is, shuffle even harder, baby.

WHY MEN MAINTAIN THE MYTH

1. *Sexual Penetration is Preferred*—The best stimulant for the penis is the woman's vagina. It supplies the necessary friction and lubrication. From a strictly technical point of view this position offers the best physical conditions, even though the man may try other positions for variation.

2. *The Invisible Woman*—One of the elements of male chauvinism is the refusal or inability to see women as total, separate human beings. Rather, men have chosen to define women only in terms of how they benefitted men's lives. Sexually, a woman was not seen as an individual wanting to share equally in the sexual act, any more than she was seen as a person with independent desires when she did anything else in society. Thus, it was easy to make up what was convenient about women; for on top of that, society has been a function of male interests, and women were not organized to form even a vocal opposition to the male experts.

3. *The Penis as Epitome of Masculinity*—Men define their lives greatly in terms of masculinity. It is a *universal*, as opposed to racial, ego boosting, which is localized by the geography of racial mixtures.

The essence of male chauvinism is not the practical, economic services women supply. It is the psychological superiority. This kind of negative definition of self, rather than positive definition based upon one's own achievements and development, has of course chained the victim and the oppressor both. But by far the most brutalized of the two is the victim.

An analogy is racism, where the white racist compensates his feelings of unworthiness by creating an image of the black man (it is primarily a male struggle) as biologically inferior to him. Because of his power in a white power structure, the white man can socially enforce this mythical division.

To the extent that men try to rationalize and justify male superiority through physical differentiation, masculinity may be symbolized by being the *most* muscular, the most hairy, the deepest voice, and the biggest penis. Women, on the other hand, are approved of (i.e., called feminine) if they are weak, petite, shave their legs, have high soft voices, and no penis.

Since the clitoris is almost identical to the penis, one finds a great deal of evidence of men in various societies trying to either ignore the clitoris and emphasize the vagina (as did Freud), or, as in some places in the Mideast, actually performing clitoridectomy. Freud saw this ancient and still practiced custom as a way of further "feminizing" the female by removing this cardinal vestige of her masculinity. It should be noted also that a big clitoris is considered ugly and masculine. Some cultures engage in the practice of pouring a chemical on the clitoris to make it shrivel up into proper size.

It seems clear to me that men in fact fear the clitoris as a threat to their masculinity.

4. *Sexually Expendable Male*—Men fear that they will become sexually expendable if the clitoris is substituted for the vagina as the center of pleasure for women. Actually this has a great deal of validity if one considers *only* the anatomy. The position of the penis inside the vagina, while perfect for reproduction, does not necessarily stimulate an orgasm in women because the clitoris is located externally and higher up. Women must rely upon indirect stimulation in the "normal" position.

Lesbian sexuality could make an excellent case, based upon anatomical data, for the extinction of the male organ. Albert Ellis says something to the effect that a man without a penis can make a woman an excellent lover.

Considering that the vagina is very desirable from a man's point of view, purely on physical grounds, one begins to see the dilemma for men. And it forces us as well to discard many "physical" arguments explaining why women go to bed with men. What is left, it seems to me, are primarily psychological reasons why women select men at the exclusion of women as sexual partners.

5. *Control of Women*—One reason given to explain the Mideastern practice of clitoridectomy is that it will keep the woman from straying. By removing the sexual organ capable of orgasm, it must be assumed that her sexual drive will diminish. Considering how men look upon their women as property, particularly in very backward nations, we should begin to consider a great deal more why it is not in the men's interest to have women totally free sexually. The double standard, as practiced for example in Latin America, is set up to keep the woman as total property of the husband, while he is free to have affairs as he wishes.

6. *Lesbianism and Bisexuality*—Aside from the strictly anatomical reasons why women might equally seek other women as lovers, there is a fear on men's part that women will seek the company of other women on a full, human basis. The establishment of clitoral orgasm as fact would threaten the heterosexual *institution*. For it would indicate that sexual pleasure was obtainable from either men *or* women, thus making heterosexuality not an absolute, but an option. It would thus open up the whole question of *human* sexual relationships beyond the confines of the present male-female role system.

BOOKS MENTIONED IN THIS ESSAY

Sexual Behavior in the Human Female, Alfred C. Kinsey, Pocketbooks

Female Sexuality, Marie Bonaparte, Grove Press

Sex Without Guilt, Albert Ellis, Grove Press

Sexual Feelings in Married Men and Women, G. Lombard Kelly, Pocketbooks

I Accuse (*Jeg Anklager*), Mette Ejlersen, Chr. Erichsens Forlag (Danish)

The Sexually Adequate Female, Frank S. Caprio, Fawcett Gold Medal Books

Thinking About Women, Mary Ellman, Harcourt, Brace & World

Human Sexual Response, Masters and Johnson; Little, Brown

Also see:

The ABZ of Love, Inge and Sten Hegeler, Alexicon Corp.

38

AUDRE LORDE

Uses of the Erotic: The Erotic as Power (1978)

There are many kinds of power, used and unused, acknowledged or otherwise. The erotic is a resource within each of us that lies in a deeply female and spiritual plane, firmly rooted in the power of our unexpressed or unrecognized feeling. In order to perpetuate itself, every oppression must corrupt or distort those various sources of power within the culture of the oppressed that can provide energy for change. For women, this has meant a suppression of the erotic as a considered source of power and information within our lives.

We have been taught to suspect this resource, vilified, abused, and devalued within western society. On the one hand, the superficially erotic has been encouraged as a sign of female inferiority; on the other hand, women have been made to suffer and to feel both contemptible and suspect by virtue of its existence.

It is a short step from there to the false belief that only by the suppression of the erotic within our lives and consciousness can women be truly strong. But that strength is illusory, for it is fashioned within the context of male models of power.

As women, we have come to distrust that power which rises from our deepest and nonrational knowledge. We have been warned against it all our lives by the male world, which values this depth of feeling enough to keep women around in order to exercise it in the service of men, but which fears this same depth too much to examine the possibilities of it within themselves. So women are maintained at a distant/inferior position to be psychically

From Audre Lorde, *Sister Outsider* (Trumansburg, N.Y.: Crossing Press, 1984). Originally delivered as a paper at the Fourth Berkshire Conference on the History of Women, Mount Holyoke College, August 25, 1978. Reprinted by permission of The Crossing Press.

milked, much the same way ants maintain colonies of aphids to provide a life-giving substance for their masters.

But the erotic offers a well of replenishing and provocative force to the woman who does not fear its revelation, nor succumb to the belief that sensation is enough.

The erotic has often been misnamed by men and used against women. It has been made into the confused, the trivial, the psychotic, the plasticized sensation. For this reason, we have often turned away from the exploration and consideration of the erotic as a source of power and information, confusing it with its opposite, the pornographic. But pornography is a direct denial of the power of the erotic, for it represents the suppression of true feeling. Pornography emphasizes sensation without feeling.

The erotic is a measure between the beginnings of our sense of self and the chaos of our strongest feelings. It is an internal sense of satisfaction to which, once we have experienced it, we know we can aspire. For having experienced the fullness of this depth of feeling and recognizing its power, in honor and self-respect we can require no less of ourselves.

It is never easy to demand the most from ourselves, from our lives, from our work. To encourage excellence is to go beyond the encouraged mediocrity of our society is to encourage excellence. But giving in to the fear of feeling and working to capacity is a luxury only the unintentional can afford, and the unintentional are those who did not wish to guide their own destinies.

This internal requirement toward excellence which we learn from the erotic must not be misconstrued as demanding the impossible from ourselves nor from others. Such a demand incapacitates everyone in the process. For the erotic is not a question only of what we do; it is a question of how acutely and fully we can feel in the doing. Once we know the extent to which we are capable of feeling that sense of satisfaction and completion, we can then observe which of our various life endeavors bring us closest to that fullness.

The aim of each thing which we do is to make our lives and the lives of our children richer and more possible. Within the celebration of the erotic in all our endeavors, my work becomes a conscious decision—a longed-for bed which I enter gratefully and from which I rise up empowered.

Of course, women so empowered are dangerous. So we are taught to separate the erotic demand from most vital areas of our lives other than sex. And the lack of concern for the erotic root and satisfactions of our work is felt in our disaffection from so much of what we do. For instance, how often do we truly love our work even at its most difficult?

The principal horror of any system which defines the good in terms of profit rather than in terms of human need, or which defines human need to the exclusion of the psychic and emotional components of that need—the principal horror of such a system is that it robs our work of its erotic value, its erotic power and life appeal and fulfillment. Such a system reduces work to a travesty of necessities, a duty by which we earn bread or oblivion for ourselves and those we love. But this is tantamount to blinding a painter and then telling her to improve her work, and to enjoy the act of painting. It is not only next to impossible, it is also profoundly cruel.

As women, we need to examine the ways in which our world can be truly different. I am speaking here of the necessity for reassessing the quality of all the aspects of our lives and of our work, and of how we move toward and through them.

The very word *erotic* comes from the Greek word *eros,* the personification of love in all its aspects—born of Chaos, and personifying creative power and harmony. When I speak of the erotic, then, I speak of it as an assertion of the lifeforce of women; of that creative energy empowered, the knowledge and use of which we are now reclaiming in our language, our history, our dancing, our loving, our work, our lives.

There are frequent attempts to equate pornography and eroticism, two diametrically opposed uses of the sexual. Because of these attempts, it has become fashionable to separate the spiritual (psychic and emotional) from the political, to see them as contradictory or antithetical. "What do you mean, a poetic revolutionary, a meditating gunrunner?" In the same way, we have attempted to separate the spiritual and the erotic, thereby reducing the spiritual to a world of flattened affect, a world of the ascetic who aspires to feel nothing. But nothing is farther from the truth. For the ascetic position is one of the highest fear, the gravest immobility. The severe abstinence of the ascetic becomes the ruling obsession. And it is one not of self-discipline but of self-abnegation.

The dichotomy between the spiritual and the political is also false, resulting from an incomplete attention to our erotic knowledge. For the bridge which connects them is formed by the erotic—the sensual—those physical, emotional, and psychic expressions of what is deepest and strongest and richest within each of us, being shared: the passions of love, in its deepest meanings.

Beyond the superficial, the considered phrase, "It feels right to me," acknowledges the strength of the erotic into a true knowledge, for what that means is the first and most powerful guiding light toward any understanding. And understanding is a handmaiden which can only wait upon, or clarify, that knowledge, deeply born. The erotic is the nurturer or nursemaid of all our deepest knowledge.

The erotic functions for me in several ways, and the first is in providing the power which comes from sharing deeply any pursuit with another person. The sharing of joy, whether physical, emotional, psychic, or intellectual, forms a bridge between the sharers which can be the basis for understanding much of what is not shared between them, and lessens the threat of their difference.

Another important way in which the erotic connection functions is the open and fearless underlining of my capacity for joy. In the way my body stretches to music and opens into response, hearkening to its deepest rhythms, so every level upon which I sense also opens to the erotically satisfying experience, whether it is dancing, building a bookcase, writing a poem, examining an idea.

That self-connection shared is a measure of the joy which I know myself to be capable of feeling, a reminder of my capacity for feeling. And that deep and irreplaceable knowledge of my capacity for joy comes to demand from all of my life that it be lived within the knowledge that such satisfaction is possible, and does not have to be called *marriage,* nor *god,* nor *an afterlife.*

This is one reason why the erotic is so feared, and so often relegated to the bedroom alone, when it is recognized at all. For once we begin to feel deeply all the aspects of our lives, we begin to demand from ourselves and from our life-pursuits that they feel in accordance with that joy which we know ourselves to be capable of. Our erotic knowledge empowers us, becomes a lens through which we scrutinize all aspects of our existence, forcing us to evaluate those aspects honestly in terms of their relative meaning within our lives. And this is a grave responsibility, projected from within each of us, not to settle for the convenient, the shoddy, the conventionally expected, nor the merely safe.

During World War II, we bought sealed plastic packets of white, uncolored margarine, with a tiny, intense pellet of yellow coloring perched like a topaz just inside the clear skin of the bag. We would leave the margarine out for a while to soften, and then we would pinch the little pellet to break it inside the bag, releasing the rich yellowness into the soft pale mass of margarine. Then taking it carefully between our fingers, we would knead it gently back and forth, over and over, until the color had spread throughout the whole pound bag of margarine, thoroughly coloring it.

I find the erotic such a kernel within myself. When released from its intense and constrained pellet, it flows through and colors my life with a kind of energy that heightens and sensitizes and strengthens all my experience.

We have been raised to fear the *yes* within ourselves, our deepest cravings. But, once recognized, those which do not enhance our future lose their power and can be altered. The fear of our desires keeps them suspect and indiscriminately powerful, for to suppress any truth is to give it strength beyond endurance. The fear that we cannot grow beyond whatever distortions we may find within ourselves keeps us docile and loyal and obedient, externally defined, and leads us to accept many facets of our oppression as women.

When we live outside ourselves, and by that I mean on external directives only rather than from our internal knowledge and needs, when we live away from those erotic guides from within ourselves, then our lives are limited by external and alien forms, and we conform to the needs of a structure that is not based on human need, let alone an individual's. But when we begin to live from within outward, in touch with the power of the erotic within ourselves, and allowing that power to inform and illuminate our actions upon the world around us, then we begin to be responsible to ourselves in the deepest sense. For as we begin to recognize our deepest feelings, we begin to give up, of necessity, being satisfied with suffering and self-negation, and with the numbness which so often seems like their only alternative in our society. Our acts against oppression become integral with self, motivated and empowered from within.

In touch with the erotic, I become less willing to accept powerlessness, or those other supplied states of being which are not native to me, such as resignation, despair, self-effacement, depression, self-denial.

And yes, there is a hierarchy. There is a difference between painting a back fence and writing a poem, but only one of quantity. And there is, for me, no difference between writing a good poem and moving into sunlight against the body of a woman I love.

This brings me to the last consideration of the erotic. To share the power of each other's feelings is different from using another's feelings as we would use a kleenex. When we look the other way from our experience, erotic or otherwise, we use rather than share the feelings of those others who participate in the experience with us. And use without consent of the used is abuse.

In order to be utilized, our erotic feelings must be recognized. The need for sharing deep feeling is a human need. But within the european-american tradition, this need is satisfied by certain proscribed erotic comings-together. These occasions are almost always characterized by a simultaneous looking away, a pretense of calling them something else, whether a religion, a fit, mob violence, or even playing doctor. And this misnaming of the need and the deed gives rise to that distortion which results in pornography and obscenity—the abuse of feeling.

When we look away from the importance of the erotic in the development and sustenance of our power, or when we look away from ourselves as we satisfy our erotic needs in concert with others, we use each other as objects of satisfaction rather than share our joy in the satisfying, rather than make connection with our similarities and our differences. To refuse to be conscious of what we are feeling at any time, however comfortable that might seem, is to deny a large part of the experience, and to allow ourselves to be reduced to the pornographic, the abused, and the absurd.

The erotic cannot be felt secondhand. As a Black lesbian feminist, I have a particular feeling, knowledge, and understanding for those sisters with whom I have danced hard, played, or even fought. This deep participation has often been the forerunner for joint concerted actions not possible before.

But this erotic charge is not easily shared by women who continue to operate under an exclusively european-american male tradition. I know it was not available to me when I was trying to adapt my consciousness to this mode of living and sensation.

Only now, I find more and more women-identified women brave enough to risk sharing the erotic's electrical charge without having to look away, and without distorting the enormously powerful and creative nature of that exchange. Recognizing the power of the erotic within our lives can give us the energy to pursue genuine change within our world, rather than merely settling for a shift of characters in the same weary drama.

For not only do we touch our most profoundly creative source, but we do that which is female and self-affirming in the face of a racist, patriarchal, and anti-erotic society.

39

Susan Griffin

Rape: The All-American Crime (1971)

I have never been free of the fear of rape. From a very early age, I, like most women, have thought of rape as part of my natural environment—something to be feared and prayed against like fire or lightning. I never asked why men raped; I simply thought it one of the many mysteries of human nature.

I was, however, curious enough about the violent side of humanity to read every crime magazine I was able to ferret away from my grandfather. Each issue featured at least one "sex crime," with pictures of a victim, usually in a pearl necklace, and of the ditch or the orchard where her body was found. I was never certain why the victims were always women, nor what the motives of the murderer were, but I did guess that the world was not a safe place for women. I observed that my grandfather was meticulous about locks and quick to draw the shades before anyone removed so much as a shoe. I sensed that danger lurked outside.

At the age of eight, my suspicions were confirmed. My grandmother took me to the back of the house where the men wouldn't hear, and told me that strange men wanted to do harm to little girls. I learned not to walk on

From *Ramparts*, September 1971.

dark streets, not to talk to strangers, or get into strange cars, to lock doors, and to be modest. She never explained why a man would want to harm a little girl, and I never asked.

If I thought for a while that my grandmother's fears were imaginary, the illusion was brief. That year, on the way home from school, a schoolmate a few years older than I tried to rape me. Later, in an obscure aisle of the local library (while I was reading *Freddy the Pig*) I turned to discover a man exposing himself. Then, the friendly man around the corner was arrested for child molesting.

My initiation to sexuality was typical. Every woman has similar stories to tell—the first man who attacked her may have been a neighbor, a family friend, an uncle, her doctor, or perhaps her own father. And women who grow up in New York City always have tales about the subway.

But though rape and the fear of rape are a daily part of every woman's consciousness, the subject is so rarely discussed by that unofficial staff of male intellectuals (who write the books which study seemingly every other form of male activity) that one begins to suspect a conspiracy of silence. And indeed, the obscurity of rape in print exists in marked contrast to the frequency of rape in reality, for *forcible rape is the most frequently committed violent crime in America today*. The Federal Bureau of Investigation classes three crimes as violent: murder, aggravated assault and forcible rape. In 1968, 31,060 rapes were *reported*. According to the FBI and independent criminologists, however, to approach accuracy this figure must be multiplied by at least a factor of ten to compensate for the fact that most rapes are not reported; when these compensatory mathematics are used, there are more rapes committed than aggravated assaults and homicides.

When I asked Berkeley, California's Police Inspector in charge of rape investigation if he knew why men rape women, he replied that he had not spoken with "these people and delved into what really makes them tick, because that really isn't my job. . . ." However, when I asked him how a woman might prevent being raped, he was not so reticent, "I wouldn't advise any female to go walking around alone at night . . . and she should lock her car at all times." The Inspector illustrated his warning with a grisly story about a man who lay in wait for women in the back seats of their cars, while they were shopping in a local supermarket. This man eventually murdered one of his rape victims. "Always lock your car," the Inspector repeated, and then added, without a hint of irony, "Of course, you don't have to be paranoid about this type of thing."

The Inspector wondered why I wanted to write about rape. Like most men he did not understand the urgency of the topic, for, after all, men are not raped. But like most women I had spent considerable time speculating on the true nature of the rapist. When I was very young, my image of the "sexual offender" was a nightmarish amalgamation of the bogey man and Captain Hook: he wore a black cape, and he cackled. As I matured, so did my image of the rapist. Rape, I came to believe, was only one of many unfortunate evils produced by sexual repression. Reasoning by tautology, I concluded that any man who would rape a woman must be out of his mind.

Yet, though the theory that rapists are insane is a popular one, this belief has no basis in fact. According to Professor Menachem Amir's study of 646 rape cases in Philadelphia, *Patterns in Forcible Rape*, men who rape are not abnormal. Amir writes, "Studies indicate that sex offenders do not constitute a unique or psychopathological type; nor are they as a group invariably more disturbed than the control groups to which they are compared." Alan Taylor, a parole officer who has worked with rapists in the prison facilities at San Luis Obispo, California, stated the question in plainer language, "Those men were the most normal men there. They had a lot of hang-ups, but they were the same hang-ups as men walking out on the street."

Another canon in the apologetics of rape is that, if it were not for learned social controls,

all men would rape. Rape is held to be natural behavior, and not to rape must be learned. But in truth rape is not universal to the human species. Moreover, studies of rape in our culture reveal that, far from being impulsive behavior, most rape is planned. Professor Amir's study reveals that in cases of group rape (the "gangbanger" of masculine slang) 90 percent of the rapes were planned; in pair rapes, 83 percent of the rapes were planned; and in single rapes, 58 percent were planned. These figures should significantly discredit the image of the rapist as a man who is suddenly overcome by sexual needs society does not allow him to fulfill.

Far from the social control of rape being learned, comparisons with other cultures lead one to suspect that, in our society, it is rape itself that is learned. (The fact that rape is against the law should not be considered proof that rape is not in fact encouraged as part of our culture.)

This culture's concept of rape as an illegal, but still understandable form of behavior is not a universal one. In her study *Sex and Temperament*, Margaret Mead describes a society that does not share our views. The Arapesh do not ". . . have any conception of the male nature that might make rape understandable to them." Indeed our interpretation of rape is a product of our conception of the nature of male sexuality. A common retort to the question, why don't women rape men, is the myth that men have greater sexual needs, that their sexuality is more urgent than women's. And it is the nature of human beings to want to live up to what is expected of them.

And this same culture which expects aggression from the male expects passivity from the female. Conveniently, the companion myth about the nature of female sexuality is that all women secretly want to be raped. Lurking beneath her modest female exterior is a subconscious desire to be ravished. The following description of a stag movie, written by Brenda Starr in Los Angeles' underground paper, *Everywoman*, typifies this male fantasy. The movie "showed a woman in her underclothes reading on her bed. She is interrupted by a rapist with a knife. He immediately wins her over with his charm and they get busy sucking and fucking." An advertisement in the *Berkeley Barb* reads, "Now as all women know from their daydreams, rape has a lot of advantages. Best of all it's so simple. No preparation necessary, no planning ahead of time, no wondering if you should or shouldn't; just whang! bang!" Thanks to Masters and Johnson even the scientific canon recognizes that for the female, "whang! bang!" can scarcely be described as pleasurable.

Still, the male psyche persists in believing that, protestations and struggles to the contrary, deep inside her mysterious feminine soul, the female victim has wished for her own fate. A young woman who was raped by the husband of a friend said that days after the incident the man returned to her home, pounded on the door and screamed to her, "Jane, Jane. You loved it. You know you loved it."

The theory that women like being raped extends itself by deduction into the proposition that most or much of rape is provoked by the victim. But this too is only myth. Though provocation, considered a mitigating factor in a court of law, may consist of only a "gesture," according to the Federal Commission on Crimes of Violence, only 4 percent of reported rapes involved any precipitative behavior by the woman.

The notion that rape is enjoyed by the victim is also convenient for the man who, though he would not commit forcible rape, enjoys the idea of its existence, as if rape confirms that enormous sexual potency which he secretly knows to be his own. It is for the pleasure of the armchair rapist that detailed accounts of violent rapes exist in the media. Indeed, many men appear to take sexual pleasure from nearly all forms of violence. Whatever the motivation, male sexuality and violence in our culture seem to be inseparable. James Bond alternately whips out his revolver and his cock, and though there is no known connection between the skills of gun-fighting and love-

making, pacifism seems suspiciously effeminate.

In a recent fictional treatment of the Manson case, Frank Conroy writes of his vicarious titillation when describing the murders to his wife:

"Every single person there was killed." She didn't move.

"It sounds like there was torture," I said. As the words left my mouth I knew there was no need to say them to frighten her into believing that she needed me for protection.

The pleasure he feels as his wife's protector is inextricably mixed with pleasure in the violence itself. Conroy writes, "I was excited by the killings, as one is excited by catastrophe on a grand scale, as one is alert to pre-echoes of unknown changes, hints of unrevealed secrets, rumblings of chaos. . . ."

The attraction of the male in our culture to violence and death is a tradition Manson and his admirers are carrying on with tireless avidity (even presuming Manson's innocence, he dreams of the purification of fire and destruction). It was Malraux in his *Anti-Memoirs* who said that, for the male, facing death was *the* illuminating experience analogous to childbirth for the female. Certainly our culture does glorify war and shroud the agonies of the gunfighter in veils of mystery.

And in the spectrum of male behavior, rape, the perfect combination of sex and violence, is the penultimate act. Erotic pleasure cannot be separated from culture, and in our culture male eroticism is wedded to power. Not only should a man be taller and stronger than a female in the perfect love-match, but he must also demonstrate his superior strength in gestures of dominance which are perceived as amorous. Though the law attempts to make a clear division between rape and sexual intercourse, in fact the courts find it difficult to distinguish between a case where the decision to copulate was mutual and one where a man forced himself upon his partner.

The scenario is even further complicated by the expectation that, not only does a woman mean "yes" when she says "no," but that a really decent woman ought to begin by saying "no," and then be led down the primrose path to acquiescence. Ovid, the author of Western Civilization's most celebrated sex-manual, makes this expectation perfectly clear: ". . . and when I beg you to say 'yes,' say 'no.' Then let me lie outside your bolted door. . . . So Love grows strong. . . ."

That the basic elements of rape are involved in all heterosexual relationships may explain why men often identify with the offender in this crime. But to regard the rapist as the victim, a man driven by his inherent sexual needs to take what will not be given him, reveals a basic ignorance of sexual politics. For in our culture heterosexual love finds an erotic expression through male dominance and female submission. A man who derives pleasure from raping a woman clearly must enjoy force and dominance as much or more than the simple pleasures of the flesh. Coitus cannot be experienced in isolation. The weather, the state of the nation, the level of sugar in the blood—all will affect a man's ability to achieve orgasm. If a man can achieve sexual pleasure after terrorizing and humiliating the object of his passion, and in fact while inflicting pain upon her, one must assume he derives pleasure directly from terrorizing, humiliating and harming a woman. According to Amir's study of forcible rape, on a statistical average the man who has been convicted of rape was found to have a normal sexual personality, tending to be different from the normal, well-adjusted male only in having a greater tendency to express violence and rage.

And if the professional rapist is to be separated from the average dominant heterosexual, it may be mainly a quantitative difference. For the existence of rape as an index to masculinity is not entirely metaphorical. Though this measure of masculinity seems to be more publicly exhibited among "bad boys" or aging bikers who practice sexual initiation through group rape, in fact, "good boys" engage in the same rites to prove their manhood. In Stockton, a small town in California which epitomizes silent-majority Amer-

ica, a bachelor party was given last summer for a young man about to be married. A woman was hired to dance "topless" for the amusement of guests. At the high point of the evening the bridegroom-to-be dragged the woman into a bedroom. No move was made by any of his companions to stop what was clearly going to be an attempted rape. Far from it. As the woman described, "I tried to keep him away—told him of my Herpes Genitalis, et cetera, but he couldn't face the guys if he didn't screw me." After the bridegroom had finished raping the woman and returned with her to the party, far from chastizing him, his friends heckled the woman and covered her with wine.

It was fortunate for the dancer that the bridegroom's friends did not follow him into the bedroom for, though one might suppose that in group rape, since the victim is outnumbered, less force would be inflicted on her, in fact, Amir's studies indicate, "the most excessive degrees of violence occurred in group rape." Far from discouraging violence, the presence of other men may in fact encourage sadism, and even cause the behavior. In an unpublished study of group rape by Gilbert Geis and Duncan Chappell, the authors refer to a study by W. H. Blanchard which relates, "The leader of the male group . . . apparently precipitated and maintained the activity, despite misgivings, because of a need to fulfill the role that the other two men had assigned to him. 'I was scared when it began to happen,' he says. 'I wanted to leave but I didn't want to say it to the other guys—you know—that I was scared.'"

Thus it becomes clear that not only does our culture teach men the rudiments of rape, but society, or more specifically other men, encourage the practice of it.

II

Every man I meet wants to protect me.
Can't figure out what from.
                                        —Mae West

If a male society rewards aggressive, domineering sexual behavior, it contains within itself a sexual schizophrenia. For the masculine man is also expected to prove his mettle as a protector of women. To the naive eye, this dichotomy implies that men fall into one of two categories: those who rape and those who protect. In fact, life does not prove so simple. In a study euphemistically entitled "Sex Aggression by College Men," it was discovered that men who believe in a double standard of morality for men and women, who in fact believe most fervently in the ultimate value of virginity, are more liable to commit "this aggressive variety of sexual exploitation."

(At this point in our narrative it should come as no surprise that Sir Thomas Malory, creator of that classic tale of chivalry, *The Knights of the Round Table*, was himself arrested and found guilty for repeated incidents of rape.)

In the system of chivalry, men protect women against men. This is not unlike the protection relationship which the mafia established with small businesses in the early part of this century. Indeed, chivalry is an age-old protection racket which depends for its existence on rape.

According to the male mythology which defines and perpetuates rape, it is an animal instinct inherent in the male. The story goes that sometime in our pre-historical past, the male, more hirsute and burly than today's counterparts, roamed about an uncivilized landscape until he found a desirable female. (Oddly enough, this female is *not* pictured as more muscular than the modern woman.) Her mate does not bother with courtship. He simply grabs her by the hair and drags her to the closest cave. Presumably, one of the major advantages of modern civilization for the female has been the civilizing of the male. We call it chivalry.

But women do not get chivalry for free. According to the logic of sexual politics, we too have to civilize our behavior. (Enter chastity. Enter virginity. Enter monogamy.) For the female, civilized behavior means chastity before marriage and faithfulness within it. Chivalrous behavior in the male is supposed to protect that chastity from involuntary defilement. The fly in the ointment of this otherwise peaceful system is the fallen woman. She does not behave. And therefore she does not deserve protection. Or, to use another argument, a major tenet of the same value system: what has once been defiled cannot again be violated. One begins to suspect that it is the behavior of the fallen woman, and not that of the male, that civilization aims to control.

The assumption that a woman who does not respect the double standard deserves whatever she gets (or at the very least "asks for it") operates in the courts today. While in some states a man's previous rape convictions are not considered admissible evidence, the sexual reputation of the rape victim is considered a crucial element of the facts upon which the court must decide innocence or guilt.

The court's respect for the double standard manifested itself particularly clearly in the case of the *People v. Jerry Plotkin*. Mr. Plotkin, a 36-year-old jeweler, was tried for rape last spring in a San Francisco Superior Court. According to the woman who brought the charges, Plotkin, along with three other men, forced her at gunpoint to enter a car one night in October 1970. She was taken to Mr. Plotkin's fashionable apartment where he and three other men first raped her and then, in the delicate language of the *S.F. Chronicle*, "subjected her to perverted sex acts." She was, she said, set free in the morning with the warning that she would be killed if she spoke to anyone about the event. She did report the incident to the police who then searched Plotkin's apartment and discovered a long list of names of women. Her name was on the list and had been crossed out.

In addition to the woman's account of her abduction and rape, the prosecution submitted four of Plotkin's address books containing the names of hundreds of women. Plotkin claimed he did not know all of the women since some of the names had been given to him by friends and he had not yet called on them. Several women, however, did testify in court that Plotkin had, to cite the *Chronicle*, "lured them up to his apartment under one pretext or another, and forced his sexual attentions on them."

Plotkin's defense rested on two premises. First, through his own testimony Plotkin established a reputation for himself as a sexual libertine who frequently picked up girls in bars and took them to his house where sexual relations often took place. He was the Playboy. He claimed that the accusation of rape, therefore, was false—this incident had simply been one of many casual sexual relationships, the victim one of many playmates. The second premise of the defense was that his accuser was also a sexual libertine. However, the picture created of the young woman (fully 13 years younger than Plotkin) was not akin to the lighthearted, gay-bachelor image projected by the defendant. On the contrary, the day after the defense cross-examined the woman, the *Chronicle* printed a story headlined, "Grueling Day For Rape Case Victim." (A leaflet passed out by women in front of the courtroom was more succinct, "rape was committed by four men in a private apartment in October; on Thursday, it was done by a judge and a lawyer in a public court-room.")

Through skillful questioning fraught with innuendo, Plotkin's defense attorney James Martin MacInnis portrayed the young woman as a licentious opportunist and unfit mother. MacInnis began by asking the young woman (then employed as a secretary) whether or not it was true that she was "familiar with liquor" and had worked as a "cocktail waitress." The young woman replied (the *Chronicle* wrote "admitted") that she had worked once or twice as a cocktail waitress. The attorney then asked if she had worked as a secretary in the financial district but had "left that employment after it was discovered that you had sexual intercourse on a couch in the office." The woman replied, "That is a lie. I left because I didn't like working in a one-girl office. It was too lonely." Then the defense asked if, while working as an attendant at a health club, "you were accused of having a sexual affair with a man?" Again the

woman denied the story. "I was never accused of that."

Plotkin's attorney then sought to establish that his client's accuser was living with a married man. She responded that the man was separated from his wife. Finally he told the court that she had "spent the night" with another man who lived in the same building.

At this point in the testimony the woman asked Plotkin's defense attorney, "Am I on trial? . . . It is embarrassing and personal to admit these things to all these people . . . I did not commit a crime. I am a human being." The lawyer, true to the chivalry of his class, apologized and immediately resumed questioning her, turning his attention to her children. (She is divorced, and the children at the time of the trial were in a foster home.) "Isn't it true that your two children have a sex game in which one gets on top of another and they—" "That is a lie!" the young woman interrupted him. She ended her testimony by explaining, "They are wonderful children. They are not perverted."

The jury, divided in favor of acquittal ten to two, asked the court stenographer to read the woman's testimony back to them. After this reading, the Superior Court acquitted the defendant of both the charges of rape and kidnapping.

According to the double standard a woman who has had sexual intercourse out of wedlock cannot be raped. Rape is not only a crime of aggression against the body; it is a transgression against chastity as defined by men. When a woman is forced into a sexual relationship, she has, according to the male ethos, been violated. But she is also defiled, if she does not behave according to the double standard, by maintaining her chastity, or confining her sexual activities to a monogamous relationship.

One should not assume, however, that a woman can avoid the possibility of rape simply by behaving. Though myth would have it that mainly "bad girls" are raped, this theory has no basis in fact. Available statistics would lead one to believe that a safer course is promiscuity. In a study of rape done in the District of Columbia, it was found that 82 percent of the rape victims had a "good reputation." Even the Police Inspector's advice to stay off the streets is rather useless, for almost half of reported rapes occur in the home of the victim and are committed by a man she has never before seen. Like indiscriminate terrorism, rape can happen to any woman, and few women are ever without this knowledge.

But the courts and the police, both dominated by white males, continue to suspect the rape victim, *sui generis*, of provoking or asking for her own assault. According to Amir's study, the police tend to believe that a woman without a good reputation cannot be raped. The rape victim is usually submitted to countless questions about her own sexual mores and behavior by the police investigator. This preoccupation is partially justified by the legal requirements for prosecution in a rape case. The rape victim must have been penetrated, and she must have made it clear to her assailant that she did not want penetration (unless of course she is unconscious). A refusal to accompany a man to some isolated place to allow him to touch her does not in the eyes of the court, constitute rape. She must have said "no" at the crucial genital moment. And the rape victim, to qualify as such, must also have put up a physical struggle—unless she can prove that to do so would have been to endanger her life.

But the zealous interest the police frequently exhibit in the physical details of a rape case is only partially explained by the requirements of the court. A woman who was raped in Berkeley was asked to tell the story of her rape four different times "right out in the street," while her assailant was escaping. She was then required to submit to a pelvic examination to prove that penetration had taken place. Later, she was taken to the police station where she was asked the same questions again: "Were you forced?" "Did he penetrate?" "Are you sure your life was in danger and you had no other choice?" This woman had been pulled off the street by a man who held a 10-inch knife at her throat and forcibly raped her. She was raped at midnight and was not able to return to her home until five in the morning. Police contacted her twice again in the next week, once by telephone at two in the morning and once at four in the morning. In her words, "The rape was probably the least traumatic incident of the whole evening. If I'm ever raped again, . . . I wouldn't report it to the police because of all the degradation. . . ."

If white women are subjected to unnecessary and often hostile questioning after having been raped, third world women are often not believed at all. According to the white male ethos (which is not only sexist but racist), third world women are defined from birth as "impure." Thus the white male is provided with a pool of women who are fair game for sexual imperialism. Third world women frequently do not report rape and for good reason. When blues singer Billie Holliday was 10 years old, she was taken off to a local house by a neighbor and raped. Her mother brought the police to rescue her, and she was taken to the local police station crying and bleeding:

"When we got there, instead of treating me and Mom like somebody who called the cops for help, they treated me like I'd killed somebody. . . . I guess they had me figured for having enticed this old goat into the whorehouse. . . . All I know for sure is they threw me into a cell . . . a fat white matron . . . saw I was still bleeding, she felt sorry for me and gave me a couple of glasses of milk. But nobody did anything for me except give me filthy looks and snicker to themselves."

"After a couple of days in a cell they dragged me into a court. Mr. Dick got sentenced to five years. They sentenced me to a Catholic institution."

Clearly the white man's chivalry is aimed only to protect the chastity of "his" women.

As a final irony, that same system of sexual values from which chivalry is derived has also provided womankind with an unwritten code of behavior, called femininity, which makes a feminine woman the perfect victim of sexual aggression. If being chaste does not ward off the possibility of assault, being feminine certainly increases the chances that it will succeed. To be submissive is to defer to masculine strength; is to lack muscular development or any interest in defending oneself; is to let doors be opened, to have one's arm held when crossing the street. To be feminine is to wear shoes which make it difficult to run; skirts which inhibit one's stride; underclothes which inhibit the circulation. Is it not an intriguing observation that those very clothes which are thought to be flattering to the female and attractive to the male are those which make it impossible for a woman to defend herself against aggression?

Each girl as she grows into womanhood is taught fear. Fear is the form in which the female internalizes both chivalry and the double standard. Since, biologically speaking, women in fact have the same if not greater potential for sexual expression as do men, the woman is taught that she must behave differently from a man and must also learn to distrust her own carnality. She must deny her own feelings and learn not to act from them. She fears herself. This is the essence of passivity, and of course, a woman's passivity is not simply sexual but functions to cripple her from self-expression in every area of her life.

Passivity itself prevents a woman from ever considering her own potential for self-defense and forces her to look to men for protection. The woman is taught fear, but this time fear of the other; and yet her only relief from this fear is to seek out the other. Moreover, the passive woman is taught to regard herself as impotent, unable to act, unable even to perceive, in no way self-sufficient, and, finally, as the object and not the subject of human behavior. It is in this sense that a woman is deprived of the status of a human being. She is not free to be.

III

Since Ibsen's Nora slammed the door on her patriarchical husband, woman's attempt to be free has been more or less fashionable. In this 19th century portrait of a woman leaving her marriage, Nora tells her husband, "Our home has been nothing but a playroom. I have been

your doll-wife just as at home I was papa's doll-child." And, at least on the stage, "The Doll's House" crumbled, leaving audiences with hope for the fate of the modern woman. And today, as in the past, womankind has not lacked examples of liberated women to emulate: Emma Goldman, Greta Garbo and Isadora Duncan all denounced marriage and the double standard, and believed their right to freedom included sexual independence; but still their example has not affected the lives of millions of women who continue to marry, divorce and remarry, living out their lives dependent on the status and economic power of men. Patriarchy still holds the average woman prisoner not because she lacks the courage of an Isadora Duncan, but because the material conditions of her life prevent her from being anything but an object.

In the *Elementary Structures of Kinship*, Claude Levi-Strauss gives to marriage this universal description, "It is always a system of exchange that we find at the origin of the rules of marriage." In this system of exchange, a woman is the "most precious possession." Levi-Strauss continues that the custom of including women as booty in the marketplace is still so general that a "whole volume would not be sufficient to enumerate instances of it." Levi-Strauss makes it clear that he does not exclude Western Civilization from his definition of "universal" and cites examples from modern wedding ceremonies. (The marriage ceremony is still one in which the husband and wife become one, and "that one is the husband.")

The legal proscription against rape reflects this possessory view of women. An article in the 1952–53 *Yale Law Journal* describes the legal rationale behind laws against rape: "In our society sexual taboos, often enacted into law, buttress a system of monogamy based upon the law of 'free bargaining' of the potential spouses. Within this process the woman's power to withhold or grant sexual access is an important bargaining weapon." Presumably then, laws against rape are intended to protect the right of a woman not for physical self-determination, but for physical "bargaining." The article goes on to explain explicitly why the preservation of the bodies of women is important to men:

"The consent standard in our society does more than protect a significant item of social currency for women; it fosters, and is in turn bolstered by a masculine pride in the exclusive possession of a sexual object. The consent of a woman to sexual intercourse awards the man a privilege of bodily access, a personal "prize" whose value is enhanced by sole ownership. An additional reason for the man's condemnation of rape may be found in the threat to his status from a decrease in the "value" of his sexual possession which would result from forcible violation."

The passage concludes by making clear whose interest the law is designed to protect. "The man responds to this undercutting of his status as *possessor* of the girl with hostility toward the rapist; no other restitution device is available. The law of rape provides an orderly outlet for his vengeance." Presumably the female victim in any case will have been sufficiently socialized so as not to consciously feel any strong need for vengeance. If she does feel this need, society does not speak to it.

The laws against rape exist to protect the rights of the male as possessor of the female body, and not the right of the female over her own body. Even without this enlightening passage from the *Yale Law Review*, the laws themselves are clear: In no state can a man be accused of raping his wife. How can any man steal what already belongs to him? It is in the sense of rape as theft of another man's property that Kate Millett writes, "Traditionally rape has been viewed as an offense one male commits against another—a matter of abusing his woman." In raping another man's woman, a man may aggrandize his own manhood and concurrently reduce that of another man. Thus a man's honor is not subject directly to rape, but only indirectly, through "his" woman.

If the basic social unit is the family, in which the woman is a possession of her husband, the super-structure of society is a male hierarchy, in which men dominate other men (or patriarchal families dominate other patriarchal families). And it is in no small irony that, while the very social fabric of our male-dominated culture denies women equal access to political, economic and legal power, the literature, myth and humor of our culture depict women not only as the power behind the throne, but the real source of the oppression of men. The religious version of this fairy tale blames Eve for both carnality and eating of the tree of knowledge, at the same time making her gullible to the obvious devices of a serpent. Adam, of course, is merely the trusting victim of love. Certainly this is a biased story. But no more biased than the one television audiences receive today from the latest slick comedians. Through a media which is owned by men, censored by a State dominated by men, all the evils of this social system which make a man's life unpleasant are blamed upon "the wife." The theory is: were it not for the female who waits and plots to "trap" the male into marriage, modern man would be able to achieve Olympian freedom. She is made the scapegoat for a system which is in fact run by men.

Nowhere is this more clear than in the white racist use of the concept of white womanhood. The white male's open rape of black women, coupled with his overweening concern for the chastity and protection of his wife and daughters, represents an extreme of sexist and racist hypocrisy. While on the one hand she was held up as the standard for purity and virtue, on the other the Southern white woman was never asked if she wanted to be on a pedestal, and in fact any deviance from the male-defined standards for white womanhood was treated severely. (It is a powerful commentary on American racism that the historical role of blacks as slaves, and thus possessions without power, has robbed black women of legal and economic protection through marriage. Thus black women in Southern society and in the ghettoes of the North have long been easy game for white rapists.) The fear that black men would rape white women was, and is, classic paranoia. Quoting from Ann Breen's unpublished study of racism and sexism in the

South, *The New South: White Man's Country*, "Frederick Douglass legitimately points out that, had the black man wished to rape white women, he had ample opportunity to do so during the civil war when white women, the wives, sisters, daughters and mothers of the rebels, were left in the care of Blacks. But yet not a single act of rape was committed during this time. The Ku Klux Klan, who tarred and feathered black men and lynched them in honor of the purity of white womanhood, also applied tar and feathers to a Southern white woman accused of bigamy, which leads one to suspect that Southern white men were not so much outraged at the violation of the woman as a person, in the few instances where rape was actually committed by black men, but at the violation of his property rights." In the situation where a black man was found to be having sexual relations with a white woman, the white woman could exercise skin-privilege, and claim she had been raped, in which case the black man was lynched. But if she did not claim rape, she herself was subject to lynching.

In constructing the myth of white womanhood so as to justify the lynching and oppression of black men and women, the white male has created a convenient symbol of his own power which has resulted in black hostility toward the white "bitch," accompanied by an unreasonable fear on the part of many white women of the black rapist. Moreover, it is not surprising that after being told for two centuries that he wants to rape white women, occasionally a black man does actually commit that act. But it is crucial to note that the frequency of this practice is outrageously exaggerated in the white mythos. Ninety percent of reported rape is intra- not inter-racial.

In *Soul on Ice*, Eldridge Cleaver has described the mixing of a rage against white power with the internalized sexism of a black man raping a white woman. "Somehow I arrived at the conclusion that, as a matter of principle, it was of paramount importance for me to have an antagonistic, ruthless attitude toward white women. . . . Rape was an insurrec-

tionary act. It delighted me that I was defying and trampling upon the white man's law, upon his system of values and that I was defiling his women—and this point, I believe, was the most satisfying to me because I was very resentful over the historical fact of how the white man has used the black woman." Thus a black man uses white women to take out his rage against white men. But in fact, whenever a rape of a white woman by a black man does take place, it is again the white man who benefits. First, the act itself terrorizes the white woman and makes her more dependent on the white male for protection. Then, if the woman prosecutes her attacker, the white man is afforded legal opportunity to exercise overt racism. Of course, the knowledge of the rape helps to perpetuate two myths which are beneficial to white male rule—the bestiality of the black man and the desirability of white women. Finally, the white man surely benefits because he himself is not the object of attack—he has been allowed to stay in power.

Indeed, the existence of rape in any form is beneficial to the ruling class of white males. For rape is a kind of terrorism which severely limits the freedom of women and makes women dependent on men. Moreover, in the act of rape, the rage that one man may harbor toward another higher in the male hierarchy can be deflected toward a female scapegoat. For every man there is always someone lower on the social scale on whom he can take out his aggressions. And that is any woman alive.

This oppressive attitude towards women finds its institutionalization in the traditional family. For it is assumed that a man "wears the pants" in his family—he exercises the option of rule whenever he so chooses. Not that he makes all the decisions—clearly women make most of the important day-to-day decisions in a family. But when a conflict of interest arises, it is the man's interest which will prevail. His word, in itself, is more powerful. He lords it over his wife in the same way his boss lords it over him, so that the very process of exercising his power becomes as important an act as obtaining whatever it is his power can get for him. This notion of power is key to the male ego in this culture, for the two acceptable measures of masculinity are a man's power over women and his power over other men. A man may boast to his friends that "I have 20 men working for me." It is also aggrandizement of his ego if he has the financial power to clothe his wife in furs and jewels. And, if a man lacks the wherewithal to acquire such power, he can always express his rage through equally masculine activities—rape and theft. Since male society defines the female as a possession, it is not surprising that the felony most often committed together with rape is theft. As the following classic tale of rape points out, the elements of theft, violence and forced sexual relations merge into an indistinguishable whole.

The woman who told this story was acquainted with the man who tried to rape her. When the man learned that she was going to be staying alone for the weekend, he began early in the day a polite campaign to get her to go out with him. When she continued to refuse his request, his chivalrous mask dropped away:

"I had locked all the doors because I was afraid, and I don't know how he got in; it was probably through the screen door. When I woke up, he was shaking my leg. His eyes were red, and I knew he had been drinking or smoking. I thought I would try to talk my way out of it. He started by saying that he wanted to sleep with me, and then he got angrier and angrier, until he started to say, 'I want pussy,' 'I want pussy.' Then, I got scared and tried to push him away. That's when he started to force himself on me. It was awful. It was the most humiliating, terrible feeling. He was forcing my legs apart and ripping my clothes off. And it was painful. I did fight him—he was slightly drunk and I was able to keep him away. I had taken judo a few years back, but I was afraid to throw a chop for fear that he'd kill me. I could see he was getting more and more violent. I was thinking wildly of some way to get out of this alive, and then I said to him, 'Do you want money. I'll give you money.' We had money but I was also thinking that if I got to the back room I could telephone the police—as if the police would have even helped. It was a stupid thing to think of because obviously he would follow me. And he did. When he saw me pick up the phone, he tried to tie the cord around my neck. I screamed at him that I did have the money in another room, that I was going to call the police because I was scared, but that I would never tell anybody what happened. It would be an absolute secret. He said, okay, and I went to get the money. But when he got it, all of a sudden he got this crazy look in his eye and he said to me, 'Now I'm going to kill you.' Then I started saying my prayers. I knew there was nothing I could do. He started to hit me—I still wasn't sure if he wanted to rape me at this point—or just kill me. He was hurting me, but hadn't yet gotten me into a strangle-hold because he was still drunk and off balance. Somehow we pushed into the kitchen where I kept looking at this big knife. But I didn't pick it up. Somehow, no matter how much I hated him at that moment, I still couldn't imagine putting the knife into his flesh, and then I was afraid he would grab it and stick it into me. Then he was hitting me again and somehow we pushed through the back door of the kitchen and onto the porch steps. We fell down the steps and that's when he started to strangle me. He was on top of me. He just went on and on until finally I lost consciousness. I did scream, though my screams sounded like whispers to me. But what happened was that a cab driver happened by and frightened him away. The cab driver revived me—I was out only a minute at the most. And then I ran across the street and I grabbed the woman who was our neighbor and screamed at her, 'Am I alive? Am I still alive?'"

Rape is an act of aggression in which the victim is denied her self-determination. It is an act of violence which, if not actually followed by beatings or murder, nevertheless always carries with it the threat of death. And finally, rape is a form of mass terrorism, for the victims of rape are chosen indiscriminately, but the propagandists for male supremacy broadcast that it is women who cause rape by being unchaste or in the wrong place at the wrong time—in essence, by behaving as though they were free.

The threat of rape is used to deny women employment. (In California, the Berkeley Public Library, until pushed by the Federal Employment Practices Commission, refused to hire female shelvers because of perverted men in the stacks.) The fear of rape keeps women off the streets at night. Keeps women at home. Keeps women passive and modest for fear that they be thought provocative.

It is part of human dignity to be able to defend oneself, and women are learning. Some women have learned karate; some to shoot guns. And yet we will not be free until the threat of rape and the atmosphere of violence is ended, and to end that the nature of male behavior must change.

But rape is not an isolated act that can be rooted out from patriarchy without ending patriarchy itself. The same men and power structure who victimize women are engaged in the act of raping Vietnam, raping Black people and the very earth we live upon. Rape is a classic act of domination where, in the words of Kate Millet, "the emotions of hatred, contempt, and the desire to break or violate personality," takes place. This breaking of the personality characterizes modern life itself. No simple reforms can eliminate rape. As the symbolic expression of the white male hierarchy, rape is the quintessential act of our civilization, one which, Valerie Solanis warns, is in danger of "humping itself to death."

40

BARBARA MEHRHOF AND
PAMELA KEARON

Rape: An Act of Terror (1971)

To see rape within the system of female oppression is to understand its non-accidental and non-arbitrary nature and to gain insight into its

From *Notes from the Third Year*, 1971.

special purpose for the class of men. There is no group other than slaves that has been singled out for such systematic and total exploitation and suppression as the class of women. The condition of women exceeds the bounds of the definition of oppression and in the modern Western world her situation is unique.

We are given to understand that in Western society the rule of law operates in contradistinction to the rule of men. This implies that society is build upon *principles* derived from Nature or God which are generally assented to by the governed. By its nature law deals with generalities; the governed are viewed as equal and indistinguishable. Women and slaves, however, have traditionally existed outside this rule of law since law is the means by which the public affairs of freemen are stabilized. The public realm is where male interest groups vie with each other to create history and the world of things. Its essence is visibility and therefore it constitutes accepted Reality. Women and slaves are relegated to the private sphere which is the vague, hidden, unseen world of superior/inferior relationships. The definitive activity of the private sphere is labor—that is, the maintenance of biological life for oneself and others. This is the function of women and slaves.

The imposition of the duty to labor exemplified in marriage cancels out whatever "paper rights" (i.e., legal or public) women might possess because it maintains her private status—servant to the male. It is in this that women are distinguished as a group and subjected to a rule of governance by which they are treated differently from other citizens. This rule of governance is the direct rule of men. This fact, that woman qua woman exists outside the protection of the law, is crucial in understanding rape and how it can be used by men as a terror tactic.

The justification of this rule of women by men is the *Ideology of Sexism*, which from a single assumption seeks to explain the meaning of human life. It posits the human male as the highest expression of Nature, his destiny as Nature's development. Thus, anything which

interferes with this destiny or his needs or desires, must be controlled or suppressed—all of
the natural world including the human female.
Male dominance over the female is therefore a
natural condition. If man is the highest expression of Nature, it follows that man is the Good.
Woman, having a will and her own self-interest,
is a potential obstruction to male destiny and is
therefore *a priori* Bad, Evil, the Criminal—and
consequently the justifiable Victim.

The Ideology of Sexism is totally inured to
experience or history. Its basis is not male
achievement but rather maleness itself. So the
ideology is not subject to criticism or adjustment despite the obvious existence of droves of
grotesque or pathetic male individuals. Like
Nazism and racism which also posit superiority
a priori, sexism is grounded in a physical manifestation of the assumed superiority. For
Nazism it is blond hair and blue eyes, for racism
skin color, for sexism the penis. But skin, eye,
and hair color are physical traits which are—
simply exist. They cannot engage in activity.
There is, then, no unique *act* which affirms the
polarity Aryan/Semite or white/black. Sexual
intercourse, however, since it involves the gen-
itals (that particular difference between sexes
selected by the Ideology of Sexism to define
superiority/inferiority), provides sexism with
an inimitable act which perfectly expresses the
polarity male/female. The Reality created by
the Ideology makes the sexual act a renewal of
the feeling of power and prestige for the male,
of impotence and submission for the female.
Rape adds the quality of terror.

Terror is an integral part of the oppression
of women. Its purpose is to ensure, as a final
measure, the acceptance by women of the inevitability of male domination. The content of
terror includes the threat of death, destitution,
and/or inhuman isolation for the female. The
most important aspect of terrorism is its indis-
criminateness with respect to members of the
terrorized class. There are no actions or forms
of behavior sufficient to avoid its danger. There
is no sign that designates a rapist since each
male is potentially one. While simple fear is

utilitarian, providing the impetus to act for
one's safety, the effect of terror is to make all
action impossible.

The earlier and more thoroughly the
woman is terrorized, the more completely she
is incapable of acting against the existing Reality modeled on the Sexist Ideology and brought
into being by the power of the male class. As
long as one is free to act one can invalidate and
transform reality. When free action is eliminated one can only incorporate reality as created by others, or go mad or die. The woman
assaulted by a rapist is not merely hampered by
real or imagined lack of kinetic energy relative
to the attacker; she is also restricted by her
fragile sense of her own reality and worth.
Rape is a punishment without crime or guilt—
at least subjective guilt. It is punishment rather
for the *objective* crime of femaleness. That is
why it is indiscriminate. It is primarily a lesson
for the whole class of women—a strange lesson, in that it does not teach a form of behavior
which will save women from it. *Rape teaches instead the objective, innate, and unchanging subordination of women relative to men.*

Rape supports the male class by projecting
its power and aggressiveness on the world. For
the individual male, the possibility of rape remains a prerogative of his in-group; its perpe-
tration rekindles his faith in maleness and his
own personal worth.

Rape is only a slightly forbidden fruit. It is
assumed to be condemned by law in our society, yet an examination of law reveals that its
forbidden quality is more of a delectable fantasy than reality. In New York State, for instance, the law stipulates that the woman must
prove she was raped by force, that "penetration" occurred, and that someone witnessed the
rapist in the area of the attack. Although the
past convictions of the defendant are not admissible evidence in a rape trial, the "reputation" of the rape victim is. The police will refuse to accept charges in many cases, especially
if the victim is alone when she comes in to file
them. In New York City only certain hospitals
will accept rape cases and they are not bound to

release their findings to the courts. Finally, the courts consistently refuse to indict men for rape.

It is clear that women do not come under the law on anything like an equal footing with men—or rather, that women as women do not enjoy the protection of law at all. Women as victims of rape, unlike the general victim of assault, are not assumed to be independent, indistinguishable, and equal citizens. They are viewed by the law as subordinate, dependent, and an always potential hindrance to male action and male prerogative. Rape laws are designed to protect males against the charge of rape. The word of a peer has a special force; the word of a dependent is always suspicious, presumed to be motivated by envy, revenge, or rebellion.

Rape, then, is an effective political device. It is not an arbitrary act of violence by one individual on another; it is a political act of *oppression* (never rebellion) exercised by members of a powerful class on members of the powerless class. Rape is supported by a consensus in the male class. It is preached by male-controlled and all pervasive media with only a minimum of disguise and restraint. It is communicated to the male population as an act of freedom and strength and a male right never to be denied.

Women, through terror unable to act, do not test the Reality dictated by Sexist Ideology. When an individual woman manages to experience rape as an act which oppresses and degrades her and limits her freedom, when she sees it as political and useful to all males, she cannot count upon support from other women. Many women believe that rape is an act of sick men or is provoked by the female. Thus women as a class do not yet have a consensus on a counter-reality which defines the true meaning of rape for us. Women do not yet have the means of communication to build such a consensus. We have no media providing instant and constant communication; we are physically, economically, and socially isolated by the institution of marriage which requires lonely labor in service to the male and primary loyalty to him.

The first step toward breaking the debilitating hold on us of the Sexist Ideology is the creation of a counter-reality, a mutually guaranteed support of female experience undistorted by male interpretation. We must build a consensus among us. Power for a group is consensus and organization. Terror depends upon the scattered, confused character of the terrorized class. We *must* understand rape as essentially an act of terror against women—whether committed by white men or minority group males. This is the only means of freeing our imagination so that we can act together—or alone if it comes to it—against this most perfect of political crimes.

41

ANGELA Y. DAVIS

Rape, Racism and the Myth of the Black Rapist (1981)

Some of the most flagrant symptoms of social deterioration are acknowledged as serious problems only when they have assumed such epidemic proportions that they appear to defy solution. Rape is a case in point. In the United States today, it is one of the fastest-growing violent crimes.[1] After ages of silence, suffering and misplaced guilt, sexual assault is explosively emerging as one of the telling dysfunctions of present-day capitalist society. The rising public concern about rape in the United States has inspired countless numbers of women to divulge their past encounters with actual or would-be assailants. As a result, an awesome fact has come to light: appallingly few

From Angela Y. Davis, *Women, Race and Class* (New York: Random House, 1981). Reprinted by permission of Random House, Inc.

1. Nancy Gager and Cathleen Schurr, *Sexual Assault: Confronting Rape in America* (New York: Grosset & Dunlap, 1976), p. 1.

women can claim that they have not been victims, at one time in their lives, of either attempted or accomplished sexual attacks.

In the United States and other capitalist countries, rape laws as a rule were framed originally for the protection of men of the upper classes, whose daughters and wives might be assaulted. What happens to working-class women has usually been of little concern to the courts; as a result, remarkably few white men have been prosecuted for the sexual violence they have inflicted on these women. While the rapists have seldom been brought to justice, the rape charge has been indiscriminately aimed at Black men, the guilty and innocent alike. Thus, of the 455 men executed between 1930 and 1967 on the basis of rape convictions, 405 of them were Black.[2]

In the history of the United States, the fraudulent rape charge stands out as one of the most formidable artifices invented by racism. The myth of the Black rapist has been methodically conjured up whenever recurrent waves of violence and terror against the Black community have required convincing justifications. If Black women have been conspicuously absent from the ranks of the contemporary anti-rape movement, it may be due, in part, to that movement's indifferent posture toward the frame-up rape charge as an incitement to racist aggression. Too many innocents have been offered sacrificially to gas chambers and lifer's cells for Black women to join those who often seek relief from policemen and judges. Moreover, as rape victims themselves, they have found little if any sympathy from these men in uniforms and robes. And stories about police assaults on Black women—rape victims sometimes suffering a second rape—are heard too frequently to be dismissed as aberrations. "Even at the strongest time of the civil rights movement in Birmingham," for example, "young activists often stated that nothing could protect Black women from being raped by Birmingham

police. As recently as December, 1974, in Chicago, a 17-year-old Black woman reported that she was gang-raped by 10 policemen. Some of the men were suspended, but ultimately the whole thing was swept under the rug."[3]

During the early stages of the contemporary anti-rape movement, few feminist theorists seriously analyzed the special circumstances surrounding the Black woman as rape victim. The historical knot binding Black women—systematically abused and violated by white men—to Black men—maimed and murdered because of the racist manipulation of the rape charge—has just begun to be acknowledged to any significant extent. Whenever Black women have challenged rape, they usually and simultaneously expose the use of the frame-up rape charge as a deadly racist weapon against their men. As one extremely perceptive writer put it:

"The myth of the black rapist of white women is the twin of the myth of the bad black woman—both designed to apologize for and facilitate the continued exploitation of black men and women. Black women perceived this connection very clearly and were early in the forefront of the fight against lynching."[4]

Gerda Lerner, the author of this passage, is one of the few white women writing on the subject of rape during the early 1970s who examined in depth the combined effect of racism and sexism on Black women. The case of Joan Little,[5] tried during the summer of 1975, illustrates Lerner's point. Brought to trial on murder charges, the young Black woman was accused of killing a white guard in a North Carolina jail where she was the only woman inmate. When Joann Little took the stand, she told how the guard had raped her in her cell

2. Michael Meltsner, *Cruel and Unusual: The Supreme Court and Capital Punishment* (New York: Random House, 1973), p. 75.

3. "The Racist Use of Rape and the Rape Charge." *A Statement to Women's Movement from a Group of Socialist Women* (Louisville, Ky.: Socialist Women's Caucus, 1974), pp. 5–6.

4. Gerda Lerner, *Black Women in White America*, (New York: Pantheon, 1972), p. 193.

5. See Angela Davis, "Joan Little—The Dialectics of Rape." *Ms. Magazine*, Vol. III, No. 12 (June, 1975).

and how she had killed him in self-defense with the ice pick he had used to threaten her. Throughout the country, her cause was passionately supported by individuals and organizations in the Black community and within the young women's movement, and her acquittal was hailed as an important victory made possible by this mass campaign. In the immediate aftermath of her acquittal, Ms. Little issued several moving appeals on behalf of a Black man named Delbert Tibbs, who awaited execution in Florida because he had been falsely convicted of raping a white woman.

Many Black women answered Joan Little's appeal to support the cause of Delbert Tibbs. But few white women—and certainly few organized groups within the anti-rape movement—followed her suggestion that they agitate for the freedom of this Black man who had been blatantly victimized by Southern racism. Not even when Little's Chief Counsel Jerry Paul announced his decision to represent Delbert Tibbs did many white women dare to stand up in his defense. By 1978, however, when all charges against Tibbs were dismissed, white anti-rape activists had increasingly begun to align themselves with his cause. Their initial reluctance, however, was one of those historical episodes confirming many Black women's suspicions that the anti-rape movement was largely oblivious to their special concerns.

That Black women have not joined the anti-rape movement en masse does not, therefore, mean that they oppose anti-rape measures in general. Before the end of the nineteenth century pioneering Black clubwomen conducted one of the very first organized public protests against sexual abuse. Their eighty-year-old tradition of organized struggle against rape reflects the extensive and exaggerated ways Black women have suffered the threat of sexual violence. One of racism's salient historical features has always been the assumption that white men—especially those who wield economic power—possess an incontestable right of access to Black women's bodies.

Slavery relied as much on routine sexual abuse as it relied on the whip and lash. Exces-

sive sex urges, whether they existed among individual white men or not, had nothing to do with this virtual institutionalization of rape. Sexual coercion was, rather, an essential dimension of the social relations between slavemaster and slave. In other words, the right claimed by slaveowners and their agents over the bodies of female slaves was a direct expression of their presumed property rights over Black people as a whole. The license to rape emanated from and facilitated the ruthless economic domination that was the gruesome hallmark of slavery.[6]

The pattern of institutionalized sexual abuse of Black women became so powerful that it managed to survive the abolition of slavery. Group rape, perpetrated by the Ku Klux Klan and other terrorist organizations of the post–Civil War period, became an uncamouflaged political weapon in the drive to thwart the movement for Black equality. During the Memphis Riot of 1866, for example, the violence of the mob murders was brutally complemented by the concerted sexual attacks on Black women. In the riot's aftermath, numerous Black women testified before a Congressional committee about the savage mob rapes they had suffered.[7] This testimony regarding similar events during the Meridian, Mississippi, Riot of 1871 was given by a Black woman named Ellen Parton:

"I reside in Meridian; have resided here nine years; occupation, washing and ironing and scouring; Wednesday night was the last night they came to my house; by "they" I mean bodies or companies of men; they came on Monday, Tuesday and Wednesday; on Monday night they said they came to do us no harm; on Tuesday night they said they came for the arms; I told them there was none, and they said they would take my word for it; on Wednesday night they came and broke open the wardrobe and trunks, and committed rape upon me; there

---

6. See Chapter 1.

7. Aptheker, *A Documentary History,* Vol. 2, pp. 552ff.

were eight of them in the house; I do not know how many there were outside. . . ."[8]

Of course, the sexual abuse of Black women has not always manifested itself in such open and public violence. There has been a daily drama of racism enacted in the countless anonymous encounters between Black women and their white abusers—men convinced that their acts were only natural. Such assaults have been ideologically sanctioned by politicians, scholars and journalists, and by literary artists who have often portrayed Black women as promiscuous and immoral. Even the outstanding writer Gertrude Stein described one of her Black women characters as possessing ". . . the simple, promiscuous unmorality of the black people."[9] The imposition of this attitude on white men of the working class was a tri-umphant moment in the development of racist ideology.

Racism has always drawn strength from its ability to encourage sexual coercion. While Black women and their sisters of color have been the main targets of these racist-inspired attacks, white women have suffered as well. For once white men were persuaded that they could commit sexual assaults against Black women with impunity, their conduct toward women of their own race could not have remained unmarred. Racism has always served as a provocation to rape, and white women in the United States have necessarily suffered the ricochet fire of these attacks. This is one of the many ways in which racism nourishes sexism, causing white women to be indirectly victimized by the social oppression aimed at their sisters of color. . . .

8. Lerner, *Black Women in White America*, pp. 185–186.

9. Gertrude Stein, *Three Lives* (New York: Vintage Books, 1970. First edition: 1909), p. 86.

IV. The Personal Is Political: Some Second-Wave Issues

"THE PERSONAL IS POLITICAL"—THAT STOCK PHRASE of 1960s and 1970s women's liberation—sums up the way many women understood the hopes, aspirations, and purpose of second-wave feminism— even though it does not encompass the totality of this complex social movement. Because extremely divergent groups and agendas were involved, important exceptions need to be made for almost any historical generalization about second-wave feminism. For one thing, the National Organization for Women (NOW), representative of liberal feminism, concerned itself most with the civic-corporate goal of gaining equality under the law, certainly not a solely personal matter. In fact, Betty Friedan, NOW president from 1966 to 1969, believed that the sexual politics of radical feminism was distracting and harmful to the women's movement. Even NOW, though, pushed for progress in areas seen as personal, including in its program a call for lesbian rights in 1971 and a homemakers' bill of rights in 1979. Overall, second-wave feminism during the 1970s was most distinctive for its work at the local, personal, and practical level, even as this same time period can be seen as the most prolific stage in U.S. feminist theorizing and intellectual production.

"Our feelings will lead us to our theory, our theory to our action, our feelings about that action to new theory and then to new action": so Kathie Sarachild summarizes her ideas for "A Program for Feminist 'Consciousness Raising'" (1968), a founding document of what would become one of the most emblematic and practical features of second-wave feminism. Rather than working from an explanatory framework—a pre-existent ideal of women's liberation—consciousness raising started with "bitch session" cell groups in which individual women took turns speaking emotionally, trying to locate the deep-rooted sources of their discontent and oppression. "Active listening" and a broader group discussion ensued in which once-isolated personal feelings and experiences evolved into collective problems and causes for action; then came the identification of the historical forces responsible for women's subordination, and finally, specific strategies to oppose those forces. This bottom-up approach to consciousness raising not only proved to be personally liberating but also created a new unity among women around their subjection to sexism and the shared meanings of feminism. It changed their worldview. Indeed, many women described consciousness raising as a conversion experience of near-religious dimension.

A final stage of consciousness raising, as Sarachild outlines it, was to move out of the living room cell groups and go public with feminist concerns. One of the first second-wave "zap actions"—the dramatization of women's issues through the media—happened in September of 1968 in Atlantic City at the Miss America Contest, where a "freedom trash can" was set up on the boardwalk, and into which high heels, bras, girdles, fashion magazines, stenographers' pads, and other such tools of oppression were discarded (although *not* lit on fire—the myth of bra-burning began here). The demonstrators crowned a live sheep Miss America; posters read "Up Against the Wall Miss America," "Miss America Is a Big Falsie," and "Miss America Sells It"; and protestors inside interrupted the pageant itself by unfurling a feminist banner from the balcony and yelling during the announcement of the winner and the farewell speech of the outgoing Miss America. In "A Critique of the Miss America Protest" (1968), Carol Hanisch, one of the zap action organizers, takes stock of the demonstration in light of her understanding of the two goals of women's liberation: awakening feminist consciousness and building sisterhood. She believes that the second cause was damaged through the "antiwomanism" of some of their tactics. "Miss America and all beautiful women," Hanisch writes, "came off as our enemy instead of our sisters who suffer with us." On the positive side, though, the mass media's coverage of the protest helped awaken many women—it "told the nation that a new feminist movement is afoot in the land."

When speaking together about their personal experiences, women began to uncover and identify the patterns of discrimination, exploitation, social control, lies, violence, and other forms of
oppression that set the parameters of their lives. Men, individually and as a group, were easily
identified as the oppressors. For some feminists, the resultant "man hating" was not only deeply
felt, but was seen as a logical political stance in the drive to right the wrongs of sexist society. This
distinct aspect of second-wave feminism was hardly seen (at a collective level, at least) before the
late 1960s. With the radical feminist and lesbian feminist impetus toward separatism and aggressive attempts to subvert male power came the consideration—introduced by Valerie Solanas in
"SCUM Manifesto" (1967)—of whether or not men should be treated with any respect at all, and
in Solanas's sociopathic treatise, whether or not they should even be allowed to continue to exist
(SCUM stands for "Society to Cut Up Men"). The concept and practice of man hating worked at
different levels; for Solanas (who shot the pop artist Andy Warhol in 1968) and Pamela Kearon, author of "Man-Hating" (1970), the concept had literal meaning and promised a real material "hatred
as empowerment" payoff; for others, like Jayne West in "Are Men Really the Enemy?" (1970), man
hating worked in a less-than-serious metaphorical manner—as a vivid allusion to a woman's position in the "battle between the sexes"; and for most, as in Dana Densmore's "Who Is Saying Men
Are the Enemy?" (1970), man hating was a misdirected although well-intentioned strategy from
the beginning—it focused hostility toward the most immediate embodiments of female oppression
rather than on its systemic culturally determined source. Overall, for the few years it was discussed, man hating helped feminism pinpoint the ways in which men kept women down, although
it was far from effective in coming to terms with the coercive complex of masculinity—a concern
taken up by pro-feminist men's groups in the early 1970s.

As some feminists came to view men as "the enemy" and especially as awareness flourished about
the previously unspoken crime of rape, self-protection from men became a goal for many women.
"Women are attacked, beaten up and raped every day," say the authors of "Karate as Self-Defense for
Women" (1970). Rather than depend on other men for protection, women like Susan Pascalé, Rachel
Moon, and Leslie B. Tanner took it upon themselves to learn such skills as a martial art or the use of
firearms. In many cases this was not easy: self-defense training helped women extend their own notions of their abilities and strengths in part because they also had to surmount obstacles created by
male attitudes—ranging from indifference to hostility—about what women could or should do. As
Pascalé, Moon, and Tanner tell it, their story is as interesting for its insights into the trials and tribulations of integrating women into traditionally male arenas as it is for its description of learning
karate. Women have faced similar attitudes and obstacles when working on such feminist issues as
dress reform, women's service in the military, and the advent of female intercollegiate and professional sports.

Building respect for women's physical autonomy and capacity was also an issue that affected the
workplace. In contrast to the intense but limited issue of man hating, women's struggle in the workplace has been a continuing part of American feminism. By the 1960s women workers in heavy industry had made some gains in trade unionism. Later, Title VII of the Civil Rights Act of 1964 would
prove to be effective in fighting both sexual discrimination in hiring and promotion decisions and sexual harassment in the workplace (application of this law did not start to develop until the early to
mid-1970s). Meanwhile, many of the thirty million or so American women workers in the late 1960s
still had to cope with inequality and hostile work environments on their own. In some places, though,
the women's movement inspired grassroots rebellions such as those described in the "Poems and Articles" (1969) of *Switchbored,* an underground newspaper mimeographed at the office by New York
City AT&T clerical workers and founders of the secret organization Women Incensed at Telephone
Company Harassment—one of the autonomous and unhierarchical WITCH "covens" that arose

within the women's liberation movement (WITCH for Women's International Terrorist Conspiracy from Hell; for Women Interested in Toppling Consumption Holidays; for Women Inspired to Commit Herstory, and so on). In 1970 the Equal Employment Opportunity Commission created by Title VII started a massive sexual discrimination suit against the AT&T monolith—what it called "without doubt, the largest oppressor of women workers in the United States" (the company at the time was the country's single largest employer of women). AT&T settled the suit in 1973 out of court, agreeing to pay women employees $38 million in back pay and wage increases.

The idea that domestic work should be a responsibility equally shared by women and men came relatively late to American feminism. Charlotte Perkins Gilman discussed the professionalization of housework and child care in *Women and Economics* (1898), but she assumed that women would fill those jobs; and feminists throughout the twentieth-century labor movement have reminded men of working women's double duty at the workplace and at home, but it was not until the second wave that feminists publicly contested the assumption that women "naturally" do the shopping, cooking, cleaning, child care, laundry, and so on. In "The Politics of Housework" (1968/1970), Pat Mainardi draws from her own experiences in trying to get her husband to do his share of the work. Her enumeration of the many subterfuges he uses to escape what he considers to be the too-menial and inconsequential jobs of housework is only partially satirical, as Mainardi does insist that men taking up housework is an indispensable part of women's liberation. Before being included in *Notes from the Second Year* (1970), "The Politics of Housework," circulated widely in mimeographed form among young feminists, including Alix Kates Shulman, who in turn wrote "The Shulmans' Marriage Agreement" (1971), which was widely published in feminist journals as well as women's magazines.

As Shulman's marriage agreement suggests, second-wave feminism involved, among other things, encouraging conscious decision making in areas previously accepted as women's duties, burdens, or simply as necessities. As the Shulmans outline it, husband and wife take turns cooking, shopping, and cleaning. They draw clear lines of responsibility for specific tasks and times of child care. The intent is to equalize both the work and the responsibility involved in running a household and raising a family—without regard to which partner brings home the bigger paycheck, or any paycheck at all. The equal sharing of day-to-day responsibility of children by father and mother remains a radical, albeit more widely considered, proposal for most American families.

An even more radical consideration is that the work of caring for children could be seen as a desirable profession for men (as well as women) and at the same time serve as a way to revolutionize society. Although an upsurge in the number of day care facilities accompanied the increase in two-income families during the last thirty-five years of the twentieth century, the overall quality of child care available to most children remains inadequate. This situation is due in part to the low pay and high turnover among the mainly female workforce and generally the lack of institutional support and cultural value assigned to the service. As seen in both Lisa Leghorn's article "Child-Care for the Child" (1970) and Louise Gross's and Phyllis MacEwan's "On Day Care" (1970), radical feminists once saw the possibility that things could develop quite differently: public day care could not only be indispensable for women, but if understood as a rewarding and creative occupation for both sexes, it could also be liberating for children by providing a more stimulating and open environment than the constancy of the home where an overworked and perhaps less-than-happy mother presides. Indicative of early second-wave feminist idealism and ambition, Leghorn, Gross, and MacEwan see day care as nothing less than a tool to start remaking the world. For instance, early child development could and should include exposure to people from different racial and socioeconomic backgrounds. Also, gender stereotypes could be avoided, they argue, by employing men in the day care staffs.

Notwithstanding such broadly viewed conceptions, practical considerations weighed heavily in women's demands for day care. For many, the possibility of earning a living, let alone building a career, rested on the availability of day care. Of course, day care by itself was no panacea. In "Welfare Is a Woman's Issue" (1972), Johnnie Tillmon, a forty-five-year-old African American woman from the Watts section of Los Angeles and the first chairwoman of the National Welfare Rights Organization (NWRO), compares the realities to the public perception of living under the federal program Aid to Families with Dependent Children (AFDC). Designed by feminists concerned with child welfare, AFDC grew from a relatively minor part of the New Deal Social Security Act of 1935 to become the heart of what would be understood as the U.S. welfare system—a five-billion-dollar per year program by the mid-1970s. Despite these expenditures, Tillmon writes, AFDC brings with it a myriad of problems for poor women, not the least of which is the taint of dependency and the necessity to "trade in *a* man for *the* man" (half of the states at this time would not make payments to families with "able-bodied" men). The biggest problem, Tillmon adds, is structural: women would prefer to work, but there are simply not enough jobs for women, especially black women, that pay a living wage. In lieu of reorganizing the American economy, the NWRO and Tillmon propose Guaranteed Adequate Income—a gender-neutral program which would make payments according to need and family size.

In examining how male-based institutions treat women, some second-wave feminists focused particularly on the practice of medicine and the U.S. health care system overall. This makes perfect sense, as the Women's Health Collective points out in "The Male-Feasance of Health" (1970), since women use and depend on the system more than men. Yet the vast majority of doctors, research scientists, medical school deans, hospital administrators, and pharmaceutical and insurance company executives have been and continue to be men—virtually all of them mystified by if not indifferent to the specific needs of women. This problem is most egregious in gynecological care. Here women are especially endangered by the broad-based cultural objectification of women: "The sick person who enters the gynecology clinic is the same sex as the sexual object who sells cars in the magazine ads," say Group II, the authors of "Are Our Doctors Pigs?" (1970). These two articles, both published in the radical feminist journal *Rat,* urge women to organize for change. Since large numbers of women are employed in the health care system as nurses, technicians, and administrative assistants, there is opportunity for an alliance between female consumers and workers. The authors also propose gathering information and creating blacklists on specific doctors, clinics, and hospitals. They suggest more women doctors would make a big difference. In this regard, there has been dramatic change since 1970: the percentage of female medical doctors in the United States increased from 7 to 8 percent in 1970 to 32.4 percent in 1987.

Women who underwent illegal abortions before 1973 faced the possibility of particularly negative experiences with the health care system if medical complications developed—and abortion was not uncommon, even though it was an illegal act. "In the 1950s about a million illegal abortions a year were performed in the United States, and over a thousand women died each year as a result," according to *Our Bodies Ourselves*—the self-help reference by The Boston Women's Health Book Collective, whose first edition in 1969 was itself a product of second-wave activism. As awareness about abortion grew, a handful of states adopted more liberal abortion laws. In 1970 New York State legalized abortion through the second trimester, but most women who lived outside of New York and couldn't afford to leave their jobs and homes or travel still did not have the right to choose whether or not to bring a pregnancy to term. In the late 1960s feminist organizations mobilized against restrictive abortion laws that violated women's rights, pushing test cases through the courts until the U.S. Supreme Court decided to hear a challenge to a Texas criminal statute outlawing abortion. In the landmark case *Roe v. Wade* (1973) the Court declared that state laws restricting abortion were unconstitutional, except during the third trimester of pregnancy when the interests of the fetus start to supersede those of the mother; the opinion defined abortion as a "fundamental right" of women, protected by the right of privacy, founded upon the Fourteenth Amendment's concept of personal liberty and restrictions upon state power. The origins of the still-contested principle of a fundamental right to have an abortion can be found in the "Brief for Appellants" (1970) and "Brief Amicus Curiae on Behalf of New Women Lawyers, Women's Health and Abortion Project, Inc., National Abortion Action Coalition" (1971), both from *Roe v. Wade.*

The extremely controversial *Roe v. Wade* decision sparked a neoconservative "pro-life" populist movement in the mid-1970s. Its first victory came when Congress passed the Hyde Amendment, which prohibits use of Medicaid funding for abortions unless a woman's life is in danger. (Before the Hyde Amendment, one third of abortions were Medicaid funded.) Thus access to abortions was once again restricted for poor women. In 1980 the Supreme Court upheld the Hyde Amendment (*Harris v. McRae*) and women began to lose constitutional protection for abortion rights. Ronald Reagan's election to the presidency in 1980 and his appointment of antiabortion-rights judges to the federal courts meant that the guarantee of a woman's fundamental right to choose to have an abortion would be further challenged and ultimately reconsidered by the Supreme Court. The test case *Webster v. Reproductive Health Services* (1989) involved a 1986 Missouri statute that among other things prohibited public funding for abortion counseling and the use of public facilities and public employees to perform abortions. Fearing that the Court would use the opportunity to overturn *Roe v. Wade* and thereby make illegal the approximately 1.6 million abortions per year, pro-choice supporters rallied forces, organizing a march in Washington, D.C., in April 1988 of more than three hundred thousand women and men insisting "We Won't Turn Back." Several amicus curiae briefs were filed in support of the right to choose to have an abortion, including "The Historians' Brief" (1988), funded by a large group of academic women's historians and other professional historians. Despite such pro-choice support, the Supreme Court upheld the Missouri law. More important, the Court suggested in its decision that it may no longer consider abortion to be a fundamental constitutional right, although Justice Sandra Day O'Connor, the swing figure, said she was not ready to scrap the *Roe* decision. After *Webster,* while the Court upheld other state laws further restricting access to abortion, it also reaffirmed the "essence" of the constitutional right to abortion in *Planned Parenthood v. Casey* (1992).

Even before Ronald Reagan won the White House, it was clear to many feminists that the growth and success of second-wave feminism depended on their ability to understand and neutralize the increasing power of the New Right in American political culture. For, as Linda Gordon and Allen Hunter explain in "Sex, Family and the New Right: Anti-Feminism as a Political Force" (1977), neo-conservatism rose in direct response and in opposition to the gains that women and minorities made through the civil rights and women's movements. The *Roe v. Wade* decision brought particular consternation to conservatives as they apprehended the breakup of patriarchal authority over reproduction and the family. A certain prudishness was also involved: pro-life activism, like the increase in gay bashing, demonstrated "hostility to freer sexual standards" and fear of that freedom, as Gordon and Hunter put it in "Sex, Family and the New Right," a wide-ranging essay examining eight main impetuses to neoconservative reactionaryism: antifeminism, antisexualism, hostility to youth, homophobia, family preservation, pro-religion, pro-work ethic, and anticivil liberties. It also calls for a more distinct feminist component in socialist thought and activism.

"One example of New Right power is the campaign against the Equal Rights Amendment," write Gordon and Hunter, and according to their analysis, "It is the feminist impulse behind ERA, not its specific content, that is most feared." The resurgence of the women's movement in the 1960s had brought new life to the decades-long effort to add an Equal Rights Amendment to the U.S. Constitution. The proposed amendment simply read: "Equality of rights under the law shall not be abridged by the United States or any state on account of sex." The National Organization for Women's "ERA Position Paper" (1967) offers a brief history of the amendment, states NOW's unequivocal support for the ERA, and—attempting to disarm critics—analyzes the main reasons that have been offered in opposition to it. Although both the Republican and Democratic Parties endorsed the ERA, and even as Congress approved it (passing it on to the state legislatures, three-quarters of which had to accept the amendment for it to become law), a firestorm of opposition emerged. Led by the politically adroit conservative Phyllis Schlafly and her organization Stop ERA (founded in 1972), it included such unlikely allies as the AFL-CIO and the Communist Party. The battle was joined. Working on a deadline of 1979, ERA supporters had won approval of two-thirds of the states by 1978. With six more states needed, NOW petitioned Congress to extend the time for ratification, as explained in the National Organization for Women's "ERA: Declaration of State of Emergency" (1978). Three more states approved the amendment, but the deadline for ratification passed on June 30, 1982, leaving the ERA dead in the water. (NOW would reintroduce it to Congress in the 1990s.)

There was still hope for the ERA, though, in November 1977, when feminists gathered in Houston, Texas, for the National Women's Conference. By this time women's conferences had become common to second-wave feminism, but the Houston gathering was a conference with a number of differences: funded by the federal government, planned by a presidential commission, charged under law to assess the status of women, the National Women's Conference (which took place after fifty state conferences) hosted more than two thousand delegates and eighteen thousand attendees—a racially, sexually, religiously, and economically heterogeneous group that reflected the breadth of the American women's movement. "At last," Gloria Steinem writes in "What Women Want: An Introductory Statement" (1978), "there were enough minority women (more than a third of all delegates) to have a strong voice—not only black women, but Hispanic women as the second largest American minority, Asian American women, American Indian women and many more." The primary product of the conference—in addition to the experience itself—was the National Plan of Action, presented to President Jimmy Carter and Congress as a near comprehensive survey of feminist goals. Steinem's statement appears in a volume that reprints the plan along with background materials on the National Women's Conference. The plan's preamble, "Declaration of American Women" (1977), reviews the "positive changes that have occurred in the lives of women since the founding of our nation" and points out that, nevertheless, women's "dream of equality is still withheld." The National Plan of Action includes these areas of concern: arts and humanities, battered women, business, child abuse, child care, credit, disabled women, education, elective and appointive office, employment, the ERA, health, homemakers' insurance, international affairs, media, minority women, offenders, older women, rape, reproductive freedom, rural women, sexual preference, statistics and women, welfare, and poverty.

In conjunction with and alongside the informal education going on at all kinds of women's meetings and gatherings, including conferences, feminists in the academy (and at other educational levels, too) were working in the classroom trying to integrate insights, questions, methods, and analyses garnered from their research and activism. Women's studies—the name, the field, the undertaking— emerged as a direct outgrowth of second-wave feminism, influenced also by 1960s student activism, the Southern Freedom Schools, and the teach-ins of the anti–Vietnam War movement. Beginning with a few scattered classes in the late 1960s, the enterprise took off in the 1970s, growing to more than thirty thousand courses and three hundred women's studies programs in colleges and universities by the early 1980s, and five hundred programs by the early 1990s. The National Women's Studies Association was founded in 1977 and remains a vibrant organization. In the early years especially, women's studies course offerings throughout the country went far in shaking up traditional classroom structure and experience. Nan Bauer-Maglin's "Journal of a Women's Course" (1973–1975) aptly demonstrates the process of questioning and learning that takes place in such a course—from its description of students revamping the syllabus on the first day to its recounting of small-group discussions and the general extemporaneous quality of the semester. Founded as an arm of the women's liberation movement—with a self-conscious feminist agenda—the ultimate success of women's studies remains an open question. Its acceptance into the academy suggests the foreboding possibility of co-optation in tension with the potential of making long-term changes in how and what American college students learn.

The great promise of women's studies has been seen in the production of new knowledge based on the acceptance of gender as an essential category for analysis as well as on women's perspectives, social experiences, and needs. In its first years, women's studies, while interdisciplinary, benefited in particular from the fields of feminist literary criticism, anthropology, and (perhaps most of all) history. Examination of the past not only uncovered female heritage or "herstory," it brought a working knowledge of the structures that have impeded achieving sexual equality and, of equal importance, the strategies that have worked in fighting those forces. The writing of women's history certainly did not begin with the second wave. Since the mid-nineteenth century, writing history for others to read has been a leading way to make explicit and thereby politicize the demands of women; the multi-volume *History of Woman Suffrage* (1891–1922), for example, was always meant to be both a detailed accounting of that topic and an active agent in its achievement. While the predominantly male and masculine American history profession was decidedly inactive in early-twentieth-century feminism, historical methods and practice consolidated their place in the social movement, as a new generation of intellectuals co-opted Darwinian evolutionary theory to expose the archaic and destructive routines, customs, and stereotypes governing relations between the sexes. Pioneering nonacademic historians like Mary Ritter Beard and Eleanor Flexner provided something of a bridge to Gerda Lerner, Ann Firor Scott, Joan Kelly, and Natalie Zemon Davis—some of the first women's historians to earn Ph.D.s (in the late 1950s and early 1960s), take up academic posts, and start forging a place for the field of women's history within the profession.

Gerda Lerner has been perhaps the most instrumental figure in the growth of academic women's history. After earning a Columbia University Ph.D. in 1966, for which she wrote and published her dissertation *The Grimké Sisters from South Carolina: Rebels Against Slavery,* Lerner joined the faculty of Sarah Lawrence College, where she cofounded with Joan Kelly in 1972 the first women's history master's degree program. Her promotion of graduate study continued after moving in 1980 to the University of Wisconsin, Madison, where she headed a new Ph.D. program in women's history. Lerner has been a prolific writer, publishing fiction, screenplays, and memoirs in addition to her scholarly books and articles on women's history. Gerda Lerner's "New Approaches to the Study of Women in American History" (1969) provides an example of the early effort to break down traditional male-based history by reconceptualizing a sexually inclusive and holistic view of the past. This would not be easy. Lerner recognizes any number of obstacles, including earlier feminists' reliance on the "oppressed group model" of women's history; she argues that, while subordinated, women have wielded considerable power within the home and family as well as in public spheres of political and social reform. Originally published in *The Journal of Social History,* the essay anticipated academic women's history's widespread turn toward social history in the 1970s.

Amid the great and divergent outpouring of women's history scholarship in the 1970s and 1980s, one historiographical strand can be followed among those who came of intellectual and political age during the 1960s and who went on to define themselves in the profession as socialist feminists. The genesis of socialist-feminist women's history can be traced back to the oppositionalist politics of the New Left and the birth of radical feminism. Compared to Gerda Lerner, for instance, who came to women's history in the 1960s as a self-described "post-Marxist," many socialist-feminist women's historians began with Marxism or at least a sharpened critique of capitalism and therefore made a deliberate effort to square socialism with feminism. One of the best examples of a historian whose intellectual-biographical sequence runs from New Left Marxism to radical feminism to socialist-feminist historian is Linda Gordon. Working in the antiwar movement and with Friends of the Student Non Violent Coordinating Committee, joining the staff of the journal *Radical America* in 1971, she could say as late as 1981 that "Marxism remains the single most important intellectual influence on my work." And, yet, in "What Should Women's Historians Do: Politics, Social Theory, and Women's History" (1978), Gordon insists that focus on class and economic materialism must be joined by the examination of the "sex/gender system." Gordon goes on to say that despite the continued need for women's historians to make their scholarship politically productive (engaging the most pressing women's issues of the day), that scholarship should also resist the form of propaganda—it must meet the research requirements and interpretive standards of the profession. Ellen Carol DuBois is another prominent scholar who moved from radical feminism in the late 1960s to socialist-feminist women's history. After working in the Boston Draft Resistance Group, DuBois started her Ph.D. work at Northwestern University in the fall of 1968 (a month after the violence at the Democratic Convention in Chicago), while also helping to form the Chicago Women's Liberation Union. Author of, among other works, *Feminism and Suffrage: The Emergence of an Independent Women's Movement in America, 1848–1869* (1978), and *Harriot Stanton Blatch and the Winning of Woman Suffrage* (1997), DuBois explains in "The Last Suffragist: An Intellectual and Political Autobiography" (1998) how her politics brought her to the topic of U.S. women winning the right to vote.

42

KATHIE SARACHILD

A Program for Feminist "Consciousness Raising" (1968)

We always stay in touch with our feelings.

Our feelings (emotions) revolve around our perceptions of our self-interest.

We assume that our feelings are telling us something from which we can learn . . . that our feelings mean something worth analyzing . . . that our feelings are saying something *political*, something reflecting fear that something bad will happen to us or hope, desire, knowledge that something good will happen to us.

Feelings aren't something we assume ahead of time that we should be on top of or underneath. Feelings are something that, at first anyway, we are *with*, that is, we examine and try to understand before we decide it's the kind of feeling to stay on top of (that is, control, stifle, stop), or the kind of feeling to be underneath (that is, let ourselves go with, let it lead us into something new and better . . . at first to a new and better *idea* of where we want to go and then to action which might help us get there).

Now male culture assumes that feelings are something that people should stay on top of and puts women down for being led by their feelings (being underneath them).

We're saying that women have all along been generally *in touch* with their feelings (rather than underneath them) and that their being in touch with their feelings has been their greatest strength, historically and for the future. We have been so in touch with our feelings, as a matter of fact, that we have used our feelings as our best available weapon—

From *Notes from the Second Year*, 1970, as presented at the First National Women's Liberation Conference outside Chicago, November 27, 1968.

hysterics, whining, bitching, etc.—given that our best form of defense against those with power to control our lives was their feelings toward us, sexual and otherwise, feelings which they always tried to fight themselves.

We're saying that for most of history sex was, in fact, both our undoing and our only possible weapon of self-defense and self-assertion (aggression).

We're saying that when we had hysterical fits, when we took things "too" personally, that we weren't underneath our feelings, but responding with our feelings correctly to a given situation of injustice. I say correctly because at that time in history (and maybe even still), by first feeling and then revealing our emotions we were acting in the best strategical manner. And this may be the reason we learned how to be so in touch with our feelings to begin with.

In our groups, let's share our feelings and pool them. Let's let ourselves go and see where our feelings lead us. Our feelings will lead us to ideas and then to actions.

Our feelings will lead us to our theory, our theory to our action, our feelings about that action to new theory and then to new action.

This is a consciousness-raising program for those of us who are feeling more and more that women are about the most exciting people around, at this stage of time, anyway, and that the seeds of a new and beautiful world society lie buried in the consciousness of this very class which has been abused and oppressed since the beginning of human history. It is a program planned on the assumption that a mass liberation movement will develop as more and more women begin to perceive their situation correctly and that, therefore, our primary task right now is to awaken "class" consciousness in ourselves and others on a mass scale. The following outline is just one hunch of what a theory of mass consciousness raising would look like in skeleton form.

I. The "bitch session" cell group
    A. Ongoing consciousness expansion
        1. Personal recognition and testimony
            a. Recalling and sharing our bitter experiences
            b. Expressing our feelings about our experiences both at the time they occurred and at present
            c. Expressing our feelings about ourselves, men, other women
            d. Evaluating our feelings
        2. Personal testimony—methods of group practice
            a. Going around the room with key questions on key topics
            b. Speaking our experience—at random
            c. Cross examination
        3. Relating and generalizing individual testimony
            a. Finding the common root when different women have opposite feelings and experiences
            b. Examining the negative and positive aspects of each woman's feelings and her way of dealing with her situation as a woman
    B. Classic forms of resisting consciousness, or: How to avoid facing the awful truth
        1. Anti-womanism
        2. Glorification of the oppressor
        3. Excusing the oppressor (and feeling sorry for him)
        4. False identification with the oppressor and other socially privileged groups
        5. Shunning identification with one's own oppressed group and other oppressed groups
        6. Romantic fantasies, utopian thinking and other forms of confusing present reality with what one wishes reality to be
        7. Thinking one has power in the traditional role—can "get what one wants," has power behind the throne, etc.
        8. Belief that one has found an adequate personal solution or will be able to find one without large social changes
        9. Self-cultivation, rugged individualism, seclusion, and other forms of go-it-alonism
        10. Self-blame!!
        11. Ultra-militancy; and others??
    C. Recognizing the survival reasons for resisting consciousness
    D. "Starting to Stop"—overcoming repressions and delusions
        1. Daring to see, or: Taking off the rose-colored glasses
            a. Reasons for repressing one's own consciousness
                1) Fear of feeling the full weight of one's painful situation
                2) Fear of feeling one's past wasted and meaningless (plus wanting others to go through the same obstacles)
                3) Fear of despair for the future
            b. Analyzing which fears are valid and which invalid
                1) Examining the objective conditions in one's own past and in the lives of most women throughout history
                2) Examining objective conditions for the present
            c. Discussing possible methods of struggle
                1) History of women's struggle and resistance to oppression
                2) Possibilities for individual struggle at present
                3) Group struggle
        2. Daring to share one's experience with the group

a. Sources of hesitancy
   1) Fear of personal exposure (fear of being thought stupid, immoral, weak, self-destructive, etc. by the group)
   2) Feeling of loyalty to one's man, boss, parents, children, friends, "the Movement"
   3) Fear of reprisal if the word gets out (losing one's man, job, reputation)
   4) Fear of hurting the feelings of someone in the group
   5) Not seeing how one's own experience is relevant to others, or vice versa
b. Deciding which fears are valid and which invalid
c. Structuring the group so that it is relatively safe for people to participate in it

E. Understanding and developing radical feminist theory
   1. Using above techniques to arrive at an understanding of oppression wherever it exists in our lives—our oppression as black people, workers, tenants, consumers, children, or whatever as well as our oppression as women
   2. Analyzing whatever privileges we may have—the white skin privilege, the education and citizenship of a big-power (imperialist) nation privilege, and seeing how these help to perpetuate our oppression as women, workers

F. Consciousness-raiser (organizer) training—so that every woman in a given bitch session cell group herself becomes an "organizer" of other groups
   1. The role of the consciousness-raiser ("organizer")
      a. Dares to participate; dares to expose herself, bitch
      b. Dares to struggle

2. Learning how to bring theory down to earth
   a. Speaking in terms of personal experience
3. Learning to "relate"
   a. To sisters in the group
   b. To other women
   c. Friends and allies
   d. Enemies
4. Particular problems of starting a new group

II. Consciousness-raising actions
   A. Zap actions
      1. Movie benefits, attacks on cultural phenomena and events, stickers, buttons, posters, films
   B. Consciousness programs
      1. Newspapers, broadsides, storefronts, women's liberation communes, literature, answering mail, others . . . ??
   C. Utilizing the mass media

III. Organizing
   A. Helping new people start groups
   B. Intra-group communication and actions
      1. Monthly meetings
      2. Conferences

43

CAROL HANISCH

A Critique of the Miss America Protest (1968)

The protest of the Miss America Pageant in Atlantic City in September told the nation that a new feminist movement is afoot in the land. Due to the tremendous coverage in the mass media, millions of Americans now know there is a Women's Liberation Movement. Media coverage ranged from the front pages of several newspapers in the United States to many articles in the foreign press.

The action brought many new members into our group and many requests from women outside the city for literature and information. A recurrent theme was, "I've been waiting so long for something like this." So have we all, and the Miss America protest put us well on our way.

But no action taken in the Women's Liberation Struggle will be all good or all bad. It is necessary that we analyze each step to see what we did that was effective, what was not, and what was downright destructive.

At this point in our struggle, our actions should be aimed primarily at doing two interrelated things: 1) awakening the latent consciousness of women about their own oppression, and 2) building sisterhood. With these as our primary immediate goals, let us examine the Miss America protest.

The idea came out of our group method of analyzing women's oppression by recalling our own experiences. We were watching *Schmearguntz*, a feminist movie, one night at our meeting. The movie had flashes of the Miss America contest in it. I found myself sitting there remembering how I had felt at home with my family watching the pageant as a child, an adolescent, and a college student. I knew it had evoked powerful feelings.

When I proposed the idea to our group, we decided to go around the room with each woman telling how she felt about the pageant. We discovered that many of us who had always put down the contest still watched it. Others, like myself, had consciously identified with it, and had cried with the winner.

From the communal thinking came the concrete plans for the action. We all agreed that our main point in the demonstration would be that all women were hurt by beauty competitions—Miss America as well as ourselves. We opposed the pageant in our own self-interest, e.g., the self-interest of all women.

Yet one of the biggest mistakes of the whole pageant was our anti-womanism. A spirit of every woman "doing her own thing"

began to emerge. Sometimes it was because there was an open conflict about an issue. Other times, women didn't say anything at all about disagreeing with a group decision; they just went ahead and did what they wanted to do, even though it was something the group had definitely decided against. Because of this egotistic individualism, a definite strain of anti-womanism was presented to the public to the detriment of the action.

Posters which read "Up Against the Wall, Miss America," "Miss America Sells It," and "Miss America is a Big Falsie" hardly raised any woman's consciousness and really harmed the cause of sisterhood. Miss America and all beautiful women came off as our enemy instead of as our sisters who suffer with us. A group decision had been made rejecting these anti-woman signs. A few women made them anyway. Some women who had opposed the slogans were in the room when the signs were being made and didn't confront those who were making the anti-woman signs.

A more complex situation developed around the decision of a few women to use an "underground" disruptive tactic. The action was approved by the group only after its adherents said they would do it anyway as an individual action. As it turned out, we came to the realization that there is no such thing as "individual action" in a movement. We were linked to and were committed to support our sisters whether they called their action "individual" or not. It also came to many of us that there is at this time no real need to do "underground" actions. We need to reach as many women as possible as quickly as possible with a clear message that has the power of our person behind it. At this point women have to see other women standing up and saying these things. That's why draping a women's liberation banner over the balcony that night and yelling our message was much clearer. We should have known, however, that the television network, because it was not competing with other networks for coverage, would not put the action on camera. It did get on the radio and in newspapers, however.

The problem of how to enforce group decisions is one we haven't solved. It came up in a lot of ways throughout the whole action. The group rule of not talking to male reporters was another example.

One of the reasons we came off anti-woman, besides the posters, was our lack of clarity. We didn't say clearly enough that we women are all *forced* to play the Miss America role—not by beautiful women but by men who we have to act that way for, and by a system that has so well institutionalized male supremacy for its own ends.

This was none too clear in our guerrilla theater either. Women chained to a replica, red, white and blue bathing-suited Miss America could have been misinterpreted as against beautiful women. Also, crowning a live sheep Miss America sort of said that beautiful women *are* sheep. However, the action did say to some women that women are *viewed* as auction-block, docile animals. The grandmother of one of the participants really began to understand the action when she was told about the sheep, and she ended up joining the protest.

There is as great a need for clarity in our language as there is in our actions. The leaflet that was distributed as a press release and as a flyer at the action was too long, too wordy, too complex, too hippy-yippee-campy. Instead of an "in" phrase like "Racism with Roses" (I still don't know exactly what that means), we could have just called the pageant RACIST and everybody would have understood our opposition on that point. If we are going to reach masses of women, we must give up all the "in-talk" of the New Left/Hippie movements—at least when we're talking in public. (Yes, even the word FUCK!) We can use simple language (*real* language) that everyone from Queens to Iowa will understand and not misunderstand.

We should try to avoid the temptation to say everything there is to say about what is wrong with the world and thereby say nothing that a new person can really dig into and understand. Women's liberation itself is revolu-

tionary dynamite. When other issues are interjected, we should clearly relate them to our oppression *as women*.

We tried to carry the democratic means we used in planning the action into the actual *doing* of it. We didn't want leaders or spokesmen. It makes the movement not only *seem* stronger and larger if everyone is a leader, but it actually *is* stronger if not dependent on a few. It also guards against the time when such leaders could be isolated and picked off one way or another. And of course many voices are more powerful than one.

Our first attempt at this was not entirely successful. We must learn how to fight against the media's desire to make leaders and some women's desire to be spokesmen. Everybody talks to the press or nobody talks to the press. The same problem came up in regard to appearances on radio and television shows after the action. We theoretically decided no one should appear more than once, but it didn't work out that way.

The Miss America protest was a zap action, as opposed to person-to-person group action. Zap actions are using our presence as a group and/or the media to make women's oppression into social issues. In such actions we speak to men as a group as well as to women. It is a rare opportunity to talk to men in a situation where they can't talk back. (Men must begin to learn to listen.) Our power of solidarity, not our individual intellectual exchanges, will change men.

We tried to speak to individual women in the crowd and now some of us feel that it may not have been a good tactic. It put women on the spot in front of their men. We were putting them in a position which we choose to avoid ourselves when we don't allow men in our discussion groups.

It is interesting that many of the non-movement women we talked to about the protest had the same reaction as many radical women. "But I'm not oppressed" was a shared response. "I don't care about Miss America" was another. If more than half the television viewers in the country watch the pageant, somebody cares! And many of us admitted watching it too, even while putting it down.

It's interesting, too, that while much of the Left was putting us down for attacking something so "silly and unimportant" or "reformist," the Right saw us as a threat and yelled such things as "Go back to Russia" and "Mothers of Mao" at the picket line. Ironically enough, what the Left/Underground press seemed to like best about our action was what was really our worst mistake—our anti-woman signs.

Surprisingly and fortunately, some of the mass media ignored our mistakes and concentrated on our best points. To quote from the *Daily News*, " . . . some women who think the whole idea of such contests is degrading to femininity, took their case to the people. . . . During boardwalk protest, gals say they're not anti-beauty, just anti-beauty contest." Shana Alexander wrote in a *Life* magazine editorial that she "wished they'd gone farther." Together, *Life* and the *Daily News* reach millions of Americans.

We need to take ourselves seriously. The powers that be do. Carol Giardino of Gainesville, Florida, was fired from her job because of her activities in women's liberation and her participation in the protest. Police cars were parked outside the planning meeting one night. The next day we got a call from the Mayor of Atlantic City questioning us about just what we planned to do. Pepsi-Cola is withdrawing as a sponsor of the pageant. They produce a diet cola and maybe see themselves as next year's special target.

Unfortunately, the best slogan for the action came up about a month after, when Roz Baxandall came out on the David Susskind show with "Every day in a woman's life is a walking Miss America Contest." We shouldn't wait for the best slogan; we should go ahead to the best of our understanding. We hope all our sisters can learn something as we did from our last foray.

44

VALERIE SOLANAS

SCUM Manifesto (1967)

Life in this society being, at best, an utter bore and no aspect of society being at all relevant to women, there remains to civic-minded, responsible, thrill-seeking females only to overthrow the government, eliminate the money system, institute complete automation, and destroy the male sex.

It is now technically possible to reproduce without the aid of males (or, for that matter, females) and to produce only females. We must begin immediately to do so. Retaining the male has not even the dubious purpose of reproduction. The male is a biological accident: the Y (male) gene is an incomplete X (female) gene, that is, has an incomplete set of chromosomes. In other words, the male is an incomplete female, a walking abortion, aborted at the gene stage. To be male is to be deficient, emotionally limited; maleness is a deficiency disease and males are emotional cripples.

The male is completely egocentric, trapped inside himself, incapable of empathizing or identifying with others, of love, friendship, affection, or tenderness. He is a completely isolated unit, incapable of rapport with anyone. His responses are entirely visceral, not cerebral; his intelligence is a mere tool in the service of his drives and needs; he is incapable of mental passion, mental interaction; he can't relate to anything other than his own physical sensations. He is a half-dead, unresponsive lump, incapable of giving or receiving pleasure or happiness; consequently, he is at best an utter bore, an inoffensive blob, since only those capable of absorption in others can be charming. He is trapped in a twilight zone halfway between humans and apes, and is far worse off than the apes because, unlike the apes, he is ca-

From Valerie Solanas, *SCUM Manifesto* (San Francisco: AK Press, 1996). The *SCUM Manifesto* was originally self-published in New York in 1967.

pable of a large array of negative feelings—hate, jealousy, contempt, disgust, guilt, shame, doubt—and moreover he *is aware* of what he is and isn't.

Although completely physical, the male is unfit even for stud service. Even assuming mechanical proficiency, which few men have, he is, first of all, incapable of zestfully, lustfully, tearing off a piece, but is instead eaten up with guilt, shame, fear, and insecurity, feelings rooted in male nature, which the most enlightened training can only minimize; second, the physical feeling he attains is next to nothing; and, third, he is not empathizing with his partner, but is obsessed with how he's doing, turning in an A performance, doing a good plumbing job. To call a man an animal is to flatter him; he's a machine, a walking dildo. It's often said that men use women. Use them for what? Surely not pleasure.

Eaten up with guilt, shame, fears, and insecurities and obtaining, if he's lucky, a barely perceptible physical feeling, the male is, nonetheless, obsessed with screwing; he'll swim a river of snot, wade nostril-deep through a mile of vomit, if he thinks there'll be a friendly pussy awaiting him. He'll screw a woman he despises, any snaggletoothed hag, and, furthermore, pay for the opportunity. Why? Relieving physical tension isn't the answer, as masturbation suffices for that. It's not ego satisfaction; that doesn't explain screwing corpses and babies.

Completely egocentric, unable to relate, empathize, or identify, and filled with a vast, pervasive, diffuse sexuality, the male is physically passive. He hates his passivity, so he projects it onto women, defines the male as active, then sets out to prove that he is ("prove he's a Man"). His main means of attempting to prove it is screwing (Big Man with a Big Dick tearing off a Big Piece). Since he's attempting to prove an error, he must "prove" it again and again. Screwing, then, is a desperate, compulsive attempt to prove he's not passive, not a woman; but he is passive and does want to be a woman.

Being an incomplete female, the male spends his life attempting to complete himself, to become female. He attempts to do this by constantly seeking out, fraternizing with, and trying to live through and fuse with the female, and by claiming his own all female characteristics—emotional strength and independence, forcefulness, dynamism, decisiveness, coolness, objectivity, assertiveness, courage, integrity, vitality, intensity, depth of character, grooviness, etc.—and projecting onto women all male traits—vanity, frivolity, triviality, weakness, etc. It should be said, though, that the male has one glaring area of superiority over the female—public relations. (He has done a brilliant job of convincing millions of women that men are women and women are men.) The male claim that females find fulfillment through motherhood and sexuality reflects what males think they'd find fulfilling if they were female.

Women, in other words, don't have penis envy; men have pussy envy. When the male accepts his passivity, defines himself as a woman (males as well as females think men are women and women are men), and becomes a transvestite he loses his desire to screw (or to do anything else, for that matter; he fulfills himself as a drag queen) and gets his cock chopped off. He then achieves a continuous diffuse sexual feeling from "being a woman." Screwing is, for a man, a defense against his desire to be female. Sex is itself a sublimation.

The male, because of his obsession to compensate for not being female combined with his inability to relate and to feel compassion, has made of the world a shitpile. . . .

Incapable of a positive state of happiness, which is the only thing that can justify one's existence, the male is, at best, relaxed, comfortable, neutral, and this condition is extremely short-lived, as boredom, a negative state, soon sets in; he is, therefore, doomed to an existence of suffering relieved only by occasional, fleeting stretches of restfulness, which state he can achieve only at the expense of some female. The male is, by his very nature, a leech, an emotional parasite and, therefore, not ethically entitled to live, as no one has the right to live at someone else's expense.

Just as humans have a prior right to existence over dogs by virtue of being more highly evolved and having a superior consciousness, so women have a prior right to existence over men. The elimination of any male is, therefore, a righteous and good act, an act highly beneficial to women as well as an act of mercy.

However, this moral issue will eventually be rendered academic by the fact that the male is gradually eliminating himself. In addition to engaging in the time-honored and classical wars and race-riots, men are more and more either becoming fags or are obliterating themselves through drugs. The female, whether she likes it or not, will eventually take complete charge, if for no other reason than that she will have to—the male, for practical purposes, won't exist.

Accelerating this trend is the fact that more and more males are acquiring enlightened self-interest; they're realizing more and more that the female interest is *their* interest, that they can live only through the female and that the more the female is encouraged to live, to fulfill herself, to be a female and not a male, the more nearly *he* lives; he's coming to see that it's easier and more satisfactory to live *through* her than to try to *become* her and usurp her qualities, claim them as his own, push the female down and claim she's a male. The fag, who accepts his maleness, that is, his passivity and total sexuality, his femininity, is also best served by women being truly female, as it would then be easier for him to be male, feminine. If men were wise they would seek to become really female, would do intensive biological research that would lead to men, by means of operations on the brain and nervous system, being able to be transformed in psyche, as well as body, into women.

Whether to continue to use females for reproduction or to reproduce in the laboratory will also become academic: what will happen when every female, twelve and over, is routinely taking the Pill and there are no longer any accidents? How many women will deliberately get or (if an accident) remain pregnant?

No, Virginia, women don't just adore being brood mares, despite what the mass of robot, brainwashed women will say. When society consists of only the fully conscious, the answer will be none. Should a certain percentage of women be set aside by force to serve as brood mares for the species? Obviously this will not do. The answer is laboratory production of babies.

As for the issue of whether or not to continue to reproduce males, it doesn't follow that because the male, like disease, has always existed among us that he should continue to exist. When genetic control is possible—and it soon will be—it goes without saying that we should produce only whole, complete beings, not physical defects or deficiencies, including emotional deficiencies, such as maleness. Just as the deliberate production of blind people would be highly immoral, so would be the deliberate production of emotional cripples.

Why produce even females? Why should there be future generations? What is their purpose? When aging and death are eliminated, why continue to reproduce? Why should we care what happens when we're dead? Why should we care that there is no younger generation to succeed us?

Eventually the natural course of events, of social evolution, will lead to total female control of the world and, subsequently, to the cessation of the production of males and, ultimately, to the cessation of the production of females.

But SCUM is impatient; SCUM is not consoled by the thought that future generations will thrive; SCUM wants to grab some thrilling living for itself. And, if a large majority of women were SCUM, they could acquire complete control of this country within a few weeks simply by withdrawing from the labor force, thereby paralyzing the entire nation. Additional measures, any one of which would be sufficient to completely disrupt the economy and everything else, would be for women to declare themselves off the money system, stop buying, just loot and simply refuse to obey all laws they don't care to obey. The police force, National Guard, Army, Navy, and Marines combined couldn't squelch a rebellion of over half the population, particularly when it's made of people they are utterly helpless without.

If all women simply left men, refused to have anything to do with any of them—ever—all men, the government, and the national economy would collapse completely. Even without leaving men, women who are aware of the extent of their superiority to and power over men, could acquire complete control over everything within a few weeks, could effect a total submission of males to females. In a sane society the male would trot along obediently after the female. The male is docile and easily led, easily subjected to the domination of any female who cares to dominate him. The male, in fact, wants desperately to be led by females, wants Mama in charge, wants to abandon himself to her care. But this is not a sane society, and most women are not even dimly aware of where they're at in relation to men.

The conflict, therefore, is not between females and males, but between SCUM—dominant, secure, self-confident, nasty, violent, selfish, independent, proud, thrill-seeking, freewheeling, arrogant females, who consider themselves fit to rule the universe, who have freewheeled to the limits of this "society," and are ready to wheel on to something far beyond what it has to offer—and nice, passive, accepting, "cultivated," polite, dignified, subdued, dependent, scared, mindless, insecure, approval-seeking Daddy's Girls, who can't cope with the unknown; who want to continue to wallow in the sewer that is, at least, familiar, who want to hang back with the apes; who feel secure only with Big Daddy standing by, with a big, strong man to lean on and with a fat, hairy face in the White House; who are too cowardly to face up to the hideous reality of what a man is, what Daddy is; who have cast their lot with the swine, who have adapted themselves to animalism, feel superficially comfortable with it and know no other way of "life"; who have reduced their minds, thoughts and sights to the male level; who, lacking sense, imagination, and wit can have value only in a male "society"; who can have a place in the sun, or, rather, in the slime, only as soothers, ego-boosters, relaxers, and breeders; who are dismissed as inconsequents by other females, who project their deficiencies, their maleness, onto females and see the female as a worm.

But SCUM is too impatient to hope and wait for the debrainwashing of millions of assholes. Why should the swinging females continue to plod dismally along with the dull male ones? Why should the fates of the groovy and the creepy be intertwined? Why should the active and imaginative consult the passive and dull on social policy? Why should the independent be confined to the sewer along with the dependent who needs Daddy to cling to?

A small handful of SCUM can take over the country within a year by systematically fucking up the system, selectively destroying property, and murder:

SCUM will become members of the unwork force, the fuck-up force; they will get jobs of various kinds and unwork. For example, SCUM salesgirls will not charge for merchandise; SCUM telephone operators will not charge for calls; SCUM office and factory workers, in addition to fucking up their work, will secretly destroy equipment.

SCUM will unwork at a job until fired, then get a new job to unwork at.

SCUM will forcibly relieve bus drivers, cab drivers, and subway-token sellers of their jobs and run buses and cabs and dispense free tokens to the public.

SCUM will destroy all useless and harmful objects—cars, store windows, "Great Art," etc.

Eventually SCUM will take over the airwaves—radio and TV networks—by forcibly relieving of their jobs all radio and TV employees who would impede SCUM's entry into the broadcasting studios.

SCUM will couple-bust—barge into mixed (male-female) couples, wherever they are, and bust them up.

SCUM will kill all men who are not in the Men's Auxiliary of SCUM. Men in the Men's Auxiliary are those men who are working diligently to eliminate themselves, men who, regardless of their motives, do good, men who are playing ball with SCUM. A few examples of the men in the Men's Auxiliary are: men who kill men; biological scientists who are working on constructive programs, as opposed to biological warfare; journalists, writers, editors, publishers, and producers who disseminate and promote ideas that will lead to the achievement of SCUM's goals; faggots who, by their shimmering, flaming example, encourage other men to de-man themselves and thereby make themselves relatively inoffensive; men who consistently give things away—money, things, services; men who tell it like it is (so far not one ever has), who put women straight, who reveal the truth about themselves, who give the mindless male females correct sentences to parrot, who tell them a woman's primary goal in life should be to squash the male sex (to aid men in this endeavor SCUM will conduct Turd Sessions, at which every male present will give a speech beginning with the sentence: "I am a turd, a lowly, abject turd," then proceed to list all the ways in which he is. His reward for so doing will be the opportunity to fraternize after the session for a whole, solid hour with the SCUM who will be present. Nice, clean-living male women will be invited to the sessions to help clarify any doubts and misunderstandings they may have about the male sex); makers and promoters of sex books and movies, etc., who are hastening the day when all that will be shown on the screen will be Suck and Fuck (males, like the rats following the Pied Piper, will be lured by Pussy to their doom, will be overcome and submerged by and will eventually drown in the passive flesh that they are); drug pushers and advocates, who are hastening the dropping out of men.

Being in the Men's Auxiliary is a necessary but not a sufficient condition for making SCUM's escape list—it's not enough to do good—to save their worthless asses men must also avoid evil. A few examples of the most obnoxious or harmful types are: rapists, politicians, and all who are in their service (campaigners, members of political parties, etc.); lousy singers and musicians; Chairmen of Boards; Breadwinners; landlords; owners of greasy spoons and restaurants that play Musak; "Great Artists"; cheap pikers and welchers; cops; tycoons; scientists working on death and destruction programs or for private industry (practically all scientists); liars and phonies; disc jockeys; men who intrude themselves in the slightest way on any strange female; real-estate men; stockbrokers; men who speak when they have nothing to say; men who loiter idly on the street and mar the landscape with their presence; double-dealers; flim-flam artists; litterbugs; plagiarizers; men who in the slightest way harm any female; all men in the advertising industry; psychiatrists and clinical psychologists; dishonest writers, journalists, editors, publishers, etc.; censors on both the public and private levels; all members of the armed forces, including draftees (LBJ and McNamara give orders, but service men carry them out) and particularly pilots (if the bomb drops, LBJ won't drop it; a pilot will). In the case of a man whose behavior falls into both the good and bad categories, an overall, subjective evaluation of him will be made to determine if his behavior is, in the balance, good or bad.

It is most tempting to pick off the female "Great Artists," liars and phonies, etc., along with the men, but that would be inexpedient, as it would not be clear to most of the public that the female killed was a male. All women have a fink streak in them, to a greater or lesser degree, but it stems from a lifetime of living among men. Eliminate men and women will shape up. Women are improvable; men are not, although their behavior is. When SCUM gets hot on their asses it'll shape up fast. . . .

SCUM will not picket, demonstrate, march, or strike to attempt to achieve its ends. Such tactics are for nice, genteel ladies who scrupulously take only such action as is guaranteed to be ineffective. In addition, only decent, clean-living, male women, highly trained in submerging themselves in the species, act on a mob basis. SCUM consists of individuals; SCUM is not a mob, a blob. Only as many SCUM will do a job as are needed for the job. Also, SCUM, being cool and selfish, will not subject itself to getting rapped on the head with billy clubs; that's for the nice, "privileged, educated" middle-class ladies with a high regard for the touching faith in the essential goodness of Daddy and policemen. If SCUM ever marches, it will be over the President's stupid, sickening face; if SCUM ever strikes, it will be in the dark with a six-inch blade.

SCUM will always operate on a criminal as opposed to a civil-disobedience basis, that is, as opposed to openly violating the law and going to jail in order to draw attention to an injustice. Such tactics acknowledge the rightness of the overall system and are used only to modify it slightly, change specific laws. SCUM is against the entire system, the very idea of law and government. SCUM is out to destroy the system, not attain certain rights within it. Also, SCUM—always selfish, always cool—will always aim to avoid detection and punishment. SCUM will always be furtive, sneaky, underhanded (although SCUM members will always be known to be such).

Both destruction and killing will be selective and discriminate. SCUM is against half-crazed, indiscriminate riots, with no clear objective in mind, and in which many of your own kind are picked off. SCUM will never instigate, encourage, or participate in riots of any kind or any other form of indiscriminate destruction. SCUM will coolly, furtively, stalk its prey and quietly move in for the kill. Destruction will never be such as to block off routes needed for the transportation of food and other essential supplies, contaminate or cut off the water supply, block streets and traffic to the extent that ambulances can't get through or impede the functioning of hospitals.

SCUM will keep on destroying, looting, fucking-up, and killing until the money-work system no longer exists and automation is completely instituted or until enough women cooperate with SCUM to make violence unnecessary to achieve these goals, that is, until enough women either unwork or quit work, start looting, leave men, and refuse to obey all laws inappropriate to a truly civilized society. Many women will fall into line; but many others, who surrendered long ago to the enemy, who are so adapted to animalism, to maleness, that they like restrictions and restraints, don't know what to do with freedom, will continue to be toadies and doormats, just as peasants in rice paddies remain peasants in rice paddies as one regime topples another. A few of the more volatile will whimper and sulk and throw their toys and dishrags on the floor, but SCUM will continue to steamroller over them.

A completely automated society can be accomplished very simply and quickly once there is a public demand for it. The blueprints for it are already in existence, and its construction will only take a few weeks with millions of people working at it. Even though off the money system, everyone will be most happy to pitch in and get the automated society built; it will make the beginning of a fantastic new era, and there will be a celebration atmosphcrc accompanying the construction. The elimination of money and the complete institution of automation are basic to all other SCUM reforms; without these two the others can't take place; with them the others will take place very rapidly. The government will automatically collapse. With complete automation it will be possible for every woman to vote directly on every issue by means of an electronic voting machine in her house. Since the government is occupied almost entirely with regulating economic affairs and legislating against purely private matters, the elimination of money and with it the elimination of males who wish to legislate "morality" will mean that there will be practically no issues to vote on.

After the elimination of money there will be no further need to kill men; they will be stripped of the only power they have over psychologically-independent females. They will be able to impose themselves only on the doormats, who like to be imposed on. The rest of the women will be busy solving the few remaining unsolved problems before planning their agenda for eternity and Utopia—completely revamping educational programs so that millions of women can be trained within a few months for high-level intellectual work that now requires years of training (this can be done very easily once our educational goal is to educate and not to perpetuate an academic and intellectual elite); solving the problems of disease and old age and death and completely redesigning our cities and living quarters. Many women will for awhile continue to think they dig men, but as they become absorbed in their projects, they will eventually come to see the utter uselessness and banality of the male.

The few remaining men can exist out their puny days dropped out on drugs or strutting around in drag or passively watching the high-powered female in action, fulfilling themselves as spectators, vicarious livers,* or breeding in the cow pasture with the toadies, or they can go off to the nearest friendly suicide center where they will be quietly, quickly, and painlessly gassed to death.

Prior to the institution of automation, to the replacement of males by machines, the male should be of use to the female, wait on her, cater to her slightest whim, obey her every command, be totally subservient to her, exist in perfect obedience to her will, as opposed to the completely warped, degenerate situation we have now of men not only not existing at all, cluttering up the world with their ignominious presence, but being pandered to and groveled before by the mass of females, millions of women piously worship-

ping before the Golden Calf, the dog leading the master on the leash, when in fact the male, short of being a drag queen, is least miserable when his dogginess is recognized— no unrealistic emotional demands are made of him and the completely together female is calling the shots. Rational men want to be squashed, stepped on, crushed, and crunched, treated as the curs, the filth that they are, have their repulsiveness confirmed.

The sick, irrational men, those who attempt to defend themselves against their disgustingness, when they see SCUM barreling down on them, will cling in terror to Big Mama with her Big Bouncy Boobies, but Boobies won't protect them against SCUM; Big Mama will be clinging to Big Daddy, who will be in the corner shitting in his forceful, dynamic pants. Men who are rational, however, won't kick or struggle or raise a distressing fuss, but will just sit back, relax, enjoy the show, and ride the waves to their demise.

45

Jayne West

Are Men Really the Enemy? (1970)

Please use a No. 2 lead ~~penis~~ pencil when taking this test. Look only at your own paper except in an emergency. No talking, gum chewing, swearing, or primping during the test. In case of fire or nuclear attack, the above rules will be suspended. You are now ready to begin. Don't. We'll tell you when to start. You may begin in exactly a few minutes.

TRUE OR FALSE

1. _____ Woman's work is never done.
2. _____ You can't tell a book by its cover.
3. _____ Housework can be fun.
4. _____ Women make the best mothers.

From *Rat: Subterranean News*, February 6, 1970.

---

*It will be electronically possible for him to tune in to any specific female he wants to and follow in detail her every movement. The females will kindly, obligingly consent to this, as it won't hurt them in the slightest and it is a marvelously kind and humane way to treat their unfortunate handicapped fellow beings.

5. _____ A female dog is referred to as a bitch.

6. _____ One of the more degrading terms that can be applied to a man is "son of a bitch."

7. _____ The discovery that she is castrated is a turning point in a girl's life. (Freud)

8. _____ Life is a bowl of cherries.

9. _____ A little loving goes a long way.

10. _____ The ten most wanted men are men.

11. _____ The opposite of a tomboy is sissy.

12. _____ Beauty is as beauty does.

13. _____ Intelligent women are often ugly.

14. _____ The best chefs in the world are men.

15. _____ A girl should find out what a man's interests are and learn about them so as to have more pleasant conversations with him.

16. _____ I can do a pushup.

17. _____ When the blank says check one M_F_, I do so without hesitation or contemplation.

18. _____ Some of the finest athletes in the world are women.

19. _____ Sen. Margaret Chase Smith could have been President if she had only remained in the race.

20. _____ Women when angered are capable of extreme forms of violence and insanity.

21. _____ I find it very convenient to carry a purse since I haven't any pockets.

22. _____ The way to a man's heart is through his stomach.

23. _____ *Flighty* is often used when referring to men.

24. _____ A permanent isn't really.

25. _____ Gentlemen prefer blondes.

26. _____ I think that it was certainly necessary that the Mormons had many wives.

27. _____ I often envy the convenience men enjoy in regard to urination.

28. _____ Women are made not born.

MULTIPLE CHOICE

1. Most rapes are committed by
   a. women
   b. children
   c. men (perverts)
   d. I am unable to distinguish rape from ordinary sexual relations.

2. When I am yelled at on the street I am
   a. flattered
   b. annoyed
   c. astonished
   d. sure I have been recognized

3. When I am yelled at on the street I respond by
   a. lowering my head and walking quicker
   b. smiling sweetly and nodding
   c. addressing myself to the specific content of the yeller and applying appropriately
   d. pretending that it was not I who was yelled at and that I am not in that place and that he is not real and I am not real and thus simply extracting myself from the situation.

4. Which of these things do you prefer to be called?
   a. lady
   b. woman
   c. female
   d. girl
   e. none of the above

5. The reason I keep my legs together when sitting is
   a. some of my underwear has holes in it
   b. my legs get cold if I don't
   c. my mother always told me to and it's a hard to break habit
   d. I like to keep my privates private

6. When I was a little girl I wanted to be a
   a. nurse
   b. cowgirl
   c. teacher
   d. secretary
   e. boy

7. If I had a baby girl, I would be
   a. disappointed
   b. I wouldn't care as long as it was healthy

c. burdened

d. quite annoyed with the Pill

8. When I play games or sports with a man

a. I let him win

b. He always beats me

c. I try to be athletic and healthy so he will play with me again

d. I just play the best I can and don't worry about the outcome

9. Which of the following things can a man do better than a woman?

a. cook

b. sew

c. masturbate

d. all of the above

10. If I could do away with anything I wanted, the first thing I would do away with is

a. the family

b. the state

c. private property

d. menstrual periods

e. all the above

DRAW A MAN

Fill the Blank.

1. _____ is never _____

2. Make a list of famous women who are not known by Mrs. _____

3. My most embarrassing moment was when _____

4. My least embarrassing moment was when _____

5. In the Orthodox Jewish worship it is said by men: "Thank God that I was not born a _____

MATCHING

a. shorts   ___ 1. boy or girl who plays like a girl

b. panties   ___ 2. unmarried woman

c. bachelor   ___ 3. woman who is somewhat free sexually

d. old maid   ___ 4. men's underwear

e. sissy   ___ 5. unmarried man

f. tomboy   ___ 6. women's underwear

w. three   ___ 7. man who is free sexually

t. unlimited   ___ 8. number of dribbles allowed in girl's basketball

q. playboy   ___ 9. man who sheds tears

h. compassionate ___10. number of dribbles allowed in men's basketball

u. whining   ___11. woman who sheds tears

                 ___12. boy who plays like a girl

ESSAY

1. Discuss the variations in tone possible when asking a male druggist this question: "Do you have Tampax Super?"

2. Discuss the population distribution along sexual lines were parents able to determine the sex of their offspring.

3. Discuss your motive for taking this test.

4. Discuss how a woman can have her cake and eat it too.

5. Discuss anything you want.

6. Erase all marks from this paper (except your responses) and pass the paper up to the person to your left. If there is no one on your left, walk to the center aisle and place your paper on the floor and sit upon it. Anyone doing anything that strange is certain to be noticed and helped.

GOOD LUCK! YOU HAVE BEEN A GOOD TESTER
AND THAT IS NOT NOTHING

46

PAMELA KEARON

Man-Hating (1970)

The question of man-hating among radical women seems like the most difficult one to get up a serious discussion on. And you really feel

From *Notes from the Second Year*, 1970.

crummy dragging it all out again only to encounter the raised eyebrows, the surprised expressions, voices vibrating with moral indignation; or worse yet, some cute joke and a round of hearty chuckles—completely destroying your point. But hold on! Before you get indignant, before you make your little joke, allow me to try to convince you that man-hating is a valid and vital issue.

Hatred is certainly an observable human fact. And since women are human—not a link between man and the ape—not some innocuous, shadowy, fairy-tale version of the Man—since this is so, hatred, hostility and resentment probably exist somehow in us. And, further, since many of us have already come to the conclusions of feminism—that equal status and opportunity with the male is necessary to our full human existence—the realization of our past and continued subjugation has most likely aroused in us some sentiment resembling hatred. Now, each of us, in denying our hatred and explaining our astonishing magnanimity, relies upon some common argument. Among the most common:

Argumentum ad Sexus:

"Men and women are made for each other sexually. I am perfectly 'normal.' Therefore, I must certainly love men."

Answer:

Many men engage in sexual intercourse, often extensively, even marry, while yet hating women. These men are called misogynists. Now, there is no shame in being a misogynist. It is a perfectly respectable attitude. Our whole society (including too many of the women in it) hates women. Perhaps we need a Latin or Green derivative in place of "man-hating" to make the perfect symmetry of the two attitudes more obvious.[1]

Argumentum ad Superioritus:

"Hate man? No! Definitely not! We must understand them; they depend upon us to show them how to love."

Answer:

This argument is based upon the "Natural Superiority of Women."[2] We are congenitally incapable of hatred. It is our mysterious XX chromosomal structure. Failing to "understand" the man is a perversion of our second nature. Brushing aside forever the utterly unprovable fiction of our second nature, and speaking purely from personal experience, it would seem, on the whole, that people do not react to oppression with Love. I mean the poison seeps out somehow. Sometimes aggressively on those in an even meaner position; sometimes taking the form of an all-pervading and impotent resentment—a petty and spiteful attitude. When women take their hatred out on others, those others are likely to be other women, particularly their own daughters. In doing so they reconcile their own impulse for an object of hate with the demands of an authoritarian system which requires all hate and spite to be directed downward, while respect and "understanding" are reserved for higher-ups, thus keeping nearly everyone supplied with pre-ordained and relatively powerless victims.

Anyway, all arguments which tend to suppress the recognition of man-hating in our midst are reducible to this: *fear*. Man-hating is a subversive and therefore dangerous sentiment. Men, who control definition, have made of it a disgusting perversion. We have been unable to get out from under their definition. I've been at meetings where women actually left because they thought that "man-haters" were on the loose. One woman talked to me in awe and disgust about a woman who she felt had made an anti-male statement at a meeting. It has been the cause of a deep rift within Women's Liberation. It is a vital issue because it involves

---

1. It is interesting that while the Greeks had a word for both man-hating and woman-hating, only the latter has been anglicized and incorporated into English—A likely word would be "misandry."

2. From the book of that title by Ashley Montague.

ultimately the way we feel about ourselves, and how far we are willing to go in our own behalf.

Hatred and Man-Hating

There is no dearth of hatred in the world, I agree. But the thing is, people keep on hating the wrong people. For instance, a lot of people apparently believe that we must fight to preserve our freedom against little Vietnam. Whites, just now stepping out of poverty themselves, arm against the "menace" of the Poor and the Blacks. Upper-middle-class radical snobs despise the class of Whites just beneath them. And men hate women. Our hatred is such a shoddy and confused emotion. We indulge in the most circuitous and illogical prejudices. We have never given the idea of hating someone who has actually done something hateful to us a chance. Oh, I know we ought to hate the sin and love the sinner. But too often we end up loving the sinner and hating his victim (as when one woman seeing another put down, or hearing about her unhappy affair, calls it masochism and that's the end of it).

If hatred exists (and we know it does), let it be of a robust variety. If it is a choice between woman-hating and man-hating, let it be the latter. Let us resolve to respond immediately and directly to injury instead of taking it all out on a more likely victim. It is a difficult stance because it requires a fidelity to what is real in us and neither innocuous nor attractive to oppressors, to that part of you which turned you on to feminism in the first place. That part which is really human and cannot submit.

47

Dana Densmore

Who Is Saying Men Are the Enemy? (1970)

The question "Are men the enemy?" has always struck me as a curious one.

From *The Female State*, April 1970.

If enemies are perceived as that force against which one does battle and against whom (having killed off sufficient numbers) one wins, the concept is obviously inappropriate.

It is clear to me that in its form "I object to your attitude that men are the enemy" the issue is a dishonest one: it is an attempted smear or a defensive counterattack against the force of our analysis (whether delivered by frightened men or frightened women).

It makes it appear that if we do anything but embrace all men, whatever their individual attitude, as our friends and allies, treating them as allies however they treat us, if we so much as speak of men generally as "our oppressors," then it must be that we regard them as "enemies" in the sense of an opponent so all-powerful and implacable that he must be killed in order to be neutralized.

Of course we couldn't kill off all men if we wanted to, but the point is that it isn't necessary and we all know it. It is the situation men and women find themselves in, the structures of society and the attitudes of women, that make it *possible* for men to oppress.

Given power and privileges, told by society that these are not only legitimate but the essence of his manhood, it is not surprising that a man should accept an oppressor's role. But if women refused to cooperate, and if they demanded changes in the structures, institutions and attitudes of society, then men, whatever their desires, could not and therefore would not oppress women.

An industrialist, seeking to maximize profits, might wish to pay his human labor subsistence wages rather than minimum legal or contract-negotiated wages. But laws, unions, and attitudes of the society about social justice together prevent him from doing so. The same would apply to men's oppression of women. It could become illegal, impossible, and unfashionable. And it will.

The distinction is often made in the female liberation movement between an "enemy" and an "oppressor." The real enemy, I think we all agree, is sexism and male supremacy; a set of attitudes held by men and women and institutionalized in our society (and in all societies throughout history).

The origin of these attitudes and institutions is immaterial. Whether they were instituted by men acting out of fear of women or by society as a whole for the survival of the species is irrelevant. Whether it was some kind of "plot" or "just the way things evolved" need not concern us. All we care about are the conditions right now, because it is right now that we propose to change. If traditional attitudes are inappropriate or unjust today in our experience, then they must be replaced.

I think we will learn more about the origins of sexism, and what role men will play in the revolution that will destroy it, by watching how men deal with our call for liberation than by setting up *a priori* categories of enemy and ally.

Men clearly function as oppressors in a sexist society. But it may be just the situation, something they can't help. It may be because women permit and even encourage such oppression. But if that is the case, and men are innocent and well-meaning, then we will see that demonstrated in their response to our rejection of our role as victim and our criticism of the institutions that cast men into the role of oppressor.

They will probably be surprised at first, showing the signs of being forced to think completely new thoughts (e.g., maybe women *are* just smart, maybe it's *not* appropriate for them to live for "their man," etc.). But, given encouragement, education, and demonstrations of how strongly we feel, they will declare themselves our allies.

They will not continue to ridicule us (if indeed they ever did), they will not play dumb and demand that the same thing be explained over and over as if we had never said a word to them, they will not set *themselves* up as an "enemy." They will show respect for us as persons and for our cause as appropriate and legitimate.

In fact it turns out that men sort themselves out into allies and "enemy."

A man who senses himself to be our "enemy" will say certain things that reveal his attitude. One standard approach of the less subtle school is "Why do you want to kill off all the men?"

This man may be just attempting to smear you or the movement. He may even couch it in pseudo-sympathetic terms such as "I agree with you completely, but why do you want to kill off all the men?" This is to alarm all people standing around and to let you know what sort of image the movement has (or will have when he gets through shooting off his mouth).

Or, he may just be making a bid for attention. You've long since given up discussing these issues with men out of acute boredom, but he knows that by throwing in something like this he can scare you into defending your image, into protesting that you do *not* want to kill off all the men. Once his foot is in the door, he can trap you into a long conversation about the merits of the movement and give you a great deal of unsolicited advice about how you should really be proceeding.

But sometimes this statement is made honestly, that is, out of an honest fear. This sort of man reveals his sense of his own enmity just as much as the others. What he means is: "I will fight to the death to maintain my privileges and my power; if you intend to take them away from me you will have to kill me."

Another ploy, a little more subtle, is "Why do you want to get rid of sex?" Again, this may be a smear, a bid for attention, or an honest fear.

When it is an honestly felt fear, what he means is: "I cannot conceive of sex, cannot be sexually interested in a woman, unless I am in a superior-to-inferior, active-to-passive, aggressor-to-victim relationship with her. If you are going to insist that we must approach each other as equals you will have destroyed sex and you might as well demand permanent celibacy."

Such men set themselves up as enemies by their actions and attitudes, but still it is inappropriate to *us* to conceive of them as such.

They are not enemies. They are irrelevant. And they are foolish, because they are going to lose in the end anyway, and they have passed up their chance to be heroes.

If a man with whom we are involved emotionally acts that way, naturally we will leave him, not to punish him or strike back at him, but because we have important things to do and he is a drag (or worse). But our work is with ourselves, with other women, and with society as a whole, with the established, institutionalized attitudes of society.

It is demoralizing, self-defeating, and ultimately boring to try to convert individual men who are determined to hold on to their power (and a liberal man who grants *almost* everything but is willing to fight viciously for the last 2% of superiority can be even more dangerous than the man who won't give at all).

And as far as *killing* the men—there are so many self-styled enemies that the disposal of the bodies alone would be a national problem, not to mention the problem of "womanning" the slaughter houses when there are so many more interesting things to do in a world women are just discovering. It would be quite impractical.

Fortunately, it is not necessary either to convert or to kill all the would-be oppressors, however ready they appear to be to defend their honer with their lives. A majority can be oppressed by a minority only with the assent of the victim, the belief by the victim that she is inferior, that it is appropriate that she be oppressed.

If the minds of the women are freed from these chains, no man will be able to oppress any woman. No man can, even now, in an individual relationship; all the woman has to do is walk out on him. And ironically enough, that is exactly what would force the men to shape up fastest. Not very many men could tolerate being deserted, especially over a political issue. And all that's needed is for the woman to learn enough respect for herself to be unwilling to live with a man who treats her with contempt.

Men are not our "enemies" and we should refuse to play "enemy" games with them. If they

ridicule us or try to smear us or isolate us, we must laugh and walk out. "Winning rounds" with individual men will not bring our final victory closer and cannot change contempt and terror into a generous respect. Challenges by individual women to individual men have always been met the same way; threats, ridicule, smears, repression. These are the prescribed ways for men to defend their "manhood" against "castrating females."

Only the march of the whole movement can force the deep re-evaluation that will enable such men to adjust to the reality of women as people and learn to deal in an adult way with their fears and insecurities.

48

Susan Pascalé, Rachel Moon, and Leslie B. Tanner

Karate as Self-Defense for Women (1970)

Women are attacked, beaten and raped every day. By Men. Women are afraid to walk certain streets after dark, and even afraid to walk into buildings where they live. It's about time that we as Women get strong in order to defend ourselves! Two of us (ages 29 and 43) and three children decided to learn Karate. We went to watch a class before signing up and if we hadn't been so determined, the class (consisting of about 25 frighteningly strong men) would have scared us into quitting before we started. We had yet to learn how really weak we were!

One reason for taking Karate, other than strictly learning self-defense, was a matter of health—women seem to smoke more than men, and certainly we never give our bodies physical exercise except for cleaning house, chasing kids and fucking. Both of us smoked too much and hadn't moved in over ten years. Another reason for one of us getting in to Karate was the fact that she has 3 children and the fam-

From *Women: A Journal of Liberation*, Winter 1970.

ily structure being what it is, we had hopes that if she and her children took Karate together it might relieve some of the emotional bull-shit that goes on, not only between children but also between the mother and the children.

In the middle of August the five of us (two women, one girl aged 15, and two boys, ages 11 and 6) started classes.

PSYCHOLOGICAL OPPRESSION

When we went to our first class, we huddled in a corner, feeling inferior and somehow as though we were trespassing. The men stood directly in front of the mirrors, totally unselfconscious, to practice. We, after 3 months, are still self-conscious. Interestingly, the 15-year-old girl is not. She has not yet been completely conditioned to be "feminine." We have discussed this among ourselves and feel it must stem from numerous causes: We are conditioned to see ourselves other than as a tough puncher—we don't really want to see ourselves looking like that, and yet we do want to. We see our little fists in the mirror, and they look like shit. We punch with our left hand, and it looks and feels like a piece of spaghetti. We are totally unaccustomed to looking in the mirror, contemplating our own gorgeous muscles. It makes us feel like fools. We are conditioned to feel that what we're doing is unfeminine. We have been taught to be passive all our lives— even for the two of us, who were sportswomen and dancers, the punching is just a little too much.

A corollary of this is falling into "female" patterns as a sort of defense against feeling inadequate. When being instructed in small groups, or working out with each other, we often start laughing, playing around and not really doing it seriously. This attitude has become particularly noticeable now that we have begun, after 3 months, to learn Komite (or free fighting). Up to this time, we have really been punching air, and not engaging in actual combat. This is tremendously difficult: not only do we laugh as a protective mechanism, but we

also tend to do the traditional womanly thing of backing away and covering our faces. It is our first instinct not to fight back.

The trouble is, even now, after actually learning how to punch, we don't really want to punch at men. The first thing we think about is: "But I don't want to hurt him." Then we realize that this is really a traditional feminine cover-up for the truth which is that we are afraid of men. Women have always known that to hit a man seriously means risking getting killed. We have acknowledged these "feminine attributes" to ourselves and we try every day to overcome them. It is clear that the longer our attitudes persist, the less we learn.

MALE CHAUVINISM IN THE DOJO, OR "WE ARE ALL BROTHERS HERE"

Non-tricky, Obvious Forms of Male Chauvinism

Our experiences, as Women, at the Dojo (the place where you learn and practice Karate) have shown us how very deep and oppressive the attitudes of men are towards Women. We have been tolerated to the point that we have sometimes felt like the "Invisible Woman." The men treat us with a patronizing air that seems to say they wish we weren't there.

The first and most obvious example of discrimination is that women are charged only half price. We don't know the actual reason for this, perhaps it's because we're considered only half-persons, or because the teacher feels guilty because he figures we'll never learn Karate anyway. We decided to take advantage of this form of oppression, and have not yet challenged it.

Secondly, the Sensei (Teacher) originally addressed the class as "Gentlemen." We let this pass for a couple of days, thinking it would take him a lesson or two to get used to us. But he continued and we confronted him, stating that we didn't care how he wished to address us, just as long as our existence was recognized, either as "ladies" with "gentlemen," or as "women" with "men," or just part of "everybody." The Sensei admitted his oversight and agreed to make amends.

Throughout the next week he continued to address everyone as "gentlemen," and we confronted him again, calling him "Mrs." and explaining that if he didn't like that, we didn't like being called "gentlemen." He apologized and said he would stop it. In the next few lessons he occasionally let one or two "gentlemen" slip but usually no more than once per lesson.

Then, quite recently, Sensei got angry at the class and let loose a loud: "Don't punch like that. It's too weak. You're punching like girls!" (Obviously the worst insult that can be given to a man.) At one time, we probably wouldn't have been insulted by this, thinking that he couldn't possibly mean us. The 15-year-old girl didn't understand our anger: we explained that any insult toward women is an insult to *us*, since we *are*, in fact, women.

Immediately after class we went to the Sensei with the words, "Remember, don't punch like a . . . " which he interrupted with, "Yes, I know, I'm sorry. I realized the minute I said it." We replied, "If women punch weak, it's precisely because of such male attitudes."

Finally, after three and a half months of attending the Dojo four to six times a week, a breakthrough came at least on this issue. Sensei let a "gentlemen" slip from his mouth and after a slight hesitation, followed it with "and ladies." Whether this will remain a permanent feature in the Dojo remains to be seen, but because two more women will soon be in our class, it probably will. Our feeling has been that we may not be able to change these men's attitudes, but at least we don't have to hear them. This much at least is relatively easy to win.

Tricky, Unobvious Forms of Male Chauvinism

Much more difficult to identify, and hence to combat, is the deep-seated, unobvious male chauvinism in the Dojo. While knowing that close to 100 percent of the men have traditional attitudes, this is complicated, first, by the fact that the Karate codes says that women should be trained on an equal basis with men.

In Karate no distinctions are made in instruction between men and women. We are expected to do everything the men do: to learn the positions as fast and to do them as well. We have been rewarded on that assumption. We have advanced in rank beyond some men who were ahead of us when we started. (We are now advanced white belts and by December we should have our green belts.) It seems to be simply a matter of time spent working in the Dojo. We can say categorically that it is possible to participate in a mixed Dojo on physical considerations. Women entering a male Dojo should watch that they are not discriminated against by having less demanded of them. Women taking Karate with an all women's group should check their instruction against all-male or mixed classes.

The only real difficulty we had was with push-ups. None of us could do more than one or two, when we started. We are now doing fourteen or sixteen, at least. Twenty are done in every class and we are expected to work up to this number. If anyone tells you that Women should not do push-ups, you can tell them that you certainly should and will. Or just tell them they're full of shit.

Second, male chauvinism is masked by the fact that the code of the Dojo is that everyone be treated with great respect and humility, regardless of rank. The slogan is: "We are all brothers." We are treated *very politely*, formally and respectfully. In terms of human relationships, however, we are avoided as much as possible because the Sensei and all the other men in the Dojo know how to treat us only in the traditional sense, i.e. as sex objects. Since we have not allowed ourselves to be treated as sex objects, we are not "women" in their eyes. And obviously we are not brothers. Hence we are in some undefined, neuter area. We are INVISIBLE!

Third, it is very difficult to figure out whether we are being treated in a certain manner because we are beginners (and weak) or because we are women. The men have tried to avoid all physical contact with us. It's a mindblower! When we need a partner for sit-ups (which means entangling our legs with theirs), they immediately try to find someone other than one of us, using the excuse (when questioned directly) that we're too light-weight or too weak. When Sensei makes the rounds to test our "stance," by touching the "butt" and thigh muscles, he just doesn't touch ours. After three months he finally did touch the 15-year-old's "butt," but he still avoids us older women like the plague. It seems clear that 25-year-old Sensei cannot see us as other than females who can be touched for one purpose and one purpose only.

Finally, the actual free-fighting exercise we do is ridiculous. One man refused to make any contact at all, and stayed at least five feet away, punching at the air. Nobody can learn to fight if they're invisible. The rationale that's given is that we're still too weak to defend ourselves. One male member of the Dojo told us that a lot of the men take us as a sort of joke, and that we must be very careful, for if we think we'll "show them" by really giving them some good strong punches, they then might retaliate far beyond what we can handle at this stage and really beat us up badly. He advised playing it soft until we could handle rough dealing. This is an obvious case of oppression. Men think we're a joke until we prove otherwise, at which point they're out to demolish us.

We seem to have only scratched the surface of the male chauvinism in the Dojo. This is so partly because we never intended to make the Dojo an area of attack. It is very difficult to carry on any fight in the Dojo because of the traditional authoritarianism which we accepted in order to get our training. Chauvinist attitudes have been attacked only when *blatant* and where we felt directly offended. We don't know what changes the future will bring. As we get stronger and more confident, issues of chauvinism which are murky to us now because of our own insecurities, will become clear, and may necessitate a real fight. The men probably will do anything (within reason) to protect the traditional "brotherhood" of the Dojo.

POSITIVE ASPECTS AND IMPLICATIONS FOR WOMEN'S LIBERATION

1. Karate has indeed affected the attitude the children have towards each other, and toward their mother. They no longer fight and throw sneak punches at each other the way they used to, but use Karate, bowing to each other, and being courteous and thoughtful of each other. The 15-year-old girl is getting very strong and is feeling confident enough to walk city streets alone, after dark. Let her speak for herself:

"There are several reasons why I wanted to learn the art of self-defense. The two most important reasons were 1) in the society we live in today I feel a great need for women to be strong, 2) karate and kata (dance forms) are really most beautiful and exciting. In the very beginning I felt inhibited, but not because I am a woman (as did my mother and friend). It was because being a white belt in a dojo you get treated like "brand new beginners." I didn't know that much about karate, but as the months passed I began to feel confident. At the end of 3 months I was put up against men to do free fighting. I felt inferior again, basically because I had never fought before; also again it was the feeling of low rank and less experience. All in all, I feel I am getting stronger, and I feel all women should get strong and learn to fight."

2. Karate has made us feel much healthier and stronger than we were before (we've even cut our smoking in half). Stronger hands and arms enable us to do things we usually rely on men to do, such as carrying heavy loads from the store.

3. Karate gets us out of the house 3 nights (or days) a week, and because we like it, it becomes something we'll do *no matter what*. It's good for freeing us from household chores/waiting around for a man to call/ waiting around for the man to come home/waiting around because the man *is* home/creating a good reason why a man must fit his schedule into ours, i.e. see us when *we're*

available/or take care of his own children three nights a week!

4. Karate has mentally increased our confidence in ourselves as human beings. Simone De Beauvoir says, "Not to have confidence in one's body is to lose confidence in oneself" (*The Second Sex*, p. 310). As a result of Karate, we are gaining confidence in our bodies and are going through some fantastic changes in terms of our feelings of self-worth. Our confidence has increased not only in confrontations with "dirty-old-men" in the streets, but in non-physical confrontations with our own men and society in general. We do feel as though we have more control over our own lives because of our new potential physical power.

5. After participating in a few Women's Liberation actions, we see more clearly than ever, the need for women to get strong. We demonstrated against blatant sexual exploitation of women in front of the "Electric Circus" on the Lower East Side, New York City, and we almost went sprawling several times as people tried to trip us. We wished then that we were Black Belts so we could defend ourselves. Recently we helped take over a panel at Cooper Union that was going to discuss Abortion—a panel consisting of four men! The men gave up the stage very quickly to the women, but shortly after came back on stage and slowly removed four mikes (that were switched off anyway) from the speakers' table, acting all the time as if no one were there. Invisible again! The men should have been forcibly escorted off the scene. We were not strong enough to confront them and make them meet our demands.

Women's Liberation has a long tough political fight before it, and our oppression, which is ultimately maintained by force, can only be overcome by force. Women will be needed as fighters.

Finally, Simone De Beauvoir says that "Violence is the authentic proof of each one's loyalty to himself, to his passions, to his own will; radically to deny this is to deny oneself any objective truth, it is to wall oneself up in an ab-

stract subjectivity; anger or revolt that does not get into the muscles remains a figment of the imagination. It is a profound frustration not to be able to register one's feelings upon the fact of the world." This we agree with completely. But she continues, "It remains true that her physical weakness does not permit woman to learn the lessons of violence." This we categorically reject. We, once as physically weak as any average female, *are* learning the lessons of violence, and learning them well. We strongly recommend that anyone else who is interested do the same.

Women must get strong!

49

SWITCHBORED

Poems and Articles (1969)

AS I SIT HERE SHARPENING PENCILS

As I sit here sharpening pencils,
I wonder about the world.
And if they know what I'm doing—
Or has my mind curled?

I'm 18 years old
With a diploma of academic degree
I wish I knew that it would make
A human pencil sharpener of me.

I wonder if anybody in the company knows
    that a girl sharpens pencils for them
And not just a few, but hundreds of them.

I wonder if this job was especially designed for
    me
Or could it be
I fell out of a tree.

Did Mrs. Larson make this job or Mrs. Bauer
    or maybe Mr. Romnes
Somebody has to know
Because I really have to see
That people feel this has to be done for them.

From *Switchbored*, August 1969.

Something they can do themselves
Because of their executive laziness
A newly created shit job it helps.

Why can't people sharpen their own pencils?
But maybe then, always having sharpened
    pencils
Is the "businesslike" way.

Anyway, I suffer from it
But automation helps a bit
Maybe I'm the human pencil holder
But the sharpener's electric.

Have one in every office
Sharpen your own if you need
Because of your not doing this
Someone's losing her dignity.

GRAVEYARD MEETING

Monday, 5:00 P.M., August 10 . . . was the first meeting of AT&T W.I.T.C.H. (WOMEN INCENSED AT TELEPHONE COMPANY HARASSMENT).

About 25 women attended, at the graveyard, across from 195 B'way. The meeting was interrupted when the priest asked us why we were there. He said, "I know this is a meeting. I insist you tell me what you are talking about. Or I'll have to ask you to leave." We refused, because he had no right to know what we were talking about, and also that we were all children of God and it was our right to stay there since it wasn't closing time and we weren't causing anyone inconvenience. The priest then threatened to call the police.

We then got into an argument about who does the church belong to, but we left. By the priest's questions, it was obvious that he was contacted by AT&T who told him to get rid of us. The AT&T bosses are scared when "their" workers get together. We left because we wanted to talk to each other more than hassle the police.

We went to City Hall Park and discussed many topics such as the need for organizations of clerical workers, the psychological training

our supervisors get in how to manipulate us, sticking together in work situations, low wages eaten up by inflation, being asked to dress for the men to get a higher position (a form of prostitution). The most important thing we discussed was our problems as women, and how to start relating to each other as women.

Our next meeting will be next Monday, August 25, right after work at City Hall Park (left side), Park Place & Broadway.

Note: There were no spies or supervisors present. There is no need of fear. We all talked as women, and *we* don't have to fear that.

WOMEN ARE GETTING TOGETHER ALL OVER THE WORLD

All our lives, we have been taught that women are a little weaker, a little dumber, a little less serious, a little less able to take care of themselves than men. Now suddenly all over the world, women have stopped accepting those old myths and started to get together with their sisters and to fight for freedom and equality. Why have things changed?

Because working people everywhere have begun to question and resist the rich and powerful people who make decisions for everyone else. People are tired of being pushed around.

High school kids are fighting against the stupid rules and robot education that prepare them to be pushed around in the army—or at AT&T. Black people are tired of getting the worst houses, the worst education, and the worst jobs and have been getting together to force this country to change so they can have decent lives. In Vietnam, the people have been together for years, slowly winning their independence against the biggest military machine in the world. And the gears of the machine, the GI's, are getting fed up too and resisting the big brass and the government that force them to kill and be killed so big companies like AT&T can continue to make billions of dollars in defense contracts. And we workers at AT&T are starting to get together too because while AT&T is making all that money and people pay higher and higher phone bills, our salaries don't even keep up with the rising cost of living and they keep trying to get more work out of us.

And more and more, women have been part of all these struggles and through them have begun to refuse to be kept down by all the old myths about women. They found that they could fight as well as men and that the men were forced to respect them and take them seriously. In black communities, welfare mothers have demanded the right to raise healthy children under safe and decent conditions. At Pan Am, 8,000 women clerical workers went on strike and won salary increases of more than 30%. In a community college in Detroit, nine women barricaded the doors of a classroom and talked to the students about the things that are going on in the world that they never tell you about in school—about people fighting for their freedom around the world, and about how women are kept down and need to join the struggle. When some man tried to call the cops, the women beat him up.

In Vietnam, the women who were fighting against the U.S. troops had to learn to do everything for themselves—to grow the rice and to defend their homes.

We *are* strong. We are through hiding our women's strength behind girly masks. We *can* turn the world around. And we will not be afraid because we will give strength to each other.

THE WORST THING THAT EVER HAPPENED TO ME

The worst thing that ever
Happened to me
I got a job at
AT&T.

Took a written test that was easy
Typing was bad
But after working
I got very mad.

The job is degrading
And such a bore

And if I question
They say "there is the door."

Never question service
Is what they say to me
But I'm sorry when it
Comes to slavery.

They call you "girl"
They overwork you
But we are women
Who won't be fooled.

By all the garbage
They hand to us
We refuse to take it
And we're gonna fuss.

So if you're tired, women
Of all this don't bitch
Just come and join us
AT&T W.I.T.C.H.

50

Pat Mainardi

The Politics of Housework (1968 / 1970)

> *Though women do not complain of the power of husbands, each complains of her own husband, or of the husbands of her friends. It is the same in all other cases of servitude; at least in the commencement of the emancipatory movement. The serfs did not at first complain of the power of the lords, but only of their tyranny.*
>
> —John Stuart Mill,
> *On the Subjection of Women*

Liberated women—very different from Women's Liberation! The first signals all kinds of goodies, to warm the hearts (not to mention other parts) of the most radical men. The other signals—HOUSEWORK. The first brings sex

From *Notes from the Second Year*, 1970.

without marriage, sex before marriage, cozy housekeeping arrangements ("I'm living with this chick") and the self-content of knowing that you're not the kind of man who wants a doormat instead of a woman. That will come later. After all, who wants that old commodity anymore, the Standard American Housewife, all husband, home and kids. The New Commodity, the Liberated Woman, has sex a lot and has a Career, preferably something that can be fitted in with the household chores—like dancing, pottery, or painting.

On the other hand is Women's Liberation—and housework. What? You say this is all trivial? Wonderful! That's what I thought. It seemed perfectly reasonable. We both had careers, both had to work a couple of days a week to earn enough to live on, so why shouldn't we share the housework? So I suggested it to my mate and he agreed—most men are too hip to turn you down flat. You're right, he said. It's only fair.

Then an interesting thing happened. I can only explain it by stating that we women have been brainwashed more than even we can imagine. Probably too many years of seeing television women in ecstasy over their shiny waxed floors or breaking down over their dirty shirt collars. Men have no such conditioning. They recognize the essential fact of housework right from the very beginning. Which is that it stinks.

Here's my list of dirty chores: buying groceries, carting them home and putting them away; cooking meals and washing dishes and pots; doing the laundry; digging out the place when things get out of control; washing floors. The list could go on but the sheer necessities are bad enough. All of us have to do these things, or get someone else to do them for us. The longer my husband contemplated these chores, the more repulsed he became, and so proceeded the change from the normally sweet considerate Dr. Jekyll into the crafty Mr. Hyde who would stop at nothing to avoid the horrors of—housework. As he felt himself backed into a corner laden with dirty dishes, brooms, mops

and reeking garbage, his front teeth grew longer and pointier, his fingernails haggled and his eyes grew wild. Housework trivial? Not on your life! Just try to share the burden.

So ensued a dialogue that's been going on for several years. Here are some of the high points:

"I don't mind sharing the housework, but I don't do it very well. We should each do the things we're best at." MEANING: Unfortunately I'm no good at things like washing dishes or cooking. What I do best is a little light carpentry, changing light bulbs, moving furniture (how often do *you* move furniture? ALSO MEANING: Historically the lower classes (black men and us) have had hundreds of years experience doing menial jobs. It would be a waste of manpower to train someone else to do them now. ALSO MEANING: I don't like the dull stupid boring jobs, so you should do them.

"I don't mind sharing the work, but you'll have to show me how to do it." MEANING: I ask a lot of questions and you'll have to show me everything every time I do it because I don't remember so good. Also don't try to sit down and read while I'm doing my jobs because I'm going to annoy the hell out of you until it's easier to do them yourself.

"We used to be so happy!" (Said whenever it was his turn to do something.) MEANING: I used to be so happy. MEANING: Life without housework is bliss. No quarrel here. Perfect Agreement.

"We have different standards, and why should I have to work to your standards? That's unfair." MEANING: If I begin to get bugged by the dirt and crap I will say, "this place sure is a sty" or "How can anyone live like this?" and wait for your reaction. I know that all women have a sore called "Guilt over a messy house" or "Household work is ultimately my responsibility." I know that men have caused that sore—if anyone visits and the place *is* a sty, they're not going to leave and say, "He sure is a lousy housekeeper." You'll take the rap in any case. I can outwait you. ALSO MEANING: I can provoke innumerable scenes over the housework issue. Eventually doing all the housework yourself will be less painful to you than trying to get me to do half. Or I'll suggest we get a maid. She will do my share of the work. You will do yours. It's woman's work.

"I've got nothing against sharing the housework, but you can't make me do it on your schedule." MEANING: Passive resistance. I'll do it when I damned well please, if at all. If my job is doing dishes, it's easier to do them once a week. If taking out laundry, once a month. If washing the floors, once a year. If you don't like it, do it yourself oftener, and then I won't do it at all.

"I hate it more than you. You don't mind it so much." MEANING: Housework is garbage work. It's the worst crap I've ever done. It's degrading and humiliating for someone of *my* intelligence to do it. But for someone of *your* intelligence. . . .

"Housework is too trivial to even talk about." MEANING: It's even more trivial to do. Housework is beneath my status. My purpose in life is to deal with matters of significance. Yours is to deal with matters of insignificance. You should do the housework.

"This problem of housework is not a man-woman problem. In any relationship between two people one is going to have a stronger personality and dominate." MEANING: That stronger personality had better be *me*.

"In animal societies, wolves, for example, the top animal is usually a male even where he is not chosen for brute strength but on the basis of cunning and intelligence. Isn't that interesting?" MEANING: I have historical, psychological, anthropological and biological justification for keeping you down. How can you ask the top wolf to be equal?

"Women's Liberation isn't really a political movement." MEANING: The Revolution is coming too close to home. ALSO MEANING: I am only interested in how I am oppressed, not how I oppress others. Therefore the war, the draft and the university are political. Women's Liberation is not.

"Man's accomplishments have always depended on getting help from other people, mostly women. What great man would have accomplished what he did if he had to do his own housework?" MEANING: Oppression is built into the system and I, as the white American male, receive the benefits of this system. I don't want to give them up.

Participatory democracy begins at home. If you are planning to implement your politics, there are certain things to remember.

1. He *is* feeling it more than you. He's losing some leisure and you're gaining it. The measure of your oppression is his resistance.

2. A great many American men are not accustomed to doing monotonous repetitive work which never issues in any lasting, let alone important, achievement. This is why they would rather repair a cabinet than wash dishes. If human endeavors are like a pyramid with man's highest achievements at the top, then keeping oneself alive is at the bottom. Men have always had servants (us) to take care of this bottom strata of life while they have confined their efforts to the rarefied upper regions. It is thus ironic when they ask of women—where are your great painters, statesmen, etc. Mme Matisse ran a millinery shop so he could paint. Mrs. Martin Luther King kept his house and raised his babies.

3. It is a traumatizing experience for someone who has always thought of himself as being against any oppression or exploitation of one human being by another to realize that in his daily life he has been accepting and implementing (and benefiting from) this exploitation; that his rationalization is little different from that of the racist who says "Black people don't feel pain" (women don't mind doing the shitwork); and that the oldest form of oppression in history has been the oppression of 50% of the population by the other 50%.

4. Arm yourself with some knowledge of the psychology of oppressed peoples everywhere, and a few facts about the animal kingdom. I admit playing top wolf or who runs the gorillas is silly but as a last resort men bring it up all the time. Talk about bees. If you feel re-

ally hostile bring up the sex life of spiders. They have sex. She bites off his head.

The psychology of oppressed peoples is not silly. Jews, immigrants, black men and all women have employed the same psychological mechanisms to survive; admiring the oppressor, glorifying the oppressor, wanting to be like the oppressor, wanting the oppressor to like them, mostly because the oppressor held all the power.

5. In a sense, all men everywhere are slightly schizoid—divorced from the reality of maintaining life. This makes it easier for them to play games with it. It is almost a cliche that women feel greater grief at sending a son off to a war or losing him to that war because they bore him, suckled him, and raised him. The men who foment those wars did none of those things and have a more superficial estimate of the worth of human life. One hour a day is a low estimate of the amount of time one has to spend "keeping" oneself. By foisting this off on others, man has seven hours a week—one working day more to play with his mind and not his human needs. Over the course of generations it is easy to see whence evolved the horrifying abstractions of modern life.

6. With the death of each form of oppression, life changes and new forms evolve. English aristocrats at the turn of the century were horrified at the idea of enfranchising working men—were sure that it signalled the death of civilization and a return to barbarism. Some working men were even deceived by this line. Similarly with the minimum wage, abolition of slavery, and female suffrage. Life changes but it goes on. Don't fall for any line about the death of everything if men take a turn at the dishes. They will imply that you are holding back the Revolution (their Revolution). But you are advancing it (your Revolution).

7. Keep checking up. Periodically consider who's actually *doing* the jobs. These things have a way of backsliding so that a year later once again the woman is doing everything. After a year make a list of jobs the man has rarely if ever done. You will find cleaning pots, toilets,

refrigerators and ovens high on the list. Use time sheets if necessary. He will accuse you of being petty. He is above that sort of thing (housework). Bear in mind what the worst jobs are, namely the ones that have to be done every day or several times a day. Also the ones that are dirty—it's more pleasant to pick up books, newspapers, etc., than to wash dishes. Alternate the bad jobs. It's the daily grind that gets you down. Also make sure that you don't have the responsibility for the housework with occasional help from him. "I'll cook dinner for you tonight" implies it's really your job and isn't he a nice guy to do some of it for you.

8. Most men had a rich and rewarding bachelor life during which they did not starve or become encrusted with crud or buried under the litter. There is a taboo that says women mustn't strain themselves in the presence of men—we haul around 50 lbs of groceries if we have to but aren't allowed to open a jar if there is someone around to do it for us. The reverse side of the coin is that men aren't supposed to be able to take care of themselves without a woman. Both are excuses for making women do the housework.

9. Beware of the double whammy. He won't do the little things he always did because you're now a "Liberated Woman," right? Of course he won't do anything else either. . . .

I was just finishing this when my husband came in and asked what I was doing. Writing a paper on housework. Housework? he said, *Housework?* Oh my god how trivial can you get. A paper on housework.

"Little Politics of Housework Quiz"

1. The lowest job in the army, used as punishment, is a) *working 9–5* b) *kitchen duty.*

2. When a man lives with his family, his a) *father* b) *mother* does the housework.

3. When he lives with a woman, a) *he* b) *she* does the housework.

4. a) *His son* b) *His daughter* learns [in] preschool how much fun it is to iron daddy's handkerchief.

5. From the *New York Times*, 9/21/69: "Former Greek Official George Mylonas pays the penalty for differing with the ruling junta in Athens by performing household chores on the island of Amorgos where he lives in forced exile" (with hilarious photo of a miserable Mylonas carrying his own water). What the *Times* means is that he ought to have a) *indoor plumbing* b) *a maid.*

6. Dr. Spock said (*Redbook*, 6/69): "Biologically and temperamentally I believe, women were made to be concerned first and foremost with child care, husband care, and home care." Think about a) *who made us* b) *why?* c) *what is the effect on their lives* d) *what is the effect on our lives?*

7. From *Time*, 1/5/70: "Like their American counterparts, many housing project housewives are said to suffer from neurosis. And for the first time in Japanese history, many young husbands today complain of being henpecked. Their wives are beginning to demand detailed explanations when they don't come home straight from work and some Japanese males nowadays are even compelled to do housework." According to *Time*, women become neurotic a) *when they are forced to do the maintenance work for the male caste all day every day of their lives* or b) *when they no longer want to do the maintenance work for the male caste all day every day of their lives.*

51

Alix Kates Shulman

The Shulmans' Marriage Agreement (1971)

I. PRINCIPLES

We reject the notion that the work which brings in more money is more valuable. The

ability to earn more money is a privilege which must not be compounded by enabling the larger earner to buy out of his/her duties and put the burden on the partner who earns less or on another person hired from outside.

We believe that each partner has an equal right to his/her own time, work, values, choices. As long as all duties are performed, each of us may use his/her extra time any way he/she chooses. If he/she wants to use it making money, fine. If he/she wants to spend it with spouse, fine.

As parents we believe we must share all responsibility for taking care of our children and home—and not only the work but also the responsibility. At least during the first year of this agreement, *sharing responsibility* shall mean dividing the *jobs* and dividing the *time.*

II. JOB BREAKDOWN AND SCHEDULE

(A) Children

1. Mornings: Waking children; getting their clothes out; making their lunches; seeing that they have notes, homework, money, bus passes, books; brushing their hair; giving them breakfast (making coffee for us). Every other week each parent does all.

2. Transportation: Getting children to and from lessons, doctors, dentists (including making appointments), friends' houses, etc. Parts occurring between 3 and 6 P.M. fall to wife. She must be compensated by extra work from husband (see 10 below). Husband does all weekend transportation and pick-ups after 6.

3. Help: Helping with homework, personal questions; explaining things. Parts occurring between 3 and 6 P.M. fall to wife. After 6 P.M. husband does Tuesday, Thursday and Sunday; wife does Monday, Wednesday and Saturday. Friday is free for whoever has done extra work during the week.

4. Nighttime (after 6 P.M.): Getting children to take baths, brush their teeth, put away their toys and clothes, go to bed; reading with them; tucking them in and having nighttime

talks; handling if they wake in the night. Husband does Tuesday, Thursday and Sunday. Wife does Monday, Wednesday and Saturday. Friday is split according to who has done extra work.

5. Baby sitters: Baby sitters must be called by the parent the sitter is to replace. If no sitter turns up, that parent must stay home.

6. Sick care: Calling doctors; checking symptoms; getting prescriptions filled; remembering to give medicine; taking days off to stay home with sick child, providing special activities. This must still be worked out equally, since now wife seems to do it all. In any case, wife must be compensated (see 10 below).

7. Weekends: All usual child care, plus special activities (beach, park, zoo). Split equally. Husband is free all Saturday, wife is free all Sunday.

(B) Housework

8. Cooking: Breakfasts during the week are divided equally; husband does all weekend breakfasts (including shopping for them and dishes). Wife does all dinners except Sunday nights. Husband does Sunday dinner and any other dinners on his nights of responsibility if wife isn't home. Whoever invites guests does shopping, cooking and dishes; if both invite them, split work.

9. Shopping: Food for all meals, housewares, clothing and supplies for children. Divide by convenience. Generally, wife does daily food shopping; husband does special shopping.

10. Cleaning: Husband does dishes Tuesday, Thursday and Sunday. Wife does Monday, Wednesday and Saturday. Friday is split according to who has done extra work during week. Husband does all the housecleaning in exchange for wife's extra child care (3 to 6 daily) and sick care.

11. Laundry: Home laundry, making beds, dry cleaning (take and pick up). Wife does home laundry. Husband does dry cleaning delivery and pick-up. Wife strips beds, husband remakes them.

52

LISA LEGHORN

Child-Care for the Child (1970)

The primary reason that we are concerned with the development of child-care facilities is that we feel there's a desperate necessity for a more human means of raising children in order to free mothers and children alike. Also, every child *must* be provided with adequate nutritional, medical and educational facilities. When children are reared privately there is no guarantee that these needs will be met. In this "affluent society" too many children aren't even provided with basic necessities. Most of the opposition that we have received has been concerned that child-care centers would deprive children of the individual attention and love that they so greatly need. Yet although the family ideal may have at one time provided for these needs, it has no longer been able to fulfill this function.

Raising children is the sole occupation of many women. This could be an extremely rewarding and creative occupation if the culture regarded it as such and provided facilities to allow the fulfillment of creative energies. But because women as a group have no choice in the raising of children, it thus becoming "women's work," it has become a degraded occupation. Degradation is inherent when one doesn't have a choice. Even if women were to overcome the psychological barriers involved in making other choices, there are no alternative institutions for the raising of children. Once married, women begin to feel stranded in a situation they have no control over. This culture has made it extremely difficult for women to choose not to bear children, what with unsafe contraception, rigid abortion laws and the loathed image of the unfertile woman. Raising children can't help but become a resented

From *The Female State*, April 1970.

occupation when it involves 24 hours a day responsibility. A great deal of frustration, anger and creative energy with no outlet must be either suppressed or find destructive outlets. Under these conditions of implied hostility the child does not receive much love and affection. Most mothers exert tyrannical authority over their children because it's the only form of authoritative power they are allowed to hold. The child needs individual love and attention. Only in a situation where those around her are free to provide for these needs, and have chosen to fulfill this function because they love children, will the child receive this love without conflict.

In a family situation one also finds that for the most part the child is submitted to the whims of the one or two parents. If the parents are pre-occupied with other problems, in bad spirits or can't give their time to the child, she will experience it emotionally as a lack of affection or in some cases as outright rejection. This can't help but be a destructive situation. Parents have to be free to place their personal needs first. Yet it's only natural that the child react negatively. The only way that the contradiction can be resolved is if the child is cared for by more people—men and women who have chosen to care for children during a portion of their lives as an occupation that they enjoy and want to learn from while teaching others.

If a child is exposed to more influences than those of her parents, she will remain open to different kinds of life-styles. It is a great deal more humane to provide a child with a greater number of life-styles and moralities from which to choose. Obviously, less possibilities are offered by two parents who have made similar basic choices (or with whom his choice dominates). Parents have made fundamental choices for their children simply by not allowing that other possibilities be available to them. They offer only one or two life-styles with which to identify, rather than a wider choice or the possibility of identifying with a community.

Oppression can be defined not only by the inability of a group of people to make free choices but also by the fact that they are defined by someone other than themselves. In this culture, children as well as women and blacks are not given the opportunity to define themselves. They sense when very young that if they don't accept the definitions of themselves that their parents have given them, that they will not receive the approbation they so greatly need. Children must be presented with a variety of self-definitions from which they can choose freely. In this way, the course of their maturity will be characterized by their efforts toward narrowing many possibilities to those they wish to pursue.

Another argument against child-care centers has been that they would deprive the child of needed continuity in her life. The assumption is, of course, that the continuity provided by her parents is a desirable one. The only continuity they provide is in their life choices. And we see children all the time fighting these choices, attempting to assert other choices, or being hurt by their parents' insistence that these choices must be followed. Parents' presence provides, in a sense, a superficial continuity. Children must be encouraged to establish inner continuity based on a growing establishment of what they want their lives to be. This is only possible if they feel free to do so, knowing that the choice hasn't already been made for them.

One is often astonished by the insight and frankness of very young children. Very often their clear-headedness can provide humane solutions to seemingly complex problems. Children can afford to be open and truthful and give conscientious and constructive thought to all issues for they have not yet made their choices. They are the only group of people who don't have vested interests in maintaining things a certain way or in seeing things occur in preconceived patterns. This becomes clouded because they are pressured to make given choices too early, not having gone through the processes of self-definition. The pressure arises from an intense desire for the approbation of those around them. They sense that to receive approbation from their parents, they must fulfill their parents' expectations of them. Subconsciously they make fundamental choices. If children were instead encouraged to take responsibility for their own decisions, they could maintain an honest and open evaluation of situations confronting them. This could lead to an extraordinary process of maturation producing adults concerned with establishing the truth, providing for the moral and the humane and contributing to the establishment of a culture that meets the needs of all.

It means a great deal to children to be treated "as adults." In a child-care center, children and adults of all ages could learn from each other. They would regard each other as individuals needing varying kinds of attentions rather than as persons with pre-conceived functions or pre-established needs. Children would have as great a voice in determining their futures as those around them. In this way, feeling personal responsibility for their lives, children would be encouraged in finding the best possible means of integrating their wishes with reality. If this process were encouraged in all humans from such an early age, one can't help but envision the development of an extraordinary civilization.

The idea that children are the future of the couple (of the man) and should be the responsibility of the couple (the woman) rather than the society as a whole serves only men's interests. In the animal kingdom the survival of the species rather than the survival of the individual has been nature's ruling concern. The young are cared for in the most efficient way possible and then leave their "parents" to fend for themselves. In many "primitive" cultures we see the children cared for communally—the responsibility as well as the rewards of child-rearing belonging to the culture as a whole. The importance of the private raising of children lies in the services it performs for the male. The family institution ensures that men aren't responsible for the drudgery involved in raising kids privately. Women take care of that. Yet children (mostly male children, the more important) are the future of the husband—his immortality. That's why they must follow his footsteps—carry on his occupation or concern for him. His sons will carry on the "family" name—his name. And they will inherit the "family" property—mostly his. This insures that man's fear of death can be dealt with. He never really dies as long as his children are perpetuated in his image. We have seen what this security for the male has done for the women and children.

53

LOUISE GROSS AND PHYLLIS MACEWAN
On Day Care (1970)

INTRODUCTION

Day Care has become one of the central issues of the Women's Liberation Movement. It is quite clear that free and public day care centers would be an important means for liberating women from the traditional tasks of child rearing. It has been suggested—and in some places carried out—that women should demand day care services from the institutions in which they work or study and from the large corporations which profit from and expand into the communities in which they live.

The authors of this discussion paper think it is a mistake to view day care solely as an issue of Women's Liberation. We would like to assert that day care centers in which children are raised in groups by men and women could be as important for the liberation of children as it would be for the liberation of women. Group child care—if well conceived—has a radical potential through the impact it could have on children's early development. It is therefore necessary that people in the movement gain a deeper understanding of the day care center as an environment for child rearing.

We consider this paper to be an introduction to the problems of existing day care centers and the possibilities for future centers.

From *Women: A Journal of Liberation*, Winter 1970.

Although we have pointed out some specific areas for radicalizing a day care center, we certainly have not developed a comprehensive model describing what an ideal day care program would look like.

We hope to develop this paper into a more thorough pamphlet and we welcome groups that are presently organizing day care centers or teachers who are working in centers to send us their ideas and suggestions.

WHY DAY CARE HAS EXISTED IN THE U.S.

Historically in the United States full-day care programs, as contrasted to half-day nursery schools, have been provided in periods of economic stress—during World War II and the depression—when women were required in the work force.[1] These programs were created primarily as a service to the corporations which needed woman-power, not as an educational and social opportunity for children. Although wartime day care centers often became educational opportunities for children, their rapid closing following World War II was a clear indication that these centers had not been organized primarily to benefit children or even to liberate women. Rather they had been organized to facilitate the carrying out of needed production.

In the past few years there has been an upsurge of state and national government interest in developing day care facilities for welfare mothers. This current interest parallels the expansion of day care during earlier periods of economic crisis. Today the main impetus behind the new drive for day care is the goal of lowering welfare costs by channeling welfare recipients into "desirable" occupations (like key punch operating). In both periods the official drive for day care has been motivated by the "needs" of the economy rather than by a concern for the welfare of either women or children.

1. For example, the Kaiser Child Service Centers in Portland, Oregon, which served more than 4,000 children from Nov. 8, 1943, to Sept. 1, 1945.

WHY DAY CARE HAS NOT DEVELOPED IN THE U.S.

The underlying reason for the failure of day care programs to develop in this country exists in the traditional idealogy that young children and their mothers belong in the home. Even today a strong bias exists against the concept that day care is potentially good for children and mothers. That women should *have* to work and therefore *have* to put their children in day care centers are circumstances which are generally considered to be necessary evils in this society.[2]

THE DEMAND FOR DAY CARE OF THE WOMEN'S LIBERATION MOVEMENT

The current demand for day care by the Women's Liberation Movement springs from a rejection of the ideology which says that women belong in the home. Yet the Movement's present demand parallels the historical attitude toward day care in its non child-centered approach. The primary reason for demanding day care is the liberation of women. While recognizing that day care is essential for women's liberation, the authors want the Movement to further recognize that day care is essential for the liberation of children. Group child care, in contrast to the more isolating private home environment, has the potential of providing an environment in which children will have more opportunity to develop social sensitivity and responsibility, emotional autonomy and trust, and a wider range of intellectual interests.

The struggle for day care centers must be considered a people's liberation issue, not just a

2. Today in the U.S. there are 4 million working women who have children under the age of 6 years, out of a total of 30 million working women. There presently are enough day care facilities to take care of 500,000 children. Compared to a number of other western industrialized countries the U.S. is backward in the field of day care. (Figures from *New York Times*, Oct. 16, 1969)

women's issue, because children are people. Both men and women who are concerned with children's development must demand day care.

WHAT IS A DAY CARE CENTER LIKE TODAY?

The majority of existing U.S. day care centers, which are run as profit-making enterprises, are glorified baby sitting services—dumping grounds—where children are bored most of the time. In these centers children are emotionally brutalized; they learn the values of obedience and passivity. They are programmed through a daily routine in which opportunities for personal choice and meaningful social relationships with adults and other children are minimal. Eating and naptime are managed in a mass production style which values efficiency over dignity. The adults as well as the children become routinized and enslaved to the daily schedule.

In contrast, there are a few day care centers where children have meaningful social and educational experiences, and where they participate in non-alienating play/work activities. In these centers self-directed learning and discovery are valued, and curriculum is developed in terms of the children's interests. Social cooperation is based on a rational group-problem-solving approach, rather than on rules impersonally established. Eating and resting activities are designed to be responsive to children's individual and group needs, rather than to meet the efficiency goals of the day care operation.

WHY WE MUST DEMAND SPACE AND MONEY AND NOT THE DAY CARE CENTERS THEMSELVES

We feel the differences among existing day care centers reflect a conflict in values and attitudes toward human development. This conflict in the care and education of young children is directly related to conflicting values and attitudes expressed in the economic and political behavior of adults. Values in competitive enterprise and individual rather than social achievement, respect for private property, adoration of the nuclear family—are attitudes that are nurtured in childhood and expressed in adult society.

As radicals we must understand that *our* goals for children are in conflict with those of the institutions—corporations and universities—from whom we will be demanding day care services. This implies that when we make demands for day care they should be solely in terms of money and space. The corporations and universities should have no control.

THE HIDDEN CURRICULUM

In organizing day care centers, we need to become aware of how values and attitudes are translated into programs for young children. We need to be aware of the existence of the day care center curriculum—hidden or explicit—and how it affects children's development.

It is well documented that attitudes toward work, race, sex (including male/female roles), initiative, and cooperation are being formed during the first five years of life. It follows that as radicals, concerned with developing a radical consciousness on these issues, we need to be seriously concerned with what happens inside the day care center.

The kind of interaction that takes place between the child and the human and physical environment (be it a home or a day care center) affects the kind of capacities that the child will have as an adult. The capacity to feel deeply and be sensitive toward other people, the capacity to trust oneself and use one's initiative, the capacity to solve problems in a creative and collective way—these are all capacities that can be given their foundation or stifled in the first five years.

By the age of 4, children are assimilating the idea that a woman's place is in the home. Three- and four-year-old children are already learning that it's better to be white. They are learning to follow directions and rules without asking why. They are learning how to deny their own feelings and needs in order to win approval from adults.

These are examples of learnings that most commonly result from early childhood experiences. These are elements of the hidden curriculum that usually characterize the child's environment in our society.

THE CHILD'S PERSPECTIVE

To a young child curriculum in a day care center is everything that he or she experiences: painting a picture, having to take a nap, experimenting with sand and water, wetting your pants or making it there on time, listening to an interesting story, eating lunch, riding a trike, being socked in the nose and having it bleed, observing one teacher being bossed by the other teacher, being told that blue is called blue, figuring out a hard puzzle, being hugged by the teacher, watching a building be demolished, seeing the mother guinea pig give birth, having everyone sing happy birthday to you, hammering a nail hard, and waiting to be picked up.

Although as adults we can place these events into categories of social, intellectual, emotional and physical experiences, for the young child each event is experienced in a total way. That is, the experience of painting a picture simultaneously involves emotional, intellectual, physical, and even social capacities. Emotionally a child may be using paint to express feelings of anger, lonliness, contentment, or boredom. Intellectually a child may be using the paint to discover what happens when different colors are mixed or learning how to write different letters. Physically, the child uses the paint brush to explore her/his own coordination, movement, and rhythm. Socially, painting can give the child an opportunity to be alone, with a friend, or in a group—depending on how the teacher has structured the painting experience.

The adult can seldom know the value that a particular experience has for a particular child. The same experience (e.g., painting a picture) will have a different value for different children, a different value to the same child at different times.

THE TEACHER'S IDEOLOGY

The teacher's values and attitudes form the base from which the structure and therefore the style of the group are formed. A single activity such as "juice time" illustrates how a teacher's goals and attitudes affect the way the situation is structured. One teacher might have three year olds pour her/his own juice from a pitcher, whereas another would have the children take already filled cups from a tray. What underlies the difference? Presumably both teachers know that three year olds are in the process of developing muscle as well as eye-hand coordination. Also, three year olds are usually concerned with becoming independent and self-sufficient. By letting children pour their own juice the teacher is structuring the situation to allow for growth—however groping—in the areas of self reliance and manual dexterity. By filling cups for the children, the other teacher is structuring the situation for maximum efficiency and neatness: to keep the routine running smoothly. One teacher uses juice time as an opportunity for children to gain some control over their activity, while the other teacher uses juice time to take control. In the first case the child gets to act upon the environment, while in the second case the child is treated as a passive recipient.

The traditional "housekeeping corner" of the nursery school and day care center is another dramatic illustration of how the teacher's values expressed in actions can have impact.

Let us take two teachers who have undergone similar training in early childhood education and have learned that the housekeeping corner provides an opportunity for children to "act out" adult roles thus contributing to their "ego growth" and "sex identification." One of the teachers sets up a housekeeping corner which encourages girls to be Mommy, the Housewife, and boys to be Daddy, the Worker.

The other teacher sets up an area in the classroom in which both boys and girls are given opportunities to cook, play with dolls and trucks, sew, hammer, build with blocks, wash clothes and dishes, dress up as doctors, firemen and firewomen, construction workers, and other interesting occupations. In other words, one teacher uses the housekeeping corner to promote the learning of traditional stereotyped roles, while the other transforms the housekeeping corner into an area where children can explore and test out various adult activities.

MEN IN THE DAY CARE CENTER/ WORK IN THE DAY CARE CENTER

Another way that children learn the traditional stereotyped roles is through observing that almost all day care teachers are women. The children quickly comprehend the concept that there is "women's work" and "men's work." This in itself would be sufficient argument for us to insist that men be included at all levels in the day care staff.

Furthermore, without including men in the day care program, the demand for day care runs the risk of contradicting the goals of women's liberation. Women should not demand simply that there be special institutions for child care, but also that men take an equal role in child care.

There is another good reason that *both* men and women should be involved in the day care center. Teaching working/playing with children can be an extraordinarily creative and non-alienating job. What often makes the caretakers of young children—teachers and mothers—feel apologetic about their occupation and what deprives men the opportunity of working with children is the fact that our society considers child care "women's work"—a low-status/cheap labor occupation biologically relegated to the weaker, "sensitive" sex.

A day care program which had a sexually integrated staff—and salaries in keeping with the value of this work—would make child-rearing a desirable and rewarding occupation. Finally, it seems self-evident that it's best for children—

emotionally, socially and politically—that they be cared for equally by both men and women.

SOME CONCLUSIONS

Day care is a people's liberation issue. Women, of course, will gain from a good day care program, but in the final analysis women's liberation depends on an entire transformation of society, not just on one institution. However, that one institution, if radically structured, can help obtain that transformation of society. The way children develop is part of that transformation.

In order to develop a radically structured day care program we must not allow any control to be in the hands of the universities and corporations. Our demand to these institutions for day care must be a demand solely for space and money. Control must rest with those who struggle for and use the day care center.

One of our prime tasks in that struggle is to develop an awareness of what a good day care program can be. We have simply attempted to make clear in this paper that day care is a complex issue.[3] The self-education which the movement must undergo on day care should be as thorough as on more obviously political issues.

54

JOHNNIE TILLMON (WITH NANCY STEFFAN)

Welfare Is a Women's Issue (1972)

I'm a woman. I'm a black woman. I'm a poor woman. I'm a fat woman. I'm a middle-aged woman. And I'm on welfare.

From Liberation News Service, February 26, 1972

3. There are numerous implications of day care organizing which we have not included in this paper such as the questions of developing the day care centers as a base for community political action, the day care center as a place to organize parents around their children's rights in the public school system, and the whole issue of day care for infants and collective child-rearing.

In this country, if you're any one of those things—poor, black, fat, female, middle-aged, on welfare—you count less as a human being. If you're all those things, you don't count at all. Except as a statistic.

I am a statistic.

I am 45 years old. I have raised six children.

I grew up in Arkansas, and I worked there for fifteen years in a laundry, making about $20 or $30 a week, picking cotton on the side for carfare. I moved to California in 1959 and worked in a laundry there for nearly four years. In 1963 I got too sick to work anymore. Friends helped me to go on welfare.

They didn't call it welfare. They called it A.F.D.C.—Aid to Families with Dependent Children. Each month I get $363 for my kids and me. I pay $128 a month rent; $30 for utilities, which include gas, electricity, and water; $120 for food and non-edible household essentials; $50 for school lunches for the three children in junior and senior high school who are not eligible for reduced-cost meal programs.

There are millions of statistics like me. Some on welfare. Some not. And some, really poor, who don't even know they're entitled to welfare. Not all of them are black. Not at all. In fact, the majority—about two-thirds—of all the poor families in the country are white.

Welfare's like a traffic accident. It can happen to anybody, but especially it happens to women.

And that is why welfare is a women's issue. For a lot of middle-class women in this country, Women's Liberation is a matter of concern. For women on welfare it's a matter of survival.

Forty-four per cent of all poor families are headed by women. That's bad enough. But the *families* on A.F.D.C. aren't really families. Because 99 per cent of them are headed by women. That means there is no man around. In half the states there really can't be men around because A.F.D.C. says if there is an "able-bodied" man around, then you can't be on welfare. If the kids are going to eat, and the man can't get a job, then he's got to go. So his kids can eat.

The truth is that A.F.D.C is like a super-sexist marriage. You trade in *a* man for *the* man. But you can't divorce him if he treats you bad. He can divorce you, of course, cut you off anytime he wants. But in that case, *he* keeps the kids, not you.

The man runs everything. In ordinary marriage, sex is supposed to be for your husband. On A.F.D.C. you're not supposed to have any sex at all. You give up control of your own body. It's a condition of aid. You may even have to agree to get your tubes tied so you can never have more children just to avoid being cut off welfare.

The man, the welfare system, controls your money. He tells you what to buy, what not to buy, where to buy it, and how much things cost. If things—rent, for instance—really cost more than he says they do, it's just too bad for you.

There are other welfare programs, other kinds of people on welfare—the blind, the disabled, the aged. (Many of them are women, too, especially the aged.) Those others make up just over a third of all the welfare caseloads. We A.F.D.C.s are two-thirds.

But when the politicians talk about the "welfare cancer eating at our vitals," they're not talking about the aged, blind, and disabled. Nobody minds them. They're the "deserving poor." Politicians are talking about A.F.D.C. Politicians are talking about us—the women who head up 99 per cent of the A.F.D.C. families—and our kids. We're the "cancer," the "undeserving poor." Mothers and children.

In this country we believe in something called the "work ethic." That means that your work is what gives you human worth. But the work ethic itself is a double standard. It applies to men and to women on welfare. It doesn't apply to all women. If you're a society lady from Scarsdale and you spend all your time sitting on your prosperity paring your nails, well, that's okay.

The truth is a job doesn't necessarily mean an adequate income. A woman with three kids—not twelve kids, mind you, just three kids—that woman earning the full Federal minimum wage of $1.60 an hour, is still stuck in poverty. She is below the Government's own official poverty line. There are some ten million jobs that now pay less than the minimum wage, and if you're a woman, you've got the best chance of getting one.

The President keeps repeating the "dignity of work" idea. What dignity? Wages are the measure of dignity that society puts on a job. Wages and nothing else. There is no dignity in starvation. Nobody denies, least of all poor women, that there is dignity and satisfaction in being able to support your kids through honest labor.

We wish we could do it.

The problem is that our country's economic policies deny the dignity and satisfaction of self-sufficiency to millions of people—the millions who suffer everyday in underpaid dirty jobs—and still don't have enough to survive.

People still believe that old lie that A.F.D.C. mothers keep on having kids just to get a bigger welfare check. On the average, another baby means another $35 a month— barely enough for food and clothing. Having babies for profit is a lie that only men could make up, and only men could believe. Men, who never have to bear the babies or have to raise them and maybe send them to war.

There are a lot of other lies that male society tells about welfare mothers; that A.F.D.C. mothers are immoral, that A.F.D.C. mothers are lazy, misuse their welfare checks, spend it all on booze and are stupid and incompetent.

If people are willing to believe these lies, it's partly because they're just special versions of the lies that society tells about *all* women.

For instance, the notion that all A.F.D.C. mothers are lazy: that's just a negative version of the idea that women don't work and don't want to. It's a way of rationalizing the male policy of keeping women as domestic slaves.

The notion that A.F.D.C. mothers are immoral is another way of saying that all women are likely to become whores unless they're kept

under control by men and marriage. Even many of my own sisters on welfare believe these things about themselves.

On TV, a woman learns that human worth means beauty and that beauty means being thin, white, young and rich.

She learns that her body is really disgusting the way it is, and that she needs all kinds of expensive cosmetics to cover it up.

She learns that a "real woman" spends her time worrying about how her bathroom bowl smells; that being important means being middle class, having two cars, a house in the suburbs, and a minidress under your maxicoat. In other words, an A.F.D.C. mother learns that being a "real woman" means being all the things she isn't and having all the things she can't have.

Either it breaks you, and you start hating yourself, or you break it.

There's one good thing about welfare. It kills your illusions about yourself, and about where this society is really at. It's laid out for you straight. You have to learn to fight, to be aggressive, or you just don't make it. If you can survive being on welfare, you can survive anything. It gives you a kind of freedom, a sense of your own power and togetherness with other women.

Maybe it is we poor welfare women who will really liberate women in this country. We've already started on our own welfare plan.

Along with other welfare recipients, we have organized together so we can have some voice. Our group is called the National Welfare Rights Organization (N.W.R.O.). We put together our own welfare plan, called Guaranteed Adequate Income (G.A.I.) which would eliminate sexism from welfare.

There would be no "categories"—men, women, children, single, married, kids, no kids—just poor people who need aid. You'd get paid according to need and family size only— $6,500 for a family of four (which is the Department of Labor's estimate of what's adequate), and that would be upped as the cost of living goes up.

If I were president, I would solve this so-called welfare crisis in a minute and go a long

way toward liberating every woman. I'd just issue a proclamation that "women's" work is real
work.

In other words, I'd start paying women a
living wage for doing the work we are already
doing—child-raising and housekeeping. And
the welfare crisis would be over, just like that.
Housewives would be getting wages, too—a
legally determined percentage of their husband's salary—instead of having to ask for and
account for money they've already earned.

For me, Women's Liberation is simple. No
woman in this country can feel dignified, no
woman can be liberated, until all women get
off their knees. That's what N.W.R.O. is all
about—women standing together, on their
feet.

55
WOMEN'S HEALTH COLLECTIVE
The Male-Feasance of Health
(1970)

The American health care system is a disaster
for almost everyone who tries to use it. All
consumers face continually escalating prices for
services which are increasingly fragmented, de-
personalized and just plain hard to find. All
health workers face a rigid, doctor-dominated
hierarchy, where all but the top jobs are low-
paid dead-ends. But certain groups are especially oppressed by the American health system, both as workers and as consumers. Black
and brown people suffer not only because they
are poor but because of the built-in racism of
most medical institutions. Less appreciated, but
potentially just as explosive, is the specific oppression of women—of all classes and races—
by the health system.

To start with, women are much more dependent on the health system than are men.
Women consume the bulk of America's health
services: They make, on the average, 25 percent

From *Rat: Subterranean News*, March 7–21, 1970.

more visits to the doctor per year than men,
and more than 100 percent more if mothers'
visits to take their children to the doctor are
counted. Women consume 50 percent more
prescription drugs than men and are admitted
to hospitals much more frequently than men.
As workers, women have always depended on
the health system as one of the few places
where a woman could always find a job. About
70 percent of all health workers, and 75 percent of all hospital workers, are women. Thus
whatever goes wrong with the health system is
a problem, by and large, for women.

As in almost every other institution of
American life, however, it is men—doctors,
medical school deans, hospital directors and
trustees, and drug and insurance company
executives—who make the decisions. Men decide which jobs will be available to women
health workers, how much they will be paid
and even what kind of uniform they will wear.
For women health consumers, men decide on
the most personal issues of health care—what
form of birth control a woman should use,
whether she should have an abortion, what
method of childbirth she should use, and of
course, how much she should be told about the
risks and options. In their exercise of power
over women, men in medicine are no more objective and scientific than any other men. They
start with an irrational image of women as ignorant and passive dependents of men, and
they reinforce that image in every aspect of the
health system.

For women health workers, this means being type-cast into jobs which are subordinate
and subservient to men. Throughout the health
system, men occupy the scientifically interesting, or authoritative, position; women do the
scut work. Women, not men, are nurses, not
because women are more "nurse-like" than
men, but because from grade school on,
women are encouraged to aim no higher than
nursing. Women are not encouraged to take science courses in high school and college, and
they are actively discouraged from entering
medical school. Nursing itself is supposed to be

a specifically feminine occupation, requiring no initiative or ability to reason. And as one medical school dean put it, "The reason that nurses are all women is that men couldn't put up with the kind of relationship that a nurse has to doctors." The doctor-nurse relationship is always authoritarian, and often characterized by subtle or overt sexual manipulation of the nurse-handmaid.

Even the women who enter the more "masculine" occupations of technicians, administrators or physicians do not find equality. Category by category, women earn 10 to 15 percent less than men in the same job. And the few women who become physicians (only seven percent of American physicians are women) are primarily concentrated in the lower prestige, lower paying specialties, especially pediatrics, rather than the "high-technology" specialties, such as surgery.

Women as health consumers are oppressed by the same male supremacist attitudes and institutionalized practices which oppress women as health workers. When they enter a hospital or a doctor's office, women encounter a hierarchy dominated by men, in which they see women playing only subservient roles. Then, as patients, they encounter all the male supremacist superstitutions which characterize American society in general. Women are assumed to be emotional and "difficult," so they are often classified as "neurotic" well before physical illness has been ruled out. (A glance at the tranquilizer ads in medical journals shows that women are, in the drug companies' view, the heaviest consumers.) And women are assumed to be vain so they are the special prey of the paramedical dieting, cosmetics, and plastic surgery businesses.

Everyone who enters the medical system in search of care quickly finds himself transformed into an object, a mass of organs and pathology. Women have a special handicap—they start out as "objects." The sick person who enters the gynecology clinic is the same sex as the sexual object who sells cars in the magazine ads. When it comes to dealing with women's bodies, physicians are no less likely to be hung up than other American men. What makes it worse is that a high proportion of routine medical care for women centers on the most superstitious and fantasy-ridden aspect of female physiology—the reproductive system. Women of all classes almost uniformly hate or fear the gynecologist. He plays a controlling role in that aspect of their lives society values most—the sexual aspect—and he knows it. Middle class women find a man who is either patronizingly over-jolly, or cold and condescending. Poorer women, using clinics, are more likely to encounter outright brutality and sadism.

Women's encounters with the health system do not end with their own health needs. In this society women bear the chief responsibility for the health of their children. Wherever the health system is inadequate or inaccessible, it is up to the mother to fill in. Even when the mother succeeds in substituting for the failing health system, she has to contend with continually proliferating household hazards. Drugs and food additives are only perfunctorily regulated by the Food and Drug Administration: It is up to the mother to determine whether monosodiumglutamate, or before that, cyclamates, are harmful for infants, and to choose among a dozen brightly advertised, but potentially dangerous cough syrups or eye drops or lotions.

Health is only one among many issues that women must face in their struggle for equality and self-determination. Male supremacism runs as deep in our society as racism, governing the way we are educated, entertained, employed and ultimately determining the ways we see ourselves and other people. It cannot be uprooted from the health system without changes in every social institution which now oppresses women—from the family to the major corporate bureaucracy. If so many women are turning first to health institutions, it is because that is where they are are—as workers, as patients, as mothers.

For the health system, the onslaught of women's insurgency could have a revolutionary impact. Women are strategically placed within the health system, holding most of the jobs and using most of the services. As consumers, the very nature of women's dependence on the health system (chiefly for preventive care for themselves and their children) is a strategic advantage: women more often than not, are healthy when they confront the health system. As workers, women have been consistently denied positions of administrative or professional authority, so that for most women workers there is little barrier of "professionalism" to prevent them from taking action around their demands. Finally, the institutional and attitudinal sources of oppression are the same for both women workers and consumers. Already there are the first signs of an alliance between women workers and consumers—an alliance which will shake the male-dominated health system to its foundations.

56
THE GROUP II
Are Our Doctors Pigs? (1970)

Biologists (but not always doctors) know that women are medically stronger than men. Women heal faster from accidents, get almost all diseases less often than men, suffer from them for a shorter period of time, and have a higher survival rate for serious diseases. The life expectancy for women is much longer than for men, and this is not occupational—female infants survive better than male.

There is only one major kind of disease we suffer from more than males—diseases affecting the female reproductive organs. For this reason, and because we are the ones capable of bearing children, the one kind of doctor we are really dependent on is the gynecologist. For many women, this is the only kind of doctor regularly seen. We depend on these doctors to help us bear children or to avoid it, to correct

From *Rat: Subterranean News*, June 5, 1970.

menstrual disorders, and check for cancer. These are not only life and death matters, they are also completely connected with our conceptions of ourselves as women. Women are both psycholgoically and physically dependent on these doctors. Gynecologists are the products of a sexist and a class society, like everybody else, and their contempt (or patronizing concern) for women as women, and as patients (humble non-professionals begging for the godly wisdom of the professionals) leads to continual abuses at times when we are most vulnerable to it.

Up to now, women have probably felt powerless to protest because we felt shame and even contempt for our own women's bodies. We also accepted that medical skill was almost magical, and went along with the doctor's own conceptions of their superiority. But lately women have begun to protest. They have found that gynecologists and obstetricians are providing them with callous disinterest and actual maltreatment, and that in a service that deals exclusively with women, medical male chauvinism is made most obvious.

Ob-gyn clinics are often the only clinics in a hospital where appointments are not made, and patients are simple expected to come in and wait. Private gynecologists seem to expect that women will accept or even enjoy waits in their offices—women's time is considered to be of little value.

Nor is her dignity honored. A woman often can get *no* gynecological treatment without answering moral, marital, and sexual questions irrelevant to her medical problem. We are made to feel embarrassed and even guilty about our medical conditions. In no other medical branch is this generally true. No one asks questions about your morality when you break a leg.

Doctors generally enhance their privileged positions by keeping medical knowledge as secret as possible. They try to convey the impression that only they, and not the patient, can understand anything about the patient's body and what is to be done to it. Gynecologists are probably the worst in this respect. They encourage women to feel ashamed to seek information about their own bodies. If a woman does ask questions she is patronizingly asked to leave everything in the doctor's hands—it is unsuitable for women to know too much. Thus gynecologists and obstetricians decide on a method of contraception for a woman without asking her preferences, or informing her of the risks; they choose a method of delivery, rather than giving a woman the relevant information and letting her make her own choice. Much of the pain of childbirth stems from the fear of a woman who has no idea what is going on, or what will happen next. Obstetricians encourage this. The high fees can more easily be collected if women believe that only the doctor will enable them to bear a child—the doctor even acts as if he does more to bear the child than the woman.

The arrogant and inhuman attitude expressed by many doctors reaches absurd extremes in gynecologists. But if as women we are proud of ourselves, of our bodies and our minds, we don't have to take this kind of shit. We can demand to be served as equals by those whose training gives them special skills, just as we use our abilities to serve others. We must demystify the doctors and take away the main tool they use to oppress us. Medical service is a right, not a privilege. We must honor only those doctors who dedicate themselves to informing us, so that we can take better care of our bodies, and to using their special skills when we are in need of assistance. We must honor them as we honor all people who act morally, not because they have a profession that makes them superior to us. Control of our bodies must be in our hands, not theirs.

Complaints are not enough. We must force these doctors to treat us properly, or to find another job. Blacklists are one tool at our disposal. The doctors won't check up on each other's behavior. We have to do it ourselves. We can submit questionnaires on all gynecologists and clinics with which we have come in contact and publish the results urging our sisters to

seek treatment only by those doctors and clinics which consensus proves are medically and humanly fit.

To this end THE GROUP II has put together the following questionnaire . . . distributed to Women's Lib groups throughout the city, but we will not have reached you all. Unfortunately we do not have the funds to fill all requests for copies of this questionnaire (save in Spanish), so we must ask those individuals and groups participating to reproduce this questionnaire themselves. You may clip it out, or write out only the answers to each category in the questionnaire, or reproduce it *in toto* (please do! It takes exactly two pages 8½ x 11 single spaced, double between categories). Results will be collated and published in RAT and in pamphlet form. Please help! The validity and usefulness of this study [are] dependent upon the *quality* of response.

TELL ALL! Please mail to: THE GROUP, II; Apt. 2A; 172 East 7th Street; New York, N.Y. 10009. (Use a separate questionnaire for each doctor or clinic.)

Doctor's name
Sex
Address
Telephone no.
Hospital Afiliation
Specialty
Clinic name
Address
Telephone no.
Is there a geographic or residence requirement?
   Yes No
If so, explain.
Is registration closed? Yes No
Same doctor each visit? Yes No

Clinic Appointments: Excellent Good Fair Horrible
One should be able to make appointments instead of coming in and waiting. Appointments ought to be made within two weeks and in the event of disturbing symptoms should be made immediately without necessitating an emergency room visit.

Clinic Care: Excellent Good Fair Horrible

If you use the health service of your college or company, gynecological problems should receive equal attention. Records should be thorough enough and personal enough for the examining doctor(s) to know you even in a clinic situation. Both medical care and communication should be comparable to what is expected and needed from a private doctor.

Discrimination: Yes No

Neither doctor nor clinic should discriminate on the basis of sex, homosexuality, class, race, age, marital status, manner of dress, etc.

Medicaid / Insurance

Does doctor/clinic accept Medicaid? Yes No
Are Medicaid patients treated differently? Yes No
Does doctor/clinic accept all insurance plans? Yes No

Finances: Excellent Good Fair Horrible

Are fees set according to patient's ability to pay or are they standard? If standard are they reasonable? Do pills, diaphragms, Pap tests cost extra?

Abortions

Under the new law will doctor/clinic perform abortions? Yes No. What is the fee?

Birth control: Excellent Good Fair Horrible

All methods should be offered. The use, risks, benefits of each should be thoroughly explained. If pills are prescribed, six month visits should be required. Contraception should be provided regardless of age or marital status.

Obstetrics: Excellent Good Fair Horrible

Patients should be permitted choice in delivery methods—natural childbirth, anesthesia, home delivery, induction of labor, and choice in breast or bottle feeding. The welfare of the mother should take precedence over that of the unborn child.

Venereal Disease: Excellent Good Fair Horrible

Examinations and tests should be given promptly and treatment instituted immediately without threats regardless of your ability to provide information on past sexual contacts. The problem should be treated with dignity.

Quality of Medical Care: Excellent Good Fair Horrible

Thorough personal and family histories must be taken and maintained. The Pap test must be administered *routinely* at least once a year. Painkillers should be given for painful out-patient procedures. Adequate follow-up care should be insisted upon. A doctor, even through a clinic, should be available by phone at any time.

Waiting Room and Personnel: Excellent Good Fair Horrible

Appointments should be made and kept at least approximately. If waiting time is unreasonable, courteous apology should be made. The non-medical staff should be courteous, sympathetic, and helpful.

Doctor-Patient Communication: Excellent Good Fair Horrible

The doctor, even in a clinic, should demonstrate interest in your total human situation, emotional, physical, and financial, as it affects your medical problem and be willing to discuss it without being patronizing. To facilitate this, such information should be kept in your records so that the doctor is always aware of your personal circumstances.

57

ROE V. WADE

Brief for Appellants (1970)

In The
Supreme Court of the United States
October Term, 1970

No. 70-18

Jane Roe, John Doe, and Mary Doe,
Appellants,

James Hubert Halleford, M.D.,
Appellant-Intervenor

v.

Henry Wade, Appellee.

From *Roe v. Wade*, No. 70-18, Brief for Appellants, U.S. Supreme Court, October Term 1970.

On Appeal from the United States District Court for the Northern District of Texas

Brief for Appellants

. . . SUMMARY OF ARGUMENT

This case presents three separate actions: (1) that of Jane Roe, an unmarried pregnant woman, who sues on behalf of herself and other women unable to obtain a legal abortion because of the Texas abortion laws; (2) that of John and Mary Doe, a childless married couple who sue on behalf of themselves and others similarly situated complaining of the adverse effect of the Texas abortion law on their marital relations; and (3) that of James Hubert Hallford, M.D., a Texas physician who intervenes on behalf of himself and other doctors similarly situated, alleging the constraint of the Texas abortion law on the practice of medicine.

The parties requested that articles 1191–1194 and 1196 of the Texas Penal Code, which make abortion a crime unless performed "upon medical advice for the purpose of saving the life of the mother," be declared unconstitutional and that Defendant Henry Wade be enjoined from instituting future prosections thereunder.

The three-judge federal court declared the statutes unconstitutional on two grounds: first "because they deprive single women and married couples of their right, secured by the Ninth Amendment, to choose whether to have children" and are overbroad and not supported by compelling state interests; and second because they are unconstitutionally vague. The court, however, refused to grant an injunction and found that John and Mary Doe had no standing.

Appellants appeal to this Court from the denial of injunctive relief and from the holding that John and Mary Doe have no standing; they urge the Court to go beyond jurisdictional points to a consideration of the merits of the statute in question. . . .

As to the merits, appellants contend that the Texas abortion law is unconstitutional since it interferes with the exercise of fundamental rights and is neither narrowly drawn nor supported by a compelling state interest. *Griswold v. Connecticut*, 381 U.S. 479 (1965). The law abridges rights emanating from the First, Fourth, Ninth, and Fourteenth Amendments to seek and receive health care, to privacy and autonomy in deciding whether to continue pregnancy, and, as to physicians, to administer medical care according to the highest professional standards. The right of personal and marital privacy has been recognized by this Court and by numerous state and lower federal courts, and is grievously infringed by the statute in question. The law is unconstitutional since it is overbroad and since it does not support any compelling state interest.

The primary interest asserted by appellee in the lower court was an interest in protecting fetal life, yet appellants have clearly shown that the state's position is fatally inconsistent since it does not exhibit any interest in or provide any protection of fetal life in any circumstance other than the medical procedure of abortion.

Additionally, the Texas abortion law is unconstitutionally vague since it gives no meaningful indication to physicians of the conditions under which an abortion may legally be performed.

Finally, the law in question imposes an unconstitutional burden of proof on a physician accused of having performed an abortion to establish that an alleged abortion was within the statutory exception established by article 1196.

In summary, appellants urge this Court to render a decision holding that the three-judge court erred in refusing to grant injunctive relief; that the three-judge court erred in holding that John and Mary Doe presented no case or controversy and did not have standing to challenge the Texas abortion law; and affirming the decision of the three-judge court that articles 1191–1194 and 1196 of the Texas Penal Code are unconstitutional. . . .

IV. The Provisions in the Texas Penal Code, Articles 1191–1194 and 1196, Which Prohibit the Medical

Procedure of Induced Abortion Unless "procured or attempted by medical advice for the purpose of saving the life of the mother," Abridge Fundamental Personal Rights of Appellants Secured by the First, Fourth, Ninth, and Fourteenth Amendments, and Do Not Advance a Narrowly Drawn, Compelling State Interest.

As former Supreme Court Justice Tom C. Clark has said:

"The result of [Griswold and its predecessors] is the evolution of the concept that there is a certain zone of individual privacy which is protected by the Constitution. Unless the State has a compelling subordinating interest that outweighs the individual rights of human beings, it may not interfere with a person's marriage, home, children, and day-to-day living habits. This is one of the most fundamental concepts that the Founding Fathers had in mind when they drafted the Constitution." Clark, *Religion, Morality, and Abortion: A Constitutional Appraisal*, 2 Loyola Univ. (L.A.) L. Rev. 1, 8 (1969).

The Constitution does not specifically enumerate a "right to seek abortion," or a "right of privacy." That such a right is not enumerated in the Constitution is no impediment to the existence of the right. Other rights not specifically enumerated have been recognized as fundamental rights entitled to constitutional protection[1] including the right to marry,[2] the right to have offspring,[3] the right to use contraceptives to avoid having offspring,[4] the right to direct the upbringing

and education of one's children,[5] as well as the right to travel.[6]

The difficulty in identifying the precise sources and limits of these rights has long been evident. In 1923 in *Meyer* v. *Nebraska*, 262 U.S. 390 (1923), this Court outlined some of the protections afforded by the Due Process Clause of the Fourteenth Amendment:

"While this court has not attempted to define with exactness the liberty thus guaranteed, the term has received much consideration and *some of the included things have been definitely stated.* Without doubt, it denotes not merely freedom from bodily restraint but also the right of the individual to contract, to engage in any of the common occupations of life, to acquire useful knowledge, to marry, establish a home and bring up children, to worship God according to the dictates of his own conscience, and generally to enjoy those privileges long recognized as essential to the orderly pursuit of happiness by free men." 262 U.S. at 399. [Emphasis added.]

The 1965 Court, in *Griswold* v. *Connecticut*, 381 U.S. 479 (1965), demonstrated the variety of sources of these fundamental rights.[7]

---

1. "The association of people is not mentioned in the Constitution nor in the Bill of Rights. The right to educate a child in a school of the parents' choice—whether public or private or parochial—is also not mentioned. Nor is the right to study any particular subject or any foreign language. Yet the first Amendment has been construed to include certain of those rights." *Griswold* v. *Connecticut*, 381 U.S. 479, 482 (1965).

2. *Loving* v. *Commonwealth*, 388 U.S. 1, 12 (1967) (alternate ground of decision).

3. *Skinner* v. *Oklahoma*, 316 U.S. 535, 536 (1942).

4. *Griswold* v. *Connecticut*, 381 U.S. 479 (1965).

5. *Pierce* v. *Society of Sisters*, 268 U.S. 510 (1925).

6. *United States* v. *Guest*, 383 U.S. 745 (1966). What was said by Mr. Justice Stewart in that opinion may be aptly paraphrased to apply in the present context:

"The Constitutional right [of marital privacy] . . . occupies a position fundamental to the concept of our Federal Union * * * [T]hat right finds no explicit mention in the Constitution. The reason, it has been suggested, is that a right so elementary was conceived from the beginning to be . . . necessary. . . ." 383 U.S. at 757.

7. Justice Douglas, delivering the opinion of the Court that Connecticut could not constitutionally outlaw the use of contraceptives, relied upon the penumbras of specific guarantees in the Bill of Rights, "formed by emanations from those guarantees that help give them life and substance." 381 U.S. at 484. Justice Goldberg, joined by Chief Justice Warren and Justice Brennan, concurred, relying upon the Ninth Amendment. Justice Harlan's concurring opinion stated the inquiry to be whether the statute infringed the Due Process Clause of the Fourteenth Amendment by violating basic values implicit in the concept of liberty. 381 U.S. 500. Justice White found that the law deprived plaintiffs of "liberty" without due process, as used in the Fourteenth Amendment. 381 U.S. 502.

Appellants contend that fundamental rights[8] entitled to constitutional protection are involved in the instant case, namely the right of individuals to seek and receive health care unhindered by arbitrary state restraint; the right of married couples and of women to privacy and autonomy in the control of reproduction; and the right of physicians to practice medicine according to the highest professional standards. These asserted rights meet constitutional standards arising from several sources and expressed in decisions of this Court. The Texas abortion law infringes these rights, and since the law is not supported by a compelling justification, it is therefore unconstitutional. . . .

A. The Fundamental Rights to Marital and Personal Privacy Are Acknowledged in Decisions of This Court as Protected by the First, Fourth, Ninth, and Fourteenth Amendments.

1. The Right to Marital Privacy

The importance of the institution of marriage and of the family has long been recognized by this Court. Consequently the Court and its members have often affirmed the sanctity of the marital relationship and of the family union. In *Maynard* v. *Hill*, 125 U.S. 190, 211 (1888), marriage was called "the foundation of the family and of society, without which there would be neither civilization nor progress." The opinion of the Court in *Skinner* v. *Oklahoma*, 316 U.S. 535, 541 (1942), spoke of marriage

8. The complaints of appellants invoked the jurisdiction of the district court under the First, Fourth, Fifth, Eighth, Ninth and Fourteenth Amendments (A. 10-11, 15-16, 24). The district court confined its consideration to the Ninth Amendment and vagueness arguments and did not pass upon the "array of constitutional arguments" (A. 116). Appellants have chosen in this brief to stress the application of the First, Ninth, and Fourteenth Amendments. However, the arguments relating to application of other Amendments and particularly the Eighth Amendment, as well developed in the Brief *Amicus Curiae* filed in this case by Attorney Nancy Stearns. Brief *Amicus Curiae* on Behalf of New Women Lawyers, Women's Health and Abortion Project, Inc. National Abortion Coalition, at 34 et seq. (Eighth Amendment)

and procreation as being "fundamental to the very existence and survival of the race." Mr. Justice Harlan, for example, has written:

"[T]he integrity of [family] life is something so fundamental that it has been found to draw to its protection the principles of more than one explicitly granted Constitutional right. . . . Of this whole 'private realm of family life' it is difficult to imagine what is more private or more intimate than a husband and wife's marital relations." *Poe* v. *Ullman*, 367 U.S. 497, 551–52 (1961) (Mr. Justice Harlan, dissenting).

Mr. Justice Douglas, in delivering the opinion of the Court in *Griswold* v. *Connecticut*, 381 U.S. 479 (1965), wrote of marriage as being "a coming together for better or for worse, hopefully enduring, and intimate to the degree of being sacred. It is an association that promotes a way of life, not causes; a harmony in living, not political faiths; a bilateral loyalty, not commercial or social projects. Yet it is an association for as noble a purpose as any involved in our prior decisions." 391 U.S. at 486.

Most recently in *Boddie* v. *Connecticut*, 401 U.S. 371 (1971), this Court reaffirmed "the basic position of the marriage relationship in this society's hierarchy of values," 401 U.S. at 374, and reiterated that "[a]s this Court on more than one occasion has recognized, marriage involves interests of basic importance in our society." 401 U.S. at 376.

Recognition of the sanctity of the marital relationship has resulted in recognition of a right of marital privacy, or as the *Griswold* decision states, "notions of privacy surrounding the marriage relationship," 381 U.S. at 486, and of rights attendant to the marital state. Protection has been extended to such rights as the rights to marry and have offspring because of their fundamental nature, even though such rights are not expressly enumerated in the Bill of Rights. These decisions support the proposition that there is a sphere of marital privacy and that important interests associated with marriage and the family are, and should be, protected from arbitrary government intrusion.

Loving v. *Commonwealth*, 388 U.S. 1, 12 (1967) (alternate ground of decision), specifically held that the due process clause of the Fourteenth Amendment protects "[t]he freedom to marry . . . as one of the vital personal rights essential to the orderly pursuit of happiness by men." *Loving* stands for the proposition that "the right to marry" is protected by the due process clause although not specifically mentioned in the Bill of Rights. Yet the right *to* marry is meaningful only to the extent that there are rights *of* marriage, *i.e.*, rights attendant to the marital state which promote the happiness of the couple.

Associated with the right to marry is the right to have children, if one chooses, without arbitrary governmental interference. This Court unanimously held that "the right to have offspring" is a constitutionally protected "human right" which cannot be taken away by a discriminatory statute requiring the sterilization of some persons convicted of crime, but not of others similarly situated. *Skinner* v. *Oklahoma*, 316 U.S. 535, 536 (1942). The *Skinner* Court recognized a constitutionally protected right *to have* offspring even though such right is not mentioned in the Bill of Rights; a right *not to have* offspring should be of equal constitutional stature.

Further cases supporting these family rights include *Pierce* v. *Society of Sisters*, 268 U.S. 510 (1925), and *Meyer* v. *Nebraska*, 262 U.S. 390 (1923), both of which were reaffirmed in *Griswold* v. *Connecticut*, 381 U.S. 479, 483 (1965). A unanimous Court in *Pierce* recognized a right to send one's children to private school. This right derived from "the liberty of parents and guardians to direct the upbringing and education of children under their control." 268 U.S. at 534–35. This liberty, and the responsibility it implies, suggests a concomitant right of persons to determine the number of children whose "upbringing and education" they will direct.

Similar in principle is *Meyer*, a 7–2 decision invalidating a State statute which prohibited teaching German to pupils below the eighth grade. The *Meyer* Court stated that the due process clause included "the right . . . to marry, establish a home and bring up children." 262 U.S. at 399. Again the Court recognized a fundamental right not enumerated in the Constitution entitled to Constitutional protection.

Griswold reaffirms these privacy concepts, and makes it clear that a husband and wife are constitutionally privileged to control the size and spacing of their family at least by contraception.

Taken together, the *Griswold, Loving, Skinner, Pierce* and *Meyer* decisions illustrated that the Constitution protects certain privacy and family interests from governmental intrusion unless a compelling justification exists for the legislation. The right of a family to determine whether to have additional children, and to terminate a pregnancy in its early stages if a negative decision is reached, is such a right and is fully entitled to protection.

The number and spacing of children obviously have a profound impact upon the marital union. Certainly the members of the Court know from personal experience the emotional and financial expenditures parenthood demands. For those couples who are less fortunate financially and especially for those who are struggling to provide the necessities of life, additional financial responsibilities can be economically disastrous. For families who require two incomes for economic survival, the pregnancy can be ruinous since the wife will generally have to resign her job. In many other situations, such as where husband and wife are working to put themselves through school, pregnancy at a particular time can present a crisis.

Pregnancy can be a significant added problem in marriages. The added pressures of prospective parenthood can be "the last straw."

This Court has previously upheld the right to use contraceptives to avoid unwanted pregnancy.

"[I]t would seem that if there is a right to use contraception, this right must also take account of the fact that most techniques are not 100 per cent protective. If the contraceptive method fails and the *Griswold* right of choice is preserved, it is a strong argument toward recognizing the right to an abortion."[9]

As did the law considered in *Griswold*, "[t]his law . . . operates directly on an intimate relation of husband and wife and their physician's role in one aspect of that relation." 381 U.S. 482. The Texas abortion law in forbidding resort to the procedure of medical abortion, has a maximum destructive impact upon the marriage relationship.

2. The Related Rights to Personal Privacy and Physical Integrity

In addition to rights associated with marital privacy, an overlapping body of precedent extends significant constitutional protection to the citizen's sovereignty over his or her own physical person.

As early as 1891 this Court stated:

"No right is more sacred, [n]or is more carefully guarded . . . than the right of every individual to the possession and control of his own person, free from all restraint or interference of others unless by clear and unquestionable authority of law. As well said by Judge Cooley, 'The right to one's person may be said to be a right of complete immunity: to be let alone.'" *Union Pac. Ry.* v. *Botsford*, 141 U.S. 250, 251 (1891), quoted in *Terry* v. *Ohio*, 392 U.S. 1, 8–9 (1968).

This right, like all rights, does have some limitations, as illustrated by *Jacobson* v. *Massachusetts*, 197 U.S. 11 (1904), *supra* at 94 *et seq.* Nonetheless, absent a compelling justification, one is entitled to personal autonomy.

In family matters relating to child rearing and procreation, the Court has recognized and sustained individual rights on a constitutional plane. "The freedom to marry . . .," *Loving* v. *Commonwealth*, 388 U.S. 1, 12 (1967); "the right to have offspring," *Skinner* v. *Oklahoma*, 316 U.S. 535, 536 (1942); "the liberty of parents and guardians to direct the upbringing and education of children under their control," *Pierce* v. *Society of Sisters*, 268 U.S. 510, 534–35

9. Brodie, *Marital Procreation,* 49 Ore. L. Rev. 245, 256 (1970).

(1925); as well as the right, at least of a married woman, to use contraceptives, *Griswold* v. *Connecticut*, 381 U.S. 479 (1965), are all protected constitutionally.

Most recently the Court reaffirmed the "fundamental . . . right to be free, except in very limited circumstance, from unwanted governmental intrusions into one's privacy," *Stanley* v. *Georgia*, 394 U.S. 557, 564 (1969) (Marshall, J.), and embraced with approval Mr. Justice Brandeis' dissent in *Olmstead* v. *United States*:

"The makers of our Constitution undertook to secure conditions favorable to the pursuit of happiness. They recognized the significance of man's spiritual nature, of his feeling and of his intellect. They knew that only a part of the pain, pleasure and satisfactions of life are to be found in material things. They sought to protect Americans in their beliefs, their thoughts, their emotions and their sensations. They conferred as against the Government, the right to be let alone—the most comprehensive of rights and the right most valued by civilized man." 277 U.S. at 478.

The Chief Justice, then a Circuit Judge, in *Application of Georgetown College, Inc.*, 331 F.2d 1010, 1016–17 (D.C. Cir.) (en banc), *cert. Denied*, 377 U.S. 978 (1964), also urged a right to be let alone, in the context of a religious objection to blood transfusions, which could include "even absurd ideas which do not conform, such as refusing medical treatment even at great risk." 331 F.2d at 1017.

Pregnancy obviously does have an overwhelming impact on the woman. The most readily observable impact of pregnancy, of course, is that of carrying the pregnancy for nine months. Additionally there are numerous more subtle but no less drastic impacts.[10]

10. For a discussion of the impacts of pregnancy on women *see* Brief *Amici Curiae* on Behalf of New Women Lawyers, Women's Health and Abortion Project, Inc., National Abortion Action Coalition filed herein by Nancy Stearns as follows: employment, at 17–21, 27–28; education, at 21–22; responsibility for the child, at 29–30; emotional, at 38–42.

3. The Right to Terminate Unwanted Pregnancy Is an Integral Part of Privacy Rights

Without the right to respond to unwanted pregnancy, a woman is at the mercy of possible contraceptive failure, particularly if she is unable or unwilling to utilize the most effective measures.[11] Failure to use contraceptives effectively, if pregnancy ensues, exacts an exceedingly high price.

The court in *Baird* v. *Eisenstadt*, 429 F.2d 1398 (1st Cir. 1970), *prob. juris. noted*, 401 U.S. 934 (U.S. No. 70–17, 1971 Term), recognized the inhumane severity of laws which impose continued pregnancy and compulsory parenthood as the cost of inadequate contraception. The statute there proscribed distribution of contraceptives to unmarried women, but the deciding principle applies to restrictive abortion laws as well.[12]

". . . [P]ersons must risk for themselves an unwanted pregnancy, for the child, illegitimacy, and for society, a possible obligation of support. Such a view of morality is not only the very mirror image of sensible legislation; we consider that it conflicts with fundamental human rights." 429 F.2d at 1402.

Baird involved contraceptives unavailable to unmarried women; this case involves measures unavailable to all women. The impact of the two statutes is identical for the women affected. Moreover, the magnitude of the impact is substantial.

When pregnancy begins, a woman is faced with a governmental mandate compelling her to serve as an incubator for months and then as an ostensibly willing mother for up to twenty or more years. She must often forego further education or a career and often must endure economic and social hardships. Under the present law of Texas she is given no other choice.

Continued pregnancy is compulsory, unless she can persuade the authorities that she is potentially suicidal or that her life is otherwise endangered. TEXAS PENAL CODE, arts. 1191–1194, 1196 (1961). The law impinges severely upon her dignity, her life plan and often her marital relationship. The Texas abortion law constitutes an invasion of her privacy with irreparable consequences. Absent the right to remedy contraceptive failure, other rights of personal and marital privacy are largely diluted.

Commentators and courts have articulated and recognized the privacy which restrictive abortion laws invade:

"[A]bortion falls within that sensitive area of privacy—the marital relation. One of the basic values of this privacy is birth control, as evidenced by the *Griswold* decision. Griswold's act was to prevent formation of the fetus. This, the Court found, was constitutionally protected. If an individual may prevent conception, why can he not nullify that conception when prevention has failed?"[13]

The decisions of this Court which implicitly recognize rights of marital and personal privacy have been followed by state and federal court decisions expressly holding the decision of abortion to be within the sphere of constitutionally protected privacy.

That there is a fundamental constitutional right to abortion was the conclusion of the court below in the instant case:

"On the merits, plaintiffs argue as their principal contention that the Texas Abortion Laws must be declared unconstitutional because they deprive single women and married couples of their right, secured by the Ninth Amendment to choose whether to have children. We agree.

"The essence of the interest sought to be protected here is the right of choice over events which, by their character and consequences, bear in a fundamental manner of the privacy of individuals." (A. 116)

11. *See* Brief *Amici Curiae* for Planned Parenthood Federation of America, Inc. and American Association of Planned Parenthood Physicians filed herein, "The Facts About Contraception," pp. 12–21.

12. *See* Lamm & Davison, *Abortion Reform*, 1 YALE REV. L. & Soc'l Action, No. 4, at 55, 58–59 (spring 1971).

13. Tom C. Clark, *Religion, Morality, and Abortion: A Constitutional Appraisal*, 2 LOYOLA UNIV. (L.A.) L. REV. 1, 9 (1969).

That view has been shared by a number of other courts which have considered the question and have affirmed that this is a fundamental right.[14] The progression of decisions by courts which have indicated their recognition of abortion as an aspect of protected privacy rights includes the following:

"The fundamental right of the woman to choose whether to bear children follows from the Supreme Court's and this court's repeated acknowledgment of a 'right of privacy' or 'liberty' in matters related to marriage, family, and sex." *California* v. *Belous*, 71 Cal. 2d 954, 458 P.2d 194, 199, 80 Cal. Rptr. 354 (1969), *cert. denied*, 397 U.S. 915 (1970).

"For whatever reason, the concept of personal liberty embodies a right to privacy which apparently is also broad enough to include the decision to abort a pregnancy. Like the decision to use contraceptive devices, the decision to terminate an unwanted pregnancy is sheltered from state regulation which seeks broadly to limit the reasons for which an abortion may be legally obtained." *Doe* v. *Bolton*, 319 F. Supp. 1048, 1055 (N.D. Ga. 1970) (per curiam).

"It is true after conception as before that 'there is no topic more closely interwoven with the intimacy of the home and marriage than that which relates to the conception and bear-

ing of progeny.' We believe that *Griswold* and related cases establish that matters pertaining to procreation, as well as to marriage, the family, and sex are surrounded by a zone of privacy which protects activities concerning such matters from unjustified governmental intrusion." *Doe* v. *Scott*, 321 F. Supp. 1385, 1389–90 (N.D. Ill.) *appeal docketed sub nom. Hanrahan* v. *Doe*, 39 U.S.L.W. 3438 (U.S. Mar. 29, 1971) (No. 70–105, 1971 Term).

Without the ability to control their reproductive capacity, women and couples are largely unable to control determinative aspects of their lives and marriages. If the concept of "fundamental rights" means anything, it must surely include the right to determine when and under what circumstance to have children. . . .

14. E.g., *Doe* v. *Bolton,* 319 F. Supp. 1048 (N.D. Ga. 1970) (per curiam), ques. of juris. postponed to merits, 91 S. Ct. 1614 (1971) (No. 971, 1970 Term; renumbered No. 70-40, 1971 Term); *Doe* v. *Scott,* 321 F. Supp. 1384 (N.D. Ill.), appeals docketed sub noms *Hanrahan* v. *Doe* and *Heffernan* v. *Doe,* 39 U.S.L.W. 3438 (U.S. Mar. 29, 1971) (Nos. 1522, 1523, 1970 Ter; renumbered Nos. 70-105, 70-106, 1971 Term); *Babbitz* v. *McCann,* 310 F. Supp. 29 (E.D. Wis.) (per curiam), appeal dismissed, 400 U.S. 1 (1970) (per curiam); *California* v. *Belous,* 71 Cal. 2d 954, 458 P.2d 194, 80 Cal. Rptr. 354 (1969), cert. denied, 397 U.S. 915 (1970); *People* v. *Barksdale,* _____ Cal. App. 3d _____, _____ Cal. Rptr. _____, 1 Crim. 9526 (Calif. Dist. Ct. App. July 22, 1971); contra, *Corkey* v. *Edwards,* 322 F. Supp. 1248 (W.D. N.C. 1971), appeal docketed, 40 U.S.L.W. 3048 (U. S. July 17, 1971) (No. 71-92); *Rosen* v. *Louisiana State Bd. Of Medical Examiners,* 318 F. Supp. 1275 (E.D. La. 1980), appeal docketed, 39 U.S.L.W. 3247 (U. S. Nov. 27, 1970) (No. 1010, 1970 Term; renumbered No. 70-42, 1971 Term).

58

ROE V. WADE

Brief *Amicus Curiae* on Behalf of New Women Lawyers, Women's Health and Abortion Project, Inc., National Abortion Action Coalition (1971)

In The
Supreme Court of the United States
October Term, 1971

No. 70-18

Jane Roe, John Doe, and Mary Doe,
Appellants

James Hubert Halleford, M.D.,
Appellant-Intervenor

v.

Henry Wade, Appellee

From *Roe* v. *Wade*, No. 70-18 and *Doe* v. *Bolton*, No. 70-40, Brief *Amicus Curiae* on Behalf of New Women Lawyers, Women's Health and Abortion Project, Inc., National Abortion Action Coalition, U.S. Supreme Court, October Term 1971.

On Appeal from the United States District Court for the Northern District of Texas

No. 70-40

Mary Doe, et al., appellants

v.

Arthur K. Bolton, et al., Appellees

On Appeal from the United States District Court for the Northern District of Georgia

Motion for Permission to File Brief and Brief *Amicus Curiae* on Behalf of New Women Lawyers, Women's Health and Abortion Project, Inc., National Abortion Action Coalition

STATEMENT OF INTEREST

During the past two years the question of the constitutionality of abortion laws—of the right of a woman to control her own body and life—has become one of the most burning issues for women throughout the country. As women have become aware of the myriad levels of unconstitutional discrimination they face daily, they have become most acutely aware of the primary role which restrictions on abortions play in that discrimination. As a result, women throughout the country have become determined to free themselves of the crippling and unconstitutional restrictions on their lives. As a major part of their efforts, thousands of women, have sought and continue to seek the aid of federal and state courts in their challenges to abortion statutes. In New York State, more than three hundred persons, primarily women, sued to have their state laws declared unconstitutional . . .

Similar efforts to challenge the abortion laws of their states are being developed by women in other states throughout the country. These women have sought the assistance of the federal courts because of the degree to which restrictions on the availability of abortion have crippled and even destroyed their own lives and lives of many other women.

The organizations listed below share the concern of these thousands of women who have sought the assistance of the courts. Each of the groups has a particular concern to see that these unconstitutional burdens and restrictions on a woman's life be removed.

The issues raised by the Texas and Georgia cases presently before this Court are not local but national issues. The problems raised by restrictive abortion laws are problems of millions of pregnant women.[1]

Therefore, *amici* have drawn on cases and statutes throughout the country in order to aid this Court in deeply and fully understanding the problem before it.

The New Women Lawyers is an unincorporated membership association of women lawyers and law students in the New York City area.

Amongst its purposes is to work through the courts to redress the discrimination and oppression which women face under the law.

As women lawyers and law students *amici* are both members of the class whose interests are before this Court and advocates for that class. Therefore, *amici* have special insight into the problems and issues presented in the two abortion cases which may be of assistance to the Court.

The Women's Health and Abortion Project, Inc., is a non-profit corporation in the State of New York which grew out of the challenge to the constitutionality of the former New York abortion statute. Amongst the purposes of the Project is to counsel, and provide information to women concerning family plan-

---

1. There are three basic types of laws used throughout the United States to prevent the performance of abortion, laws permitting the performance of abortion, a) only when necessary to save the life of the women, b) when necessary to preserve her life and health and c) the "reform" type law which permits abortion for reasons of life and health, as well as when the fetus resulted from rape, incest or when there is a likelihood of fetal deformity, etc. In discussing the constitutional infirmities of abortion laws, *amici* have not distinguished amongst the different types of laws because regardless of their wording their effect has all been the same—to deny an abortion to nearly every woman who wishes one.

ning and abortion without fee. Since the liberalized New York abortion law went into effect on July 1, 1970, the Project has counselled thousands of desperate women from across the country who came to New York seeking abortions. The Women's Health and Abortion Project therefore has particular concern for and understanding of the problems of women in need of abortion and is particularly concerned with the infringement of women's rights by laws such as those of Georgia and Texas restricting the availability of abortion to women.

The Women's National Abortion Action Coalition is a coalition of women's groups and individual women throughout the country who have united in efforts to eliminate all abortion laws. Many of the individual women within the Coalition are plaintiffs in class action litigation challenging the constitutionality of the abortion laws of their own states. Many others work with pregnancy counseling groups and are members of women's groups whose prime concern is the elimination of discriminatory laws such as abortion laws.

Therefore, the Coalition is particularly concerned about the issues presented in the two cases before this Court and well suited to understand and present to this Court, to the fullest extent, the tolls which these laws take on the lives of women.

Amici believe that their special perspective on the constitutional issues before this Court will be of assistance to this Court in its deliberations on one of today's most sensitive issues— an issue of overwhelming importance to more than 50% of the nation's population. *Amici* have sought to present aspects of the issue involving the constitutional rights of women which they believe have not been treated by the parties to this litigation or by other amici such as the manner in which the challenged Texas and Georgia statutes deprive women of their rights to life, liberty and the equal protection of the laws guaranteed by the Fourteenth Amendment and the degree to which they constitute cruel and usual [*sic*] punishment in violation of the Eighth Amendment to the Constitution.

Amici, therefore, urge this Court to accept their Brief Amicus in the hope that it will be of assistance in unravelling the crucial constitutional issues before this Court.

SUMMARY OF ARGUMENT

This is a brief *Amicus* in support of actions challenging the constitutionality of the abortion statutes of Georgia, Georgia Code Annotated, secs. 26–1201 *et seq.* (1969); and Texas, Texas Penal Code Articles 1191, 1193, 1194 and 1196. The Texas statute permits abortion only when necessary to preserve the life of the pregnant woman. Under the Georgia statute a woman may obtain an abortion only with the approval of a committee of doctors where the abortion is necessary to preserve her life or health, or when the pregnancy resulted from rape, or would result in a deformed child.

Amici have argued that both statutes are void in that they violate the most basic constitutional rights of women.

First, the Texas and Georgia statutes and other statutes which restrict the availability of abortion, deny to women their right to control and direct their lives and bodies as protected by the Fourteenth Amendment's guarantees of life and liberty. *Amici* have attempted to set forth for the Court the manner in which the status of pregnancy and motherhood severely restricts the life of a woman, the way in which an unwanted pregnancy can unalterably change and even destroy her life.

Amici have next shown that despite the fact that both man and woman are responsible for any pregnancy, it is the woman who bears the disproportionate share of the *de jure* and *de facto* burdens and penalties of pregnancy, child birth and child rearing. Thus, any statute which denies a woman the right to determine whether she will bear those burdens denies her the equal protection of the laws.

Carrying, giving birth to, and raising an unwanted child can be one of the most painful and longlasting punishments that a person can endure. *Amici* have argued that statutes which condemn women to share their bodies with another organism against their will, to be child breeders and rearers against their will, violate the Eighth Amendment's proscription against cruel and unusual punishment.

Finally, *amici* contend there is no compelling state interest in forcing a woman to these deprivations of her constitutional rights. For, it is no longer possible to justify a ban on abortions to protect a woman's health and such a ban is a constitutionally unacceptable method to use to establish a particular moral standard. Furthermore, the argument that the state must protect the life of the fetus when examined closely is in reality a codification of a particular religious doctrine and therefore constitutionally insufficient.

In closing, *amici* have urged that the doctrine of *Younger* v. *Harris* does not bar the Court from deciding this matter before it for in fact Mary Doe in *Doe* v. *Bolton* and Jane Roe in *Roe* v. *Wade* may not challenge the abortion statutes of Georgia and Texas in state criminal proceedings as envisioned in *Younger* and must turn to the Federal Courts to safeguard their constitutional rights.

The Right to Liberty

If the Fourteenth Amendment and its guarantees are to have any real meaning for women, they must not be read to protect only women's physical survival. The Fourteenth Amendment speaks not merely of life, but of life and liberty. For the framers of our constitution recognized well that it is not life alone which must be protected, but also personal liberty and freedom. Because of that fact, the Constitution has established requirements that neither life nor liberty may be denied a person without the guarantees of due process. As the Court of Appeals for the Second Circuit stated in *Madera* v. *Board of Education of the City of New York*, 386 F.2d 778, 783–4 (2nd Cir., 1967), invoking a long-standing constitutional principle: ". . . The 'liberty' mentioned in [the Fourteenth] Amendment

means, not only the right of the citizen to be free from the mere physical restraint of his person by incarceration, but the term is deemed to embrace the right of the citizen to be free in the enjoyment of all his faculties; to live and work where he will; to earn his livelihood by any lawful calling; to pursue any livelihood or avocation. . . ."

The right of liberty is one which is complex and closely related to other rights protected by the Constitution. As stated by this Court in *Smith* v. *Texas*, 233 U.S. 630, 636 (1914), "Liberty means more than freedom from servitude, and the constitutional guaranty is an assurance that the citizen shall be protected in the right to use [her] powers of mind or body in any lawful calling."

The right of liberty has long been seen by this Court as one which is basic to matters of family and children. In *Meyer* v. *Nebraska*, 262 U.S. 390, 399 (1823), this Court stated, "Without doubt 'liberty' denotes not merely freedom from bodily restraint but also the right of the individual to contract, to engage in any of the common occupations of life, and acquire undue knowledge, to marry, establish home and bring up children, to worship God according to the dictates of his own conscience, and generally to enjoy those privileges long recognized at common law as essential to the orderly pursuit of happiness by free men."

It should go without saying that the liberty to establish a home and bring up children is nearly meaningless if it does not include the liberty to decide when and whether to have those children. Of course, this right to control the timing of one's family is now expressed in *Griswold* v. *Connecticut*, 381 U.S. 479 (1965).

Even this does not circumscribe the limits of liberty, however. As Justice Douglas expressed in his dissent in *Poe* v. *Ulman*, 367 U.S. 497, 516 (1961): "Though I believe that 'due process' as used in the Fourteenth Amendment includes all of the first eight Amendments, I do not think it is restricted and confined to them. . . . The right 'to marry, establish a home and bring up children' was said, in *Meyer* v. *Ne-*

braska, . . . to come within the 'liberty' of the person protected by the Due Process Clause of the Fourteenth Amendment. . . . 'Liberty' is a conception that sometimes gains content from the examinations of other specific guarantees . . . or from experience with the requirements of a free society."

Most recently the understanding of personal liberty has come to include such matters as physical appearance—the way in which a person presents himself or herself to the world. In *Breen v. Kahl*, 296 F.Supp. 702, 706 (W.D.Wisc., 1969), aff'd 419 F.2d 1034 (7th Cir., 1969), the court ordered the reinstatement of high school students whose hair length did not conform to the school board standard stating: "The freedom of an adult male or female to present himself or herself physically to the world in the manner of his or her own choice is a highly protected freedom. . . .

For the state to impair this freedom, in the absence of a compelling subordinating interest in doing so, would offend a widely shared concept of human dignity, would assault personality and individuality, would undermine identity, and would invade human 'being'. It would violate a basic value 'implicit in the concept of ordered liberty.' *Palko v. Connecticut*, 302 U.S. 219, 325. . . .

It would deprive a man or woman of liberty without due process of law in violation of the Fourteenth Amendment. See *Griswold*, 381 U.S. at 499–500 (Harlan, J., concurring)."

Accord, *Griffin v. Tatum*, 300 F.Supp. 60 (M.D. Ala., 1969); *Westley v. Rossi*, 305 F.Supp 706 (D. Minn., 1969); *Durham v. Pulsiter*, 312 F.Supp. 411 (D. Ut., 1970); *Reichenberg v. Nelson*, 310 F.Supp. 248 (D. Nebr., 1970).

The concept of the right to liberty is one which has developed from the right to contract in *Allgeyer*, to the right to raise a family in *Meyer*, to the right to control one's own appearance in *Breen*. Surely none of these rights can be seen as more basic, fundamental or worthy of protection than a woman's right to control her body and the nature, direction and quality of her life.

In light of this understanding of the meaning of the guarantees of the Fourteenth Amendment, it is even more critical that this Court carefully examine the ways in which women are systematically deprived of their rights by the abortion laws of Texas and Georgia as well as those of nearly every state in the nation.

It should be obvious that from the moment a woman becomes pregnant her status in society changes as a result of both direct and indirect actions of the government and because of social mores. Except in very rare cases (primarily among the wealthy) she is certainly no longer "free in the enjoyment of all [her] faculties; . . . free to use them in all lawful ways; to live and work where [she] will; to earn [her] livelihood by any lawful calling; to pursue any livelihood or avocation. . . ." *Madera v. Board of Education of the City of New York*, *Supra* at 783–4.

Pregnancy, from the moment of conception, severely limits a woman's liberty. In many cases of both public and private employment women are forced to temporarily or permanently leave their employment when they become pregnant. The employer has no duty to transfer a pregnant woman to a less arduous job during any stage of pregnancy (should the woman or her doctor consider this advisable); nor is there any statutory duty to rehire the woman after she gives birth. For example, under the New York State Civil Service Law, Rule 3, a female employee must report her pregnancy to the appointing authority not later than the fourth month. The appointing authority then may in his discretion ". . . place the employee on leave *at any time* when in its judgement the *interest of either the department* or the employee would be best served" [emphasis supplied]. There is no indication that the employee's medical condition is the critical factor and there are no standards on which the decision is made. What is plain is that regardless of whether the woman wishes and/or needs to continue working, regardless of whether she is physically capable of working, she may nonetheless be required to stop working solely because of her pregnancy. In many if not most states women who are public employees are compelled to terminate their employment at some arbitrary date during pregnancy regardless of whether they are capable of continuing work. See for example *Cohen* v. *Chesterfield County School Board*, Civ. Action No. 678–70-R (E.D.Va.) May 17, 1971; *Schattman* v. *Texas Employment Commission*, Civil Action No. A-70-CA-75 (W.D.Tex.) February 25, 1971; and *LaFleur* v. *Cleveland School Board of Education*, Civil Action N. C-71–292 N.D. Ohio, May 27, 1971.

In Connecticut a directive from the Attorney General in 1938 stated that a pregnant woman could not be employed "during the four weeks previous to and following her confinement." This rule still exists. In fact, such employment is a criminal offense (directed against the employer). This denial of liberty in one's work is accompanied by an unconstitutional taking of property, for Connecticut provides no maternity benefits. A woman is also denied unemployment compensation during her last two months of pregnancy, even when her unemployment is due to some reason other than pregnancy. CGST 31–236(5). *Janello* v. *Administrator*, *Unemployment Compensation Act*, 178 A.2d 282, 23 Conn. Supp. 155 (1961). If "total or partial unemployment is due to pregnancy," the woman is completely ineligible for benefits. *Janello*, *supra* at 156. Even worse, the employer has the absolute, arbitrary right to fire a pregnant woman when, in his estimation, her pregnancy would interfere with her work. *Janello*, *supra* at 157.

In Louisiana a recent amendment in 1968 of L.S.A.-R.S. 23:1601(6)(b) enables a woman who is forced to leave her employment either by contract or otherwise on account of pregnancy, to qualify for unemployment compensation. But, as illustrated in the case of *Grape* v, *Brown*, 231 So. 2d 663 (Ct. App. La., 1970) the unemployment compensation in no way adequately compensates either for the actual wages lost, or for the denial of liberty which forces a woman to receive unemployment compensation. Mary Grape was employed as a key punch operator by Southwestern Electric Power Co.

When she became pregnant she was advised that the company policy required that expectant mothers terminate employment no later than the end of the 150th day of pregnancy and that no leaves of absence would be granted. Thus she was forced onto unemployment compensation and had lost her job.

Mississippi laws curtail even more severely the liberty of a woman and her property. Sec. 7379(a), Miss. Code 1942 Rec. states that a married woman who has left work because of pregnancy is considered to have voluntarily severed her employment without good cause and therefore is not even entitled to unemployment compensation. See *Mississippi Employment Security Commission* v. *Corley*. 148 So.2d 715 (Miss., 1963). Thus, the pregnant woman loses her job, her source of income, and is *forced* to become economically *dependent* on others. The law is most harsh on pregnant women who are heads of households, and depended upon as breadwinners. Statistics show that a very high percent of all working women are in this position, i.e., they *must* work to support themselves and/or their children.

But restrictions on a woman's liberty and property only *begin* with pregnancy. A woman worker with children is considered "unavailable for work" (which means that she cannot qualify for unemployment compensation), if she restricts her hours of availability to late afternoon and night shifts so that she may care for her children during the day. Connecticut courts have often held that "domestic responsibilities" are "personal reasons unrelated to employment," *Lukienchuk* v. *Administrator*, *Unemp. Comp. Act*, 176 A.2d 892, 23 Conn. Sup. 85 (Super. Ct., 1961) or "entirely disconnected from any attribute of employment" *Lenz* v. *Administrator*, *Unemp. Comp. Act*, 17 Conn. Sup. 315 (Super. Ct., 1951). In one decision the court said that a woman had just *five weeks* to try to rearrange her life and her domestic responsibilities to try to make herself "available for work" according to Connecticut standards (i.e., ready to work at all hours of the day). There is only one case that held that a woman who restricted her availability for personal reasons was entitled to unemployment compensation. The woman had *seven* children. *Carani* v. *Danaher*, 13 Conn. Supp. 109 (Super. Ct., 1943).

But the dominant belief is that a woman's "personal reasons" (in most cases, "domestic responsibilities") for seeking work during specific hours are not relevant to employment. Thus, women with home responsibilities (children or husband)—who need or want to work—are considered "unavailable for work." They are denied the freedom "to live and work where they will, to earn their livelihood by any lawful calling" *Allgeyer* v. *Louisiana*, *supra* and "to engage in any of the common occupations of life" *Meyer* v. *Nebraska*, *supra*—freedoms that are implicitly in the Fourteenth Amendment's "concept of ordered liberty." *Palko* v. *Connecticut*, 302 U.S. 319 (1937). It becomes clear from Connecticut decisions on pregnant working women that the State of Connecticut considers pregnancy a "malady," *Adams* v. *American Fastener Co.*, 7 Conn. Supp. 379 (1939). Under these circumstances, a case can well be made that the anti-abortion law, in compelling a pregnant woman to continue this condition against her wishes, is not merely a denial of liberty, but also an imposition of cruel and unusual punishment on the woman. See Section III *infra*. "Confinement" well describes the situation of the pregnant woman, or mother, who is denied work, or restricted in her work because of an employer's decision on her ability to work.

Here we see how inextricably the rights to life and liberty are mixed and even more how laws restricting abortion deny women both.

Once a woman has given birth, according to the Court of Appeals for the Fifth Circuit, she may still be barred from employment as long as she has pre-school children. *Phillips* v. *Martin Marietta Corp.*, 411 F.2d 1. (5th Cir., 1969). See Section II, *infra*, for a discussion of the treatment of *Phillips* by this Court. Furthermore, if she needs or merely wishes to work while she has pre-school children she cannot unless she is fortunate enough to have family who will care for the children or is wealthy enough to hire help.

And, though a housekeeper, nurse, or baby sitter is a necessary expense enabling her to work, she may not deduct the salary of that person from her income tax 26 U.S.C. 214 and thus is normally left with little if any of her pay after those expenses are covered.

Thus as long as a woman has young children she is denied the right to obtain employment though her ". . . power to earn a living for [herself] and those dependent upon [her] is in the nature of personal liberty." *Smith* v. *Hill*, 285 F.Supp. 556, 560 (D.N.C., 1968).

A further denial of liberty results from the fact that women are generally forced to arbitrarily end their education because of pregnancy. Until recently, girls who became pregnant were forced to drop out of public school in New York. In New York City, Central Harlem, more than forty percent of the girls who leave school before graduation do so because of pregnancy. Haryou, 1964, *Youth in the Ghetto*, N.Y. Orans Press, p. 185. This still happens in countless other cities throughout the country as well. See, for example, *Perry* v. *Grenada Municipal Separate School District*, 300 F.Supp. 748 (N.D.Miss., 1969). Many women are also deprived of higher education because of college rules requiring that pregnant women leave school.

The importance of education in modern society has been stressed and restressed in recent years, since Chief Justice Warren stated in *Brown* v. *Board of Education*, 347 U.S. 483, 493 (1954): "Today, education is perhaps the most important function of state and local governments. . . . It is required in the performance of our most basic public responsibilities. . . . It is the very foundation of good citizenship. Today it is a principal instrument in awakening . . . cultural values, in preparing . . . for later professional training and in helping . . . to adjust normally to his environment.

It has been recognized more recently that there are special problems for women in obtaining education for though "men and women are equally in need of continuing education . . . at present women's opportunities are more limited than men's." *American Women*: *Report of the President's Commission on the Status of Women,* 1963, p. 11. Nonetheless, women are robbed of their education and opportunity for any development and self-fulfillment; robbed of their rights to be "free in the enjoyment of all (their) faculties," Madera, *supra,* at 783–4, by chance of an unwanted pregnancy.

The incursions on the liberty of an unmarried woman who becomes pregnant are even more severe. She too may be fired from her job and is even more likely to be compelled to discontinue her education. Unable to terminate her pregnancy, she is often forced into marriage against her will and better judgment in an attempt to cope with the new economic and social realities of her life. Such marriages are forced on women despite the fact that the right to marry or *not to marry* may not be invaded by the state. *Loving* v. *Virginia,* 388 U.S. 1 (1967).[2]

Of course, frequently, the man who is responsible for the pregnancy refuses to marry her. Then unable to support herself she may be forced to become a welfare recipient, become part of that cycle of poverty, and expose herself to the personal humiliation, loss of personal liberty and inadequate income that entails.

To further add to her difficulties, the mere fact of her out-of-wedlock pregnancy or child resulting from that pregnancy may be used as "some evidential or presumptive effect" to a decision to exclude or remove her from public housing. *Thorpe* v. *Housing Authority,* 393 U.S. 268, 271 (1969). Thus, having been forced to bear a child she did not want, she may be deprived of her right and ability to provide for herself and her child either because of employer policies or because of her inability to leave the child. Surviving on at least marginal income, she who is most obviously in need of public housing is then deprived of decent shelter because of the existence of that very same child.

For a woman perhaps the most critical aspect of liberty is the right to decide when and whether she will have a child—with all the burdens and limitations on her freedom which that entails. But that has been robbed from her by men who make the laws which govern her.

As early as 1848 women spoke out against the way in which men controlled their lives—denied them of any meaningful liberty. At the Women's Rights Convention held in Seneca Falls, New York, on July 14, 1848, the women spoke of men as follows: "He has compelled her (woman) to submit to laws in the formation of which she has no voice. . . . He has taken all her rights to property, even to the wages she earns. . . . In the covenant of marriage . . . the law (gives) him power to deprive her of her liberty and to administer chastisement. . . . He closes against her all the avenues of wealth and distinction which he considers most honorable to himself. . . . He has denied her the facilities for obtaining a thorough education. . . . He has endeavored in every way that he could to destroy her confidence in her own powers, to lessen her self-respect, and to make her willing to lead an abject life. *Victory, How Women Won It,* National American Woman Suffrage Association, A Centennial Symposium, 1840–1940, H. W. Wilson Co., 1940, pp. 15–25.

Restrictive laws governing abortion such as those of Texas and Georgia are a manifestation of the fact that men are unable to see women in any role other than that of mother and wife. Furthermore,

"So long as he continues to think and write, to speak and act, as if maternity was the one and sole object of a woman's existence—so long as children are conceived in weariness and disgust—you must not look for high-toned men and women capable of accomplishing any great and noble achievement."[3]

As recently as July 12, 1971 the Supreme Court of the State of Florida reversed three convictions for conspiracy to commit abortion.

2. The reaction of forcing a pregnant girl or woman into marriage as a "solution" to an unwanted out-of-wedlock pregnancy is exemplified by the ruling of a Maryland court in 1955, waiving the marriage age requirements to permit a thirteen year old pregnant girl to marry. Harold Rosen, M.D., *Psychiatric Implications of Abortion, A Case Study of Social Hypocrisy,* 17 Wes. R.L. Rev. 454, at 454.

3. Elizabeth Stanton to Gerrit Smith, December 21, 1857, Stanton papers, LC, quoted in Andrew Sinclair, *The Emancipation of the American Woman,* Harper Colphon Book, New York, 1966, p. 259.

In the concluding sentence of its opinion the Court stated: "In sum the [abortion] statute intrudes into the area of personal liberty of women and does it crudely in vague, uncertain, archaic language." *Walsingham* v. *Florida*, *supra*, slip opinion, p. 15, Ervin, J., Concurring.

The Florida statute does not alone abridge a woman's fundamental right to liberty. The statutes of Georgia, Texas and nearly every other state in the nation similarly deny to women throughout the country their most precious right to control their lives and bodies.

59

WEBSTER V. REPRODUCTIVE HEALTH SERVICES
The Historians' Brief (1988)

This brief was filed as part of *William L.Webster, et al., v. Reproductive Health Services, et al*. in the Supreme Court of the United States, October Term, 1988, on appeal from the United States Court of Appeals for the Eighth Circuit. *Note*: Numerous additional historians signed the brief after it was filed, bringing the total number to over 400.

Interest of Amici

Amici are two hundred and eighty-one American historians who, with the permission of the parties, here seek to provide a rich and accurate description of our national history and tradition in relation to women's liberty to choose whether to terminate a pregnancy. Never before have so many professional historians sought to address this Honorable Court in this way. Amici have widely diverse perspectives and knowledge, but are united in the conviction that *Roe v.Wade* is essential to women's liberty and equality and consistent with the

From "Brief on 281 American Historians as *Amici Curiae* Supporting Appellees," in *The Public Historian*, Summer 1990, re *Webster v. Reproductive Health Services*, 492 U.S. 490 (1989).

most noble and enduring understanding of our history and traditions.

SUMMARY OF ARGUMENT

Established constitutional principles require examination of our history and tradition as a Nation to determine the existence and contours of fundamental constitutional rights. The United States asserts that our history unambiguously supports the constitutionality of laws restricting women's access to abortion.

This brief will demonstrate that for much of our nation's history abortion was not illegal; that for much of the nineteenth century abortion remained legal prior to quickening; and that, in most states, the statutes regulating abortion did not punish women. It discusses the prevalence and visibility of abortion in the nineteenth century. It shows that a variety of complex factors underlay the nineteenth-century laws restricting abortion: concern for women's health, the medical profession's desire to control the practice of medicine, openly discriminatory concepts of the appropriate role of women, opposition to non-procreative sexual activity and to the dissemination of information concerning birth control, and hostility to those who did not fit the white Anglo-Saxon Protestant model. Our brief shows that concern for the fetus has become a central argument for anti-abortion laws only as these earlier justifications have become either anachronistic or constitutionally and culturally impermissible.

Restricting access to abortion imposes ponderous burdens on the liberty and equality of women. A state cannot constitutionally justify the imposition of such burdens by adopting one, highly contested, metaphysical concept of the value of fetal life. This Court should affirm *Roe v. Wade*.

Argument

I. Our traditions and history define the contours of the constitutional right to privacy.

Since John Marshall, no Justice of this Court has seriously disputed that the wise and intended meaning of our Constitution is determined by interpreting its words in light of our nation's history and traditions.[1] Our history and tradition shape the meaning of the relatively concrete provisions of the Constitution, such as the First Amendment.[2] History and tradition also give content to the more open-textured provisions of our Constitution— the prohibition of the Fifth and Fourteenth Amendments of state actions that deprive citizens of life, liberty or property without due process of law; the Fourteenth Amendment's guarantee of equal treatment under the law; and the Ninth Amendment's command that the "enumeration in the Constitution, of certain rights, shall not be construed to deny or disparage others retained by the people."

Judge Frankfurter, a staunch defender of judicial restraint, underscored the role of history and tradition, joining this Court's invalidation of "released-time" religious instruction in public schools:

"Accommodation of legislative freedom and constitutional limitations upon that freedom cannot be achieved by a mere phrase. We cannot illuminatingly apply the 'wall-of-separation'

metaphor until we have considered the relevant history of religious education in America, the place of the 'released time' movement in that history, and its precise manifestation in the case before us."

In *McCollum v. Board of Education*, 333 U.S. 203, 213 (1948)(Frankfurter, J., concurring), Justice Frankfurter frankly acknowledged that "'released time' ha[d] attained substantial proportions," but recognized that that fact did not decide the case. *Id.* at 224. A more exhaustive examination of our traditions led Justice Frankfurter, and seven other Justices, to strike down Illinois' "released-time" program.

While there is little disagreement that history and tradition are important guides to decision in this area of the law, there is significant dispute about what our history actually demonstrates.[3] This Court's 1973 decision in *Roe v. Wade* provided a rich and sound description of the history of abortion. Since 1973 much historical work has expanded and deepened this understanding. An important part of American historical inquiry has shifted from the study of wars, formal legal rules, economics and elections, to provide a fuller and far more rounded account of American social history through exploration of diaries, letters, and other artifacts of what "ordinary people" did and believed.

In searching our nation's history for evidence of our society's basic beliefs, practices, and understandings, statutes are neither the only sources nor the best ones. As legal historian Hendrik Hartog has pointed out, "[I]n defining law as the command of the sovereign we ordinarily deny the legitimacy of inter-

---

1. See, e.g., *McCulloch v. Maryland,* 17 U.S. (4 Wheat.) 316, 400–6 (1819) (Marshall, C.J.); *Poe v. Ullman,* 367 U.S. 497, 542–44 (1961)(Harlan, J., dissenting); *Roe v. Wade,* 410 U.S. 113 (1973); *Moore v. East Cleveland,* 431 U.S. 494, 503–5 (1977)(plurality opinion). Justice White has expressed this view eloquently:

"[T]his Court does not subscribe to the simplistic view that constitutional interpretation can possibly be limited to the 'plain meaning' of the Constitution's text of the subjective intention of the Framers. The Constitution is not a deed setting forth the precise metes and bounds of its subject matter; rather it is a document announcing fundamental principles in value-laden terms that leave ample scope for the exercise of normative judgment by those charged with interpreting and applying it." *Thornburgh v. American College of Obstetricians and Gynecologists,* 476 U.S. 747, 789 (1986)(White, J., dissenting).

2. See, e.g., *Martin v. Struthers,* 319 U.S. 141, 145 (1943)(door-to-door distribution of literature protected by First Amendment because "in accordance with the best tradition of free discussion").

3. The brief *amicus curiae* of the United States, in the instant case, seeks to show that our history does not support women's claim of right to terminate pregnancy. It relies upon only one historical work: James Mohr's *Abortion in America: The Origins and Evolution of National Policy* (1978). Brief *amicus curiae* of the United States at 13, 16–17. Among historians this book is widely regarded as accurate and comprehensive. Professor Mohr is among the historians on whose behalf our brief is submitted. Yet, as we shall demonstrate, the United States misapprehends both Mohr's work and the historical record.

pretive stances other than those . . . which have the benefit of formal authoritativeness."[4] In any calculus of traditions and "fundamental" values, the moral beliefs and practices of ordinary people are entitled to consideration.[5]

II. At the time the federal constitution was adopted, abortion was known and not illegal.

As the Court demonstrated in *Roe v. Wade*, abortion was not illegal at common law.[6] Through the nineteenth century American common law decisions uniformly reaffirmed that women committed no offense in seeking abortions.[7] Both common law and popular American understanding drew distinctions depending upon whether the fetus was "quick," *i.e.*, whether the *woman* perceived signs of independent life.[8] There was some dispute whether a common law misdemeanor occurred when a third party destroyed a fetus, after quickening, without the woman's consent. But

early recognition of this particular crime against pregnant women did not diminish the liberty of the woman herself to end a pregnancy in its early stages.[9]

Abortion was not uncommon in colonial America.[10] Herbal abortifacients were widely known,[11] and cookbooks and women's diaries of the era contained recipes for medicines.[12] Recent studies of the work of midwives in the 1700s report cases in which the midwives provided women abortifacient compounds. More significantly, these cases are described as routine and are unaccompanied by any particular disapproval.[13]

The absence of legal condemnation of abortion in colonial America is all the more remarkable because both families and society valued children and population growth in a rural economy, with vast unsettled lands, where diseases of infancy claimed many lives. For these reasons, single women more often sought

4. Hartog, *Pigs and Positivism,* 1985 Wis. L. Rev. 899, 934–35.

5. See Veysey, "Intellectual History and the New Social History," in *New Directions in American Intellectual History* 3–26 (J. Higham & P. Conkin, eds., 1979).

6. *Roe v. Wade,* 410 U.S. 113, 132–36 & n.21 (1973). See also J. Mohr, supra note 3, at 3–19.

7. For example, in 1845, Chief Judge Shaw of Massachusetts held that abortion, with the woman's consent, is not punishable at common law unless the fetus were quick. *Commonwealth v. Parker,* 50 Mass. (9 Met.) 263, 43 Am. Dec. 396 (1845). In 1892 the Massachusetts Supreme Judicial Court held that, despite statutory enactments regulating abortion, the woman having an abortion was not a principal or an accomplice. *Commonwealth v. Follansbee,* 155 Mass. 274, 29 N.E. 471 (1892). In *Abrams v. Foshee,* 3 Iowa 274, 278, 66 Am. Dec. 77, 80 (1856), the Iowa Supreme Court held that abortion, prior to quickening, was no crime. *Hatfield v. Gano,* 15 Iowa 177 (1863), held that Iowa's statutory enactment did not apply to abortion produced by a woman herself. See C. Smith-Rosenberg, Disorderly Conduct 219–20 (1985).

8. See *Roe v. Wade,* 410 U.S. at 134–36; J. Mohr, supra note 3, at 24–26. In ordinary language in the eighteenth century and much of the nineteenth century the term "abortion" meant the termination of pregnancy after the point of quickening. *Id.* at 3–5.

9. See *Roe v. Wade,* 410 U.S. at 134–36; J. Mohr, supra note 3, at 24–26. Means, *The Phoenix of Abortional Freedom,* 17 N.Y. L. Forum 335, 336–53 (1971) demonstrates that commentators who asserted that a misdemeanor could be charged against third parties who destroy a fetus by assaulting women late in pregnancy misread the common law precedents upon which they purported to rely. Even in cases involving brutal beatings of women in the late stages of pregnancy, common-law courts refused to recognize abortion as a crime, independent of assault upon the woman, or in one case "witchcraft." See A. McLaren, *Reproductive Rituals* 119–121 (1983).

10. "[O]bservers in the seventeenth and eighteenth centuries made repeated references to employment of abortifacients by both the single and the married." A. McLaren, *supra* note 9, at 114 and generally at 113–44.

11. The classic work was N. Culpeper, *The English Physician* (1799). See J. Brodie, *Family Limitations in American Culture,* Ph.D. dissertation, University of Chicago 1982, at 224–30.

12. C. Smith-Rosenberg, *supra* note 7, at 228.

13. For example, a midwife reported, "She is suffering from obstructions and I prescribed the use of particular herbs." Diary of Martha Moore Ballard, Sept. 27, 1789, Maine State Manuscript Library. For a general discussion, see Ulrich, "Martha Moore Ballard and the Medical Challenge to Midwifery," in *From Revolution to Statehood: Maine in the Early Republic, 1783 to 1920* (J. Leamon & C. Clark, eds., 1988).

abortions in the Colonial era.[14] The absence of legal condemnation is particularly striking in the New England culture of tight-knit, religiously homogeneous communities in which neighbor observed the private behavior of neighbor and did not hesitate to chastise those who violated pervasive moral norms of the community.[15] In an era characterized by extensive oral and written moral prescripts from community and religious leaders, birth control and abortion were rarely the subject for moralizing. Where abortion is noted, it is not the practice itself that is subject of comment, but rather the violation of other social/sexual norms that gave rise to the perceived need to attempt to abort.[16]

In the late eighteenth century, strictures on sexual behavior loosened considerably. The incidence of pre-marital pregnancy rose sharply; in the late eighteenth century, one third of all New England brides were pregnant at the time of marriage, compared to less than ten percent in the seventeenth century.[17] Falling birth rates in the 1780s suggest that, at the same time our founders drafted the Constitution, including the Ninth Amendment's guarantee that the enumeration of certain rights "shall not be construed to deny or disparage others retained by the people," the use of birth control and abortion increased.[18]

III. Through the nineteenth century, abortion became even more widely accepted and highly visible.

Through the nineteenth century and well into the twentieth, abortion remained a widely accepted popular practice, despite increasingly vigorous efforts to prohibit it after 1860.[19] Changing patterns of abortion practice and at-

14. M. Grossberg, *Governing the Hearth* 159 (1985). J. D'Emilio and E. Freedman, *Intimate Matters: A History of Sexuality in America* (1988), report, "Cases of attempted abortion usually involved illicit lovers, not married couples. 'When a single woman,' Margaret Lakes later confessed, she 'used means to destroy the fruit of her body to conceal her sin and shame.' Elizabeth Robins of Maryland confessed that she had twice taken savin, an abortifacient; her husband suspected that she had an incestuous relationship with her brother." *Id.* at 26.

15. Adultery, incest, insubordination by children, and even "living alone not subject to the governance of family life," were condemned by the criminal law, when abortion was not. See Cott, *Eighteenth-Century Family and Social Life Revealed in Massachusetts Divorce Records,* 10 J. of Soc. Hist. 20, 22–24, 33 (1976); P. Laslett, *The World We Have Lost* 37–38 (1973); D. Flaherty, *Privacy in Colonial New England* 42–43, 76 (1972); P. Aries, *Centuries of Childhood: A Social History of Family Life* 405–7 (R. Baldick trans. 1962). For a more popular, fictional treatment, see N. Hawthorne, *The Scarlet Letter* (1850).

16. J. D'Emilio & E. Freedman, *supra* note 14, at 12, report the following case from the 1600s. "Captain William Mitchell, an influential Marylander who served on the governor's council, not only impregnated Mrs. Susan Warren and gave her a 'physic' to abort the child, but he also 'lived in fornication' with his pretended wife, Joan Toaste. Even so, the first charge filed against Mitchell by the Maryland attorney was that he professed himself to be an Atheist and openly mocked all Religion."

17. M. Gordon, *The American Family: Past, Present, and Future* 173 (1978). For comprehensive discussions see D. Smith & M. Hindus, *Premarital Pregnancy in America,* 1640–1971: An Overview and Interpretation, 5 J. Interdisciplinary Hist. 537, 553-57 (1975); Hoff-Wilson, "The Illusion of Change: Women and the American Revolution," in The American Revolution: Explorations in the History of American Radicalism 404 (A. Young, ed. 1976).

18. Wells, *Family Size and Fertility Control in Eighteenth Century America: A Study of Quaker Families,* 25 Population Studies 73 (1971); M. Norton, *Liberty's Daughters: The Revolutionary Experience of American Women, 1750–1800* 232 (1980).

19. C. Degler, *At Odds: Women and the Family in America from the Revolution to the Present* 243–46 (1980). Several studies by physicians in various parts of the U.S. suggest that in the mid-nineteenth century one abortion was performed for every four live births. See J. Mohr, *supra* note 3, at 76–80. Reports from the late 1870s estimated even greater numbers. *Id.* at 81–82. The Michigan Board of Health estimated in 1898 that one-third of all pregnancies in that state ended in abortion. Haggard, *Abortion: Accidental, Essential, Criminal, Address Before the Nashville Academy of Medicine,* Aug. 4, 1898, at 10, discussed in C. Smith-Rosenberg, *supra* note 7, at 221.

titudes towards it can only be understood against a more general background of dramatic change in American economic and family life. During the period between ratification of the Constitution and adoption of the Civil War Amendments, Americans moved to cities and increasingly worked for wages.[20] In 1787, the average white American woman bore seven children; by the late 1870s, the average was down to fewer than 5; by 1900 it was 3.56.[21] Carl Degler calls this decline in fertility "the single most important fact about women and the family in American history."[22]

Economic reasons motivated urban couples to limit their family size. Working-class married women, faced with the material difficulty of managing a family budget on a single male wage, resorted to abortion as the most effective available means of "conscious fertility control."[23]

But more than economic factors were at work in the restriction of fertility.[24] White middle-class Americans were, in particular, influenced by changing family conceptions and definitions of motherhood. As men's work patterns deviated farther from those of women, "wife" and "home" became powerful symbols of men's economic security and social standing.[25]

Nineteenth-century women faced sharply conflicting demands. "The True Woman was domestic, docile, and reproductive. The good bourgeois wife was to limit her fertility, symbolize her husband's affluence, and do good within the world."[26]

To limit the number of children they bore, women adopted a range of strategies, including abortion.[27] Through the 1870s abortion was "common," a "matter of fact" and often "safe and successful."[28] The most common methods of abortion in the nineteenth century involved herbs and devices that women could purchase from pharmacists and use themselves.[29] Nevertheless, in 1871, New York City, with a population of less than one million, supported two hundred full-time abortionists, not including doctors who sometimes performed abortions.[30]

For most of the nineteenth century, abortion was highly visible. "Beginning in the early 1840s abortion became, for all intents and purposes, a business, a service openly traded in the free market. . . . [Pervasive advertising told Americans] not only that many practitioners would provide abortion services, but that some

---

20. See C. Degler, *supra* note 19.

21. Smith, "Family Limitation, Sexual Control, and Domestic Feminism in Victorian America," in *A Heritage of Her Own* 226 (N. Cott & E. Pleck, eds., 1979). For discussion of continual decline in family size in the eighteenth and nineteenth centuries, see R. Petchesky, *Abortion and Woman's Choice* 73–74 (1986).

22. C. Degler, *supra* note 19, at 191.

23. See R. Petchesky, *supra* note 21, at 53.

24. The size of rural families also declined sharply during the nineteenth century. Faragher, *History From the Inside-Out: Writing the History of Women in Rural America,* 33 Am. Q. 536, 549 (1981); R. Petchesky, *supra* note 21, at 74. James Mohr observes that by the 1860s abortion "seemed to thrive as well on the prairies as in large urban centers." J. Mohr, *supra* note 3, at 100.

25. The home was conceived as "a bastion of peace, of repose, of orderliness, of unwavering devotion to people and principles beyond the self . . . safe from the grind-

ing pressures and dark temptations of the world at large. . . . The husband-father undertook an exclusive responsibility for productive labor. . . . [F]amily life was wrenched apart from the world of work—a veritable sea-change in social history. . . . [T]he wife-mother . . . became the centerpiece in a developing cult of Home." Demos, "Images of The American Family, Then and Now," in *Changing Images of the Family* 51, 52 (V. Tufte and B. Myerhoff, eds., 1979).

26. C. Smith-Rosenberg, supra note 7, at 225.

27. One physician wrote that "abortion is not always associated with crime and disgrace; it may arise from causes perfectly natural and altogether beyond the control of the female." T. Beck, 1 *Elements of Medical Jurisprudence* 207 (1823), quoted in M. Grossberg, *supra* note 14, at 160.

28. L. Gordon, *Woman's Body, Woman's Right: A Social History of Birth Control in America,* 51–52 (1976).

29. See LaSorte, *Nineteenth Century Family Planning Practices,* 41 *J. of Psychohistory* 163, 166–70 (1976).

30. *New York Times,* Aug. 23, 1871, at 6.

practitioners had made the abortion business their chief livelihood. Indeed, abortions became one of the first specialties in American medical history."[31]

IV. Nineteenth-century abortion restrictions sought to promote objectives that are today plainly either inapplicable or constitutionally impermissible.

Between 1850 and 1880, the newly formed American Medical Association, through some of its vigorously active members, became the *"single most important factor in altering the legal policies toward abortion in this country."*[32] Nineteenth-century "regular" physicians enlisted state power to limit access to abortion for reasons that are, in retrospect, parochial, and have long since been rejected by organized medicine.[33] The doctors found an audience for their effort to restrict abortion because they appealed to broader concerns: maternal health, consumer protection, a discriminatory idea of the natural subordination of women, nativist fears generated by the fact that elite Protestant women often sought abortions. Some of those seeking these diverse objectives also sought to attribute moral status to the fetus.

A. From 1820–1860, abortion regulation in the states rejected broader English restrictions and sought to protect women from particularly dangerous forms of abortion.

In 1803, English law made all forms of abortion criminal.[34] Despite this model, for two decades, no American state restricted access to abortion. In 1821, when one state, Connecticut, acted, it prohibited only the administration of a "deadly poison, or other noxious and destructive substance."[35] Moreover, the act applied only after quickening,[36] and punished only the person who administered the poison, not the woman who consumed it. In the late 1820s, three other states followed the Connecticut model, prohibiting the use of dangerous poisons *after* quickening. Most American states did not see abortion as a problem demanding legislative attention.

In 1830, Connecticut became the first state to punish abortion after quickening.[37] In the same year, New York, also animated by a concern for patient safety, considered a law to prohibit *any* surgery, unless two physicians approved it as essential. Prior to scientific understanding of germ theory and antisepsis, any surgical intervention was likely to be fatal. The act finally adopted applied only to surgical abortion and included the first "therapeutic" exception, approving abortion where two physicians agreed that it was "necessary."[38] As the Court recognized in *Roe v. Wade*, until the twentieth century, abortion, particularly when done through surgical intervention, remained significantly more dangerous to the woman than

---

31. J. Mohr, *supra* note 3, at 47. "[A] genuinely flourishing market in abortion services existed in the United States from the 1840s through the 1870s. *Id.* at 98. In the 1860s and 1870s both the popular press and medical journals were full of advice about abortion services. *Id.* at 67–68. See also C. Degler, *supra* note 19, at 230.

32. J. Mohr, *supra* note 3, at 157 (emphasis supplied). See also R. Petchesky, *supra* note 21, at 79.

33. See brief *amicus curiae* of the American Medical Association in the instant case.

34. The law was passed as part of a comprehensive revision of the criminal code, urged by Lord Ellenborough, broadening the sweep of the criminal law and increasing penalties. J. Mohr, *supra* note 3, at 23; *Roe v. Wade*, 410 U.S. 113, 136–38 (1973).

35. The Public Statute Laws of the State of Connecticut 152–53 (1821). See J. Mohr, *supra* note 3, at 22. See also Quay, *Justifiable Abortion—Medical and Legal Foundations,* 49 Georgetown L. Rev. 395 (1960–61).

36. Missouri adopted such a statute in 1825, Illinois in 1827, and New York in 1828. See J. Mohr, *supra* note 3, at 25–27.

37. Conn. Stat. Tit. 22, [Sec.] 14 at 152 (1821), reported by Quay, *supra* note 35, at 453.

38. See N.Y. Rev. Stat., pt. IV, Ch. I, tit. VI [Sec.] 21, at 578 (1828–1835), reported by Quay, *supra* note 35, at 499.

childbirth.[39] Because nineteenth-century abortion laws were drafted and justified to protect women, they did not punish women as parties to an abortion.[40]

None of these early laws, restricting forms of abortion thought to be particularly unsafe, were enforced.[41] That absence itself speaks powerfully, particularly since abortion was prevalent. Despite legislative action and medical opposition, common, openly tolerated practice suggests that many Americans did not perceive abortion as morally wrong.[42]

B. From the mid-nineteenth century, a central purpose of abortion regulation was to define who should be allowed to control medical practice.

Without exception, physicians were the principal nineteenth-century proponents of laws to restrict abortion. A core purpose of the nineteenth-century laws, and of doctors in supporting them, was to "control medical practice in the interest of public safety."[43] This is not to deny that some doctors had moral objections to abortion, as well as moral and social views about women and race. But the most significant explanation for the drive by medical doctors for statutes regulating abortion is the fact that these doctors were undergoing the historical process of professionalization.

Medicine was not then the organized, highly regulated profession we know today. It was an occupation in which conventional and scientifically authoritative modes of practice still contended for stature and authority with more popular modes, such as botanic medicine, homeopathy, herbalists, midwives and abortionists. Allopathic physicians sought to establish and consolidate professional sovereignty.[44] This struggle was not easy, nor was its outcome certain. The professionalizing spirit, illustrated by pressures to require licensure for doctors, was contrary to the egalitarian spirit of public life in Jacksonian America.[45] It was only by mid-century, with the founding of the American Medical Association, that professional sovereignty was tentatively established for "scientific" medicine.[46]

Most nineteenth-century Americans did not seek the help of physicians in dealing with pregnancy, abortion and childbirth.[47] Childbirth remained an affair of family, friends, and midwives until well into the nineteenth

---

39. See *Roe v. Wade,* 410 U.S. at 148–50; Means, *supra* note 9, at 353-54, 358–59, 382–96.

40. *Roe v. Wade,* 410 U.S. at 151–52; M. Grossberg, *supra* note 14, at 163–64.

41. J. Mohr, *supra* note 3, at 37.

42. C. Degler, *supra* note 19, at 233–34, cites physicians who observe that women who are "otherwise quite intelligent and refined, with a keen sense of their moral and religious obligations to themselves and to others, deem it nothing amiss to destroy the embryo during the first few months of its growth."

43. J. Mohr, *supra* note 4, at 31–32.

44. See P. Starr, *The Social Transformation of American Medicine: The Rise of a Sovereign Profession and the Making of a Vast Industry* (1982).

45. From the 1820s through the 1840s, the prevailing political ideology in the United States was strongly opposed to all forms of monopoly or elitism. Thus, exclusive political clubs or economic associations were regarded with suspicion. See *Antebellum American Culture* 187–95 (D. Davis, ed., 1977).

46. See generally P. Starr, *supra* note 44; W. Rothstein, *American Physicians in the Nineteenth Century: From Sects to Science* (1972). The phenomenon of professionalization in American culture has been much studied. See, e.g., T. Haskell, *The Emergence of Professional Social Science: The American Social Science Association and the Nineteenth-Century Crisis of Authority* (1977); G. Geison, ed., *Professions and Professional Ideologies in America* (1983); Bender, "The Erosion of Public Culture: Cities, Discourses, and Professional Disciplines," in *The Authority of Experts: Studies in History and Theory* 84–106 (T. Haskell, ed., 1984); and B. Bledstein, *The Culture of Professionalism: The Middle Class and the Development of Higher Education in America* (1976). Although some historians celebrate the effects of professionalization on our culture and others criticize them, all agree on two basic propositions: the professionalizing impulse is a response to needs perceived by practitioners regarding the establishment and maintenance of legitimate social authority, and the nature of those disciplines. The development of the medical profession in America is a vivid example of these larger developments.

47. No group of physicians was more insecure than those specializing in problems of women's reproductive health. C. Smith-Rosenberg, *supra* note 7, at 231.

century.[48] The process by which childbirth became associated with doctors and hospitals, and with a heightened degree of medical intervention, is a well-documented example of the medical profession's gradual consolidation of authority. This development was not necessarily coercive or conspiratorial. Women were eager for services and knowledge that might lessen the risks and pain of childbirth. But the physician's effort to move childbirth to the hospital involved more than clinical considerations. Similarly, the deep involvement of doctors in the early abortion statutes was intimately connected with professional struggles between proponents of "scientific medicine" and those who practiced less conventional modes of healing.

As we have seen, the first anti-abortion laws were "anti-poisoning" statutes rather than sweeping prohibitions on all abortions. Because certain abortifacients derived from herbs and purgatives could be fatal if taken in overly large quantities, it became a crime to "administer" such remedies.[49] These laws did not express an abhorrence of abortion any more than current laws banning the unauthorized practice of law represent an abhorrent of legal representation. Rather, they served the dual function of protecting the public and solidifying the bounds of professional authority.

More significant, the nineteenth-century movement to regulate abortions was one chapter in a campaign by doctors that reflected a professional conflict between "regulars" (those who ultimately became the practitioners and proponents of scientific medicine) and "irregulars." As James Mohr explains:

"Practically, the regular physicians saw in abortion a medical procedure that not only gave the competition an edge but also undermined the solidarity of their own regular ranks.

If a regular doctor refused to perform an abortion he knew the woman could go to one of several types of irregulars and probably receive one. . . . As more and more irregulars began to advertise abortion services openly, especially after 1840, regular physicians grew more and more nervous about losing their practices to healers who would provide a service that more and more American women after 1840 began to want. Yet, if a regular gave in to the temptation to perform an occasional discreet abortion, and physicians testified repeatedly that this frequently happened among the regulars, he would be compromising his own commitment to an American medical practice that would conform to Hippocratic standards of behavior. *The best way out of these dilemmas was to persuade state legislatures to make abortion a criminal offense. Anti-abortion laws would weaken the appeal of the competition and take the pressure off the more marginal members of the regulars' own sect.*"[50]

To be sure, some "regulars" were morally troubled by abortion, and not all "irregulars" were willing to perform them. A variety of reasons explains why "regular physicians became interested in abortion policy from an early date and repeatedly dragged it into their prolonged struggle to control the practice of medicine in the United States."[51] In the larger context, however, public consideration of abortion in antebellum America was more an issue of medical authority and professional sovereignty than of any particular social or moral attitude toward abortion. Without such an explanation centering on professional imperatives, it is difficult to account for the fact that the American Medical Association and its members became primary proponents of twentieth-century statutes legalizing abortion. *See* Section V, *infra.*

C. *Enforcement of sharply differentiated concepts of the roles and choices of men and women underlay regulation of abortion and contraception in the nineteenth century.*

The American Medical Association's campaign to restrict access to abortion succeeded

---

48. See J. Leavitt, *Brought to Bed: Child-Bearing in America, 1750–1950* (1986); R. Wertz & D. Wertz, *Lying-In: A History of Childbirth in America* (1977); B. Ehrenreich & D. English, *For Her Own Good: 150 Years of the Experts' Advice to Women* (1979).

49. J. Mohr, *supra* note 3, at 21–22.

50. *Id.* at 37 (citation omitted, emphasis added).

51. *Id.*

for many reasons. Concerns over the dangers of surgical abortion to women were well founded. Further, physicians persuaded male political leaders that "abortion constituted a threat to social order and to male authority."[52] Since the 1840s, a growing movement for women's suffrage and equality had generated popular fears that women were departing from their purely maternal role.[53] These fears were fueled by the fact that family size declined sharply in the nineteenth century.[54]

In 1871, the American Medical Association's Committee on Criminal Abortion described the woman who sought an abortion:

"She becomes unmindful of the course marked out for her by Providence, she overlooks the duties imposed on her by the marriage contract. She yields to the pleasures— but shrinks from the pains and responsibilities of maternity; and, destitute of all delicacy and refinements, resigns herself, body and soul, into the hands of unscrupulous and wicked men. Let not the husband of such a wife flatter himself that he possesses her affection. Nor can she in turn ever merit even the respect of a virtuous husband. She sinks into old age like a withered tree, stripped of its foliage; with the stain of blood upon her soul, she dies without the hand of affection to smooth her pillow."[55]

The nineteenth-century American Medical Association's view of women is strikingly similar to that adopted by this Court in 1872, when women were denied the right to practice law because "divine ordinance," and "the nature of things," prescribed a "family institution [that] is repugnant to the idea of a woman adopting a distinct and independent career from that of her husband."[56] This Court has, of course, now come to see this view as part of our "long and unfortunate history of sex discrimination," and as constitutionally illegitimate.[57]

The women's movement of the nineteenth century affirmed that women should always have the right to decide whether to bear a child and sought to enhance women's control of reproduction through "voluntary motherhood," ideally to be achieved through periodic abstinence.[58] Anxieties about changing family functions and gender roles were critical factors motivating the all-male legislatures that adopted restrictions on abortion.[59]

In contrast to the feminist demand for control of reproduction, the federal government, in 1873, took the lead in banning access to information about both contraception and abortion. The Comstock law[60] restricted not

52. C. Smith-Rosenberg, *supra* note 7, at 235.

53. The moral fervor of the abolitionist cause drew Northern women more deeply into public life than ever before in our history. See E. Flexner, *Century of Struggle: The Woman's Rights Movement in the United States*, Ch.13 (rev. ed. 1975). Some of the women who were active in the anti-slavery movement perceived parallels between the subjugation and disenfranchisement of black people and the oppression of women. In 1848, the first Women's Rights Convention, held in Seneca Falls, New York, issued a proclamation that closely tracked the original Declaration of Independence. Stanton, "Declaration of Sentiments 1848," reprinted in L. Kerber & J. Mathers, *Women's America: Refocusing the Past* 431–33 (1982).

54. M. Ryan, *Cradle of the Middle Class: The Family in Oneida County, New York, 1790–1865* 155–57 (1983).

55. Atlee & O'Donnell, *Report of the Committee on Criminal Abortion*, 22 *Transactions of the American Medical Association 241* (1871), quoted in C. Smith-Rosenberg,

supra note 7, at 236–37. Smith-Rosenberg observes that, although middle-class husbands were undoubtedly active participants in their wives' decisions about abortion, the nineteenth-century "AMA linked doctor and husband as the equally wronged and innocent parties. The aborting wife, in contrast, was unnaturally selfish and ruthless." *Id.* at 236.

56. *Bradwell v. Illinois,* 83 U.S. (16 Wall.) 130, 141 (1872) (Bradley, J., concurring).

57. *Frontiero v. Richardson,* 411 U.S. 677, 684 (1973).

58. *See* L. Gordon, *supra* note 28, at 109. During this period much scientific and folk wisdom held a flatly inaccurate view of the cycle of female fertility. *Id.* at 101. This inaccurate belief, combined with hard data on declining birthrates, see notes 21–33 *supra,* underscore how common abortion must have been.

59. C. Smith-Rosenberg, *supra* note 7, at 218.

60. The act prohibits mailing, transporting or importing "obscene, lewd or lascivious" items, specifically including all devices and information pertaining to "preventing conception and producing abortion." See Comstock Act, Ch. 258, [Sec.] 1, 17 Stat. 598 (1873). It was

only medical information on abortion and contraception, such as a medical text on physiology written by an eminent Harvard scientist, but also literary depictions, such as Leo Tolstoy's disapproving tale of infidelity, *The Kreutzer Sonata*, as well as moral literature, including a pamphlet urging total chastity.[61] An 1876 federal court decision rejected a claim that physicians should have the right to distribute contraceptive information.[62]

In the nineteenth century, opposition to abortion and contraception were closely linked, just as political and doctrinal support for this Court's decisions in *Griswold v. Connecticut* and *Roe v. Wade* are linked in this century. Michael Grossberg observes that "Anthony Comstock had labeled as abortionists everyone who advocated or dealt in family-limitation materials and services."[63]

The core purposes of the Comstock Act were to enforce chastity on the young and unmarried and to preserve the subservient position of women within a "traditional" family structure. Nineteenth-century restrictions on abortion and contraception can only sensibly be understood as a reaction to the uncertainties generated by large shifts in family functions and anxieties generated by women's challenges to their historic roles of silence and subservience.

D. Nineteenth-century contraception and abortion regulation also reflected ethnocentric fears about the relative birthrates of immigrants and yankee protestants.

not until 1971 that an amendment was passed deleting the prohibition as to contraception. Pub. L. 91-662, 84 Stat. 1973 (1971). The ban as to information about abortion remains. See 18 U.S.C. [Sec.] 1461 (1988)(current version of Act).

61. See M. Grossberg, *supra* note 14, at 190.

62. *United States v. Foote*, 25 Fed. Cas. 1140, 1141 (S.D.N.Y. 1876), discussed in M. Grossberg, *supra* note 14, at 191. Edward Bliss Foote, the defendant, was an advocate of free-thought, civil liberties, women's rights and birth control. After his arrest, Foote wrote, "It is my conscientious conviction that every married woman should have it within her power to decide for herself just when and just how often she will receive the germ of a new offspring." See *id.*; L. Gordon, *supra* note 28, at 168.

63. M. Grossberg, *supra* note 14, at 193.

Nativism, notably anti-Catholicism, had been part of American politics and culture as early as the Jacksonian period.[64] The Civil War and Reconstruction Era dramatically raised consciousness about national identity and citizenship. Social conservatives in the 1850s articulated an "organicist" ideal in which social unity would predominate over diversity.[65] By the 1870s social though was turning the insights of Charles Darwin toward racist ends.[66] The political ideology of "free labor," forged in the nascent Republican Party in the years preceding the Civil War,[67] was severely challenged by an influx of foreign labor in the latter part of the nineteenth century. The discriminatory immigration policies and nativist fears of the late nineteenth and early twentieth centuries had their roots in a far earlier period, when Americans first became concerned about the creation of an urban population of wage workers.[68]

Beginning in the 1890s, and continuing through the first decades of the twentieth century, these nativist fears coalesced into a drive against what was then called "race suicide."[69] The "race suicide" alarmists worried that women of "good stock"—prosperous, white, and Protestant—were not having enough children to maintain the political and social supremacy of their group.[70] Anxiety

64. D. Davis, *From Homicide to Slavery: Studies in American Culture* 137–54 (1986); S. Lipset & E. Raab, *The Politics of Unreason: Right-Wing Extremism in America, 1790–1970* (1970).

65. See G. Frederickson, *The Inner Civil War: Northern Intellectuals and the Crisis of the Union* (1965).

66. See R. Hofstadter, *Social Darwinism in American Thought* (1955).

67. E. Foner, *Free Soil, Free Labor, Free Men: The Ideology of the Republican Party Before the Civil War* (1970).

68. The classic work on this issue is J. Higham, *Strangers in the Land: Patterns of American Nativism 1860–1925* (1988).

69. See L. Gordon, *supra* note 29, at 136–58.

70. See C. Degler, *supra* note 19, at 229–30, on the concern of physicians that women of "good stock" were particularly likely to obtain abortions. In Buffalo in 1855, the fertility ratio of Irish women of ages 30–34 was over twice that of native white women. *Id.* at 134.

over the falling birth rates of Protestant whites in comparison with other groups helped shape policy governing both birth control and abortion.[71] As James Mohr points out, "The doctors both used and were influenced by blatant nativism. . . . There can be little doubt that Protestants' fears about not keeping up with the reproductive rates of Catholic immigrants played a greater role in the drive for anti-abortion laws in nineteenth-century America than Catholic opposition to abortion did."[72]

V. Enforcement of abortion restrictions in the first half of the twentieth century followed historic ethnic and class differentiations, affirmed historic concerns about enforcing gender roles, and imposed enormous costs upon women, their families and physicians.

Statutory restrictions on abortion remained virtually unchanged until the 1960s. Physicians were allowed to perform abortions only "to preserve the mother's life." Nonetheless, the incidence of abortion remained high, ranging from one pregnancy in seven at the turn of the century, to one in three in 1936.[73]

Most abortions were performed illegally.[74] Legal restrictions did not stop abortion, but made it furtive, humiliating, and dangerous.[75]

In the first half of the twentieth century, a two-tiered abortion system emerged in which services depended on the class, race, age and residence of the woman. Poor and rural women obtained illegal abortions, performed by people, physicians and others, who were willing to defy the law out of sympathy for the woman or for the fee. More privileged women steadily pressed physicians for legal abortions and many obtained them. Some doctors could be persuaded that deliveries would endanger women's health; the dilation and curetage procedure was indicated for numerous other gynecological health problems.

Shifts in the definition of "therapeutic" abortion responded to larger social forces.[76] Early in the century, "race suicide" fears fueled efforts to suppress both abortion and birth control.[77] During the depression, abortions increased as the medical profession recognized impoverishment as an indication for therapeutic abortion.[78] In the 1940s and 1950s the definition of therapeutic abortion expanded to

71. J. Reed, *From Private Vice to Public Virtue: The Birth Control Movement and American Society Since 1830* (1978); D. Kevles, *In the Name of Eugenics: Genetics and the Users of Human Heredity* (1985); D. Kennedy, *Birth Control in America: The Career of Margaret Sanger* (1971).

72. See J. Mohr, *supra* note 3, at 167. Horatio Robinson Storer, who spearheaded the American Medical Association's mid–nineteenth century anti-abortion campaign, frequently referred to racial themes. See *id.* at 180–90. One doctor lamented in 1874 that, owing to the prevalence of abortion among Protestant women, "the Puritanic blood of '76 will be but sparingly represented in the approaching centenary." *Id.* at 167. Carl Degler also documents that physicians of the 1850s and 1860s expressed particular concern that abortion was increasingly sought by married women of "high repute." C. Degler, *supra* note 19, at 229.

73. See F. Taussig, *Abortion, Spontaneous and Induced: Medical and Social Aspects* 338, and Appendix A, 453–75 (1936). See also *Stix, A Study of Pregnancy Wastage,* 13 Milbank Memorial Fund Q. 347 (1935); *Stix & Wiehl, Abortion and Public Health,* 28 Am. J. Pub. Health 622, Table I (1938).

74. See K. Luker, *Abortion and the Politics of Motherhood* 48–54 (1984).

75. See brief *amicus curiae* of the National Abortion Rights Action League in the instant case.

76. L. Reagan, *When is Abortion Necessary to Save a Woman's Life?: The Political Dimension of Therapeutic Abortion During the Period of Criminalized Abortion in the United States, 1880–1973* (unpublished paper, Univ. of Wisconsin, Madison, June 20, 1987).

77. On November 20, 1912, 390 federal postal inspectors arrested 173 people for using the mails to disseminate information about abortion and contraception in violation of the Comstock Act. The campaign was called the "federal war on race suicide." "Take Chicagoans in Federal War on Race Suicide," *Chicago Tribune,* Nov. 21, 1912, p. 1.

78. In 1931 an American Medical Association editorial noted that "poverty . . . does not constitute an indication for abortion, [but] there is no doubt that in the United States many abortions are performed for borderline cases in which there is a strong ethical indication plus a more or less minor medical ailment." *Abortion or Removal of Pregnant Uterus,* 95 J. Am. Med. Ass'n 1169 (1931).

include psychiatric indications.[79] Physicians were caught in a double bind: abortion was criminal, but the reasons women sought them were so multiple and compelling that they were difficult to resist.

In the 1950s, more restrictive attitudes toward both legal and illegal abortions[80] were part of a conservative response to growing female labor-force participation and independence.[81] The 1960s movement to legalize abortion arose in response to this, rather brief, wave of anti-abortion enforcement. Physicians, particularly those who worked in public hospitals and clinics, saw women who needlessly suffered and died as a consequence of illegal abortions.[82] Others were disturbed that most of those women were poor and black.[83] Many were distressed by the class bias inherent in the psychiatric indications for therapeutic abortions.[84] In the late 1960s, concerned physicians were joined by women who had come to understand that control of reproductive capacity is the *sine qua non* of women's self-governance and moral personhood.[85]

As a number of states acted to legalize abortion, additional concerns heightened pressure for recognition of constitutional protection for the basic right of abortion choice. Debate over abortion, now revolving around insoluble metaphysical disputes about the moral status of the fetus, preoccupied state legislatures and often prevented them from ad-

dressing other vital issues.[86] Class and regional differentiations were accentuated as it became possible for women with resources to travel to states where abortion was legal. In *Roe v. Wade*, this Court responded to all of these forces in holding that constitutional rights of liberty and privacy protect the right of woman and her physician to choose abortion.

VI. The moral value attached to the fetus became a central issue in American culture and law only in the late twentieth century, when traditional justifications for restricting access to abortion became culturally anachronistic or constitutionally impermissible.

Some of those seeking to enlist the power of the state to deny women's liberty to choose abortion have long articulated a concern for the fetus.[87] Yet until the late twentieth century, this concern was always subsidiary to more mundane social visions and anxieties. The mid-nineteenth century physicians' campaign sought to prohibit the practice of botanic medicine and chiropractic, as well as abortion. Protection of fetal life is plainly not the driving concern of such a movement. Those who opposed abortion and birth control to staunch "race suicide" sought to protect the privilege of elite white Anglo-Saxon Protestants, not to protect fetuses.

Religious support for the physicians' campaign to bar abortion was practically non-existent.[88] Physicians vigorously sought to enlist moral authority and organized religion in their

---

79. K. Luker, *supra* note 74, at 45–47, 54–57.

80. L. Lader, *Abortion* 42–51 (1966).

81. M. Ryan, *Womanhood in America: From Colonial Times to the Present,* 198–215 (1975); *America's Working Women: A Documentary History—1600 to the Present,* 299–308 (R. Baxandal, L. Gordon & S. Reverly, eds., 1976).

82. See brief *amicus curiae* of the American Public Health Association and brief *amicus curiae* of the Attorneys General in Support of Appellees.

83. See brief *amicus curiae* of Organizations of Women of Color.

84. See *McRae v. Califano,* 391 F. Supp. 630, 668–76 (E.D.N.Y. 1980).

85. K. Luker, *supra* note 74, at 92–125.

86. See J. Mohr, *Iowa's Abortion Battles of the Late 1960s and Early 1970s,* Annals of Iowa 50 (summer 1989), 63–89; K. Luker, *supra* note 74, at 66–91.

87. See J. Mohr, *supra* note 3, at 165–66.

88. The extensive religious press of the United States, both Catholic and Protestant, "maintained a total blackout on the issue of abortion from the beginning of the nineteenth century through the end of the Civil War." J. Mohr, *supra* note 3, at 183. It was not until 1869 that a papal declaration condemned abortion as a violation of the fetus prior to "ensoulment," held to be 40 days gestational age for a male fetus and 80 days for a female. Before that time, Catholic theology condemned early abortion

campaign to restrict abortion, and "were openly disgusted when the established voices of moral authority refused to speak on their behalf. . . . Medical journals accused the religious journals of valuing abortifacient advertising revenue too highly to risk criticizing the practice."[89]

Further, the small support that physicians found among Protestant religious leaders appeared to be "more worried about falling birthrates among their adherents than about the morality of abortion itself."[90] The conspicuous absence of religious support for the physicians' anti-abortion crusade is particularly striking compared to extensive religious involvement in other nineteenth-century movements for changing social morality, such as temperance.[91]

Nineteenth-century laws restricting access to abortion were not based on a belief that the fetus is a human being. To the contrary, New Jersey Chief Justice Green expressed the prevailing judicial opinion in 1849 when he asserted that although it was "true, for certain purposes, [that] the law regards an infant as *in being* from the time of conception, yet it seems nowhere to regard it as *in life*, or to have respect to its preservation as a living being."[92] Michael Grossberg summarizes the nineteenth-century cases, saying, "[A] fetus enjoyed rights only in property law and then only if successfully born. It had no standing in criminal law

until quickening, and none at all in tort. The law highly prized children, not fetuses."[93]

Judith Walzer Leavitt's analysis of medical decisions about the procedure of craniotomy (a surgical mutilation of the live fetal head to permit vaginal extraction) provides one complex window on the moral status of the fetus, during the period from 1880 to 1920. At this time, most women gave birth at home. When a woman's pelvis was too small to permit delivery, two alternatives were possible.[94] A Cesarean section would ordinarily save the fetus, but posed high risks to the woman's life. A craniotomy killed the fully formed fetus, but with significantly less risk to the woman.

Most physicians thought craniotomy, which could save the life of the woman, the more appropriate choice in this difficult situation.[95] Others based their assessment on their judgment of the social and moral worth of the woman.[96] But the core issue for physicians was the principle that "the obstetrician alone must be the judge of what is to be done."[97] Roman Catholic writers widely condemned craniotomy in popular medical journals, informing obstetricians in 1917 that it was "[b]etter that a

on precisely the same terms as it had condemned masturbation and contraception, i.e., a distrust of sexuality and an interference with natural processes. In Catholic doctrine late abortions were always held to be a form of homicide. No American diocesan newspaper reported the Pope's 1869 statement. *Id.* at 187. In that same year, the Bishop of Baltimore issued the only formal nineteenth-century Catholic condemnation of abortion in America, *id.* at 186, and the Old School Presbyterians became the only major Protestant denomination to condemn abortion. *Id.* at 192. No other religious denominations or leaders followed.

89. J. Mohr, *supra* note 3, at 184.

90. *Id.* at 195.

91. *Id.* at 182–96.

92. *Cooper v. State,* 22 N.J. L. (2 Zab.) 52, 56–57 (1849) (emphasis in the original), discussed in M. Grossberg, *supra* note 14, at 165.

93. M. Grossberg, *supra* note 14, at 165.

94. In some cases, physicians could attempt to avoid this dilemma by stretching or breaking the woman's pelvis. See Leavitt, *The Growth of Medical Authority: Technology and Morals in Turn-of-the-Century Obstetrics,* 1 Med. Anthropology Q. 230, 233–35 (1987).

95. Craniotomy was, of course, a brutal and distasteful procedure. Nonetheless, one medical leader, speaking to a medical society audience, in 1892 explained:

"I should much prefer Cesarean section in these cases, but I scarcely expect in the near future that a larger number will consent to it. The husband, if told the truth [about the dangers to the woman of Cesarean section], will demand craniotomy, and I think moreover that every one of us would do the same under similar circumstances. I know I should, and I feel confident that every gentleman here to-night would too, if his own wife were in question."

T. Barker, *When is Emryotomy Justifiable? Proceedings of the Philadelphia County Medical Society* 132–39 (1892), quoted in Leavitt, *supra* note 94, at 240.

96. Leavitt, *supra* note 94, at 246.

97. *Id.* at 244.

million mothers die than that one innocent creature be killed."[98] But continued medical practice and dialogue demonstrate that neither patients nor physicians attached such high, absolute value to the fetus, even when it was plainly viable.

As this Court observed in *Roe v. Wade*, the pattern of American abortion laws does not support the view that they were designed principally to incorporate a view of the fetus as a person. Both the lesser punishment for abortion than for homicide, and the various exceptions allowing the physician to determine that abortion is justified, rebut the assumption that laws against abortion reflect that belief.[99]

Further, increasing "scientific" understanding does not support attributing enhanced moral value to the fetus. That pregnancy is a biologically continuous process has long been recognized by Americans even when the common law recognized a woman's right to choose abortion. For example, a popular home medical book published in 1871 and dedicated to the *Wives of the Ministers of the Gospel of the United States*, stated: "[T]he contents of the pregnant womb, formed in miniature at conception, are the child, the waters, the membranes holding them, the navel cord, and afterbirth."[100] The book goes on to describe in detail embryonic and fetal development. Historically, claims that startling advances in medical knowledge about pregnancy and fetal development should alter attitudes toward abortion have consistently been highly exaggerated.[101]

98. *Id*. at 239–40.

99. See *Roe v. Wade*, 410 U.S. 113, 132–50 (1973).

100. Quoted in K. Luker, *supra* note 74, at 23.

101. See K. Luker, *supra* note 74, at 23–25. Other parties before this Court are better able than historians to address current claims of technical advances. See brief *amicus curiae* of the American Medical Association, refuting the claim that it is now possible to maintain fetal life outside the womb at ever earlier stages of gestation. See also brief *amicus curiae* of American Law Professors in Support of Appellees.

One technological development that has spurred the effect to attach moral value to the fetus is the technology that allows the imaging of the fetus *in utero*.

VII. A presumed interest in protecting fetal life does not justify denying women their historic liberty to choose abortion.

A culture can, of course, allow growing humanistic impulses to attach greater moral value to fetuses or to potential human life, even if these moral judgments are not triggered by new scientific understanding. But, for two core reasons, this Court should reject state efforts to invoke the protection of fetal life to justify restrictions upon women's access to abortion.

First, as this brief has demonstrated, the complex historic grounds for restricting access to abortion are now either socially irrelevant or recognized as constitutionally illegitimate. Both culturally and legally, it is today impossible to defend abortion restrictions as a means of enforcing an absolutist religious belief, grounded in natural law, that intimate relations must always remain open to the possibility of procreation.[102] Similarly, abortion restrictions cannot be justified by desires to keep women in traditional roles.[103] Likewise, our social consensus, embodied in principles of legal equality, would not permit the Court to defend restrictions on abortion as a means of encouraging the propagation of white Yankee stock or of punishing racial or religious minorities. But any sophisticated understanding of American history and traditions must recognize that such motivations do not disappear simply because they are

B. Katz Rothman observes that "the fetus *in utero* has become a metaphor for 'man' in space, floating free, attached only by the umbilical cord to the spaceship. But where is the mother in that metaphor? She has become empty space." B. Rothman, *The Tentative Pregnancy: Prenatal Diagnosis and the Future of Motherhood* 114 (1986). Rosalind Petchesky observes, "[I]mages by themselves lack 'objective' meanings; meanings come from the interlocking fields of context, communication, application and reception. . . ." Petchesky, *Fetal Images: The Power of Visual Culture in the Politics of Reproduction*, 13 *Feminist Studies* 263, 286 (1987).

102. See *Griswold v. Connecticut*, 381 U.S. 479 (1965); *Eisenstadt v. Baird*, 405 U.S. 438 (1972).

103. See *Stanton v. Stanton*, 421 US. 7 (1975); *Orr v. Orr*, 440 U.S. 268, (1979).

no longer culturally or constitutionally legitimate. In this context, we must therefore question whether protection of unborn life has become a surrogate for other social objectives that are no longer tolerated.

Second, and decisively, this Court must affirm *Roe v. Wade*, and reject asserted state interests in protecting prenatal life, because the costs of denying constitutional protection to abortion choice are simply too enormous. Our experience from the 1890s until 1973 amply demonstrates that if women are denied access to legal abortions, many will turn in desperation to self-abortion, folk remedies, or illegal practitioners. Many will die. Others will suffer permanent damage to their reproductive capacity. Still others will bear children for whom they cannot provide adequate care. Apart from these devasting consequences to the lives and health of women, restricting access to abortion will again deny the fundamental legitimacy of women as moral decision-makers.

Conclusion

The judgment of the Court of Appeals and this Court's decision in *Roe v. Wade* should be affirmed.

60

LINDA GORDON AND ALLEN HUNTER

Sex, Family and the New Right: Anti-Feminism as a Political Force (1977)

"Traditionally a man's role as head of the family takes him away from the hearthstone. A woman is like many stones: She is the hearthstone from which warmth and light are reflected throughout the home; she is the decorative, exotic stones hedging and protecting precious and

From *Radical America*, November 1977. Reprinted by permission of the author.

beautiful growth; she is graceful as marble, preserving culture and tradition; and, she is as hard as granite with anything that threatens her home and children. She is soapstone and pumice, ever-cleansing and smoothing; She is a touchstone; a close comfort to her mate and little ones. And she sometimes feels like a well-worn cobblestone, over which have passed the tribulations of all she holds dear. Woman is at once like the sunny sand that warms, and like the heart and sinew of the sandbags that keep the home secure from intruding torrents in crisis. She can be ruby-lipped, onyx-eyed, pearl-skinned, and topaz-tressed. But always she shines like the symbol of her marriage, the perfect diamond that will reflect her growth from bride to grandmother."

—Ron Wright,
A Man Looks at the Equal Rights Amendment,
John Birch Society pamphlet.

A mere five years ago we probably would have dismissed such a statement as representing a defeated past, a man's fantasy projected onto a past that never really existed.* But this kind of anti-feminism is now propelling a strong and growing New Right. The New Right cultural politics of sex and family are not only a backlash against women's and gay liberation movements—seen in the opposition to abortion, affirmative action, and gay rights—but are also a reassertion of patriarchal forms of family structure and male dominance. Furthermore, this conservative

*Most of the ideas in this article should be regarded as hypotheses. Our views are not based on extensive research, but on reading the popular press, talking to other socialists concerned with these issues, and our own participation in various political projects. We hope that readers with concrete information about New Right groups, whether it supports or contradicts our argument, will send it to us; and that readers with different points of view will write letters for publication in *Radical America*. We want to acknowledge the substantial help given us by Frank Brodhead, Marla Erlien, Ann Withorn, and Sheli Wortis. Needless to say, they are not responsible for this final version, especially since we could not or would not accept some of their criticisms.

cultural politics is a direct challenge to class conscious politics. The inadequate response by the Left is largely due to its prevalent economism and an insufficient appreciation of feminism. In Part I of this article we will look at the specific issues of the New Right, describe the ideological coherence of the separate campaigns and locate that coherence in the conservative response to broad social change. We will also hazard some guesses about the class and cultural basis of the reaction. In Part II we describe what a socialist program about sex and family issues could be.

THE NEW RIGHT: ITS ISSUES

Until recently it seemed that racism, especially anti-busing, was the heart of the conservative backlash. This fit with the central role of racism in the history of right-wing politics. The growth of anti-busing organizations in the last several years and the more recent reinvigoration of the Nazis and the KKK reinforced this view. Racism has not diminished as a political force, but has been joined—and the whole right-wing thereby strengthened—by a series of conservative campaigns defending the family, a restrictive and hypocritical sexual morality, and male dominance.

These campaigns, waged largely by single-issue organizations, identify their enemies most often as liberals, feminists and blacks. The "old Right" groups, such as the John Birch Society or the American Nazi Party, identified their enemy as communists, since theirs was a backlash against an earlier period of left political activity. Despite these differences however, many "old rightists" are leaders of new-right groups. The New Right, however, has attracted many thousands of new grass roots adherents and may develop a power and dynamism the old Right lacked. Recently there has been an important shift from the periodic electoral manipulation of backlash sentiments to well-organized con-

servative mass movements with the national capability of mobilizing thousands. This large following will increase right-wing influence in both political parties and may help cement a rightward political realignment in national politics.[1]

One example of New Right power is the campaign against the Equal Rights Amendment. Anti-ERA organizing has been going on for several years in many states and has been able to prevent its passage. This constitutional amendment appears to most radicals a minimal and symbolic gesture. It offers little if won, but will represent a big defeat if lost. In a sense the opposition to ERA reflects conservative agreement that it would not make much economic difference. For example, the anti-ERA arguments are not usually about economic competition, but focus on silly comments about lack of privacy in toilets and a hypocritical abhorrence for drafting women. It is the feminist impulse behind ERA, not its specific content, that is most feared; it is less the equality than the independence of women that is opposed.

Like opposition to the ERA, opposition to abortion has been growing in the past few years, but its focus has recently shifted. Legally the strategy has been altered by the Supreme Court decision, and then by state administrative and legislative action, to the question of the use of public welfare and medical funds for abortion. Politically the anti-abortionists have increasingly revealed their deepest motives—fear of women's independence rather than concern for the unborn. Many anti-abortionists (and many pro-abortionists) have a genuine moral concern about abortion. But right-wing leaders have been able to manipulate these con-

1. Karl Mannheim made a distinction between traditional and conservative thought that we find useful for understanding the social bases of grass-roots support for conservative politics. See his essay "Conservative Thought" in *Essays on Sociology and Social Psychology* (Oxford University Press, 1953), pp. 74–164, or *From Karl Mannheim* edited by Kurt Wolff (Oxford University Press, 1971), pp. 132–222.

cerns into moral righteousness, and to join anti-feminist politics to racist, anti-working class, and especially anti-welfare politics. As the feminist movement seeks to regain access to abortion for poor women and to prevent further defeats, abortion opponents will continue to push for further restrictions.

The anti-abortion campaign shares with the backlash against gay rights a hostility to freer sexual standards generally. The primary complaints of those who supported Anita Bryant at the polls are against "public display" and the social influence of homosexuals. Resistance to gay rights is especially strong on questions of employment (notably in public schools and agencies) and access to housing. Private, unseen behavior does not seem to be as threatening. It is the system of male-dominated heterosexuality that is at stake. Homophobia, like woman-hating, also rests on deep, often subconscious, often irrational feeling. Consider the fear so many have of young boys being sexually abused by older gay men, while in fact heterosexual child abuse is much more common; because men raping women is part of the system of male dominance it is less shocking than men assaulting men.

Opponents also see homosexuality as a total attack on the family, although in fact it is mostly an attack on the family as the only legitimate social unit. Coming out of the closet means ceasing to pretend to fit into the family system. The difference between a bachelor or a spinster and a homosexual is that the former is perceived as a deprived, lacking individual, a person missing something. The latter may be called a pervert, but she or he seems complete. Furthermore, what is different about homosexual relationships, even when they mimic marriage and the family, is that they are not based on the "special" qualities of a female member of the couple, qualities which are used to justify and perpetuate the exploitation of women. Homosexuals may and often do replicate conventional sexual divisions of labor, but they do not do so on the basis of alleged biological necessity. Thus the

social and alterable quality of these divisions is evident.

The anti-busing movement is nourished by some of the same fears for the loss of family. The loss of neighborhood schools is perceived as a threat to community, and therefore family stability by many people, particularly in cities where ethnically homogenous communities remain. The image of the neighborhood school may be a romanticized or even fake recollection; but fears for children's safety and objections to the inaccessibility of their schools and teachers reflect both family love and parental desire for control. The opponents of busing are usually quick to point out that school integration would likely produce an increase in interracial sex, and they are right. While they call upon images of black men raping white girls, the possibility of sex based in intimate and loving relations is equally frightening to them. And the fear of black power, "reverse discrimination," at the community level—associated with fear of crime, property devaluation, dirtiness and noisiness—reflects not only the direct economic crunch on white working-class people but also a less tangible sense of cultural disintegration.

A strong addition to this panoply of Right causes is the campaign against "reverse discrimination," or affirmative action. Affirmative action requirements and judicial decisions are victories won by the black and women's liberation movements. They have not, actually, altered employment or educational discrimination very much. But affirmative action has provided the basis for the organization and struggle of women and minority groups. The grievance mechanisms available under Title VII of the 1964 Civil Rights Act, Executive Order 11246 of 1968, and the Equal Pay Act of 1963, have been used more by working-class than by professional and managerial people (in contrast to a current Left view which holds that these are the tools of "bourgeois feminism"). The current focus in the affirmative action struggle is the case of Allan Bakke, who sued the University of California for admitting some minority students allegedly less qualified than he. His case was heard by the U.S. Supreme Court in October 1977 and a decision is expected in the spring of 1978. A ruling for Bakke, by legitimizing the concept of reverse discrimination, could thereby also legitimize openly racist and anti-woman pronouncements and decisions, greatly strengthening the Right.

This is not an exhaustive list. Other issues may, in other parts of the country, already loom larger. Opposition to foreign undocumented workers, to welfare, to the Panama Canal Treaty, to sex education and liberal textbooks, to the importation of foreign goods are examples. If the New Right develops into a strong reactionary movement it will, no doubt, incorporate anti-communism and jingoism. But we think the issues we have mentioned show that the New Right is picking up great strength from a defense of a threatened patriarcalism.

THE NEW RIGHT: DEFENSE OF PATRIARCHY

"Abortion is only one of many issues. The whole picture includes drug abuse, alienation of youth, disrespect for authority, religious decline, decay of the family structure, destruction of traditional education, revolution on the campus, racial strife, undermining of law enforcement and the judicial system, increase in homosexuality and perversion, inflation, repudiation of our currency, registration and confiscation of firearms, no-win wars, destruction of national pride and prestige, deliberate loss of United States military superiority and economic strength, planned and fabricated shortages of fuel and food leading to rationing and increasing control over the American people. . . to fight abortion without understanding and fighting the total conspiracy is to ensure certain and total defeat."
—John L. Grady, M.D., *Abortion Yes or No,*
American Public Opinion pamphlet
(a John Birch Society publication)

One of the key sources of coherence in the New Right is, we think, a reactionary response to the continued dissolution of patriarchal forms. By patriarchy we do not simply mean male supremacy, and we dissociate ourselves from a prevalent feminist use of the term to describe a transhistorical system of male domination. We mean by patriarchy a specific organization of the family and society, in which heads of families controlled not only the reproductive labor, but also the production by all family members.

Patriarchy was a system that prevailed throughout the world in agrarian societies. As commerce and handicraft production became increasingly important in Europe and the U.S., the patriarchal family remained the unit of production. It was only industrialism—specifically the removal of production from the home-workshop and the introduction of individual wage labor—that undercut patriarchy's economic basis. Without property or skills to pass on to sons, proletarianized fathers lost much of their power. At first the transformation of many working-class women into non-producing housewives increased their dependence on their husbands, but in the twentieth century widespread employment of women has given them more economic independence.

But industrial capitalism did not automatically or immediately make patriarchy obsolete. First, the effects of industry were experienced differently by different classes, religions, regional and ethnic groups. As we will argue in the next section, we think that the New Right represents particular social groups for whom patriarchy has remained viable into the present. Second, there was a great deal of resistance among working-class people to the individualizing tendency of capitalism, and even for women and children the patriarchal family in many circumstances represented a vital source of economic and emotional support, as well as a basis for anti-capitalist struggles—as in strikes, community boycotts and cultural rituals. Still, the main trend has been the weakening of family and community power and the increased autonomy of women, young people and single people. Today the political reassertion of the family is usually a reactionary, not a progressive, force.

Nevertheless, part of the feminist confusion about the term "patriarch" stems from a failure to recognize that there have been losses as well as gains in its dissolution. Individual independence and the right to dissent have been gained at the cost of loneliness, rootlessness, and disintegration of social order.[2] Many of the services that families provided—ranging from cooking to healing to entertainment—must now be purchased or paid for through taxes, and the services available are an inadequate approximation of more personally provided services. This means of providing services increases the isolation within and between families, thereby deepening the inability of families to produce what their members need. And the inadequacy of families to meet sharpening personal crises in turn provides the occasion for increased bureaucratic intervention and control.

But to meet these problems the Right proposes programs to preserve patriarchal forms. Their clinging to ineffective "solutions" (such as the prohibition on abortion, which can never stop abortion), and their support for repression of proponents of alternatives, comes from their misunderstanding of the source of these problems. True to their backlash orientation, the New Rightists blame Left political movements. While the Left could respond by claiming proudly to have furthered the decline of patriarchy, it is the process of capitalism itself which has been primarily responsible.

Here we want to call attention to eight major themes of the New Right's patriarchalism, all interrelated but analytically separable: anti-feminism, hostility to youth, anti-

sexualism, homophobia, the defense of conventional family, an anti-civil libertarian bias, the work ethic, and religion.

Anti-feminism is in many ways the basis of the patriarchal defense. The "specialness" of women appears to be the foundation of the family, the sexual system, the system of work. Women's social uniqueness is produced by a family organization in which women provide motherly and wifely love and services. The abolition of the gender differences that recreate women's specialness threatens to deprive men and children of home-making, men of sexual satisfaction upon demand, and everyone of stable living units. These services and stabilities are genuinely needed; they are not "false" needs imposed from above. The problem is that capitalist industrial society could not replace patriarchal stability. And now women's supposedly natural function—providing that stability—seems so tenuous that her specialness must be guarded by law, her access to the last male preserves (such as the army, sports) forbidden.

While there are many themes in the anti-abortion struggle, the fear of women's power seems the strongest. Power over reproduction has historically been defended by men because it is a source of class (property-holding) as well as sexual power. The spectre of women's rejection of motherhood has characterized anti-birth control propaganda for over a century, and population control fears cannot erase the more terrifying vision of facing a world without womanly tenderness. It seems to us that the images of the aborted fetuses, the emphasis on the cruelty of abortion, reflects a fear for the withdrawal of motherly compassion. But while nurturance is a value to be cherished, for the Right it usually means self-sacrifice, as in the anti-abortionist's contention that women should put the life of the unborn child first. No political-economic explanation can alone explain the virulence of the anti-abortion movement; its passion shows that male dominance is also embedded in personality.

Male fear of loss of control over the family is also expressed through anti-youth biases of

2. We are not suggesting patriarchal societies were free of such problems. However, stronger communities provided collective forms for restraining anti-social behavior and supporting its victims, while accepting the inevitability of such problems. By contrast capitalist society has raised the hope of abolishing such social misery at the same time as its destruction of community power makes it more difficult to control these forms of violence.

the New Right. Like the New Left, this movement represents generational struggle—but the parents' side. While the New Left was anti-authoritarian, the New Right stands for obedience. There are real grounds for concern about the passivity, pessimism and cynicism of many young people; many youthful responses to their problems are personally and socially disruptive; no one likes vandalism and car theft. But the Right has no positive program for youth, merely a lament for a lost past. Fathers who in fact are unable to pass on a culture to their children are blaming their impotence on liberal intellectuals, school teachers, etc.

Protests about loss of control over women and children are indistinguishably mixed in with hostility to sexual freedom. Anti-abortion spokespeople increasingly state explicitly their view that female chastity, not better contraception, is the solution to unwanted pregnancies. The anti-gay reaction is also a reaction against sex itself. The effeminate/exhibitionist style of *some* gay men that has come to be their *collective* image represents the desertion of the repressed, serious and under-emotional style that has been "masculine." Instead gays offer a style that is playful, pleasure-seeking, indeed gay, a style that is symbolically a rejection of the work ethic.

The work ethic is, of course, outmoded in the sense that sticking to its guidelines no longer particularly promotes economic success. But it protects many people from the recognition of their incapacity for pleasure. Thus anti-sexual feelings of the New Right also mask widespread sexual misery. The feminist movement has popularized the understanding that many—perhaps most—women do not experience orgasm. Less well understood is the fact that the sex clinics are as often faced with men who suffer sexual dysfunction and unhappiness. Nor is sexual "failure" limited to those who can afford therapy. One of the worst errors common among Leftists is the idea that busy, overworked and underpaid working-class people do not have time to "indulge" themselves in neuroses, or in longing to be rid of

their neuroses. Sexual misery may be caused in part by class exploitation but it apparently affects all classes.

The sexual part of Right-wing repressiveness is largely hypocritical. Plenty of the anti-abortion, anti-gay men are anxious to lead active sexual lives, without much regard for the needs of their women. But we suspect that the longing for a stable family with clearly understood sex and generational roles represents in part a vision of a calm that will reduce sexual anxiety. The new assertions of female sexuality cannot fail to threaten conventional sources of masculine sexual confidence and the traditional family system is a familiar sexual turf. And the family system must be understood as including a continued double standard.

CLASS POLITICS AND THE NEW RIGHT

We have not rushed to offer a "class analysis" of the New Right because we think that Left analyses of phenomena like this have often been held back by hurrying towards reductionist, safely familiar, categorization. In fact the sex-and-family sources of much of the New Right energy suggest that class groupings in the U.S. can be so divided and heterogeneous that other bonds—such as sexual, ethnic, and kinship ties—can provide the solidarity for collective political expression.

Nevertheless the New Right *is* part of class struggle. Even if the campaigns have amassed significant working-class support (and we are not sure that they have), they are dominated by leaders from the petite bourgeoisie, and politicians, churchmen, and some professionals.[3] A unity between class and male-supremacist politics is possible because it is often among the petite bourgeoisie that it has been possible for

3. We do not mean to underemphasize the role of capitalists in the Right and in funding ultra-conservative politics. We have not discussed the capitalist funding, participation in, and even political leadership of Right politics because we want to emphasize the social dynamic of the Right as a movement.

patriarchy to survive longest. Men who are self-employed, or whose work like that of politicians can at times be handed down to successors, retain the economic power of patriarchs long after factory workers' sons rebel and/or become estranged from the family. Furthermore small businessmen, politicians, churchmen and the like more often integrate their wives into their careers, creating a functional basis for wifely subordination and an organic image of an integrated family. Political machines are often organized as small patriarchates, much like criminal machines. There are still some skilled craftsmen who, through exclusionary craft unions, can pass on vocations to their sons.

Anti-gay, anti-welfare, racist, and anti-youth feelings have been used to hark back to an older ideology, a distinction between the "deserving" and "undeserving" poor. This division allows a subjective narrowing of the *working* class to exclude the unemployed, the under-employed, single mothers—the marginal in general. With this in view the New Right calls for the further victimization of these who are already the main victims of capitalist class relations, and tries to split the working class into antagonistic factions.

At the same time "white ethnics," usually Catholics, have sometimes provided new constituencies for the Right campaigns. Cohesive ethnic communities and patriarchal forms have been mutually supportive, and both have been especially provoked by the violation of community autonomy through such interventions as busing. The Catholic Church has been important in several ways. It has provided a religious ideology that is anti-sexual and anti-feminist, as well as a moralistic rhetoric for making political demands. The Church also reinforces authoritarian values. The wealth and national organization of the Church make it an effective political mobilizer. Fundamentalist Protestantism has also contributed many enthusiasts to the New Right campaigns. In general, church-based politics, at least among whites, reinforces cross-class alliances.

Conservative sections of the working class share some values with business and managerial people that allow for cross-class political cohesiveness as well. These values are primarily individualism, the work ethic, and hostility toward liberal professionals, the bureaucratic state, and governmental intrusion into community and family life.

But despite its anti-big-government bias, there are ways in which the Right mobilization is useful for the capitalist class in the current recession. The pro-working-*man* sentimentality provides ideological cover for attacks on the working class. Two things seem to be happening. First, a squeeze on working-class living standards is being directed not primarily at the point of production, except among public employees, but at delivery of social services by the state. Second, with the decline of the black movement and increased conservative mobilization in some white "ethnic" communities, the decreased funds available are being redirected accordingly. There is a "fit" between anti-sexual, anti-woman, racist and work-ethic attitudes, and these attacks on social services.

The threatened collapse of the traditional Democratic coalition—labor, minorities, and liberal professionals—is one of the explanations for the "new populism" that is associated with the celebration of (white) middle America, and also for the criticisms *by* politicians *of* politicians for fostering the growth of the state. Thus Carter and other politicians will make use of the attacks on the big government to reduce social welfare but not to reduce the size of government itself. The capitalist state will be "retooled" and its class nature strengthened, and one of the legitimations for this will be the kind of anti-statism articulated by the Right.

At the simplest level the right-wing causes have the advantage of not making demands that will cost taxpayers money. In fact, they oppose many programs that cost money. They are against federal spending on abortion and busing, against federal enforcement of affirmative action and occupational safety. They are against day care and adequate health care especially if paid for by public funds. Their opposition to governmental intervention and big-ness does not, however, extend to opposition to military spending, to nuclear power, or to further beefing up of domestic police forces.

ORGANIZATIONAL FORM OF THE NEW RIGHT

The organizational unity of the Right is growing along with its ideological coherence, and certain factors promoting that unity should be noticed.[4]

While we have focussed here on the sex-and-family issues which form the basis of many Right campaigns, we want to emphasize the great force of racism as a unifying belief. In addition, the simple fact that the Right groups are virtually all white—and feel happy with that constituency—is also an organizational strength. Their racial homogeneity makes it easier to organize on a cross-class basis; the fear of reverse discrimination creates a unified sense of victimization among many white working-class Rightists which aligns them with capitalists and managers opposed to affirmative action for their own reasons.

Furthermore, the Right can use traditional community structures—such as ethnic neighborhoods, churches and church organizations, political party networks. Although socialists should surely look for progressive aspects of community networks, community organization today more readily lends itself to domination by petit-bourgeois leaders.

Related to the community strength of the Right is the important role of women in many campaigns. Women who espouse the most conservative views about woman's "place" are often the most active speakers, agitators, demonstrators. Women are active, of course, because these campaigns represent a natural political extension of woman's work: family, children, church and morality. However, it is already no-

ticeable that as some campaigns grow from local community resistance to city, let alone national forms (as in the anti-busing movement), men reassert control.[5]

Another important source of strength for the Right is its hierarchical form. That structure, while it may have alienated a few rebels, is initially comfortable for the majority because it replicates the dominant structure of the society.

At this time the single-issue approach of the New Right is also an organizational advantage. It allows lowest-common-denominator unity and seeks to create feeling of acceptance and solidarity. Even should the New Right coalesce into multi-issue organizations, larger than the far-right John Birch or Nazi models, its opportunism and rigid top-down form may immunize it against the sectarianism that fosters splits in the Left. Left sectarianism is partly the result of dogmatic thinking, but it is also partly the result of the socialist necessity to develop an analysis that encompasses an entire world and an entire revolutionary strategy. By contrast the Right gains adherents through manipulation of emotional and cultural symbols by a well-funded and corrupt leadership. On the other hand, we can expect divisions within the Right based on power struggles and on the conflicting needs of different interest groups. This will be especially common in electoral politics which invites competition for votes and for control of patronage. (A recent split in ROAR, an anti-busing organization in Boston, is an example of this.)

SOCIALISM AGAINST PATRIARCHY

Socialists of various tendencies, both reformist and revolutionary, have been burdened with a tradition of economism. By economism we mean encouraging working-class struggles for *more* of the same, focusing on the redistrib-

4. For a good description of the New Right and some sense of its organizational ties see Andrew Kopkind, "America's New Right," *New Times*, September 30, 1977.

5. Kathleen McCourt, in *Working-Class Women and Grass-Roots Politics* (Indiana University Press, 1977), describes the conservative activity of white working-class women on Chicago's southwest side.

ution of what is already delivered by the capitalist system without questioning *what* is produced nor *how* it is produced.[6] The economistic conception of socialism demands redivision of the pie and neglects the basic recipe. Socialists have too often neglected the social relations of production and they also have been resistant to radical perspectives on sex and family issues on the grounds they were not "basic." We are here concerned with the latter which we reject as a mechanistic two-stage model—first people struggle for high wages and then they think about better sexual relationships—because it is so evidently not true.

Socialists have also neglected sex and family issues on the grounds that working-class people *as a class* have conservative views on these issues. We do not accept this evaluation for two reasons. First, it is time socialists stopped imagining a working class composed of white patriarchs. Second, we see no reason why socialists should be more willing to compromise on, say, women's rights than on any number of other currently unpopular socialist principles. Finally, socialists have neglected sex and family issues because radical views on these subjects often came from the middle classes. But so did most socialist theory. The question is not whether or not there will be class alliances; the question is toward what end and with what outlook.

The issues currently being raised so successfully by the right justify as strong a socialist response as possible. We think socialists ought to develop programs and organizations that address the dissolution of patriarchy, and the left will also have to make sex, family and women's liberation among our primary issues.

It is not easy to be pro-sex in our culture. The prevailing cultural and commercial manipulation is saturated with sexuality to a degree that simultaneously tantalizes and repels. Not only pornography, but also advertising, slick

books, fashion, sado-masochistic rock—all these cash in on repressed sexuality. At times people try to hold on to a sense of morality and propriety by arguing that sex should be less important, by prefering to focus on work, friends, or "higher" endeavors. Some socialists and feminists, especially because of their anger about the sexual exploitation of women, adopt anti-sexual or anti-heterosexual attitudes. For many women all heterosexual relations are distorted by male dominance; the view that heterosexual relations are too trying, too full of inequality to be worth attempting, is surely a reasonable one for many women; some substitute homosexual relations, some masturbation, some celibacy. The last—celibacy—is a traditional response, for in the nineteenth century feminism was associated with prudery. As a personal choice the rejection of sexual activity may be appropriate for some, but as a political line it is a loser. Similarly, the substitution of masturbation for a relationship seems unlikely to satisfy complex human sexual needs, mixed as they are with desires for love and intimacy.

It is important, if at times difficult, to project a view that endorses, even celebrates, the pleasures of sex; and emphasizes the affinity of sexual delight with free, mutual, sensitive and responsible relationships. The capacity for sexual pleasure and sexual relationships is a universal and creative human capacity. Furthermore, the instinct for sex is related to the capacity for play, in turn closely connected to the imagination of a good life which spurs people to struggle for socialism. Sexual restraint was and still is in some respects, necessary for survival. It is a part of the development of human self-control which maximizes the possibility of human freedom and creativity. But sexual prudery today is a tool of domination of men over women, of old over young, and of class over class. In political practice these questions will be matters for judgment and it would be futile to search for clean and simple sexual morals. Such a search would lead to either moralistic repression or irresponsible individualism. But to deny the importance of the

6. This is broader than the Leninist definition of economism because we connect the drive for working-class *political* power (emphasized by Lenin in his criticism of economism) with transforming *social* relations.

widespread search for sexual pleasure will only blind the Left to a tremendous amount of energy, anti-authoritarian sentiments, and capacity for greater honesty and cooperation already existing in society.

If a socialist politics of sex must be complex, a politics of the family must be even more so. We can be in principle unequivocally pro-sex because sex itself is a human activity that has its own worth and which can be separated from those oppressive power relations that invade it. We do not know whether the family can be separated from its oppressive aspects and remain a stable institution. The family is a remarkably universal social creation. It is so weaved into the systems of domination that it has been extremely difficult for socialists to distinguish its oppressive from its supportive possibilities. We think that a socialist politics should clearly oppose the systematically oppressive relations that the family helps to maintain: age, male, and heterosexual domination. But we also think that socialists should support the search for the satisfactions that families can sometimes provide: emotional and sexual intimacy, child-rearing by caring people, cooperation and sharing. Some people are not searching for and finding these outside of families. Others are living in families in which they are struggling—often with good results—against inequality; many others have no choice but to remain in oppressive families. To denounce the family in our circumstances is at best an abstraction; at worst it may seem contemptuous. But without condemning many people's love and need for their families we can fight against the romantic, reactionary, reassertion of family as an ideal model of authority and community.

Women's liberation is a threat that must run through capitalist politics of sex and the family, but it also needs an independent focus. To view feminism as only a politics of sexual and family change would be to vastly underestimate the breadth of the feminist critique. Commitment to women's liberation also requires changing conditions for women in economic and social structures beyond the family.

Opposing discrimination against women in jobs and in the law is part of the struggle against women's oppression in the home and vice versa. The relationship between oppression in family and other institutions is a mutually determining dynamic.

NOTES TOWARD A SOCIALIST PROGRAM

1. Gay Rights

Politically it is important to recognize that the gay rights movement may still be on an upswing; gay liberation pressure has produced clear advances in recent years and Anita Bryant has stimulated a revival of gay liberation energy. A serious problem, however, particularly among male gays, is the increasing class divisions within the movement. (Male homosexuals, unlike women, include many men of quite privileged social position.) It is important for socialists enthusiastically to support campaigns to end legal, residential and job discrimination against homosexuals, for unbiased health and mental care, and for homosexuals' right as couples and as parents. By not addressing the needs of homosexuals, the Left has missed opportunities to help build socialist and class consciousness among working-class homosexuals.

The civil libertarian and simple-justice arguments for gay rights are not minor and should not be relinquished. But we are struck that much socialist support for homosexuals' freedom has been liberal—that is, it does not consider how open homosexuality can contribute to building a socialist movement for all. Homosexuals have been in the forefront of building alternative forms of living and non-family support networks. Lesbians contribute, we think, a particularly strong challenge to male supremacy. As women who do not choose to live with men they are not, on the whole, as easily "managed." Working-class lesbians, at least those without options for upward mobility, may have less stake in getting male approval, and thus more easily assume leadership in workplace and community struggles. In most communities, the presence of women maintaining themselves without men is vital to the fight against male supremacy. Whether the women are gay or straight, they offer support and strong models to other women and place sexist men on the defensive. Strong, independent single women and their friendships, whether gay or straight, offer single women alternatives to compromising their own work and identity for men, and offer married women the strength to struggle to change their situations when that struggle requires taking risks. Lesbians have an objective, unchanging interest in the maintenance of supportive women's communities, and mixed communities that do not assume the heterosexual couple as the normal unit for social life. We all gain a more viable, militant community from the freedom of homosexuals.

2. Reproductive Self-Determination and Sexual Freedom

Today the abortion issue is the leading point of political contest in the areas of both women's liberation and sexual freedom. But the grounds of the struggle may shift very quickly so it is important to enunciate a full socialist program for reproductive self-determination even as we continue working actively for abortion rights. Historically, the separation of sex and reproduction has been a basic material condition for women's liberation and for sexual freedom.

Abortion, safe contraception and related medical care should be top-priority among the free social services socialists fight for. At the same time, women's freedom to *have* children should be defended as vigorously; this means stringent guidelines to prevent coercive sterilization, abortion, or surrendering of children for adoption, as well as good day care, pediatric care, and welfare aid without which women are not free to choose.

Ultimately the best way of giving women control over their reproduction will be good sex education. A socialist sex-education program cannot be merely physiology; it must be a

political women's liberation education as well as one based on pro-sex attitudes.

3. Violence Against Women

The implicit cultural licensing of violence against women helps maintain male supremacy. Revoking the license must be done by increasing women's power. While we need not applaud the sexual exhibitionism of clothing styles—largely dictated to women by sexist fashion and media industries—we must absolutely defend the right of freedom of dress, freedom of mobility, even freedom to be flirtatious and friendly without "deserving" violence. It is time to deny men the right to define the limits of women's good behavior. The ideology that men cannot control their sexual urges has been called upon to support male supremacy for centuries. The pathological sex murderers of recent years are in part products of the general insanity and violence of our culture, but in part too they are the demented extensions of "normal" male ideas that sexual domination is their right. The association of sex and violence is promoted by advertising, rock-music promotion, television, as well as "hard" smut.

4. Affirmative Action

With the Bakke case pending in the Supreme Court, the left is in a position that is uniquely American: immediate political issues are dictated by the judicial system. But, like abortion, we cannot ignore this. The defeat of affirmative action (even more than the possible defeat of the ERA) would be a severe setback. Though it is hard to know what to do right now except march, propagandize, and pressure particular institutions, the Left should maintain the view that the ERA, affirmative action, school desegregation and equal employment opportunities form important parts of any socialist program.

FEMINISM AND SOCIALISM

The importance of these issues, and the inadequacy of the Left's response, moves us to argue for the necessity of a feminist approach more strongly than ever. The inability of the non-feminist Left to incorporate the successes of the recent women's movement has produced a greater distance between socialist and feminist individuals and organizations than is healthy. A splintering of feminism itself into different political tendencies has of course promoted this separation. There was hope that the separation might be reduced by the development of an autonomous socialist-feminist tendency in the last five years, and in the long run it is the most promising development in the contemporary women's movement. But in the short run it has not been able to offer much general leadership, and within socialist feminism there have been setbacks. One was the reassertion of a crude Leninist, reductionist view of the "woman question" that was essentially anti-feminist, even though often coming from within socialist-feminist organizations. In reducing the question of sexism to a class question, and restricting the current program of women's liberation to one of "democratic rights," these Leninists tacitly accepted, at least in current organizing, the most conservative views of proper sexual and family behavior. At the same time many other socialist feminists, in their understandable concern to bring a class politics to their women's liberation program, also avoided sex-and-family issues in favor of an emphasis on organizing women around labor-market and job grievances. This emphasis reflected an economistic tendency even among feminists, a tendency to neglect "quality" in favor of "quantity" issues. This mistaken emphasis sometimes leads to the undervaluing of two strengths of the women's liberation movement: the understanding that the "personal is political," and the development of organizational forms that prefigure socialist social relations. We would like briefly to reconsider these important feminist contributions, and to suggest that their value does not run counter to, and even supports, the building of a working-class socialist movement.

One meaning of the "personal is political" is that politics is not a "thing" external to people's own inner lives. Political relations invade, shape, and help constitute inner life. For instance, the relationship between a worker and a boss— "labor and capital"—is not just one of wages, hours, and working conditions, but is experienced through actual relationships between workers and their "superiors," relationships encapsulated in patterns of deference and domination, refracted through posture, tone of voice, dress, and influencing such "personal" qualities as self-image. Another meaning of the "personal is political" is that many personal problems have social, economic and political causes, and their solutions require social and political change. If this is a truism, the Left is not acting on it. Personal problems, if they continue to be perceived as private, will be obstacles to political participation. By contrast, personal problems subjected to a radical analysis can reveal the pervasive power relations in society, and can encourage people toward political strategies for change. The fact is that access to political concerns is usually initially through direct experience. For instance, it is maddening that affirmative action is felt as more of a threat to many people than nuclear power plants. The reason, perhaps, is that affirmative action upsets traditional social relations and personal expectations, while nuclear power does not, at least not directly or immediately. Yet once people do connect deeply felt personal problems to larger political structures, they often go on to make political sense out of the whole society rather quickly. This is not merely hypothetical; many women in the last decade moved rapidly from complaints about sexual relationships to feminism to socialism.

This transition is of course not automatic. The transition is more likely to take place when personal experiences are collectively explored and politically experienced people participate in the process. Furthermore, saying that the "personal is political" does not deny individuals' responsibility for their own lives. Not all personal problems necessitate political solutions, nor can all be solved politically. But virtually all aspects of personal life have social dimensions, just as all political power relations have personal dimensions.

Another major contribution of feminism is the development of forms of organization and thereby of community in which new kinds of social relations predominate. The collective investigation of personal oppressions can lead to a clearer understanding that the social distribution of power affects everyday life, and that the elimination of oppression necessitates new social relationships. Feminist groups, for example, have struggled to minimize internal inequalities and to create friendships and living communities in which all members felt valued and central. If feminist groups sometimes were idealist and attempted to create democracy simply by declaring it, that is no reason to undervalue the importance of struggle for democratic communities. In fact feminist groups have been able to create organizations that were far more democratic and participatory than most of what the Left had previously done. There is, however, an inherent tension between the struggle for political power and the development of community solidarity; between the drive to organize more people and confront those with power, and paying attention to internal group dynamics. We are not suggesting that the struggle for power through outreach, organizing and confrontation should be sacrificed. But many on the Left are not attentive enough to how internal aspects of their own organization tend to reproduce some of the very oppressive power relations, feelings of isolation and passivity that maintain capitalist domination.

The women's liberation movement has not been alone on the Left in attaching importance to the "personal is political" and to pre-figurative forms of struggle. But these themes are central to feminism. They have been most clearly expressed in two organizational forms: consciousness raising and self-help groups.

In consciousness-raising groups, people share their personal experiences, often about things which they have been previously ashamed to discuss. In most homogenous groups, people have been able quickly to learn that even their worst shames and miseries were not so uncommon, were parts of social patterns, created by social relationships. There is a difference, however, between CR and support groups. Good CR groups should be supportive, through the enormously comforting gift of solidarity, but they should also challenge existing relations and defenses against change. The fact that many CR groups did create such challenges is illustrated by the fact that many dissolved after a year or two, despite deep personal commitments, because their members felt the need for larger and more action-directed political groups.

It is also important to note that CR groups were a particular form uniquely appropriate to women's liberation. "Men's liberation" groups have a greater tendency to become merely supportive, to reinforce existing patterns, and at worst to provide cover for backlash grievances against women's anger. But we are not convinced that CR groups are useless for anyone except women. Like any political form, they are not magic; they require clear political goals, structure and leadership. But it seems to us that all political organizations ought to create some space, formal or informal, where people can talk politically about their personal lives.

Although "self-help" has come to refer mainly to gynecological clinics, in fact it denotes a more general organizational form in which people work collectively to help themselves deal with social problems. Perhaps the best way to appreciate the significance of these kinds of service projects is to contrast them with the more standard, welfare-state model of rendering services as commodities (paid for either directly or through taxes) delivered by bureaucrats or professionals. Recently, the women's movement itself has brought many social problems into the open: rape, incest, wife-beating, for examples. In response, institutions such as hospitals, police forces, judicial systems, mental health clinics and universities are intervening ever more extensively and deeply into family life. The well-known distaste with which most welfare recipients regard their social workers is an accurate indication of the attitudes that many service workers (including, unfortunately, many workers objectively in the working class) have been socialized into. But even well-meaning social workers often only deepen despair because of the inability of the institutions they work within to offer alternatives better than even the most oppressive families and neighborhoods.

A further complexity in developing a Left response to bureaucratic intervention is that we cannot simply denounce it. The feminists' power of disclosure, for example, went far beyond the capacity of the women's movement to deal with problems. A man's home is not his torture chamber, after all. There is a great deal that therapy and counselling can do to help unhappy people. Even the capitalist state can sometimes protect people from worse, or more pressing, evils.

Self-help groups cannot replace the state, but they can offer radical alternatives for some. Through projects such as rape crisis centers, alcoholics groups, and shelters for abused wives, the victims of oppressive men and institutions are encouraged to change their lives with the aid of other women, often previously victims.

The model of collective self-help, while not in itself a socialist strategy, strengthens the connection between personal and social change. In the best of cases, self-help groups combine consciousness-raising with material aid and an opening to a new community of people; thus providing not only the ideas but some of the conditions for adopting a less passive stance towards the world. The self-help model is a way of dealing with the fact that politics often becomes a part of one's life only when a political problem is directly experienced.

Of course there are wide variations in such projects, and the most famous of these—the gynecological clinics—are now frequently hierarchically run. Furthermore, self-help ideology has sometimes promoted an unqualified anti-professionalism and disregard of helpful expertise. But the shunning of such work by socialists has also contributed to the low political level of many projects. Self-help groups are susceptible to all the political problems of service projects; attracting people with a client orientation towards the project, conflict of interest and energy between performing services and political outreach, bureaucratization forced by state licensing requirements, among others. But all political work has problems and we are not convinced that these are greater than the potential benefits.

It is also important to keep self-help projects and consciousness-raising groups in mind when evaluating the current state of the Left. While many sectors of the Left do not seem active now, such self-help groups are spreading among working-class women. Indeed, a good part of the most dynamic political activity in the working class today is among women who have been changed by feminism.

Still, it is important to remind ourselves again that many working-class women are in the Right, too. We are alarmed at the growth of the Right, and think it should be answered. But our primary reason for arguing that the Left should make sex-and-family, "personal," issues important in our work is not simply a desire to respond to the Right. On the contrary we have several more long-run and positive reasons for urging that course. We think that the development of a fuller socialist-feminist program on these issues would contribute greatly to a socialist program that would be attractive and realistic for our country. We think that many people, and perhaps especially working-class people, are troubled and looking for solutions to problems of personal tension, violence, and loneliness. We do not mean to suggest that this is a whole socialist program or even the basic part of one. But we think that family and personal instability is a weak spot in capitalism, and that socialists can participate in and develop political responses attractive to much of the working class.

61

NATIONAL ORGANIZATON FOR WOMEN

ERA Position Paper (1967)

An informational memorandum prepared
for the National Organization for
Women (NOW) regarding the Equal Rights
Amendment and similar proposals.

NOW's Statement of Purpose endorses the
principle that women should exercise all the
privileges and responsibilities of American society in equal partnership with men and states
that:

"the power of American law, and the protection guaranteed by the U. S. Constitution to
the civil rights of all individuals, must be effectively applied and enforced to isolate and remove patterns of sex discrimination, to ensure
equality of opportunity in employment and education, and equality of civil and political rights
and responsibilities on behalf of women, as well
as for Negroes and other deprived groups."

The Fourteenth Amendment to the United
States Constitution provides that no State shall
"deprive any person of life, liberty or property,
without due process of law; nor deny to any
person within its jurisdiction the equal protection of the laws." The Fourteenth Amendment
restricts the *States* and the "due process" clause
of the Fifth Amendment similarly restricts the
Federal Government from interfering with
these individual rights. These are the constitutional provisions under which much of the civil
rights for Negroes litigation has been brought
and it is now clear that any radical distinction in
law or official practice is unconstitutional.

THE PRESIDENT'S COMMISSION
ON THE STATUS OF
WOMEN RECOMMENDATION

The issue of constitutionality of sex distinctions in the law has been raised in a number

Documents produced for and circulated at National
Organization for Women Annual Meeting, 1978.

of cases under the 5th and 14th Amendments.
However, the Civil and Political Rights Committee of the President's Commission found in
1963 (Report, p.34):

"The courts have consistently upheld
laws providing different treatment for
women than for men, usually on the basis of
the State's special interest in protecting the
health and welfare of women. In no 14th
Amendment case alleging discrimination on
account of sex has the United States Supreme
Court held that a law classifying persons on
the basis of sex is unreasonable and therefore
unconstitutional. Until such time as the
Supreme Court reexamines the doctrine of
'sex as a basis for legislative classification' and
promulgates the standards determining which
types of laws and official practices treating
men and women differently are reasonable
and which are not, it will remain unclear
whether women can enforce their rights under the 14th amendment or whether there is
a constitutional gap which can only be filled
by a Federal constitutional amendment."

The President's Commission on the Status
of Women in its report to President Kennedy
in October, 1963, declared:

"Equality of rights under the law for all
persons, male or female, is so basic to democracy and its commitment to the ultimate value
of the individual that it must be reflected in the
fundamental law of the land."

The Commission went on to say that it believed that the principle of equal rights for men
and women was embodied in the 5th and 14th
amendments, and accordingly, "a constitutional
amendment need not now be sought in order
to establish this principle." The Commission
states further:

"Early and definitive court pronounce-
ment, particularly by the U.S. Supreme Court,
is urgently needed with regard to the validity
under the 5th and 14th amendments of laws
and official practices discriminating against
women, to the end that the principle of equality become firmly established in constitutional
doctrine" (*American Women*, pages 44–45).

The Commission report optimistically does not include any recognition of the possibility that the Court might rule against women seeking to invoke the protection of the Constitution.

HISTORY OF THE
EQUAL RIGHTS AMENDMENT

The constitutional amendment which the Commission stated it did not deem necessary to endorse in 1963 was the proposed Equal Rights Amendment. That amendment, which has been introduced in every Congress since 1923, in its present form would provide (see S.J. Res. 43, 90th Congress. 1st Sess.):

"Equality of Rights under the law shall not be denied or abridged by the United States or by any State on account of sex."

Congress has in the past held hearings on the Equal Rights Amendment, most recently in 1948 and in 1956, and the amendment has twice passed the Senate, but with a provision added that the amendment "shall not be construed to impair any rights, benefits, or exemptions now or hereafter conferred by law, upon persons of the female sex." The effect of the added provision, known as the "Hayden rider," has been to kill the Equal Rights Amendment, since proponents of the amendment obviously would not wish to support the addition. The Senate Judiciary Committee has frequently reported favorably on the amendment and the recent reports specifically oppose the "Hayden rider" pointing out that the qualification "is not acceptable to women who want equal rights under the law. It is under the guise of so-called 'rights' or 'benefits' that women have been treated unequally and denied opportunities which are available to men."

EFFECT OF THE
EQUAL RIGHTS AMENDMENT

Constitutional amendments, like statutes, are interpreted by the courts in light of intent of Congress. Committee reports on a proposal are regarded by the courts as the most persuasive evidence of the intended meaning of a provision. Therefore, the probable meaning and effect of the Equal Rights Amendment can be ascertained from the Senate Judiciary Committee reports (which have been the same in recent years):

1. The amendment would restrict only governmental action, and would not apply to purely private action. What constitutes "State action" would be the same as under the 14th amendment and as developed in the 14th amendment litigation on other subjects.

2. Special restrictions on property rights of married women would be unconstitutional; married women could engage in business as freely as a member of the male sex; inheritance rights of widows would be the same as for widowers.

3. Women would be equally subject to jury service and to military service, but women would not be required to serve (in the Armed Forces) where they are not fitted any more than men are required to so serve.

4. Restrictive work laws for women only would be unconstitutional.

5. Alimony laws would not favor women solely because of their sex, but a divorce decree could award support to a mother if she was granted custody of the children. Matters concerning custody and support of children would be determined in accordance with the welfare of the children and without favoring either parent because of sex.

6. Laws granting maternity benefits to mothers would not be affected by the amendment, nor would criminal laws governing sexual offenses become unconstitutional.

SUPPORT OF AND OPPOSITION TO
THE EQUAL RIGHTS AMENDMENT

The National Woman's Party, which continued to carry on the feminist movement following the adoption of the Nineteenth Amendment, has led the fight for an Equal Rights Amendment. Other organizations which have supported the amendment include the National Federation of Business and Professional Women's Clubs, the General Federation of Women's Clubs, National Association of Women Lawyers, National Association of Colored Business and Professional Women, St. Joan's Alliance, American Federation of Soroptimist Clubs, and various women's professional and civic organizations. Strong opposition to the amendment has come from the labor unions. Other organizations opposing the amendment have included the Americans for Democratic Action, National Council of Jewish Women, National Council of Catholic Women, National Council of Negro Women.

The most recent Congressional hearings on the amendment were held in 1956. There does not appear to be any record which would indicate that any of the opponents of the amendment who objected to the amendment's effect of eliminating special labor laws for women, have re-examined their position since the enactment of Title VII of the Civil Rights Act of 1964. Some of the organizations opposed to the amendment have urged the Equal Employment Opportunity Commission not to enforce Title VII in a manner which would affect State laws restricting the employment of women. On the other hand, some labor unions, notably the U.A.W., Chemical Workers and Typographical Workers, have urged the EEOC to rule that the equal employment opportunity provisions of the Federal law supersede special hours and weight lifting restrictions on women workers.

CURRENT SEX DISCRIMINATION CASES

In a 1966 case, *White v. Crook*, a three judge federal court in Alabama held the Alabama law excluding women from serving on juries violate the 14th amendment. The court said that "the plain effect (of the equal protection clause of the 14th amendment) is to prohibit prejudicial disparities before the law. This means prejudicial disparities for all citizens—including

women." The State did not appeal to the U.S. Supreme Court and the Alabama legislature amended its law to permit women to serve on juries on the same basis as men. A similar case challenging the constitutionality of a Mississippi jury law excluding women is currently pending before a three judge federal court in Mississippi (*Willis v. Carson*). The Mississippi jury law is also at issue in *Bass v. Mississippi*, pending before the Fifth Circuit U.S. Court of Appeals. The Mississippi Supreme Court, in the case of *Hall v. Mississippi*, declined to apply the doctrine of *White v. Crook* and held that the Mississippi law did not violate the 14th amendment. The U.S. Supreme Court dismissed the appeal in that case on jurisdictional grounds and did not hear the case.

The exclusion of women from draft boards under selective service regulations (which have recently been amended to permit women to serve) is at issue in a conscientious objector case in Georgia.

In *Mengelkoch v. Industrial Welfare Commission* the constitutionality of the California hours restriction law for women workers is being challenged. This case is pending before a three judge federal court in Los Angeles. NOW attorneys Marguerite Rawalt and Evelyn Whitlow are representing the plaintiff women workers. A Federal court in Indiana recently ruled in *Bowe v. Colgate-Palmolive Co.* that Title VII does not prohibit an employer from excluding women from jobs which require the lifting of more than 35 pounds. Although Indiana does not have a weight lifting restriction law for women, the court reasoned that some States do and this justifies employers in other States in adopting the same "protective" practices. A California weight lifting limitation on women workers is alleged as violating their right to equal employment opportunity under Title VII in *Regguinti v. Rocketdyne and North American Aviation*, pending in a Federal court in the State. However, the plaintiff's attorney did not raise the issue of a violation of the 14th amendment. There may be other Title VII cases as well which could involve testing the validity under the

14th amendment of State restrictive laws, but in which the attorneys have failed to raise the issue.

A Pennsylvania State court held that a statute providing longer prison sentences for women than for men does not deny to women the equal protection of the laws under the 14th amendment (*Commonwealth v. Daniels*). This case is currently being appealed to the Pennsylvania Supreme Court. A county court in Oregon held, in January, 1967, that a city ordinance providing for punishment of female prostitutes is unconstitutional because it does not apply equally to males.

This listing of pending litigation does not, of course, purport to be exhaustive.

SUGGESTED NEW INTERPRETATIONS OF THE 5TH AND 14TH AMENDMENTS

In "Jane Crow and the Law" (34 G.W. Law Rev. 232) (1965) authors Murray and Eastwood suggest that the doctrine that sex is a reasonable basis for classifying persons under the law, which has been used to justify upholding the constitutionality of laws which treat women differently from men, should be discarded by the courts. They point out that it could be argued that *any sex* differentiation in law or official practice today is inherently unreasonable and discriminatory and therefore violates the Constitution. The prospective effect of such an interpretation of the Constitution by the courts is outlined on pages 240 and 241 of that article.

NOW's brief in the *Mengelkoch* case asserts that the doctrine that sex is a valid basis for classifying persons does not even apply where there is involved the right to pursue lawful employment, since this is an *individual* right and a liberty and property which the State cannot restrict.

If these suggested constitutional interpretations are adopted by the courts in all areas of sex discrimination, the principle of equality set forth in the Equal Rights Amendment might in effect be "read into" the 5th and 14th amendments.

ANALYSIS OF ARGUMENTS AGAINST THE EQUAL RIGHTS AMENDMENT

Reasons which have been given for opposing the Equal Rights Amendment are as follows:

1. The amendment would be difficult to interpret and would result in a great deal of litigation.

2. The amendment is not necessary because women can achieve constitutional equality through litigation under the 5th and 14th amendments.

3. Any constitutional requirement of equal treatment of the sexes is undesirable because it would require equal treatment of men and women in (a) state labor laws, (b) family law, (c) criminal laws, (d) social benefits law, and (e) obligations to the State and to the Nation.

1. "The amendment would be difficult to interpret and would result in a great deal of litigation."

The meaning of "equality of rights under the law" would be a question for interpretation by the courts. The language of the Equal Rights Amendment is patterned after the 19th Amendment:

ERA: "Equality of rights under the law shall not be denied."

19th: "The right of citizens of the United States to vote shall not be denied or abridged by the United States or by any State on account of sex."

However, the 19th amendment is specific and applies only to the right to vote. Its meaning is therefore more clear than the Equal Rights Amendment, which applies to all "rights." Excessive litigation (and possible undesirable decisions) under the Equal Rights Amendment might be avoided if "equality of rights" were more clearly defined in the legislative history of the amendment as meaning *the right to equal treatment without differentiation based on sex.*

As noted in the cases mentioned above, women are now seeking to invoke the protection of the 14th amendment in the courts. In part because of the enactment of Title VII of the Civil Rights Act of 1964, it is likely that litigation under the 14th amendment will increase. It is possible that the adoption of the Equal Rights Amendment would actually have the effect of reducing the amount of litigation necessary to secure equal treatment of the sexes under the law. Of course, litigation is not necessarily bad. Indeed under our legal system litigation is a proper means for correcting discriminatory treatment.

2. "The amendment is not necessary because women can achieve constitutional equality through litigation under the 5th and 14th amendments."

Women have been seeking equal rights under these amendments since 1872. (For a summary of the cases see the Report of the Committee on Civil and Political Rights, Appendix B, President's Commission on the Status of Women.) Women can and should continue to do so until discrimination in laws and official practices is eliminated. In "Jane Crow and the Law" (op. cit. supra) Murray and Eastwood state (page 237):

"Although the Supreme Court has in no case found a law distinguishing on the basis of sex to be a violation of the fourteenth amendment, the amendment may nevertheless be applicable to sex discrimination. The genius of the American Constitution is its capacity, through judicial interpretation, for growth and adaptation to changing conditions and human values. Recent Supreme Court decisions in cases involving school desegregation, reapportionment, the right to counsel, and the extension of the concept of state action illustrate the modern trend towards insuring equality of status and recognizing individual rights. Courts have not yet fully realized that women's rights are a part of human rights; but the climate appears favorable to renewed judicial attacks on sex discrimination. . . ."

Supporters of the Equal Rights Amendment believe that the potential of the 14th amendment is too unclear and that women's constitutional rights to equality are too insecure to rely exclusively on the possibility of getting more enlightened court decisions under that amendment.

In a 1963 case, the Supreme Court stated: "The Fifteenth Amendment prohibits a State from denying or abridging a Negro's right to vote. The Nineteenth Amendment does the same for women. . . . Once a geographical unit for which a representative is to be chosen is designated, all who participate in the election are to have an equal vote—whatever their race, whatever their sex. . . . This is required by the Equal Protection Clause of the Fourteenth Amendment." *Gray v. Sanders, 371 U.S. 368, 379.*

This interpretation of the 14th amendment reinforced and made doubly secure the right to vote. There are numerous cases in which the Supreme Court has interpreted the 14th amendment to reinforce or to extend rights guaranteed by earlier or, as in the above case, later amendments to the Constitution. For example, the more general due process and equal protection concepts of the Fifth and Fourteenth Amendments have been used to strengthen more specific rights of individuals to freedom of speech, assembly and religion guaranteed by the First Amendment; and the right to a speedy trial and right to counsel guaranteed by the Sixth. If the Equal Rights Amendment is adopted, the courts might well subsequently interpret the Fourteenth Amendment as reinforcing constitutional equality for women.

A question might be asked as to why there should be a special equality guarantee for women and not for Negroes or for the aged. As a result of successful litigation under the Fifth and Fourteenth Amendments, Negroes today *have* the constitutional right to equal treatment and both the Federal Government and the States are absolutely prohibited from treating persons differently because of race. The same is true as to national origin and religion. With respect to age, absolute equality of rights and responsibilities is *not* desirable. If age were added to the Equal Rights Amendment, child labor laws would be rendered void, as would social security and government retirement systems. Selective service laws could not place the responsibility to serve in military service on a certain age group, and state requirements that children attend school could not be based on age.

If the Fourteenth Amendment had been drafted so as to absolutely and unequivocally require equal treatment without differentiation based on race, Negroes would not have had to painstakingly, step by step, achieve equality of rights under the law through litigation and legislation. The general language of the 14th amendment guarantees of due process and equal protection of the law for all persons has enabled the courts to give recognition to important human rights concepts of freedom of speech and religion and protection of the rights of persons accused of crimes. These are unrelated to race and it is not suggested that the 14th amendment should have been limited to requiring racial equality. Nevertheless, one might ask those who oppose the Equal Rights Amendment on the ground that equality of rights for women might ultimately be achieved under the present constitutional framework whether, at this day in history, women should be asked to repeat the painful, costly and uncertain course of litigation which Negro Americans had to endure.

3. "Any constitutional requirement of equal treatment of the sexes is undesirable because it would require equal treatment of men and women in (a) state labor laws, (b) family law, (c) criminal laws, (d) social benefits law, and (e) obligations to the State and to the Nation."

At the time of the last Congressional hearings on the amendment (1956) it was assumed by both proponents and opponents of the amendment that there is no existing constitutional requirement that women be accorded equal rights and responsibilities under the law. The debate centered on whether the constitution *should* require equal treatment of the sexes. Those who opposed the amendment simply opposed equal treatment of men and women.

It is assumed that all members of NOW favor equal rights and responsibilities for women. Nevertheless, before endorsing or rejecting the Equal Rights Amendment one would want to know the consequences and effects of the amendment.

The precise effect in a particular case alleging denial of equal rights under the amendment would be a question for the courts. As noted above, the courts, in making their determinations, would be guided by the intended meaning of the "legislative history" of the amendment. Organizations such as NOW could help in shaping the legislative history and in clarifying the effect the amendment is intended to have.

The President's Commission on the Status of Women and the various State Commissions have outlined the areas of law and official practice which treat men and women differently. All of these studies have been made *since* the last hearings on the amendment.

The Equal Rights Amendment would require equal treatment without differentiation based on sex. Purely private discrimination, whether based on race, religion, sex or national origin, is not reached and is not prohibited by the U.S. Constitution. Laws and actions of agents of the Government are clearly reached. The question in each instance would be whether the right to equal treatment is denied or abridged by the State or Federal Government.

The precise effect of the amendment in a given situation cannot be predicted with absolute certainty since this would be determined by the courts. The following discussion indicates how the amendment might affect various laws and practices which treat men and women differently.

(a) State Labor Laws

(1) Minimum wage laws and other laws giving rights to women workers. If the State guarantees to women workers a minimum wage, men workers would be entitled to equal treatment by virtue of the Equal Rights

Amendment. The same reasoning applies as to any state protected guarantees of seating facilities, lunch periods, or similar benefits provided for women workers. These laws or regulations would be automatically extended to persons of both sexes in the same way the State voting laws which applied only to men were automatically extended to women by virtue of the 19th amendment.

(2) State laws limiting and restricting the hiring and employment of female workers—hours restrictions, night work restrictions and weight lifting limitations. These laws are all limitations on the freedom of women workers because of their sex. They limit the right to pursue lawful employment and to work when and how long they choose. They confer *no* rights on women. Both men and women are, of course, free to not work longer than they so choose or at such times as they choose, by virtue of the 13th amendment's prohibition against slavery and forced labor. State restrictive laws would not be extended to men; they would be nullified by the Equal Rights Amendment because they place restrictions on women not placed on men.

(3) Laws totally prohibiting the employment of women in certain occupations, such as bar tending and mining, likewise would be void, because they clearly deprive women, because of their sex, of the right to employment in these occupations. State laws providing a higher minimum age for employment for girls would be affected by the amendment by reducing the age to that provided for boys.

(4) Maternity laws would not be affected by the amendment because such laws are not based on sex; they do not apply women as a class. (See "Jane Crow and the Law," pages 239–240.)

(b) Family Law

(1) Both mothers and father are now generally responsible for the support of children under state laws. This would not be changed by the Equal Rights Amendment. In case of di-

vorce or separation, where the mother (or father, as the case may be) has custody and care of the children, courts could continue to require the other parent, be it mother or father, to contribute to the financial support of the children. Present laws do not give recognition to the financial worth of homemaking and child care. The Equal Rights Amendment would probably not require that such worth be recognized in determining the relative responsibilities of parents in case of divorce. However, recognizing the value of child care and homemaking would be consistent with the principle of equality of rights under the amendment.

(2) Alimony for wives solely because they are female would be prohibited by the Equal Rights Amendment. However, continued support by one spouse for the other after divorce or separation based on actual necessary economic dependency, relative ability to provide family support or past relationships and obligations of the particular parties would not be prohibited by the amendment because the alimony or support would not be based on sex but upon some other criteria. The states would continue to be free to establish these values and criteria; they would simply be prohibited from discriminating against either men or women because of sex.

(3) Minimum age for marriage. Some states provide a lower minimum age for marriage for women than for men. The amendment would prohibit treating men and women differently in regard to age for marriage. If under state law women have the right to marry at age 18 and men at age 21, the amendment would give men the right to marry at 18. The state could, of course, amend its law to provide that the age be 21 for both sexes.

(4) Age of right to parental support. Some states give girls a right to be supported to age 18 and boys to age 21. Since the girls would have the right to be treated equally under the amendment, their right in these states would be automatically extended to age 21. The states would be free, of course, to provide a different age, so long as it is the same for boys and girls.

(5) State laws placing special limitations and restrictions on married women but not on married men would be nullified by the amendment.

(c) Criminal Law

States would be prohibited from providing greater penalties for female law violators than for males. There are certain sex crimes, such as rape, which apply only to males. These would not be affected by the the Equal Rights Amendment since the state in enacting these laws has not made any classification of persons by sex; if these laws were drafted so as to refer to persons instead of males, their meaning would be the same. (See "Jane Crow and the Law," page 240.)

(d) Social Benefits Laws

There are certain differences in benefits which men and women receive under the social security and government retirement laws. There may be similar state retirement systems which give greater or lesser benefits to women. Legislation is currently pending in Congress to correct some of the inequities in the Federal law (see, e.g., H.R. 643, 90th Congress, to eliminate differences in government employees' fringe benefits). It could reasonably be expected that by the time an Equal Rights Amendment became effective, differences between the sexes in these laws would have been corrected. However, insofar as differences remained, the State or Federal Government, as the case may be, would be obligated by the Equal Rights Amendment to give the same benefits to both sexes.

(e) Service to the State and to the Nation

(Government employment, jury service and military service.) The Equal Rights Amendment would prohibit discrimination against women in public employment at all levels of government. The Administration's Civil Rights Bill would prohibit any sex discrimination in juror qualification or in selection of jurors. This would eliminate laws excluding or discouraging women from serving on juries. It is generally agreed that a state law relieving women from jury service responsibilities relegated them to second class citizenship and should be forbidden. The Equal Rights Amendment would make women eligible to serve on all juries on the same basis as men. With regard to military service the same reasoning might apply. It could be argued that failure of a nation to give its women the same responsibilities as it requires of its men makes women second class citizens. The Military Selective Service Act of 1967 requires men but not women to register for military service. The Equal Rights Amendment would have the effect of extending this requirement to women and make women eligible for selection just as women would be eligible for jury selection on the same basis as men. The present selective service law will automatically expire on July 1, 1971.

Some lawyers might disagree that the Equal Rights Amendment would have the effects outlined above. However, to the extent that supporters of the amendment can agree on the desired effects of the amendment on existing laws, such effects could be made more certain if they are carefully set forth and made a part of the amendment's legislative history.

62

NATIONAL ORGANIZATION FOR WOMEN

ERA: Declaration of State of Emergency (1978)

We declare a State of Emergency for the National Organization for Women in which we turn all our resources to the ratification effort and to extension of the deadline for ratification an additional seven years.

Documents produced for and circulated at National Organization for Women Annual Meeting, 1978.

There comes a time when the harsh political realities must be recognized: the major interests of our country have hypocritically given lip service to the ERA while sabotaging its ratification by political deals, tradeoffs and do-nothingness.

There comes a time when a movement must decide its own destiny—when it must determine on what line it will stand and fight.

The ERA is the foundation on which all our gains rest. If the ERA is defeated, it will be perceived as a vote against equality for women. The gains women have made in the past 15 years will be eroded and erased. Worse yet, every future effort we make will be dismissed with the excuse that when the ERA failed, it proved that the women of this country didn't want equality.

Never mind that only 7% of those voting on the ERA in their state legislatures—where it counts—have been women.

Never mind that 80% of those women at the National Women's Conference—where it could have no binding effect—voted for the ERA.

Never mind that public opinion polls have time again proved majority support.

Never mind that ⅔ of the states with ¾ of the population have ratified the ERA.

Political leaders do not want to be diverted by the truth or confused by the facts. And an indifferent national press refuses to consider the life and death issues facing women as hard news.

The burden on those of us who know the truth is to explode the myths, to confront the realities.

There comes a time to stand and fight and it is NOW.

The ERA is the last best hope in this century of committing this country to the principle of human equality—regardless of sex. It has been 55 years since the ERA was first introduced in Congress as the second step in guaranteeing full citizenship to women.

Two generations of women have now struggled for its ratification. If it fails, it will take 2 more generations to recover from the loss. There comes a time when we must have the courage to declare "This ABOVE ALL."

If we do not say this, *who will?*

If we who believe most passionately that all women and men are created equal are not willing to fight when the last chance to realize that dream in our lifetime is in dire peril, *who will?*

If we who know the hypocrisy that has almost turned our victory into defeat will not expose it, *who will?*

If we do not rise to the challenge of going the extra mile, of giving all that we can in the last critical days, *who will?*

If we back away from a last ditch, all-out fight for the ERA today, what compromise of our convictions will we tolerate tomorrow?

WE MUST NOT REFUSE THIS CHALLENGE.

We must not deceive ourselves into believing that we can proceed with business as usual while the victory we have so nearly won is stolen from us.

Most of the traitors who switched votes and sold us out cannot be held accountable until after March, 1979 because they are not up for election until 1980. There is no longer one full legislative session left before the deadline is reached and our opposition is stalling with parliamentary delaying tactics and is prepared to stonewall it until time runs out. We cannot fool ourselves. We have done less than the best. We cannot fail to recognize that we in fact have not adequately alerted our own membership and indeed the nation to the peril to those of us who dream of full equality for women.

Therefore we declare a State of Emergency for the National Organization for Women in which we turn all our resources to the ratification effort and to extension of the deadline for ratification of the ERA an additional 7 years.

That we emphatically state that the extension of the deadline is necessary. Necessary for the real impact of the ERA boycott of convention business in unratified states; necessary for an electoral strategy to have full impact; necessary to remove time as the issue and to place the ERA before the public in an atmosphere in which the merits of the ERA itself are the only issue, necessary to erase the half-truths and distortions of the opposition and that we state emphatically that we are not willing to accept the false hope or reintroduction on March 23, 1979 that erases 55 years of work.

Rather we recognize that a vote against extension of the deadline is a vote *against* equality for women in this century.

There comes a time to gather the courage of our convictions, the strength of our unity, the passion of our commitment and declare we are pledged to do all that is humanly possible to pass H.J. Res. 638—the extension of time line in this session of Congress. We are determined to be victorious because we will not tolerate the possibility of living lives in which there is no realistic hope of sisters and brothers, wives and husbands, mothers and fathers, women and men, living together, working together as equals.

WE HAVE PASSED THE POINT OF NO RETURN!

63

GLORIA STEINEM

What Women Want: An Introductory Statement (1978)

If this book survives to be read by our relatives of the distant future, it will have two virtues.

First, it will be one of the few accounts of history made and recorded from the bottom up. We have only to think of our school texts that concentrated on the uppermost few— royal marriages, official treaties, presidential candidates, foreign policy debates—to understand how rarely we heard of what most people were actually doing. Even those records were often filtered by distant historians, with the re-

From U.S. National Commission on the Observance of International Women's Year, *What Women Want* (New York: Simon and Schuster, 1979), 10–17.

sult that ideas and movements among ordinary people, whose massive pressures may have been the genesis of actions at the top, had to reach the stage of violent revolution before we learned about them at all.

This volume is one of the exceptions. It is a documentation of history being made from the bottom up, by populist process, and described here for posterity by those who were there and who made it happen.

Second, *What Women Want* may be something even more rare: a published record of the political agenda of women as a group. Certainly, its scope goes beyond the usual bow toward women who married or gave birth to important men, or who excel in male spheres of interest as exceptions. To complete the agenda that is documented here, women had first to conceive a series of open "town meetings" in each state and territory of the United States (many were to involve 10,000 to 20,000 women and to be the biggest political meetings ever held in their states) plus a national, delegated conference to follow. They had to press Congress for legislation and public funds to finance the meetings—and that was just the beginning. They then built bridges among economic, racial, ethnic, religious and interest groups in order to achieve a representative planning body for each of the fifty-six meetings, and evolved a debate and balloting procedure that would allow the participants to vote on all the basic issues, to recommend other issues for national consideration, and to elect the proportionate number of delegates allotted for each area's population.

Great energy, skill, caring and inventiveness went into this coalition-building and into the solving of endless logistical problems on a shoestring budget. (The $5 million that Congress had appropriated was only about 7 cents per adult American woman; Congressional opponents and skeptics had slashed the original modest request for $10 million by half.) It's impossible to calculate the personal sacrifice and time invested, but agreement was finally reached, in a massive national assembly on the majority goals and on priorities of and for the female half of America.

It was as if women had recreated for themselves a temporary version of the national political structure that had substantially excluded them for 200 years—with little money or conventional experience, and with no promise of personal award or political jobs at the end. Equally important, they accepted a commitment to democratic inclusiveness that the original ideas of this country did not address. True, the American definition of democracy has broadened since our founders created a constitution for a limited constituency of white, property-owning males, but the state meetings that led up to Houston were generally more representative by race, age, economic status, ethnicity and religion than the official legislatures making decisions in those same states. And the Houston Conference was more representative by those measures than either the House of Representatives or the Senate, and more democratic in its procedures—from allowing floor debate, amendments and substitute motions to encouraging voting by individual conscience rather than by geographical blocs or for political reward—than the political conventions that were its closest model.

This long and complex process was often frustrating and never perfect, but it surprised many Americans, including some of the women who worked hardest to make it happen, by far surpassing the standards set by comparable Establishment events. It raised hopes for a new openness and inclusiveness in national political events to come.

"Houston was a kind of Constitutional Convention for American women," explained one European observer. "They ratified the existing Constitution by demanding full inclusion in it, and then outlined the legislative changes that must take place if female citizens are to fully enjoy those rights for the first time."

This mammoth project begins to sound unprecedented—and there are many factual ways in which that is true. But comparable events *have* happened in the past. Women have taken action against the political system of male dominance for as many centuries as it has existed, and some of those actions have been at least as impressive in their own contexts, and more courageous. If we are to preserve the events recorded in this book, we should be aware that similar changeful, challenging, woman-run events have been unrecorded, suppressed, or even been ridiculed in the past.

As a student reading American history in the schools of the 1950s, I read that white and black women had been "given" the vote in 1920—an unexplained 50 years after black men had achieved that right. I learned nothing about the more than 100 years of struggle by nationwide networks of women who organized and lectured around the country at a time when they were not supposed to speak in public; who lobbied their all-male legislatures, demonstrated in the streets, went on hunger strikes and went to jail; who publicly burned the speeches of President Wilson in order to protest their government's insistence that it was fighting "for democracy" in World War I— when half of American citizens had no political rights at all. In short, I did not learn that several generations of my foremothers had nearly brought the country to its knees in order to win a separate legal identity, including the right to vote, for women as a group.

At least the right to vote was cited in history books, however, as one that American women had not always enjoyed. Other parts of that legal identity—the goal of the long, first wave of feminism—were not mentioned. How many of us were taught what it meant, for instance, for women to struggle against their status as the human property of husbands and fathers? It was a condition of chattel so clear that the first seventeenth-century American slaveholders adopted it, as Gunnar Myrdal has pointed out, as the "nearest and most natural analogy" for the legal status of slaves.[1] As young students, how many of us understood that the

1. Gunnar Myrdal, *An American Dilemma*. New York: Harper and Brothers, 1944, p. 1073.

right of an adult female American to own property, to sue in court or to sign a will, to keep a salary she earned instead of turning it over to a husband or father who "owned" her; to go to school, to have legal custody of her own children, to leave her husband's home without danger of being forcibly or legally returned; to escape a husband's right to physical discipline; to challenge the social prison of being a lifelong minor if she remained unmarried or a legal non-person if she did marry—how many of us were instructed that all of these rights had been won through generations of effort by an independent women's movement?

When we studied American progress toward religious freedom, did we read about the many nineteenth-century feminists who challenged the patriarchal structure of the church; who dared question such scriptural rhetoric as the injunction of the Apostle Paul to "Wives, submit yourselves unto your husbands as unto the Lord"? Were we given a book called *Woman's Bible*, a scholarly and very courageous revision of the scriptures undertaken by Elizabeth Cady Stanton?

If we read about religious and political persecution in America, did we learn that the frenzy of the New England witch trials, tortures and burnings were usually the persecutions of independent or knowledgeable women, of midwives who performed abortions and taught contraception, of women who challenged the masculine power structure in various ways?

When we heard about courageous people who harbored runaway slaves, did they include women like Susan B. Anthony who helped not only black slaves, but runaway wives and children escaping the brutality of white men who "owned" them?

Of course, to record the fact that blacks and women were both legally chattel, or that the mythology of "natural" inferiority was (and sometimes still is) used to turn both into a source of cheap labor, is not to be confused with equating these two groups. Black women and men suffered more awful restrictions on

their freedom, a more overt cruelty and violence, and their lives were put at greater risk. Angelina Grimké, one of the white Southern feminists who worked against both race and sex slavery, always pointed out that "We have not felt the slave-holder's lash . . . we have not had our hands manacled."[2] White women were sometimes injured or killed in "justified" domestic beatings, or sold as indentured workers as a punishment for poverty or for breaking a law. Hard work combined with the years of coerced childbearing designed to populate this new land may have made white women's life expectancy as low as half that of white males. (The average frontier family seems to have been a two-mother family: when a woman died after multiple childbirths, her husband married again to have another worker and more children. Early American graveyards full of young women who died in childbirth testify both to the desperation with which many women sought out midwives for contraception or abortion, and to the motives for punishing such practices as immoral, dangerous; perhaps even the work of witches.) Nonetheless, white women were far less likely than black slaves to risk or lose their lives, and particularly less so than black women who were used as breeders of more slaves as well as workers. In contrast, the more typical white female punishment was the loss of her identity, or to have her spirit broken. As Angelina Grimké explained, "I rejoice exceedingly that our resolution should combine us with the Negro. I feel that we have been with him; that the iron has entered into our souls . . . our *hearts* have been crushed."[3]

But why did so many history books assume that women and blacks could have no issues in common; so much so that they failed to report coalitions of the past? Historians seem to pay little attention to movements among the powerless. Or perhaps the intimate challenge presented by a majority coalition of women of all

2. Grimké, in Elizabeth Cady Stanton, et al., *The History of Woman Suffrage*, Vol. II. Rochester: Charles Mann, 1899.

3. Grimké, *op. cit.*

races and minority men was (and still is) too threatening to the profound politics of a caste system based on sex and race.

Certainly, the lessons of history were not ignored because they were not explicit. Much of the long struggle against black slavery and for women's rights had been spent as a functioning, conscious coalition. (*"Resolved*, There never can be a true peace in this Republic until the civil and political rights of all citizens of African descent and all women are practically established."[4] That statement was made at a New York convention in 1863.) Like most early feminists, Elizabeth Cady Stanton believed that sex and race prejudice had to be fought together; that both were "produced by the same cause, and manifested very much in the same way. The Negro's skin and the woman's sex are both [used as] *prima facie* evidence that they were intended to be in subjection to the white Saxon man."[5] Frederick Douglass, the fugitive slave who became an important national leader of the movement to abolish slavery, vowed in his autobiography that, "When the true history of the antislavery cause shall be written, women will occupy a large space in its pages, for the cause of the slave has been peculiarly women's cause."[6] And there were many more such conscious lessons and statements.

If more of us had learned the parallels and origins of the abolitionist and suffragist movements, there might have been less surprise when a new movement called Women's Liberation grew from the politicization of white and black women in the civil rights movement of the 1960s. If we had been taught that women's connections to other powerless groups were logical, that women lacked power as a caste, and that we might be understandably relieved when men rejected domination and violence as proofs of manhood, certainly I and many other women of my generation would have wasted less time being mystified by our frequent, odd and unexplained

sense of identification with all the "wrong" groups—the black movement, migrant workers, or with our male contemporaries defying the "masculine" role by refusing to fight in Vietnam.

As it was, however, suffragists were often portrayed as boring, ludicrous blue-stockings; certainly no heroines you would need in modern America where we were "the most privileged women in the world." We were further discouraged from exploring our strengths by accusations of penis-envy, the dominating-mother syndrome, careerism, black matriarchy and other punishable offenses. Men emerged from World War II, Freudian analysis and locker rooms with vague threats that they could and should replace uppity women with more subservient ones—an Asian or European war bride instead of a "spoiled" American, a "feminine" white woman to replace a black "matriarch" or just someone younger as "the other woman."

There were many painful years of reinventing the wheel before we re-learned organically what our foremothers had discovered and could have taught us: that a false mythology—limited ability, childlike natures, special job skills (always the poorly paid ones), greater emotionalism and more sexual natures, less respect for members of our own group, chronic lateness and irresponsibility, and happiness with our "natural" place—was being used to keep all women and minority men in the role of cheap labor and support system.

"The parallel between women and Negroes is the deepest truth of American life, for together they form the unpaid or underpaid labor in which America runs."[7] That was Gunnar Myrdal writing in 1944 in a rather obscure appendix to his landmark study on racism, *An American Dilemma*. Even in the '60s when I discovered those words—and wished devoutly that I had read them years earlier—I still did not know that Susan B. Anthony had put the issue even more succinctly almost a century before Myrdal. "Woman," she said, "has been the great unpaid laborer of the world."[8]

4. Stanton, *op. cit.*

5. Stanton, *op. cit.*

6. *Life and Times of Frederick Douglass,* written by himself (1892). New York: Collier, 1962, p. 469.

7. Myrdal, *op. cit.*, p. 1077.

8. Susan B. Anthony, in Stanton, *op. cit.*, Vol. 1.

The current movements toward racial justice and feminism have had some success in pressuring for courses in women's history, black history, the study of Hispanic Americans, American Indians and many others (perhaps all better collectively referred to as "remedial history"), but these subjects still tend to be special studies taken only by the interested. They are rarely an integrated, inescapable part of the American history texts read by all students.

And if the recent past of our own country is still incomplete for many of us, how much less do we learn about other countries and more distant pasts?

What do we know about the African warrior queens of Dahomey, for instance, who led armies against colonial invaders? Or the merchant women of modern West Africa who dominate the consumer markets of their countries? If we know little about the relationship of our own New England witch hunts to patriarchal politics, how much less do we know about the more than eight million women who were burned at the stake in medieval Europe, perhaps as an effort to wipe out remains of prehistoric woman-goddess religions? If the exceptional American women who were explorers, outlaws, doctors, pirates, soldiers, and inventors are only just being rediscovered, what about those American Indian nations that honored women in authority more than the "advanced" cultures that were to follow?

How are we to interpret the discovery that many of the "pagan idols," "false gods" and "pagan temples" so despised by Judeo-Christian teachings and the Bible in particular were representations of a female power: a god with breasts? How will our vision of pre-history change now that archeologists have discovered that some skeletons—assumed to be male because of their large-boned strength, or because they were buried with weapons and scholarly scrolls—are really female? (In America, the archeological find described as the Minnesota Man has recently been redesignated the Minnesota Woman. In Europe, some warrior-skeletons have turned out to be female.) Now that

we are beginning to rediscover the interdependency of sexual and racial caste systems in our own history, and in our own lives, will political science courses begin to explain that a power structure dependent on race or class "purity"—whether it is women and blacks in the American South and South Africa, or women and Jews in Nazi Germany—will also restrict freedom of women because our bodies are the means of production, the necessary perpetuators of race and class lines?

This revelatory, mind-expanding era is worldwide: the international movements against caste—against all systems that dictate power and lifetime roles based on sex or race—are the most profound and vital movements of this century. They are changing both our hopes for the future and our assumptions about the past.

Sometimes those revelations can be angering. It seems that our ancestors knew much that we have had to re-learn with such pain.

In the National Plan of Action adopted at Houston, there are many echoes of the first wave of feminism. The high incidence of battered women and the reluctance of police to interfere are shocking facts that struck many Americans as new discoveries. Knowing more about the history of a husband's legal right to "own" and discipline a spouse could have helped to uncover those facts sooner. A wife's loss of her own name, legal residence, credit rating and many other rights might have seemed less "natural" and inevitable if we had known that our marriage laws were still rooted in the same English common law precedent ("husband and wife are one person in law . . . that of the husband")[9] that nineteenth- century feminists had struggled so hard to escape. We would have been better prepared for arguments that the Equal Rights Amendment would "destroy the family" or force women to become "like men" if we had known that the same accusations, almost word for word, were leveled against the suffrage movement. (Our own foremothers were called "unsexed women," "en-

9. *Blackstone, Commentaries.*

tirely devoid of personal attraction," who had only been "disappointed in their endeavors to appropriate breeches.")[10] Even the charge that the ERA would be contrary to states' rights and constitute a "federal power grab" is a repeat of the argument that a citizen's right to vote should be left entirely up to the states; a problem that caused suffragists to proceed state by state, and to delay focusing on the Nineteenth Amendment for many years.

In a way, the unity represented by the minority women's resolution—perhaps the single greatest accomplishment of the Houston Conference—was also the greatest example of the high price of lost history. After all, black women had been the flesh-and-blood links between abolition and suffrage; yet they had suffered double discrimination and invisibility, even at the time. ("There is a great stir about colored men getting their rights," explained Sojourner Truth, the great black feminist and anti-slavery leader, "but not a word about colored women.")[11] Then American leaders destroyed the great coalition against the caste systems of sex and race by offering the vote and a limited acceptance to black men, but refusing the majority and intimate challenge presented by females as a group. Black women were forced to painfully and artificially slice up their identities by choosing to support their brothers at their own expense, or, like Sojourner Truth, to advocate "keeping the thing going . . . because if we wait till it is still, it will take a great while to get things going again."[12] Once it was clear that black men were going to get the vote first, black women were further isolated by some white suffragists who, embittered by the desertion of white and black male allies, used the racist argument that the white female "educated" vote was necessary to outweigh the black male "uneducated" vote. Divisions deepened. Sojourner Truth's argument that it would "take a great while to get things going again" if the

two great parallel causes were divided turned out to be true. It was a half century later, and many years after her death, before women of all races won the vote.

When the first, reformist prelude to feminism started up again in the early and mid '60s, it was largely a protest of middle-class, white housewives against the "feminine mystique" that kept them trapped in the suburbs. For black women who often had no choice but to be in the labor force, that was a lifestyle that some envied and few could afford. Only after the civil rights movement and feminism's real emergence again in the later '60s—after the analysis of women as a caste, not just as an integrationist few—did the organic ties between the movements against racial and sexual caste begin to grow again. In spite of great racial divisions in the country, and in spite of an economic and social structure that exploits racial tensions among women, the Women's Movement is now the most integrated and populist force for change in the country.

Houston was the first public landmark in a long, suspicion-filled journey across racial barriers. At last, there were enough minority women (more than a third of all delegates) to have a strong voice—not only black women, but Hispanic women as the second largest American minority, Asian American women, American Indian women and many more. But how much less perilous this journey would have been if we had known about those bridges of the past; if we had not had to build new coalitions through what seemed a wilderness.

Houston was part of a second wave, a continuation—but it also provided historical lessons of its own.

Reproductive freedom finally joined such accepted rights as freedom of speech or assembly. Some women came to that conclusion out of a simple, personal concern for health, or an understanding that, if they did not control their bodies from the skin in, they could never control their lives from the skin out. Others felt that women's role as the most basic means of production would remain the source of their

10. *New York Herald,* September 7, 1853.

11. Sojourner Truth, in Stanton, *op. cit.*, Vol. II, p. 193.

12. *Ibid.*

second-class status as long as outside forces were allowed to either restrict or compel that production. For both reasons, the feminist-invented phrase of "reproductive freedom" was chosen over "population control." The first signifies an individual's basic human right to decide to have or not have children, but the second legitimizes some external force or power over women's lives. This affirmation of reproductive freedom as a basic human right was a long way from the burning of healers, midwives and witches, but there is still a long way to go before the stated goal of reproductive freedom becomes a reality in women's lives.

"Sexual preference," the second issue of sexuality, included the issue of lesbianism. Ironically, the effort to frighten women off was exactly what caused many to vote for civil rights for lesbians, even though they might not have supported that issue before. Until the label of "lesbian" no longer holds the threat of lost jobs, child custody or a place to live—until women can no longer be punished for their private sexual choices—all women will continue to be threatened into conformity by the potential danger of being called "lesbian." Furthermore, it is the patriarchal societies that wish to control women's bodies as a means of producing children that also try to control and condemn any sexual forms that cannot end in conception. Whether it's male homosexuality, lesbianism, contraception or any heterosexual forms of expression that cannot lead to conception, it is the same political motive that tries to restrict them all.

The politics of sexuality and reproduction had been the most difficult for the first wave of feminists to discuss publicly, much less to change. But these issues of such importance to women's lives and survival were brought out into the open in Houston, and recognized as fundamental to women's self-determination.

Houston also symbolized an end to much of the split between the younger or more radical feminists who had come out of the Left (and who mistrusted efforts "inside the system") and those reformers or older, more conservative women (who mistrusted efforts to work "outside the system"). If one person made that bonding possible, it was probably Bella Abzug, a main author of the idea for the Conference, and the presiding officer of its Commissioners. As one of the few American political leaders to rise through social movements, not through political party structures, she had gained trust and colleagues on both sides: with more radical feminists because of her devotion to issues, and with more conservative women she had served in Congress and gained Government support for the Conference. Houston was the result of hard work by thousands of women, but Bella Abzug may be the one person without whom there would have been no such event.

In fact, one of the most moving and impressive experiences of Houston was its blending of tactics and styles. Prefeminist, either/or, polarized thinking seemed to give way to an understanding that victory was more likely if we surrounded a goal from all sides.

For myself, Houston and all the events surrounding it have become a personal landmark in history; the sort of event one measures all other dates in life as being "before" or "after."

I had mistrusted it as an idea. (What sort of conference could be supported by the Government without betraying women's real issues and needs?) And I had feared it as an approaching trial. (Might not the anti-woman, right-wing minority turn it into a public battleground?) Though I finally came to work very hard in its preparation, I would have given almost anything to be able to avoid the possible conflict, to stop worrying, to stay home, to delay this event that I cared about too much.

I thought my fears were rational, but in retrospect, I realize that they were not.

Yes, I had learned, finally, that individual women could be competent, courageous and loyal to each other. In spite of growing up without the sight of women being honored in authority, and without a knowledge of women's hidden history, I had learned that from my sisters in this second wave of feminism. But I still did not know that *women as a group* could be competent, courageous and loyal to each other; that we could conduct large, complex events and honor each other's diversity; that we could literally make a history that was our own.

But we can. Houston taught me that. And I hope that this lesson will not be lost, but carried into the future.

64

NATIONAL COMMISSION ON THE OBSERVANCE OF INTERNATIONAL WOMEN'S YEAR

Declaration of American Women (1977)

We are here to move history forward.

We are women from every State and Territory in the Nation

We are women of different ages, beliefs, and life-styles.

We are women of many economic, social, political, racial, ethnic, cultural, educational, and religious backgrounds.

We are married, single, widowed, and divorced.

We are mothers and daughters.

We are sisters.

We speak in varied accents and languages but we share the common language and experience of American women who throughout our Nation's life have been denied the opportunities, rights, privileges, and responsibilities accorded to men.

For the first time in more than 200 years of our democracy, we are gathered in a National Women's Conference, charged under Federal law to assess the status of women in our country, to measure the progress we have made, to identify the barriers that prevent us from participating fully and equally in all aspects of national life, and to make recommen-

From U.S. National Commission on the Observance of International Women's Year, *What Women Want* (New York: Simon and Schuster, 1979), 85–86.

dations to the President and to the Congress for means by which such barriers can be removed.

We recognize the positive changes that have occurred in the lives of women since the founding of our nation. In more than a century of struggle from Seneca Falls 1848 to Houston 1977, we have progressed from being nonpersons and slaves whose work and achievements were unrecognized, whose needs were ignored, and whose rights were suppressed to being citizens with freedoms and aspirations of which our ancestors could only dream.

We can vote and own property. We work in the home, in our communities and in every occupation. We are 40 percent of the labor force. We are in the arts, sciences, professions, and politics. We raise children, govern States, head businesses and institutions, climb mountains, explore the ocean depths, and reach toward the moon.

Our lives no longer end with the childbearing years. Our lifespan has increased to more than 75 years. We have become a majority of the population, 51.3 percent, and by the 21st Century, we shall be an even larger majority.

But despite some gains made in the past 200 years, our dream of equality is still withheld from us and millions of women still face a daily reality of discrimination, limited opportunities, and economic hardship.

Man-made barriers, laws, social customs, and prejudices continue to keep a majority of women in an inferior position without full control of our lives and bodies.

From infancy throughout life, in personal and public relationships, in the family, in the schools, in every occupation and profession, too often we find our individuality, our capabilities, our earning powers diminished by discriminatory practices and outmoded ideas of what a woman is, what a woman can do, and what a woman must be.

Increasingly, we are victims of crimes of violence in a culture that degrades us as sex objects and promotes pornography for profit.

We are poorer than men. And those of us who are minority women—blacks, Hispanic Americans, Native Americans, and Asian Americans—must overcome the double burden of discrimination based on race and sex.

We lack effective political and economic power. We have only minor and insignificant roles in making, interpreting, and enforcing our laws, in running our political parties, businesses, unions, schools, and institutions, in directing the media, in governing our country, in deciding issues of war or peace.

We do not seek special privileges, but we demand as a human right a full voice and role for women in determining the destiny of our world, our nation, our families, and our individual lives.

We seek these rights for all women, whether or not they choose as individuals to use them.

We are part of a worldwide movement of women who believe that only by bringing women into full partnership with men and respecting our rights as half the human race can we hope to achieve a world in which the whole human race—men, women, and children—can live in peace and security.

Based on the views of women who have met in every State and Territory in the past year, the National Plan of Action is presented to the President and the Congress as our recommendations for implementing Public Law 94–167.

We are entitled to and expect serious attention to our proposals.

We demand immediate and continuing action on our National Plan by Federal, State, public, and private institutions so that by 1985, the end of the International Decade for Women proclaimed by the United Nations, everything possible under the law will have been done to provide American women with full equality.

The rest will be up to the hearts, minds, and moral consciences of men and women and what they do to make our society truly democratic and open to all.

We pledge ourselves with all the strength of our dedication to this struggle "to form a more perfect Union."

65
NAN BAUER-MAGLIN
Journal of a Women's Course (1975)

In the Spring of 1971 and the Fall of 1973 I taught a women's studies course at a largely third-world school, The Borough of Manhattan Community College (BMCC). BMCC is a two year Open Admission college in the City University system whose students are mainly working-class Blacks and Puerto Ricans. Except for its focus on women, the 1971 course, "Images of Women in English and American Literature," might seem from its syllabus rather like a traditional English course. . . . Readings from the essay anthology *Sisterhood is Powerful* were interlaced with five assigned novels: *The House of Mirth* by Edith Wharton, *Sons and Lovers* by D. H. Lawrence, *The Awakening* by Kate Chopin, *Browngirl, Brownstones* by Paule Marshall, and *The Spy in the House of Love* by Anais Nin.

The 1971 course was initiated by a group of women teachers and students, and was the only women's course at BMCC. It generated a lot of excitement and controversy because it implicitly raised the question of the relevance of women's liberation to the third-world people. Consciousnesses were raised—or at least jolted—as a result of the course. I think it was a success, but there were certain problems that are important to comment upon.

I was one of the problems. I am a white, middle-income, married woman. At the time, I was new to feminism and to teaching. And the syllabus reflects a bias left over from English graduate school. In retrospect, I realize that because of my newness to feminism I was partially teaching myself rather than fully addressing myself to the needs of the students. Another

From *Papers in Women's Studies*, June 1975, published by students and faculty at the Women's Studies Program, University of Michigan, Ann Arbor. Reprinted by permission of the author.

problem was the tension which existed be-tween the diverse types of people concerned with politically and emotionally charged issues implicit in any women's studies class: third-world people vs. Whites, radicals vs. apolitical people, "serious" literature students vs. the rest of the class, students vs. teacher, and men vs. women. But division and tension are some-times positive teaching values, and much learn-ing did take place that semester, although not in the intimate and warm atmosphere of my con-sciousness-raising group that I had so wanted to duplicate.

When I walked into my "Images of Women in English and American Literature" class in September, 1973, I had nagging doubts about whether a women's literature course made much sense in a community college. Despite my fears, the course was fantastic! It worked for me and it worked for all twenty-two stu-dents, although in different ways.

One reason for this success was that I had become more comfortable with my feminism and my teaching. Like others in the movement, I had grown from a narrowly-focused concep-tion of feminism that concentrated on re-ex-amining my personal life and analyzing women's socialization and male-female rela-tions, to an understanding of the interconnec-tions between class, race, and sex oppression. The 1973 syllabus, an important part of which was developed by my sister teachers, Kathy Chamberlain and Naomi Woronov, emphasizes the writings of Black and Puerto Rican women, women of other countries, and working women. . . .

I had also rethought classroom structure, the role of the teacher, and the teaching of lit-erature. I no longer felt guilty about not teach-ing "great" literature. I no longer felt that I had to teach literature as an isolated subject whose specialized jargon removes it from the world rather than puts it into the world. My objective in the women's studies course is, in the words of Louis Kampf and Paul Lauter:

"to make literature a vital part of stu-dents' lives rather than an antiquarian or for-mal study or a means of forcing them into feelings of 'cultural deprivation.' In other words, we want to change the relationship of students to literature in a classroom from that of passive consumption of culture to an active engagement with the emotions, ideas, poli-tics, and sensibilities of writers and of others. When a book supports or challenges our own lives, we may convey the sense that what's at stake is not a job of laying on 'monuments of unageing intellect' but a life-process in which books do shape what we see or hope for or do" (p. 44).

A survey of the class . . . suggests its make-up. My journal, which traces the day-to-day interaction in the class, gives a sense of how serious, sensitive, open, and anxious to listen and explore the students were. In the beginning, not all of them wanted to be in a women's studies course, and most of them did not identify with the women's liberation movement. Many struggled with reading and writing difficulties, yet their responses throughout the four-month course and their evaluations . . . indicate that they grew in their understanding of the issues of women's liberation. My journal indicates that third-world and working-class students can and do relate to women's issues. Many were moved to read, to write, to change their situations, that is, to apply the ideas discussed in this class to their own lives.

September 18, 1973

We responded to the four images of women I handed out with the syllabus: "Blue Woman," an anonymous folk ballad; a sixteenth century Chinese poem; Sojourner Truth's "Ain't I a Woman"; and the words of a revolu-tionary Vietnamese woman. The folk ballad evoked a lot of personal sharing. We went around the room describing what we did when we were blue. Patterns were discovered: the men tended to move—to walk, go out for a drink, date a woman—while the women tended to become passive—withdraw, cry, or to clean or to shop. We talked about the phenomenon of directing anger towards oneself rather than the oppressor; we drew a parallel between women and Blacks.

September 19, 1973

In small groups the syllabus was discussed and reordered. It was decided that after the initial weeks of introductory discussion we should begin with the topic of Black women. All opposed my suggestion of using every Tuesday for group discussions and, on some occasions, to have the men in a separate group and Black and White in separate groups. Is this a sign of advanced consciousness on their parts or a refusal to acknowledge differences or just an indication that they feared the intimacy and hard work of group process?

September 24 and 25, 1973

Great classes! I played tapes of Helen Reddy singing "I Am Woman" and Carole King singing "Where You Lead" and "A Natural Woman." This stimulated Cathy and Charlotte to bring in a Yoko Ono record, to type out the lyrics for everyone and to have Rita lead the Oct. 4 class on Yoko Ono's songs. Everyone loves "I Am Woman." The men do not see it as hostile to men, rather Eddie felt it was hostile to the establishment; James drew a picture of women marching together proudly. We free-associated about the words " 'cause I've been down there on the floor" and saw that to mean everything from sexual oppression, to slavery, to housework, to emotional put-downs. One male visitor praised the song "Where You Lead" to be a REAL love song. We then argued whether it was a love song or a slave song. What is dependence and independence? The question was raised about how the song would strike us if a man sang it; in other words, this emphasized how the song glorified the typical woman's role of follower, server, sacrificer. It would be ridiculous to imagine a man singing it.

The "Woman Poem" by Nikki Giovanni focussed the issue of whether all women are alike and have common problems. Many felt that this was a poem for and about Black women. After a lot of discussion we agreed that poor women felt some of these problems also and that the poem outlined issues for all women such as being a sex object, needing love, acting as a martyr, being discriminated against at work, defining one's life as suffering and unhappiness.

October 2, and 9, 1973

The class at first resisted my suggestion that we break into groups and discuss the assignment of interviewing an older woman. I think the general feeling is that no one wants to miss anything that is said but it also reflects a tendency to focus on men and to fear participation. I pushed them into groups. Afterwards everyone acknowledged that the groups were quite successful in coming up with good and different questions for the interview. Lee Hom plans to interview her mother, a Chinese immigrant; Lillian Holt is interviewing her grandmother, a Blackfoot Indian; Carolyn wants to interview Melba Tolliver, a Black newscaster; and Rita Fraser wants to interview me.

We began to examine the issues of age, aging, and growing up, using Rose Lichtman's interview with her grandmother "From One Generation to Another" and poems by Siv Widerberg from the book *I'm Like Me.*

October 11, 1973

Augie was excited by his discovery of the magazine *Ms;* he told the class to check it out.

We returned to the problem of aging in relation to the Erica Jong poem. Ruby talked about how she felt old at 22; I talked about being 31 and how sickness and age seem real to me now. Charlotte said some men also worry about aging and appearance: her boyfriend worries about balding.

Began *The Autobiography of Miss Jane Pittman;* for the next two weeks we will be referring to this book and other literature related to Black women. Everyone read the book—a rare phenomenon at Manhattan Community College. Most of the students were quite upset to discover that the book was fiction; this prompted a long discussion about the relation of fiction to reality. Lillian said her grandmother, a Blackfoot Indian, had a very similar life; therefore, the book does reflect reality. She said that based on her own experiences, her grandmother's history, and the story of Miss Jane Pittman she has grown to hate Whites.

I gave my first extended lecture on the history of Black people in America as outlined in *The Autobiography*. Charlotte was amazed at the false history taught in high school. We outlined topics to discuss for the next week in relation to the novel such as: strength and survival, Black/White relations, the role of religion, the role of Black men, the present day for Black women.

October 15, 1973

Some reactions to Newsreel's *The Woman's Film*: Denise said it was good to see poor White women speak up. Ruby was surprised that White, Black, and Chicano women came out directly for change by the gun; she approves of that. Silvia and Carolyn did not like the Black woman's remark that White women will have to come to Black women for help; they (they are Black) both felt that Black women have to reach out as well.

October 16, 1973

First I read a leaflet about the plight of Farah workers, 85 percent of whom are women, and related this to the Chicanos in the film.

Our discussion today centered around the notion of strength and the myth of the Black matriarchy. We talked about how all the outspoken men in *The Autobiography* were killed and what that implied about the role for Black women. A comparison was made with many

Black men who are either in jail, on drugs, killed in Vietnam, or killed for political reasons.

October 18, 1973

In relation to *The Autobiography* and the topic of strong women, we read "Miss Rosie" by Lucille Clifton and "lineage" by Margaret Walker. "My grandmothers were strong./Why am I not as they?"

Question: Who is stronger, your grandmother or yourself?
Joan: My grandmother; she is an Italian immigrant. She lived on the Lower East Side and had to work all her life. She had none of the conveniences, affluence, education we have today.
Emmaline [shaking her head]: I grew up in the South and had just as tough a life as my grandmother.
Julia: My grandmother worked in the fields in Puerto Rico; nothing in my life compares to that.
Joan [rethinking it]: In some ways we are stronger today, at least psychologically. We don't take any shit; I always open my mouth.
Me: You mean that even if your grandmother had a difficult life, she was trapped in the lady role to some extent?

Later on Lillian brought up her grandmother's advice to have babies so that Indians and Blacks will not be wiped out. A long emotional debate ensued; I urged women to depend on themselves to fight oppression and not look to the next generation as a solution.

Back to *The Autobiography*. Why was "the one," the leader-savior only conceived of as a man? Were there any Black women leaders in history? Along with this we read Sonia Sanchez's poem "Queens of the Universe" which praises Black women for being and urges them to be "the only QUEENS OF THE UNIVERSE, even though we be stepping unqueenly sometimes." Harvey was critical of the line: "and the job of blk/woooomen is to deal with this under the direction of blk/men." Silvia related this line to Sonia Sanchez's Black

Muslim beliefs. I suggested that most religions put women "under" men. We pursued the idea of religion and male chauvinism; I mentioned *The Woman's Bible* by Elizabeth Cady Stanton; Dale and Silvia wanted to explore that on their own.

October 23, 1973

Listened to a tape of Fran Beale's (of Third World Women's Alliance) speech (at the May 25, 1973 Guardian Forum) "Black Women, a History of Resistance." Some people were bored, partly due to poor acoustics. Despite this, a heavy discussion followed when Julia wanted to know if Beale meant that male chauvinism was a result of capitalism and imperialism. I was amazed; during my four years of teaching at this school, no class has taken ideas so seriously. We discussed socialism in other countries and the problems and successes of women in places like China, Cuba, Russia. We talked about feudalism and pre-capitalist times, and discussed whether there ever was a matriarch or at least equality; Robert said that was impossible for man always dominated as the HUNTER. Harvey and I exploded that myth; we talked about the more important role of agriculture and the early inventions attributed to women. Harvey decided to do his project on tribes such as the Pygmies where it is said men and women are equal.

October 25, 1973

Five women (Rita, Ruby, Lydia, Lillian and Charlotte) took sections of the Beulah Richardson poem "A Black Woman Speaks" and led the discussion. James' opening comment moved me: he said that the poem made him realize that White women are also enslaved. He read a section of the poem aloud:

> They said, the white supremacist said
> you were better than me,
>   that your fair brow should never know
>   the sweat of slavery.
> They lied.

> "White womanhood" too is enslaved
> the difference is degree.
> They brought me here in chains.
> They brought you here unwitting slaves
>   to man. . . .
> Mind you, I speak not mockingly
> but I fought for freedom,
> I'm fighting now for our unity.
> We are women all,
> and what wrongs you murders me,
> eventually marks your grave
> so we share a mutual death at the hand of
>   tyranny.

After class, Denise told me she wanted to talk about poor White women soon. I have noticed a certain impatience among the White students when we concentrate on Black subjects; they do not see the racism involved in that. It is important from my point of view to begin with Black women (or third-world women) because the connection of sex, race, and class puts the woman question on a political plane. I gave Denise a reading list and suggested that she do her project on literature about poor White women by Olsen, Stead, Oates, Smedley, and Arnow.

October 30, 1973

Read Carolyn Rodger's poem "U Name This One" and Helen Mendes' essay "Who I Am." Discussion: How were you brought up? What images of women were held up before you? From Mendes: "Although women around us may have given lip service to the fact that women were supposed to be 'delicate, fragile, sweet,' and all that, they presented us children with living models of women being strong and virile." Were you a lady? Did you fight? Julia described her parents' relationship; her mother must serve her father in every way; her father keeps telling Julia that she must learn her place and that her husband, if she gets one, will slap her around for she is too rebellious. I said I hoped she would talk more about this when we discussed Puerto Rican women.

November 1, 1973

Annette read "Negro Mother" by Langston Hughes. She said she brought it in because she was moved by it; everyone seemed affected. I said it was a good summary of our discussion related to the novel, *The Autobiography of Miss Jane Pittman*, and it reiterated the theme (the suffering and strength of Black women over history) of the poem "I Am a Black Woman" by Mari Evans in the Helen King article, "The Black Woman and Women's Lib." The two lines "But God put a song and a prayer in my mouth. / God put a dream like steel in my soul" led to a discussion of the positive and negative uses of religion in slavery time. It was a survival mechanism; it gave people hope. Also it was sometimes used as a front for planning rebellions and learning to read and write. However, sometimes it encouraged people to give up the struggle for a good life here on earth. Following this, we tried to analyze the role of religion in the Black community today. Several people recalled their mothers "dragging" them to religious meetings.

Related to the poem "Nikki Rosa" by Nikki Giovanni we mulled over the idea that Black love equals Black wealth. Is love wealth? Is Black love special? Do poor people love more than rich people?[1]

From here we will share our interviews with older women and then discuss *The Awakening* by Kate Chopin. The syllabus I began with is too ambitious; it is terribly frustrating—there is so much to talk about. I have to see this class as a beginning and hope that students will go on to explore (actively as well as mentally) the issues further on their own. I hope the class can come to my house some evening.

November 8, 1973

After a week's break, it was good to see everyone. Each one told about the older woman she/he interviewed:

1. For a good discussion of this poem, see Howe, Florence, with Carol Ahlum, Mary Kai Howard, and others, "Why Teach Poetry?—An Experiment," in Kampf and Lauter, pp. 259–307.

Charlotte: Bonnie Cooper, age 35, her grandmother was Lucretia Mott.

Harvey: His mother, age 50, lower middle class, Polish.

Cathy: Her girlfriend's mother, age 39, with 5 children.

Vito: His sister, age 28.

Denise: Spoke to her uncle's mother about her Italian grandmother.

Eddie: A friend, age 30, divorced, who has gone through a lot of changes.

Joan: Her father's ex-wife, who was her mother from age 2–10.

Augie: A Greek woman from the Post Office.

Lydia: Her mother from the Ukraine, age 47 or so.

Maxine: Her sister-in-law's mother, age 45 with 5 children.

Carolyn: Could not get Melba Tolliver, so she stopped a Black woman on the street near Equitable life insurance.

Ruby: A counselor at school.

Lee: Her mother, age 42, from Hong Kong, with 6 children.

Julia: Her aunt from Puerto Rico, the oldest of 10 children; she has one son.

Rita: (She and I could never work out an interview time; she seemed somewhat hesitant about interviewing me.) A friend, Black, a nurse, with 5 children, deserted by her husband and now living with another woman. She was quite disappointed that the woman did not want to talk about bi-sexuality, which Rita feels is the case.

Lillian: A woman in her late twenties, a bi-sexual prostitute. She was hard to interview for she was always getting calls. Lillian did not interview her Indian grandmother, who did not want her life written down.

James: A 34 year old Black woman with 3 children; she was open and free although he did not know her well before.

Silvia: 60 year old Spanish woman; she focused on her married life.

Emmaline: Her mother from the South.

Several people talked about or read parts of their interviews. Lee seemed desperate to speak. She described her mother's hard, long days in the laundry; her father's control of the purse strings and his "cruelty" to her mother; the gap between herself and her mother especially concerning sexual behavior. I think she felt good about talking.

November 12, 1973

Film—"Women on the March." It had serious flaws but it does show how passionately women felt about the vote.

November 13 and 15, 1973

The Awakening did not turn everyone on as *Miss Jane Pittman* had. However, after getting their impressions and then giving a "pep" talk about the book, especially about its reception among the critics, and after telling about Kate Chopin's life, I think the class seemed more receptive. We listed topics to focus on: sexuality, role models for Edna, her children and her husband, etc. The discussion often wandered (something Silvia objected to when she called me that night; my reply: "you are responsible; do something about it" and "wandering is not so bad"). The following is an outline of the discussion, combining all our voices:

Why did she awaken at 29? I asked each one to write me a letter at 30.

Why did she marry? She went from one bad situation to another. Would you take this marriage? What is wrong with it anyway? She had money, an attentive husband (he brought her candy), servants. Most people in the class said no to the marriage.

Why did she just move out without any attempt on her part to discuss, explain, work out a compromise or an understanding? I raised the question as to which man understood her—Robert, her father, her husband, the doctor, her lover? Some added that even the male critics did not understand her.

What does it mean to awaken?

Can spiritual hunger hurt as much as physical hunger?

What about Edna and her ring? What does the ring symbolize?

Who in the class wants a ring? Eddie said that a ring is half of a handcuff. Rita asked me about my ring, which I wore for the first time since September. I described how I first felt at about age 22 the need for a ring, that is, for love and marriage; I described how I now see the ring as a defense, and how not wearing it gives me more freedom; I cannot fall back on or be classified in terms of a role. Charlotte was quite candid. She wants a diamond ring; she'll even take it from her father.

Discussion of Edna's affairs evoked our own attitudes toward marriage as a life-long commitment and toward sexual fidelity. Most class members express high hopes for marriage, and expect complete fulfillment and fidelity from their partners.

Why did she kill herself? We kept returning to this question. I posed it another way. What were her choices? We tried to understand what Edna meant when she said she would never give up herself for her children. The discussion touched on her revolutionary attitude toward sex. She did not love Alex; she had pleasure.

November 19, 1973

I returned the interviews and described to the class parts of each interview which fascinated me, moved me, or whatever: Julia's Puerto Rican aunt's fight to avoid pregnancy; Lydia's mother's time in a concentration camp; the interest in bi-sexuality on the part of several interviewers; Lee's mother's advice—"Do not get married"; the similarity of Denise's Sicilian grandmother's story to *Gold Flower's Story*; Harvey's mother's anger towards her children and her attempts to rewrite the interview; Lillian's subject, prostitution. I am hoping with rewrites some can be sent to *Up From Under* or the Feminist Press.

Back to the theme of marriage, I read aloud Kate Chopin's "The Story of An Hour" in which a longtime married woman dances for joy upon learning that her husband has been killed. She collapses when he appears; it *all* had been a mistake.

Joan responded so totally to Erica Jong's poem "Here Comes" that she led the class in analyzing it; obviously she has flipped through a lot of *Bride*'s magazines. "What happens there/is merely icing since/a snakepit of dismembered/douchebag coils (all writhing)/awaits her on the tackier back pages." "Back pages" we agreed meant literally the back pages of the magazine where the less romantic, more practical items are sold and also the back pages of life, life behind and beyond the wedding ceremony. We all shared wedding experiences; I told of Arthur's shoes being too tight. I brought in a *Newsweek* ad—"Nothing makes markets like marriage"—which exposed marriage as an economic arrangement for consumption.

November 20, 1973

"Housewife" by Anne Sexton. What does the title mean? Do women marry houses?

Rita: Her mother taught her no matter what you must cook and clean the house for your husband. Harvey described a house that is a museum; the family lives in the basement. That reminded me of my mother's living room; I tiptoed on the carpet and never sat on the big, puffy couch. Joan's 73 year old grandmother still cleans from morning to night. Charlotte told how she has to make the bed and clear the table while her brother is treated like a prince. Her brother's girlfriend butters his bread. Silvia urges Charlotte to rebel. *Me:* Don't put women down for cleaning. Why do they clean?

Eventually Denise asks us a question which brings us back to the poem: What parts of the house correspond to the body? "Some women marry houses./It's another kind of skin; it has a heart/a mouth a liver and bowel movements/The walls are permanent and pink/See how she sits on her knees all day/faithfully washing herself down. . . . "

Explain "A woman is her mother." She is a mother to the house and to the man; she is her mother for she is the house; the house is like a baby; she mothers herself.

"A Sailor at Midnight" by Elizabeth Sargent. Respond to the "I," what is she like?

Harvey: She is sensitive, a poet; when she picks up a sailor, she likes the way he observes and describes things. *Silvia:* She is not a whore; she is free (liberated) about sex. *Annette:* Is she a virgin? Lots of nos. *Eddie explains:* The whole poem points to the last line: "'What are you anyway,' he whispered, /'Are you a virgin?'/ 'No, I'm a poet,' I said. 'Fuck me again.'" She is saying that women do rather than just be. *Joan, all excited:* I understand! Women are usually never doctors or lawyers or Indian chiefs, rather they are legs or breasts, etc.

We related this poem to *The Awakening*: do women initiate sex? Most of the class seemed very "into" this discussion, especially when Silvia said that as a Spanish woman she had been trained to please the man exclusively; she was amazed to discover that women can masturbate. The men in the class gave their feelings about initiation and passivity, finally saying that they would love to be at a dance and have a woman approach and ask for that dance, and—(hesitation)—reject her. A lot of laughter in the class. The conclusion: sex roles hurt men as well as women.

I introduced the Tillie Olsen story "I Stand Here Ironing" by telling about her life and how her work and children interrupted her writing. Denise asked me if it would be ok to ask a personal question: Do I like children? I seem hostile to children. So I talked about my own ambivalence and concern about having children, talked quite personally about my age and about Arthur, but also tried to relate my concerns to the Olsen story. The problem and expense of childcare, the isolation of the family unit, the seeming inevitability of the woman's responsibility for children, even in non-malechauvinist homes, among other issues, have made me hesitant about "raising a family." It felt good to share a problem which is not utmost in my mind.

November 27, 1973

Today everyone wrote an essay in class; some people brought in evaluations. James' (he is, by the way, the only Black male in the class) really moved me, and so I want to include part of it in my journal:

"When I first entered the class, I was a little pessimistic about will it be a very good class. I found it not only to be very interesting and rewarding but something essential or mandatory to my learning experience. The subjects, thoughts, and facts discussed really made me aware that there really is a definite difference in the roles that the society has put into us.

"This class experience has made me very conscious and sometimes too conscious of the roles of the women today. Sometimes I may go to a movie and see the oppression of the woman and this would make me question how this role came about and who's at fault and how could this have been avoided. This just spoils my movie, but I guess this will balance off somehow. . . ."

November 29, 1973

I brought in material for projects: for Ruby, *Tomorrow's Tomorrow: The Black Woman* by Joyce Ladner; an Indian bibliography for Lydia; for Sarah, stories by Olsen, Lessing and Oates; for Silvia, an interview with Anais Nin; for several people *Witches, Midwives and Nurses*; for Julia, some Puerto Rican literature.

I have been bragging about the class to friends and colleagues and so predictably the class was not so good today. It should have been great because *Gold Flower's Story* by Jack Belden is so powerful and everyone loved it. The reason for the reserve was that I criticized the in-class essays, and asked those with a low mark to rewrite their essays. They were hurt and angry (at me and themselves). Also as a result of the evaluations I urged more people to talk up in class so I think there was a feeling of awkwardness.

One of the interesting aspects of the discussion based on *Gold Flower* was the role of religion and culture in general in projecting a negative image of women and in keeping them down. We picked out Chinese proverbs quoted in *Gold Flower* reflecting this:

"Officials depend on seals; tigers depend on moutains; women depend on their husbands" (p. 39).

"If I buy a horse, I can beat it; if I marry a wife, I can do as I like" (p. 39).

"When a woman is angry, her husband beats her; when he is angry, he also beats her" (p. 39).

"Women are like wheelbarrows; if not beaten for three days they can not be used" (p. 40).

"The thread controls the needle; a husband controls his wife" (p. 40).

We then tried to explore our own religion and culture for parallels. I quoted the Jewish Orthodox daily prayer: "I thank Thee, O Lord, that Thou has not created me a woman" and the Commandment: "Thou shalt not covet thy neighbour's house, thou shalt not covet thy neighbour's wife, nor his man-servant, nor his ox, nor his ass, nor anything that is thy neighbour's." The class was aghast. *Gold Flower's Story* and the wish of Chinese women to be born as dogs no longer seemed so far away.

December 3, 1973

A comparison of *Gold Flower* with "The River-Merchant's Wife: A Letter" by Rihaku (8th century) yielded a bright observation: Unlike Gold Flower, the River-Merchant's wife can write and express herself. I related this to one of the underlying themes of this class: Why women have not written or spoken out. And will *you* begin to write and speak?

From there, we looked at Anne Sexton's poem "For My Lover, Returning to His Wife," another letter to a man. It was fun to work on the imagery associated with wife and "mistress"; the mistress came out looking more exciting yet having no power.[2]

2. Ira Shor's "Anne Sexton's 'For My Lover . . .': Feminism in the Classroom," in Hoffman, et al., pp. 57–67, is a good article on how to teach this poem.

December 6 and 11, 1973

When I arrived late, Joan was entertaining the class with an enthusiastic and detailed account of a stripper she saw this weekend at a bar. Next came talk of peep shows, men's and women's magazines, and rape.

After giving a brief summary of the three assigned readings ("Puerto Rican Women Rap about Women's Liberation"—from BMCC, "Que Viva Puerto Rico Libre!—The Fighting Women" by Noemi Velazquez, and the poem "To Julia De Burgos" by Julia De Burgos) and showing the class the newspaper *Triple Jeopardy* put out by Third World Women's Alliance, I turned the class over to Julia. At first she was shy, but as she read her interview about her aunt's life in Puerto Rico, she relaxed and added a lot of personal details. She talked about how her father has isolated her mother from all her friends, even women. He will not let her work, and is suspicious even when she goes to the supermarket. Julia believes that machismo comes from an inferiority complex.

The class questioned whether machismo is peculiar to Puerto Rican or Spanish culture, whether we see it in all cultures, or whether it's a class phenomenon rather than a cultural one.

On December 11, I listed seven Puerto Rican women's names on the board—Maria de las Barbudo, Mariana Bracetti, Lola Rodriques de Tio, Ana Roque de Duprey, Concepcion Torres, Luisa Capetillo and Lolita Lebron. Everyone, especially Julia and Silvia, was excited over the discovery of new women. A quote from Luisa Capetillo about free love brought amazement—Think of a Puerto Rican woman speaking out publicly like this in the early 1900s!—and it led to a long discussion of the history and origins of the marriage contract. Annette changed her project to marriage contracts and Silvia is debating whether to switch from Anais Nin to Luisa Capetillo.

We read the poem "To Julia De Burgos" aloud and I asked who "you" and "I" were. "The word is out that I am your enemy/that is my poetry I am giving you away." Many thought "you" and "I" were two different people. We listed the characteristics of the two on the board: the lady vs. the woman, the server vs. the creator, the house vs. the world. We mulled over the schizophrenic nature of women, the ambivalence of women, especially women who want to create, act, be whole and feel that struggle between the "you" and the "I."

December 10, 1973

Beautiful slides by Kathy Chamberlain, an English teacher, on women in China; a Chinese saying: "Women hold up half the sky."

December 13, 1973

We voted to make the final exam optional—probably a mistake. We went around the room for project reports; most have not started work on theirs; it worries me.

I do not think I will assign *The Long Day* by Dorothy Richardson again; something like Agnes Smedley's *Daughter of the Earth* would be better. Many found *The Long Day* boring and difficult. They are not, as I am, interested in women and their work. Annette picked up on the author's elitism. As we went around the room for initial ideas and reactions, several good discussion topics arose despite the general negativity:

1. *Why women and immigrants came to the cities and how the media portrayed them.* We compared the domestic novels the shop girls read to our soap operas and love comics. The name Rose Fortune given to the author by one of the working women, Eddie pointed out, was symbolic of all the "girls'" dreams of meeting a rich man and escaping from the sweat shops. Julia found a parallel with her Puerto Rican aunt's hopes as she came to New York, and what she actually found. Eddie recommended *The Jungle*.

2. *Sexual oppression and prostitution.* I gave statistics about working women in 1890 and 1910 and explained how any woman (especially white) was considered to be "fallen" just because she worked.

3. *The author's attitude and how it reflected a white, middle-class bias.* Her moralism (blames the women rather than the system), her racism, her sexism, her educated elitism were all noted. The passages describing the laundry pinpoint the integral aspects of the still-existing racism and sexism on the job:

"Don't any men work in this place except the foreman?" . . .

"Love of Mary!" she exclaimed indignantly; "and d'ye think any white man that called hisself a white man would work in sich a place as this, and with naygurs?" (p. 243).

4. *How work done by women outside the home mirrors that done inside the home.* That seemed like a new and fascinating idea for most. Ruby wanted to know how typing was like a home job. Someone saw the similarity between office work and housekeeping. Housekeeping, serving, sewing, nursing, teaching, child-raising, sexual serving—we matched jobs inside and outside the home.

From here the discussion veered into a heated debate about homosexuality; I gave up trying to steer it back to women and work.

December 20, 1973

The last day of class before vacation and almost everyone is here, hurrah! First we talked about the film, *Angela Davis: Portrait of a Revolutionary*. I talked about the strong image Angela Davis presented despite the three strikes against her—she is Black, a woman, and a Communist. Joan liked the shot of Angela smoking a pipe but she criticized the film for not giving enough information to understand why Angela was arrested. We reviewed the events; I recommended George Jackson's letters, especially for his changing attitude towards women.

Back to *The Long Day*. The conditions in 1901 were contrasted to conditions today— long hours, little pay, accidents, fires, no unions, child labor, poor housing, sexual assaults, etc. The choices then: suffer and endure, go crazy, marry, turn to prostitution or commit

suicide. Then Lee described her desperation to get a job and how some boss promised her one if she would "cooperate"; she felt Black women had to face this more often than White women.

I handed out leaflets from the Women's Bureau, Department of Labor, and we analyzed statistics on the salary of minority women, White women, minority men, White men. It is always amazing to see women on the bottom, although the statistics leave out the fact that many minority men cannot find work at all.

January 3, 1974

Getting back into touch with each other after Christmas vacation is hard; it was somewhat of a mistake to assign "heavy" reading for the first day back: "Silences: When Writers Don't Write" by Tillie Olsen and "Shakespeare's Sister" by Virginia Woolf. Joan, Eddie, Charlotte and Cathy responded to the Virginia Woolf article which prompted me to ask, "Who feels like Shakespeare's sister?" Silence. "How do you feel about writing? How do you feel about speaking? For instance, do the men in your classes usually speak out more? Why?" Many responses and then Eddie asked me, "Are you Shakespeare's sister?" Yes, I was and still am to some extent; I compared Arthur's confidence in his voice—speaking and writing—to my own lack of confidence. It has been a 30-year struggle, and I am a relatively privileged woman. I reiterated the parallel made by both Woolf and Olsen between women and the working class:

". . . the silence where the lives never came to writing. Among these, the mute inglorious Miltons: those whose waking hours are all struggle for existence; the barely educated; the illiterate; women. Their silence the silence of centuries as to how life was, is, for most of humanity. Traces of their making, of course, in folk song, lullaby, tales, language itself, jokes, maxims, superstitions, but we know nothing of the creators or how it was with them" (Olsen, p. 101).

A note to myself: next time I'd like to use *Growing Up Female in America: Ten Lives* edited by Eve Merriam for it includes a good cross-section of women including Mother Jones; Mountain Wolf Woman, a Winnebago Indian; a pioneer woman; two well-known suffrage women; Susie King Taylor, born a slave; and others.

January 7, 1974

A nice party!

January 8, 10, and 14, 1974

These last three days were somewhat frustrating. Everyone was involved in last minute work for other classes as well as mine. Because we had project reports, the class did not have the same kind of intimacy of before. I was depressed because some of the projects were not really that good—I have such high expectations for this class—and because I do not like endings and that feeling of loss. Of particular note: Eddie's children's story "Wanderlust: The Adventures of Younge Childe Edward and Nanny Mag," Ruby's "Black Women from Ancient Times to Slavery in America," and "The Gospel According to Harvey," an analysis of women's roles in the Bible. Some of the projects not in yet which I expect will be good: Silvia on Anais Nin, Julia on nuns, and Denise's children's story. The day of reports on sexuality was a provocative one: James on rape, Rita and Cathy on homosexuality, Lillian on unwed mothers, and Joan on prostitution. Ruby quoted a Gullah language proverb which summed up Black women's lives:

"Ah done been in sorrow's kitchen
and ah licked the pots clean."

She wrote two poems, "Black Woman" and "To Be a Slave."

To end the class, I asked Ruby to read out-loud "A Chant for My Sisters" and "Turning" . . . which I hoped summed up some of the ideas of the course and would inspire everyone to struggle further.

The class is now over; there were last minute contacts and intimacies; I know I will be seeing some beyond this last day. Charlotte's joining a women's group. Cathy called me on the phone to give me a recipe for the cake she made for the party; we joked about relating over a recipe.

One thing which struck me as I reviewed the class and compared it to other classes, past and present, was that there were no withdrawals and few absences—an incredible record for BMCC. I would criticize myself for not stressing writing enough, but on the whole I see this class as a good/great experience for me and for the students, personally, educationally, and politically.

Final thoughts—

A CHANT FOR MY SISTERS

Marilyn Lowen Fletcher

> it's all right to be a woman
> dishwasher, big belly, sore back
> swollen ankles
>
> it's all right to be woman
> the listener the waiter/sailor's wife
> patient
> by the seashore/looking out
>
> it's all right to be woman
> coquette
>   seductress
>   conniving bitch
>
> it's all right to be woman
> a chant for my sisters
> strong before me
> harriet sojourner emma and rosa
> harriet sojourner emma and rosa
>
> a chant for my sisters
> rifke sorel rochel and mary
> yemaya yemaya yemaya yemaya
>
> yemaya yemaya yemaya yemaya
> oshun. . . . .
> oshun. . . . .
>
> a chant for my sisters
> strong in battle
> la bandita killing generals with zapata
> maria in mexico and mississippi

haydee with the rest at moncada
a chant for my sisters
dead before I could meet them
victorious
in havana
and dien bien phu

TURNING[3]

Lucille Clifton

turning into my own
turning on in
to my own self
at last
turning out of the
white cage turning out of the
lady cage
turning at last
on a stem like a black fruit
in my own season
at last

66

GERDA LERNER

New Approaches to the Study of Women in American History (1969)

The striking fact about the historiography of women is the general neglect of the subject by historians. As long as historians held to the traditional view that only the transmission and exercise of power were worthy of their interest, women were of necessity ignored. There was little room in political, diplomatic, and military history for American women, who were, longer than any other single group in the population, outside the power structure. At best their relationship to power was implicit and peripheral and could easily be passed over as in-

From *Journal of Social History*, Fall 1969. Reprinted by permission of the author.

3. Reprinted from *The Massachusetts Review* © 1972 The Massachusetts Review, Inc.

significant. With the rise of social history and increasing concern with groups out of power, women received some attention, but interest was focused mainly on their position in the family and on their social status.[1] The number of women featured in textbooks of American history remains astonishingly small to this day, as does the number of biographies and monographs by professional historians.

The literature concerning the role of women in American history is topically narrow, predominantly descriptive, and generally devoid of interpretation. Except for the feminist viewpoint, there seems to be no underlying conceptual framework.

Feminist writers, not trained historians, were the first to undertake a systematic attempt to approach the problem of women's role in American life and history. This took the forms of feminist tracts, theoretical approaches, and compilations of woman's "contributions."[2] The early compilers attacked the subject with a missionary zeal designed, above all, to right wrong. Their tendency was to praise anything women had done as a "contribution" and to include any women who had gained the slightest public attention in their numerous lists.[3] Still, much positive work was done in simply recounting the

1. Cf. Arthur Schlesinger, Sr., *New Viewpoints in American History* (New York, 1992), chap. 6. For a contemporary historian's viewpoint, see David M. Potter, "American Women and the American Character," in *American History and Social Sciences*, ed. Edward N. Saveth (New York, 1964), pp. 427–428.

2. The most important feminist tracts before the launching of the woman's rights movement are: Charles Brockden Brown, *Alcuin: A Dialogue* (Boston, 1798); Sarah M. Grimke, *Letters on the Equality of the Sexes and the Condition of Woman* (Boston, 1838); and Margaret Fuller, *Woman in the Nineteenth Century* (Boston, 1844). The publications of the feminist movement are too numerous to list here; a representative collection is incorporated in Elizabeth C. Stanton, Susan B. Anthony, and Matilda J. Gage, *History of Woman Suffrage* (6 vols.; New York, 1881–1922).

3. Typical of the "compilers" are: Lydia M. Child, *History of the Condition of Women* (2 vols.; New York, 1835); Sarah J. Hale, *Woman's Record . . .* (New York, 1853); Phebe A. Hanaford, *Daughters of America, or Women of the Century* (Augusta, Me., n.d.); and Frances E. Willard and Mary A. Livermore, *American Women* (New York, 1897).

history of the women's rights movement and some of its forerunners and in discussing some of the women whose pioneering struggles opened opportunities to others. Feminist writers were hampered by a two-fold bias. First, they shared the middle-class, nativist, moralistic approach of the Progressives and tended to censure out of existence anyone who did not fit into this pattern. Thus we find that women like Frances Wright and Ernestine Rose received little attention because they were considered too radical. "Premature feminists" such as the Grimké sisters, Maria Weston Chapman, and Lydia Maria Child are barely mentioned. The second bias of the feminists lies in their belief that the history of women is important only as representing the history of an oppressed group and its struggle against its oppressors.

This latter concept underlies the somewhat heroic, collectively authored *History of Woman Suffrage*. This work, probably because it represents an easily available though disorganized collection of primary sources, has had a pervasive influence on late historians. Following the lead and interpretation of the feminists, professional historians have been preoccupied with the woman's rights movement in its legal and political aspects. Modern historians, too, think that what is important to know about women is how they got the ballot.[4]

The only serious challenge to this conceptual framework was offered by Mary Beard in the form of a vigorous though often fuzzy polemic against the feminists.[5] What is important about women, said Mary Beard, is not that they were an oppressed group—she denied that they ever were—but that they have made a continuous and impressive contribution to society throughout all of history. It is a contribution, however, which does not fit into the value system generally accepted by historians when they made decisions as to who is or is not important to history. Mary Beard undertook in several of her books to trace the positive achievements of women, their social role, and their contributions to community life. Her concepts are most successfully reflected in *The Rise of American Civilization*, which she coauthored with her husband Charles Beard. In it the position of women is treated throughout in an integrated way with great attention to the economic contributions made by women.[6] But the Beards's approach to the subject of women had little influence on the historical profession. Perhaps this was due to the fact that in the 1930's and 1940's both the general public and historians became somewhat disenchanted with the woman's rights movement.

The winning of suffrage had made only a slight change in the actual status of women, and other factors—technological and economic changes, access to higher education, changing sexual mores—now loomed a great deal larger. The impact of Freudianism and psychology had made reformers in general somewhat suspect. Feminism was not infrequently treated with the same humorous condescension as that other successful failure: temperance.

Women have received serious attention from economic historians. There is a good deal of excellent literature dealing with the problem of women workers. Women as contributors to the economy from colonial times on, the laws affecting them, their wage and working conditions, and their struggle for protective legislation have been fully described.[7] Although

---

4. Cf. Eleanor Flexner, *Century of Struggle: The Woman's Rights Movement in the United States* (Cambridge, Mass. 1959); Aileen S. Kraditor, *The Ideas of the Woman Suffrage Movement* (New York, 1965).

5. *Woman as Force in History* (New York, 1946).

6. Mary R. Beard, *America Through Women's Eyes* (New York, 1934), *On Understanding Women* (New York, 1931), and *Women's Work in Municipalities* (New York, 1915); Charles R. and Mary R. Beard, *The Rise of American Civilization* (New York, 1927).

7. For the economic life of colonial women see: Elisabeth A. Dexter, *Colonial Women of Affairs: Women in Business and Professions in America before 1776* (Boston, 1931), and *Career Women of America: 1776–1840* (Francestown, N.H., 1950); Richard B. Morris, *Government and Labor in Early America* (New York, 1946); and Julia C. Spruill, *Women's Life and Work in the Southern Colonies* (Chapel Hill, 1938). For women's economic role in nineteenth- and twentieth-century America, see: Edith Abbott, *Women in Industry*

female labor leaders have not generally been given much attention, their activities are on record. Excellent collections of material pertaining to women at Radcliffe and Smith College are available but remain insufficiently explored.

Modern historians of the reform movements have done much to restore a sane balance to female achievement in reform; yet one still finds excluded from notice certain women who would have been included as a matter of course had they been men. Sophie Loeb, Grace Dodge, and Mary Anderson could be cited as examples.[8]

The historical literature on the family in America is quite scanty, but there seems to be a revival of interest in the subject. Several interesting monographs have begun to deal with the family role of women in its various aspects. This approach is promising and will hopefully be pursued by other historians.[9]

A new conceptual framework for dealing with the subject of women in American history is needed. The feminist frame of reference has become archaic and fairly useless. The twentieth-century revolution in technology, morality, education, and employment patterns has brought enormous changes in the status and role of American women; these changes demand a historical perspective and understanding. The emergence of a recent "new feminism"

is a social phenomenon requiring interpretation. Most importantly, women themselves are as entitled as minority group members are to having "their" history fully recorded.

Yet the subject is complex. It is difficult to conceptualize women as a group, since they are dispersed throughout the population. Except for special interest organizations, they do not combine together. The subject is full of paradoxes which elude precise definitions and defy synthesis.

Women at various times and places were a majority of the population, yet their status was that of an oppressed minority, deprived of the rights men enjoyed. Women have for centuries been excluded from positions of power, both political and economic, yet as members of families, as daughters and wives, they often were closer to actual power than many a man. If women were among the most exploited of workers, they were also among the exploiters. If some women were dissatisfied with their limited opportunities, most women were adjusted to their position in society and resisted efforts at changing it. Women generally played a conservative role as individuals and in their communities, the role of conserving tradition, law, order, and the status quo. Yet women in their organizations were frequently allied with the most radical and even revolutionary causes and entered alliances with the very groups threatening the stats quo.

If women themselves acted paradoxically, so did society in formulating its values for women. The rationale for women's peculiar position in society has always been that their function as mothers is essential to the survival of the group and that the home is the essential nucleus of society as we know it. Yet the millions of housewives and homemakers have throughout our history been deprived of the one tangible reward our society ranks highest: an income of their own. Neither custom, law, nor changes of technology, education, or politics have touched this sacred tradition. The unpaid housewife-and-mother has affected attitudes toward the women who perform homemaking

(New York, 1918); J. B. Andrews and W. D. P. Bliss, *Report on Condition of Woman and Child Wage-Earners in the United States* (19 vols; Doc. No. 645, 61st Congress, 2nd Session; Washington, 1910); and Elizabeth Baker, *Technology and Women's Work* (New York, 1964).

8. For women in reform movements, see: Robert Bremner, *American Philanthropy* (Chicago, 1960); Clarke E. Chambers, *Seedtime of Reform: American Social Service and Social Action, 1918–1933* (Ann Arbor, 1963); Christopher Lasch, *The New Radicalism in America: 1889–1963* (New York, 1965); and Daniel Levine, *Varieties of Reform Thought* (Madison, Wis., 1964).

9. For a history of the family, see Arthur W. Calhoun, *A Social History of the American Family* (3 vols.; Cleveland, 1918); Sidney Ditzion, *Marriage, Morals, and Sex in America* (New York, 1953); Paul H. Jacobson, *American Marriage and Divorce* (New York, 1959); and William O'Neill, *Divorce in the Progressive Era* (New Haven, 1967).

services for strangers. Traditionally women in the service trades have been the lowest paid among all workers. Nor has this pattern been restricted to the unskilled groups. When women have entered an occupation in large numbers, this occupation has come to be regarded as low status and has been rewarded by low pay. Examples for this are readily found in the teaching and nursing fields. Even intellectual work has been treated with the same double standard. Creative fields in which women excel—poetry, the short story—have been those carrying the lowest rewards in money and esteem. Only in the performing arts has individual female talent had the same opportunity as male talent. Yet a cursory glance at the composition of any major symphony orchestra even today will reveal that in this field, too, opportunities for women have been restricted.

In dealing with the subject of women, studies frequently use other distinctive groups in our society as models for comparison. Women's position has variously been likened to that of the slaves, oppressed ethnic or racial minorities, or economically deprived groups. But these comparisons quickly prove inadequate. The slave comparison obviously was a rhetorical device rather than a factual statement even at the time when Harriet Martineau first made it.[10] While the law denied women equal citizenship and for certain purposes classed them with "Indians and imbeciles," it never denied them physical freedom nor did it regard them as "chattel personnel." In fact, even within the slavery system, women were oppressed differently from men. The "minority group model" is also unsatisfactory. All members of a minority group which suffers discrimination share, with a very few exceptions, in the low-status position of the entire group. But women may be the wives of Cabinet members, the daughters of Congressmen, the sisters of business leaders, and yet, seen simply as persons, they may be disfranchised and suffer from economic and educational discrimination. On the other hand, a lower class woman may advance to a position of economic or social power simply by marriage, a route which is generally not open to members of racial minority groups. In one particular respect the minority group comparison is illuminating: like Negroes, women suffer from "high visibility"; they remain more readily identifiable for their group characteristics than for their personal attainments.[11]

Modern psychology, which has offered various conflicting theories about the role and place of women, has further complicated the task of the historian. If a social historian wishes to study a particular ethnic or religious minority, he can study its location and economy, its culture, leadership, adjustment to American society, and contributions. The question of psychology would only arise in dealing with personal biographies. But the historian of women is at once faced with the necessity of making psychological judgments. Is it not a basic fact that the psychology as well as the physiology of women is different from that of men? Therefore they must of necessity have different expectations, needs, demands, and roles. If so, is the difference in "rights" not simply natural, a reflection of reality? The problems become more vexing when dealing with individual women. The biographer feels obliged first of all to concern himself with his subject's sexual role. Was she married? A mother? If she was not, this indicates that whatever she achieved was the result of sexual frustration. If she was married, one is under an obligation to explain that she did not neglect her children or perhaps that she did. And always there is the crucial question: "What was her relationship to her father?" This is not intended to disparage the efforts of those biographers who wish to enlist the aid of modern psychology for their work. But it should be pointed out that a great deal of excellent history about men has been written without the author's feeling compelled to discuss his subject's sex life or relationship to his mother in

10. *Society in America* (New York, 1837), I, 158.

11. Helen Hacker, "Women as a Minority Group," *Social Forces*, XXX (1951–52), 60–69.

explaining his historical significance. In dealing with women, biographers are impeded by the necessity of dealing first with sex, then with the person. This is an approach which must be examined in each case for its applicability: where it is useful, it should be retained; where it is not, it should be discarded without apology.

In order to broaden the study of women in American history, it is not really necessary to suggest new sources. Primary research material is readily available, not only in the several manuscript collections devoted to the subject, but in the usual primary sources for social historians: local historical records, letters, diaries, the organizational records of women's clubs, religious and charitable organizations, labor unions in fields employing women workers. There are numerous magazines, especially written for women, which provide good source material. Archives of Congress and of state governments contain petitions and statements made at hearings which can yield valuable information about the activities and interests of women. Many of these readily available sources remain neglected.

A fresh approach to known material and to available sources could provide valuable new insights. The following suggestion might make a useful beginning:

First, the subject "Women" is too vast and diffuse to serve as a valid point of departure. Women are members of families, citizens of different regions, economic producers, just as men are, but their emphasis on these various roles is different. The economic role of men predominates in their lives, but women shift readily from one role to another at different periods in their lives. It is in this that their function is different from men and it is this which must form the basis for any conceptual framework. In modern society the only statement about women in general which can be made with validity concerns their political status. Therefore the subject should be subsumed under several categories and any inquiry, description, and generalization should be limited to a narrower field. It is useful to deal with the *status* of women at any given time—to distinguish among their economic status, family status, and political-legal status. There must also be a consideration of class position, as has been usefully proven in recent studies of the feminist movement.[12]

Second, we should look at different aspects of women's role in American history. We must certainly be concerned with the woman's rights movement, but only as part of the total story. Historians must painstakingly restore the actual record of women's contributions at any given period in history. It is interesting that the history of women before the advent of the feminist movement has been more fully recorded and in a more balanced way than it has afterward, so that the story of colonial women can be quite fully traced through secondary literature.[13] But when we deal with the period after 1800, it often proves difficult to establish even descriptive facts. During the early national period, women organized elaborate welfare and relief systems which they staffed and administered. This story should be part of the history of the period; it is not now. Women were the teachers in most of the nation's public schools during the nineteenth century; this is worth recording and exploring. Women made a significant contribution to the growth and development of frontier communities. These are but a few of the many areas in which more research and uncovering of factual information are needed.

Third, we might well discard the "oppressed group model" when discussing women's role in the political life of the nation. Instead, we might start with the fact that one generalization about women which holds up is that they were, longer than any other group in the nation, deprived of political and economic power. Did this mean they actually wielded no power or did they wield power in different

12. See Kraditor and Lasch.
13. A full bibliography of colonial women is to be found in Eugenie A. Leonard, Sophie H. Drinker, and Miriam Y. Holden, *The American Woman in Colonial and Revolutionary Times: 1565–1800* (Philadelphia, 1962).

forms? My research has led me to believe that they wielded considerable power and in the middle of the nineteenth century even political power. They found a way to make their power felt through organizations, through pressure tactics, through petitioning, and various other means; these later became models for other mass movements for reform.

Fourth, another important fact is that women are a group who for a considerable period of history were deprived of equal access to education. While they were not illiterate, their education was limited, usually to below the high school level. This was true of the majority of women until the end of the nineteenth century. It might be very useful to investigate what impact this had on female behavior and more specifically, women's performance as a group in terms of outstanding achievement. To put it another way, how many generations of educated women are necessary to produce a significant number of outstanding women academicians? How many generations of college-trained women are necessary before women in sizable numbers make contributions in the sciences? When do women begin to move from the small-scale, home-centered creative forms, the fiction, poetry and article-writing, to the larger-scale work within the framework of cultural institutions? Is the proverbial dearth of female philosophers really a result of some innate distinctiveness of female mental function or rather the product of centuries of environmental and institutional deprivation? This type of inquiry lends itself to a comparative cross-cultural approach. A comparison between the educational deprivation of women and that suffered by certain minority groups might lead us to a demonstrable correlation between educational deprivation and a gap of several generations before adequate and competitive performance is possible. This could explain a great deal about some of our problems with minority groups, public schooling, and academic achievement.

Fifth, it would be most worthwhile to distinguish the ideas society held at any given moment in regard to woman's proper "place" from what was actually woman's status at that time. The two do not necessarily overlap. On the contrary, there seems to be a considerable gap between the popular myth and reality. Social historians might legitimately be concerned with the significance of this gap, how to account for it, and whether it fits any distinguishable pattern. It would also be important to understand the function of ideas about women in the general ordering of society. Was the fact that colonial women were idealized as thrifty housewives and able helpmeets cause or effect of the labor shortage in the colonies? Are the idealized suburban housewife, the fashion-conscious teenager, the sex-symbol model, causes or effects of our consumer-oriented society? And what effect does the socially held concept of woman's role have on the development of female talent, on woman's contribution to the society?

Finally, we come back to the initial problem of how to judge the contribution of women. Are women noteworthy when their achievement falls exactly in a category of achievement set up for men? Obviously not for this is how they have been kept out of the history books up to now. Are women noteworthy then, as the feminists tended to think, if they do anything at all? Not likely. The fact remains that women are different from men and that their role in society and history is different from that of men. Different, but equal in importance. Obviously their achievements must also be measured on a different scale. To define and devise such a scale is difficult until the gaps in our historical knowledge about the actual contributions of women have been filled. This work remains to be done.

But we already know enough about the subject to conclude that the role women played at different times in our history has been changing. The patterns and significance of these changes, the continuities and discontinuities, the expectations and strivings of the pioneers, and the realities of the social scene—all these await study and new interpretations. One would hope at once for a wider framework and a narrower focus—a discarding of old categories and a painstaking search of known sources for unknown meanings. It is an endeavor that should enlist the best talents of the profession and, hopefully and at long last, not primarily female talent.

67

LINDA GORDON

What Should Women's Historians Do: Politics, Social Theory, and Women's History (1978)

I want to focus in this talk on the kinds of questions we women's historians are working on and how we choose them. Since choices must be made within our political context, whether or not we know it, it may be appropriate to begin with the reminder that the feminist movement, and the gains women have made because of it, are today facing a strong and possibly growing resistance and backlash. Primarily, we face a strong, new, rightwing political movement, ranging from such single-issue campaigners as antiabortionists to ideological fascists. To some extent this rightwing resurgence is an international phenomenon, paralleled in England, Germany, and other European countries as well as in the Third World. But the Right in the United States alone has made antifeminism its central concern and rallying cry.[1] The character of the Right in this country in part reflects the power of the women's movement, just as in the last century feminism reached its greatest strength here.

From *Marxist Perspectives*, Fall 1978; originally presented as a speech at the International Conference in Women's History, November 16–18, 1977, Univesity of Maryland. Reprinted by permission of the author.

1. Linda Gordon and Allen Hunter, "Sex, Family and the New Right: Anti- Feminism as a Political Force," *Radical America*, XI (1977) and XII (1978).

The women's movement has produced another kind of backlash among liberals and even leftists, among intellectuals and professionals. This antifeminist response, like that of the Right, is being conditioned by economic recession and the return to a scarcity mentality after the optimism of the 1960s. But, while it is the Right that adopts the direct-action techniques of the New Left—witness the recent sit-ins at abortions clinics—and even threatens us with a taste of gang violence (fire-bombings, gang beatings of gays), Left and liberal antifeminism have moderation, caution, and calm as their standards. We are experiencing a return to the myth of academic objectivity; a return to unanalyzed empiricism and narrow focus in scholarship; a return to the fetish of strict boundaries not only between the disciplines but within them—e.g., social, political, and intellectual history.

These and other changes have spurred me to rethink the relationship of scholars who work in women's studies to the feminist movement. What seemed an adequate relationship eight years ago will no longer do. During the late 1960s the women's historians with whom I met and talked in Boston imagined ourselves simply propagandists for the women's liberation movement. I myself wrote some polemical pieces that I do not like very much now and, indeed, soon came to reject. We quickly recognized that we could not serve up history upon demand or produce heroines, inspirationals, or laments for victims to serve immediate tactical needs, especially as the women's movement's own lack of clarity and unity became clear. But we should also note the importance of some of those ill-founded early polemics about women in history. That kind of world-turned-upsidedown thinking, suggesting that everything was really its opposite, has been characteristic of many powerful social movements. This turning of reality inside-out is a way of supplying the vision of a changed future, even if it is described in fantasies about the past.

Needed not, however, is a more complex relationship of commitment to the feminist movement, with a relative autonomy as scholars. One characteristic of this relationship might be that we should take our questions from the movement but not our answers. Certainly, we recognize that the questions do not always emerge from the research itself—that without radical political demands we may not dare to wonder the things we should be wondering. At the least, women's history may dry up as its practitioners lose touch with the polemical and theoretical writings of activists. We will get our answers primarily from the analysis of historical data, but if our questions are dictated by the methods and procedures of our profession, they may not be the most revealing. Obvious as this may seem, we do not always discipline ourselves to choose our topics thoughtfully. The availability of a cache of source material, and of a method for analyzing it, often creates our topics for us.

But this distinction—questions from one place, answers from another—is too simple. We cannot, after all, prepare a list of questions and categories of analysis and then apply it to data, as some social scientists do. We need a mutual relation between our historical era and our subjects and their era. If you listen quietly and intently to the people who appear in your historical source material, it sometimes happens that they begin to speak to you. It is a surprising experience at first, for, as one stares at these women of the past, one is often taken aback at their strange ways: Their language seems incomprehensible, their manners odd, their responses bewildering; and then they suddenly reach out to offer a new word, a new concept, a new phrase or analogy, to explain themselves. Now this experience, at least for me, is most of what is wonderful about being a historian, and I should not like to smother those voices. Approaching them with preformed questions will do just that, will prevent them from speaking, whether the preformed questions come from methodological or political determinism.

Still, historical material, dead people, will not dictate to us what to write. We must bring

to it not only questions but also hunches, even theories, based on other parts of our knowledge. And, let us be honest, we are also usually and unavoidably hoping for certain answers. The idea is to keep our expectations and contributions flexible, to remain humble about what we know, and to expect and learn to love surprises.

The small degree of feminist academic success achieved in the United States—and nowhere else I might add—has both advantages and disadvantages for those who want to attempt this two-sided task. It is a great victory that so many of us teach women's history and some of us even sponsor Ph.Ds. We should understand the history of our own professionalization and see that our work rests, both intellectually and professionally, on the bases of work done by at least a century and a half of previous feminist scholars. In this regard I would like to recommend Kathryn Sklar's article about women's historians of the nineteenth-century United States.[2] She shows that material need—that of "respectable" women who had to earn their own livings—provided much greater impetus for serious historical research and writing than pure conviction did. To recall the circumstance that propelled Mary Wollstonecraft into her career as a writer is to notice an important part of material conditions for the birth of modern feminism.

Thus, for most of us professionalization is not a political choice but an economic, and now social, necessity. While women's history remains at the fringes of the discipline—indeed, still outside it in the view of most historians—many of us were trained in the more central concerns and methods of the discipline of history from which we have gained some methodological and critical rigor. But professionalization has also encouraged among us an increasing specialization that make it harder and harder to relate to a social movement which, after all, demands opinions about

2. Kathryn Sklar, "American Female Historians in Context, 1770–1930," *Feminist Studies*, II (1975), 171–184.

everything. Professionalism makes us busier and busier. It is all we can do to keep up with the scholarship in our "field," let alone read about or participate in social action. Professionalism makes us more and more antiutopian, practical, modest in our demands, as it makes us more estranged from the situation of the majority of women.

Let me make explicit the conclusions inherent in a historical understanding of our professionalization. We cannot, nor should we, reject it. We are stuck with it and are lucky to be stuck with it at this historical moment. We should learn everything possible from this elite, male-dominated discipline called history. But we can also support and maintain confidence in those women trying to do similar work without the advantages and limitations of membership in the profession. A good beginning, at least intellectually, towards that humility might be some critical reading about professionals in general: C. Wright Mills has a lot to say in his *White Collar* and in his essay, "The Professional Ideology of the Social Pathologist";[3] more recently Barbara and John Ehrenreich offered a post-1960s view—one I disagree with but think essential to consider—in their essay "The Professional Managerial Class."[4]

To move now from the general to the specific, how do professional women's historians try to maintain a living, tense, and stubborn relationship to the women's movement in our intellectual work? I have argued that our historical questions ought to be formed in relation to current politics as well as to open-minded exploration of the past "as it really was." A difficult double task, but let me offer three thoughts about useful questions.

First, we need to be concerned with both objective and subjective reality. We have recently experienced great advances in the availability of objective data: family size and struc-ture, fertility, employment, criminal activity, health, consumption. As a result, we are experiencing a sort of bottleneck in the study of subjective experience, especially since it is difficult to find the historical voices of the common people. But, to resign oneself to this difficulty can lead to dreadful distortions. In contrast to some of the great traditional biographies and intellectual histories of the elite, some "social" historians have recently produced studies of working people who seem to have no emotional or mental life, no cravings for "higher" things. The product is historically false and has a conservative political impact. The point is not that it is illegitimate to collect and analyze objective data, but that the neglect of subjectivity, politics, and intellectual history can create a misleading impression of the totality and a distorted interpretation of reality.

Perhaps some examples may illuminate these problems. We know that in the United States there has been a rather steady shift from the employment of daughters to that of mothers, but we know little about the attendant intrafamily conflict. Similarly, subjective material can lead to misinterpretation if not set in the context of objective conditions. Thus, we would be puzzled by nineteenth-century women's effusive expressions of love for each other if we could not set those feelings within the context of women's family and friendship networks.

Sources that reveal subjective experience among common people may remain scarce. We will have to squeeze them hard and to refine our systems of interpretation. Cultural anthropology has offered useful methods of analysis as illustrated by Natalie Davis' use of the complex and indirect meanings of cultural symbols.[5] We can also turn "psychohistory" to our use. Kathryn Sklar's biography of Catharine Beecher[6] demonstrates that, without detaching the individual from her social and intellectual

3. C. Wright Mills, "The Professional Ideology of the Social Pathologist," *American Journal of Sociology*, XLIX (1943), 165–180.

4. Barbara and John Ehrenreich, "The Professional Managerial Class," *Radical America* XI (1977).

5. Natalie Zemon Davis, *Society and Culture in Early Modern France: Eight Essays* (Stanford, 1975).

6. Sklar, *Catharine Beecher: A Study in American Domesticity* (New Haven, 1973).

context, it is possible to enter ego conflicts to illuminate the situation of womanhood at a specific historical moment.

Second, we need to ask questions about change over time. This problem increases as we collect more objective data, which almost always pertains to particular moments. Even comparison of data from two points in time remains an observation of two static points. Change can only be inferred, and a common inference in liberal capitalist society is that it happened gradually. In fact, social change often occurs in bursts. Its study requires close observation and analysis of the process of transformation itself: moments of revolution or of other social disturbances, and social and ideological movements themselves. We shall lose a great deal if the static, conflict-denying myths that now dominate some social sciences—e.g., modernization theory—begin to determine historical research.

So, at least part of women's history must remain committed to an older tradition of social history—the study of social conflict. We can use some insights of other recent social history—e.g., that social conflict is part of culture, often invisible to the outsider. Nevertheless, I am still convinced that the moments of overt conflict express, condense, and ever clarify the conflict latent at other times. They do so not only through struggle, but through the social ideologies they both use and create. Underestimation of the importance of ideology in women's past encourages, and is encouraged by, over-objectivism.

Third, I do not see how one can study social conflict without doing what has been called political history. Since social change only happens through power conflict, it cannot be apprehended without attention to politics. A social history that excludes politics risks becoming ahistorical.

This third observation remains abstract because it immediately encounters a large theoretical problem: the definition of politics, one of the greatest concerns for Marxism at this time. Much current Marxist writing about the

State, and the Genoveses' article "The Political Crisis of Social History,"[7] seem to me to miss one of the lessons of the New Left and the women's movement—that one can no longer define politics only in terms of struggle for the State. The State is central to political power in modern society, and political strategies must ulitmately focus upon it; but groups can also wield political power through structures and processes distant from government. I suspect that on this question confusion may be more correct than clarity at the current time, and that an important reconceptualization is in process. But the necessity to include politics in social history still holds. Social findings about women must be situated in relation to political structures or they lose significance.

The Marxist tradition has offered the most accurate analysis of capitalism and of the particular situation of women in it, and the best strategy for a liberating revolution. Nevertheless, during the past decade the most penetrating new analyses of women's situation have not come from Marxists but from independent feminists who, in the United States, adhere to tendencies sometimes identified as "radical-feminist," concerned with patriarchy as an alternative to class. These ideological tendencies have called our attention to questions of reproduction; to the centrality of mothering in determining the female gender; to social networks, family and community, sex and friendship. These are the subjects the development of which has contributed most to women's history and has allowed women's history to contribute so much to history in general.

There are several reasons for this lack of Marxist leadership in feminist theory and scholarship. One is the persecution of Marxist intellectuals—the driving of radical scholarship and thought out of those institutions which allow intellectuals to live, teach, and write. Another is the suppression of creative Marxist thought for

7. Elizabeth Fox-Genovese and Eugene D. Genovese, "The Political Crisis of Social History," *Journal of Social History*, X (1976), 205–220.

many decades by the Stalinist domination of the Communist movement. Had we had a different Marxism thriving into the 1930s, 1940s, and 1950s, we might have avoided the near total suppression of the feminist movement during those decades. And we might have had a more lively and creative social history from which to learn. A third reason has been a Marxist tendency to overemphasize industrial production; ironically, the capitalist class rather than the working class; and formal organization. These emphases are inadequate for a good history of men and almost eliminate women from view.

More deeply, however, it may also be that the situation of women cannot be fully explained in terms of the capitalist mode of production—the subject central to Marxist thought. Our sex/gender system has roots in the organization of reproduction, which appears to have predated all forms of class society. Capitalism has not itself completely individualized people, and production relations are often mediated by other social relations created by reproductive forms of organization—by friendship, kinship, informal work groups.

We need to construct materialist analyses of patriarchal and reproduction forms, which should not be understood as patriarchal "survival." The relationships that are not directly dictated by capital accumulation are as vital—as "modern"—as capital itself, though not usually as powerful. In some cases such social patterns, including the sex/gender system, may even prove strong enough to react back upon the process of capital accumulation—for example, through conditioning the kind of labor force available, the forms of worker resistance, even the kinds of demands directed against the State.

As an example of the practicability of such a project, take some recent work on the impact of industrialization on women, which has proven particularly fruitful by trying to encompass both reproductive and productive forms of social organization.[8] The complex patterns that emerge might be viewed as the continuation of a patriarchal economy of reproduction with a capitalist economy of production. This rather old-fashioned use of the word "economy" to include child-raising, kinship, and social cooperation, has the advantage of suggesting that the "old values" were not merely a cultural overlay but also a kind of worker consciousness, different from capitalist-industrial class consciousness but formed in the same way: Materially, by the social relations of labor.

This line of research and analysis means an enormous collective labor but need not lead to "jumbo history." Small-scale studies may even prove more beneficial since more amenable to the sketching of women's lives in total context. Women's history has a special need to maintain the sense of totality. If the focus on women is to be understood as merely another specialization within a profession, the legitimacy of our enterprise might indeed be challenged. The most radical assertion we have to make may be the (apparently) simplest: As Joan Kelly[9] pointed out a few years ago, sex must be taken as a fundamental social category, not reducible to any other category, not even "ultimately." In practice, all kinds of topics in social history— family, trade unions, riots, entertainment,

8. For example, Joan W. Scoot and Louise A. Tilly, "Women's Work and the Family in Nineteenth-Century Europe," *Comparative Studies in Society and History*, XVII (1975); Leonore Davidoff, "Mastered for Life: Servant and Wife in Victorian and Edwardian England," *Journal of Social History*, VII (1974), 406–428; Batya Weinbaum and Amy Bridges, "The Other Side of the Paycheck: Monopoly Capital and the Structure of Consumption," in *Capitalist Patriarchy and the Case for Socialist Feminism*, ed., Zillah R. Eisenstein (N.Y., 1978); Judith Walkowitz, "The Making of an Outcast Group: Prostitutes and Working Women in Nineteenth-Century Plymouth and Southampton," in *A Widening Sphere*, ed., Martha Vicinus (Bloomington, Ind., 1977); Peter N. Stearns, "Working-class Women in Britain, 1890–1914," in *Suffer and Be Still*, ed., Martha Vicinus (Bloomington, Ind., 1972). This is, no doubt, a most idiosyncratic list of personal preferences. Nevertheless, that such a high proportion of these articles are about European history indicates, I think, the weak theoretical tradition in American historiography.

9. Joan Kelly-Gadol, "The Social Relation of the Sexes: Methodological Implications of Women's History," *Signs*, I (1976), 809–823.

housing, nutrition—will have to be analyzed so as to include two sexes, and then put back together with the experience of both sexes included. Sex and gender are not merely analytic categories that one can choose to apply, but basic parts of the human experience that one may neglect only at the risk of great historical distortion.

Politics in the United States today is demonstrating that the sex/gender struggle has the potential to become, once again, a vital historical force. This is the context in which I hope we can place our discoveries about women in the past.

68

ELLEN CAROL DUBOIS

The Last Suffragist: An Intellectual and Political Autobiography (1998)

From the beginning, my decision to focus my scholarship on woman suffrage ran against the grain of the developing field of women's history. In 1969, the year I selected my dissertation topic, women's history was only an aspiration, albeit a widespread one. Feminism was still a word with which even those of us who would go on to revive it were uncomfortable using. In graduate history programs all over the country, young women like myself were realizing that the history of women in the U.S. was an enormous unexplored territory, rich with compelling analytical questions. In buildings other than the ones where we took our graduate seminars, on evenings when we were not reading in preparation for our qualifying exams, we were writing feminist manifestos, attending meetings, calling demonstrations, and forming women's organizations. Determined to unify our political and scholarly selves (and

Revised from Ellen Carol DuBois, *Women Suffrage and Women's Rights* (New York: New York Univ. Press, 1998), 1–29. Reprinted by permission of the author.

protected by a robust economy from too great anxieties about our future careers), my generation wanted to contribute to a historical practice that would be useful, that would not only document social change but help to realize it. Meanwhile, in the streets alongside men, we were committed to stopping the war in Vietnam.

For the most part, women's historians of the late 60s and early 70s were directing their energies toward women's private lives—family, childrearing, sexuality. This was a perspective that was shaped by many factors. First of all, the entire practice of history was in the midst of a tremendous paradigm shift that would eventually go by the term "social history." Itself an intellectual response to the larger politics and culture of "the sixties," social history directed historians' attention away from the designated rulers to the masses of common folk, with whom we believed the real fate of society lay. We were as dedicated to a democratic approach to the power to make history in our roles of historians as those of citizens. For the time being politics in the formal sense of elections, office holding and government, was outside of young historians' purview.

In addition, there was the strong sense that politics was not the place to find women's overlooked and suppressed historical importance, their "agency," to use the word that was coming to symbolize social historians' intent to subvert old-fashioned notions of historical significance. Questions of the relation between "public" and "private" life would soon surface as one of the fundamental conundrums of modern feminist thought, but initially women's historians observed the distinction even as they began to challenge it. Public life, where women had been the objects of sustained and multifaceted discrimination, did not seem the arena in which women were going to be restored to history at the level of which we aspired. Given the frameworks of social history, to identify women's "agency" historians would have to focus on the things that most women did most of the time, on the very private and family concerns that had been considered too trivial and personal for historical investigation.

A major factor in the lack of interest in political history was the larger disillusionment and contempt that surrounded formal politics in these years. The rise and fall of hopes for modern liberalism during the Kennedy-Johnson years, the inexorable growth of the war in Vietnam, the electoral corruption and executive criminality of Watergate left many convinced of the uselessness of choosing between parties and of the impossibility of controlling the arrogance of power at the ballot box. I voted in November, 1968, shortly after my twenty-first birthday, but cannot remember which minor candidate I preferred to Hubert Humphrey and the Democrats. In 1980, I reluctantly voted for Jimmy Carter over Ronald Reagan but most of my friends refused this lesser evil ploy. The twelve years of reactionary Republicanism ushered in at that point eventually forced renegades from Democratic liberalism back into electoral politics, but not until unbelievable damage was wrought on the social fabric and feminists and progressives of all sorts learned the painful lesson that who voted for what could make a difference.

From the very beginning of my work on suffrage, therefore, I felt compelled to explain why the long struggle to win the vote was worth studying, what it could contribute to the field of women's history. The question, as I posed it then, still seems to me to be a valid and crucial one: why was woman suffrage the demand around which women's boldest aspirations for emancipation coalesced in the nineteenth century? Why was political equality at the core of radical feminism in this period? My answer, structured in response to the feminist focus on private life of those years, was that precisely by bypassing the private sphere and focusing on the male monopoly of the public sphere, pioneering suffragists sent shock waves though the whole set of structures that relegated women to the family. If I had had access to the terms developed twenty years later, I would have written that women's demands for

suffrage uniquely threatened to disrupt and reorganize the relations of gender.

We called ourselves "radial feminists" then. By "radical feminism," we meant a movement that challenged the social order as profoundly as the labor and civil rights movements. This was a complex claim, that both assumed the link between feminism and other radical movements, and insisted on feminism's distinctiveness. The determination in these years to establish what we called the "autonomy" of women's historic struggle for liberation is difficult to recall, inasmuch as feminism is infinitely more legitimate now than it was then, far stronger than the politics of class and race towards which we felt, in the 1970s, so much like junior partners. Over the years, as feminism grew while the larger enthusiasm for "radical" change withered, I became less concerned with insisting on autonomy, and more with drawing attention to the connection between feminism and other battles for social justice.

In general, I was becoming concerned that the whole political dimension of women's history was getting short shrift, and with it attention to the character of women's subordination. The women's liberation movement had opened up the meaning of the word "political" via its claim that "the personal is the political," that is, that power relationships characterized even the most seemingly private of encounters between men and women, from lovemaking to housekeeping. I embraced this expanded definition but also wanted to restore something of the more organized, collective and public dimension to politics, and to indicate that ultimately feminist goals had to be won at this level. Even though the young field of women's history was beginning to achieve academic legitimacy, the idea of a historical practice influenced by a political movement outside the university was by no means seen as professionally acceptable. I was concerned that just as women's history was beginning to find acceptance in the academy, the intellectual legitimacy of bringing openly feminist questions to the field was under attack.

I was critical of women's history practice which I thought conceded too much to, or co-incided too closely with the apolitical spirit of academic history. In particular, I argued that women's history was taking shape around an interpretive framework, associated with the term "women's culture," which left little room for the place of feminist politics. "Women's culture," I contended, was an interpretation that focused on women's ability to relocate themselves away from the pressures and limitations of male dominance into an environment defined more by their own repressed needs and perspectives; I preferred a more frontal attack on male privilege. At a more general level, my argument was that some of the resources necessary to envision and forge truly different power relations between the sexes needed to be taken from the hands of men themselves. To rely on an expression that came later, I was disagreeing with Audre Lord's famous slogan that "the master's tools" could never "dismantle the master's house." In this, I was influenced by the venerable Caribbean historian, C. L. R. James, whose approach was the opposite of Lord's: the tools the oppressed most needed, he argued, were precisely those of the master, turned to their own purposes.

But where to begin my own study of woman suffrage? My generation's feminism had been forged in the era of civil rights, the "mother movement" of the 1960s. So locating the origins of the women's rights perspective in the 1830s, at the point at which abolitionism led "nominally free" women (to use Angelina Grimke's words) to recognize and protest their own kind of enslavement, was so obvious as to be virtually automatic. Over the years, I would find in the impact of abolitionism on the history of American feminism clues to everything from the ability of women's rights pioneers to critique the ideology of woman's separate sphere, to their insights into the sexual dimensions of women's subordination, to the enduring, if contradictory, link between race and gender in the American feminist tradition. In the 1970s, I emphasized the dissenting perspective on sexual difference that emerged among abolitionist women, the insistence that male and female, like black and white, faded in the face of human and moral oneness before God.

The narrative line on which I was concentrating at this point, like the political process I was living through, was that of "the emergence of an independent women's movement." While committed to the dialectic of radicalism and feminism, my account was decidedly tilted toward separation rather than attachment. To me at that point, abolitionist-feminists, like women's liberationists a hundred and thirty years later, appeared as junior partners in an extraordinary radical enterprise, profiting from the conviction that fundamental social relationships could be revolutionized, and yet held back by not yet being first and foremost a women's movement.

Impatient for nineteenth century suffragism to appear in all its initial boldness, I hurried forward, moving too quickly through the women's rights battles of the eighteen-fifties that would catch my eye two decades later. I was eager to get to the years after the Civil War, when the franchise became the focus of the feminist struggle. In my finished dissertation and subsequent book as a member of a determinedly anti-war generation I virtually ignored the Civil War to concentrate my attention on Radical Reconstruction. I not only wanted to emphasize the primacy of the suffrage demand, I also wanted to confront the fundamental mischaracterization that has always dogged it: that political equality was a "single issue," which ignored all the other dimensions—sexual, economic—of women's emancipation. As evidence to the contrary, I demonstrated the dramatic expansion of interest in wage-earning women and in the sexual dimension of women's subordination that accompanied the rise of attention to woman suffrage in the late 1860s.

My biggest analytic challenge was to understand that moment when the priorities of blacks' and women's emancipation came into conflict and choices between them had to be made; this became the focus of my dissertation and of the book that resulted from it. The 1867–1869 crisis that occurred once woman suffragists realized their inability to win inclusion in the Fourteenth and Fifteenth amendments not only led to animosity between suffragists and defenders of freedmen's rights; it also split suffragists into competing camps just at the moment that they launched a serious drive for political equality. This episode is one of those turning points in history that requires, indeed deserves, continuously revised interpretation, so fundamental were the issues involved, so irresolvable the conflicts facing the participants, so painful the choices they faced. When first confronting the conflict within the suffrage movement over the Fourteenth and Fifteenth amendments, my judgment was that this was a necessary, productive, and though painful, positive development in the history of American feminism. I returned to these questions later, at which time I had much more to say about the negative imapct of the reconstruction shifts in the woman suffrage movement on the historic link between black freedom and women's emancipation.

My original argument about woman suffrage had always been vulnerable to charges that it underplayed the racism unleashed among feminists by their break with abolitionists, and now these criticisms hit their mark. By the 1980s, black feminism had reached a sort of critical mass in terms of visibility and distinctiveness of political message. Now I saw how the shift away from universal suffragism and towards an exclusive focus on (to use Stanton's words) "an aristocracy of sex" worked in reactionary ways to constrict the movement's reach. In the place of its original high minded universality, suffrage arguments focused exclusively on the need for the vote among white, middle class, educated women which was inevitably counterposed against what they regarded as the unwarranted political power of men who were their natural inferiors. Political conditions around me were now alerting me to the importance, no longer merely of legitimat-

ing feminism, but of insuring that its reach was broad and its impact democratic.

My rereading of reconstruction suffragism was also a reaction to an all-encompassing, paradigm-rattling debate about whether "equality" was an adequate theoretical basis for challenging women's subordination or whether it just led to minor integrations of women into a still male-defined world. In the late 1970s, a wing of feminism had begun to develop instead around the celebration and elaboration of women's "difference" from men as a means to deeper sorts of change. Elaborations of "difference feminism" called into question basic elements of progressive political theory including individualism, the desirability of expanded rights, and liberal thought itself.

The debate over equality and difference in feminism was crucially shaped by the larger atmosphere of Reagan-era politics, notably the collapse of progressive politics and the demonization of liberal ideas. The further we get from these years, the more obvious it seems to me that feminists and progressives of all sorts were under a terrible cloud of political impossibility during them. Insurgent conservativism rode all too easily over what little there was of an openly leftwing opposition and went on to drive liberalism itself into full-fledged retreat. Feminists really had only two alternatives: to pull back our forces and defend liberal premises we had once sought to transcend, or to change direction and question our liberal roots altogether. Both had their dangers; I elected the former.

A crucial event that illuminates the political context of the feminist turn against "equality" was the "Sears case," an episode of great significance for feminist scholarship in the early 1980s. The case began when the Equal Employment Opportunity Commission charged the Sears Company with sexual discrimination. The case had been filed in the final months of the Carter administration, but it was heard in 1982, before a judge appointed by President Reagan, and Sears shaped its defense accordingly. Sears reasoned that arguments about the historical "difference" in women's values, choices and lifestyles could be used to attribute women's current absence from high-paying sales positions to their own women's choices rather than the corporation's discriminatory employment policies. This was a painful irony for the field of women's history. The notion of women's agency was here being marshalled against the commitment to social change with which it had originally been paired. What had once been called inequality was now being labeled as difference. The sorry truth was that the defense's historical case was consistent with the emphasis women's historians had placed on nineteenth century women's role in creating their own distinct "sphere" and the satisfaction it had provided them.

Nowhere was the intersection of the right wing insurgencies of the 1980s and the path of women' history more important than with respect to the family and sexuality, the history and political significance of which modern feminists had been the first to explore. A "new" right, like the "new" left and the "new" feminism it had spawned, had learned to focus on the frustrations and yearnings fostered within private life and the political possibilities these offered. The badge of feminism was now claimed by those who argued that women's interests were not served by liberalized divorce laws, an all-out drive for equality in the labor force, increased sexual choices or even the easy availability of legal abortion.

In the early years of the Republican insurgency, the most explosive of these cross-over feminist issues was pornography. In the late 1970s, a feminist attack on pornography began to grow in influence. Women's liberation had done important work in opening up and politicizing the issues of rape, which so many women had suffered in shame and isolation. The anti-rape movement metamorphasized into the anti-pornography movement, a development which was very much encouraged by the growing power of the right wing, which found it more useful and malleable than the campaign to eliminate rape. So promising was distaste for

pornography as a concern which could draw women into politics that feminists had a difficult time maintaining control over it. I became a full-fledged participant in what became nicknamed "the feminist sex wars." I joined with other feminists who were determined to challenge the conservative drift of contemporary sexual politics and especially the anti-pornography movement.

The figure of Elizabeth Cady Stanton has consistently been at the forefront of my writings on nineteenth century suffragism. I have always found Stanton's insights into women's subordination so extraordinarily rich, the meanings of her words so multiple, that returning to them time after time seems no more limited to me than concentrating on the study of any other timeless thinker. Stanton died in 1902, eighteen years before woman suffrage finally found its place in the constitution. If I was going to follow the woman suffrage movement through to its conclusion, I would have to find another figure to trace. This is how I first settled on a study of Harriot Stanton Blatch, as a surrogate for her mother.

A great deal has been written by feminist biographers about the intensity of identification between themselves and their subjects, but it was precisely because of my reverence for Elizabeth Cady Stanton that I did not want to write her biography. I did not think I had enough critical distance on her ideas to write a book with an edge to it, which is the kind of history I do best. By writing a life of the daughter instead of the mother, I found a much better vehicle, one which both represented my own position as fictive daughter more accurately and allowed me the emotional and historical distance necessary to put my subject's contributions in their proper place. As it turned out, Harriot Stanton Blatch had her own historical riches to offer me, as she led me through the revival of suffrage militancy and feminist vision that reappeared in the last decade of women's drive for the vote. Her leadership helped the movement to shift from a nineteenth century women's rights ideology, born of natural rights ideas and focused on political notions of independence and power, to a twentieth century feminist version, reflecting social democratic ideas, and concentrating on economics.

My work on Harriot Blatch led me from the winning of the Nineteenth Amendment directly into the process by which the woman suffrage movement was incorporated into the historical record. I came to see that the very question with which I had begun my own work—what made the suffrage demand so radical at its inception—was part of a historical debate that reached this far back. This phase of my work had its own political context. By the late 1980s, Republican politicians and officials had come to appreciate how much the writing and teaching of U.S. history had changed under the influence of the social history paradigm of the late 1960s. Shielding their own political purposes behind a "just-the-facts" appeal for objectivity, conservative forces attacked American historians for advancing a left-wing agenda that taught students to hate their country and distrust their government. This was a compliment of sorts: apparently reinterpretations of American history had made enough of an impact to deserve such an all-out reaction.

From this perspective, my account of the early stages of woman suffrage historiography was a rumination on the relationship of history making and political engagement. On the one hand, I criticized the amateur, politically-motivated feminist historians of suffrage in the 1920s for simplifying the historical narrative and suppressing debate over its meaning. Yet I also appreciated that it was precisely because of their own feminist commitment that they had begun the work of preserving the suffrage record, of turning the past into history; without them there might not be an historical record over which to argue. Taken together, these observations suggested a standard for responsible history, one that was both politically engaged and committed to full disclosure and democratic debate.

For most of the time that I have been working on the history of woman suffrage, few have shared my interest. The word "suffrage" remained as antiquated (and regularly misspelled) as it had been when I wrote my first graduate paper on the subject. But in the 1990s, women and politics has become a popular issue. On the coattails of Bill Clinton's presidency, many more women were elected to public office, constituting the famous "year of the woman" in 1992. Politics at the highest level turned increasingly on "women's issues," most notably abortion rights. A gender gap in voting, which had been a factor at least since 1980, now drew pundits' attention. Women's greater liberalism (pacificism, Democrat preference, inclination to social spending) was noticed and appreciated, though attributed to fundamentally female inclinations, rather than the widespread impact of twenty years of liberal feminism.

In the last half decade, the scholarship on suffrage has blossomed. By a very rough estimate, already in the 1990s there have been more monographs and collections of articles published on the woman suffrage movement in the United States than in the entire period between 1960 and 1990. Even more remarkable is a renaissance of interest in the subject outside the academy. The seventy-fifth anniversary of the Nineteenth Amendment in 1995 and the sesquicentennial of the Seneca Falls Convention in 1998 were marked by widespread, grassroots celebration; by contrast, the fiftieth anniversary, occurring during the infancy of the modern feminist revival, went virtually unobserved.

Three decades ago, I became both an historian and a feminist as part of a generation trying to face down modern contempt for feminism. Then I focused on the political independence of feminism from other movements. Later, as modern feminism grew more confident, I defined feminism so as to strengthen the left wing of it, in which I placed myself, by emphasizing the interplay between struggles for political power in the public sphere and association with other insurgent political movements. When the sexual politics of modern feminism began to take a turn which I thought conservative, I did my best to make history serve the case of a "pro-sex" feminism. Then in the face of heated contests about family life, sexuality, and the scope and future of marriage, I put myself in the camp which sought to push the limit of politically possible sexual and familial change. Hopefully, through all this, I have met my own standards for historical responsibility as well as political engagement.

It has become a commonplace to say that how we approach the past has everything to do with where we are located in the present. The historian has to stand someplace to generate her questions of the past. But investigating the past is also connected to what we want from the future, for the historian is also trying to understand the trajectory of change of which she is a part. And if committed to intervening through political action to affect the contemporary trajectory, that is to being an active citizen, the historian's perspective must be part of that effort, intended to affect or alter what the future brings. In virtually all my writings, I have insisted on the intimate relationship between the practice of women's history and the possibilities of modern feminist politics. Although the rhetorical character of some of these claims now causes me some embarrassment, I am unwilling to give up my own personal "metanarrative," which is a sort of wishful progressivism seeking to recruit adherents, an insistence that things might get better, if only people refuse to be discouraged about making them so.

Suggestions for Further Reading

Boxer, Marilyn. "For and About Women: The Theory and Practice of Women's Studies in the United States." *Signs* (Spring 1982).

Carabillo, Toni, Judith Meuli, and June Bundy Csida. *Feminist Chronicles: 1953–1993*. Los Angeles: Women's Graphics, 1993.

Collins, Patricia Hill. *Black Feminist Thought: Knowledge, Consciousness, and the Politics of Empowerment*. New York: Routledge, 1991.

Davis, Flora. *Moving the Mountain: The Women's Movement in America Since 1960*. New York: Simon and Schuster, 1991.

Dill, Bonnie Thornton. "Race, Class, and Gender: Prospects for an All-Inclusive Sisterhood." *Feminist Studies* 9 (1983): 131–50.

Echols, Alice. *Daring to Be Bad: Radical Feminism in America, 1967–1975*. Minneapolis: Univ. of Minnesota Press, 1989.

Eisenstein, Hester. *Contemporary Feminist Thought*. Boston: G. K. Hall, 1983.

Evans, Sara. *Born for Liberty: A History of Women in America*. New York: Free Press, 1989.

Faderman, Lillian. *Odd Girls and Twilight Lovers: A History of Lesbian Life in Twentieth-Century America*. New York: Columbia Univ. Press, 1991.

Ferree, Myra Marx, and Beth B. Hess. *Controversy and Coalition: The New Feminist Movement across Three Decades of Change*. New York: Twayne, 1994.

Freeman, Jo. *The Politics of Women's Liberation*. New York: David McKay, 1975.

Gatlin, Rochelle. *American Women Since 1945*. Jackson: Univ. Press of Mississippi, 1987.

Giddings, Paula. *When and Where I Enter: The Impact of Black Women on Race and Sex in America*. New York: William Morrow, 1984.

Gordon, Linda. *Pitied but Not Entitled: Single Mothers and the History of Welfare*. New York: Free Press, 1994.

Hine, Darlene Clark, and Kathleen Thompson. *A Shining Thread of Hope: The History of Black Women in America*. New York: Broadway Books, 1998.

Katz, Jonathan Ned. *Gay American History: Lesbians and Gay Men in the U.S.A.* New York: Meridian, 1992.

Kitzinger, Celia. *The Social Construction of Lesbianism.* London, U.K.: Sage, 1987.

Mathews, Donald G., and Jane Sherron De Hart. *Sex, Gender, and the Politics of ERA.* New York: Oxford Univ. Press, 1990.

Miller, Neil. *Out of the Past: Gay and Lesbian History from 1869 to the Present.* New York: Vintage, 1995.

Minnich, Elizabeth, Jean O'Barr, and Rachel Rosenfeld. *Reconstructing the Academy: Women's Education and Women's Studies.* Chicago: Univ. of Chicago Press, 1988.

Palmer, Phyllis Marynick. "White Women/Black Women: The Dualism of Female Identity and Experience in the United States." *Feminist Studies* 9 (1983): 151–70.

Pettegrew, John. "Matching Practice with Theory: Is There a Role for Pragmatism in U.S. Women's History?" Unpublished paper delivered at the American Historical Association Conference, New York City, 1997.

Polatnick, M. Rita. "Diversity in Women's Liberation Ideology: How a Black and a White Group of the 1960s Viewed Motherhood." *Signs* 21 (1996): 679–706.

Ryan, Barbara. *Feminism and the Women's Movement: Dynamics of Change in Social Movement, Ideology and Activism.* New York: Routledge, 1992.

Simons, Margaret A. "Racism and Feminism: A Schism in the Sisterhood." *Feminist Studies* 5 (1979): 384–401.

Taylor, Verta, and Leila J. Rupp. "Women's Culture and Lesbian Feminist Activism: A Reconsideration of Cultural Feminism." *Signs* 19 (1993): 32–61.

Tobias, Sheila. *Faces of Feminism: An Activist's Reflections on the Women's Movement.* Boulder, Colo.: Westview, 1997.

PART II

Of Continuity and Discontent: Late-Twentieth-Century Feminism

I. Feminism in a Multicultural World

THE SUCCESSES AND THE DIFFICULTIES ENCOUNTERED BY women of different races and ethnicities confronting each other—confronting the residues of pervasive sexist and racist ideologies in themselves and in each other—were central in constructing what has come to be called "third-wave feminism." As Leslie Heywood and Jennifer Drake—the editors of *Third Wave Agenda: Being Feminist, Doing Feminism* (1997)—assert, "the definitional moment of third wave feminism has been theorized as proceeding from critiques of the white women's movement that were initiated by women of color, as well as from the many instances of coalition work undertaken by U.S. third world feminists." In other words, feminism in the 1990s emerged from a complex multicultural analysis of the ways in which feminist theory and practice *must* extend beyond consideration of relations between the sexes, how it must involve exploring complex relations *among women* and the often contradictory and shifting positions within which women are located along the axes of gender, race, ethnicity, class, and sexuality.

The 1980s saw the rise of "multiculturalism" as an ideal in the United States. This broad movement held that the United States ought not only to respect but also to value and sustain the distinctive cultures carried by the myriad ethnic and racial groups within its borders. At the practical level, multiculturalism was manifest primarily in educational policies that rejected the long-tolerated bias of Eurocentric curricula and affirmed the history, art, language, and even learning styles of African Americans, Asian Americans, Native Americans, and Hispanic Americans. Bilingual education and Afrocentric classrooms were two particular projects created within the rubric of multicultural education, as was the widespread revision of literature and history curricula to include people of color and present a more balanced learning experience for students.

Multiculturalism won a foothold in the United States in part because of increased immigration. As a result of the Immigration and Nationality Act of 1965—the first loosening of restrictions since 1924—immigration rates almost quadrupled between 1960 and 1990, fed especially by newcomers from Asian and Latin American countries. Also, the 1960s and 1970s spawned more or less successful nationalist movements within all the major racial/ethnic groups in the United States as each demanded recognition and social justice.

The widespread acknowledgment of these Blacks, Asian Americans, Native Americans, Hispanics, and other distinct groups in popular culture and education in the 1980s represented a success for multiculturalism, but also in some ways the dispersal of social and political concerns—a kind of watering down. A school board's mandate to celebrate Black History Month, for instance, obviously does not address the increasing impoverishment of an "underclass" of African Americans. Nor does introducing a novel by Amy Tan into a high school literature class challenge U.S. foreign policy in Asia. Nevertheless, to draw from a concept popularized by feminism's second wave, multiculturalism raised people's consciousness, at the least.

Multicultural feminism rests on both a broad-based multiculturalism and second-wave feminism. Like Black women activists in the 1960s and 1970s who often developed a feminist consciousness as a result of experiences with sexism in the civil rights and Black power movements, other women of color began to define their own interests as intersecting with but no longer identical to the interests of their brothers in revolutionary struggle. African American, Chicana, Native American, and Asian American feminists all insisted on their identity as *women* of *color* (and they emphasized *both* terms), seeking to end sexist *and* racist oppression and gain visibility and social equality for themselves. As Alma Garcia puts it in her discussion of Chicana feminism, women of color faced ideological questions in three areas: "the relationship between feminism and the ideology of cultural nationalism or racial pride, feminism and feminist-baiting within the larger movements, and the relationship between their feminist movements and the white feminist movement." In other words, in their fundamental struggle to achieve an authentic sense of identity and to have that identity recognized by the wider society, feminists of color had to negotiate the politics both of their gender and of their race; they had to face the denial and often distortion of their personhood by both nationalist and feminist organizations.

A groundbreaking text in the flowering of a multicultural feminism was the collection *This Bridge Called My Back: Writings by Radical Women of Color*, edited by Cherríe Moraga and Gloria Anzaldúa and published first in 1981 by the small feminist publishing house Persephone Press. (After Persephone closed its doors, Kitchen Table, Women of Color Press took over publication, which continues to date). The central characteristics of this anthology epitomize the ideals of multicultural feminism: first, each writer addresses in some way the need for women of color to name themselves, to embark on the often painful process of self-discovery, and then to insist that others acknowledge and respect that identity; second, the collection is based on a new sense of the primacy of relations *between women* and of the importance of accepting differences *among women*. Women of color were fighting the sexism of men, including men of color, and the racism of American society in general, but a hard reality, often provoking despair, was that they also had to face the racism, denial, and discrimination of other women, even other feminists, whether white or women of color. The title *This Bridge Called My Back* expresses both the hope and the pain of women connecting across the chasm of their differences: "bridge" suggests possibility, but it is a possibility for empathy done on the "backs" of women who must lay themselves down to enable other women to make the journey toward them—to allow other women to "walk across" their experience. As Donna Kate Rushin writes in "The Bridge Poem," which opens the collection, "I've had enough/I'm sick of seeing and touching/Both sides of things/ Sick of being the damn bridge for everybody." She has to explain everybody to everybody, she writes, and is "sick of filling in your gaps."

The "Preface to *This Bridge Called My Back*" (1981), by Cherríe Moraga, a Chicana lesbian feminist, illustrates the ideology of the book as a whole. The essay is a kind of journal showing the progress of her framing the book and her evolving sense of the lessons it must instill—and has instilled in her as she has worked through it. Using the Boston train line as an analogue to the metaphor of the bridge, Moraga—herself light-skinned—writes that this collection must make sense of the difference between the white suburb of Watertown (where she begins the essay) and Black Roxbury (one of her destinations). It must also make sense of her own and others' differently fraught journeys (both literal and metaphoric) from white to color and from color to white. To white women who, as Moraga sees it, have made the subject of feminism a unified white subject, who have never bothered to ride the train to Roxbury or anywhere else, and who have thus made the feminist movement exclusive and reactionary, she angrily challenges: "*I call my white sisters on this*." The writings in *Bridge* repeatedly stress that it is up to each individual woman to educate herself about difference and to build her own bridge. Moraga's essay is also infused with the idea that understanding difference is predicated on understanding and accepting oneself and on recognizing within oneself the internalization of the broader social hatred of differences.

Merle Woo's "Letter to Ma" (1981), another essay in *This Bridge Called My Back*, also illuminates the struggles of women of color to battle racism and sexism as well as their own internalized invisibility and victimization on the way to arriving at an empowered sense of their true self. A Chinese/Korean American writer and "Yellow Feminist," Woo writes in a letter to her mother about the essence of her feminism—battling the complacency and ignorance of white women and the sexism of the whole society, including Asian men. But the letter is framed by a much more troubling problem for Woo, that is, her separation from her mother—a Korean immigrant whom she loves and respects but with whom she often finds it difficult to connect. Mother and daughter have, Woo writes, chosen different reactions to racism: while Woo herself has made the deliberate choice to acknowledge her anger and to fight for change, her mother's response "has been one of silence, self-denial, self-effacement." Trying to get her mother to understand her daughter's course of action and conviction, and even to realize the heroism in her history, is the real purpose of this letter—reinforcing the focus of this collection on relationships among women, especially women of color.

Letty Cottin Pogrebin, a founding editor of *Ms.*, enters the common project of rendering the invisible woman visible with her article "Anti-Semitism in the Women's Movement" (1982). Pogrebin's specific focus is mainstream feminism's blind spot for Jewish women and, much worse, the active anti-Semitism of many feminists. This discrimination stems, according to Pogrebin, from built-in biases in the women's movement. The Jewish experience, she argues, does not conform easily to preexisting feminist categories and is not easily explained by the commonplace feminist framework, even after the sustained introjection of relatively recent theories of race and class. In fact, Pogrebin claims that analyses of women's economic oppression based on assumptions about women's poverty and analyses of race based primarily on the experiences of African American women have in part contributed to the imperceptibility of Jewish women's oppression. Pogrebin draws a connection between Jews and women in general in that many members of each group have achieved an economic privilege that does not, however, signify an absence of oppression: "neither misogyny nor anti-Semitism always results in economic privations," she writes. Pogrebin also explains how non-Jewish feminists, ideologically opposed to imperialism and nationalism, have been unable to understand Zionism and have made "Israel a macho imperial stand-in for all the world's male-supremacy." Similarly, feminists have misunderstood Jewish women's faith, having targeted Judaism as the supremely patriarchal religion, responsible for the death not only of a loving and (as some see it) feminist Jesus but also of numerous pre-Judaic goddess-centered religions. In sum, arguing from the specific location of her own particular identity against any totalizing feminist ideologies—whether of class, race, religion, or nation—Pogrebin shows how even the most commonly accepted leftist feminist beliefs (for instance, opposition to imperialism) can contribute to discrimination against a particular group when applied universally.

Emphasizing the importance of acknowledging differences between various ethnic and racial groups of women, Rayna Green's "Diary of a Native-American Feminist" (1982) underlines the rich woman-centered culture that Native American women have inherited from their varied tribes. While the feminism of women of color was often impelled in large part by sexism inherent in the history of intraracial relationships—and even in so-called revolutionary movements to end racism—Green focuses on the consistently empowering historical and contemporary aspects of tribal cultures. Green describes a Mohawk woman proclaiming at a meeting: "'I'm certainly for a return to the old ways. . . . In the old days the women in my tribe ran things, and in some tribes, they still do.'" Paula Gunn Allen's essay, "Who Is Your Mother? Red Roots of White Feminism" (1986), is an elaboration of how many of the dearest feminist tenets have their origins in Native American practices, an influence that has, along with American Indian culture itself, been overlooked. Allen's argument—which is that Indian society, like many contemporary feminists, believed in "the central importance of female energies, autonomy of individuals, cooperation, human dignity, human freedom, and egalitarian distribution of status, goods, and services"—forces a recognition of the particularity of the Native American woman while at the same time forging a bridge between Indians and other groups.

bell hooks, feminist theorist and Professor of English at the City College of the City University of New York, has been a central figure both in pointing out the ways in which women oppressed in one situation can become the oppressor in another—and in calling for coalitions of women who are willing to engage in self-criticism and reach for a feminist solidarity across the many fissures and fractures that divide them. In "Third World Diva Girls: Politics of Feminist Solidarity" (1990), hooks discusses one of the particular problems that risks eroding the feminist community: the creation of token superstars among women of color. Such a practice, and the unthinking adoration of white women directed toward the idealized scholar on which it depends, makes encounters between black women/women of color outside home communities "one of the real danger zones," where the illusion of a feminist coalition utterly breaks down. As hooks describes it, powerful black female "stars" trash other black women whom they have been trained to regard as a threat, and Third World women "stars" ignore their own historical position as colonizers of Africa and reinscribe the colonial paradigm in their relations with Black women. The answer, hooks explains, is a return to a feminist ethics that recognizes "the way in which patriarchal feminist thinking distorts women's relation to one another."

Another aspect of so-called third-wave feminism that emerged in the context of multiculturalism is a fundamental suspicion of clearly demarcated and unchanging categories of identity. Increasingly toward the end of the twentieth century, feminists eschewed "identity politics"—that is, labeling themselves and permanently marking themselves as members of one or even two classes of people (indelibly and only Black Woman, for instance, and thus ignoring the ways that construct may be unsettled by lesbianism, wealth, white blood, Native American ancestry, etc.). A groundbreaking book that challenged the permanence and fixity of identity categories was Gloria Anzaldúa's *Borderlands/La Frontera: The New Mestiza*. In a chapter entitled "*La conciencia de la mestiza*: Towards a New Consciousness" (1987), Anzaldúa describes a new feminist consciousness derived from the geographic, spatial, and cultural location of "*la mestiza*"—the woman inhabiting the borders of white, Mexican, and indigenous cultures; she calls this new way of being "the consciousness of the borderlands." While the beliefs of each of these cultures (white, Mexican, indigenous) attack, contradict, and negate each other, Anzaldúa calls for an acceptance, even an embrace of the ambiguity and fluidity inherent in their confluence; she calls for a rejection of inflexible and clear-cut categories. Denying either-or choices in terms of culture, *la mestiza* serves as a model for all feminists who must destroy the subject-object duality, and all dualistic thinking that emanates from it, which separates "me" from "them," and which results in the projection of unwanted aspects of the self onto others; such dualism is at the root of the split between white and colored, between men and women. A refusal to inhabit the borderlands, to recognize one's own and others' intermingling of identities, has been fatal, Anzaldúa argues. Whites have ignored any reality, any identity, but their own (narrowly, even falsely defined); they have chosen to remain in ignorance, to reject and negate Chicano/as, Mexicans, and Native Americans, and they have, moreover, forced people of color to "barricade ourselves behind our separate tribal walls so they can pick us off one at a time." Walls and borders, like the rigid categories they represent, are literally deadly. Both the internal terrain of the psyche and the external landscape need, for everyone's sake, to resemble instead the fluid borderlands of *la mestiza*.

Anzaldúa's notion of a perpetually shifting and multiple consciousness/borderlands has been labeled by feminist theorist Susan Stanford Friedman "hybridity"—"the cultural grafting that is the production of geographical migration." Hybridity, or cultural grafting, depends on "migration through space" and a "movement through different cultures." The flexibility and ephemerality of this model of identity reflects a distinct shift from the model implicit in *This Bridge Called My Back*, in which women were defined by more fixed categories—Chicana, Black women, dyke, white woman—and in which they traveled *from* their own position *to* that of another, a process that suggests a relatively stable originating and ending point and a meeting of two clearly defined and separate cultural locations. A product of poststructuralist theory, which through the 1980s began to destabilize any notion of categories, whether of gender or race, Anzaldúa's essay, and its notion of hybridity, begins to cast doubt on the permanence or fixity of those categories of identity (now recast as cultural constructions) that structured feminism in the 1970s and early 1980s.

Perhaps as a result of shifting borders, increased immigration, and broader imaginings, American feminists in the 1990s showed a renewed interest in global feminism—a necessary development for the reenvisioning of feminism as a movement that recognizes and celebrates the multitude of differences among *all* women. Global feminism is not new; in 1902 woman suffrage became an international movement with the formation of the International Woman Suffrage Alliance, headed by Carrie Chapman Catt. Throughout the nineteenth century, women had formed international socialist and labor parties such as the Women's Socialist International and the International Ladies Garment Workers Union. In the nineteenth and early twentieth centuries, however, alliances formed were mostly between U.S. and European women—with English women's campaign for the vote, for instance, being of most direct concern to American suffragists. In the 1980s and 1990s global feminism was equally concerned with the state of women in the so-called Third World.

June Jordan, poet and professor of African American studies at the University of California-Berkeley, asks, in "Where Is the Sisterhood?" (1996), published in *The Progressive*, about the worldwide lack of respect for female lives. In doing so, she demonstrates that a familiar concept of American feminism—sisterhood—can and should have global implications. Jordan's title has a double meaning, since she is not only calling for women to band together to end the violence against women who have "no name"—an invisible sisterhood—but she is also pointing out a literal shortfall of women globally. The United Nations' 1995 Report on the World's Women announced there were fewer women in the world than men, and in 1990 economist Amartya Sen wrote that more than 100 million women are "missing" from the world—the result of unequal employment, unequal nutrition, and unequal health care. It is also the result, as Jordan points out, of aborted, murdered, and abandoned baby girls in cultures where boys matter more than girls—and also of the universal violence against women.

One of the most important steps forward in global feminism was a series of world conferences on women organized by the United Nations. The last one of the twentieth century was the United Nations Fourth World Conference on Women held for ten days in Beijing, China, in 1995. Representatives from 189 countries (more than 47,000 people) met and unanimously agreed that inequalities between men and women persist worldwide, with serious consequences for the well-being of all humans. As a result of the conference, by early 1998, 70 percent of 187 national governments had drawn up plans to improve women's rights in their countries. The "Beijing Declaration" (1995), drafted by organizers of the conference as a blueprint for the global advancement of women, persistently connects women's equality with the interests of humanity; "women's rights are human rights," is a refrain of the document. The declaration also connects women with the interests of children and thus with the future.

First Lady Hillary Rodham Clinton's "Remarks to the NGO Forum on Women" (1995) was given as part of a forum that ran concurrently with the Beijing United Nations Conference. NGOs are nongovernmental organizations and, as Clinton points out, they are crucial to the process of change—

putting pressure on often reluctant governments and planning and implementing programs that concretely improve women's lives. Interested in practical change, Clinton exhorts that the outcome of
the conference should be distilled into one easily comprehensible page, so women can carry it into
every village in the world, and so every woman in every village can understand it. The theme of the
conference and the forum, she states, "is about making sure that women, their children, their families, have the opportunities for health care and education, for jobs and political participation, for lives
free of violence, for basic legal protections, and, yes, for internationally recognized human rights no
matter where they are or where they live."

In the group of short essays "Getting There" (1997), published in the twenty-fifth anniversary
issue of *Ms*. magazine, four women of color—Rebecca Adamson, Veronica Chambers, Urvashi
Vaid, and Mari J. Matsuda—manifest a late-twentieth-century feminism that is not white, middle
class, or driven by U.S. and European interests, and that is not even primarily about gender. Instead all four writers recognize a world riven by a poverty and injustice that cross national and
racial boundaries—and yet a world divided by an increasing isolation and atomization. All four
nevertheless imagine the possibility of a global community shaped by feminist values such as tolerance and interdependence.

The two striking, and discouraging, motifs of all four pieces are poverty and isolation. Adamson,
Chambers, and Matsuda all highlight, drawing on their unique experiences as women of color as well
as national and global statistics, the shocking increase of poverty in recent decades. In an essay reminiscent of Paula Gunn Allen's, Adamson, a Cherokee Indian, compares the tribal tradition of a sustainable economy, driven by the values of cooperation, reciprocity, equal relationships, and communal ownership and distribution, with the actuality of a global economy driven by the basic and
self-fulfilling free-market mantra of scarcity of resources. As a result of a world economy driven by
profit, inequality of material wealth has skyrocketed, with the richest 20 percent of the world's population consuming 80 percent of the world's resources. Chambers, an African American, writes of
growing up in a world where everyday hate and poverty literally tried to kill her and her community.
And finally, Matsuda laments the ways in which the manipulation of myths and images ("lies") about
a distinctly racialized poverty—"hardworking Asians and lazy blacks, the erasure of white poverty,
and the women-blaming image of the welfare queen"—has made poverty acceptable in the United
States and has ensured that there will be no "New Deal for our times."

The four women contributing to this forum also all emphasize division and isolation (which is
itself both a cause and effect of global economic equality and the realities and myths of a racialized
poverty). As Adamson points out, it is because the world has denied the interdependence of all people and all nations—their intrinsic responsibilities to each other and to their earth—that resources
and land are depleted, poverty is spreading, and fifty of the top economies in the world are corporations driven by no sense of responsibility but to their own profit margin. Matsuda, similarly, insists
that the problems of poverty and hatred stem from "living in a nation divided" by wealth, patriarchy,
racism, and homophobia. "We don't know much about each other," Matsuda writes, "across lines of
race, class, and sexuality." Chambers, too, writes extensively not only about the division of racism
within the still-mostly white women's movement but also the divisions that obtain among women of
color—homophobia, ageism, discrimination against those with disabilities. Communication has broken down, Chambers writes, over the fault lines of anger and guilt. And, lastly, Vaid also lists breaches
within feminism, asserting that many feminists have simply "abandoned the ideal of a multiracial society." Vaid identifies how the feminist movement has become a series of "ever-narrowing problem
movements": the problems of race devolve on a few groups, as do the problems of abortion, domestic violence, sexual harassment, and so on.

All of the writers call for a comprehensive feminist program that will reach across the rapidly escalating number of divides and isolated specialized groups. As Vaid puts it, "What we need is a progressive platform—a clear economic agenda linked to a cultural vision. In short, a common movement that makes visible the possibility of a democratic future." From Moraga's "bridge," to Anzaldúa's "borderlands," to hooks' "diva girls," feminists of the 1980s and 1990s turned the lens sharply inward, illuminating the differences among women, but then tried to imagine a means of breaching those differences. A refrain of all is that a feminist revolution is *only* possible if women *do* reach across the multitude of ways in which they are separated. In some ways, the unremitting focus on splits among groups of women, and their healing as a precondition for any kind of action against the oppressive system of sexism, seems like a step back from the decades before 1950 when white feminists consistently and directly tackled their oppression by men and patriarchal institutions. But the dream of feminism in which the subject of that movement was unified, and white, was always doomed to fail. Recognizing the multiple subject of feminist movements *is* a precondition to ending sexism.

69

CHERRÍE MORAGA

Preface to *This Bridge Called My Back* (1981)

Change does not occur in a vacuum. In this preface I have tried to recreate for you my own journey of struggle, growing consciousness, and subsequent politicization and vision as a woman of color. I want to reflect in actual terms how this anthology and the women in it and around it have personally transformed my life, sometimes rather painfully but always with richness and meaning.

I TRANSFER AND GO UNDERGROUND

(Boston, Massachusetts—July 20, 1980)

It is probably crucial to describe here the way this book is coming together, the journey it is taking me on. The book is still not completed and I have traveled East to find it a publisher. Such an anthology is in high demand these days. A book by radical women of color. The Left needs it, with its shaky and shabby record of commitment to women, period. Oh, yes, it can claim its attention to "color" issues, embodied in the male. Sexism is acceptable to the white left publishing house, particularly if spouted through the mouth of a Black man.

The feminist movement needs the book, too. But for different reasons. Do I dare speak of the boredom setting in among the white sector of the feminist movement? What was once a cutting edge, growing dull in the too easy solution to our problems of hunger of soul and stomach. The lesbian separatist utopia? No thank you, sisters. I can't prepare myself a rev-

olutionary packet that makes no sense when I leave the white suburbs of Watertown, Massachusetts and take the T-line to Black Roxbury.

Take Boston alone, I think to myself and the feminism my so-called sisters have constructed does nothing to help me make the trip from one end of town to another. Leaving Watertown, I board a bus and ride it quietly in my light flesh to Harvard Square, protected by the gold highlights my hair dares to take on, like an insult, in this miserable heat.

I transfer and go underground.

Julie told me the other day how they stopped her for walking through the suburbs. Can't tell if she's a man or a woman, only know that it's Black moving through that part of town. They wouldn't spot her here, moving underground.

The train is abruptly stopped. A white man in jeans and tee shirt breaks into the car I'm in, throws a Black kid up against the door, handcuffs him and carries him away. The train moves on. The day before, a 14-year-old Black boy was shot in the head by a white cop. And, the summer is getting hotter.

I hear there are some women in this town plotting a *lesbian* revolution. What does this mean about the boy shot in the head is what I want to know. I am a lesbian. I want a movement that helps me make some sense of the trip from Watertown to Roxbury, from white to Black. I love women the entire way, beyond a doubt.

Arriving in Roxbury, arriving at Barbara's.[1] . . . By the end of the evening of our first visit together, Barbara comes into the front room where she has made a bed for me. She kisses me. Then grabbing my shoulders she says, very solid-like "we're sisters." I nod, put myself into bed, and roll around with this word, *sisters,* for two hours before sleep takes on. I earned this with Barbara. It is not a given between us—Chicana and Black—to come to

From Cherríe Moraga and Gloria Anzaldúa, eds., *This Bridge Called My Back: Writings by Radical Women of Color,* 2nd ed. (New York: Kitchen Table, Women of Color Press, 1983), xiii–xix.

1. I want to acknowledge and thank Barbara Smith for her support as a sister, her insights as a political activist and visionary, and especially for her way with words in helping me pull this together.

see each other as sisters. This is not a given. I keep wanting to repeat over and over and over again, the pain and shock of difference, the joy of commonness, the exhilaration of meeting through incredible odds against it.

But the passage is *through,* not over, not by, not around, but through. This book, as long as I see it for myself as a passage through, I hope will function for others, colored[2] or white, in the same way. How do we develop a movement that can live with the fact of the loves and lives of these women in this book?

I would grow despairing if I believed, as Rosario Morales refutes, we were unilaterally defined by color and class. Lesbianism is then a hoax, a fraud. I have no business with it. Lesbianism is supposed to be about connection.

What drew me to politics was my love of women, the agony I felt in observing the straight-jackets of poverty and repression I saw people in my own family in. But the deepest political tragedy I have experienced is how with such grace, such blind faith, this commitment to women in the feminist movement grew to be exclusive and reactionary. *I call my white sisters on this.*

I have had enough of this. And, I am involved in this book because more than anything else I need to feel enlivened again in a movement that can, as my friend Amber Hollibaugh states, finally ask the right questions and admit to not having all the answers.

A BRIDGE GETS WALKED OVER

(Boston, Massachusetts—July 25, 1980)

I am ready to go home now. I am ready. Very tired. Couldn't sleep all night. Missing home. There is a deep fatigue in my body this morning. I feel used up. Adrienne asks me if I can write of what has happened with me while here in Boston. She asks me if I *can* not *would.* I

2. Throughout the text, the word "colored" will be used by the editors in referring to all Third World peoples and people of color unless otherwise specified.

say, yes, I think so. And now I doubt it. The pain of racism, classism. Such overused and trivialized words. The pain of it all. I do not feel people of color are the only ones hurt by racism.

Another meeting. Again walking into a room filled with white women, a splattering of women of color around the room. The issue on the table, Racism. The dread and terror in the room lay like a thick immovable paste above all our shoulders, white and colored, alike. We, Third World women in the room, thinking back to square one, again.

How can we—this time—not use our bodies to be thrown over a river of tormented history to bridge the gap? Barbara says last night: "A bridge gets walked over." Yes, over and over and over again.

I watch the white women shrink before my eyes, losing their fluidity of argument, of confidence, pause awkwardly at the word, "race," the word, "color." The pauses keeping the voices breathless, the bodies taut, erect—unable to breathe deeply, to laugh, to moan in despair, to cry in regret. I cannot continue to use my body to be walked over to make a connection. Feeling every joint in my body tense this morning, used.

What the hell am I getting myself into? Gloria's voice has recurred to me throughout this trip. A year and a half ago, she warned and encouraged: "This book will change your life, Cherríe. It will change both our lives." And it has. Gloria, I wish you were here.

A few days ago, an old friend said to me how when she first met me, I seemed so white to her. I said in honesty, I used to feel more white. You know, I really did. But at the meeting last night, dealing with white women here on this trip, I have felt so very dark: dark with anger, with silence, with the feeling of being walked over.

I wrote in my journal: "My growing consciousness as a woman of color is surely seeming to transform my experience. How could it be that the more I feel with other women of color, the more I feel myself Chicana, the more susceptible I am to racist attack!"

A PLACE OF BREAKTHROUGH: COMING HOME

(San Francisco, California—September 20, 1980)

When Audre Lorde, speaking of racism, states: "I urge each one of us to reach down into that deep place of knowledge inside herself and touch that terror and loathing of any difference that lives there,"[3] I am driven to do so because of the passion for women that lives in my body. I know now that the major obstacle for me, personally, in completing this book has occurred when I stopped writing it for myself, when I looked away from my own source of knowledge.

Audre is right. It is also the source of terror—how deeply separation between women hurts me. How discovering difference, profound differences between myself and women I love has sometimes rendered me helpless and immobilized.

I think of my sister here. How I still haven't gotten over the shock that she would marry this white man, rather than enter onto the journey I knew I was taking. (This is the model we have from my mother, nurturing/waiting on my father and brother all the days of her life. Always how if a man walked into the room, he was paid attention to [indulged] in a particular Latin-woman-to-man way.) For years, and to this day, I am still recovering from the disappointment that this girl/this sister who had been with me everyday of my life growing up—who slept, ate, talked, cried, worked, fought with me—was suddenly lost to me through this man and marriage. I still struggle with believing I have a right to my feelings, that it is not "immature" or "queer" to refuse such separations, to still mourn over this early abandonment, "this homesickness for a woman."[4] So few people re-

ally understand how deep the bond between sisters can run. I was raised to rely on my sister, to believe sisters could be counted on "to go the long hard way with you."

Sometimes for me "that deep place of knowledge" Audre refers to seems like an endless reservoir of pain, where I must continually unravel the damage done to me. It is a calculated system of damage, intended to ensure our separation from other women, but particularly those we learned to see as most different from ourselves and therefore, most fearful. The women whose pain we do not want to see as our own. Call it racism, class oppression, men, or dyke-baiting, the system thrives.

I mourn the friends and lovers I have lost to this damage. I mourn the women whom I have betrayed with my own ignorance, my own fear.

The year has been one of such deep damage. I have felt between my hands the failure to bring a love I believed in back to life. Yes, the failure between lovers, sisters, mother and daughter—the betrayal. How have we turned our backs on each other—the bridge collapsing—whether it be for public power, personal gain, private validation, or more closely, to save face, to save our children, to save our skins.

"See whose face it wears,"[5] Audre says. And I know I must open my eyes and mouth and hands to name the color and texture of my fear.

I had nearly forgotten why I was so driven to work on this anthology. I had nearly forgotten that I wanted/needed to deal with racism because I couldn't stand being separated from other women. Because I took my lesbianism that seriously. I first felt this the most acutely with Black women—Black dykes—who I felt ignored me, wrote me off because I looked white. And yet, the truth was that I didn't know Black women intimately (Barbara says "it's about who you can sit down to a meal with, who you can cry with, whose face you can touch"). I had such strong "colored hunches" about our potential connection, but was basi-

---

3. From "The Master's Tools Will Never Dismantle The Master's House" (from the text).

4. Adrienne Rich, "Transcendental Etude," *The Dream of a Common Language* (New York: Norton, 1978), p. 75.

5. From "The Master's Tools Will Never Dismantle The Master's House" (from the text).

cally removed from the lives of most Black women. The ignorance. The painful, painful ignorance.

I had even ignored my own bloodline connection with Chicanas and other Latinas. Maybe it was too close to look at, too close to home. Months ago in a journal entry I wrote: "I am afraid to get near to how deeply I want the love of other Latin women in my life." In a real visceral way I hadn't felt the absence (only assumed the fibers of alienation I so often felt with anglo women as normative). Then for the first time, speaking on a panel about racism here in San Francisco, I could physically touch what I had been missing. There in the front row, nodding encouragement and identification, sat five Latina sisters. Count them! Five avowed Latina Feminists: Gloria, Jo, Aurora, Chabela y Mirtha. For once in my life every part of me was allowed to be visible and spoken for in one room at one time.

After the forum, the six of us walk down Valencia Street singing songs in Spanish. We buy burritos y cerveza from "La Cumbre" and talk our heads off into the night, crying from the impact of such a reunion.

Sí, son mis comrades. Something my mother had with her women friends and sisters. Coming home. For once, I didn't have to choose between being a lesbian and being Chicana; between being a feminist and having family.

I HAVE DREAMED OF A BRIDGE

(San Francisco, California—September 25, 1980)

Literally, for two years now, I have dreamed of a bridge. In writing this conclusion, I fight the myriad voices that live inside me. The voices that stop my pen at every turn of the page. They are the voices that tell me here I should be talking more "materialistically" about the oppression of women of color, that I should be plotting out a "strategy" for Third World Revolution. But what I really want to write about is faith. That without faith, I'd dare not

expose myself to the potential betrayal, rejection, and failure that lives throughout the first and last gesture of connection.

And yet, so often I have lost touch with the simple faith I know in my blood. My mother. On some very basic level, the woman cannot be shaken from the ground on which she walks. Once at a very critical point in my work on this book, where everything I loved—the people, the writing, the city—all began to cave in on me, feeling such utter despair and self-doubt, I received in the mail a card from my mother. A holy card of St. Anthony de Padua, her patron saint, her "special" saint, wrapped in a plastic cover. She wrote in it: "Dear Cherríe, I am sending you this prayer of St. Anthony. Pray to God to help you with this book." And a cry came up from inside me that I had been sitting on for months, cleaning me out—a faith healer. Her faith in this saint did actually once save her life. That day, it helped me continue the labor of this book.

I am not talking here about some lazy faith, where we resign ourselves to the tragic splittings in our lives with an upward turn of the hands or a vicious beating of our breasts. I am talking about believing that we have the power to actually transform our experience, change our lives, save our lives. Otherwise, why this book? It is the faith of activists I am talking about.

The materialism in this book lives in the flesh of these women's lives: the exhaustion we feel in our bones at the end of the day, the fire we feel in our heart when we are insulted, the knife we feel in our backs when we are betrayed, the nausea we feel in our bellies when we are afraid, even the hunger we feel between our hips when we long to be touched.

Our strategy is how we cope—how we measure and weigh what is to be said and when, what is to be done and how, and to whom and to whom and to whom, daily deciding/risking who it is we can call an ally, call a friend (whatever that person's skin, sex, or sexuality). We are women without a line. We are women who contradict each other.

This book is written for all the women in it and all whose lives our lives will touch. We are a family who first only knew each other in our dreams, who have come together on these pages to make faith a reality and to bring all of our selves to bear down hard on that reality.

It is about physical and psychic struggle. It is about intimacy, a desire for life between all of us, not settling for less than freedom even in the most private aspects of our lives. A total vision.

For the women in this book, I will lay my body down for that vision. *This Bridge Called My Back.*

In the dream, I am always met at the river.

70
MERLE WOO
Letter to Ma (1981)

January, 1980

Dear Ma,

I was depressed over Christmas, and when New Year's rolled around, do you know what one of my resolves was? Not to come by and see you as much anymore. I had to ask myself why I get so down when I'm with you, my mother, who has focused so much of her life on me, who has endured so much; one who I am proud of and respect so deeply for simply surviving.

I suppose that one of the main reasons is that when I leave your house, your pretty little round white table in the dinette where we sit while you drink tea (with only three specks of Jasmine) and I smoke and drink coffee, I am down because I believe there are chasms between us. When you say, "I support you, honey, in everything you do except . . . except . . ." I know you mean except my speaking out and writing of my anger at all those things that have caused those chasms. When you say I shouldn't be so ashamed of Daddy, former gambler, re-

From Moraga and Anzaldúa, *This Bridge Called My Back,* 140–47.

tired clerk of a "gook suey" store, because of the time when I was six and saw him humiliated on Grant Avenue by two white cops, I know you haven't even been listening to me when I have repeatedly said that I am not ashamed of him, not you, not who we are. When you ask, "Are you so angry because you are unhappy?" I know that we are not talking to each other. Not with understanding, although many words have passed between us, many hours, many afternoons at that round table with Daddy out in the front room watching television, and drifting out every once in a while to say "Still talking?" and getting more peanuts that are so bad for his health.

We talk and we talk and I feel frustrated by your censorship. I know it is unintentional and unconscious. But whatever I have told you about the classes I was teaching, or the stories I was working on, you've always forgotten within a month. Maybe you can't listen—because maybe when you look in my eyes, you will, as you've always done, sense more than what we're actually saying, and that makes you fearful. Do you see your repressed anger manifested in me? What doors would groan wide open if you heard my words with complete understanding? Are you afraid that your daughter is breaking out of our shackles, and into total anarchy? That your daughter has turned into a crazy woman who advocates not only equality for Third World people, for women, but for gays as well? Please don't shudder, Ma, when I speak of homosexuality. Until we can all present ourselves to the world in our completeness, as fully and beautifully as we see ourselves naked in our bedrooms, we are not free.

After what seems like hours of talking, I realize it is not talking at all, but the filling up of time with sounds that say, "I am your daughter, you are my mother, and we are keeping each other company, and that is enough." But it is not enough because my life has been formed by your life. Together we have lived one hundred and eleven years in this country as yellow women, and it is not enough to enunciate words and words and words and then to have them only mean that we have been keeping each other company. I desperately want you to understand me and my work, Ma, to know what I am doing! When you distort what I say, like thinking I am against all "caucasians" or that I am ashamed of Dad, then I feel anger and more frustration and want to slash out, not at you, but at those external forces which keep us apart. What deepens the chasms between us are our different reactions to those forces. Yours has been one of silence, self-denial, self-effacement; you believing it is your fault that you never fully experienced self-pride and freedom of choice. But listen, Ma, only with a deliberate consciousness is my reaction different from yours.

When I look at you, there are images: images of you as a little ten-year-old Korean girl, being sent alone from Shanghai to the United States, in steerage with only one skimpy little dress, being sick and lonely on Angel Island for three months; then growing up in a "Home" run by white missionary women. Scrubbing floors on your hands and knees, hauling coal in heavy metal buckets up three flights of stairs, tending to their younger children, putting hot bricks on your cheeks to deaden the pain from the terrible toothaches you always had. Working all your life as maid, waitress, salesclerk, office worker, mother. But throughout there is an image of you as strong and courageous, and persevering: climbing out of windows to escape from the Home, then later, from an abusive first husband. There is so much more to these images than I can say, but I think you know what I mean. Escaping out of windows offered only temporary respites; surviving is an everyday chore. You gave me, physically, what you never had, but there was a spiritual, emotional legacy you passed down which was reinforced by society: self-contempt because of our race, our sex, our sexuality. For deeply ingrained in me, Ma, there has been that strong, compulsive force to sink into self-contempt, passivity, and despair. I am sure that my fifteen years of alcohol abuse have not been forgotten by either of us, nor my suicidal depressions.

Now, I know you are going to think that I hate and despise you for your self-hatred, for your isolation. But I don't. Because in spite of your withdrawal, in spite of your loneliness, you have not only survived, but been beside me in the worst of times when your company meant everything in the world to me. I just need more than that now, Ma. I have taken and taken from you in terms of needing you to mother me, to be by my side, and I need, now, to take from you two more things: understanding and support for who I am now and my work.

We are Asian American women and the reaction to our identity is what causes the chasms instead of connections. But do you realize, Ma, that I could never have reacted the way I have if you had not provided for me the opportunity to be free of the binds that have held you down, and to be in the process of self-affirmation? Because of your life, because of the physical security you have given me: my education, my full stomach, my clothed and starched back, my piano and dancing lessons—all those gifts you never received—I saw myself as having worth; now I begin to love myself more, see our potential, and fight for just that kind of social change that will affirm me, my race, my sex, my heritage. And while I affirm myself, Ma, I affirm you.

Today, I am satisfied to call myself either an Asian American Feminist or Yellow Feminist. The two terms are inseparable because race and sex are an integral part of me. This means that I am working with others to realize pride in culture and women and heritage (the heritage that is the exploited yellow immigrant: Daddy and you). Being a Yellow Feminist means being a community activist and a humanist. It does not mean "separatism," either by cutting myself off from non-Asians or men. It does not mean retaining the same power structure and substituting women in positions of control held by men. It does mean fighting the whites and the men who abuse us, straightjacket us and tape our mouths; it means changing the economic class system and psychological forces (sexism, racism, and homophobias) that really hurt all of us. And I do this, not in isolation, but in the community.

We no longer can afford to stand back and watch while an insatiable elite ravages and devours resources which are enough for all of us. The obstacles are so huge and overwhelming that often I do become cynical and want to give up. And if I were struggling alone, I know I would never even attempt to put into action what I believe in my heart, that (and this is primarily because of you, Ma) Yellow Women are strong and have the potential to be powerful and effective leaders.

I can hear you asking now, "Well, what do you mean by 'social change and leadership'? And how are you going to go about it?" To begin with we must wipe out the circumstances that keep us down in silence and self-effacement. Right now, my techniques are education and writing. Yellow Feminist means being a core for change, and that core means having the belief in our potential as human beings. I will work with anyone, support anyone, who shares my sensibility, my objectives. But there are barriers to unity: white women who are racist, and Asian American men who are sexist. My very being declares that those two groups do not share my complete sensibility. I would be fragmented, mutilated, if I did not fight against racism and sexism together.

And this is when the pain of the struggle hits home. How many white women have taken on the responsibility to educate themselves about Third World people, their history, their culture? How many white women really think about the stereotypes they retain as truth about women of color? But the perpetuation of dehumanizing stereotypes is really very helpful for whites; they use them to justify their giving us the lowest wages and all the work they don't want to perform. Ma, how can we believe things are changing when as a nurse's aide during World War II, you were given only the tasks of changing the bed linen, removing bed pans, taking urine samples, and then only three years ago as a retired volunteer worker in a local hos-

pital, white women gave themselves desk jobs and gave you, at sixty-nine, the same work you did in 1943? Today you speak more fondly of being a nurse's aide during World War II and how proud you are of the fact that the Red Cross showed its appreciation for your service by giving you a diploma. Still in 1980, the injustices continue. I can give you so many examples of groups which are "feminist" in which women of color were given the usual least important tasks, the shitwork, and given no say in how that group is to be run. Needless to say, those Third World women, like you, dropped out, quit.

Working in writing and teaching, I have seen how white women condescend to Third World women because they reason that because of our oppression, which they know nothing about, we are behind them and their "progressive ideas" in the struggle for freedom. They don't even look at history! At the facts! How we as Asian American women have always been fighting for more than mere survival, but were never acknowledged because we were in our communities, invisible, but not inaccessible.

And I get so tired of being the instant resource for information on Asian American women. Being the token representative, going from class to class, group to group, bleeding for white women so they can have an easy answer—and then, and this is what really gets to me—they usually leave to never continue their education about us on their own.

To the racist white female professor who says, "If I have to watch everything I say I wouldn't say anything," I want to say, "Then get out of teaching."

To the white female poet who says, "Well, frankly, I believe that politics and poetry don't necessarily have to go together," I say, "Your little taste of white privilege has deluded you into thinking that you don't have to fight against sexism in this society. You are talking to me from your own isolation and your own racism. If you feel that you don't have to fight for me, that you don't have to speak out against capital-

ism, the exploitation of human and natural resources, then you in your silence, your inability
to make connections, are siding with a system
that will eventually get you, after it has gotten
me. And if you think that's not a political
stance, you're more than simply deluded,
you're crazy!"

This is the same white voice that says, "I am
writing about and looking for themes that are
'universal.'" Well, most of the time when "universal" is used, it is just a euphemism for
"white": white themes, white significance,
white culture. And denying minority groups
their rightful place and time in U.S. history is
simply racist.

Yes, Ma, I am mad. I carry the anger from
my own experience and the anger you couldn't
afford to express, and even that is often misinterpreted no matter how hard I try to be clear
about my position. A white woman in my class
said to me a couple of months ago, "I feel that
Third World women hate me and that *they* are
being racist; I'm being stereotyped, and I've
never been part of the ruling class." I replied,
"Please try to understand. Know our history.
Know the racism of whites, how deep it goes.
Know that we are becoming ever more intoler-
ant of those people who let their ignorance be
their excuse for their complacency, their liberalism, when this country (this world!) is going
to hell in a handbasket. Try to understand that
our distrust is from experience, and that our
distrust is power*less*." Racism is an essential part
of the status quo, power*ful,* and continues to
keep us down. It is a rule taught to all of us
from birth. Is it no wonder that we fear there
are no exceptions?

And as if the grief we go through working
with white women weren't enough; so close to
home, in our community, and so very painful,
is the lack of support we get from some of our
Asian American brothers. Here is a quote from
a rather prominent male writer ranting on
about a Yellow "sister":

". . . I can only believe that such blatant
sucking off of the identity is the work of a Chinese American woman, another Jade Snow

Wong Pochahontas yellow. Pussywhipped
again. Oh, damn, pussywhipped again."

According to him, Chinese American
women sold out—are contemptuous of their
culture, pathetically strain all their lives to be
white, hate Asian American men, and so marry
white men (the John Smiths)—or just like
Pochahontas: we rescue white men while betraying our fathers; then marry white men, get
baptized, and go to dear old England to become curiosities of the civilized world. Whew!
Now, that's an indictment! (Of all women of
color.) Some of the male writers in the Asian
American community seem never to support
us. They always expect us to support them, and
you know what? We almost always do. Anti-
Yellow men? Are they kidding? We go to their
readings, buy and read and comment on their
books, and try to keep up a dialogue. And they
accuse us of betrayal, are resentful because we
do readings together as Women, and so often
do not come to our performances. And all the
while we hurt because we are rejected by our
brothers. The Pochahontas image used by a
Chinese American man points out a tragic
truth: the white man and his ideology are still
over us and between us. These men of color,
with clear vision, fight the racism in white society, but have bought the white male definition of "masculinity": men only should take on
the leadership in the community because the
qualities of "originality, daring, physical
courage, and creativity" are "traditionally masculine."[1]

Some Asian men don't seem to understand that by supporting Third World women
and fighting sexism, they are helping themselves as well. I understand all too clearly how
dehumanized Dad was in this country. To be a
Chinese man in America is to be a victim of
both racism and sexism. He was made to feel
he was without strength, identity, and purpose. He was made to feel soft and weak,

---

1. *AHEEEEE! An Anthology of Asian American Writers,*
editors Frank Chin, Jeffrey Paul Chan, Lawson Fusao In-
ada, Shawn Wong (Howard University Press, 1974).

whose only job was to serve whites. Yes, Ma, at one time I was ashamed of him because I thought he was "womanly." When those two white cops said, "Hey, fat boy, where's our meat?" he left me standing there on Grant Avenue while he hurried over to his store to get it; they kept complaining, never satisfied, "That piece isn't good enough. What's the matter with you, fat boy? Don't you have respect? Don't wrap that meat in newspapers either; use the good stuff over there." I didn't know that he spent a year and a half on Angel Island; that we could never have our right names; that he lived in constant fear of being deported; that, like you, he worked two full-time jobs most of his life; that he was mocked and ridiculed because he speaks "broken English." And Ma, I was so ashamed after that experience when I was only six years old that I never held his hand again.

Today, as I write to you of all these memories, I feel even more deeply hurt when I realize how many people, how so many people, because of racism and sexism, fail to see what power we sacrifice by not joining hands.

But not all white women are racist, and not all Asian American men are sexist. And we choose to trust them, love and work with them. And there are visible changes. Real tangible, positive changes. The changes I love to see are those changes within ourselves.

Your grandchildren, my children, Emily and Paul. That makes three generations. Emily loves herself. Always has. There are shades of self-doubt but much less than in you or me. She says exactly what she thinks, most of the time, either in praise or in criticism of herself or others. And at sixteen she goes after whatever she wants, usually center stage. She trusts and loves people, regardless of race or sex (but, of course, she's cautious), loves her community and works in it, speaks up against racism and sexism at school. Did you know that she got Zora Neale Hurston and Alice Walker on her reading list for a Southern Writers class when there were only white authors? That she insisted on changing a script done by an Asian

American man when she saw that the depiction of the character she was playing was sexist? That she went to a California State House Conference to speak out for Third World students' needs?

And what about her little brother, Paul? Twelve years old. And remember, Ma? At one of our Saturday Night Family Dinners, how he lectured Ronnie (his uncle, yet!) about how he was a male chauvinist? Paul told me once how he knew he had to fight to be Asian American, and later he added that if it weren't for Emily and me, he wouldn't have to think about feminist stuff too. He says he can hardly enjoy a movie or TV program anymore because of the sexism. Or comic books. And he is very much aware of the different treatment he gets from adults: "You have to do everything right," he said to Emily, "and I can get away with almost anything."

Emily and Paul give us hope, Ma. Because they are proud of who they are, and they care so much about our culture and history. Emily was the first to write your biography because she knows how crucial it is to get our stories in writing.

Ma, I wish I knew the histories of the women in our family before you. I bet that would be quite a story. But that may be just as well, because I can say that *you* started something. Maybe you feel ambivalent or doubtful about it, but you did. Actually, you should be proud of what you've begun. I am. If my reaction to being a Yellow Woman is different than yours was, please know that that is not a judgment on you, a criticism or a denial of you, your worth. I have always supported you, and as the years pass, I think I begin to understand you more and more.

In the last few years, I have realized the value of Homework: I have studied the history of our people in this country. I cannot tell you how proud I am to be a Chinese/Korean American Woman. We have such a proud heritage, such a courageous tradition. I want to tell everyone about that, all the particulars that are left out in the schools. And the full awareness of being a woman makes me want to sing. And I do sing with other Asian Americans and women, Ma, anyone who will sing with me.

I feel now that I can begin to put our lives in a larger framework. Ma, a larger framework! The outlines for us are time and blood, but today there is a breadth possible through making connections with others involved in community struggle. In loving ourselves for who we are—American women of color—we can make a vision for the future where we are free to fulfill our human potential. This new framework will not support repression, hatred, exploitation and isolation, but will be a human and beautiful framework, created in a community, bonded not by color, sex or class, but by love and the common goal for the liberation of mind, heart, and spirit.

Ma, today, you are as beautiful and pure to me as the picture I have of you, as a little girl, under my dresser-glass.

I love you,
Merle

71

LETTY COTTIN POGREBIN

Anti-Semitism in the Women's Movement (1982)

Why now? Why write about anti-Semitism and the Women's Movement when we have the Moral Majority and Ronald Reagan to worry about?

Because, very simply, it's there. And because I am a Jew who has been finding problems where I had felt most safe—among feminists.

- On hearing that I planned to write about anti-Semitism, one feminist asked, "Won't

Ms. have to give equal time to the PLO?" Incredible. When did anti-Semitism turn into a "balanced issue," with Palestine Liberation Organization interests skewed into a respectable other side? Must we remind people that those who are against anti-Semitism are against Jew-hating? The opposite is not to be pro-PLO. The opposite is to be *for* Jew-hating.

- A white civil rights activist proudly described having organized interracial groups of women in Little Rock, Arkansas. "We went out in teams," she said. "A black woman, a Jewish woman, and a white woman." She never noticed that she had made Jews a race apart.

- Midge Costanza gave me a view from the inside: "Because I'm known as an Italian-Catholic, Gentile women feel they can say anti-Semitic things to me, like 'Why should we carry the Jews on our backs,' as if Jews are responsible for the energy problem, or 'That one's a Jew so there's no arguing with her.' But the worst was at the 1980 Democratic Convention when a bunch of women were tossing around names to speak on various platform issues. I was amazed when both Jews and non-Jews discarded certain Jewish names because they thought having a Jew associated with an issue would hurt."

- A month or so before the United Nations Women's Conference in Copenhagen in 1980, I asked a black friend to sign a petition. Five years before, the PLO had monopolized the Mexico City women's conference to drag Israel through the mud and to declare Zionism racism. There were signs that Copenhagen would be exploited for a similar purpose, and some of us felt a petition warning against this time bomb might defuse it.

My friend told me the Copenhagen conference was a hot topic in the black community. Trade-offs were being negotiated; an anti-apartheid resolution might be passed in return for American blacks' compliance on a Palestinian agenda item.

"Please understand," said my friend. "I can't afford to sign."

I understand that large numbers of Jewish women, far out of proportion to our percentage in the population, have worked for civil rights, welfare rights, Appalachian relief—issues that did not necessarily affect our own lives. What I do *not* understand is how much we must live through before our non-Jewish sisters can "afford" to make anti-Semitism their concern.

• When American Jewish women returned from that Copenhagen conference stung by anti-Semitic experiences, some women here at home chose not to believe their stories or called their reactions "Jewish paranoia."

I cannot think of any feminist context in which a woman's testimony—whether about sexism or racism—would be disregarded or labeled "female paranoia." Why the gap when women speak bitterness about anti-Semitism?

Are Jewish women overreacting? Evelyn Torton Beck, professor of Women's Studies at the University of Wisconsin at Madison, thinks not: "At one community conference, our posters advertising a full-day workshop on homophobia and anti-Semitism were torn down—and this happened in locations that sponsored feminist activities, in women's bathrooms and women's bars. At the university where I teach, posters for my course on 'The Jewish Woman' were ripped and defaced. I heard someone say that Jews were 'taking over' the local chapter of the National Lesbian Feminist Organization in Madison."

Because anti-Semitism has been an issue at the National Women's Studies Conference, last summer, an ad hoc group called Feminists Against Anti-Semitism organized a panel on "Anti-Semitism as Racism." One panelist, Esther Broner, asked rhetorically "Why this eternal buzzing of the Jew?"—and then answered: "Because we Jews feel fragile. Because a third of our people have been destroyed in our own lifetimes and the ashes of mourning cling to our clothes."

Before accusing us of overreacting, our Christian sisters should try to understand the immediacy of our mourning and the 5,000 years of terror that echo in our souls.

After the great outcry against Israel's annexation of the Golan Heights, I heard a woman joke, "Israel is Hitler's last laugh on the Jews"—as if Menachem Begin's ultra-nationalism would ultimately destroy the Jewish people better than Hitler could. I do not think criticism of Begin is automatically anti-Semitic any more than criticism of Ronald Reagan is anti-American. However, now that it is open season for attacks on Israel, such criticism, often under the rubric of "anti-Zionism," is sometimes a politically "respectable" cover of anti-Semitism. Jews learn to call it as we feel it. I felt the woman's "joke" was anti-Semitic, but I did not insist that far from being a joke, Israel is a haven for a people against whom someone is always engineering the "last laugh." I said nothing. For the first time, I felt afraid. I worried about my feminist friends' commitment to Jewish survival and about their opinions of events in the Middle East.

I considered why Jewish women *are* validated by the women's movement when we trudge through Judaic subcultures ruffling beards with our demands for reform but not when we bring Jewish consciousness back the other way into feminism; or why we are cheered when we critique the Bible for its anti-woman bias but not when we criticize feminists for their anti-Jewish jokes.

I thought of how often I had noticed Jews omitted from the feminist litany of "the oppressed." And I began to wonder why the Movement's healing embrace can encompass the black woman, the Chicana, the white ethnic woman, the disabled woman, and every other female whose struggle is complicated by an extra element of "outness," but the Jewish woman is not honored in her specificity? Will feminism be our movement only so long as we agree not to make our Jewishness an issue? *Must we identify as Jews within feminism with as much discomfort as we identify as feminists within Judaism?*

I needed to know if these questions were plaguing anyone else. So for many months I talked to more than 80 women from several feminist constituencies and other than the half dozen who said they had never been made to feel uncomfortable as Jews in the Movement, every woman had a story to tell.

Of course, it should not surprise us to find anti-Semitism within feminism. Unless one consciously explores the connections between all forms of oppression, it is possible to, say, work for black rights and still be a sexist or work for women's rights and still be a racist.

Racism among feminists has long been admitted, or at least given lip service, when women assemble anthologies, courses, or conferences. My point is that anti-Semitism has not yet risen to the level of concern or talk, much less action. Maybe this is because we Jews have not made it an issue; or because Jewish women are perceived as influential within the Movement and often in the nonfeminist world as well. But are we? Or is this perception part of the stereotype and thus part of the reason why anti-Semitism remains the hidden disease of the Movement?

To cure it, we need to examine the five problems basic to Jews and sisterhood.

PROBLEM 1
FAILURE TO SEE THE PARALLELS

Time and again I heard women use the phrase "Jews are the women of the world," or its converse, "Women are the Jews of the world." Yet feminism has never systematically analyzed the similarities between anti-Semitism and sexism the way that racism and sexism are understood as twin oppressions. The parallels are striking:

- Just as woman comes in two opposing archetypes, Madonna and whore, so is the Jew split in two: victim (Anne Frank) and victimizer (Shylock).
- The myth of "female power" (in terms of sexual or maternal omnipotence) recasts the male in the vulnerable role and thus justifies discrimination against women; the myth of "Jewish power" recasts the Christian majority as pawns, and helps justify repression of the Jews.
- "Jews really control the press," "White women really control the wealth," and "Black matriarchs really control black men" are three equally inaccurate clichés invented to mask the overwhelming concentration of power and money in the hands of *white Christian men*.
- The existence of some leisured women and some affluent Jews is claimed as proof that *all* members of both groups are privileged.
- Woman (wife, prostitute, secretary) serves as a buffer between the capitalist system and the exploited male worker, thus sexism absorbs men's economic frustration by buying them off with privatized patriarchal power. Similarly, Jew (landlord, teacher, or homemaker-employer) serves as a buffer between the dominant class and the underclass, thus deflecting their rage onto a convenient scapegoat.
- All-purpose inferiors, both women and Jews are reminded incessantly of how we differ from the "norm." We are, interchangeably, the "quintessential Other," says historian Paula Hyman. Each group is hated because it demands "the right to be both equal and distinctive"—whether that distinctiveness means women's culture or Jewish culture, women's physical differences or Jewish religious differences. We make the "superior" group angry because we want to maintain our uniqueness without being penalized for it.
- Both women and Jews have to struggle to have their oppression recognized, even by its victims, because neither misogyny nor anti-Semitism always results in economic privations. Instead, these hatreds are their own weapons honed by age-old mystical fears. The mystique of the *intrinsic* sexual-psychic evil of both women and Jews makes plausible periodic purges of Jews and bizarre accusations against women.

• "Women are too powerful" was the underlying impetus for the slaughter of 9 million "witches" and the advancement of a repressive patriarchal religious establishment. "Jews are too powerful" was the argument Hitler used to promote himself as champion of the working class against rich "Jewish bankers." (Similar anti-Semitic innuendos are used today to mobilize Polish nationalism, a trick that utilizes Jew-hating even in a country that has only a handful of Jews left.)

Every so often, when times are especially hard, Jews get identified as "the problem." Lately, so do women. Times are harder now—and both anti-Semitism and antifeminism are on the rise. Nevertheless, Jewish women concerned about anti-Semitism are often scolded for raising "side issues," and are asked to wait until "larger" inequities are solved.

Here too, there is a parallel: those who would berate us for mentioning anti-Semitism at this time—for "holding the interests of Jews above the interests of women"—ignore the fact that some of all women are Jews and half of all Jews are women. Like those who berate feminists for "holding the interests of women above the interests of blacks," or poor people, or any group, such critics ignore that half of *every* group is women. In short, asking Jews to blur themselves into womankind as defined by non-Jews is like asking feminists to blur themselves into humanism as defined by males.

The failure to see these parallels and make them integral to feminist theory has meant that anti-Semitism and we who care about it are not yet taken seriously in the Women's Movement.

PROBLEM 2
THE BIG SQUEEZE:
ANTI-SEMITISM FROM THE RIGHT
AND FROM THE LEFT

In the current climate, Jewish feminists have a special need for the Women's Movement to be a safe harbor from two raging storms.

On the lunatic right, overt anti-Semitic violence, vandalism, swastika-painting and desecrations have increased in the last three years. The KKK, Nazis, White Solidarity Movement, and National States' Rights Party burn crosses and curse Jews, blacks, and feminists in one fiery breath. Such groups accuse the Women's Movement of forcing Christian women into the workplace and the military where blacks and Jews are conspiring to commit lesbianism and miscegenation. The purpose of the Equal Rights Amendment, they say, is to "destroy the white Christian family and discourage the birth of white children."

To build opposition to the ERA, the extremists appeal to anti-Semitic feelings that the Harris and Yankelovich public-opinion polls have found present in one third of Americans. At the Houston Women's Conference I remember banners saying "Kikes for Dykes" and "Abzug, Friedan, and Steinem are all anti-Christian Jews." Comedian Maxine Feldman got police protection when she performed at the conference. "There were three hundred KKK in the audience carrying placards that read, 'Kill all dykes, kikes, commies, and abortionists,'" she recalls, "and I was three out of four."

In Illinois, fliers bearing a picture of a mutilated woman warned that if the ERA passed, women would be drafted to fight in Israel and would end up looking like her. A broadside sent to each state senator lists "Zionist names" connected to the ERA plot to wreck Christian homes by "pitting wives against husbands." It cautions: "Wake up, Americans! Roll back Zionist one-worldism before . . . the ruling Jews take all the honey, leaving only the wax for you Christian Goyim."

Lyndon LaRouche's U.S. Labor Party and Willis Carto's Liberty Lobby hammer at three themes: the Jews killed Christ; the Holocaust is a hoax; and Zionism is racism.

These cranks used to be easy to ignore, but the proliferation of vandalism and assaults in "respectable" neighborhoods makes the fringe seem less remote. What's more, the lunatics have made it seem reasonable and tame when Birchers or fundamentalists call for "a Christian America" or disingenuously stigmatize Jews.

Reverend Bailey Smith, president of the Southern Baptist Convention, followed his claim that "God almighty does not hear the prayer of a Jew," with this comment in a subsequent sermon: "Why did God choose the Jews? I don't know why. I think they've got funny-looking noses myself." He later said he was misunderstood.

The Rev. Dan C. Fore, former chair of the New York Moral Majority, told the *New York Times:* "Jews have a god-given ability to make money. . . . They control the media; they control this city."

Confounding the landscape on the right are:

- Neoconservative Jews like Norman Podhoretz and Irving Kristol who, along with Reagan Republicans, are smugly anti-affirmative action and antifeminist.
- Anti-ERA, antichoice Orthodox Jews, such as the organization of rabbinical wives who invited Phyllis Schlafly to be their dinner speaker.
- Fundamentalist Christians like Jerry Falwell who claim to support Israel, but whose support does not seem to be founded on any dedication to Jewish survival but on a biblical prophecy that says a Jewish state must exist in order to set the stage for Jesus' Second Coming—after which all Jews must convert or be damned.

What concerns me as much as these unholy alliances are those feminists who seem to believe that a monolithic right-leaning "Jewish vote" has been responsible for the defeat of some feminist issues or candidates when, in fact, we have our Ayatollahs and our Gandhis like every group.

While the right plays new tricks with American Jews, the problems on the left are old and familiar. Much leftist anti-Semitism stems from radicals' inability to understand that individual Jews' economic success is not the same as Jewish political power, let alone the power to assure one's own group safety.

Karen Lindsey explains: "The black struggle fits fairly comfortably into a leftist economic analysis: most U.S. blacks are poor or working class with little access to good jobs or the education that might lead to them. . . . But the oppression of Jews does not so easily lend itself to a simplistic class analysis." (As noted, neither does the oppression of women.)

Ellen Willis goes further: "The oppression of Jews is not economic oppression, it is the dynamic of anti-Semitism. It is when anti-Semitism exists and people do not admit it exists and accuse the victim of paranoia."

Another painful phenomenon on the left is the guilt of Jewish children of families who made it into the middle class; their disavowal of their parents' values and fear for their leftist credentials prevent them from identifying with other Jews. In the civil rights years, Lindsey recalls, they "identified themselves more as white oppressors than as Jewish oppressed, and their Gentile co-workers did nothing to discourage this view."

This sort of guilt-tripping and radical myopia is even more blatant in connection with Israel. "I've never recovered from hearing a woman at a feminist meeting scream, 'Golda Meir is not my sister: she's a fascist,'" says Elenore Lester. "By making Israel a macho imperial stand-in of all the world's male supremacy, the Women's Movement threw me into the arms of Judaism."

Somehow, leftists who espouse one-world transnationalism make exceptions for "national liberation" struggles and independent nation states in Latin America, Africa, or anywhere *but* Israel.

Israel is supposed to commit suicide for the sake of Palestinian "liberation." Jewish women are supposed to universalize themselves so that Palestinian women can have a national identity. Zionists have no standing on the left. Palestinians are all assumed to be have-nots and Israelis the affluent hosts—the parents who made it.

"Anti-Israel leftists have no idea of who Zionists are," says Sharone Abramowitz. "They don't know that the majority of Israeli Jews are dark-skinned, poor, and uneducated refugees from Arab and north African countries."

Asked to justify their PLO support, many leftist feminists say that they are taking sides in a clash between European imperialism and Third World anticolonialism. They do not see the Israeli-Palestinian problem as a conflict between two national movements with complex historical origins. Pressed, they show ignorance of even the vaguest outlines of Jewish experience, and yet they freely prescribe what Jews or Israel should or should not do.

"I try to give feminists a thirty-minute crash course in Jewish history, but they don't want to know," says Judy Dlugacz. "It's just not cool to be a Zionist. It makes you a pariah in radical feminist circles."

Many Jews believe that pro-PLO women in America are expressing their anti-Semitism as surely as pro-Afrikaner whites in South Africa are assumed to be expressing their racism:

- Barbara Seaman faults the Southern women's health center that displayed pro-PLO posters on the walls—as if anti-Zionist Third World solidarity went hand-in-hand with justice in health issues.
- A British feminist said anti-Zionism turns into anti-Semitism because people define "Zionism as a racial characteristic instead of a cultural phenomenon."
- Three New York women protested when the 1981 International Women's Day forum sponsored by a "Committee Against Genocide" paired a speaker decrying apartheid with a speaker decrying Zionism—implying they are comparable evils—and when *Womanews,* a feminist paper, chose to list the forum as an important *women's* event.
- Phyllis Chesler is tired of hearing women say that Israel's Law of Return is racist. (Mindful

of the time when Jewish refugees were the "Boat People" of the world, the Law grants automatic Israeli citizenship to any Jew.) "I am saddened and angered by feminists who would never call a separatist coffeehouse or women's center sexist, but who are quick to call the Law of Return racist," insists Chesler.

And I agree. If we can understand why history entitled lesbians to separatism, or minorities and women to affirmative action, we can understand why history entitles Jews to "preferential" safe space. *To me, Zionism is simply an affirmative action plan on a national scale.* Just as legal remedies are justified in reparation for racism and sexism, the Law of Return to Israel is justified, if not by Jewish religious and ethnic claims, then by the intransigence of worldwide anti-Semitism.

Because nations tend to be capricious about protecting Jewish rights, our survival has been tenuous through the ages: think about the Diaspora (the Babylonian exile of Jews from the Middle East in the sixth century B.C.), and the crushing defeats by the Romans in the first century; think about the Crusades, the Spanish Inquisitor of the 16th century, the 19th-century pogroms that drove Jews out of Eastern Europe, Stalin's purges, Hitler's "final solution," or the fact that both the Pope and Franklin Roosevelt were silent after receiving graphic early reports on the fate of European Jews in the concentration camps, and "ordinary" French, Italians, and Poles turned in their Jews to the Nazis.

Given virtually every country's record of treating us as surplus citizenry, the survival of Israel is vital to the survival of Jews. It's that simple.

Like many, I cling to hopes of a two-state solution that does not demand Israel's suicide. I long for a PLO counterpart to the Israeli peace groups so that rational dialogue may begin. But PLO moderates, rare as they are, seem to have been silenced by their own violent hardliners; I have heard that many—including some peace-seeking women—fear for their lives. In the absence of peace initiatives and open sisterhood, I am left to assume (according to PLO sentiments expressed in Copenhagen) that the average Palestinian woman would wish me dead. Until this changes, I have no tolerance for anti-Zionists even if they are feminists. Again, like many Jews, I have come to consider anti-Zionism tantamount to anti-Semitism because the political reality is that its bottom line is an end to the Jews.

Andrea Dworkin put it brilliantly: "In the world I'm working for, nation states will not exist. But in the world I live in, I want there to be an Israel." To those leftists who excuse their anti-Israel position because of the Begin administration, Dworkin answers: "I resent the expectation that, having been oppressed, Jews should exercise a higher morality running their country than anyone else. The idea that suffering purifies is Christian, not Jewish."

Some assert that anti-Zionism has become the left's socially acceptable response to "the uppity kike" the way anti-feminism is to "the uppity broad." Ellen Willis cites the case of Vanessa Redgrave, the pro-PLO actress who "exemplifies a mentality that has flourished ever since 1967, when Israel became the prime metaphor for the powerful Jew: [Redgrave] hates Bad Jews—Zionists—loves Good Jews—victims, preferably dead. . . ." But the power of Jews as emotional symbols would mean little if they were not hugely outnumbered and so in reality powerless. It is that combination that makes anti-Semitism so appealing: to kill a gnat, imagining it's an elephant, is to feel powerful indeed.

Where does all this leave us? Caught in the big squeeze. The Moral Majority uses its pro-Israel position as proof that it likes Jews. The left insists that its anti-Israel position doesn't mean it *doesn't* like Jews. "Attacked from the left for being too well-off and from the right for being too left wing, Jews lack even the contingent power of dependable political allies," says Willis, describing our classic double bind. To the Third World, we are white oppressors, but to our fellow white oppressors, we are

Jews. No wonder so many Jewish women are finding it harder and harder to find an ideological home. And no wonder we so badly need to create a feminist politic flexible enough to absorb differing views of Jewish women's issues, but firm enough to resist anti-Semitism with a single voice.

PROBLEM 3
THE THREE I'S

What women experience as anti-Semitism varies from *invisibility* (the omission of Jewish reality from feminist consciousness) to *insult* (slurs, Jew-baiting, and outright persecution) to *internalized oppression* (Jewish self-hatred, which some call the most pernicious anti-Semitism of all).

Invisibility

Andrea Dworkin calls it "being insensitive to genocides that are immediate to me." When the reality of the Holocaust is denied or trivialized or labeled "Jewish self-centeredness," Dworkin feels the chill of anti-Semitism. "My whole family in Eastern Europe was almost totally wiped out. I grew up among the few survivors. I understand when someone says, 'My great-grandmother was a slave,' but I don't feel the same understanding from others when I say 'My aunt was in Auschwitz.'"

Evie Beck described invisibility as a form of oppression that works against both Jews and lesbians. "When you're invisible, you lose your voice," she says. "But becoming visible opens you to attack. I found it easier to tell straight people I'm lesbian than to tell some feminists that I'm Jewish."

T. Drorah Setel, a student rabbi and coordinator of the Feminist Task Force of the New Jewish Agenda, laments: "I am unseen as a feminist among Jews and unseen as a Jew among feminists. Had I been black or Latina, my commitment to my community of origin would have been acceptable and my attachment to my people would have been honored."

Miriam Slifkin, a scientist and former president of North Carolina NOW, remembered a conference in her state at which some women insisted on an opening prayer that was "full of Our Fathers and Christ's name. It never occurred to them that there were Jews in the room. I asked that the prayer be struck from the record in respect for non-Christian women and the chair, Libby Koontz, made it official."

Other complaints of invisibility focus on scholars overlooking the latent anti-Semitism that fueled the nativism of some suffragists who objected that ignorant immigrants could vote while native-born *Christian* women could not. Or on women's courses and conferences that always include suffragists, slaves, Christian temperance workers, but not always Jewish garment workers, labor organizers, or ghetto social workers.

Insult

Women's testimony about anti-Semitic insults is more complex. "Everyone's so laid back out here," says Phyllis Katz of Boulder, Colorado. "When someone attacks you as an 'outspoken, intellectual female from New York,' you're not sure if they're putting you down as a feminist, a Jew, or an Easterner."

"I'm perceived as intimidating and overbearing; in other words, Jewish," says Philadelphia's Evie Litwok. "Well, my style is a result of my being the child of survivors of the Holocaust. I was brought up to take risks. That style is a threat to some women. They've tried to destroy the behavior I need to survive."

Insults often result from an ironic overlap between the typecasting of Jews and feminists: both groups are characterized by outsiders as loud, pushy, verbal, domineering, middle class. Yet, within feminism, the attributes and expressive habits culturally associated with Jewish ethnicity—such as being raised to speak our minds, to trade on education and eloquence when there is no other currency, to interrupt, or else be interrupted—contradict the ideal of (Quaker meetinghouse turn-taking) sisterhood.

Jewish stock types also present extra problems in feminism. For instance, the Jewish Mother epitomizes the self-sacrificing, maternal role that many feminists most vocally repudiate.

Pauline Bart of Chicago is troubled by this: "My Jewish qualities are as discriminated against in the lesbian movement as a height requirement would discriminate against Puerto Ricans in the fire department.

"The ideal dyke personality is in direct conflict with my socialization as a Jew. The acceptable dyke is a jock. She's into mechanical things like fixing cars or carpentry. She's tough, unemotional, nonmonogamous. In short, the model for the ideal dyke is an adolescent, working-class Gentile male—right down to the body build, the cap, and the butch jacket. There's no way I can fill that role."

The Jewish Princess stereotype—a materialistic child-woman, indulged by her parents and educated to lure a husband—runs dead against the feminist ideal of a strong, up-front, self-supporting radical who demands her rights, and makes her own life. (In 1971, *Off Our Backs* ran a comic strip lampooning "a Jewish Princess named Felicia" who had a nose job, a lawyer father, a dentist husband, three children, a split-level in Jersey, a powder-blue Mustang, and played bridge every Thursday.)

A third stereotype, the Exotic Jewess, is usually portrayed as dark, voluptuous, close to "animal" sexuality and privy to carnal mysteries. This feminized "dirty Jew" stereotype gave the Cossacks an excuse to rape women of the *shtetl* (a small ghetto village); it is useful to pornographers, sexual sadists, and even to the Christian mainstream in which Eve, the Old Testament temptress, is cast as inventor of Original Sin. Diane Gelon, administrator of Judy Chicago's "Dinner Party," says she often heard comments like "It must have been done by Jewish women; it's so blatantly sexual."

Add to these distinctly female stereotypes the old "classics," the Jewish Intellectual, the Jewish Moneymaker, and there is no room for us to be *anything* without triggering someone's preconception.

Gloria Greenfield's experiences illuminate the point:

"As publisher and treasurer of Persephone Press, I get a lot of heat. When negotiating the financial terms of a contract, I've been accused of being 'cunning,' a 'cheap Jew,' or of 'Jewing someone down.' When Evie Litwok and I gave financial workshops, several women said we were only into money because we're Jews. They reduced our revolutionary strategy for women's economic self-sufficiency to a Jewish *business*.

"As for the intellectual put-down, a lot of feminists see women's studies as an organizing tool; when I say I see it as serious research, I'm called a bourgeois Jewish intellectual. Bourgeois! My parents are Russian immigrants. Neither of them went to high school. My mother is a janitor; my father works as a cabdriver and a hospital worker. Feminists could try to understand what education means to someone like me."

Andrea Dworkin has altered her behavior to defy the stereotype: "I keep quiet at meetings more than I should because I don't like feeling singled out as the Jew with the words.

"I grew up poor in Camden, New Jersey, where Jews had to stay on our own block. For us, reading and writing was the only thing they couldn't take away from us. Even though I was a girl, my family encouraged me to become literate. And now, in the Women's Movement, I am made to feel self-conscious about being 'an intellectual.'"

As feminists should know well, stereotypes often originate in group survival techniques and coping mechanisms that have been flattened into caricature. Stereotypes are also barriers to intimacy because they deny individual complexities. They add insult to injury, transforming group pride and survival strengths into cause for shame. And they hurt.

Internalized Oppression

Both Inge Lederer Gibel and Cynthia Ozick reminded me of the words of Rosa Luxemburg, the German Communist leader who had this response to a letter about the atrocities and pogroms against the Jews in Eastern Europe: "Why do you pester me with your special Jewish sorrows? . . . I cannot find a special corner in my heart for the ghetto."

Luxemburg, a Jew, went on to speak movingly of suffering Africans, Asians, and Indians—which at the time prompted one historian to marvel at the phenomenon of a group so capable of compassion for others but only of contempt for its own. Of course, the overall record of Jewish philanthropy to other Jews disproves that generalization, but it is true enough in its particulars to rankle. (And to give me the chills, for not one Jew in Rosa Luxemburg's Polish town was left alive by the Germans in World War II.)

If today's women also slough off our "special Jewish sorrows," it is because many of us have internalized anti-Semitic views of everything Jewish—including our suffering—adding a double unworthiness for being both female and Jewish. Self-hatred and denial of a part of oneself or one's origins is a kind of *invisibility imposed from within*.

Oddly enough, internalized oppression is a luxury. Like the Queen Bee, the "only Jew in the club" functions best when denial of one's group is possible and assimilation is permitted. As factual oppression worsens, assimilated Jews have historically been forced to rediscover their Jewishness one way or another. (Although under most conditions Jews can choose to pass where blacks cannot, Hitler proved that a society can rout out its Jews regardless of their denial or disguise.)

I think the current rebirth of Jewish identity among feminists—or at least the desire to confront anti-Semitism—is a repudiation of that internalized oppression that kept us closeted.

It is no accident that this Jewish "coming out" process has in many feminist communities been spearheaded by lesbians. Having opened the windows on one secret identity and not only survived but flourished, lesbians seem less willing to live with another part of their identity repressed—and more willing to brave the consequences within feminism of calling attention to those "special Jewish sorrows."

No matter how "un-Jewish" we are, no matter how unobservant, atheistic, disconnected to the Jewish community or the State of Israel, more and more women who were *born* Jewish are coming to believe they must deal with what that identity means to them and how they feel about other Jews and Jewish issues.

On January 11, 1981, at the San Francisco Women's Building, 350 Bay Area feminists showed up for a forum on "Anti-Semitism in the Women's Community." Fifty had been expected. The women who organized the event—Sharone Abramowitz, Marsha Gildin, Chaya Gusfield, and Pnina Tobin—filled the program with a history of anti-Semitism, a short skit on women resistance fighters in the Warsaw ghetto, a presentation on Jewish women in the labor movement, another on anti-Semitism in the early suffrage movement, and a listing on a blackboard of all the Jewish stereotypes called out by women in the crowd. But it was the speak-out on "passing" that brought forth visceral pain and dammed-up tears.

Rising from the audience, woman after woman told of how she hated her "Jewish nose" and had it "fixed"; how she straightened her despised kinky "Jewish hair"; how she allowed herself to be mistaken for Italian or Puerto Rican; how hard she worked to get rid of her "Jewish accent" or to force herself to stop talking with her hands; or how inevitably she preferred to identify as a civil rights worker, a Marxist, a veggie, a radical feminist—anything but a Jew.

Tobin felt that the forum was important to build Jewish awareness and strength in the face of the rise of the right. She, too, had been denying her roots. "In the 1960s, I tried to be a hippie mother—white Anglo Southern California mellow," says Tobin. "Only now am I reclaiming the positive qualities of the Jewish mother in me: the strength, the warmth, the characteristics of the *shtetl*. They may seem outmoded here, but when children's lives are in danger, like in the pogroms, it's important for women to hover and protect. Also I was finally able to admit that the feminist format for consciousness-raising is not right for me; it's frustrating for anyone whose training is to get excited, interrupt, argue within the '*mishpacha*' [family], and expect enough love and warmth to absorb it all."

Another common symptom of internalized oppression is described by Maxine Feldman: "As a kid, I was the only Jew on my block to keep my own nose, and in the Movement's early days, I was the only one to keep my own name. Women were changing their names if they had a 'man' ending. They said it was to deny the patriarchy, but they were also denying their Jewish identities. Feldman is a Jewish name, not a male name. When they asked why I didn't change it, I answered, 'Why don't Margie *Adam* and Cris *Williamson* change theirs?'"

Pianist-composer Davida Goodman also uses the name Ishatova, which is "good woman" in Hebrew. She chose to identify as a Jewish woman for the first time at the West Coast Women's Music Festival at Yosemite. To a hushed audience she talked about her pianist mother, a survivor of Auschwitz; she played the same Chopin piece that her mother played in the concentration camp and read a poem about her mother.

"People came up to me crying," said Goodman. "They told me, 'I'm Jewish' or 'I live with a Jew' or tried to make some connection. Since then I have a feeling of 'my people' with Jewish women."

"I feel reborn as a Jew in the Women's movement," said Arlene Raven, founder of Chrysalis and the L.A. Woman's building. "What had been shushed out of me is up front now."

For poet and writer Louise Bernikow, the absence of negativism is enough of a positive: "I came from a lower-class Jewish family and I had an image of a Jewish girl locked in the attic with the Nazis outside her door. I obliterated my own Jewishness. Most of my friends were Christian. The night I went to the New York feminist seder was the first time I'd ever been at an organized Jewish women's event. I was deeply moved by the ceremony. But I was more moved by the fact that Gloria Steinem was there talking about her Jewish grandmother and identifying as a Jew when she is half-Jewish and had the choice *not* to."

This business of *identifying* was posited in a new way by a Gentile friend: "Would you say to your c-r group 'I'm a Jew' or 'I'm Jewish?'" she asked. "Why does 'Jew' seem to be a racial slur, and 'Jewish' the polite liberal term?"

Her questions made me realize that almost all the women I interviewed called themselves "Jewish"; few said, "I'm a Jew." Is this a clue to our self-hatred? Do we avoid the noun as too strong an embodiment, too central an identity? Is the adjective a means of diminishing or taming the Jew-part of our identity? (Jewish woman is as bland in its way as working woman, Democratic woman, Southern woman.) Have we absorbed the anti-Semite's invective use of "Jew" to the point where we cannot speak our tribal name without fear?

PROBLEM 4
RELIGION, GODS, AND GODDESSES: THE 5,000-YEAR-OLD MISUNDERSTANDING

There is a morning prayer in which every Orthodox Jewish man thanks God for not creating him a woman. "I wish I had a nickel for every time a feminist has quoted that prayer to argue the supreme sexism of the Jewish faith," says Pnina Tobin. "That prayer has probably been spoken more often by anti-Semitic non-Jews than by Jewish worshipers."

Several years ago, Leonard Swidler wrote an essay that has become the basic catechism of Christian feminists. In it he argued that "Jesus was a feminist" because he broke with many Jewish customs that mistreated women. However comforting this thesis may be for some (especially in view of the misogyny of the religious right), it leaps over all the Christian sexism perpetrated in Jesus' name, from the mas-

culinist liturgy to the lack of women apostles, to the Catholic refusal to ordain women priests—and it has been used to make Judaism the heavy among patriarchal religions. In fact, a major focus of attention at the December, 1981, convention of Catholic, Jewish, and Protestant Feminists of Faith was the "disconcerting trend toward anti-Semitism" in the writings of some Christian feminists.

"The more negative they can make Judaism," explains Judith Plaskow, who teaches religion at Manhattan College, "the more feminist Jesus appears for veering away from it."

When asked if she was flatly denying the sexism in Judaism's origins, Plaskow replied: "Obviously Judaism is patriarchal. This hurts us deeply. Yet it's one thing when we articulate it in our terms and another when it is taken up by Christians as evidence that Jews are *more* patriarchal than any other people. Just as Jews have been called *more* Communist, or *more* stiff-necked, or more whatever, this kind of projection of humanity's ills onto one group has been used against women. It is what we as feminists are committed to destroy."

Speaking of projection, a feminist who believes menstrual blood is sacred told me flatly one day that Jews killed the pagan glories of the female religion by inventing the patriarchal God of Abraham. As I listened to this spiritualist "sister," the commonality of our menstrual blood disappeared. It was my Jewish blood that ran cold. We "Christ-killers" had become "Goddess-killers." Feminism or not, how far have I come if I am still called murderer?

Miriam Schneir points out that ancient Judaism was against polytheism, rather than against women, and that it took Christianity to articulate the rabid woman-hating that culminated in church-led witch-hunts. Yet, Judaism takes the rap for the death of the female deity in several Spiritualist/Matriarchist books, most notably *The First Sex,* by Elizabeth Gould Davis (Putnam's, 1971), and *A Different Heaven and Earth,* by Sheila D. Collins (Judson, 1974).

Plaskow, who is also coeditor of *Womanspirit Rising: A Feminist Reader in Religion* (Harper &

Row, 1979), says of those authors: "They over-look the fact that many goddess-worshiping cults were themselves patriarchal or that the Goddess was being dethroned long before Judaism came along."

Goddesses may have become important symbols to many feminists for whom both Christianity and Judaism are beyond the pale. But, warns Cynthia Ozick, "Let's not romanticize them. Their purpose was often human sacrifice. Babies were killed to appease them. Mothers were brainwashed to want their children chosen for death."

"The present feminist spirituality movement wipes out the fact that for its time, Judaism was a tremendous step forward," insists Tillie Olsen. "The old religions were terrible. And who needs goddesses anyway? Why not dignify ourselves with the actual achievements of real women: shelter, food gathering, the invention of language. Why let men's definition of religion be the source of our spirituality?"

PROBLEM 5
BLACK-JEWISH RELATIONS

If parallels between women and Jews are sometimes missed, parallels between Jews and blacks are almost too obvious—so close, in fact, that rather than inspire coalitions, they incite what Susan Weidman Schneider calls "a competition of tears."

I think the reason we often fail to identity together is the same for both black women and Jewish women: we do not always have the ability to be feminists *first*. Right now, for example, I feel more vulnerable in America as a Jew than as a woman.

Many black women have suffered more for their race than their sex. Many Jewish women, from biblical times through the Holocaust, have been slaughtered not because they were female but because they were Jewish. As a result, both groups have often chosen to stand in solidarity with their men against a hostile world rather than explore shared circumstances and synthe-

size an analysis that includes racism, sexism, *and* anti-Semitism.

Black women have been criticized by some white feminists for putting race ahead of sex. From my new perspective and with my sense of Jewish vulnerability, I understand this and I wonder whether the feminist world view needs to be expanded to recognize times when sisterhood must bow to "peoplehood" for blacks and Jews.

Instead we do little more than compare burdens and police one another's privileges. Historically, we have been pitted against each other: in ghetto slums as the poorest housing passes to the lowliest newcomer group; in competition for liberal philanthropic dollars; in transitional neighborhoods and suburbs; in schools and jobs where a finite number of slots is reserved for all non-WASPs to divide amongst themselves. That this game of blacks versus Jews is continued in the Women's Movement is one of the gravest failures of feminism.

Many Jewish women specifically resent that, for years, they have talked openly about "confronting" their racism, while with a few noteworthy exceptions black women's anti-Semitism has been largely unmentionable.

My interviews suggest this is changing. Jewish women are asking their black sisters to deal with the fact that they (like other Gentiles) stereotype, scapegoat, and stigmatize Jews—not just because we are white, but because we are Jews. Don McEvoy of the National Conference of Christians and Jews puts it succinctly: "Being anti-Semitic is one way for blacks to buy into American life."

Jewish women I interviewed mentioned certain grievances more than once. For example, this passage from Iva E. Carruthers' "War on African Familyhood," an essay in the anthology *Sturdy Black Bridges* (Anchor, 1979): "*Today one of the most serious assaults to African familyhood is being forged by the white feminist movement; the theory for which is emerging from a predominantly Jewish elite group . . .*"

Carruthers goes on to identify "Aryan intrusion" as the means by which Jewish feminists destroy African familyhood; the grating irony of equating Jew and Aryan is evidently lost on her.

Also cited by some Jews as deeply offensive were two poems in *Conditions 5,* the issue on racism. In Carole Clemmons Gregory's poem, "Love Letter," a black Delilah suggests that the Jewish Samson would use his God-given strength to kill black people. And these lines from Judy Simmons' poem, "Minority," seemed gratuitously divisive:

> mine is not a People of the Book / taxed but acknowledged;
>
> their distinctiveness is
>
> not yet a dignity; their Holocaust
>
> is lower case

That "competition of tears" foolishly pits slavery against the Nazi genocide as though inhumanity was a zero-sum phenomenon and there was only so much moral outrage to go around.

"Over and over again I heard blacks complain that 'The Holocaust' film on television was the Jews' way of stealing the spotlight from 'Roots,'" said a black friend. "The average black is not sympathetic toward any white person who is brutalized or discriminated against. A lot of black women resist the Women's Movement because they think it's full of pushy Jewish women who have nothing to do but complain; but when the going gets rough they have their men to protect them."

Barbara Smith, the black feminist writer and activist, said: "I think it's important for Jewish women to claim their oppression but acknowledge their white-skin privilege. At the same time I understand why women of color find it hard to accept that anyone with white-skin privilege can be oppressed. It is necessary for both groups to make an effort to comprehend each other's situation."

Renée Franco runs workshops on black-Jewish issues in Boston and Atlanta. "Anti-Semitism from minority groups, as well as from people in general, is based on misinformation about Jews," she maintains. "Women say to me, 'You don't look or act Jewish,' and when I challenge them they say they mean I'm not loud or rich and I don't have a Jewish accent." Franco is a Sephardic Jew who was raised in the American South.

Inge Lederer Gibel spent most of her adult life in the civil rights movement. At a retreat organized to discuss sexism and racism, Gibel raised the problem of elderly Jewish women living in poor neighborhoods. "If they have been mugged and robbed by black teenage boys and they are now afraid of black males, do we tell them they are racists?" she asked. Gibel reported that one black woman fliply answered: "Nobody gets mugged unless they're looking for trouble."

"I said, 'I don't think mugging old women is funny,'" Gibel continued. "The black woman yelled back at me, 'That's why you people have always been in trouble, and are always going to be in trouble.' I asked her, "What do you mean by 'you people?'" She snarled, "You know what I mean." She called me a racist, and suggested I go into the next room with her and fight it out physically.

"Some people see white racism as the *only* evil on earth, but ignore anti-Semitism, which is the oldest form of racism."

In 1979, when United Nations Ambassador Andrew Young resigned after admitting he had met secretly with a PLO representative, many blacks blamed his ouster on "the Jews." Among those heard from were several important black women. Esther E. Edwards, director of the Regional Office of the National Black Human Rights Caucus, said, "Young was used as a scapegoat to appease Jewish ethnics here and in Israel. . . ."

Sherry Brown, president of the Frederick Douglass Community Improvement Council of Anacostia, told the Washington *Post:* "We have to understand who our true enemies are. Jews have historically profited as slumlords and merchants from the suffering of black people."

Most disturbingly, Thelma Thomas Daley, then president of Delta Sigma Theta, a predominantly black sorority of some 100,000 members, took off from the Young affair to accuse Jewish groups of "subverting affirmative action programs." She showed no awareness of the great numbers of Jewish *women's* groups who have worked for affirmative action from the very start.

In an interview in the *NewYork Times,* Daley said of Jews: "We have been patient and forbearing in their masquerading as friends under the pretense of working for the common purpose of civil rights. . . . [T]heir loyalties are not compatible with the struggle of black Americans for equal opportunity under the law. Indeed, we question whether their loyalties are first to the State of Israel or to the United States." Given black Americans' special support for African Americans' special support for African nations, this statement seemed especially insensitive.

Of course, while our groups remain divided, our most violent enemies continue to see us as one and the same. According to Klanwatch, a project of the Southern Poverty Law Center, men and women in the KKK are "prepared to kill black people and Jews in the 'race war' their leaders say is coming." And pornographers, sadists, and rapists make interchangeable use of black women and Jewish women as the ultimate sexualized victim. As Susan Brownmiller points out, "the reputation of lasciviousness and promiscuity" is black women's and Jewish women's historic common bond. Unless we ourselves forge a healthier, more life-enhancing bond, we leave it to our enemies to tell us who we are and what we have in common.

Some readers may be relieved that this report corroborates their own experiences. Others may feel disheartened and wish for some hopeful proposals for dealing with anti-Semitism in the Women's Movement so that it doesn't divide us. I'm sorry to say I have no such proposals. Instead, I feel suddenly akin to the many black women I know who have refused to take responsibility for curing white racism. I feel angry and sad and I find myself agreeing with Cynthia Ozick: "It is for decent persons to come forward and sound that note of hope, either through self-repair or through declarations of

abhorrence for anti-semitism. We Jews can't get rid of anti-Semitism by ourselves."

72

RAYNA GREEN

Diary of a Native-American Feminist (1982)

The vignettes that follow tell a story—about Native-American women, about what they're doing and thinking these days, about the many parts that make up the American Indian Women's Movement. These scenes don't tell the whole story, but in my travels as the director of the Native-American Science Resources Center at Dartmouth College, I have listened to (and recorded in journal form) the stories of Native-American women. I have seen their health and vitality, their toughness and the tragedy of their need to be so tough. Those stories will be told by voices that remain soft, in numbers that stay small. Sometimes they are humorous or heartening; sometimes they are hard to hear at all. But they give strength to Native people in this country. Perhaps they also will mean something to others.

FALL, 1977, BILLINGS, MONTANA

Three hundred Indians from Montana tribes assemble in a hotel conference room to discuss energy development on reservation lands. Far from enthusiastic about the economic gains promised by that development, most Native people remain skeptical of its "benefits." A middle-aged man from one of the Plains tribes stands to lament the detrimental effects that economic and environmental change will bring to Indian cultures. He cites a perceived shift in sex-role behavior as one example of the passion of the old ways, noting how some women are even running for tribal council and defying traditional male leadership to do so. But an older Mohawk woman, a fed-

From *Ms.*, July/August 1982. Reprinted by permission of the author.

eral official from a long tradition of matriarchal leadership, rises to rebut him and brings down the house. "I'm certainly for a return to the old ways," she tells the audience. "In the old days, the women in my tribe ran things, and in some tribes, they still do. So bring back the old days." My friends and I are delighted. Her speech isn't exactly the opening shot of the revolution, but it puts Indian women where I don't always believe we are—squarely in the feminist consciousness. Later, some of us talk about the upcoming National Women's Conference in Houston and the planned participation of Indian women. Several of them feel we'll have as hard a time persuading majority feminists to listen to us as we did with the old boys out in the audience earlier today. Some think the real problem will be in getting the multitribal delegation of Native women together in this forum really quite new to us. Tribal differences and the press of other life-and-death issues may rob us of what majority feminists call "sisterhood," we worry. "Perhaps," I say, "but Indian women will be seen and heard in the context of the Women's Movement." Bring on the new days. Bring on the new days.

SPRING, 1979, LAWRENCE, KANSAS

Hundreds of women gather in Lawrence for the National Women's Studies Association meeting, and the organizers are justifiably celebratory. As at the IWY Conference in Houston, the presence of so many native women stirs interest. While no one fetes us, we do feel much like the visiting delegation from the People's Republic of China—a welcomed oddity. Staff photographers cannot resist photographs of tribal women, and we find ourselves elated at our success. People attend our panels and workshops, and we work with other Third World women on mutual concerns. Still, as usual, we struggle to explain who and what we are to women who think that the term "minority" explains us and who know very little about the state of Indian people in this country. But it works for now.

The scholar-activists among us, including Clara Sue Kidwell (Chippewa-Choctaw) and Twila Martin Kekabah (Chippewa), have just formed a new national consortium called "Ohoyo" (Choctaw for "woman"), and we are trying our new wings at NWSA.

Owanah Anderson (Choctaw) says we must determine what we can adapt and use from the Women's Movement, and so we try here. There are as many versions of Indian feminism as there are tribes, we tell other women at Lawrence, and we are grateful that we have some new friends to tell it to.

FALL, 1980, ALBUQUERQUE, NEW MEXICO

After the opening day of Ohoyo's first national meeting, we talk in my hotel room about the *Martinez* v. *Santa Clara* case, just decided by the Supreme Court in favor of Santa Clara Pueblo.

Shirley Hill Witt (Akwesasne Mohawk), an anthropologist and director of the Rocky Mountain Regional Office of the U.S. Commission on Civil Rights, Carol Connor (Assiniboine/Sioux), just out of law school, Marjorie Bear Don't Walk (Salish-Chippewa), a Montana nutritionist and designer whose clothes some of us wear, and Ada Deer (Menominee), legislative liaison for the Native-American Rights Fund, go over the case, not altogether in harmony. Mrs. Martinez sued her tribe on sex discrimination because, married to a non-Indian, she and her children were denied tribal health and education benefits. Yet Pueblo males who married non-Indians still retained rights to benefits as did their children. Tribal lawyers argued the case on tribal sovereignty (the right of a tribe, under guarantees by treaty, to govern itself and determine its own forms and statutes of governance). All of us agree that based on this decision, the Santa Clara might extend that discrimination to employment, credit and other areas. Yet, all of us are grateful that the court upheld tribal sovereignty. We are, as the saying goes, between a rock and a hard place.

Someone points out that the Indian Health Service still denies benefits to non-Indian spouses of Indian women while offering them to non-Indian spouses of men. We debate whether such rules are traditional with Indian cultures or whether they have been "imported" from European "patriarchal" traditions. And we debate whether we should attack Native tradition the way majority feminists have attacked their own and the traditions of other non-Western peoples. If we tamper with things, some of us think we'll be worse off than ever, and Indian experience with programs developed to "benefit" us certainly affirms that position. Whatever the source of the problem, some say, the tribes should now honor the women equally.

The argument cannot be resolved here, and to ease the impasse, we joke. But as we laugh in that Albuquerque hotel room, Mrs. Martinez and all the others haunt us. The double bind of race and sex is too real. Two powerful words—tradition and equality—do battle with one another in Indian country. But whose version of tradition and whose version of equality should we fight for?

FALL AND WINTER, 1980, ON THE ROAD

As usual, I'm traveling on business. In Spokane, Washington, I go to an Indian political meeting and spend a lot of time with an old friend, LaDonna Harris (Comanche). Her latest incarnation as hell-raiser is her candidacy for Vice-President of the United States on the Citizens' Party ticket. She has carried her longtime advocacy for Indian people into a national forum where Indian women are virtually nonexistent or ignored. She describes the strangeness of being in that milieu, but talks about the strong support of Indian women—the group of Ute women whose poster announced that they were "Round and Brown for LaDonna." She won't win the election, but she will have broken one more barrier.

On to the Daybreak Star Center in Seattle, Washington, where the newly formed Women of All Red Nations (WARN) has convened. I recall recent visits with Katsi Cook (Akwesasne Mohawk), a former WARN member, whose "women's dance health project" works to restore women's traditional knowledge of their bodies. "In a traditional world Native women understood their bodies in terms of the earth and the moon." Katsi says, "They walked holding hands with Grandmother Moon. The women's dance reminded them of their close relationship to Mother Earth, a reflection of their own power to give and sustain life. The consciousness of the women's dance has to be the consciousness of our survival as women. We need to take back our power as human beings on the female side of life."

For Katsi and others like her at Akwesasne, the return to traditional patterns of living will allow Indian people to take back their power as human beings. They reject the authority of modern, elected governments, and have reconstructed older and enduring forms of traditional governance that include women in major decision-making roles. They live communally under clan systems, stressing self-sufficiency and environmentally conservative economic systems. When Katsi says that "the nuclear family is the moral equivalent of nuclear power," she makes two points important to the people she represents.

Women like Katsi are the "radicals" of Indian country. The WARN women, with many behind them, signal Indian women's major involvement in the important Indian issues of our time—water, fishing, and treaty rights, tribal termination, and self-determination, Indian cultural retention. Women's issues fit easily into these rubrics. Women like Katsi, gentle but assured, fit into the mold of sixties' and seventies' militant leadership exercised by women like Kahn Tineta Horn (Mohawk) at the takeover of Alcatraz Island, Lorelei Means (Lakota Sioux) at the battle of Wounded Knee II, Ramona Bennett (Puyallup) and Janet Mc-

Cloud (Tulalip), who lead the battles for aboriginal fishing rights in Washington State. They follow the strong tradition of Constance Redbird Pinkerman-Uri (Cherokee/Choctaw), a physician-lawyer who first blew the whistle on sterilization abuse of Indian women and lobbied for the new federal sterilizations regulations that benefit all women.

But these are strange "radicals" who insist on upholding the Constitution by upholding treaties and who wish to return to old ways of behavior, not overthrow them. These are strange radicals—some of whom believe that abortion is as wrong as unnecessary sterilization, while genuinely conservative Indian women may be profoundly prochoice. Looking for feminist or radical orthodoxy will be a fruitless search in Indian country and I know that my mainstream isn't that far apart from WARN's revision of the world. If "left" and "right" don't mean much—in terms of the issues basic to Indian survival—to Indian women, perhaps we have something important to share with other feminists.

EARLY SPRING, 1981, TAHLEQUAH, OKLAHOMA

The second national Ohoyo meeting, and I wander from room to room in a university student union. In one, women from 30 different tribes talk about getting the Equal Rights Amendment passed in Oklahoma, and they see no conflict of interest between justice for Indian women and tribal sovereignty. With satisfaction, they note that the Indian Health Service recently amended its ruling on denial of services to women's non-Indian spouses. I breathe easier than I did in Albuquerque.

In another room, Thelma Forrest (Cherokee) shows some women the products of her successful crafts program for women of the Cherokee Nation. I think of my grandmother as I hold up each of these new revivals of traditional rivercane, honeysuckle, oak, and buckbrush baskets. The book display and film show-

ings draw me and others to see ourselves reflected in print and cinematic versions.

Directed by Owanah Anderson and with assistance from the U.S. Women's Education Equity Act Program, Ohoyo has become the center of activity for a number of Indian women throughout the country. This year in Tahlequah, the historic and present capital of the Cherokee Nation, grandmothers, tribal council women, and chairwomen, tribal and urban community developers, national and local political leaders have come here to talk and plan for the future of Native women. Most here would not describe themselves as "feminists" or as part of the "Women's Movement." But they are all quite clear about the need for attention to Native women, and they are vocal about the burdens they bear because they are female. Here, as Ada says, "we are mobilizing our strength to survive."

73

Paula Gunn Allen

Who Is Your Mother? Red Roots of White Feminism (1986)

At Laguna Pueblo in New Mexico, "Who is your mother?" is an important question. At Laguna, one of several of the ancient Keres gynocratic societies of the region, your mother's identity is the key to your own identity. Among the Keres, every individual has a place within the universe—human and nonhuman—and that place is defined by clan membership. In turn, clan membership is dependent on matrilineal descent. Of

From Paula Gunn Allen, *The Sacred Hoop: Recovering the Feminine in American Indian Traditions* (Boston: Beacon Press, 1986); reprinted in Rick Simonson and Scott Walker, eds., *The Graywolf Annual Five: Multicultural Literacy* (St. Paul, Minn.: Graywolf Press, 1988), 13–27. Copyright 1986, 1992 by Paula Gunn Allen. Reprinted by permission of Beacon Press, Boston.

course, your mother is not only that woman whose womb formed and released you—the term refers in every individualcase to an entire generation of women whose psychic, and consequently physical, "shape" made the psychic existence of the following generation possible. But naming your own mother (or her equivalent) enables people to place you precisely within the universal web of your life, in each of its dimensions: cultural, spiritual, personal, and historical.

Among the Keres, "context" and "matrix" are equivalent terms, and both refer to approximately the same thing as knowing your derivation and place. Failure to know your mother, that is, your position and its attendant traditions, history, and place in the scheme of things, is failure to remember your significance, your reality, your right relationship to earth and society. It is the same thing as being lost—isolated abandoned, self-estranged, and alienated from your own life. This importance of tradition in the life of every member of the community is not confined to Keres Indians; all American Indian Nations place great value on traditionalism.

The Native American sense of the importance of continuity with one's cultural origins runs counter to contemporary American ideas: in many instances, the immigrants to America have been eager to cast off cultural ties, often seeing their antecedents as backward, restrictive, even shameful. Rejection of tradition constitutes one of the major features of American life, an attitude that reaches far back into American colonial history and that now is validated by virtually every cultural institution in the country. Feminist practice, at least in the cultural artifacts the community values most, follows this cultural trend as well.

The American idea that the best and the brightest should willingly reject and repudiate their origins leads to an allied idea—that history, like everything in the past, is of little value and should be forgotten as quickly as possible. This all too often causes us to reinvent the wheel continually. We find ourselves discovering our collective pasts over and over, having to retake ground already covered by women in the preceding

decades and centuries. The Native American view, which highly values maintenance of traditional customs, values, and perspectives, might result in slower societal change and in quite a bit less social upheaval, but it has the advantage of providing a solid sense of identity and lowered levels of psychological and interpersonal conflict.

Contemporary Indian communities value individual members who are deeply connected to the traditional ways of their people, even after centuries of concerted and brutal effort on the part of the American government, the churches, and the corporate system to break the connections between individuals and their tribal world. In fact, in the view of the traditionals, rejection of one's culture—one's traditions, language, people—is the result of colonial oppression and is hardly to be applauded. They believe that the roots of oppression are to be found in the loss of tradition and memory because that loss is always accompanied by a loss of a positive sense of self. In short, Indians think it is important to remember, while Americans believe it is important to forget.

The traditional Indians' view can have a significant impact if it is expanded to mean that the sources of social, political, and philosophical thought in the Americas not only should be recognized and honored by Native Americans but should be embraced by American society. If American society judiciously modeled the traditions of the various Native Nations, the place of women in society would become central, the distribution of goods and power would be egalitarian, the elderly would be respected, honored, and protected as a primary social and cultural resource, the ideals of physical beauty would be considerably enlarged (to include "fat," strong-featured women, gray-haired, and wrinkled individuals, and others who in contemporary American culture are viewed as "ugly"). Additionally, the destruction of the biota, the life sphere, and the natural resources of the planet would be curtailed, and the spiritual nature of human and nonhuman life would become a primary organizing principle of human society. And if the traditional tribal systems that are emulated included pacifist ones, war would cease to be a major method of human problem solving.

RE-MEMBERING CONNECTIONS
AND HISTORIES

The belief that rejection of tradition and of history is a useful response to life is reflected in America's amazing loss of memory concerning its origins in the matrix and context of Native America. America does not seem to remember that it derived its wealth, its values, its food, much of its medicine, and a large part of its "dream" from Native America. It is ignorant of the genesis of its culture in this Native American land, and that ignorance helps to perpetuate the long-standing European and Middle Eastern monotheistic, hierarchical, patriarchal cultures' oppression of women, gays, and lesbians, people of color, working class, unemployed people, and the elderly. Hardly anyone in America speculates that the constitutional system of government might be as much a product of American Indian ideas and practices as of colonial American and Anglo-European revolutionary fervor.

Even though Indians are officially and informally ignored as intellectual movers and shapers in the United States, Britain, and Europe, they are peoples with ancient tenure on this soil. During the ages when tribal societies existed in the Americas largely untouched by patriarchal oppression, they developed elaborate systems of thought that included science, philosophy, and government based on a belief in the central importance of female energies, autonomy of individuals, cooperation, human dignity, human freedom, and egalitarian distribution of status, goods, and services. Respect for others, reverence for life, and, as a by-product, pacifism as a way of life; importance of kinship ties in the customary ordering of social interaction; a sense of the sacredness and mystery of existence; balance and harmony in relationships both sacred and secular were all features of life among the tribal confederacies

and nations. And in those that lived by the largest number of these principles, gynarchy was the norm rather than the exception. Those systems are as yet unmatched in any contemporary industrial, agrarian, or postindustrial society on earth.

There are many female gods recognized and honored by the tribes and Nations. Femaleness was highly valued, both respected and feared, and all social institutions reflected this attitude. Even modern sayings, such as the Cheyenne statement that a people is not conquered until the hearts of the women are on the ground, express the Indians' understanding that without the power of woman the people will not live, but with it, they will endure and prosper.

Indians did not confine this belief in the central importance of female energy to matters of worship. Among many of the tribes (perhaps as many as 70 percent of them in North America alone), this belief was reflected in all of their social institutions. The Iroquois Constitution or White Roots of Peace, also called the Great Law of the Iroquois, codified the Matrons' decision-making and economic power:

"The lineal descent of the people of the Five Fires [the Iroquois Nations] shall run in the female line. Women shall be considered the progenitors of the Nation. They shall own the land and the soil. Men and women shall follow the status of their mothers" (Article 44).

"The women heirs of the chieftainship titles of the League shall be called Oiner or Otinner [Noble] for all time to come" (Article 45).

"If a disobedient chief persists in his disobedience after three warnings [by his female relatives, by his male relatives, and by one of his fellow council members, in that order], the matter shall go to the council of War Chiefs. The Chiefs shall then take away the title of the erring chief *by order of the women in whom the title is vested*. When the chief is deposed, the women shall notify the chiefs of the League . . . and the chiefs of the League shall sanction the act. The women will then select another of their sons as a candidate and the chiefs shall elect him" (Article 19) (Emphasis mine).[1]

The Matron held so much policy-making power traditionally that once, when their position was threatened they demanded its return, and consequently the power of women was fundamental in shaping the Iroquois Confederation sometime in the sixteenth or early seventeenth century. It was women

"who fought what may have been the first successful feminist rebellion in the New World. The year was 1600, or thereabouts, when these tribal feminists decided that they had had enough of unregulated warfare by their men. Lysistratas among the Indian women proclaimed a boycott on lovemaking and childbearing. Until the men conceded to them the power to decide upon war and peace, there would be no more warriors. Since the men believed that the women alone knew the secret of childbirth, the rebellion was instantly successful."

"In the Constitution of Deganawidah the founder of the Iroquois Confederation of Nations had said: 'He caused the body of our mother, the woman, to be of great worth and honor. He purposed that she shall be endowed and entrusted with the birth and upbringing of men, and that she shall have the care of all that is planted by which life is sustained and supported and the power to breathe is fortified: *and moreover that the warriors shall be her assistants.*'"

"The footnote of history was curiously supplied when Susan B. Anthony began her 'Votes for Women' movement two and a half centuries later. Unknowingly the feminists chose to hold their founding convention of latter-day suffragettes in the town of Seneca [Falls], New York. The site was just a stone's throw from the old council house where the Iroquois women had plotted their feminist rebellion" (Emphasis mine).[2]

Beliefs, attitudes, and laws such as these became part of the vision of American feminists and of other human liberation movements around the world. Yet feminists too often believe that no one has ever experienced the kind of society that empowered women and made that empowerment the basis of its rules of civilization. The price a feminist community must pay because it is not aware of the recent presence of gynarchical societies on this continent is unnecessary confusion, division, and much lost time.

THE ROOT OF OPPRESSION IS LOSS OF MEMORY

An odd thing occurs in the minds of Americans when Indian civilization is mentioned: little or nothing. As I write this, I am aware of how far removed my version of the roots of American feminism must seem to those steeped in either mainstream or radical versions of feminism's history. I am keenly aware of the lack of image Americans have about our continent's recent past. I am intensely conscious of popular notions of Indian women as beasts of burden, squaws, traitors, or, at best, vanished denizens of a long-lost wilderness. How odd, then, must my contention seem that the gynocratic tribes of the American continent provided the basis for all the dreams of liberation that characterize the modern world.

We as feminists must be aware of our history on this continent. We need to recognize that the same forces that devastated the gynarchies of Britain and the Continent also devastated the ancient African civilizations, and we must know that those same materialistic, antispiritual forces are presently engaged in wiping out the same gynarchical values, along with the peoples who adhere to them, in Latin America. I am convinced that those wars were and con-

---

1. The White Roots of Peace, cited in *The Third Woman: Minority Women Writers of the United States,* ed. Dexter Fisher (Boston: Houghton Mifflin, 1980), p. 577. Cf. Thomas Sanders and William Peek, eds., *Literature of the American Indian* (New York: Glencoe Press, 1973), pp. 208–239. Sanders and Peek refer to the document as "The Law of the Great Peace."

2. Stan Steiner, *The New Indians* (New York: Dell, 1968), pp. 219–220.

tinue to be about the imposition of patriarchal civilization over the holistic, pacifist, and spirit-based gynarchies they supplant. To that end the wars of imperial conquest have not been solely or even mostly waged over the land and its resources, but they have been fought within the bodies, minds, and hearts of the people of the earth for dominion over them. I think this is the reason traditionals say we must remember our origins, our cultures, our histories, our mothers and grandmothers, for without that memory, which implies continuance rather than nostalgia, we are doomed to engulfment by a paradigm that is fundamentally inimical to the vitality, autonomy, and self-empowerment essential for satisfying, high-quality life.

The vision that impels feminists to action was the vision of the Grandmothers' society, the society that was captured in the words of the sixteenth-century explorer Peter Martyr nearly five hundred years ago. It is the same vision repeated over and over by radical thinkers of Europe and America, from François Villon to John Locke, from William Shakespeare to Thomas Jefferson, from Karl Marx to Friedrich Engels, from Benito Juarez to Martin Luther King, from Elizabeth Cady Stanton to Judy Grahn, from Harriet Tubman to Audre Lorde, from Emma Goldman to Bella Abzug, from Malinalli to Cherríe Moraga, and from Iyatiku to me. That vision as Martyr told it is of a country where there are "no soldiers, no gendarmes or police, no nobles, kings, regents, prefects, or judges, no prisons, no lawsuits. . . . All are equal and free," or so Friedrich Engels recounts Martyr's words.[3]

Columbus wrote:

"Nor have I been able to learn whether they [the inhabitants of the islands he visited on his first journey to the New World] held personal property, for it seemed to me that whatever one had, they all took shares of. . . . They are so ingenuous and free with all they have, that no one would believe it who has not seen it; of anything that they possess, if it be asked of

them, they never say no; on the contrary, they invite you to share it and show as much love as if their hearts went with it."[4]

At least that's how the Native Caribbean people acted when the whites first came among them; American Indians are the despair of social workers, bosses, and missionaries even now because of their deeply ingrained tendency to spend all they have, mostly on others. In any case, as the historian William Brandon notes,

"the Indian *seemed* free, to European eyes, gloriously free, to the European soul shaped by centuries of toil and tyranny, and this impression operated profoundly on the process of history and the development of America. Something in the peculiar character of the Indian world gave an impression of classlessness, of propertylessness, and that in turn led to an impression, as H. H. Bancroft put it, of 'humanity unrestrained . . . in the exercise of liberty absolute.'"[5]

A FEMINIST HEROINE

Early in the women's suffrage movement, Eva Emery Dye, an Oregon suffragette, went looking for a heroine to embody her vision of feminism. She wanted a historical figure whose life would symbolize the strengthened power of women. She found Sacagawea (or Sacajawea) buried in the journals of Lewis and Clark. The Shoshoni teenager had traveled with the Lewis and Clark expedition, carrying her infant son, and on a small number of occasions acted as translator.[6]

Dye declared that Sacagawea, whose name is thought to mean Bird Woman, had been the

---

3. William Brandon, *The Last Americans: The Indian in American Culture* (New York: McGraw-Hill, 1974), p. 294.

4. Brandon, *Last Americans*, p. 6.

5. Brandon, *Last Americans*, pp. 7–9. The entire chapter "American Indians and American History" (pp. 1–23) is pertinent to the discussion.

6. Ella E. Clark and Margot Evans, *Sacagawea of the Lewis and Clark Expedition* (Berkeley: University of California Press, 1979), pp. 93–98. Clark details the fascinating, infuriating, and very funny scholarly escapade of how our suffragette foremothers created a feminist hero from the scant references to the teenage Shoshoni wife of the expedition's official translator, Pierre Charbonneau.

guide to the historic expedition, and through Dye's work Sacagawea became enshrined in American memory as a moving force and friend of the whites, leading them in the settlement of western North America.[7]

But Native American roots of white feminism reach back beyond Sacagawea. The earliest white women on this continent were well acquainted with tribal women. They were neighbors to a number of tribes and often shared food, information, child care, and health care. Of course little is made of these encounters in official histories of colonial America, the period from the Revolution to the Civil War, or on the ever moving frontier. Nor, to my knowledge, has either the significance or incidence of intermarriage between Indian and white or between Indian and Black been explored. By and large, the study of Indian-white relations has been fo-

cused on government and treaty relations, warfare, missionization, and education. It has been almost entirely documented in terms of formal white Christian patriarchal impacts and assaults on Native Americans, though they are not often characterized as assaults but as "civilizing the savages." Particularly in organs of popular culture and miseducation, the focus has been on what whites imagine to be degradation of Indian women ("squaws"), their equally imagined love of white government and white conquest ("princesses"), and the horrifyingly misleading, fanciful tales of "bloodthirsty, backward primitives" assaulting white Christian settlers who were looking for life, liberty, and happiness in their chosen land.

But, regardless of official versions of relations between Indians and whites or other segments of the American population, the fact remains that great numbers of apparently "white" or "Black" Americans carry notable degrees of Indian blood. With that blood has come the culture of the Indians, informing the lifestyles, attitudes, and values of their descendants. Somewhere along the line—and often quite recently—an Indian woman was giving birth to and raising the children of a family both officially and informally designated as white or Black—not Indian. In view of this, it should be evident that one of the major enterprises of Indian women in America has been the transfer of Indian values and culture to as large and influential a segment of American immigrant populations as possible. Their success in this endeavor is amply demonstrated in the Indian values and social styles that increasingly characterize American life. Among these must be included "permissive" childrearing practices, for imprisoning, torturing, caning, strapping, starving, or verbally abusing children was considered outrageous behavior. Native Americans did not believe that physical or psychological abuse of children would result in their edification. They did not believe that children are born in sin, are congenitally predisposed to evil, or that a good parent who wishes the child to gain salvation, achieve success, or earn the

---

7. The implications of this maneuver did not go unnoticed by either whites or Indians, for the statues of the idealized Shoshoni woman, the Native American matron Sacagawea, suggest that American tenure on American land, indeed, the right to be on this land, is given to whites by her. While that implication is not overt, it certainly is suggested in the image of her that the sculptor chose: a tall, heavy woman, standing erect, nobly pointing the way westward with upraised hand. The impression is furthered by the habit of media and scholar of referring to her as "the guide." Largely because of the popularization of the circumstances of Sacagawea's participation in the famed Lewis and Clark expedition, Indian people have viewed her as a traitor to her people, likening her to Malinalli (La Malinche, who acted as interpreter for Cortés and bore him a son) and Pocahontas, that unhappy girl who married John Rolfe (not John Smith) and died in England after bearing him a son. Actually none of these women engaged in traitorous behavior. Sacagawea led a long life, was called Porivo (Chief Woman) by the Comanches, among whom she lived for more than twenty years, and in her old age engaged her considerable skill at speaking and manipulating white bureaucracy to help in assuring her Shoshoni people decent reservation holdings.

A full discussion is impossible here but an examination of American childrearing practices, societal attitudes toward women and exhibited by women (when compared to the same in Old World cultures) as well as the foodstuffs, medicinal materials, countercultural and alternative cultural systems, and the deeply Indian values these reflect should demonstrate the truth about informal acculturation and cross-cultural connections in the Americas.

respect of her or his fellows can be helped to those ends by physical or emotional torture.

The early Americans saw the strongly protective attitude of the Indian people as a mark of their "savagery"—as they saw the Indian's habit of bathing frequently, their sexual openness, their liking for scant clothing, their raucous laughter at most things, their suspicion and derision of authoritarian structures, their quick pride, their genuine courtesy, their willingness to share what they had with others less fortunate than they, their egalitarianism, their ability to act as if various lifestyles were a normal part of living, and their granting that women were of equal or, in individual cases, of greater value than men.

Yet the very qualities that marked Indian life in the sixteenth century have, over the centuries since contact between the two worlds occurred, come to mark much of contemporary American life. And those qualities, which I believe have passed into white culture from Indian culture, are the very ones that fundamentalists, immigrants from Europe, the Middle East, and Asia often find the most reprehensible. Third and fourth-generation Americans indulge in growing nudity, informality in social relations, egalitarianism, and the rearing of women who value autonomy, strength, freedom, and personal dignity—and who are often derided by European, Asian, and Middle Eastern men for those qualities. Contemporary Americans value leisure almost as much as tribal people do. They find themselves increasingly unable to accept child abuse as a reasonable way to nurture. They bathe more than any other industrial people on earth—much to the scorn of their white cousins across the Atlantic, and they sometimes enjoy a good laugh even at their own expense (though they still have a less developed sense of the ridiculous than one might wish).

Contemporary Americans find themselves more and more likely to adopt a "live and let live" attitude in matters of personal sexual and social styles. Two-thirds of their diet and a large share of their medications and medical treatments mirror or are directly derived from Native American sources. Indianization is not a simple concept, to be sure, and it is one that Americans often find themselves resisting; but it is a process that has taken place, regardless of American resistance to recognizing the source of many if not most of American's vaunted freedoms in our personal, family, social, and political arenas.

This is not to say that Americans have become Indian in every attitude, value, or social institution. Unfortunately, Americans have a way to go in learning how to live in the world in ways that improve the quality of life for each individual while doing minimal damage to the biota, but they have adapted certain basic qualities of perception and certain attitudes that are moving them in that direction. . . .

The feminist idea of power as it ideally accrues to women stems from tribal sources. The central importance of the clan Matrons in the formulation and determination of domestic and foreign policy as well as in their primary role in the ritual and ceremonial life of their respective Nations was the single most important attribute of the Iroquois, as of the Cherokee and Muskogee, who traditionally inhabited the southern Atlantic region. The latter peoples were removed to what is now Oklahoma during the Jackson administration, but prior to the American Revolution they had regular and frequent communication with and impact on both the British colonizers and later the American people, including the African peoples brought here as slaves.

Ethnographer Lewis Henry Morgan wrote an account of Iroquoian matriarchal culture, published in 1877,[8] that heavily influenced Marx and the development of communism, particularly lending it the idea of the liberation of women from patriarchal dominance. The early socialists in Europe, especially in Russia, saw women's liberation as a central aspect of the socialist revolution. Indeed, the basic ideas

---

8. Lewis Henry Morgan, *Ancient Society or Researches in the Lines of Human Progress from Savagery Through Barbarism to Civilization* (New York, 1877).

of socialism, the egalitarian distribution of gods and power, the peaceful ordering of society, and the right of every member of society to participate in the work and benefits of that society, are ideas that pervade American Indian political thought and action. And it is through various channels—the informal but deeply effective Indianization of Europeans, and christianizing Africans, the social and political theory of the confederacies feuding and then intertwining with European dreams of liberty and justice, and, more recently, the work of Morgan and the writings of Marx and Engels—that the age-old gynarchical systems of egalitarian government found their way into contemporary feminist theory.

When Eva Emery Dye discovered Sacagawea and honored her as the guiding spirit of American womanhood, she may have been wrong in bare historical fact, but she was quite accurate in terms of deeper truth. The statues that have been erected depicting Sacagawea as a Matron in her prime signify an understanding in the American mind, however unconscious, that the source of just government, of right ordering of social relationships, the dream of "liberty and justice for all" can be gained only by following the Indian Matrons' guidance. For, as Dr. Anna Howard Shaw said of Sacagawea at the National American Woman's Suffrage Association in 1905:

"Forerunner of civilization, great leader of men, patient and motherly woman, we bow our hearts to do you honor! . . . May we the daughters of an alien race . . . learn the lessons of calm endurance, of patient persistence and unfaltering courage exemplified in your life, in our efforts to lead men through the Pass of justice, which goes over the mountains of prejudice and conservatism to the broad land of the perfect freedom of a true republic; one in which men and women together shall in perfect equality solve the problems of a nation that knows no caste, no race, no sex in opportunity, in responsibility or in justice! May 'the eternal womanly' ever lead us on!"[9]

9. Clark and Evans, *Sacagawea*, p. 96.

74

BELL HOOKS

Third World Diva Girls: Politics of Feminist Solidarity (1990)

THIRD WORLD DIVA GIRLS

Politics of Feminist Solidarity

Coming from a Southern black working-class background, one that remains a place I consider "home," I brought with me to feminist movement a certain style of being that grows out of black cultural traditions, like signifying. In the P.C. (politically correct) world of feminism, signifying tends to provoke negative feedback, as there has been so much emphasis on a notion of friendship and sisterly bonding that is based on principles of "seamless harmony." No one really speaks about the way in which class privilege informs feminist notions of social behavior, setting standards that would govern all feminist interaction. Often the "nice, nice" behavior privileged white women had rebelled against in their relationships with white men was transposed onto relations between white women and women of color. It was a common occurrence at feminist events for women of color to be accused of having said or done the wrong thing (especially in confrontational encounters where white women cried). Feelings of social awkwardness intensified when black women found that our social and cultural codes were neither respected nor known in most arenas of feminist movement. Moving in academic circles, spaces often inhabited by not too interesting smart people, a few intellectuals here and there, and in artistic circles peopled mainly by folks from privileged class backgrounds or the up and coming greedy folk who are wanting as much as they can get for as little cost, I often feel my class back-

From bell hooks, *Yearning: Race, Gender, and Cultural Politics* (Boston: South End Press, 1990), 89–102. Reprinted by permission of the author and South End Press.

ground. I struggle with the politics of location—pondering what it means for individuals
from underclass and poor backgrounds to enter
social terrains dominated by the ethos and values of privileged class experience.

Assimilation makes it very easy for those
of us from working-class backgrounds to acquire all the trappings that make us seem like
we come from privilege, especially if we are
college educated and talk the right kinda talk
(every time I try to get clever and throw
some vernacular black speech into my essays,
they are perceived as errors and "corrected").
Until recently I felt that was alright, I'd been
happy to keep that speech for private spaces
of my life. Now, I recognize how disempowering it is for people from underprivileged
backgrounds to consciously censor our
speech so as to "fit better" in settings where
we are perceived as not belonging. It's easy
enough for folks from working-class backgrounds to step into the world of privilege
and realize we've made a mistake and to go
right back where we came from. There's a
certain inverse status to be had by retreating
back into one's problematic roots bearing the
message that it's really better there, a more
righteous place (where you might not be fully
understood but where you at least have ties).
Better to be there than to be with those privileged "others" who don't have a clue where
you're coming from.

Faced with the choice of assimilating or returning to my roots, I would catch the first
train home. There is another more difficult and
less acceptable choice, that is to decide to
maintain values and traditions that emerge
from a working-class Southern black folk experience while incorporating meaningful knowledge gained in other locations, even in those hierarchical spaces of privilege. This choice
makes a lot of people uncomfortable. It makes
it hard for them to put you in a neat little category and keep you there. In a troubled voice,
my grandmother asked me the last time I saw
her before she died, "How can you live so far
away from your people?" In her mind, "my peo-

ple" were not synonymous with a mass of black
people, but with particular black folks that one
is connected to by ties of blood and fellowship,
the folks with whom we share a history, the
folks who talk our talk (the patois of our region), who know our background and our
ways. Her comment silenced me. I felt a pain in
my heart as though I had been pierced by a
sharp blade. My grandmother's words were
like that; they felt to me like little knives. My
silent response was tacit agreement that only
misguided confused folks would live away from
their people, their own.

I often think about my people, especially
the womenfolk, the way we were raised, when
I participate in feminist meetings and conferences. I am startled by the dichotomy between
the rhetoric of sisterhood and the vicious way
nice, nice, politically correct girls can deal with
one another, do one another in, in ways far
more brutal than I ever witnessed in shoot and
cut black communities. With no body of feminist theory shaping her actions, my mama was
determined to raise her daughters to value our
connections to one another. Often she would
"preach" on the subject of sisterhood. She would
tell us about households of women, sisters usually, where they were always quarreling with
one another, fighting, back-stabbing, working
out some "serious" female rivalry. Mama made
it clear there was gonna be none of that in our
house. We were gonna learn how to respect and
care for one another as women. It was not an
easy task; her six girls were very different. Despite her efforts, now and then envy and little
hatreds would surface, but for the most part we
learned how to bond as sisters across our differences. We all had to become grown women to
look back and see the importance of this early
home training, 'cause it takes being a woman to
know just what we can do to wound one another. Now that we are grown black women, we
can sit on the porch at family reunions and
groove on the strength of our ties, that we are
close despite differences of class, experience,
values, attitudes, sexual practice, education, and
so on. At those times I remember mama's hard

work, teaching us tolerance, compassion, generosity, sisterly ways to love one another.

Growing up in a household full of black females, it was impossible to cultivate any sense of being "exotic." 'Cause folk will laugh at you in a minute and tell you your shit is just common. This does not mean that within our collective family setting one's uniqueness was not acknowledged or valued—it was—but it did not give anybody the right to assert dominating power over other folks. Moving in and out of segregated black communities into predominantly white circles, I have observed how easy it is for individual black females deemed "special" to become exoticized, objectified in ways that support types of behavior that on home turf would just be considered out of control. Basically in white culture black women get to play two roles. We are either the bad girls, the "bitches," the madwomen (how many times have you heard folks say that a particularly assertive black woman is "crazy") seen as threatening and treated badly, or we are the supermamas, telling it like it is and taking care of everybody, spreading our special magic wherever we go. Certainly the most outstanding contemporary example of the way this particular image is codified in popular culture and commodified is in the construction of Oprah Winfrey as beloved black "mammy" icon. Everyone tries to destroy the bad girls, who are constantly checked and kept in line, and the supermamas, who are sometimes "vamps" (witness the change in Oprah's image after she lost weight—take the 1989 Revlon ad, for example) on their off time, and get to do whatever they want; after all they are "special." Unless we remain ever vigilant about the ways representations of black womanhood (especially those of successful individuals) are appropriated and exploited in white supremacist capitalist patriarchy, we may find ourselves falling into traps set by the dominant culture.

In the past few years I have received greater attention for my feminist writing, more public recognition, and it makes me understand how easy it is to become self-enthralled, to believe that somehow one deserves to be set apart from others and in some cases to "lord it over them" especially those who seem to be less enlightened, less knowing. Now and then I have to "check" myself, look at my behavior and engage in some down home critical feedback, or I have to check things with comrades to make sure I'm not getting out of line. It seems to me that one of the real danger zones is that space where one encounters black women/women of color outside home communities in predominantly white space. Often we meet in these arenas and treat each other as adversaries. Often in white settings we are like siblings fighting for the approval of "white parents" whose attention we now have. It's serious. Recently I attended a major conference on "Third World feminism" where I was one of several "women of color" invited to speak (I put that label in quotes because I rarely use it. I mostly identify myself as a black woman). When I arrived at the conference, I was mingling and heard a number of participants talk about how they had come to see the fireworks, the negative confrontations that they were confident would take place between women of color there. Their comments and expectations reminded me of the many scenes fictively portrayed in African-American literature where black people, most often males, fight one another publicly, to entertain white folks, making of themselves a dehumanized spectacle.

Fearful that just such a happening might take place at this conference, I was particularly sensitive to whether or not I and other women of color were relating to one another with recognition, care, and respect, appreciating those women who were engaged in a similar process. We were acting out an ethical commitment to feminist solidarity that begins first with our regarding one another with respect. Throughout most of the conference, as though by collective mutual consent, Third World feminist speakers maintained an impressive positive interaction with one another even in situations where dialogue was rigorously critical. Folks disagreed but not in ways that were trashing of one another, silencing or disenabling. On the final day of the conference, this sense of care was completely disrupted by the actions of one Third World woman scholar—behaving towards women of color, particularly black women, in ways that were disrespectful (for example she was always quick to point out perceived intellectual inadequacies in their comments), setting the stage for the competitive spectacle many of us had worked hard to avoid.

In the aftermath of this encounter, as folks were digging up the bodies and trying to lay blame, I was chastised by many people for having behaved in a positive respectful manner towards this critic throughout the conference. She is a scholar whose work I respect and from my cultural tradition an "elder" whom I should respect on principle. I was surprised by all this criticism directed at me for being "too nice." Suddenly the usual bourgeois insistence on decorum that is a tedious norm in most public academic settings was deemed non-applicable to this situation and participants seemed really glad to have had an occasion to witness the spectacle of one woman of color "putting down," mind you in very fancy ways, black women and black people. Indeed the girl was out of control. Of course, in the aftermath, she placed the blame on "us," more specifically me, saying it was something I said that just upset her. Naturally she could have decided to work out with me, in another setting, whatever was bothering her, but dare I say "that would have been too much, right." The point however is that this business of blaming the black women for why "you have to abuse us" sounds so familiar. Similarly, when black women challenge racism within the feminist movement the dominant response is one of hostility and anger. We are most often accused of inviting this hostility whenever we confront to resist. Black women resisting racism in feminist movement were tracked and then told "You made me do it." Frequently white women use this tactic to mask their complicity with racist structures of domination. A parallel paradigm is often enacted in interactions between powerful Third World elites and black Americans in predominantly white settings. This was certainly taking place at the conference, nor was it surprising that it was initiated by the Third World woman scholar whose work has received the most extensive legitimation in privileged white academic circles.

The current popularity of post-colonial discourse that implicates solely the West often obscures the colonizing relationship of the East in relation to Africa and other parts of the Third World. We often forget that many Third World nationals bring to this country the same kind of contempt and disrespect for blackness that is most frequently associated with white western imperialism. While it is true that many Third World nationals who live in Britain and the United States develop through theoretical and concrete experience knowledge of how they are diminished by white western racism, that does not always lead them to interrogate the way in which they enter a racialized hierarchy where in the eyes of whites they automatically have greater status and privilege than individuals of African descent. Within the feminist movement Third World nationals often assume the role of mediator or interpreter, explaining the "bad" black people to their white colleagues or helping the "naive" black people to understand whiteness. For example: in a women's studies program where the black woman is seen by white colleagues as hostile and angry, they go to the Third World national and express concern saying, "Why can't she be like you." She responds by saying: "In my country we have a long tradition of diplomacy; therefore I am in a better position to cope with the politics of difference." Confident that she cares about the fate of her black colleague, she then shares this conversation with her and offers advice. Unwittingly assuming the role of go-between, of mediator, she re-inscribes a colonial paradigm. Such an action disrupts all possibility that feminist political solidarity will be sustained between women of color cross-culturally. Certainly many of us left the conference on Third World feminism feeling as though a rift had been created between black women and Third World nationals that remained unexamined and unresolved.

Weeks after the conference ended, I was still defending my position that it was important for women of color to treat one another with respect, even if that meant extending oneself beyond what might normally be seen as appropriate behavior. Audre Lorde makes this point again and again in her insightful essay "Eye to Eye," reminding readers that in patriarchal white supremacist context, this gesture, whether it be black women dealing with one another with respect, or women of color in general, is an act of political resistance. It is an indication that we reject and oppose the internalized racism that would have us work against one another. . . .

Writing about the way black women relate to one another, about policing that leads us to vent an anger deeper than any we let loose on other groups, Audre Lorde raises these questions: "Why does that anger unleash itself more tellingly against another Black woman at the least excuse? Why do I judge her in a more critical light that any other, become enraged when she does not measure up?" Black women may "police" one another because many of us were raised in communities where we were taught that it was a gesture of care to "oversee" each other's actions. When many of us were growing up it was common for elders to monitor the behavior of those younger. Sometimes this monitoring was helpful, but it was often repressive. In different locations such gestures may be less an expression of care and more an attempt to maintain the status quo. Black women often police one another to maintain positions of power and authority, especially in professional settings. Unfortunately, the legacy of being the "exception" damages our ability to relate to one another. Usually, gifted brilliant black women work in settings where it is easy to begin thinking of oneself as different from and superior to other black women. Many of us are repeatedly told by white "superiors" that we are different, special. Internalizing this message can make it difficult to share space with another black woman. Hooked on being the "exception" this individual may need to expose or undermine other black female peers, to show that she is better. This can lead to horribly negative interactions in work settings. Since black women (like almost everyone raised in this society) are usually taught to believe competition is necessary for success, it's easy for folks to feel particularly gratified by having one-upped a colleague; that may be even more the case if that person is another black woman/woman of color. Also we appear more qualified and trustworthy in the eyes of white people when we function as overseer, willing to crack the whip harder on each other.

When asked to submit a list of ten names from which three would be chosen to evaluate me in a tenure process, I felt most wary of naming black women. I named only one, whom I felt could be trusted not to judge my work unfairly, which is not to say that I thought she would only make positive comments. My wariness is a response to negative encounters with black women peers, who often see differing opinions and lifestyles as reason to viciously trash, excommunicate, and ostracize other black women. This seems ironic since most black women, especially those of us who are reluctant to advocate feminism, often chauvinistically insist that we have had this tradition of mutual support and closeness and did not need feminist thinking to create such ties. There is some truth in this assertion, although it is usually forgotten that these ties often emerge in a homogeneous setting. Many of us learned how to bond with females who were like us, who shared similar values and experiences. Often these close-knit groups used the power of their intimacy to trash women outside the chosen circle.

Like all women within patriarchal society, black women have to develop oppositional feminist strategies that will indeed enable us to accept, respect, and even honor peers who are not like us. We must understand that through active work, such solidarity should lead to the formation of different strategies that make productive communication possible. Many women who are high achievers have learned the rugged individualist model of success. This is true of many black women. They may feel that any gestures of bonding with other women threaten that success. Sometimes black women in positions of authority and power impose internalized racist assumptions on those folks whom they have power to influence. They may share downgrading messages that they once received and used as a challenge, a goad for further productivity. Unfortunately, that is not the way most of us respond to negative feedback. In Nikki Giovanni's "Woman Poem" she has a line that reads, "I ain't shit, you must be lower than that to care." Confronting internalized racism and sexism must be a central agenda for both feminist and black liberation struggle. An important stage in this process is developing skills that enable us to look at ourselves critically and observe how we behave towards others.

Recently, at a dinner where a well-known black woman writer was present, I said in conversation with the person I was sitting next to that I had sent a novel to several publishers and it had been rejected. The famous black woman writer (whose work has inspired and excited me both as a writer and a teacher) interrupted the conversation she was having to say loudly to me, in a hostile tone of voice, "Probably it's just a bad novel." Since she had been behaving all evening as though no one had anything to say worth listening to but herself, I was not surprised by this not-so-subtle attack. I was grateful, however, that I had not met her at a time in life when I was longing for a black woman mentor, for affirmation that I should continue writing. No interaction between us indicated that she was familiar with my writing. I pondered how damaging this negative feedback could have been for a fledgling writer. Her hostility saddened me. Though we were in a group that was predominantly white and were hearing

many of the usual comments made in such settings (some of them naively racist), she did not direct critical comments to these speakers. In fact she was most gracious to the white men present. Audre Lorde's question: "Why does that anger unleash itself most tellingly against another black woman at the least excuse" came to mind. To answer that question we would need to critically examine the dynamics of black female interaction from a feminist perspective.

When I later spoke with other guests, who had again relished this spectacle, I was told that I must have done something to invite such hostility. Their need to absolve the well-known writer of responsibility of her actions seemed linked to the longing to maintain their idealized notions of powerful black womanhood. When you are well-known, surrounded by fans and adoring followers, few people offer critical feedback. Most folks tend to graciously overlook abusive and dominating behavior by famous "feminist" thinkers, even if our work is based on a critique of domination. Feminist analysis of the way patriarchy manifests itself in everyday life highlights the subtle and seemingly trivial incidents where men exercise coercive control and domination over women as important arenas of political struggle. Individual men changing their dominating behavior serve as necessary examples for their peers. Often women engaged with feminism critique behavior in men that is acceptable to them when done by women. Much of the dominating and abusive behavior that happens in feminist circles where there are gradations of power would be immediately challenged and critiqued if the perpetrators were men.

As feminist movement has progressed and individuals have even begun to talk about postfeminism, many women are forgetting one of the most important dimensions of feminist struggle, the focus on feminist ethics. That focus was rooted in the recognition of the way in which patriarchal sexist thinking distorts women's relation to one another. Commitment to feminist politics was a corrective process. Consciousness-raising groups were once settings where women engaged in dialectical exchange about these issues. Nowadays there is a tendency to act as though it is no longer important how women deal with one another. In the place of the community-based consciousness-raising group, we have feminist stars who are leaders in that they shape feminist thinking and action. Yet these women are often the least willing to participate in sessions where their feminist practice might be interrogated. The emergence of a feminist star system, one that has concrete material rewards (royalties from book publication, paid lectures, high-paying jobs, etc.), means that women jockey for power within feminist circles, and women of color are most often competing with one another.

When feminism becomes a means for opportunistic self-advancement, it means that prominent spokespeople can easily lose sight of the need to share critical feminist thought with masses of people. Much of the small amount of feminist writing done by women of color is directed towards a white audience. Thus it comes as no surprise that we are not working as hard as we should be to spread the feminist message to large groups of people of color. It also means that we are rarely engaged in the types of mentor relationships that would produce a new group of feminist thinkers and theorists who would be women and men of color. Those who are deeply committed to feminist struggle must be ever mindful of the reality that this commitment is actively manifest when we share knowledge, resources, and strategies for change with those who have the least access.

Working with a brilliant group of young women of color who are struggling to deepen their critical consciousness, to learn ways to be politically active, who are striving to develop intellectually, I lovingly called them "Third World diva girls," a title which gives expression to their uniqueness and importance. We use the word "girl" in that way it is used in traditional African-American culture as a sign of intense womanist affection, not as a put down. It is an evocation to and of intimacy, based on proud recognition of gender. And we use the term "diva" because of the special role women have had in opera. (See Catherine Clement's *Opera: The Undoing of Women*.) It both names specialness but carries with it the connotation of being just a bit out of control, stuck on oneself. We wanted it as a reminder of how easy it is to imagine we are superior to others and therefore deserve special treatment or have the right to dominate. . . .

A clear distinction must be made between receiving the respect and recognition exceptional women of color active in feminist movement rightfully deserve and the misuse of power and presence. Speaking about this in relation to black women, Lorde reminds us:

"Often we give lip service to the idea of mutual support between black women because we have not yet crossed the barriers to these possibilities, nor fully expressed the angers and fears that keep us from realizing the power of a real Black sisterhood. And to acknowledge our dreams is to sometimes acknowledge the distance between those dreams and our present situation."

If "Third World diva girls," whoever they may be—emerging writers and thinkers or the already famous and well-known—want to know whether we are cultivating the kind of sisterhood based on feminist solidarity and informed by feminist ethics, we must look and listen, observe and hear the response around us. We must engage in ongoing self-critique. When I give a talk and no one raises challenging questions, then I consider how I've represented myself. When I'm doing talks and folks tell me that I'm not the way they thought I would be, I ask them to explain. Sometimes they want to let me know that I'm not power tripping like the way they thought I might, since so many of us do. I am especially gratified when I receive a letter that clarifies how I am perceived. One came recently. After hearing me speak at the university where she works, a black woman listener wrote these words:

"Your lecture raised my consciousness of the world in which we live to a much higher level. I was so deeply touched by your words and your obvious "black pride." I have had no female or male black role models. . . . So hearing you speak was monumental. . . . I don't see you as the "celebrity figure" you are but as a true sister who knows her roots and herself and is proud of it. I believe you have appeared in my life for a reason."

This letter inspires me, strengthens the conviction that feminist solidarity has reality and substance.

Sometimes I act like a diva girl in the worst way—that is narcissistic, self-focused, or wanting others to serve me. Home with my family recently I was wanting attention and my sisters let me know it was getting out of hand. Tired from intense months of teaching, writing, and being on the lecture circuit, I did indeed want to be pampered and waited on, to get that special care the divas of our imagination merit because they are so unique. My sisters were willing to give that care, to affirm my specialness, even as they let me know there were limits, boundaries beyond which I would be placing them in the role of subordinates. The difficulties women of color face in a white supremacist capitalist patriarchy are intense. We can only respect and admire all among us who manage to resist, who become self-actualized. We need to cherish and honor those among us who emerge as "stars," not because they are above us but because they share with us light that guides, providing insight and necessary wisdom. To be a star, a diva, carries with it responsibility; one must learn to know and respect boundaries, using power in ways that enrich and uplift. In these times that are fundamentally more anti-feminist than post-feminist, feminist movement needs activists who can carry on the work of liberation, diva girls who are on the front line.

75
GLORIA ANZALDÚA
La conciencia de la mestiza/Towards a New Consciousness (1987)

Por la mujer de mi raza hablará el espíritu.[1]

Jose Vasconcelos, Mexican philosopher, envisaged *una raza mestiza, una mezcla de razas afines, una raza de color—la primera raza síntesis del globo.* He called it a cosmic race, *la raza cósmica,* a fifth race embracing the four major races of the world.[2] Opposite to the theory of the pure Aryan, and to the policy of racial purity that white America practices, his theory is one of inclusivity. At the confluence of two or more genetic streams, with chromosomes constantly "crossing over," this mixture of races, rather than resulting in an inferior being, provides hybrid progeny, a mutable, more malleable species with a rich gene pool. From this racial, ideological, cultural and biological cross-pollinization, an "alien" consciousness is presently in the making—a new *mestiza* consciousness, *una conciencia de mujer.* It is a consciousness of the Borderlands.

UNA LUCHA DE FRONTERAS / A STRUGGLE OF BORDERS

Because I, a *mestiza,*
continually walk out of one culture
and into another,
because I am in all cultures at the same
time,
alma entre dos mundos, tres, cuatro,

From Gloria Anzaldúa, *Borderlands/La Frontera: The New Mestiza* (San Francisco: Aunt Lute Books, 1987), 77–88. Copyright 1987 by Gloria Anzaldúa. Reprinted with permission from Aunt Lute Books.
1. This is my own "take off" on Jose Vasconcelos' idea. Jose Vasconcelos, *La Raza Cósmica: Misión de la Raza Ibero-Americana* (México: Aguilar S.A. de Ediciones, 1961).
2. Vasconcelos.

me zumba la cabeza con lo contradictorio.
Estoy norteada por todas las voces que me
  hablan
simultáneamente.

The ambivalence from the clash of voices results in mental and emotional states of perplexity. Internal strife results in insecurity and indecisiveness. The mestiza's dual or multiple personality is plagued by psychic restlessness.

In a constant state of mental nepantilism, an Aztec word meaning torn between ways, *la mestiza* is a product of the transfer of the cultural and spiritual values of one group to another. Being tricultural, monolingual, bilingual, or multilingual, speaking a patois, and in a state of perpetual transition the *mestiza* faces the dilemma of the mixed breed: which collectivity does the daughter of a darkskinned mother listen to?

El choque de un alma atrapado entre el mundo del espíritu y el mundo de la técnica a veces la deja entullada. Cradled in one culture, sandwiched between two cultures, straddling all three cultures and their value systems, *la mestiza* undergoes a struggle of flesh, a struggle of borders, an inner war. Like all people, we perceive the version of reality that our culture communicates. Like others having or living in more than one culture, we get multiple, often opposing messages. The coming together of two self-consistent but habitually incompatible frames of reference[3] causes *un choque,* a cultural collision.

Within us and within *la cultura chicana,* commonly held beliefs of the white culture attack commonly held beliefs of the Mexican culture, and both attack commonly held beliefs of the indigenous culture. Subconsciously, we see an attack on ourselves and our beliefs as a threat and we attempt to block with a counterstance.

But it is not enough to stand on the opposite river bank, shouting questions, challenging

patriarchal, white conventions. A counterstance locks one into a dual of oppressor and oppressed; locked in mortal combat, like the cop and the criminal, both are reduced to a common denominator of violence. The counterstance refutes the dominant culture's views and beliefs, and, for this, it is proudly defiant. All reaction is limited by, and dependent on, what it is reacting against. Because the counterstance stems from a problem with authority— outer as well as inner—it's a step towards liberation from cultural domination. But it is not a way of life. At some point, on our way to a new consciousness, we will have to leave the opposite bank, the split between the two mortal combatants somehow healed so that we are on both shores at once and, at once, see through serpent and eagle eyes. Or perhaps we will decide to disengage from the dominant culture, write it off altogether as a lost cause, and cross the border into a wholly new and separate territory. Or we might go another route. The possibilities are numerous once we decide to act and not react.

A TOLERANCE FOR AMBIGUITY

These numerous possibilities leave *la mestiza* floundering in uncharted seas. In perceiving conflicting information and points of view, she is subjected to a swamping of her psychological borders. She has discovered that she can't hold concepts or ideas in rigid boundaries. The borders and walls that are supposed to keep the undesirable ideas out are entrenched habits and patterns of behavior; these habits and patterns are the enemy within. Rigidity means death. Only by remaining flexible is she able to stretch the psyche horizontally and vertically. *La mestiza* constantly has to shift out of habitual formations; from convergent thinking, analytical reasoning that tends to use rationality to move toward a single goal (a Western mode), to divergent thinking,[4] characterized by movement

3. Arthur Koestler termed this "bisociation." Albert Rothenberg, *The Creative Process in Art, Science, and Other Fields* (Chicago, IL: University of Chicago Press, 1979), 12.

4. In part, I derive my definitions for "convergent" and "divergent" thinking from Rothenberg, 12–13.

away from set patterns and goals and toward a more whole perspective, one that includes rather than excludes.

The new *mestiza* copes by developing a tolerance for contradictions, a tolerance for ambiguity. She learns to be an Indian in Mexican culture, to be Mexican from an Anglo point of view. She learns to juggle cultures. She has a plural personality, she operates in a pluralistic mode—nothing is thrust out, the good the bad and the ugly, nothing rejected, nothing abandoned. Not only does she sustain contradictions, she turns the ambivalence into something else.

She can be jarred out of ambivalence by an intense, and often painful, emotional event which inverts or resolves the ambivalence. I'm not sure exactly how. The work takes place underground—subconsciously. It is work that the soul performs. That focal point or fulcrum, that juncture where the mestiza stands, is where phenomena tend to collide. It is where the possibility of uniting all that is separate occurs. This assembly is not one where severed or separated pieces merely come together. Nor is it a balancing of opposing powers. In attempting to work out a synthesis, the self has added a third element which is greater than the sum of its severed parts. That third element is a new consciousness—a mestiza consciousness—and though it is a source of intense pain, its energy comes from continual creative motion that keeps breaking down the unitary aspect of each new paradigm.

En unas pocas centurias, the future will belong to the mestiza. Because the future depends on the breaking down of paradigms, it depends on the straddling of two or more cultures. By creating a new mythos—that is, a change in the way we perceive reality, the way we see ourselves, and the ways we behave—*la mestiza* creates a new consciousness.

The work of *mestiza* consciousness is to break down the subject-object duality that keeps her a prisoner and to show in the flesh and through the images in her work how duality is transcended. The answer to the problem between the white race and the colored, be-

tween males and females, lies in healing the split that originates in the very foundation of our lives, our culture, our languages, our thoughts. A massive uprooting of dualistic thinking in the individual and collective consciousness is the beginning of a long struggle, but one that could, in our best hopes, bring us to the end of rape, of violence, of war.

LA ENCRUCIJADA / THE CROSSROADS

A chicken is being sacrificed
at a crossroads, a simple mound of earth
a mud shrine for *Eshu,*
Yoruba god of indeterminacy,
who blesses her choice of path.
She begins her journey.

Su cuerpo es una bocacalle. La mestiza has gone from being the sacrificial goat to becoming the officiating priestess at the crossroads.

As a *mestiza* I have no country, my homeland cast me out; yet all countries are mine because I am every woman's sister or potential lover. (As a lesbian I have no race, my own people disclaim me; but I am all races because there is the queer of me in all races.) I am cultureless because, as a feminist, I challenge the collective cultural/religious male-derived beliefs of Indo-Hispanics and Anglos; yet I am cultured because I am participating in the creation of yet another culture, a new story to explain the world and our participation in it, a new value system with images and symbols that connect us to each other and to the planet. *Soy un amasamiento,* I am an act of kneading, or uniting and joining that not only has produced both a creature of darkness and a creature of light, but also a creature that questions the definitions of light and dark and gives them new meanings.

We are the people who leap in the dark, we are the people on the knees of the gods. In our very flesh, (r)evolution works out the clash of cultures. It makes us crazy constantly, but if the center holds, we've made some kind of evolutionary step forward. *Nuestra alma el trabajo,* the opus, the great alchemical work; spiritual *mestizaje,* a "morphogenesis,"[5] an inevitable unfolding. We have become the quickening serpent movement.

Indigenous like corn, like corn, the *mestiza* is a product of crossbreeding, designed for preservation under a variety of conditions. Like an ear of corn—a female seed-bearing organ—the *mestiza* is tenacious, tightly wrapped in the husks of her culture. Like kernels she clings to the cob; with thick stalks and strong brace roots, she holds tight to the earth—she will survive the crossroads.

Lavando y remojando el maíz en agua de cal, despojando el pellejo. Moliendo, mixteando, amasando, haciendo tortillas de masa.[6] She steeps the corn in lime, it swells, softens. With stone roller on *metate,* she grinds the corn, then grinds again. She kneads and moulds the dough, pats the round balls into *tortillas.*

> We are the porous rock in the stone
>   *metate*
> squatting on the ground.
> We are the rolling pin, *el maíz y agua,*
> *la masa harina. Somos el amasijo.*
> *Somos lo molido en el metate.*
> We are the *comal* sizzling hot,
> the hot *tortilla,* the hungry mouth.
> We are the coarse rock.
> We are the grinding motion,
> the mixed potion, *somos el molcajete.*
> We are the pestle, the *comino, ajo, pimienta,*
> We are the *chile colorado,*

---

5. To borrow chemist Ilya Prigogine's theory of "dissipative structures." Prigogine discovered that substances interact not in predictable ways as it was taught in science, but in different and fluctuating ways to produce new and more complex structures, a kind of birth he called "morphogenesis," which created unpredictable innovations. Harold Gilliam, "Searching for a New World View," *ThisWorld* (January, 1981), 23.

6. *Tortillas de masa harina*: corn tortillas are of two types, the smooth uniform ones made in a tortilla press and usually bought at a tortilla factory or supermarket, and *gorditas,* made by mixing masa with lard or shortening or butter (my mother sometimes puts in bits of bacon or *chicharrones*).

the green shoot that cracks the rock.
We will abide.

EL CAMINO DE LA MESTIZA / THE MESTIZA WAY

"Caught between the sudden contraction, the breath sucked in and the endless space, the brown woman stands still, looks at the sky. She decides to go down, digging her way along the roots of trees. Sifting through the bones, she shakes them to see if there is any marrow in them. Then, touching the dirt to her forehead, to her tongue, she takes a few bones, leaves the rest in their burial place."

"She goes through her backpack, keeps her journal and address book, throws away the muni-bart metromaps. The coins are heavy and they go next, then the greenbacks flutter through the air. She keeps her knife, can opener and eyebrow pencil. She puts bones, pieces of bark, *hierbas,* eagle feather, snakeskin, tape recorder, the rattle and drum in her pack and she sets out to become the complete *toleteca.*"[7]

Her first step is to take inventory. *Despojando, desgranando, quitando paja.* Just what did she inherit from her ancestors? This weight on her back—which is the baggage from the Indian mother, which is the baggage from the Spanish father, which is the baggage from the Anglo?

Pero es difícil differentiating between *lo heredado, lo adquirido, lo impuesto.* She puts history through a sieve, winnows out the lies, looks at the forces that we as a race, as women, have been a part of. *Luego bota lo que no vale, los desmientos, los desencuentros, el embrutecimiento. Aguarda el juicio, hondo y enraízado, de la gente antigua.* This step is a conscious rupture with all oppressive traditions of all cultures and religions. She communicates that rupture, documents the struggle. She reinterprets history and, using new symbols, she shapes new myths. She adopts new perspectives toward the dark-skinned, women and queers. She strengthens

---

7. Gina Valdés, *Puentes y Fronteras: Coplas Chicanas* (Los Angeles, CA: Castle Lithograph, 1982), 2.

her tolerance (and intolerance) for ambiguity. She is willing to share, to make herself vulnerable to foreign ways of seeing and thinking. She surrenders all notions of safety, of the familiar. Deconstruct, construct. She becomes a *nahual,* able to transform herself into a tree, a coyote, into another person. She learns to transform the small "I" into the total Self. *Se hace moldeadora de su alma. Según la concepción que tiene de sí misma, así será.*

QUE NO SE NOS OLVIDE LOS HOMBRES

> "*Tú no sirves pa' nada—*
> you're good for nothing.
> *Eres pura vieja.*"

"You're nothing but a woman" means you are defective. Its opposite is to be *un macho.* The modern meaning of the word "machismo," as well as the concept, is actually an Anglo invention. For men like my father, being "macho" meant being strong enough to protect and support my mother and us, yet being able to show love. Today's macho has doubts about his ability to feed and protect his family. His "machismo" is an adaptation to oppression and poverty and low self-esteem. It is the result of hierarchical male dominance. The Anglo, feeling inadequate and inferior and powerless, displaces or transfers these feelings to the Chicano by shaming him. In the Gringo world, the Chicano suffers from excessive humility and self-effacement, shame of self and self-deprecation. Around Latinos he suffers from a sense of language inadequacy and its accompanying discomfort; with Native Americans he suffers from a racial amnesia which ignores our common blood, and from guilt because the Spanish part of him took their land and oppressed them. He has an excessive compensatory hubris when around Mexicans from the other side. It overlays a deep sense of racial shame.

The loss of a sense of dignity and respect in the macho breeds a false machismo which leads him to put down women and even to brutalize them. Coexisting with his sexist behavior is a love for the mother which takes precedence over that of all others. Devoted son, macho pig. To wash down the shame of his acts, of his very being, and to handle the brute in the mirror, he takes to the bottle, the snort, the needle, and the fist.

Though we "understand" the root causes of male hatred and we will no longer put up with it. From the men of our race, we demand the admission/acknowledgment/disclosure/testimony that they wound us, violate us, are afraid of us and of our power. We need them to say they will begin to eliminate their hurtful put-down ways. But more than the words, we demand acts. We say to them: We will develop equal power with you and those who have shamed us.

It is imperative that mestizas support each other in changing the sexist elements in the Mexican-Indian culture. As long as woman is put down, the Indian and the Black in all of us is put down. The struggle of the mestiza is above all a feminist one. As long as *los hombres* think they have to *chingar mujeres* and each other to be men, as long as men are taught that they are superior and therefore culturally favored over *la mujer,* as long as to be a *vieja* is a thing of derision, there can be no real healing of our psyches. We're halfway there—we have such love of the Mother, the good mother. The first step is to unlearn the *puta/virgen* dichotomy and to see *Coatlapopeuh-Coatlicue* in the Mother, *Guadalupe.*

Tenderness, a sign of vulnerability, is so feared that it is showered on women with verbal abuse and blows. Men, even more than women, are fettered to gender roles. Women at least have had the guts to break out of bondage. Only gay men have had the courage to expose themselves to the woman inside them and to challenge the current masculinity. I've encountered a few scattered and isolated gentle straight men, the beginnings of a new breed, but they are confused, and entangled with sexist behaviors that they have not been able to eradicate. We need a new masculinity and the new man needs a movement.

Lumping the males who deviate from the general norm with man, the oppressor, is a gross injustice. *Asombra pensar que nos hemos quedado en ese pozo oscuro donde el mundo encierra a las lesbianas. Asombra pensar que hemos, como femenistas y lesbianas, cerrado nuestros corazónes a los hombres, a nuestros hermanos los jotos, desheredados y marginales como nosotros.* Being the supreme crossers of cultures, homosexuals have strong bonds with the queer white, Black, Asian, Native American, Latino, and with the queer in Italy, Australia and the rest of the planet. We come from all colors, all classes, all races, all time periods. Our role is to link people with each other—the Blacks with Jews with Indians with Asians with whites with extraterrestrials. It is to transfer ideas and information from one culture to another. Colored homosexuals have more knowledge of other cultures; have always been at the forefront (although sometimes in the closet) of all liberation struggles in this country; have suffered more injustices and have survived them despite all odds. Chicanos need to acknowledge the political and artistic contributions of their queer. People, listen to what your *jotería* is saying.

The mestizo and the queer exist at this time and point on the evolutionary continuum for a purpose. We are a blending that proves that all blood is intricately woven together, and that we are spawned out of similar souls.

SOMOS UNA GENTE

Hay tantísimas fronteras
que dividen a la gente,
pero por cada frontera
existed también un puente.
—Gina Valdés

Divided Loyalties

Many women and men of color do not want to have any dealings with white people. It takes too much time and energy to explain to the downwardly mobile, white middle-class women that it's okay for us to want to own "possessions," never having had any nice furniture on our dirt floors or "luxuries" like washing machines. Many feel that whites should help their own people rid themselves of race hatred and fear first. I, for one, choose to use some of my energy to serve as mediator. I think we need to allow whites to be our allies. Through our literature, art, *corridos,* and folktales we must share our history with them so when they set up committees to help Big Mountain Navajos or the Chicano farmworkers or *los Nicaragüenses* they won't turn people away because of their racial fears and ignorance. They will come to see that they are not helping us but following our lead.

Individually, but also as a racial entity, we need to voice our needs. We need to say to white society: We need you to accept the fact that Chicanos are different, to acknowledge your rejection and negation of us. We need you to own the fact that you looked upon us as less than human, that you stole our lands, our personhood, our self-respect. We need you to make public restitution: to say that, to compensate for your own sense of defectiveness, you strive for power over us, you erase our history and our experience because it makes you feel guilty—you'd rather forget your brutish acts. To say you've split yourself from minority groups, that you disown us, that your dual consciousness splits off parts of yourself, transferring the "negative" parts onto us. (Where there is persecution of minorities, there is shadow projection. Where there is violence and war, there is repression of shadow.) To say that you are afraid of us, that to put distance between us, you wear the mask of contempt. Admit that Mexico is your double, that she exists in the shadow of this country, that we are irrevocably tied to her. Gringo, accept the doppelganger in your psyche. By taking back your collective shadow the intracultural split will heal. And finally, tell us what you need from us.

BY YOUR TRUE FACES
WE WILL KNOW YOU

I am visible—see this Indian face—yet I am invisible. I both blind them with my beak nose and am their blind spot. But I exist, we exist. They'd like to think I have melted in the pot. But I haven't, we haven't.

The dominant white culture is killing us slowly with its ignorance. By taking away our self-determination, it has made us weak and empty. As a people we have resisted and we have taken expedient positions, but we have never been allowed to develop unencumbered—we have never been allowed to be fully ourselves. The whites in power want us people of color to barricade ourselves behind our separate tribal walls so they can pick us off one at a time with their hidden weapons; so they can whitewash and distort history. Ignorance splits people, creates prejudices. A misinformed people is a subjugated people.

Before the Chicano and the undocumented worker and the Mexican from the other side can come together, before the Chicano can have unity with Native Americans and other groups, we need to know the history of their struggle and they need to know ours. Our mothers, our sisters and brothers, the guys who hang out on street corners, the children in the playgrounds, each of us must know our Indian lineage, our afro-*mestisaje,* our history of resistance.

To the immigrant *mexicano* and the recent arrivals we must teach our history. The 80 million *mexicanos* and the Latinos from Central and South America must know of our struggles. Each one of us must know basic facts about Nicaragua, Chile and the rest of Latin America. The Latinoist movement (Chicanos, Puerto Ricans, Cubans and other Spanish-speaking people working together to combat racial discrimination in the market place) is good but it is not enough. Other than a common culture we will have nothing to hold us together. We need to meet on a broader communal ground.

The struggle is inner: Chicano, *Indio,* American Indian, *mojado, mexicanó,* immigrant Latino, Anglo in power, working class Anglo, Black, Asian—our psyches resemble the bordertowns and are populated by the same people. The struggle has always been inner, and is played out in the outer terrains. Awareness of our situation must come before inner changes, which in turn come before changes in society. Nothing happens in the "real" world unless it first happens in the images in our heads.

El día de la Chicana
I will not be shamed again
Nor will I shame myself.

I am possessed by a vision: that we Chicanas and Chicanos have taken back or uncovered our true faces, our dignity and self-respect. It's a validation vision.

Seeing the Chicana anew in light of her history. I seek an exoneration, a seeing through the fictions of white supremacy, a seeing of ourselves in our true guises and not as the false racial personality that has been given to us and that we have given to ourselves. I seek our woman's face, our true features, the positive and the negative seen clearly, free of the tainted biases of male dominance. I seek new images of identity, new beliefs about ourselves, our humanity and worth no longer in question.

Estamos viviendo en la noche de la Raza, un tiempo cuando el trabajo se hace a lo quieto, en el oscuro. El día cuando aceptamos tal y como somos y para en donde vamos y porque—ese día será el día de la Raza. Yo tengo el conpromiso de expresar mi visión, mi sensibilidad, mi percepción de la revalidación de la gente mexicana, su mérito, estimación, honra, aprecio, y validez.

On December 2nd when my sun goes into my first house, I celebrate *el día de la Chicana y el Chicano.* On that day I clean my altars, light my *Coatlalopeuh* candle, burn sage and copal, take *el baño para espantar basura,* sweep my house. On that day I bare my soul, make myself vulnerable to friends and family by expressing my feelings. On that day I affirm who we are.

On that day I look inside our conflicts and our basic introverted racial temperament. I identify our needs, voice them. I acknowledge that the self and the races have been wounded. I recognize the need to take care of our personhood, of our racial self. On that day I gather the splintered and disowned parts of *la gente mexicana* and hold them in my arms. *Todas las partes de nosotros valen.*

On that day I say, "Yes, all you people wound us when you reject us. Rejection strips us of self-worth; our vulnerability exposes us to shame. It is our innate identity you find wanting. We are ashamed that we need your good opinion, that we need your acceptance. We can no longer camouflage our needs, can no longer let defenses and fences sprout around us. We can no longer withdraw. To rage and look upon you with contempt is to rage and be contemptuous of ourselves. We can no longer blame you, nor disown the white parts, the male parts, the pathological parts, the queer parts, the vulnerable parts. Here we are weaponless with open arms, with only our magic. Let's try it our way, the mestiza way, the Chicana way, the woman way.

On that day, I search for our essential dignity as a people, a people with a sense of purpose—to belong and contribute to something greater than our *pueblo*. On that day I seek to recover and reshape my spiritual identity. *¡Animate! Raza, a celebrar el día de la Chicana.*

76

JUNE JORDAN

Where Is the Sisterhood? (1996)

It eats at my heart. I can't get it out of my head that mothers throw away, or drown, or suffocate, their baby girls. This happens in India, and Africa, and China, which is to say that coming into the world female is extremely hazardous inside the majority cultures of our species.

Seven years ago, twelve-year-old African-American Bracola Coleman was found dead on her kitchen floor. Evidently she had been fatally wounded by a broomstick jammed into her vagina.

Chinese infant Mei Ming, which means No Name in Mandarin, was recently found decom-

posing inside a Chinese orphanage, where she had been left to perish without food or any other kind of care.

When my Uncle Teddy called his wife about their newborn baby, and when his wife, my aunt, told him she'd given birth to a baby girl, my Uncle Teddy exclaimed, "There must be some mistake!"

The violation and murder of Bracola Coleman received negligible coverage. We know the tool of her annihilation, but we do not know who she was alive:

On what street and up which stairs and near or far from what refrigerator with cheese or Pepsi or beer inside, did she live?

Where was she heading when she died?

Before, or after, watching what on TV?

What did she ever laugh about?

Why did no one protect her from this last unmitigated desecration of her body?

Her life and her death elicited equal neglect.

On the other hand, the calculated starvation and abandonment of Mei Ming has received international attention as the existence of "dying rooms" for unwanted children, particularly unwanted baby girls, becomes more and more appallingly documented.

But none of this attention will resurrect that child. She died and she lived with No Name.

And nobody knows how she was born or where, or who she might have wanted to become or why.

We know nothing about Mei Ming except the meaning of her name.

My uncle could not kill his daughter by phone, but she killed herself years later, in a tailspin of belief in her own worthlessness. My cousin carried my uncle's name, but without his love his name conferred no safety, no promise of familial esteem; she had no name of her own, no claim to legitimate, beloved standing in the world.

She was just a girl.

When it became clear that my new friend, the African-American head of the local NAACP, intended to rape me, I tried to stop him by asking: "Do you know who I am?" By which I meant that I was his new friend, his political sister: a black woman willing and able to love and admire him. He silenced me with violence.

I could not call myself a name that would compel his nonviolent recognition and respect.

I could not call myself a name that he would have to answer with his own.

I was just a girl.

India, China, Africa are not white, Western countries. Bracola Coleman and my cousin Lynnsely Rutledge did not yield to white, Western assault.

In the newsprint photo of Mei Ming, suffering has consumed her. She is emaciated, diseased. The violence of the affliction of No Name could not be more clearly conveyed. Her executioners were neither Western nor white.

We cannot say of twelve-year-old Bracola Coleman, "She's dead." We cannot even say of Mei Ming, "She's dead." "She" never existed for us. Denied and despised, these children died from No Name. And the lethal brutality that befalls those of us carrying No Name into the world is no longer, anywhere, theoretical.

I am saying America is not colorblind, but evil is. Hatred opens up an inhumane temptation for every kind of people on Earth.

These dead children should summon us to a further commitment, building upon affirmative action and its original, limited aims.

These dead children died nameless, belonging nowhere in particular. We did not know them and, therefore, could not save them from their ignominious existence.

Building upon affirmative action as we have first conceived of it, we should now move against our own legacies of acquiescence, complicity, hatefulness, and cowardice. Whoever we are, we need to interact actively with all of our cultures of origin. In this sense, self-criticism is way overdue. And we need to exorcise inertia from our notions of acceptable behavior, or even belated self-criticism will lapse into mere embroidery upon comfortable habits of self-absorption.

Every single one of us is No Name in the universe of somebody else who is No Name to you and me.

And the problem is this: Between Nobody Real and Nobody Real, every imaginable violation, every imaginable violence, seems distant, or abstract, and, therefore, possibly unreal, and, therefore, unimportant, or impossible to interdict.

I am calling for a righteous redefinition of affirmative action so that we will attend to emergency issues specific to female life, as well as issues adhering to bedeviled constructs of racial identity. I believe that righteous affirmative action means that we extirpate all historical hatred attached to our names—whether that brutal negativity points to a slavemaster, the manager of a brothel or young children for sale, an uncle, Snoop Doggy Dog, Patrick Buchanan, Timothy McVeigh, or yet another movie showing black women in BMW convertibles and expensive clothes, with zero political consciousness, zero community usefulness.

Where is the movie about Ms. Fannie Lou Hamer? (Who?)

Why are there voluminous surveys and findings pertinent to young black men but no comparable intelligence available about black women and young black girls?

Where is the sisterhood?

Why is it that all black women do not declare ourselves The Welfare Queens United?

Is there any doubt about the sadistic and boastful scapegoating of black women who raise children by ourselves and then ask for recognition, respect, and sometimes assistance?

Is there any amazingly difficult research still to be accomplished before we discover that AFDC adds up to 1 percent of the national budget, and that there are more white women on welfare than black women, and that there is no statistical proof that children raised by their single mothers do more poorly than children of Patrick Buchanan's parents?

Where is the sisterhood?

Why do we keep silent when the so-called Welfare Queen comes up?

Or when we hear about the genital mutilation of girls?

Or when we read about a young black mother terrified and bullied into jumping off a bridge?

Where is the sisterhood?

If we do not join together for the sake of the neediest among us, then what is the purpose of our unity?

The United Nations 1995 Report on the World's Women Trends and Statistics begins with this stunning announcement: "There are fewer women in the world than men." In an ancillary but earlier 1992 U.N. report, *The Sexual Age Distribution of the World's Population,* we learn that men have outnumbered women, worldwide, since 1965.

In a 1990 *New York Review of Books* article entitled, "More Than 100 Million Women Are Missing," the writer, Amartya Sen, reports that gainful employment is decisive in the determination of female longevity and that unequal nutrition and unequal health care correlate with the declining ratio of women to men.

Sen calculates the shocking, awesome, number of deaths implied by inequality and neglect, and arrives at her estimate of "more than 100 million women missing"—more than 100 million female lives extinguished by contempt.

When you interlink this contempt with female infanticide and the increasing popularity of interrupting pregnancy if, otherwise, a baby girl will be born, you guarantee the mute evaporation of hundreds of millions of female lives ahead of us.

This documented, but utterly disregarded, vanishing of female life has taken place all around us, and recently.

Where is the sisterhood?

Would you or my multicultural studies include or omit this information?

Why is this years-ago-documented loss of female life nevertheless "news" in 1996?

Any affirmative action deserving our faith and our hard work must militate against the perishing of the female of our species. That perishing, that endangerment, remains, shamelessly, hidden. And that endangerment flourishes inside the majority cultures of the world—African, Indian, and Chinese.

Systematic, careless, and traditional hatred of female life leads, inexorably, to gender genocide, and nothing less than that.

And, in the context of genocide, what will affirmative action require?

And where is the sisterhood?

As a female member of our endangered species, I am searching for relevant proof of sisterhood: I am searching for relevant proof of brotherhood hinged to that sisterhood.

I want to pursue the collective, and the creative, securement of all of our legitimate names for all of our, finally, legitimate lives.

I need to establish my legitimate name inside the consciousness of strangers. I need to learn the legitimate names of the strangers surrounding me. Then, perhaps, I can hope, at last, to find something possibly useful, possibly affirmative to say.

In the name of Bracola Coleman and Mei Ming, who perished unknown among us, I commit my heart and my mind to this further, lifelong, student undertaking.

77

UNITED NATIONS FOURTH WORLD CONFERENCE ON WOMEN

Beijing Declaration (1995)

1. We, the Governments participating in the Fourth World Conference on Women,

2. Gathered here in Beijing in September 1995, the year of the fiftieth anniversary of the founding of the United Nations,

From gopher://gopher.undp.org/00/unconfs/ women/off/a--20.en (12/31/99). Grateful acknowledgment is made to the United Nations for making documents from The Fourth World Conference on Women available on the Internet.

3. Determined to advance the goals of equality, development and peace for all women everywhere in the interest of all humanity,

4. Acknowledging the voices of all women everywhere and taking note of the diversity of women and their roles and circumstances, honouring the women who paved the way and inspired by the hope present in the world's youth,

5. Recognize that the status of women has advanced in some important respects in the past decade but that progress has been uneven, inequalities between women and men have persisted and major obstacles remain, with serious consequences for the well-being of all people,

6. Also recognize that this situation is exacerbated by the increasing poverty that is affecting the lives of the majority of the world's people, in particular women and children, with origins in both the national and international domains,

7. Dedicate ourselves unreservedly to addressing these constraints and obstacles and thus enhancing further the advancement and empowerment of women all over the world, and agree that this requires urgent action in the spirit of determination, hope, cooperation and solidarity, now and to carry us forward into the next century.

We reaffirm our commitment to:

8. The equal rights and inherent human dignity of women and men and other purposes and principles enshrined in the Charter of the United Nations, to the Universal Declaration of Human Rights and other international human rights instruments, in particular the Convention on the Elimination of All Forms of Discrimination against Women and the Convention on the Rights of the Child, as well as the Declaration on the Elimination of Violence against Women and the Declaration on the Right to Development;

9. Ensure the full implementation of the human rights of women and of the girl child as an inalienable, integral and indivisible part of all human rights and fundamental freedoms;

10. Build on consensus and progress made at previous United Nations conferences and summits—on women in Nairobi in 1985, on children in New York in 1990, on environment and development in Rio de Janeiro in 1992, on human rights in Vienna in 1993, on population and development in Cairo in 1994 and on social development in Copenhagen in 1995 with the objective of achieving equality, development and peace;

11. Achieve the full and effective implementation of the Nairobi Forwardlooking Strategies for the Advancement of Women;

12. The empowerment and advancement of women, including the right to freedom of thought, conscience, religion and belief, thus contributing to the moral, ethical, spiritual and intellectual needs of women and men, individually or in community with others and thereby guaranteeing them the possibility of realizing their full potential in society and sharing their lives in accordance with their own aspirations.

We are convinced that:

13. Women's empowerment and their full participation on the basis of equality in all spheres of society, including participation in the decision-making process and access to power, are fundamental for the achievement of equality, development and peace;

14. Women's rights are human rights;

15. Equal rights, opportunities and access to resources, equal sharing of responsibilities for the family by men and women, and a harmonious partnership between them are critical to their well-being and that of their families as well as to the consolidation of democracy;

16. Eradication of poverty based on sustained economic growth, social development, environmental protection and social justice requires the involvement of women in economic and social development, equal opportunities and the full and equal participation of women and men as agents and beneficiaries of people-centered sustainable development;

17. The explicit recognition and reaffirmation of the right of all women to control all aspects of their health, in particular their own fertility, is basic to their empowerment;

18. Local, national, regional and global peace is attainable and is inextricably linked with the advancement of women, who are a fundamental force for leadership, conflict resolution and the promotion of lasting peace at all levels;

19. It is essential to design, implement and monitor, with the full participation of women, effective, efficient and mutually reinforcing gender-sensitive policies and programmes, including development policies and programmes, at all levels that will foster the empowerment and advancement of women;

20. The participation and contribution of all actors of civil society, particularly women's groups and networks and other non-governmental organizations and community-based organizations, with full respect for their autonomy, in cooperation with Governments, are important to the effective implementation and follow-up of the Platform for Action;

21. The implementation of the Platform for Action requires commitment from Governments and the international community. By making national and international commitments for action, including those made at the Conference, Governments and the international community recognize the need to take priority action for the empowerment and advancement of women.

We are determined to:

22. Intensify efforts and actions to achieve the goals of the Nairobi Forwardlooking Strategies for the Advancement of Women by the end of this century;

23. Ensure the full enjoyment by women and the girl child of all human rights and fundamental freedoms and take effective action against violations of these rights and freedoms;

24. Take all necessary measures to eliminate all forms of discrimination against women and the girl child and remove all obstacles to gender equality and the advancement and empowerment of women;

25. Encourage men to participate fully in all actions towards equality;

26. Promote women's economic independence, including employment, and eradicate the persistent and increasing burden of poverty on women by addressing the structural causes of poverty through changes in economic structures, ensuring equal access for all women, including those in rural areas, as vital development agents, to productive resources, opportunities and public services;

27. Promote people-centered sustainable development, including sustained economic growth, through the provision of basic education, life-long education, literacy and training, and primary health care for girls and women;

28. Take positive steps to ensure peace for the advancement of women and, recognizing the leading role that women have played in the peace movement, work actively toward general and complete disarmament under strict and effective international control, and support negotiations on the conclusion, without delay, of a universal and multilaterally and effectively verifiable comprehensive nuclear-test-ban treaty which contributes to nuclear disarmament and the prevention of the proliferation of nuclear weapons in all its aspects;

29. Prevent and eliminate all forms of violence against women and girls;

30. Ensure equal access to and equal treatment of women and men in education and health care and enhance women's sexual and reproductive health as well as education;

31. Promote and protect all human rights of women and girls;

32. Intensify efforts to ensure equal enjoyment of all human rights and fundamental freedoms for all women and girls who face multiple barriers to their empowerment and advancement because of such factors as their race, age, language, ethnicity, culture, religion, or disability, or because they are indigenous people;

33. Ensure respect for international law, including humanitarian law, in order to protect women and girls in particular;

34. Develop the fullest potential of girls and women of all ages, ensure their full and equal participation in building a better world

for all and enhance their role in the development process.

We are determined to:

35. Ensure women's equal access to economic resources, including land, credit, science and technology, vocational training, information, communication and markets, as a means to further the advancement and empowerment of women and girls, including through the enhancement of their capacities to enjoy the benefits of equal access to these resources, inter alia, by means of international cooperation;

36. Ensure the success of the Platform for Action, which will require a strong commitment on the part of Governments, international organizations and institutions at all levels. We are deeply convinced that economic development, social development and environmental protection are interdependent and mutually reinforcing components of sustainable development, which is the framework for our efforts to achieve a higher quality of life for all people. Equitable social development that recognizes empowering the poor, particularly women living in poverty, to utilize environmental resources sustainably is a necessary foundation for sustainable development. We also recognize that broad-based and sustained economic growth in the context of sustainable development is necessary to sustain social development and social justice. The success of the Platform for Action will also require adequate mobilization of resources at the national and international levels as well as new and additional resources to the developing countries from all available funding mechanisms, including multilateral, bilateral and private sources for the advancement of women; financial resources to strengthen the capacity of national, subregional, regional and international institutions; a commitment to equal rights, equal responsibilities and equal opportunities and to the equal participation of women and men in all national, regional and international bodies and policy-making processes; and the

establishment or strengthening of mechanisms at all levels for accountability to the world's women;

37. Ensure also the success of the Platform for Action in countries with economies in transition, which will require continued international cooperation and assistance;

38. We hereby adopt and commit ourselves as Governments to implement the following Platform for Action, ensuring that a gender perspective is reflected in all our policies and programmes. We urge the United Nations system, regional and international financial institutions, other relevant regional and international institutions and all women and men, as well as non-governmental organizations, with full respect for their autonomy, and all sectors of civil society, in cooperation with Governments, to fully commit themselves and contribute to the implementation of this Platform for Action.

78

HILLARY RODHAM CLINTON

Remarks to the NGO Forum on Women (1995)

First Lady Hillary Rodham Clinton: Thank you. Thank you so much, I feel so much at home and so much a part of this group. I only wish that in addition to the enthusiasm and interest amongst all of the NGOs who are gathered here, the weather had been more cooperative this morning and I greatly regret that we were forced to move this occasion indoors in order to avoid any of us drowning out there. But I am very sorry that not everyone who wished to be with us this morning was able to be in, and I hope all of you will convey my personal regrets to anyone who was turned away or

From http://www.igc.org/beijing/plenary/hillary. html (3/4/97). Grateful acknowledgment is made to the United Nations for making documents from The Fourth World Conference on Women available on the Internet.

disappointed because of the size of this auditorium.

It is a great pleasure for me to be here, and I want to start by thanking Supatra and Irene for their leadership in this extraordinary and historic enterprise. But I also what to thank all of you who are here, because I know from looking at the lists of people who have come, of knowing personally many of the Americans who have come, that in this auditorium and at this Forum, there are thousands and thousands of women and men who every day work to make lives better in their communities for all people. And that is the greatest contribution any one of us is able to make, and that is why the United States and many other countries so strongly support the efforts of NGOs and have worked very hard to ensure that NGOs could participate in this Forum. As many of you know, our government and other governments recognize the important role that NGOs play in policy and planning, in development and implementation and monitoring of programs that advance the progress of women.

I wanted to come here to Huairou to salute you for your dedication to a cause greater than all of us. I know that many of you went to great efforts to be here. I know many were kept from attending this Forum. I know that for many of you who did get here, getting here was far from easy. Many of you did not even know until the last minute that you would be permitted to travel here, and others bore great personal expense in order to come. In addition to the weather, which is not in anyone's control, and is always unpredictable, I know that you have had to endure severe frustrations here as you have pursued your work, and I also want to say a special word on behalf of women with disabilities who have faced particularly challenging (inaudible) but I mostly want to thank you for your perseverance, because you did not give up, you did not stay away, you are here, and the fact that you are, will make a difference in the days and months and years to come. Because even though you may not be physically present in Beijing at the Conference during these ten days, the wisdom that is accumulated here, the experience, the energy, the ideas are on full display. Thanks to your resourcefulness, your tenacity, your sense of purpose and your spirit, you are playing an important role in this Conference, and you will be the key players in determining whether or not this Conference goes beyond rhetoric and actually does something to improve the lives of women and children.

As I said yesterday, the faces of the women who are here mirror the faces of the millions and millions who are not. It is our responsibility, those of us who have been able to attend this Conference and this NGO forum, to make sure that the voices that go unheard will be heard. This Conference is about making sure that women, their children, their families, have the opportunities for health care and education, for jobs and political participation, for lives free of violence, for basic legal protections, and yes, for internationally recognized human rights no matter where they are or where they live.

Time and time again we have seen that it is NGOs who are responsible for making progress in any society. Some of us never knew we were NGOs twenty and twenty-five and thirty years ago, that was not even a phrase that any of us had ever heard. We were people working together on behalf of all of those rights which we care about and hold dear. But when one looks at the progress that has been made throughout the world, it is clear that it is the NGOs who have charted real advances for women and children. It is the NGOs who have pressured governments and have led governments down the path to economic, social and political progress, often in the face of overwhelming hostility. Again, NGOs have persevered, just as you have by coming here and staying here and participating in this Forum. What will be important as we end the Forum and the Conference at the end of this week, is that it will be NGOs who will hold governments to the commitments that they make. And it is important that the final Platform for Action that is adopted be distilled down into words that every woman, no matter where she lives, or how much education she has, can understand. I think we should want every woman, no matter where she is, to believe that there are women all over the world who care about her health, who want her children to be educated, who want her to have the dignity and respect that she deserves to have.

When I think of the faces that I have seen in my own country, when I think of the women who did not have health care because they cannot afford it in the United States of America, when I think particularly of a woman I met in New Orleans, Louisiana, who told me that because she did not have enough money she was told by physicians there in our country, that they would not do anything about the lump in her breast, but would merely wait and watch, because if she had insurance she would have been sent to a surgeon. I think about the woman I met in a village outside Lahore, Pakistan, who had ten children, five boys and five girls, and was struggling as hard as she could to make sure her girls were educated and wanted help to get that job done. I think of the faces of the beautiful women I met at SEWA, the Self-Employed Women's Association in India, all of them had walked miles and miles, some of them for twelve and fifteen hours to get to our meeting together, and I listened as they stood up and told me what it had meant that for the first time in their lives, they having little money of their own, they could buy their own vegetable carts, they could buy their own thread and materials so that they could make income for themselves and their families.

I think of the women in the village in Bangladesh, a village of untouchables, I think of how those women who were Hindus invited to their village for my visit women from the neighboring village who were Moslems. I think of how those women sat together under a lean-to, Hindus and Moslems together in one of the poorest countries of the world, but so many of those women telling me what their lives had been changed to become because they had become borrowers that were now part of the

Grameen Bank micro-enterprise effort. I think particularly of the play that their children put on for me to see, a play in which the children acted out the refusal by a family to let a girl child to go to school, and how finally through efforts undertaken by the mother and the sister, the father agreed that the child could go to school. And then further down the road from that village, I stood and watched families coming to receive food supplements in return for keeping their girl children in school.

Those are the kinds of women and experiences that happen throughout the world, whether one talks about my country or any country. Women are looking for the support and encouragement they need to do what they can for their own lives and the lives of their children and the lives of their families. The only way this Conference will make a difference to these women, is if the results of the Conference are taken and distilled down into one page perhaps, which stages basic principles that you and I would perhaps debate and understand but may not be easily communicated. If that is done, then to carry that message into every corner of the world so there can be sharing of experiences. When I came home from Bangladesh, I visited in Denver, Colorado a program that is modeled on the Grameen Bank, helping American women who are welfare recipients get the dignity and the skills that they need to take care of themselves and their children.

So despite all of the difficulties and frustrations you have faced in coming here and being here, you are here not only on behalf of yourselves, but on behalf of millions and millions of women whose lives can be changed for the better, if you resolve along with all of us, to leave this place and do what we can together to make the changes that will give respect and dignity to every woman.

I know that today at the Women's Conference there is a special celebration of girls. The theme is investing in today's girls, tomorrow's women and the future. We know that much of what we do, we are doing not for ourselves, but we are doing for our daughters, our nieces, our granddaughters. We are doing it because we have the hope that the changes we work for will take root and flower in their lives. When I was privileged to be in New Delhi, India, I met a young woman who I think spoke for many, many women, and someone asked me yesterday at the Conference if I had a copy of the poem which this young woman wrote. And I said that I did and she asked if I could read it today, and I said that I would. Because this was a poem about breaking the silence, the silence that afflicts too many women's lives, the silence that keeps women from expressing themselves freely, from being full participants even in the lives of their own families. This poem written by a young woman, I think is particularly appropriate since we are celebrating today the future of girls. Let me read it to you:

"Too many women in too many countries speak the same language of silence. My grandmother was always silent, always agreed. Only her husband had the positive right, or so it was said, to speak and to be heard. They say it is different now. After all, I am always vocal, and my grandmother thinks I talk too much. But sometimes I wonder. When a woman gives her love as most do generously, it is accepted. When a woman shares her thoughts as some women do graciously, it is allowed. When a woman fights for power as all women would like to, quietly or loudly, it is questioned. And yet, there must be freedom if we are to speak. And yes, there must be power if we are to be heard. And when we have both freedom and power, let us not be misunderstood. We seek only to give words to those who cannot speak—too many women in too many countries. I seek only to forget my grandmother's silence."

That is the kind of feeling that literally millions and millions of women feel every day. And much of what we are doing here at this Forum and at this Conference is to give words to break the silence and then to act. When I was at Copenhagen for the Summit

on Social Development, I was pleased to announce that the United States would make an effort to enhance educational opportunities for girls so that they could attend school in Africa, Asia, and Latin America. Today that effort, funded with United States' dollars, is being organized in countries throughout those continents by NGOs.

There are so many ways we can work together. There are so many things that must be done. And let me just end with a postcard that I received from a woman who, with many, many others, wrote me her feelings and thoughts about this Conference. I don't know this woman, but she wrote to tell me that she wanted me to carry this card to Beijing. And she went on to say, "Be assured of many prayers for the success of the Conference, to better conditions for women and children throughout the world." She put on this card a prayer and the prayer was written in many languages. It's a prayer that applies and can be said by many if not all of the world's religions. And I want to end with that because I think that in many respects what we are attempting to do requires the kind of faith and commitment that this prayer represents:

Oh God, creator of the heavens and the earth, we pray for all who gather in Beijing [and I would add Huairou as well] bless them, help them and us to see one another through eyes enlightened by understanding and compassion. Release us from prejudice so we can receive the stories of our sisters with respect and attention. Open our ears to the cries of a suffering world and the healing melodies of peace. Empower us to be instruments in bringing about your justice and equality everywhere.

That is my prayer as well, and with my thanks to all of you I believe we can take the results of this Forum and this Conference and begin to translate them into actions that will count, in the lives of girls and women who will have never heard of what we have done here, by whose lives can be changed because of what you have done coming here.

79

Rebecca Adamson, Veronica Chambers, Urvashi Vaid, and Mari J. Matsuda

Getting There (1997)

REBECCA ADAMSON
"WHOLE EARTH" ECONOMY

All things are bound together, all things connect, and what happens to the Earth happens to the children of the Earth. Human beings did not weave the web of life; each of us is but one thread, and whatever she does to the web, she does to herself. For tribal people, who see the world as a whole, the essence of our work is in its entirety. In a society where all are related, where everybody is someone else's mother, father, brother, sister, aunt, or cousin, and where you cannot leave without eventually coming home, simple decisions require the approval of nearly everyone in that society. It is society as a whole—not merely any part, or parts, of it—that must survive.

This is the Native understanding that for thousands of years provided the values and belief systems for organizing our societies. While the diverse and varying results embodied reciprocity, such models are being lost at the exact time their wisdom is becoming the understanding in a global sense.

As more and more technology shrinks our planet Earth, the commonality that emerges among people is our interdependence. If we can see this clearly, within ourselves and within all creatures, the way we conduct our lives takes on larger meaning and just on the horizon lies the vision of humanity.

Where are the native nations in this vision? For the past two centuries, we have been the "miner's canary" thrust into a development process gone haywire. Today, the official unem-

ployment rate for Native Americans is 35 percent—although on many of the reservations or homelands, it runs higher than 80 percent—and only 29 percent of the entire adult Indian population earn more than $9,000 a year. The death rate from alcoholism is 5.6 times the national norm, and we are now witnessing the second generation of fetal alcohol syndrome babies.

But just as the "miner's canary" warned early coal miners of poisonous gases, what is happening to us is also happening elsewhere in the world. Poverty is expanding rapidly in the inner cities, in rural towns, on the borders, around the globe. Fueled by inequality, the number of poor people in the world continues to grow in spite of a quintupling of the global economy since 1950: the richest 20 percent of the world's population consumes 80 percent of the world's resources, and even in the wealthiest economies, 100 million people still live in poverty. In the current, skewed version of development, 51 of the top 100 economies in the world are corporations. These corporations have more wealth than 130 countries, yet they have no responsibility for education or health or social welfare, nor do they have any commitment to place. And what of the Earth in this "development" farce? Eleven percent of the earth's productive land is already degraded, and much of that degradation is irreversible in a human time scale. Nonnatural soil erosion—at a rate of 25 billion tons a year—greatly exceeds soil formation. Loss of biodiversity is reflected in the present-day extinction rate of about one species every 20 minutes.

Every society organizes itself politically, socially, and economically according to its values. In spiritual terms, this is evolution. In human terms, this is development. The issue of development, more than any other issue, is the battle line between two competing world views—Euro-American values of individualism, domination, exploitation, and separation, versus tribal values of kinship, balance, reciprocity, and interconnectedness.

In the Euro-American model, even the most basic college course in economics teaches one fundamental truth—underlying all economics theory is the idea of a scarcity of resources. This becomes a self-fulfilling prophecy because, if on that basis, you then organize your economy on accumulation, consumption, production, and growth, of course you will achieve a scarcity of resources. Environmental degradation, resource depletion, and global warming attest to that. The fundamental value of tribal peoples was sustainability; livelihoods were conducted in ways that sustained resources and limited inequalities in society. What made traditional economies so radically different and so fundamentally dangerous to Western economies were the traditional principles of sustainability versus scarcity of resources; of sharing and distribution versus accumulation; and kinship usage rights versus individual exclusive ownership rights. Indigenous societies that have not been disrupted value stability and sustainability instead of growth. They protect resources in many ways, including the promotion of anticonsumerist ethics. Juxtapose these values against the fundamental values of the individualistic society in this country, of accumulation and growth, and you can see why there has always been a conflict. . . .

In the field of economic development, economists like to think Western economics is value-neutral. But the fact is, it reflects definite values. This is the system that pays a merger acquisitionist hundreds of thousands of dollars and a teacher $40,000. Under what conditions can values be translated to a single-scale measurement such as money? Has this society that has made all these technological advances become so detached that the economic system is God? Is it the center of society's spirituality, or is society ready to take control of the economic system and use it for humanity?

Never before have we had the responsibility for our evolution—for our survival—so clearly before us. We are entering what many futurists are calling a *planetary society*—we can kill all humankind with a single bomb, we can destroy the ozone, we can blow up the planet. The current rules of the game must therefore change. These are not win-or-lose power-control scenarios any longer. We all lose. The interdependency of humans, the relevance of relationships, is returning as a fact of life. It is ancient, ancient wisdom.

Unless there is something I don't know, we are all indigenous peoples of this community called Earth. As indigenous peoples, of this planet, we have to reorganize to get along; we have to believe in a new vision of humanity. I was taught that a vision is your life. In this case, it is our survival.

VERONICA CHAMBERS
REMEMBERING THE FUTURE

won't you celebrate with me
what I have shaped into
a kind of life? i had no model
born in babylon
both nonwhite and woman
what did i see to be except myself?[1]

These brave and spirited words, from "won't you celebrate with me?" by the poet Lucille Clifton, echo the isolation and struggle of many of us who find ourselves fighting double and triple prejudices within this generation of feminism. It is no secret that the modern women's movement has been dominated by women who are straight, white, and middle-class. But it is also no secret that, all along, there have been women of color in the movement.

There have always been African Americans and Latinas who have battled both the racism of their "sisters" as well as the sexism within their own ethnic communities. There have always been Asian American women and Native American women who have battled invisibility and xenophobia. There has never been a time when there weren't gay and bisexual women in the movement, as well as poor women and disabled women. Often we talk about strategies for making the movement more "inclusive," but the

1. Copyright © 1993 by Lucille Clifton. Reprinted by permission of Copper Canyon Press.

fact is, the women we seek to "include" have been here all along. . . .

But racism is not the only divisive element in the women's movement. We know there are white women who fight against sexism while remaining completely unaware, and unconcerned, with their own racism. What we don't talk about as often are the other ways in which each of us must continue to do the difficult work of looking within and seeing the work we have to do.

How do we, as black women, begin to address the rampant homophobia in our communities? How do we modify the joyous portrait of sister-girl-friendships, à la *Waiting to Exhale,* to include gay women as well?

How do we as young women, living in a culture that overvalues youth, begin to address the question of ageism? In the workplace, where older men are seen as wise and older women are seen as crones, how do young women make alliances? When we find ourselves being pitted against older women, or when we address our sisters' suspicion and envy, how do we react?

We often speak about guilt in terms of race. But how do any of us address our own ignorance about the differences of disability? How do we face with grace—and not guilt—women who fight discrimination on the terrain of their own bodies?

Some, who are easily frustrated, say that it is not enough to ask questions. What they want, they say, are answers. But as we take this movement into the twenty-first century, I think we would do well to think like scientists. In science, the questions are always considered the most exciting part. What if, instead of anger and guilt and moral obligation, we brought our imaginations to bear on the divisions within the feminist community? If we imagined these questions as a Stephen Hawking hypothesis about the stars and the universe, where would we go from here? "Why do we remember the past and not the future?" Hawking once wrote. This is a great question for feminists, one that allows us to feel more empowered about equality as ours to

claim—not only equality with men, but also equality with other women. It's our future. Instead of thinking about what has been done and what has not been done in the past, could we think like astronomers who look at the night sky and ask how high, how far, how fast?

Beyond the factionalism that comes from any politicized organization, I look at our differences—our skin, our sexuality, our physicality—and, I wonder how do we all fit? It's not unlike the Chinese puzzle Muriel Rukeyser speaks of in her wonderful poem, "Effort at Speech Between Two People." The refrain could be the refrain of our lives: "Take my hand, speak to me." And I know the vulnerability in there, the fearless quest for communication, is intrinsic to how we can reconcile our questions of difference. My friends and I used to laugh at the talk, talk, and more talk ethic of the seventies movement—the encounter groups, the opening of one's "self." Only in the nineties have we come to realize how valuable that kind of communication process was. But it wasn't only because those seventies rap sessions seemed too earnest and corny that we didn't take them on. It was because we have been so mired in guilt and anger—the anger that stops me from talking to women in the movement whom I feel are racist; the guilt that prevents them from facing me squarely on the issues.

I don't talk much partly because a white woman once said to me, "Black women are always complaining." I had not been complaining; I had been throwing out challenges. Why didn't she want to "celebrate with me"; to view my life and all the challenges of being a black woman in a culture that lauds neither my race nor my gender as something to celebrate? Being a minority woman presents challenges that are not always so visible to the white mainstream of the movement. When Lucille Clifton says, "come celebrate with me that everyday something has tried to kill me and has failed," I know she means "something" in the largest sense of the word: hate and poverty, discrimination, and media manipulation. But I am also keenly aware, as someone who was raised in a community of poverty and violence, that "kill" is not just a metaphor.

Stories of what went down on streets I walked every day filled me with an indescribable terror. At nine and ten years old, I would try to imagine what it felt like to be shot, to be stabbed, to be killed. Every night I prayed for a quick death and not the slow-motion throb of bullet piercing layer upon layer of flesh that haunted me in my dreams. So when I think about things worth struggling for and things worth celebrating, I count the very fact of my life among them.

I know this legacy of violence sets me apart, but I tell this truth of my life not to emphasize our differences, but to bring us closer. For it's because of such things that I value not only my life, but all our lives and the work we are doing here. The bottom line is that we, and everyone and everything that we could possibly mean, are worth struggling for. The commitment we make to ourselves and each other is both the only question that matters and the answer we seek.

URVASHI VAID
SEEKING COMMON GROUND

Those of us who say we are committed to progressive social change need to find ways of reviving women's liberation and developing a broader movement—and feminists can start by repairing and rebuilding the splits in our ranks.

Take, for example, the breach between academic and activist feminists. We activists have to take some responsibility for helping to foster an anti-intellectual climate in the ranks by emphasizing personal experience over political analysis and focusing on the elitism of academia, while doing little to achieve greater access to higher education for all people. We have all contributed to the rupture by collapsing feminism into single-issue advocacy. Instead of a broad-based feminist movement for economic and social change, we work in ever-narrowing problem movements—abortion, domestic violence, sexual harassment, and so on. We have all helped to create a climate of specialization and isolation, when we should be striving for more visible feminist advocacy and making efforts to link women's problems to broader policy initiatives.

Then there are the continuing tensions between lesbian feminists and straight women, between bisexuals and lesbians, between some feminists and transgendered people—and between ex-lesbians and lesbians for that matter—when what we should be doing is restating our connections. It's not coincidental that the military argues that gays in the ranks would threaten traditional male bonding and undermine unit cohesion, while a neo-conservative woman scholar writing in the *New York Times* says women should be banned from combat because we put a damper on the chief form of male bonding—bragging in the locker room. To prove they're not fags, men have to prove they are heterosexual, which, to follow convention, means objectifying and conquering women sexually—then boasting about it.

And we must concede that many feminists—white, brown, African American, Asian, native—have abandoned the ideal of a multiracial society. We, like most people in the wider society, isolate race into its own movement, rather than striving for an understanding of how race in the United States is a subtext to most aspects of public policy and social tension.

While the Right has consolidated its coalition, developed conservative public policy options, and strategically advanced both an economic and a cultural agenda, the progressive side of the political spectrum has built movements that are disconnected from each other, isolated intellectuals from organizers, and devoted an inordinate amount of its resources to responding to right-wing attacks. The appeal of the new centrist politics espoused by many liberals and neoconservatives is directly related to the failure of progressives to offer clear and comprehensible policy alternatives, as well as to our lack of political strength and our poor level of political organization.

What we need are enhanced relationships between local-level leaders and activists and a core of progressive activists working together to create new public policy and practice. What we need to do is broaden debate by distributing more widely the policy work already done by single-issue organizations and academic scholars. What we need is a progressive platform—a clear economic agenda linked to a cultural vision. In short, a common movement that makes visible the possibility of a democratic future.

MARI J. MATSUDA
MERIT BADGES FOR
THE REVOLUTION

Late one night I visited the new Franklin Delano Roosevelt memorial in Washington, D.C., with four other law professors of color. We critical race theorists read the memorial's pledges to feed the hungry and rebuild a nation. We lamented the absence of a New Deal of our times. The monument expressed ideas we midnight visitors shared, but our admiration was coated with the irony that clings so mournfully to our point of view. Looking at the life-size figures of men in a breadline, one of us commented, "I guess no colored folks were poor during the Depression." The image of American heartbreak circa 1930 is of able-bodied white men in the stance of degraded hunger.

White men still stand in breadlines, but the perceived face of our poverty is now black, and no president comes forward to speak of ending poverty with the sober resolve reserved for times of war. The war on poverty ended the day that the image of urban children of color replaced the image of ragged white children in Appalachia in the photogravure of American poverty. Theories of genetic and cultural predisposition to poverty overtook the notion of poverty as something unfortunate that happens to people, like flood and famine, that good cit-

izens respond to with aid. Racism constructs today's poverty as bad choices: "Those people just don't want to work."

A version of racism directed against my own people shores up the belief that poverty is a choice. The model minority myth describes Asians who arrive here penniless, and uplift themselves through values of work, education, and family. Never mind that large numbers of Asian immigrants live in poverty, made worse by so-called welfare reform; and please don't remind anyone that Asian American mom-and-pops perch precariously atop the powder keg created by our abandonment of the urban poor.

The combination of lies about hard-working Asians and lazy blacks, the erasure of white poverty, and the women-blaming image of the welfare queen, has made poverty acceptable in this nation. When racism and patriarchy intersect in this way, look for heterosexism too: "Those single-parent homes are terrible. No male role model, no breadwinner, generations of children growing up poor." Instead of maldistribution of wealth, it is resistance to heterosexual coupling that causes poverty.

Given this ideological entanglement, it is clear to me that we can't fight racism, homophobia, poverty, and patriarchy as separate battles. But many allies see otherwise; good leaders in the civil rights movement who don't get why gay rights are central to our cause; heroic labor organizers who insist class is the main issue; activists in the Asian American community who say, "Push too hard on feminism and you'll alienate our grass roots"; white feminists who feel picked on when they labor to organize an event only to field complaints that the music or the food or the complexion of the proceedings was too white. Working for social change brings us right up against the basic fact of American segregation: we don't know much about each other across lines of race, class, and sexuality. We are clumsy, ignorant, and hurtful when we try to cross those lines.

Make yourself a merit badge if you were in one of those conflicts and stuck it out. Feminist work is coalition work, and in coalition work people think, and sometimes say:

"Why am I always the one educating others about my culture? Why can't they educate themselves as I have had to educate myself in order to survive?"

"Do I have to prove again that I'm not [racist] [anti-Semitic] [homophobic]? Haven't I worked long and hard to establish my solidarity?"

"If I said half of what I'm thinking, I wouldn't last an hour here."

"When are we going to get some real organizing done? I'm so tired of taking care of people who feel excluded."

"They expect me to be grateful just because I get to be here."

"I don't even have medical insurance and she's talking about her new car."

"They're going to hate me because I can afford a new car."

To the good women who will say, "Tell me more about why you feel that way, I really want to listen," when divisions rise up among us, I want to say, "I love you, I admire you, you are my sisters, and I will stay in it with you until the day I die."

We didn't invent the divisions that explode in our faces every time we try to work together; they were handed to us and we will defeat them. This is the eve of our new progressive coalition. There are too many unhappy people. All they need is some good information to realize that their misery comes from living in a nation divided, where the rich get richer, the poor get poorer, and the middle class finances the transaction. Their misery comes from patriarchy, which sets impossible standards for men and leaves scars on women's bodies. It comes from racism, which makes us ever fearful of difference. It comes from homophobia, stealing from us the selves we would discover if rigid roles in gender and sexuality faded away. A progressive coalition can put this poison out of our lives forever.

Our coalition must have feminism at its core, and share that core with a utopian vision of economic equality, dignified work for all who are able, and a promise of care for all who cannot care for themselves. Our coalition must reject homophobia and acknowledge the history of American racism, defining a good world as one in which nonsubordinating differences in culture, language, sexuality, and style are treasured and nurtured. The key to building this coalition is the fun of it. It is simply more fun, as the young people who live by the antiracist, antihomophic creed have found, to roll around in difference. Learn about it, let go the fear of it, and feel giddy from that letting go. We would never watch the same TV program over and over, all day and all night. Why would we want to live in the same TV program, over and over, all day and all night? English only, western culture, hetero *über alles,* and the litany I grew up on as a voracious reader of supermarket magazines: buy-this-gotta-look-good-getta-guy. Losing that is called freedom.

All my sisters with their merit badges, pushing an antiracist, antihomophobic, class-busting version of feminism and living to tell of it, are getting ready to bring the progressive coalition to full bloom.

Those lovely third wavers, with their clothes, their attitude, their music all so fresh and intriguing to me, will lead us. We are waiting, clusters of outsiders meeting at midnight to gaze at the monuments of American culture and whisper our truth: there is so much promise there, and so much evil.

FDR felt constrained to hide his disability; felt compelled to sign an executive order locking up my father's family along with virtually every other Japanese American living on the West Coast during World War II; and could not find a way to welcome Jewish refugees before the horror closed in. For some of us, those facts loom large when we visit the memorial. I behold FDR's gentle smile and wonder if his spirit longs to join us as we move to a place where able-bodied and disabled are one; where we shake off the curse of past hierarchies. He followed us part way there, for the true architects of the New Deal were the thousands of poor men and women who marched to Washington to erect a tent city on Roosevelt's doorstep. Black, white, yellow, brown, they demanded jobs, education, health care, and food for their children, and they refused to leave until they made history. That history reflects a compassionate, can-do sensibility that is alive and waiting for the next deal, the third wave, the great progressive coalition that you'll read about in pages of *Ms.* over the next 25 years. Someday we'll build a monument to our struggle, and old women will come to lay their badges down at its base. I'll see you there.

II. Pop Culture Feminism

THE TWENTIETH CENTURY SAW AN INCREASE IN the permeation of electronically driven popular culture into seemingly all aspects of personal and public life. Film, radio, and the popular music recording industry, television, personal computers with e-mail, the Internet and the World Wide Web—all of these mass media have combined to give women more power to both understand the world and project themselves into it, while at the same time subjecting and limiting them to the kinds of gender-based institutional biases that predate the printing press. In response, U.S. women have laid bare debilitating assumptions and stereotypes not so much by directly opposing dominant cultural forces—although there are certainly examples of this—but by infiltrating, and making a wide range of cultural forms their own. An early formalized strategy for such efforts is described in the National Organization for Women statement, "Task Force on Image of Women in Mass Media" (1967).

Are female pop-music stars and other performers who play on their physical attractiveness and sexuality just reinforcing the male gaze that objectifies women, or are they somehow subverting masculine authority, realizing their own subjectivity by pushing the bounds of decency and thereby wresting agency from heterosexual relations? In Madonna I and Madonna II (1990/1991), the iconoclastic critic Camille Paglia answers this question with a resounding affirmation of letting it all hang out, of taking advantage of "woman's sexual glamour" that has "bewitched and destroyed men since Delilah and Helen of Troy." Paglia declares war on what she considers the prudish Waspish feminists who claim that Madonna has only played into male fantasies and degraded womanhood in the process; Madonna's "flood of inner sexual personae," she counters, can free those women who embrace the "Dionysian realm"—that is, the ecstatic, orgiastic, creative intuitive power with which women are born. Notice how Paglia finds her own sexuality in Madonna's radio and music video performances—they help her "express herself." Whatever one thinks of Paglia's polemics, it must be recognized that the paradox of her embrace of Madonna for self-development was highly representative of late-twentieth-century postmodern American culture, as proved by the tens of thousands "Madonna-bes" that could be seen in the country's malls and dance clubs during the 1980s and early 1990s. Whether that self-development is feminist is another issue altogether.

While sharing Paglia's approval of Madonna, Angela Johnson's "Confessions of a Pop Culture Junkie" (1994) contrasts Paglia's unabashed exuberance for women in popular culture with a playful element of guilt in what Johnson describes as a "frivolous" and "flighty" love of Cosmopolitan magazine, the TV show Beverly Hills 90210, and other a-feminist (if not anti-feminist) forms of entertainment and fantasy. Johnson—an editor of Off Our Backs, the women's news journal in which this essay is published—wonders if these distractions are in any way consistent with her commitment to women's politics: "can I turn swords into plowshares, movie trivia into feminist activism?" She doesn't answer the question conclusively, but resigns herself to the ever-presence of popular culture and the power of its enticements—most of the Off Our Backs editorial collective have happily submitted, she reports. Johnson's attitude is probably more representative than Paglia's of how many American women approach popular culture. Her irony helps explain how there can be so many feminist lovers of soap operas, romance novels, and beauty pageants. There was a knowingness to late-twentieth-century appreciation of popular culture, although part of that mind-set was knowing full well that popular culture is still socially determinative, creating a web of meanings and expectations that oftentimes narrows the acceptable possibilities for women's identity.

When considering popular culture's paradoxically creative and coercive capacity, special attention must be given to Hollywood and the movie business, one of America's most distinct and powerful culture factories. Since its founding outside of Los Angeles in the early 1910s, Hollywood has played a large role in shaping American ideals of gender. It has proved to be especially prolific in producing larger-than-life depictions of the "real man." Whether it be in the form of the gunslinging cowboy, the hard-boiled detective, or the heroic soldier, archetypical manhood takes shape in a homosocial hypermasculine world of competitive performance—an ideological context that morally sanctions the use of violence and that casts woman as a weak and incapable other, a less-than-secondary figure whose beauty and sexuality are oftentimes the episodic reward for male dominance, cunning, and killing. Since the 1960s, however, Hollywood has also come out with films that undermine these dominant story lines. Anti-Westerns like *McCabe and Mrs. Miller* (1971) have deglamorized the genre, laying bare the selfish motivations of masculine violence and also embracing the active presence and strength of women in the history of the American West. Perhaps the most accomplished example of the "feminist Western" is *The Ballad of Little Joe* (1993), whose heroine thrives as a cross-dressing cowboy, keeping men in their place through her intelligence and skill with a gun. Another feminist-inspired appropriation of a masculine genre—as discussed by film critic Kathi Maio in "Film: Women Who Murder for the Man" (1991)—is the accomplished road movie *Thelma and Louise* (1991), in which Susan Sarandon and Geena Davis play friends setting out for a quiet weekend of fishing but end up fugitives after killing a man who raped Louise. *Thelma and Louise*, as Maio points out, can be viewed as a strategic rejection of male power or patriarchy: from Louise leaving her insipid and unfaithful husband to the two friends blowing up the rig of an abusive trucker, the film is framed as an expression of purposeful feminist anger and retribution. *Thelma and Louise* drew a great deal of backlash and criticism from male writers who only saw it as a vehicle for man hating.

Of course another powerful source of traditional gender ideals and masculine preeminence has been the post–World War II advent of television and the popularity of shows featuring male action heroes. *The Lone Ranger* (1949–1957), *Combat!* (1962–1967), *Hercules: The Legendary Journeys* (1995–1999)—to name just a few of hundreds—have all brought high danger and superhuman achievement into the American living room, where adults and children alike have come to expect the hero to selflessly risk his life, overcome the "bad guy," and generally save the day. The portrayal of women on television, on the other hand, has included few strong, independent, or heroic characters. Most female leads in television—from *The Donna Reed Show* (1958–1966) to *Roseanne* (1988–1997)—have realized power through their traditional moral authority as mother. There have been exceptions to this formula, one of the most popular being *Xena: Warrior Princess* (1995–2001)—the more successful spin-off from *Hercules*—which has achieved a cult following among a broad spectrum of American females (and males). As Wendy Bryan explains in "Xenatopia" (1998), a key to the show's appeal is the star's unique ability to display such warrior traits as courage, sacrifice, and physical prowess while remaining an undeniably feminine figure. Bryan also takes the reader inside the *Xena* fan club phenomenon, a subculture that had previously been reserved for the primarily masculine support networks of *Star Trek* (1966–1969) and its successors.

Women's limited access to television and other entertainment media improved in late-twentieth-century America. The personal freedom that can be found through performance is discussed in "Postmodern Sisters" (1993), Tom Lanham's interview with pop musicians Juliana Hatfield and Tanya Donelly, and comedian Sandra Bernhard. All three women describe their early childhood desire to be the center of attraction, the class clown, and/or simply left alone to write and explore their feelings about the world into which they were born. And now, as successful nationally-known figures, they still describe their professional motivation as the potential for onstage unencumbered self-expression—although they also speak of the gratification they receive from the "love" of the audience and the symbiotic relationship they have with their fans. Bernhard was a leading figure in the late-1980s meteoric rise of female stand-up comedy, an entertainment form that has not hesitated to turn the tables on the long-standing male stereotyping of women. In Claudia Dreifus's interview, "Cokie Roberts, Nina Totenberg, and Linda Wertheimer" (1994), these three women who came of age during the second wave of feminism describe "bottom pinching" and other daily forms of sexual discrimination and harassment they experienced when breaking into the male world of broadcast journalism and Washington, D.C., politics. This piece illustrates that what is at stake in women gaining more control of news coverage is not only influencing what information the public receives but also determining the political issues of the day, as evidenced by Totenberg's lead role in breaking the Anita Hill–Clarence Thomas story over the Supreme Court nominee's alleged sexual harassment of his aide.

In resisting the beauty myths still so pervasive in late-twentieth-century America, girls and women have found the Internet and the World Wide Web to be a potentially invaluable way to create networks of support. Relatively free from the commercially driven content of Hollywood, television, and fashion magazines; virtually instantaneous in delivering ideas and information; perfectly accessible (for those who have their own computers) from the comfort and privacy of one's own home: cyberspace could become *the* new site for initiating feminist activism, much like that of the speaker's platform for the early-twentieth-century suffragist or the mimeograph machine for the 1960s countercultural feminist—only the Internet and the Web have the potential to reach millions of people around the world. At the same time, however, there is the troublesome physical disconnect between those communicating. In any event, the hopefulness in the opening years of a medium that will likely come to dominate early-twenty-first-century culture is evident in Lynda Hinkle's "The Smash! FAQ" (1998), an Internet call to arms to those of "any age, ethnic background, dress size, class, religion, [and] political persuasion" to destroy or "smash" all the stereotypes and lies about the female body and its appearance. On the same day of 1998, June 3, Lisa Jervis's "Imperfect Beauty" (1998) article appeared in *bitchmag*—an online zine founded by a group of young women writers who, like Hinkle, were trying to raise conciousnesses and exhort their readership to accept themselves as they are and ignore the allure of the stacked-waif ideal that the mass media promulgate. Lisa exposes the lie that, despite its claims to more racial and physical inclusion, the fashion industry and its magazines have made an attempt to create a "realistic" view of women. Also on June 3, *bitchmag* included Hayley Nelson's "Dating Is Tired, Marriage Is Wired" (1998): a feature article distancing the mainstream media's romanticization of marriage from the reality that the author's twenty-something middle-class friends learned primarily from the disenchantment of their parents' lives and the young women's own interests in putting marriage off until the ambition and sexual freedom of young adulthood take their course.

The potential exists for the rapidly developing computer media to become a fulcrum for early-twenty-first-century feminism, but women would first need to overcome many of the same problems that have hindered other forms of communication—namely male predominance in the institutions that control and shape communication. The challenge involves mastering the technology: "The boys have the code," as Virginia Eubanks puts it, "and that's the way it plays." But the biggest problem, according to some, is pornography, sexual harassment, and an overarching antiwoman cast to much that can be found in cyberspace. In response, the Dandelion web project and other intersite services have been organized to facilitate women's online needs. Women Halting Online Abuse is a group founded specifically to use the law and other means to make the Web an unobstructed place for self-expression and activist organizing, as detailed in "About W.H.O.A." (1998). And, as seen in *bitchmag*'s rant by Heather Irwin, entitled "Shouting into the Vacuum" (1998), many of the new online feminist zines include manifestos opposing "geekboys'" control of the Internet. In *Brillo*, Virginia Eubanks's "A Woman's Place in Cyberspace" (1998) offers an imaginative assessment of the cultural dynamics working against women. It is not only the superstructural lewdness of cyberpunk and cyberporn that have to be dealt with. Also needing to be subdued are the underlying assumptions of online masculinity, like the equation between the objectification of women and the manipulation of computers. Eubanks continues her thoughts on how to transform cyberspace into a source of empowerment for women in "Hacking Barbie" (1998), her *Brillo* interview with the Barbie Liberation Organization. In strategizing how to subvert masculine power, the organization considers using heterosexual imagery to entice male readers into feminist sites.

Since at least the late 1980s, pop music has been an increasingly commanding venue for female expression. Women's success in rock culture and business is broad and varied, but in terms of feminism perhaps the most focused effort has been the so called Riot Grrrl movement that began in the Pacific Northwest in 1991. Originally a female response to punk rock, Riot Grrrl quickly included— as Melissa Klein describes in "Young Feminism and the Alternative Music Community" (1997)—extra-musical attention to domestic violence, racism, rape, and other women's issues at its national conventions and in its fan publications. Still, Riot Grrrl's power to inspire through head-banging music is its basic goal. In considering some of her favorite bands like L7, Babes in Toyland, and Bikini Kill, twenty-four-year-old Rachel Orviro in "I Am a Girl" (1998) testifies to Riot Grrrl's program of self-reinvention, "making Cindy Brady grow up into Courtney Love." As its name suggests, Riot Grrrl plays on the appeal of anger and visceral opposition to the masculine powers that be. It had staying power throughout the 1990s, as illustrated in short rants "I Wanna Riot!" (1998) by someone calling herself punkgrrrl, and Cynthia's "Join the Riot!" (1998).

Rap or hip-hop—originating on the streets of 1970s New York City—has also proved to be a musical form conducive to feminist expression. In fact, because of the desperate misogyny of some "gangsta rap," there seemed to be a special need for African American women to step up and change the words. The problem, though, as Joan Morgan sees it in "The Bad Girls of Hip-Hop" (1997), is that many of the most successful "sista" rappers adopted some of the same self-destructive values of their male predecessors: in "coupling highly materialistic, violent and lewd personas with deliciously infectious rhythms and rhymes," performers like DaBrat, Foxy Brown, and Lil' Kim are missing an opportunity to get out positive "images of Blackness." Morgan, author of the book *Diary of a Hip-Hop Feminist* (1999), is quick to point out that there are exceptions; Queen Latifah, Salt-N-Pepa, Yo Yo, and Lyte have all displayed "Afro-feminine regality, refined sensuality, and womanist strengths." It is time, Morgan concludes, to hold the others accountable.

An alternative to alternative rock for women was the Lilith Fair, an all-women traveling music festival, founded in the summer of 1997 by Sarah McLachlan and expanded in the summer of 1998 to include more than seventy performers in folk and pop music. The Lilith Fair helped mark the coming equality of women in mainstream music. But while the songs of performers like Natalie Merchant, Sinead O'Connor, Jewel, Tracy Chapman, and Fiona Apple certainly carried different meanings than the testosterone-driven music of male rockers, Lilith Fair was not an agenda-filled feminist enterprise. As Nancy Coulter writes in "The Lilith Fair: A Celebration of Women in Music" (1997), there were almost as many men as women in the audiences of each concert. At the same time there was a strong lesbian presence on stage and surrounding the fair.

A distinct component of American political culture in 1998 was the widespread and out-of-control opining regarding President Bill Clinton's sexual indiscretions with the White House intern Monica Lewinsky. With the countless radio and television call-in shows, daily polls taken by CNN and other news services, not to mention the round-the-clock analysis and speculation by the Washington, D.C., pundit class, the Clinton sex scandal took on a life and a will of its own, driven by the media as much as by Independent Counsel Ken Starr, with the American public consistently expressing its relative indifference to the whole affair. Is the "improper relation," as Clinton maintained, a "private matter"? Or was it sexual harassment in the workplace, or an abuse of the president's significant power? Perhaps a grossly reckless act that called into doubt the president's ability to lead? In "Dear Bill and Hillary" (1998), Andrea Dworkin makes a strong case for understanding it as an "abuse-of-power scandal"—a calculated use of the president's authority to take routinized sexual advantage of a young woman not much older than his daughter. Dworkin also takes aim at Hillary Clinton, the would-be feminist who devotes herself to protecting her husband's exploitation of other women. Dworkin's article was originally published in *The Guardian* of London, in January 1998, right after word broke of the Clinton-Lewinsky "bimbroglio"; it made its way to the Web in the summer of 1998.

80

NATIONAL ORGANIZATION FOR WOMEN

Task Force on Image of Women in Mass Media (1967)

*Submitted by: Patricia Trainor, Chairman
National Organization for Women*

Goals

We will campaign to change the stereotyped image and the denigration of women in all the mass media, by all the forms of protest and pressure on networks, advertisers and editors which have been effective in abolishing the stereotyped images of Negroes and Jews. We will campaign for the inclusion of images of women which reflect, and thus encourage, the active participation of women in all fields of American society; images which are now completely absent from school books, as well as the media. "Look, Jane, Look" should have other pictures of women than the aproned mother, waving goodbye.

Action, Follow Through

The New York Committee on Image was organized in February, 1967, under the chairmanship of Patricia Trainor, a computer programmer. Because of its geographical location in relation to the centers of the communications media, it will serve as the nucleus for a National Task Force on Image.

Twenty members have been active during the past month, setting up initial priorities, creating a structure for action, and initiating specific projects. Plans for action in the Mass Media have coalesced around three main focuses:

Monitor Subcommittee

Under the direction of Dolores Alexander, reporter on *Newsday,* this committee will monitor media, assigning priorities and suggesting

From NOW task force document, 1967.

specific communications outlets as targets for NOW action. Plans have been drawn up for an Ad Hoc Committee of the general membership to visit various Equal Employment Agencies in New York City and newspapers during April, asking that the interpretation of Title VII of the Civil Rights Act of 1964, which currently permits Help Wanted ads to be segregated by sex if a disclaimer is printed, be changed to require full integration of employment ads.

In addition to this project, plans are under way to approach specific TV networks and advertisers regarding the image of women they use to sell their air time and products.

Research Subcommittee

This Subcommittee, under the direction of Susanna Schad, sociologist at Rutgers, will perform services to the entire membership of the NOW organization, supplying facts about the role and contribution of women in the modern world. In addition, it will research the current image of women in the public mind, suggesting substitute images for NOW to foster. An In-House Education project, organizing lectures and seminars for members of NOW (and eventually the general public) is planned.

Creative Individual Participation

We wish to combine the advantages of creative individual action with the power available to an organized group. Action by membership from all geographic areas is crucially important. Members of NWO are urged to write immediately in their own names to publisher and communications executives whenever a false image of women has been promulgated. This enables immediate action, without the delay which is necessary whenever we are going to speak as a group. Then, a copy of the letter is to be forwarded to Dolores Alexander (Monitor Subcommittee). Monitor will analyze all letters received from members with a view to a subsequent statement to the addressee in the name of the NOW organization.

81

CAMILLE PAGLIA

Madonna I and Madonna II (1990/1991)

MADONNA I: ANIMALITY AND ARTIFICE

Madonna, don't preach.

Defending her controversial new video, "Justify My Love," on *Nightline* last week, Madonna stumbled, rambled, and ended up seeming far less intelligent than she really is.

Madonna, fess up.

The video is pornographic. It's decadent. And it's fabulous. MTV was right to ban it, a corporate resolve long overdue. Parents cannot possibly control television, with its titanic omnipresence.

Prodded by correspondent Forrest Sawyer for evidence of her responsibility as an artist, Madonna hotly proclaimed her love of children, her social activism, and her condom endorsements. Wrong answer. As Baudelaire and Oscar Wilde knew, neither art nor the artist has a moral responsibility to liberal social causes.

"Justify My Love" is truly avant-garde, at a time when that word has lost its meaning in the flabby art world. It represents a sophisticated European sexuality of a kind we have not seen since the great foreign films of the 1950s and 1960s. But it does not belong on a mainstream music channel watched around the clock by children.

On *Nightline,* Madonna bizarrely called the video a "celebration of sex." She imagined happy educational scenes where curious children would ask their parents about the video. Oh, sure! Picture it: "Mommy, please tell me

From Camille Paglia, *Sex, Art, and American Culture: Essays* (New York: Vintage, Random House, 1992), 3–13. "Madonna I: Animality and Artifice" originally appeared in *The New York Times,* December 14, 1990; "Madonna II: Venus of the Radio Waves" originally appeared in *The Independent Sunday Review,* London, July 21, 1991. Copyright 1992 by Camille Paglia. Reprinted by permission of Vintage Books, a Division of Random House Inc.

about the tired, tied-up man in the leather harness and the mean, bare-chested lady in the Nazi cap." Okay, dear, right after the milk and cookies.

Sawyer asked for Madonna's reaction to feminist charges that, in the neck manacle and floor-crawling of an earlier video, "Express Yourself," she condoned the "degradation" and "humiliation" of women. Madonna waffled: "But I chained myself! I'm in charge." Well, no. Madonna the producer may have chosen the chain, but Madonna the sexual persona in the video is alternately a cross-dressing dominatrix and a slave of male desire.

But who cares what the feminists say anyhow? They have been outrageously negative about Madonna from the start. In 1985, *Ms.* magazine pointedly feted quirky, cuddly singer Cyndi Lauper as its woman of the year. Great judgment: gimmicky Lauper went nowhere, while Madonna grew, flourished, metamorphosed, and became an international star of staggering dimensions. She is also a shrewd business tycoon, a modern new woman of all-around talent.

Madonna is the true feminist. She exposes the puritanism and suffocating ideology of American feminism, which is stuck in an adolescent whining mode. Madonna has taught young women to be fully female and sexual while still exercising control over their lives. She shows girls how to be attractive, sensual, energetic, ambitious, aggressive, and funny— all at the same time.

American feminism has a man problem. The beaming Betty Crockers, hangdog dowdies, and parochial prudes who call themselves feminists want men to be like women. They fear and despise the masculine. The academic feminists think their nerdy bookworm husbands are the ideal model of human manhood.

But Madonna loves real men. She sees the beauty of masculinity, in all its rough vigor and sweaty athletic reflection. She also admires the men who are actually like women: transsexuals and flamboyant drag queens, the heroes of the

1969 Stonewall rebellion, which started the gay liberation movement.

"Justify My Love" is an eerie, sultry tableau of jaded androgynous creatures, trapped in a decadent sexual underground. Its hypnotic images are drawn from such sadomasochistic films as Liliana Cavani's *The Night Porter* and Luchnio Visconti's *The Damned*. It's the perverse and knowing world of the photographers Helmut Newton and Robert Mapplethorpe.

Contemporary American feminism, which began by rejecting Freud because of his alleged sexism, has shut itself off from his ideas of ambiguity, contradiction, conflict, ambivalence. Its simplistic psychology is illustrated by the new cliché of the date-rape furor: "'No' always means 'no.'" Will we ever graduate from the Girl Scouts? "No" has always been, and always will be, part of the dangerous, alluring courtship ritual of sex and seduction, observable even in the animal kingdom.

Madonna has a far profounder vision of sex than do the feminists. She sees both the animality and the artifice. Changing her costume style and hair color virtually every month, Madonna embodies the eternal values of beauty and pleasure. Feminism says, "No more masks." Madonna says we are nothing but masks.

Through her enormous impact on young women around the world, Madonna is the future of feminism.

MADONNA II:
VENUS OF THE RADIO WAVES

I'm a dyed-in-the-wool, true-blue Madonna fan.

It all started in 1984, when Madonna exploded onto MTV with a brazen, insolent, in-your-face American street style, which she had taken from urban blacks, Hispanics, and her own middle-class but turbulent and charismatic Italian-American family. From the start, there was a flamboyant and parodistic element to her sexuality, a hard glamour she had learned from Hollywood cinema and from its devotees, gay men and drag queens.

Madonna is a dancer. She thinks and expresses herself through dance, which exists in the eternal Dionysian realm of music. Dance, which she studied with a gay man in her home state of Michigan, was her avenue of escape from the conventions of religion and bourgeois society. The sensual language of her body allowed her to transcend the over-verbalized codes of her class and time.

Madonna's great instinctive intelligence was evident to me from her earliest videos. My first fights about her had to do with whether she was a good dancer or merely a well-coached one. As year by year she built up the remarkable body of her video work, with its dazzling number of dance styles, I have had to fight about that less and less. However, I am still at war about her with feminists and religious conservatives (an illuminating alliance of contemporary puritans).

Most people who denigrate Madonna do so out of ignorance. The postwar baby-boom generation in America, to which I belong, has been deeply immersed in popular culture for thirty-five years. Our minds were formed by rock music, which has poured for twenty-four hours a day from hundreds of noisy, competitive independent radio stations around the country.

Madonna, like Venus stepping from the radio waves, emerged from this giant river of music. Her artistic imagination ripples and eddies with the inner currents in American music. She is at her best when she follows her intuition and speaks to the world in the universal language of music and dance. She is at her worst when she tries to define and defend herself in words, which she borrows from louche, cynical pals and shallow, single-issue political activists.

Madonna consolidates and fuses several traditions of pop music, but the major one she typifies is disco, which emerged in the Seventies and, under the bland commercial rubric "dance music," is still going strong. It has a terrible reputation: when you say the word *disco,* people think "Bee Gees." But I view disco, at its serious best, as a dark, grand Dionysian music with roots in African earth-cult.

Madonna's command of massive, resonant bass lines, which she heard in the funky dance clubs of Detroit and New York, has always impressed me. As an Italian Catholic, she uses them liturgically. Like me, she sensed the buried pagan religiosity in disco. I recall my stunned admiration as I sat in the theater in 1987 and first experienced the crashing, descending chords of Madonna's "Causing a Commotion," which opened her dreadful movie, *Who's That Girl?* If you want to hear the essence of modernity, listen to those chords, infernal, apocalyptic, and grossly sensual. This is the authentic voice of the *fin de siècle*.

Madonna's first video, for her superb, drivingly lascivious disco hit "Burnin' Up," did not make much of an impression. The platinum-blonde girl kneeling and emoting in the middle of a midnight highway just seemed to be a band member's floozie. In retrospect, the video, with its rapid, cryptic surrealism, prefigures Madonna's signature theme and contains moments of eerie erotic poetry.

"Lucky Star" was Madonna's breakthrough video. Against a luminous, white abstract background, she and two impassive dancers perform a synchronized series of jagged, modern kicks and steps. Wearing the ragtag outfit of all-black bows, see-through netting, fingerless lace gloves, bangle bracelets, dangle earrings, chains, crucifixes, and punk booties that would set off a gigantic fashion craze among American adolescent girls, Madonna flaunts her belly button and vamps the camera with a smoky, piercing, come-hither-but-keep-your-distance stare. Here she first suggests her striking talent for improvisational floor work, which she would spectacularly demonstrate at the first MTV awards show, when, wrapped in a white-lace wedding dress, she campily rolled and undulated snakelike on the stage, to the baffled consternation of the first rows of spectators.

I remember sitting in a bar when "Lucky Star," just out, appeared on TV. The stranger perched next to me, a heavyset, middle-aged working-class woman, watched the writhing Madonna and, wide-eyed and slightly frowning, blankly said, her beer held motionless halfway to her lips, "Will you look at this." There was a sense that Madonna was doing something so new and so strange that one didn't know whether to call it beautiful or grotesque. Through MTV, Madonna was transmitting an avant-garde downtown New York sensibility to the American masses.

In "Lucky Star," Madonna is raffish, gamine, still full of the street-urchin mischief that she would portray in her first and best film, Susan Seidelman's *Desperately Seeking Susan* (1984). In "Borderline," she shows her burgeoning star quality. As the girlfriend of Hispanic toughs who is picked up by a British photographer and makes her first magazine cover, she presents the new dualities of her life: the gritty, multiracial street and club scene that she had haunted in obscurity and poverty, and her new slick, fast world of popularity and success.

In one shot of "Borderline," as she chummily chews gum with kidding girlfriends on the corner, you can see the nondescript plainness of Madonna's real face, which she again exposes, with admirable candor, in *Truth or Dare* when, slurping soup and sporting a shower cap over hair rollers, she fences with her conservative Italian father over the phone. Posing for the photographer in "Borderline," Madonna in full cry fixes the camera lens with challenging molten eyes, in a bold ritual display of sex and aggression. This early video impressed me with Madonna's sophisticated view of the fabrications of femininity, that exquisite theater which feminism condemns as oppression but which I see as a supreme artifact of civilization. I sensed then, and now know for certain, that Madonna, like me, is drawn to drag queens for their daring, flamboyant insight into sex roles, which they see far more clearly and historically than do our endlessly complaining feminists.

Madonna's first major video, in artistic terms, was "Like a Virgin," where she began to release her flood of inner sexual personae, which appear and disappear like the painted creatures of masque. Madonna in an orchid-heavy Veronese duchess in white, a febrile Fassbinder courtesan in black, a slutty nun-turned-harlequin flapping a gold cross and posturing, bum in air, like a demonic phantom in the nose of a gondola. This video alone, with its coruscating polarities of evil and innocence, would be enough to establish Madonna's artistic distinction for the next century.

In "Material Girl," where she sashays around in Marilyn Monroe's strapless red gown and archly flashes her fan at a pack of men in tuxedos, Madonna first showed her flair for comedy. Despite popular opinion, there are no important parallels between Madonna and Monroe, who was a virtuoso comedienne but who was insecure, depressive, passive-aggressive, and infuriatingly obstructionist in her career habits. Madonna is manic, perfectionist, workaholic. Monroe abused alcohol and drugs, while Madonna shuns them. Monroe has a tentative, melting, dreamy solipsism; Madonna has Judy Holiday's wisecracking smart mouth and Joan Crawford's steel will and bossy, circusmaster managerial competence.

In 1985 the cultural resistance to Madonna became overt. Despite the fact that her "Into the Groove," the mesmerizing theme song of *Desperately Seeking Susan,* had saturated our lives for nearly a year, the Grammy Awards outrageously ignored her. The feminist and moralist sniping began in earnest. Madonna "degraded" womanhood; she was vulgar, sacrilegious, stupid, shallow, opportunistic. A nasty mass quarrel broke out in one of my classes between the dancers, who adored Madonna, and the actresses, who scorned her.

I knew the quality of what I was seeing: "Open Your Heart," with its risqué peep-show format, remains for me not only Madonna's greatest video but one of the three or four best videos ever made. In the black bustier she made famous (transforming the American lingerie industry overnight), Madonna, bathed in blue-white light, plays Marlene Dietrich straddling a chair. Her eyes are cold, distant, all-seeing. She is ringed, as if in a sea-green aquarium, by windows of lewd or longing voyeurs. Sad sacks, brooding misfits, rowdy studs, dreamy gay twins, a melancholy lesbian.

"Open Your Heart" is a brilliant mimed psychodrama of the interconnections between art and pornography, love and lust. Madonna won my undying loyalty by reviving and re-creating the hard glamour of the studio-era Hollywood movie queens, figures of mythological grandeur. Contemporary feminism cut itself off from history and bankrupted itself when it spun its puerile, paranoid fantasy of male oppressors and female sex-object victims. Woman is the dominant sex. Woman's sexual glamour has bewitched and destroyed men since Delilah and Helen of Troy. Madonna, role model to millions of girls worldwide, has cured the ills of feminism by reasserting woman's command of the sexual realm.

Responding to the spiritual tensions within Italian Catholicism, Madonna discovered the buried paganism within the church. The torture of Christ and the martyrdom of the saints, represented in lurid polychrome images, dramatize the passions of the body, repressed in art-fearing puritan Protestantism of the kind that still lingers in America. Playing with the outlaw personae of prostitute and dominatrix, Madonna has made a major contribution to the history of women. She has rejoined and healed the split halves of woman: Mary, the Blessed Virgin and holy mother, and Mary Magdalene, the harlot.

The old-guard establishment feminists who still loathe Madonna have a sexual ideology problem. I am radically pro-pornography and pro-prostitution. Hence I perceive Madonna's strutting sexual exhibitionism not as cheapness or triviality but as the full, florid expression of the whore's ancient rule over men. Incompetent amateurs have given prostitution a bad name. In my university office in Philadelphia hangs a pagan shrine: a life-size full-color cardboard display of Joanne Whalley-Kilmer and Bridget Fonda naughtily smiling in scanty, skintight gowns as Christine Keeler and Mandy Rice-Davies in the film *Scandal.* I tell visitors it is "my political science exhibit." For me, the Profumo affair symbolizes the evanescence of male government compared to woman's cosmic power.

In a number of videos, Madonna has played with bisexual innuendoes, reaching their culmination in the solemn woman-to-woman kiss of "Justify My Love," a deliciously decadent sarabande of transvestite and sadomasochistic personae that was banned by MTV. Madonna is again pioneering here, this time in restoring lesbian eroticism to the continuum of heterosexual response, from which it was unfortunately removed twenty years ago by lesbian feminist separatists of the most boring, humorless, strident kind. "Justify My Love" springs from the sophisticated European art films of the Fifties and Sixties that shaped my sexual imagination in college. It shows bisexuality and all experimentation as a liberation from false, narrow categories.

Madonna's inner emotional life can be heard in the smooth, transparent "La Isla Bonita," one of her most perfect songs, with its haunting memory of paradise lost. No one ever mentions it. Publicity has tended to focus instead on the more blatantly message-heavy videos, like "Papa Don't Preach," with its teen pregnancy, or "Express Yourself," where feminist cheerleading lyrics hammer on over crisp, glossy images of bedroom bondage, dungeon torture, and epicene, crotch-grabbing Weimar elegance.

"Like a Prayer" gave Pepsi-Cola dyspepsia: Madonna receives the stigmata, makes love with the animated statue of a black saint, and dances in a rumpled silk slip in front of a field of burning crosses. This last item, with its uncontrolled racial allusions, shocked even me. But Madonna has a strange ability to remake symbolism in her own image. Kitsch and trash are transformed by her high-energy dancer's touch, her earnest yet over-the-top drag-queen satire.

The "Vogue" video approaches "Open Your Heart" in quality. Modeling her glowing, languorous postures on the great high-glamour photographs of Hurrell, Madonna reprises the epiphanic iconography of our modern Age of Hollywood. Feminism is infested with white, middle-class, literary twits ignorant of art and smugly hostile to fashion photography and advertisement, which contain the whole history of art. In the dramatic chiaroscuro compositions of "Vogue," black and Hispanic New York drag queens, directly inspired by fashion magazines, display the arrogant aristocracy of beauty, recognized as divine by Plato and, before him, by the princes of Egypt.

In my own theoretical terms, Madonna has both the dynamic Dionysian power of dance and the static Apollonian power of iconicism. Part of her fantastic success has been her ability to communicate with the still camera, a talent quite separate from any other. To project to a camera, you must have an autoerotic autonomy, a sharp self-conceptualization, even a fetishistic perversity: the camera is a machine you make love to. Madonna has been fortunate in finding Herb Ritts, who has recorded the dazzling profusion of her mercurial sexual personae. Through still photography, she has blanketed the world press with her image between videos and concert tours. But Madonna, I contend, never does anything just for publicity. Rather, publicity is the language naturally used by the great stars to communicate with their vast modern audience. Through publicity, we live in the star's flowing consciousness.

Madonna has evolved physically. In a charming early live video, "Dress You Up," she is warm, plump, and flirty under pink and powder-blue light. Her voice is enthusiastic but thin and breathy. She began to train both voice and body, so that her present silhouette, with some erotic loss, is wiry and muscular, hyperkinetic for acrobatic dance routines based on the martial arts. Madonna is notorious for monthly or even weekly changes of hair color and style, by which she embodies the restless individualism of Western personality. Children love her. As with the Beatles, this is always the sign of a monumental pop phenomenon.

Madonna has her weak moments: for example, I have no tolerance for the giggling baby talk that she periodically hauls out of the closet, as over the final credits of *Truth or Dare*. She is a complex modern woman. Indeed, that is the main theme of her extraordinary achievement. She is exploring the problems and tensions of being an ambitious woman today. Like the potent Barbra Streisand, whose maverick female style had a great impact on American girls in the Sixties, Madonna is confronting the romantic dilemma of the strong woman looking for a man but uncertain whether she wants a tyrant or slave. The tigress in heat is drawn to surrender but may kill her conqueror.

In "Open Your Heart," Madonna is woman superbly alone, master of her own fate. Offstage at the end, she mutates into an androgynous boy-self and runs off. "What a tramp!," thundered the *New York Post* in a recent full-page headline. Yes, Madonna has restored the Whore of Babylon, the pagan goddess banned by the last book of the Bible. With an instinct for world-domination gained from Italian Catholicism, she has rolled like a juggernaut over the multitude of her carping critics. This is a kaleidoscopic career still in progress. But Madonna's most enduring cultural contribution may be that she has introduced ravishing visual beauty and a lush Mediterranean sensuality into parched, pinched, word-drunk Anglo-Saxon feminism.

82

ANGELA JOHNSON

Confessions of a Pop Culture Junkie (1994)

I have to confess something about the *off our backs* collective: lots of us are pop culture junkies. We may peruse the *Washington Post,* but a substantial subset of us devour *People Magazine,* in whose pages I was thrilled to discover that Tommy Lee Jones was Al Gore's college

From *Off Our Backs,* May 1994. Reprinted with the permission of *Off Our Backs*.

room-mate; while the other, purer feminist I imagine I "should" be is saying "Who's Tommy Lee Jones?" (and would probably be appalled to know the answer), I am well into a discussion about the connections between manly love and indifference in his performance in *The Fugitive* (a movie in which the only significant things that happen to women are: one gets murdered; one is told to shut up). And I'm not alone in this; I've found that a quiet, slightly dull evening at home with friends turns into an animated conversation when it turns out that someone in the room knows someone whose friend worked for Julia Roberts, and you should hear what she had to say about her. . . . For a surprising number of my radical friends, the Academy Awards is a must-see; and I can tell you what I was doing the day Diana and Charles got married just as vividly as I remember where I was when Nelson Mandela was released from prison.

Now, I know what my other, purist self thinks of all this, and I am imagining that you, the reader are thinking the same: Frivolous, you think; flighty; you picture me in clothes from The Gap, or even—could it be?—Benneton. Car of choice: Suzuki Samari, or maybe a convertible Mustang; or some bumper-sticker-bedecked Volvo handed down from my parents. (Or maybe you are saying to yourself "You know, in retrospect, that blue suit she wore to announce the engagement—the one with the scallops—that was just not right for the occasion." In which case you needn't even read on; we are sisters, and you can write me here at the paper to tell me about how you once met someone who'd kissed k.d. lang at a bar. Which reminds me that someone here on the collective used to know someone who played basketball with a woman who was Whitney Houston's lover. I kid you not.)

As for the flightiness and false glamour I'm imagining a sober-minded, serious, committed reader, my better half, would attribute to me and the other pop-culture feminists I know—well, I admit I've read *Cosmo* (I thought it was well accepted that reducing calorie intake was an ineffective way to lose weight, but Helen Gurley Brown has set me straight. Millions of women still, apparently, bond over hunger). Some of my friends smoke and one gets expensive haircuts. However, none of us—not one— owns a convertible. My wardrobe can best be described as late-eighties. "I can't throw this out, it's still got years of wear left in it." And we're all rabid, man-hating radical feminists. But radical feminists who watch *Beverly Hills, 90210* every Wednesday night. (We were uniformly offended that a women's studies professor would have an affair with Brandon.)

Now I, myself, indulge this passion only moderately; I subscribe to *Spy,* and to the *Utne* (face it, Eric, it's just the leftist version of *Reader's Digest,* best kept in the bathroom). But I don't subscribe to *People,* for example, I just wait to read my neighbor's; so you can see that I still have some perspective on the phenomenon. But I know feminists, right here on the *off our backs* collective in fact, who not only refuse to take phone calls between 8 and 10 p.m. Wednesday night, but who subscribe to *Entertainment Weekly*. I, myself, can't stand *Beverly Hills, 90210*—I absolutely loathe it (although observant readers will note that I follow major plot lines). Let's put it this way: after seven years of high school teaching, I feel there are major credibility problems with the show. However (I am going to bare my soul now), a show that I can really get into is *Star Trek*. How many of you have noticed that there is a certain something between Captain Picard and Q?

OK, so we've established that Generation X'ers are a frivolous bunch. That's what I first attributed my own passion for celebrity gossip and sniping to—a fact well-established by the mainstream media. Well, many of the women whom I see following this trend are in their mid-to-late twenties. However, when I presented an earlier draft of this article to the collective, the baby boomers among us were unanimously offended by it and some felt miffed that their own interest in pop culture was going unappreciated; so perhaps this is not, after all, a generational phenomenon. But so what? What

does this mean for the feminist movement, and how is Angela going to get out of the waters of ageism into which she is drifting here? (Parenthetically, the slang version of the *Oxford English Dictionary* traces the first known usage in print of the word ageism to our letters page, some time in the late seventies or early eighties— surely some of you can come up with earlier usages?)

I spent the first few years of my adulthood rigorously rejecting all mainstream culture; I listened to ten-year-old Holly Near recordings and traveled hundreds of miles to see Alix Dobkin. I lost track, in a most delightful way, of what was hot—no t.v., no radio, no magazines, just feminist lectures and lesbian parties, stimulating and bracing. I loved and followed the old feminist martyrs—Alice Paul, Jane Addams. But slowly, something happened, and I found myself creeping down to watch *Dynasty* on the dorm t.v. It was Steve and Luke that did it—it was a political act to watch their relationship unfold; but, you know, before they'd broken up I was hooked. Soon I was following Madonna—again a political act; this brazen woman, flaunting her round belly—she excited me as a symbol of female independence. By the time she was going around labeling herself Boy Toy—hooked again. And I don't want you to think these things supplanted the ardent discussions of body hair and intersecting oppressions; they didn't. I'm not sure that I could argue that they enhanced them, either; however, they are part of me, whether I like it or not.

So: can I turn swords into plowshares, movie trivia into feminist activism? Or ought I just continue on as I have been, relishing little tidbits of gossip as a break from my real, feminist work? Is there a place where these two passions of mine intersect?

The Riot Grrrls, WAC, the Lesbian Avengers—these groups are glam, they're hip, they're now, and not coincidentally, they're spreading like wildfire. Now, here at *off our backs* we're trained; we can come to consensus in minutes, we can allocate tasks, process out disagreements, break new theoretical ground, and still have time left at the end of the meeting to gossip about Rosie O'Donnell (whose name has been linked romantically with Sophie B. "Damn I wish I was your lover" Hawkens). But we suffer image problems. When I walk into a feminist bookstore or conference and say "hi, I'm from *off our backs*," I'm greeted with affection; but I can feel that image lingering— stodgy, hard-line and humorless. So: recall that I was raised up with the image of those old feminist martyrs; a very persistent voice in me suggests that if we want to draw more women into the movement, or into the *off our backs* office, me and my star-struck friends should get off our butts, quit talking about Rosie, and get out there and get to work. However, I have a feeling that this willingness to drudge may actually work against us sometimes; I have a feeling that within my attraction to the glamorous Rosie, an attraction I customarily see as ephemeral to feminism, may lie some sort of strength.

I'm not quite sure how to make use of this; how to synthesize my passion for glamour, for celebrity and celluloid, with my commitment to feminism. But I'm beginning to think it is a marriage that could work; primarily because all this gossip is fun (infuse fun into the feminist movement? We have too much work to do!) I've been seeing some tiny moves in that direction here at *off our backs*. Remember the larger-than-life photo of Cindy that we copped from R —— S —— a few months go? and whimsy keeps showing up around the periphery of our layout—I was thrilled to open the paper and find myself described as "office titan" a few months ago. We interview Riot Grrrls (and some come to layout—what a pleasure!); we report on WAC; we've been trying for about six months to make contact with the remains of the D.C. Lesbian avengers. We wear the hippest sunglasses we can find along with our feminist t-shirts. We cultivate numerous interns and volunteers (only to be asked, hostilely, "why are so many of the women here young?", when I had just been congratulating myself on combatting our old hard-line image

and appealing to newer feminists). But mostly what I do is drudge along, and debate the great questions of the feminist movement ("should transsexuals be allowed at Michigan?"), and for a nice break recount the time two of us met Mary Stuart Masterson at a pro-choice march. (She's short).

83

KATHI MAIO

Film: Women Who Murder for the Man (1991)

Back in the early 1970s, opponents of the Equal Rights Amendment claimed that if we got the ERA, women would have to fight in wars. With the Vietnam war still a nightmare, this was a potent argument—a winning one, it turned out. Women still don't have a constitutional guarantee of equal rights, but it looks like we're getting the "right" to kill for Uncle Sam anyway. The "clean," controlled media event known as the Gulf War brought us hundreds of sound bytes of women soldiers talking tough, along with countless video glimpses of women toting rifles, flying helicopters, and assembling bombs. These images of the 35,000 women who served in the war seem to have convinced U.S. audiences that women shouldn't just tote rifles, they should also shoot them at the enemy.

In a *McCall's* survey conducted last May, 84 percent of respondents approved of combat duty for women. A *Newsweek* poll revealed a less gung-ho attitude, but the majority of those surveyed felt women should be allowed in combat units. In July, the Senate voted to remove the ban on women flying combat missions: the first step toward placing women on the front lines.

Ironically, at the same time the press was covering the debate on women in combat, another media debate about women toting guns

From *Ms.*, November/December 1991. Reprinted by permission of *Ms.* Magazine, copyright 1991.

was raging. The controversy involved a movie, a tale of outlaw-buddies-on-the-run-make-believe. It was a film not unlike countless others, except for its low body count. Only one man was killed, compared to the 80 or more women, men, and children who regularly perish in the films of Arnold Schwarzenegger and his cinematic blood brothers.

What made this movie the subject of heated debate? The outlaw buddies were two *women*. And one female lead shoots a man—a *rapist*—not in self-defense; not in defense of the red, white, and blue; but in *rage*.

The film, of course, was *Thelma & Louise*. And the debate was, for the most part, an even gender split. Most women found the film cathartic and affirming. Most men responded differently. Their reactions fell somewhere on a scale from mild discomfort to hysterical outrage. Hysterics were especially in evidence among male critics.

John Robinson of the Boston *Globe* called *T & L* the "last straw" of "male bashing," and "the latest in a string of cultural strikes against manhood." In the San Francisco *Chronicle,* Herb Caen quoted another man-about-town "nutshell[ing] *Thelma & Louise* as 'Bitch Cassidy and the Sundress Kid.'" John Leo, of *U.S. News & World Report,* labeled the film "Toxic Feminism." Ralph Novak of *People* had even more of a fit: "Any movie that went as far out of its way to trash women as this female chauvinist sow of a film does to trash men would be universally, and justifiably, condemned."

Dream on, Ralph! Negative stereotyping of women is, indeed, the accepted norm in Hollywood films. And violence against women in slasher films and so-called thrillers constitutes a continual stream of female blood. So, when this level of antifeminist bombast is directed at one warm, often funny, ultimately tragic road picture, you can only conclude that though the guys like to dish it out, they sure can't take it.

But, to be fair, the boys had a right to feel threatened by this movie, which is, in its clever subversion of a male action formula, an indictment against patriarchy.

For once, in a Hollywood film, men are held accountable for their oppression of women. And not just for the crime of rape. Plenty of schlock movies like *Sudden Impact* (1983) and *Positive I.D.* (1987) have dealt with women avenging their rapes, and have caused nary a ripple of strife. The worst (1983's *I Spit on Your Grave*) tried to justify repeated and extremely exploitive depictions of rape by letting the woman get her revenge in the last reel. The better ones seemed to argue that when a woman falls victim to extraordinary violence, she has the right to answer brutality with a bullet.

Thelma & Louise portrayed male violence as an ordinary, everyday event. It's more than rape—it's a husband's verbal abuse of his wife; it's a stranger feeling he has the right to harass any woman. Thelma and Louise become outlaws not because they love violence, but because men won't leave them be. In their most spectacular "crime," they avenge themselves on a harassing trucker by blowing up his (very phallic) gasoline tanker. "Something's crossed over" inside Thelma and her friend. They are no longer willing to accept violation as their lot.

It is their ultimate rejection of patriarchy that makes Thelma and Louise such controversial movie heroes. There have been other women killers in recent movies, but they haven't raised the same frenzy of masculine ire because they remained, on some level, good girls.

The Julia Roberts star vehicle *Sleeping with the Enemy* is an example of a safe woman killer. After enduring three years of brutal marriage, Laura Burney fakes her own death and escapes to Iowa. There, in the first week, she falls in love with Mr. Right—a fuzzy, sensitive drama teacher named Ben (Kevin Anderson). When Laura (after being stalked and spooked for half the movie) at last kills her husband, she does so to protect her wounded lover. The movie makes it clear that Martin Burney (Patrick

Bergin) is a bogeyman, a Freddy Krueger with a handsome face and a good manicure. Eliminating him eliminates Laura's problems. Now she can bake homemade apple pies for her new man, happily ever after.

A bogeyman of a different type is used in *The Silence of the Lambs*—a stereotypical gay transvestite with a mincing walk and a nipple ring. Jonathan Demme plays to audience homophobia as he directs Ted Levine as "Buffalo Bill," a fiend who kills and skins women so he can sew up a fashion statement in female flesh.

Bill's noble adversary is an FBI trainee named Clarice Starling (Jodie Foster). Foster is, as always, brilliant as the stalwart but emotionally wounded heroine. This is a strong woman character, yes. But notice how in several scenes, notably the climax in the pitch-dark, hell-hole cellar, the audience (which assumes the viewpoint of the serial killer) is invited to get off on Starling's terror. There is also something exceedingly disturbing about the way Starling falls under the spell of the courtly serial killer played by Anthony Hopkins. It's as though she is a pawn to be manipulated by two male controls: the repellently powerful Hannibal the Cannibal and the father-figure FBI boss, Jack Crawford (Scott Glenn). As a woman who destroys a demonic serial murderer in the name of the FBI, Starling is the epitome of the safe and acceptable woman killer.

La Femme Nikita is also a tool of male authority. In this international hit from France, Anne Parillaud plays a punk addict turned cop killer who is saved from a clandestine execution so that she can be recruited for a secret government unit. Over months of training, weapons and martial arts experts hone her street-fighting skills, while the divine Jeanne Moreau teaches her wardrobe and make-up tips, and advises her on the clever use of "a surface sweetness." When her Pygmalion process is complete, Nikita (now called Marie) is sent out to kill on command. As a government killer in designer outfits, she has limited appeal. It's

in those early scenes, when she exhibits a feral will to live, that she is magnificent. In the end, Nikita escapes the government control of her "Uncle" Bob and the tender trap of love embodied by her lover, Marco (Jean-Hugues Anglade). Her fate is uncertain, but she definitely has a talent for survival.

Linda Hamilton plays another woman with a will to live, and the self-defense skills to ensure it, in the recent mega-hit *Terminator 2*. Pumped-up and almost psychopathic, Sarah Connor doesn't let a bullet or a stab wound stop her. But when she starts shooting, she is being the best mom she can be. Sarah must protect her young son (destined to be the savior of humankind) from the high-tech hit man sent back in time to blow him away. Sarah is about as tough as they come. But she is, in the final analysis, only the holy vessel in guerrilla garb. And since she is trying to avert nuclear holocaust as well as her son's murder, she is the mother of us all. Filmmaker James Cameron explored the same thematic material in *Aliens* (1986), when mother-figure Ripley (Sigourney Weaver) battled with a space alien "mom" to protect her young charge, Newt (Carrie Henn).

The monster a mother must do battle with isn't always a space creature or an android. One of Hollywood's favorite movie monsters is the single careerwoman. A protective wife and mother can always kill one of those and retain the sympathy of the audience. *Fatal Attraction* (1987) is the most successful example, but *Presumed Innocent* (1990) did a more refined job of bashing the unmarried employed woman. Even so, ambitious sex-crimes prosecutor Carolyn Polhemus (like Alex Forrest in *Fatal Attraction*) was the kind of "bad news" who deserved death. And it wasn't any of Carolyn's numerous male ex-lovers who smashed her skull. No, it was Bonnie Bedelia, playing yet another of her aggrieved homemaker roles. She was only protecting hearth and home, so of course her guilt-ridden husband, Rusty (Harrison Ford), never turns her in.

Hollywood's most successful movies about femmes fatales have always bolstered traditional femininity and male power. Women can shoot a gun for the government and blow away anyone who threatens their men or their kids, but any "heroine" who packs a pistol against systematic male violence is going to take some heat.

A science fiction film like *Eve of Destruction* (1991) will never do the same box office as a big-budget extravaganza like *T 2*. And part of the reason is what each film says about women. In *Eve of Destruction,* a woman scientist, Dr. Eve Simmons (Renée Soutendijk), creates a look-alike robot programmed with the doctor's own memories. When Eve VIII runs amok, she starts blowing away any man who gives her grief, as well as several of the men who gave her creator grief over the years.

Too bad! Eve VIII is eventually destroyed by the woman who gave her "life." And in *Thelma & Louise,* our heroes have no place to go but over and out. Yet these are still powerful images of women who dare to feel anger against male violence and domination. The trashy delight, *Eve of Destruction,* bombed at the box office. But *Thelma & Louise,* fueled by controversy and word-of-mouth support by women, became 1991's "sleeper hit."

And, my, how good it felt to hear the women cheer when that (very phallic) tanker blew sky-high!

84

WENDY BRYAN

Xenatopia (1998)

Once a month, as regular and vicious as PMS, swordfights break out at Meow Mix—a grrrly bar in New York's Lower East Side—over *Xena: Warrior Princess,* while the more battle-shy fans watch back-to-back episodes over cocktails.

From http://www.virago-net.com/brillo/xena.htm (6/3/98). Reprinted by permission of the author.

This gathering proves that Xena is the heroine we've all been waiting for: one who neither apologizes for her brutal behavior nor hides behind a boring, mousy, secretarial alias. One who would respond to cries of, "Why are you such a megabitch?" with a fatal stab in the gut.

There are myriad reasons why this syndicated TV show is such a phenomenon, which may or may not be as fascinating as the folks who actually watch the show. That's why the opportunity to communicate with Xenaites at the first-ever *Hercules* and *Xena:Warrior Princess* convention, held recently at the Burbank Airport Hilton in Burbank, California, was so delicious.

The writers of *Xena: Warrior Princess* have shown little regard for historical accuracy in creating this crazy mish-mash. Xena, for instance, is a warrior from ancient Greece who defeats medieval villages with fancy kung fu fighting methods, yelping her battle cry in an Arabic tongue, and ordering her army about with an American accent.

Yet this bizarre pastiche of cultures has gathered a varied and strange following for Xena, and all of the fans seemed to be present at the Hilton.

Although Xena's show is a spin-off of *Hercules,* she has clearly won the popularity contest. While tickets were still available for the day devoted to Hercules, Xena Sunday was sold out well in advance, with tenacious fans lining up outside in the rain waiting to get inside. Teenage punk girls mingled with suede-clad, paunchy Renaissance Faire freaks. Geeky men with domination leather fantasies fondled Xena cardboard cutouts while young boys deliberated between the official and unofficial Lucy Lawless Fan Clubs. Moms and daughters wore matching "Xenites Rule" T-shirts, while lesbian couples sported tees with an image of Xena and her perky blonde sidekick Gabrielle kissing. It was not the usual group of convention fans, a special breed whose obsessions bolster the U.S. economy with the purchase of overpriced T-shirts, posters, and fan club memberships.

It was disturbing to discover that medieval revivalism dominated the convention—there were a few too many obnoxious, geeky men dressed like friars. They didn't seem to understand that *Xena* uses the Middle Ages as an alternate stage for contemporary storytelling, just like *The Smurfs*. No, *Xena* is *not* intentionally trying to rehash the Dungeons and Dragons game craze of 1984.

And yes, some of Xena's fans are a little confused. But that's okay—so, apparently, is Lawless, at least judging by her onstage antics. Take, for instance, her performance at the convention's big finale: First, the blue-polyester-garbed Princess Warrior herself kindly obliged most of her fans' requests. She arched her eyebrow on command, shrieked her battle cry, and signed frisbees. When Lawless exclaimed that she ought to run for dictator of the year, the audience of thousands screamed their support.

But when asked to sing, Lawless hedged a little, then confessed, "I only know bad cowgirl songs, and there are children present." She did, however, delight her fans by singing the old standard "Deep in the Heart of Texas" and the lesser-known "I've Got a Lovely Bunch of Coconuts" (note: she sang this while hung upon a crucifix on a reel of Xena bloopers).

More properly, she also answered pressing questions about the show, such as "How come every guy Gabrielle kisses always dies?" One especially flustered little boy in a Superman T-shirt approached the stage to speak to Lawless, but became so excited that he forgot what it was he wanted to ask her and simply burst into tears, sobbing, "I love your show."

He's probably going to end up with some kind of crazy Xena fetish when he grows up.

XENA: A PICTORIAL ANALYSIS

The Cult of Xena

The show's subversive subtext has inspired quasi-intellectual debate on the Internet, bringing the postmodern literati on as faithful viewers of *Xena*. One would hope, for instance,

that The Journal of Xena Studies would be a beacon of hope in a sea of "creative anachronism," but the sentimental descriptions of on-screen kisses shared by Xena and Gabrielle, and jumbled gushing paragraphs about the wonders of Lucy are, frankly, disappointing. One bizarre rant, however, discusses the "foreshadowing" of modern day law and economics in *Xena: Warrior Princess*. Has anyone told this man that television isn't real? And that Greek mythological figures didn't run around New Zealand in the middle ages?

Xena: Bondage Queen

Xena has the strength to wield both sword (phallus) and the chakram (cootchie), and she's as much of a bondage queen as Wonder Woman is. While Wonder Woman simply works for the U.S. Army in her spare time, Xena has an army of her very own. Lynda Carter was just dandy for the bra-burning '70s, but '90s women (and men) need someone capable of burning down the White House.

Boob Power

While other popular hermaphroditic figures like RuPaul lampoon one or the other sides of his/her sexual nature, Xena seems to wear both her masculinity and her femininity with pride. There's really no question that Xena's all woman—her boobs are bustin' out all over, yet she wields the kind of power that only American men are able to obtain in today's political climate. Xena's gender interchangability has a kind of mass appeal that sexually ambiguous characters like Pat (of *Saturday Night Live*) never attained.

Xena vs. Brenda: The More Appropriate '90s Grudge Match

Instead of evil warlords, perhaps a more equal match for the Warrior Princess would be Brenda Walsh from *Beverly Hills 90210*. The battle to end all battles would've ensued if these two had occupied the same time slot in the kingdom of prime time. Their hot-blooded tempers perfectly match their high cheekbones and identical hairstyles. Bangs would fly. Sass-aby makeup cases would clash with ancient swords. But, as good outweighs evil, Xena would most likely kick Brenda's ass back into her suburban home.

85

Tom Lanham

Postmodern Sisters (1993)

As I amble into the antechamber of Los Ange-les' hip Cafe Morpheus, I wonder what Naomi Wolf would make of the scene transpiring there today. It's a fashionable magazine photo shoot featuring three very strong-minded women, perhaps—thanks to their well-documented ex-ploits in the entertainment industry—the very "beautiful heroines" of which *The Beauty Myth* spoke.

These are high-profile ladies.

There's Juliana Hatfield, darling of the col-lege radio crowd, whose new *Become What You Are* album (Atlantic) and charming flagship tracks "Supermodel" and "My Sister" are threat-ening to push the chirpy singer into the Top 40 mainstream. Here also is Tanya Donelly, doe-eyed girl-next-door and the Buddha of Belly, a kinetic four-piece combo that was just nomi-nated for MTV's award for its heavy-rotation fave "Feed the Tree" (from the *Star* album on Sire/Reprise). Donelly and Hatfield know each other, have toured together, and, in fact, are handled by the same manager. They chat peri-odically as the afternoon wears on.

The third camera subject, however, keeps to herself, and watches the countless hair-dressers, makeup specialists, and publicists with a kind of seasoned tolerance. After all, this is Sandra Bernhard, recording artist and star of stage and screen, an otherworldly beauty who's

From *Creem*, 1993.

had myriad photo spreads in national publica-tions, even a racy layout in that bible of the tacky common man, *Playboy*. Although she still has a recurring role on the *Roseanne* sitcom and a new contract with Epic Records that just came through, today she's stumping for her second book, the stream-of-consciousness di-ary/diatribe *Love Love and Love* (Harper Collins). This business of looking photogenic is *de rigeur* for Bernhard by now, and she sits pa-tiently on a stool while her people meticulously fuss over her. Even the slightest stray wisp of hair is seen to and carefully brushed, sprayed, or plastered into place before the lens can freeze it in time for posterity.

How would Wolf rationalize the woman who is not only an individual, but also possesses a beautiful public image to represent and con-firm all of her stature? It's a conundrum of monolithic proportions. Bernhard, Hatfield, and Donelly all began their careers with some latent urge to communicate, some deep need with them to turn loose the creative beast and let it assume a form at will. In simple terms, we can call this a career choice. At some point on the timeline, however, an image, a cameo por-trait, almost, became entangled with their art. An image that demands upkeep—nobody thinks of making bad photos as part of their ca-reer choice. Modigliani never had his photo on an album cover or dust jacket.

So we have hair stylists at Cafe Morpheus. We have makeup brushes and kits and creams and gels and mousses and just about everything under the glittery Shiseido sun to make a woman look her best. Donelly undergoes this treatment for an hour and a half, and emerges as something the Western world would term exquisite, her short blonde hair plastered back, haloes of forest green shadowing her hypnotic eyes. She is then positioned in a big Sidney Greenstreet plush chair (for the same amount of makeup time) as the shutter at last snaps away. Afterwards, trial Polaroids of the Belly bombshell litter the floor—Tanya with a black evening dress on; Tanya wearing a pinstriped pantsuit; Tanya with her legs draped coyly over the armrest; Tanya sitting prim and proper, hands folded in her lap.

When I arrive around noon, there's enough tension pinging around the back room to explode the Hindenburg. Hatfield hasn't shown up yet, because—reportedly—her stylist told her it would be a good idea to drop by a salon, preshoot, to get her strawberry blonde page-boy locks streaked. This has delayed the photographers. In the fashion world, this warrants death by dismemberment.

Hatfield finally saunters in, and everyone relaxes. A little."What do you think?" she asks some folks, running her hands through her new 'do. She receives compliments all around on the difference. Having hung out with the shy, somewhat mousy Hatfield a week before in San Francisco, I'm straining my eyes to notice any change in tone or texture. I didn't have the heart to tell her it looked exactly the same—if she was happy with it, the camera would be too.

Unless you're Prince, most guys don't comprehend all these facial aesthetics. Out of the shower, into the jeans, and Wham! Men are ready for the closeup.

But here's a whole subculture of the music/movie industry—the stylists, the fixits of Hollywood—that exists on the coattails of the public's desire to see its idols untarnished. In fact, whenever they got a break, the hair-and-face people paired off to talk trash about their personal travails. I asked a couple who their most difficult assignment was and both, in unison, tittered "Rebecca Demornay!" "But have you ever done Faye Dunaway?" one queried the other, rolling her eyes, "Honey, she *is* Mommie Dearest!"

Actually, Bernhard is beginning to look a little Mommie Dearest herself as this laborious shoot draws to a close. She's tired, anxious to get home by 6 PM, and—after innumerable separate poses—more than ready to take her place between Hatfield and Donelly on a wooden dais for the final group shot. But one of the hair experts won't let them be. Crouching behind the photographer like an umpire for

Calvin Klein, a beefy, earth-mothery woman in a witch-like dress continually rushes the tiny stage to pat or comb Hatfield or Donelly's trying tresses (which, to my untrained eye, seem to already be in order).

More delays.

Bernhard's stylist—a catty fellow with several tattoos—can't resist the in-joke of running up to his client and pretending to straighten her hair, too. Bernhard smiles wickedly. It's funny. The whole damn process is funny.

The original concept for this piece was to sit down with all three women at the same time and get a conversation going, some interplay happening, and have them asking each other the questions. Thanks to the taxing demands photography places on beauty, that didn't happen.

I was allowed separate half-hours with each of them. "I like it better this way," said Bernhard afterwards. "Otherwise, we would've all been influencing each other's answers, trying to say the right thing." Which made sense, because each camp was separate from the others, and looked like some harried general's tent from a Civil war scenario. Clothes decorated chairs, booths, tables, and couches as if they were fallen soldiers, wounded and waiting for someone to pump some life into them.

"Take your hat off boy, when you're talking to me/And be there when I feed the tree," Donelly sings in her optimistic voice on "Feed the Tree," which is not only one of 1993's most engaging pop songs but a demand for respect, for undying devotion from a would-be suitor.

"Love is the only shocking act left on the face of the earth," writes Bernhard in her tome, whose many protagonists seek fast physical pleasure while underneath they want only to be held, treated as human beings and not sexual objects.

"Well I wake up in the morning and the first thing that I say/Is that I hope that I can make it through another lonely day," observed Hatfield in "Everybody Loves Me But You," a conversely uptempo cut from her first post-Blake Babies solo album, '92's *Hey Babe*.

As I interview them, these women all look stunning, radiant. The kind of gals a guy'd be proud to bring home to Mom. But are they happy? Confident in their craft? Secure in their relationships? If so, what got them to those points?

Hatfield and Donelly are both in their mid-twenties, but they got into show business as teenagers and now have fully-developed instincts for survival. For Bernhard, 10 years their senior, this knowledge is rote, a credo by which to live. And—strangely enough—their separate interview answers came out remarkably similar. A camera can't give you confidence or respect. Sometimes it can't even give you a nice feeling about your appearance. That, say Juliana Hatfield, Tanya Donelly, and Sandra Bernhard, has to come from within. And no-one can help you cultivate this garden of the life-shaping morals but yourself.

All performers, at some early point, have to acknowledge that they're different from their peers.

When was the first time you took note of your creative urge?

Hatfield: You don't really get self-conscious until you get into high school, I think. So when I got into high school I started to feel weird and to deliberately isolate myself from people because I wanted to be different. I felt uncomfortable doing the things kids my age were doing. I liked the people in high school, but felt very different from them. That's when I realized that playing music was my destiny. But my whole life I'd made myself perform in some way. I'd play piano recitals and I was on the gymnastic team so I'd have to get up there in front of the gym and do my routine. I always wanted to do something in front of a crowd.

Donelly: Kristen and I started Throwing Muses when we were 15, and it just happened naturally. I think we were so young that we didn't have a concept of why we were doing it and what it is for. But I was really privileged to be born into a good situation. I have great parents and a great friend base, and I've always had good luck meeting the people I was supposed

to meet. My parents never had any structured idea for what people should do with their lives, and that helped a lot.

Bernhard: I think it's something that's just instinctive. Since I was a very small kid, I had that instinct to reach out and connect with people on that kind of entertainment level. I can't say that when you're five years old, you have a real conscious understanding of it. I liked getting attention, I liked making people laugh. But when I was in high school I became very clear on how to manipulate people in that way. I was the class commentator. Whenever there was any kind of political discussion or a discussion about sexuality or the world, I would always talk out of turn, because I couldn't control my urge to express how I felt. That always got me into a lot of trouble. But I think that's what's lacking in education—kids should be allowed to express themselves without being squelched.

Did discovering your art help you to communicate? Bring you out of your shell as a kid?

Donelly: I was nerdy, geeky, totally. I was really ugly and awkward and lonely—all the typical stuff. Kristen and I started writing and that's what I turned to. But I also wrote a lot of poetry when I was a kid, and wrote a lot of short stories later. That was the outlet for awhile. But when I discovered the guitar and songwriting, I realized that was where I had to focus. Because of all the poetry I'd written before I'd ever picked up a guitar, I was really lyrically oriented anyway.

Bernhard: [My Beauty] didn't work in the '70s. Certainly not in Scottsdale, Arizona. But I don't think I'd be as insightful or sensitive as I am if I'd been accepted without any struggle. I don't think any good artist has not had a huge struggle, either physically or emotionally. But I think it's usually a combination—people who are awkward and not held up as the typical American beauty usually become much better artists. There's a difference between a Patti Smith and a Sharon Stone—let's be real about it. Maybe Sharon Stone wasn't a drop-dead beauty in high school—I tend to believe she was. They can say whatever they want, those people, but I think they should just come clean and admit, "Yeah, I've had it a little bit easier."

Hatfield: Maybe that's why a lot of shy people want to perform—they find it hard to communicate in a normal way, so performing is easier than dealing one-on-one with people. You don't have to see any one face—you're either in front of this big mass of people or you're recording and you don't even see the people. You can communicate something that way, and you're not gonna fuck up and say the wrong thing. You've got plenty of time to plan out exactly what you want to say in your music and your writing.

Was there a strong need to be loved, a need for applause that motivated you? And is that what applause feels like—love?

Donelly: Oh, absolutely. It's something people try to deny, and I've tried to deny it for a really long time. But there's a massive gratification in being recognized and respected. I first started becoming addicted to it very recently, realizing, in an almost pathetic way, that it would be a huge loss in my life if I didn't have this outlet and the feedback.

Hatfield: Definitely. I want love from the audience, and it's so obvious. No one who performs wants to be booed; they want to be appreciated, clapped for, adored. It's instant gratification but it doesn't fulfil in the end; it doesn't last. It's a cheap thrill, and you learn that it's not enough. People don't understand how someone who sells millions of records and sells out concerts could be unhappy. But they just don't realize that this adulation cannot sustain a life.

Bernhard: It's all very glamorous, this career, but it's very hard at the same time. And I'm just not the type of person who gets caught up in being a celebrity or a star; it's not in my nature. There've been different projects along the way, like *King of Comedy,* where people like Martin Scorsese validated me, and that makes you the good person you are, hopefully. And I am a good person—I have a lot of love for people and I give a lot of myself in real honest ways. But when you have to put out that kind of

veneer of strength, it leaves you vulnerable. I'm a human being, I'm a woman, you know. I have an incredible capacity for tenderness and sensitivity. It's not like I can go on Letterman's show and he can be a prick and I'll be alright about it—it affects me. Every hurt, every assault that I have to counter, either with my career or from being a woman, it affects me.

You've all become, in various ways, storytellers. When did you first understand your gift with words, the ability to move people?

Donelly: Storytelling is the most important thing in the world and also one of the oldest forms of communication. People have always used it as a means to express themselves and as a reflection of their culture. When I was in Throwing Muses, I wrote a song called "Dragon Head" and that was the first time anybody asked me what my songs were about, and the first time I got a lot of opinions from people on what it could be about. I started to realize that I had to think more about what's coming out of my mouth—not beforehand, but in retrospect. I think it's dangerous to set a goal in your head and try to write around that goal. And if people get something out of my songs, then that's the most important thing that I ever could've done. Even weird interpretations of the songs—whatever they get out of it is as valid as whatever I meant to say.

Hatfield: When I was in high school I wrote stories. I wrote a couple of really good ones that won a couple of awards. One of them was about a day in Bolivia. But I knew that I had a real talent for writing when I wrote those stories. And now "My Sister" has influenced people in ways I've never seen before. While I was at the station this deejay in Arizona played it over the air and she started crying. It was amazing. And this other girl came up to me recently and said that her sister had died two months ago and she really wanted me to sign this piece of paper that she was going to put by her grave.

Bernhard: It happened when I started performing. When I moved here to L.A. in '74 and a year later started getting up in clubs and doing a very rudimentary version of what I do now. I think I knew I had that power. Well, I always knew I had it, but then I put it to practical use. And I've fought against the stereotypes of women who are basically self-loathing and lazy and who don't want to challenge themselves. Women who've found it simpler to live a patriarchal cliché, to be ruled, to sell themselves short. Or maybe there's just nothing there for them, they don't have any options—it's either marry well or disappear. And the stories I tell are not that against the mainstream. A lot of work I do includes those people in a way. A lot of my work is a eulogy to what people lose in their lives, what people aren't allowed to experience. Instead of banging heads with them, critiquing them or tearing them apart, I'm—in a weird way—paying last respects to the things they weren't allowed to experience because they were crushed by the confines and limitations put on them by religion and their family.

In theory, it's a Catch 22—the closer you get to fame, the further you get from normal relationships, with the end of the line being, of course, Michael Jackson, who can't even go shopping without a disguise. How do you keep yourself grounded?

Bernhard: Well, I've kept my close friends for many years and I'm very close to my family. And, especially in the past few years, I've kept sycophants and desperadoes at bay and I've retreated farther and farther back into my private life. I've kept my work as my work and backed away from it when I was done with it. But I think in the first five to ten years of your career, you want to experience those kinds of people. It's fun to have people cater to you and kiss your ass—that's part of the experience. But then you grow up. Or you don't grow up. You either mature as an artist, or you don't.

Hatfield: After awhile, you just know people. You've got instincts. You get close to certain people and you know they're good people. I've never really had a lot of close relationships, so having a lot of fans isn't gonna change anything for me. And when I see my old friends from

school, they say the same things, like "Hey, I heard you were playing," or "I saw you in a magazine—wow a big rock star!" Most people don't know what it's like being in a band—it's just my lifestyle, what I chose to do; it's normal for me. But people think that as soon as you have a record out, you're some kind of a star. The artistic lifestyle is really normal for a lot of people, but some of the folks I went to school with still think it's so foreign and exotic.

Donelly: I have a relationship right now where we're changing the rules a little bit. I'm really bad at love, I think, and wish I weren't. Plainly and logistically, though, I'm never home, and that hurts. I have my friends, and I'll meet people that I'm attracted to that I can tell are true spirits, but for the most part I have a pretty closed community of people I've always relied on. We in the band surround ourselves with people who not only don't kiss our ass but barely respect us at all. There's nobody around us who wouldn't tell us we sucked if we did. And that's important.

Are there subjects you currently feel more comfortable dealing with than you did as a novice?

Donelly: I feel more comfortable singing very straightforward, personal songs now than I ever did before. I think I used to cloak things in metaphors. I've always been very conscious of the people I'm writing about and making sure that they're not hurt; that's something I've had to give up. If I'm going to grow as a songwriter, then I've got to write about the things that come naturally to me and not edit things for fear of wounding those who've wounded me. Searching for truth is a personal quest; in a way, that's what God is. I do believe in ultimate truth, which is very unpopular in the '90s, in a world where personal truth reigns supreme. There are truths that are stronger than your truths or what your experiences have led you to believe.

Hatfield: Writing is hard. Everything about it is difficult—it's not effortless. I remember writing two songs with my friend when I was nine. One of them was this long story about meeting this guy on a beach in the summer and having a summer romance where it ended at the end of the summer. And the other one was about a man who had a blue-collar job who'd come home at the end of the day and tell his wife to leave him alone. It went, "Well I've been working all day and I'm tired tonight/ And I want you to leave me alone right now/You know a man like me gets tired sometimes/And I want you to leave me alone right now." These days, I just hope that I don't get so unhappy that I kill myself. That's my concern. I hope I never kill myself.

Bernhard: I don't think any artist is in full swing until their mid-to-late thirties. I don't think that you can really have that depth and power to reinterpret your own psyche. (The average nine-fiver) may not go into self-analysis, but that's not their job. If that was everyone's job, we'd be out of a job. Of course that's not what they do—that's what we do for them. The heart surgeon repairs the heart, the shoe repairman puts new soles on the shoe. And it's the artist's job to interpret the darker regions of the consciousness, the psyche, and the emotions for people. For me, it is—and for most people who consider themselves artists, it is. For those people who just want to make some quick money, it probably isn't. And when I said "Love is the only shocking act left" in my book I meant that I think everyone's completely numbed by the cultural barrage of information we're given each day—war, disease, famine, loss, suicide, murder. And that love is the one thing that disarms us. When someone really loves us, and is compassionate and tender with us, it's a disarming thing.

Once you've chosen this career, it seems like there's no rule book for growing up, like the entertainment business almost encourages a Peter Pan existence. How do you work through that to adulthood?

Bernhard: Again, I think you have to have a certain amount of self-examination and understanding of your psyche, especially to carry on any kind of successful relationship. But there's a point where you have the revelation that you don't want abusive relationships any more, and where you finally learn to accept yourself and what in your past has led you to this kind of redundancy in relationships. I always felt confident about performing, always knew I was gonna do this. I don't think I always felt confident about my private life and my relationships. But I'm happy now that I have some kind of resolve in my life. Of course, there's always an ongoing struggle with different aspects of your emotions. But that's what keeps you going— that kind of introspection.

Hatfield: My parents were totally cool— they never interfered, because I think they knew that I was really serious and that anyone who tried to fuck with my destiny was in danger. Once I knew what I wanted to do, no one could say anything to dissuade me. But I've matured a lot since I've been playing music. I think you've just gotta hang around with smart people and you learn from them.

Donelly: I'm trying to mold myself into the type of person who's not so obsessed with herself emotionally that she can't learn and grow spiritually. But like a lot of people, I'm obsessed with my emotional life, and it starts to get in the way of the things that you could know on this planet. It's in just trying so hard to know yourself that you stop trying to know the things that'd lead you most directly to yourself. Everyone is alone inside their own head— we come into the world alone, and we leave alone. And that's not something to be avoided. It's something to be embraced and celebrated. Your mind and your heart have to be nurtured above all else.

But since the MTV thing happened, things have gotten strange. Now we have really young kids, like 12 and younger, coming to the open air shows. A 10-year-old came to this in-store we did, and I said "I'm literally old enough to be your mother." And he looked back at me and said, "I wish!" It was so surreal. But this career was definitely a choice I made, and I honestly don't ever wish I was someone else or doing something else.

86

CLAUDIA DREIFUS

Cokie Roberts, Nina Totenberg and Linda Wertheimer (1994)

For the 14.7 million listeners of National Public Radio, Cokie Roberts, 50, Linda Wertheimer, 50, and Nina Totenberg, 49, are the Three Musketeers: gutsy, witty, informed reporters who break stories from inside the Washington political machine. As a troika they have succeeded in revolutionizing political reporting. Twenty years ago Washington journalism was pretty much a male game, like football and foreign policy. But along came demure Linda, delicately crashing onto the Presidential campaign press bus; then entered bulldozer Nina, with major scoops on Douglas Ginsberg and Anita Hill; and in came tart-tongued Cokie with her savvy Congressional reporting. A new kind of female punditry was born.

Today the three are expanding their audiences by branching out into television. Roberts, in addition to her NPR wake-up stint on "Morning Edition," is the first regular female panelist to appear on "This Week," on ABC, and is Ted Koppel's frequent understudy on "Nightline." Wertheimer anchors NPR's flagship broadcast, "All Things Considered," but also makes appearances on the CBS Sunday talkfest "Face the Nation." And Totenberg, NPR's legal affairs correspondent, does commentary and reporting for ABC.

In real life, these broadcasting Musketeers are the closest of friends, sharing vacations, theater subscriptions, everyday advice and general emotional support. They have husbands who, in varying degrees, participate in the friendship: Roberts is married to Steven Roberts, a senior writer at *U.S. News & World Report,* with whom she has two grown children; Totenberg is wed to Floyd Haskell, a former

From *The New York Times Magazine,* January 2, 1994. Reprinted by permission of the author.

Senator from Colorado; and Wertheimer's husband, Fred Wertheimer, is head of the citizens' lobbying organization Common Cause.

On a recent morning in Roberts's cramped office at ABC News in Washington, as a television set blared out C-span coverage of the Senate debate on Bob Packwood, the three reporters ruminated about the pains and pleasures of their breakthrough careers.

Q: Today the Senate discusses what to do with its most famous diarist. Do any of you stand a chance of making an unsolicited appearance in Senator Packwood's little memoir? "Today I placed my hand on Nina Totenberg's knee. . . ."

NT: Not unless he's been fantasizing.

LW: This is part of being older. I mean, I would say that in the last 10 or so years any member of Congress that came after me would be somebody with an asterisk by his name that said "senile," "demented."

CR: The Members of the House—they're just babies! They're *soooo* much younger than we are. They call us "ma'am." They see us as dowagers.

NT: Speak for yourself, Cokie!

Q: As young girls, whom did you dream of being?

NT: Nancy Drew. She was perfect. She could do everything, from perfect dives off a diving board to finding the bad guy.

CR: And she had a racy blue roadster. As for me, there was never anybody I wanted to be. I suppose I expected my life to be like my mother's. But I did not have some special heroine.

LW: Well, *your* mother counts: Lindy Claiborne Boggs, your father's closest counselor and then a Congresswoman herself, counts as a heroine. In my own case I wanted to be Pauline Frederick, the NBC correspondent to the United Nations. I remember watching television in 1956, and there was Pauline out on the steps of the United Nations when the tanks were rolling into Hungary. I was thinking, "I didn't know women could do that." And in fact, they couldn't.

Q: When did you conclude that they "couldn't."

LW: In 1967 after working for a couple years at the BBC in England, I went to NBC in New York for a job. And there this "gentleman" informed me that "women are not credible on the air." He then offered to introduce me to a woman at NBC whose career he thought I should emulate—she'd been a researcher for 10 years—and I just started yelling at him. It was in neon: "This Is the Only Job a Woman Can Have!"

CR: I had a very similar experience in that same time frame. In 1966 I left an on-air anchor television job in Washington, D.C., to get married. My husband was at the *New York Times*. For eight months I job-hunted at various New York magazines and television stations, and wherever I went I was asked how many words I could type.

NT: It was blatant. You were constantly thrown in the position of feeling like you were asking for favors when you applied for a job. Two experiences come to mind. The first was in 1965. I called the *Quincy Patriot Ledger* because I heard there was an opening, and this male editor said to me, "Oh, we don't hire women." The Civil Rights Act had recently passed. I'm not sure I knew that women were covered. It was so much the way things were that I wasn't outraged.

Ten years later, I was a somewhat accomplished journalist. I'd won prizes. I'd had jobs for a long time. And I was looking for another job. I had lunch with the bureau chief of a distinguished chain of newspapers. This man looked at me and without a moment's hesitation said, "But, Nina, we already have our woman." I felt the rage well up through my gullet and I just shoved it back down again. What could I do? Throw my food in his face?

CR: One other thing: While these men were saying we couldn't have the jobs, their hands were on our knees.

NT: There were a couple of instances that were truly awful, but most of the time if you just moved away about a foot, they got the message and there was no scene. That's all you ever wanted: to avoid a scene.

Q: And did you get the job?

NT: No. But you weren't getting the job anyway.

Q: Twenty-five years later, along comes Anita Hill. Given your own experiences, you must have empathized.

NT: Well, since Anita Hill was *my* story, I should answer that. Many, many years earlier, I had been aggressively pursued by a supervisor. That may have helped in talking to Anita Hill. But other than that, I just thought it was a good story, as much about the Judiciary Committee as anything else.

CR: I do think, though, that in some ways women of our age were less sympathetic to Anita Hill because what happened to her didn't seem so bad as compared to what happened to us. I mean, it was just talk.

CR: And she had the job. So when the hearings happened it was a very interesting moment in our offices, where the young women were truly appalled and the older women were basically saying, "Ahhh, that's nothing, babe. Let us tell you the way it used to be."

Q: Since we're talking history, how did you three meet?

LW: Cokie and I went to school together at Wellesley, but we didn't know each other there. She was in the class ahead of me, and from a famous family. Everyone said, "Oh, she's the daughter of the House majority whip, she's Hale Boggs's daughter."

NT: I was the one who drafted Cokie for NPR. That must have been 1977. Linda and I were there already, and there was an opening for another reporter. I had heard that Steve Roberts and his wife were back in Washington after living overseas for a few years, that she was looking for work. So I called him and he brought over her résumé. And I remember Linda saying, "Is that Cokie Boggs?" The rest is history.

CR: When I came in for an interview Linda and Nina were there, greeting me and encouraging me. And it just made all the difference in the world. NPR was a place where I wanted to work because they were there.

NT: NPR had quite a few women on staff. It was, and still is, a shop where a woman could get considerable visibility and responsibility. NPR's wages were at least a third lower than elsewhere in the industry, and for what they paid, they couldn't find men.

LW: Cokie joined me over on the Hill covering Congress. The hilarious thing was that I had spent years trying to develop a beat in Congress, working really hard, trying to understand what the talk meant, how the monster actually worked. I thought I was good at it. Then Cokie arrived, after living in Greece for years, and I had the feeling that she was born to understand Congress.

CR: We were a great team. Tip O'Neill always said to me, "I give you'se girls from NPR first shot at everything."

Q: How did the tag "Three Musketeers" get pinned to you?

CR: Oh, how does any of that get started? It's basically, "they all look alike." We were three women who were very good friends. We socialized together, sat together in the office, had our desks close together. We were all the same age and people just didn't distinguish between us.

Q: Are there qualities that any of the three of you envy in the others?

NT: Oh, I envy Cokie's tact. . . . Linda and I started a union at NPR. During negotiations we all had roles: I was the Screamer, Linda was the Rational One, Tactful Cokie closed the deal. We don't do this anymore because the NPR boys have become quite good at negotiations.

CR: Well, I envy Nina's guts. Sometimes when we're all sitting together at the office we see Nina working the phone, and Linda and I just look at each other and say, "Dear God. . . ." I also envy Linda's incredible persistence. I mean, when she goes in to a live event, she can tell you every little detail down to the mortar in the cracks of the building she's about to sit in.

LW: I would say I envy Nina's courage, and Cokie taught me a great deal about not blowing up. I have an awful temper.

Q: Has Cokie ever been rude to anybody?

CR: Oh, sure. Let me think. When John Tower was up for Secretary of Defense and was running into confirmation problems about his alleged womanizing and drinking. There was concern about him having his finger semi-on the button. So Senator Tower went on the Brinkley show. It was live, and it was remarkable because he came on and took the pledge not to drink. David was away, and Sam Donaldson, who was hosting, said something like, "Well, Senator, it's not just alcohol, you know. There have been charges of womanizing." So Senator Tower says, "I'm a single man. I *do* date women." And then he says, "What is your definition of womanizing, Sam?" And then, basically because I'm sitting there in a skirt, he turns to me and says, "Cokie, do you have a definition of the term?"

LW: And Cokie said, "Well, I think most women know it when they see it, Senator." I watched that and thought, "Ohhhhhhhh, my God. . . ." It was one of those moments. I had a similar one with the sportscaster Red Barber. We were on the air and he said something to me about how many really fine women there are at NPR. And then he said something like, "Speaking of the other gender, do you think Winning Colors is gonna be in trouble with the muddy track at Pimlico?"

CR: This is an attempt to sabotage. . . . A total sandbag job.

Q: I don't get it.

CR: Well, that's the point. [Laughs] You're live on the air, and you've got the world's sports expert on with you. You're a girl, right? And he just segues from this gracious thing to asking you a totally impossible question, like "What is 4,852 times 900,848—and tell me right now."

LW: And I suppose he didn't think I had any idea who Winning Colors was. Well, I just started laughing. "I'm really rooting for the filly, Red," I said, "But I think we've had a lot of rain, and you know, Pimlico is really going to be muddy, no question about it." Heh, heh. I *always* read the racing news in *The New Yorker*. The bastard didn't get me!

Q: Well, Linda, perhaps the late Red Barber could have traded notes with Ross Perot on their dislike of you?

CR: Linda spoke vicious truths to Ross Perot.

LW: Yes, I asked him about some history and he got very upset.

CR: He went nuts! I heard the broadcast while driving down Sunset Boulevard. I had been interviewing somebody and I was driving back to my hotel, and there on the radio was Ross Perot barking at Linda: "This is a classic setup. Is this a radio program? You're not just somebody calling in? Whoever you're trying to do a favor for, you've done it, and I'm sure you had a smirk on your mouth as you got me into this." It was a riot. I almost had a wreck!

NT: Here's Linda's thoroughness again. Linda had covered the tax bill, in which Perot had succeeded in getting himself a multimillion dollar loophole of the kind that he was condemning all over the country. So she had him dead to rights because she'd been there when it happened. He went ballistic.

Q: Ross Perot didn't much care for you either, Cokie.

NT: In the beginning he *loved* her. He wanted her to run for Vice President.

CR: Oh, that was just a rumor. I had written an op-ed piece that talked about why he was having the effect he was having. And I had heard from people in his organization that this was the best description of the phenomenon they had seen. But then I had him on "Nightline" and he again talked about us not asking him questions that wanted to be asked. The whole interview became just unbelievably testy, and it just got ruder and tenser and awful. We just sat there thinking. "Is he gonna get up and leave? Is he gonna throw the chair? Is he going to strangle himself on his microphone?" The next week he gave his comment about not minding reporters, just female re-

porters: "They're all trying to prove their manhood."

Q: Actually, you three have been charged with proving your *womanhood.* The conventional wisdom has it that with the increasing number of women in the Washington press corps, you have changed the nature and content of political reporting.

LW: Well, we were interested in the range of issues that have defined the role of women in politics.

CR: This was more true in covering Congress than on the campaign trail, because you're covering issues on an ongoing basis. During the 1990 budget-agreement talks, when the budget negotiators from the Bush Administration and Congress were all holed up at Andrews Air Force Base, our male colleagues would ask them, "How many M.X.'s are there still left in the budget?" And I'd ask, "Are mammograms still covered?"

In the 1988 Presidential campaign I felt that had there not been so many women on the campaign bus, Gary Hart's womanizing wouldn't have been a story. Hart's behavior was something that a lot of us had talked about in the prior election. We'd wondered: At what point were Gary Hart's relationships with women a story? Then the 1988 race came around and it looked like he might become President. Because there were a lot of women talking about this as an issue, that might have had the effect of sending *The Washington Post* and *Miami Herald* out on that story.

Q: Do you ever wonder if it was a mistake to politicize the private lives of politicians? Bill Clinton was rumored to have a Gary Hart-ish sexual life, yet he's turned out to be quite supportive of women's rights.

CR: So's Bob Packwood.

Q: Has Bob Packwood's story long been known in Washington, as Gary Hart's was?

NT: In a way. I've run into female staffers who ran Senatorial offices 10 years ago, who would, as a matter of course, instruct newcomers not to be in a room alone with him. If you were a woman on Capitol Hill, you knew who was a bottom pincher and who wasn't. If you were a female reporter you still had to interview everybody, but there were certain Senators you knew to sit *far* away from—or dress like a nun with.

CR: The point is that 10 years ago no one would have thought Packwood's behavior with women was a story.

NT: Cokie and I did "Nightline" recently with Dianne Feinstein. Senator Feinstein was the only member of the Senate we asked who would go on the program about Packwood. And she felt very strongly, as she said on the air, that there was absolutely a direct connection between Anita Hill and Bob Packwood—that the Packwood disciplinary proceeding would not have happened without the Thomas-Hill hearings.

Q: Your friendship sounds so idyllic. Do you ever get angry at one another?

NT: Oh, we have been angry, but it never lasts long.

LW: Whenever there have been stresses, it's been because somebody's had some kind of personal problem and we've had to adjust to provide the support. Mostly there's a lot of cooperation; there were plenty of times when one of us would have to go somewhere and the other one would cover. I'd go to a news conference and then come back and say, "Here's what happened, and the cut of tape you want is there." And we just had that kind of trust. And we also had the capacity to divide up the work without getting competitive.

Q: Not even a wee bit competitive?

CR: Whatever competition there is . . . is pretty healthy. I mean, there have been lots of primary nights when we'd sit there at three o'-clock in the morning exhausted, trying to out-write each other. And if the other one had not been there, you wouldn't have done it, because at moments like that you're so tired that all you want to do is go to bed.

NT: Our beats *do* overlap, but we manage it. Cokie and Linda both cover Congress and the political beat. And I certainly trample on their turf. If there's a big confirmation battle

over a Supreme Court nominee, there's no question it's my story. And they're always deferred to me on that. Totally. And if I'm covering a political story, like a Presidential campaign, I have no expectation that I'll get first dibs.

Q: In closing, how do you feel when you meet younger women in journalism who haven't any idea how rough things used to be in the "bad old days"?

NT: Murder comes to mind.

LW: I think what happens now is that the young women get the first job, and the next job, and achieve some level of success. But at some point they hit a wall and they find out that until and unless a substantial number of mostly white men die, they may not be able to move up. It's a shock to their systems.

CR: On one hand you always have to fight the feeling of saying, "Just you wait, my pretties. . . ." You don't want to be the Wicked Witch of the West, but you do know that they will run into sex discrimination as they proceed in their journalistic lives. Still, you're proud they don't have to fight as hard as we did. We opened things up—for them.

87

LYNDA HINKLE

The Smash! FAQ (1998)

What is a Smashing Girl?

A Smashing Girl is a woman of any age or background that says "NO!" to self-loathing of her body and stands up for her right to be whole and happy. She also doesn't judge other women based on their appearance and tries to encourage others to adopt a similar attitude of self acceptance. She is committed to the idea that all women are beautiful. She is . . . in the slang . . . smashing woman . . . (meaning gor-

From http://www.dandyweb.com/smash/more .html (6/2/98). Reprinted by permission of the author.

geous and breathtaking) as well as a woman capable of destroying lies and stereotypes. She is of any age, ethnic background, dress size, class, religion, political persuasion, etc.

What is the Smashing Network?

It is an organization of women committed to ending beauty prejudice in themselves and our society.

What if I want to support women by helping fight beauty prejudice but I have a Y chromosome?

Boyz are welcome to join the Smashing Auxillary and become SMASH Boyz supporting women in the fight against beauty prejudice.

Who started this and why?

Lynda Hinkle started this organization as part of the community service committment that her one woman business, Dandelion Innovations, espouses. She is a fat girl since childhood and the editor of the now defunct Phat Phree Ezine (fat acceptance quarterly).

If I became a Smashing Girl, does that mean I have to follow an agenda . . . or stop wearing makeup?

The only agenda is self acceptance and overcoming beauty prejudice. Makeup, frills and all that jazz are not the problem. Self esteem and oppression are.

What are the benefits of joining the Smashing Network?

Smashing Network members will receive occasional updates on Smash site changes, projects, giveaways, ideas and information. Their site and name will be listed on the Network URL List. They will be offered the opportunity to shape and direct this organization as it grows and improves. They will make Lynda very happy.

How do I join? Does it cost anything?

Its free! Just have to fill out a form. None of the information collected will be given to any other entity besides Smash. It will not be freely distributed in any form.

What if I would like to submit to Smash's Article/ Rant Page?

Send me email! I would be more than delighted, I would be tickled pink as it were. I am also accepting original artwork and comix (scanned only . . .), URL's for the links page, and any personal rants, raves, reviews or ideas! Also . . . I would adore to have some of you lovely ladies, especially those who think you aren't, send me scanned pictures to put up and praise publically :).

Is there other SMASH stuff I can do?

We now have a SMASH mailing list, but it focuses on "women smashing stereotypes" of all kinds, not just body image. If you would like to join, please send email to smash-list-request@ dandyweb.com with the message: subscribe.

88

Lisa Jervis

Imperfect Beauty (1998)

Hey, did you hear that standards of beauty are becoming more real? Actresses and models now supposedly look like your neighbors, that woman sitting next to you on the subway, and maybe even you!

That's the news from the fashion editors— and no doubt they believe it—but the truth is far less exciting. What we're actually seeing has changed so little and we're being told it's so big, that it only serves to lull us into complacency.

From *bitchmag*, http://www.bitchmag.com/ features/archive/imperfect/index.html (6/3/98). Reprinted by permission of the author.

May's *Glamour* trumpets "The New Idea of Beauty." They say "it's bigger, broader, more inclusive." Yeah right. Maybe about an inch bigger in the right places, of course. September's *Marie Claire* announces that "The hottest faces currently mesmerizing the fashion world are less Barbie-doll plastic and more inspirationally offbeat," and presents us with a list of "Imperfect Beauties." Both mags show us photographs of these "new" women who supposedly look more like us. So "imperfect noses," "dreadlocks," "bowed legs," "crooked lips," and "freckles" on these babes are supposed to mean that models and actresses now look like the average woman? Supposedly "women who aren't 5'11" with enormous busts and long blond hair can relate to these models and think, 'Well, this is something I could hope to possibly look like.'"

Puh-leeze. Spare me the "these-are-regular-women" pap. It's just not true.

Ethnic diversity is another supposed success story. A comment in *Marie Claire* makes me wonder how successful they really are, though. "The new look embraces a broad range of unconventional, ethnic, even odd looks. . . ." No matter how well-meaning this statement is, putting "ethnic" and "odd" in the same category is trivializing and insulting. And *Glamour's* line-up of actresses shows only two Asian-Americans, one dark-skinned African-American, and one African-American so light-skinned (at least as far as I can tell) that if you don't know who she is you'd probably think she's white. Maybe including non-white models at all is some kind of progress in their eyes, but if it is it only shows how much further we need to go. It's not even close to time for rejoicing and declaring the racism in standards of beauty gone—or even more than slightly decreased.

Glamour is also touting new and more realistic body types. Wait a minute, then how come the two women who are described as size 14 literally have their bodies blocked from view—one by a cut-off frame and the other because she's standing behind other models? This kind of hypocrisy isn't a one-shot deal: A recent ad in a San Francisco free weekly recruiting women for a *New York Times* fashion shoot says, "Do you look good in a suit? Are you an interesting woman, any age, any ethnicity?" They say they're seeking "real women, not models," and that "all types [are] welcome," but at the end of the ad they reveal that you must be a size 8 or smaller. Hello? Anyone home in there? Size 8?

Both articles go on to praise certain ad campaigns for being progressive about standards of beauty: cK One "takes the idea of realism to a new level"; Oil of Olay and Esprit are running "real-woman, testimonial-style" ads; Prescriptives "actually showcases its ordinary but nonetheless attractive employees." Make no mistake, though. With very few exceptions, these ads are sure as hell not populated by average-looking women. By pretending that they are, fashion mags and ad execs fool us into thinking that we have escaped the bad old days of rigid rules of appearance for some multicultural be-yourself paradise of naturalness.

And to get into this new Eden, you still need to obsess over your appearance and buy lots of junk to smear on your face. Now, though, it's a feminist act: "The personal is political. You support or defeat a changing ideal with your actions. That not only means buying from companies that promote many versions of beauty but refusing to conform to the unrealistic standards yourself by choosing to celebrate the differences that make your looks uniquely beautiful," says *Glamour*. The operative word here, however buried, is buy. The connection of beauty images to commerce is so wholly uncritical that in these articles about changing standards, we're also given make-up tips: paint your mouth more heavily to go with your big nose; don't try to change your skin tone with foundation.

I've got some advice of my own: don't be fooled. Things haven't changed enough as long as we're still being given directives about how to enhance our looks, no matter how "realistic" the goal is—because the fashion and beauty industry needs to sell us something in order to survive. The "changing" standard of beauty is just another sales pitch.

89

HAYLEY NELSON

Dating Is Tired, Marriage Is Wired (1998)

"Marriage is fashionable again," announced Dan Quayle speechwriter Lisa Schiffren in a March op-ed in *The New York Times.* Sure, the statistics support her claim, showing a boom in the number of weddings in the past few years. But it's still strange that popular media can classify marriage—an emotional commitment and one of the most sacred bonds between two people—as "in fashion" or "out."

The media may claim that marriage is popular right now, but I know more twenty-somethings who say that they'll never marry. Our generation has to deal with a whole new set of issues surrounding marriage, and whether we've lost our faith in marriage or we're still drawn to tying the knot, we aren't going to scurry to a chapel just because some magazine tells us it's the *now* thing to do.

Magazines like *Cosmo* offer countless features on how to land Mr. Right—and draw him in hook, line, and sinker to the pulpit. It's often implied that single women are miserable and lonely, simply biding their time before they trap an eligible bachelor. Personally, I think it's just the opposite—most women I know are single by choice, taking advantage of their youth to fully explore the world, before they decide whether or not to marry at all. Whereas when women's mags glorify single-hood, the stories still imply that marriage is a woman's final goal—an expectation that seems straight from the 1950's. Even *Mademoiselle's* story entitled "Single and Loving It" ends with the assertion that we need to "squash the idea that a single woman of 40 has a higher chance of getting kidnapped by a terrorist than of getting married."

From *bitchmag*, http://www.bitchmag.com/features/archive/imperfect/index.html (6/3/98). Reprinted by permission of the author.

It's ironic that the media focuses on marriage as the end-all-be-all, when for some of us, marriage seems like more trouble than it's worth. My generation is the first generation to grow up knowing more divorced parents than nuclear families: between 1970–1990, the number of divorces quadrupled. We were also the first generation who had parents at couples counseling, who went to family therapy, and who knew people having children out of wedlock (in the last twenty years, the number of non-marital births has risen from 5.3 percent to more than thirty percent). My parents had to work hard to stay together: they went to therapy to figure out even little problems, like my dad working long hours, or issues about disciplining the children. When I look at most marriages around me now, more than three-quarters of them appear completely dysfunctional—whether due to lack of communication or simply lack of love.

The broken marriages surrounding us have made a mark on our generation's perception of permanent union. One friend of mine was so disenchanted with the concept, he vowed not to marry until he wanted children, and then he would want his bride-to-be to sign a pre-nuptial agreement. After growing up with two sets of parents and a mother who endured miserable affairs, a binding commitment just didn't make much sense to him.

But thirty years ago, our parents were under much greater pressure to marry, and it was common to settle down to start a family right out of college. Kids got married before they really knew what they were getting themselves into. My generation is in no such rush; we're starting careers later, and getting married later. More and more of us are taking time to indulge in self-exploration and experimentation—not to mention self actualization. According to Carla, who married at 30, "When people in our generation choose to marry, it is a union between two individuals who truly know who they are and what they want out of life. Marriage in the 90's is about celebrating individual freedom and growth within the secure framework of true (selfless) love."

Jenny, a recently engaged 24-year-old law school student, puts it this way: "I think waiting to get married is a good idea because it's harder for our generation to know what we want out of marriage. Women in our generation want someone who will let us be ourselves and allow us to have a career—someone who doesn't just agree that a woman should work, but who will support all levels of achievement. We want a truly equal relationship, with stability and love—all of this sugar-coated with passion." It's this ideal of the perfect mate that keeps many of us on the dating scene, searching for a more meaningful commitment.

But still, is it in our biological cards to be faithful to one person *forever?* What if we suddenly find ourselves attracted to someone new? Lessley, 22, lives with her boyfriend, but wouldn't dream of getting married. "I don't want to get married, because I don't ever want to make any promises of life-long monogamy to anyone. I would never take a vow I could conceive of breaking, and I can all-too-easily imagine myself entering a new phase of life where I would want to be single, and would not want to deny myself that."

TV shows like *Melrose Place* and *Beverly Hills 90210* like to glorify the lives of single people, making life in your twenties seem like one big glamorous date, with great looking people all over the place hooking up right and left. In reality, I see a lot of lonely people struggling to meet a quality partner, or to just be happy on their own. The media seems to overlook the often difficult process of meeting someone and getting to know them. In real life, we take sex a lot more seriously than do our TV counterparts—we're not messing around when it comes to issues like STDs and AIDS—and we're not all hopping into the sack with the first cute face we meet. Magazines portray the dating scene in a similar fashion. It's the sexy swinging-single syndrome: the "fun" behind getting ready, what to wear, where to go, and what to do on dates. Give me a break!!

We get quite a barrage of mixed messages from the media about marriage; it's "in" to get married, but it's OK to be a swinging single, but singledom is also just a temporary fix until marriage. Pick your poison. No matter what we choose to hear, despite what the statistics may say, our generation knows that marriage isn't the bed of roses June Cleaver made it seem, and most of us are taking our time before taking the plunge. It's our freedom to decide when—and if—marriage is right for us.

90
WOMEN HALTING ONLINE ABUSE
About W.H.O.A. (1998)

Please Note:

No one outside of the President or anyone so appointed by her is authorized to give the official positions of W.H.O.A. or to speak for W.H.O.A. If you have difficulties with anyone claiming to be a member of W.H.O.A. who appears to be violating any of our policies or violating net etiquette in trying to get our message across, please let us know at whoa@femail.com.

Check out our page of banners that you can use on your web site to show your support for W.H.O.A. You can even become one of our web partners!

OUR CHARTER
MISSION STATEMENT

The mission of W.H.O.A. is to educate the Internet community about online harassment, empower victims of harassment, and formulate voluntary policies that systems administrators can adopt in order to create harassment-free environments. W.H.O.A. fully supports the right to free speech both online and off, but asserts that free speech is not protected when it involves threats to the emotional or physical

From Women Halting Online Abuse, http://whoa.femail.com/about.html (6/2/98). Reprinted by permission of the author.

safety of anyone. W.H.O.A. further asserts that online harassment is about power in a community: a power structure that has tended to accept or ignore harassment rather than actively seek to cease it. While W.H.O.A. does not wish to single any group out as an enemy, we recognize and celebrate that the tide of the community is changing as people from all walks of life begin to become active participants online. As such, we must begin to assert our power as a group of concerned individuals (no matter what our backgrounds) toward the protection of all people online against harassment targeted against them based on gender, sexual preference, race, ethnicity, age or privilege. W.H.O.A. is an organization created and founded by women, but we welcome men who demonstrate sensitivity toward the issues of harassment and a willingness to support our cause.

GOALS AND IMPLEMENTATIONS

1. Educate the Internet Community About Harassment. This will take several forms:
   a. Educating administrators of BBS's, chats, IRC servers, web sites and other interactive media about the issues of harassment and creating positive, safe communities. This will be implemented through the development of web site resources, email resource packs that can be provided upon request of administrators, and through the development of an administrators' email newsletter bulletin.
   b. Educating the community itself and providing information about how users can protect themselves against harassment situations. Part of this involves the creation of a safe-site and unsafe-site list that will allow users to make decisions about the level of protection they are comfortable with at the sites they frequent. Sites that adopt anti-harassment policies and follow through on them will be added to the safe list. Sites that have complaints pending against them in which the administrator refuses to consider arbitration or refuses to address the issue will be placed on the unsafe site list.
   c. Educating targets of harassment on how to fight back and protect themselves in the meantime against further harassment.
2. Empowering Targets of Harassment. In addition to education about what they can do to fight back, W.H.O.A. will provide advice and referral to targets of harassment.
3. Providing Policies for a Better Internet Community.

There are several policies that W.H.O.A. will seek to develop and advance.

   a. Policies against sexual harassment or intimidation through public or private means (such as email).
   b. Policies against public personal attacks, particularly involving the "outing" of private information about someone or libelous material.
   c. Policies against threats of any kind.
   d. Policies favoring the self-policing of sites.

All of these policies will seek to encourage administrators to use the control they have over the use of their resources to remove any persons causing offenses to those policies that are either severe or repeated. Administrators who choose to adopt these policies will be educated and assisted in putting them into practice. They will also be encouraged by appearance on the Safe List and permission to use the W.H.O.A. Safe Site Logo if they choose. Administrators who do not choose to adopt these policies will not be censured in any way unless there are complaints against their site.

ADMINISTRATIVE STRUCTURE

The administration of a vast program such as this requires many hands and many minds, which means that in order to continue to run effectively, W.H.O.A must have clear leadership. This will take the form of a Board of Directors possibly consisting of the following key positions:

PRESIDENT AND CEO

Responsible for the appointment of the Board of Directors. Also responsible for providing leadership on all matters relating to W.H.O.A. and for the general health and growth of the organization. Responsible for administration related to membership and dissemination of educational materials. May appoint and remove all staff and Board members.

PUBLICITY DIRECTOR

Responsible for providing direction to the publicity campaign necessary to get W.H.O.A.'s message to the Internet community and the world.

EDUCATIONAL DEVELOPMENT DIRECTOR

Responsible for the development and review of educational materials related to online abuse/harassment. Develops a contact list of professionals to refer targets of harassment to for emotional or legal counsel.

DIRECTOR OF POLICY

Responsible for the development and administration of W.H.O.A.'s anti-harassment policies. Also responsible for the development of W.H.O.A.'s own policies with the consent and assistance of the membership and the Board.

DIRECTION OF SITE INVESTIGATION

Responsible for determining the eligibility of sites for safe or unsafe site listing.

Each of these Directors may choose a committee if they wish of interested members to help them with the responsibilities that fall under their position. Directors will be appointed by the President. Directors will be chosen on the basis of sensitivity to the issue of harassment, prior administrative or related experience, and willingness to commit to the project. All Directors are responsible to fill out reports to the President in regard to their projects. Failure to do so will result in termination. As part of their duty, Directors are asked to commit to approximately two–three hours per week of volunteer service in their area. Directors may be summarily removed at any time by the President if they fall inactive. They may also be removed for other forms of misconduct but only with the consent of the remaining Board members.

In addition to the Board of Directors, an Advisory Board consisting of individuals who offer assistance on special projects or occasional advice in an area of their expertise will exist. Advisory Board members are appointed by the President for unlimited terms and are removed by a vote of the Board of Directors if their actions are contrary to the best interests of W.H.O.A.

W.H.O.A. POLICIES

1. W.H.O.A. is not a replacement for legal counsel and under no circumstances are any of its officers permitted to provide legal advice.

2. W.H.O.A. is also not a replacement for psychological counseling. While we hope to be a supportive and empowering embrace of understanding to those who come to us for help, we cannot provide advanced psychological assistance, and will also refer out in cases that seem to require it.

3. W.H.O.A., its officers and members, must agree as part of their involvement that they will never, under any circumstances, directly contact any person that is suspected of harassment. Rather, we deal with administrators and others in positions of authority who can use their influence to resolve the issue, rather than endangering any others.

4. W.H.O.A. does not demand compliance with its policies from sites. Rather, we suggest.

If harassment is taking place and site administrators refuse to address it, W.H.O.A. uses letter writing campaigns, boycotts, or publicity to fight injustices, remaining nonviolent, responsible, fair-minded, and willing to negotiate on anything but a person's right to emotional or physical safety.

5. W.H.O.A. will not advise its members to write letters or take any action against any site unless it has either seen proof from the victim that harassment is taking place or has directly spoken with or visited the site and found a culture of harassment and abuse.

6. W.H.O.A. will not give out the personal information of any of its members or anyone it tries to help under any circumstances barring court order.

MEMBERSHIP

Membership is free and open to all. Members will receive updates and information about W.H.O.A. as well as the opportunity to serve in any committees or volunteer to assist the organization in a manner with which they feel comfortable. Membership information is available.

91

HEATHER IRWIN

Shouting into the Vacuum (1998)

Okay, here's what we know. The Net has historically been predominately white, predominately male and predominately run by geeks who, upon reaching middle age and amassing enormous wealth, feel that they have something to prove—namely that they are predominately white and predominately male, and have a lot of money and power that you don't. Those

From *bitchmag*, http://www.bitchmag.com/features/archive/imperfect/index.html (6/3/98). Reprinted by permission of the author.

are the facts, and there ain't no point in debating them.

But listen up geekboys, women are coming online in record numbers and dammit, they want content. Content that doesn't go out of its way to offend, insult, alienate and repugnate. Content that addresses their interests and their concerns, and content that actually has some relevance to their lives. Content, most of all, that isn't about being white, male and mired in the testosterone-laden minefields of technobabble.

If we have to read one more story lauding the antics of those nutty suck boys, the brilliance of wired visionaries who make it a habit of demeaning women, or the likes of patronizing netchicks like Carla Sinclair, we're going to kill someone. And you better believe we know where your BMW's are parked at night.

Oddly enough, online marketing departments, editors and writers know that women want more—and certainly the women so desperately searching for relevant content know they want more—so how come no one is doing anything about it?

On the eve of the Webgrrls conference in New York, a number of sites (all run by men) have recently run columns decrying the lack of women's content on the 'Net. And while we're glad someone is listening, we can't help but roll our eyes and whisper in hoarse voices that we've been screaming into that vacuum for nearly a year now—and we're sure that there are a number of women who've been doing it even longer than the julie-come-latelies of Bitch. It's a perennial problem that no one seems to be addressing.

Why? I can sum it up in one word: advertising.

Sure, this is a major duh, but it bears explaining once again that sites that have big name advertisers (no matter what they tell you) have to conform to those advertisers' expectations, morals, standards, etc. Sites that aren't sponsored—well, they pretty much have to go it alone depending on goodwill, handout and a lot of caffeine-assisted late nights. And at this point, there is no real middle ground. Decent women's content is over and over again falling into the void, either selling out and dumbing down or remaining true to its mission and often folding due to lack of money, interest and time.

So what's a grrrl to do? Accept the milquetoast content of sites like Women's Wire (hey no offense, we love those girls, but there's no denying they've got to please their sponsors) or simply surf endlessly for indie sites that usually don't last longer than a few months?

At this point there's no real answer. Not until companies like Wired and Time Warner and Word and all the rest of the companies that are throwing money into new content decide that what's really important isn't just advertising but actually creating real content, real communities and real spaces for the rest of us. Places where people just come to be themselves, to listen, to learn, to share and to interact—not to be proselytized to about the wonders of the digital revolution (sponsored by Lexus).

But as usual, we're not holding our breath waiting.

92

VIRGINIA EUBANKS

A Woman's Place in Cyberspace (1998)

Several years go I ended up shelving an article about the representations of women in cyberpunk because I figured that everything that needs to be said about cyberpunk has been said. It was passé, mid-eighties. And I continued to think that for quite some time. However, due to my recent foray into the technological workforce, I've become more aware of the subtle and treacherous ways in which the misogynistic

From *Brillo*, Number 1, http://www.virago-net.com/rant/index.html (6/3/98). Reprinted by permission of the author.

tendencies of cyberpunk have informed how many people think about the ways that women are "supposed" to relate to technology. The genre may be dead, but the metaphorical relationships it helped create have endured.

So let's talk about one of these metaphorical relationships. Specifically, the one that equates women with the body and the white male with the mind. Nowhere is this metaphor more obviously stated as it is in many of the "great works" of cyberpunk, Gibson's novels in particular. In *Neuromancer,* considered the classic cyberpunk novel, Gibson's major female character is Molly, a technologically enhanced body-for-hire who paid for her "upgrades" by becoming a puppet, or programmable prostitute. She also has sex with the novel's protagonist, Henry Case, and acts as his body when he is in cyberspace, the realm of the mind and therefore, the male. Her role as body and tool is very explicit.

In *Count Zero,* the second in the trilogy, the situation isn't any better. Gibson's major female figures are "horses," voodoo priestesses who serve as the conduits of the (male) Loa who exist in cyberspace, and Angela Mitchell, whose brain has been replaced by circuitry of her father's design. As my first quote shows, cyberspace is constructed by Gibson as a female region to be used and controlled by men, and is highly sexualized. Only men have access to the fruits of this female region, and they receive their rewards by "jacking in" through their computers.

Women are simply resources, bodies. They are not active agents, nor users of the technology. Exploring this fictional world may seem to be just academic, especially if you think, as I did, that cyberpunk is dead. But look at any issue of *Wired,* or one of the other currently hip techno-fetish magazines and count the number of Gibson and cyberpunk references. Cyberpunk has very clearly and pervasively influenced the way we think about technology. Of course, I'm not blaming cyberpunk alone for creating this paradigm. Cyberpunk is just a particularly poignant and relevant example of this metaphor as it relates to a discussion of the inclusion of women in new technologies. The Woman = Body, Man = Mind paradigm is an old standard, and it has given rise to a lot of myths going around about how "we" feel about computers.

We are intimidated by new technology. It's not user-friendly enough for us to understand. We're just not interested. We don't understand how important it is. Any of these sound familiar? None of these assumptions have anything to do with why women are staying away from the Internet in droves. Besides the obvious issue of access—that women still make absurdly lower salaries than most white men and are often pigeonholed into jobs that give them less training with and less access to new technologies—there is a major reason that no one is talking about. The Internet and the World Wide Web are actively and aggressively hostile to women. Not the technology itself, but the attitudes of the people who are using it.

That's where the second quote, from a fairly well-known and well-respected industry magazine, comes in. Here it is in spades. Computer = Woman. Man uses and dominates computer. Therefore, man uses and dominates woman. This is the pervasive and persistent metaphor working barely beneath the patriarchal and misogynist attitudes that poison so many women's experiences with the Internet. This is how the metaphor of Woman = Body, Man = Mind is perpetuated. And it effects how men and women relate to each other on-line. It makes the Internet just a high-tech place for men to harass women. If you think I'm overstating my case here, I'm not. When I began to use the Internet, I had a fairly gender-ambiguous on-line name, Kiai. In a truly naive, newbie style, I went into public spaces, believing that would protect me, and chatted. Within 3 months I had changed my name, quit the service I was using, and had sworn off public spaces for good. Why? Rafts of unsolicited email and instant messages asking me if I "compu-dated" and asking me what I looked like, one in particular including pictures of some guy in his underwear.

If I wanted to be harassed, I can just go outside wearing a skirt. I don't need it on my computer, too, and I very much doubt that my experience with the technology is the exception and not the rule. Even when women can get past this kind of harassment and begin to use the technology in productive ways, things like the abortion clause of the Telecommunications Act happen to remind us that we are not welcome on the new frontier, and reaffirm that women's voices will not be included in any kind of substantive way on this new medium. Because to talk about issues that are important to women is flatly and simply illegal.

There's a lot of talk these days about how to get women more involved in the Internet and related technologies. A disturbing trend I've noticed is talk about adapting technological training to suit "our learning styles." That is, making the technology more simple, less technical and friendlier, so that women will be able to understand it. The concept of "dumbing-down" and "friendlying-up" technology so that women will be more comfortable with it is thoroughly offensive and ultimately counterproductive. What is at issue here is not the technology itself but the paradigms surrounding its use. Technology is simply a tool—and those of us in the margins of society need to be taught to use these tools effectively. But most importantly, the paradigms that surround the technology, the metaphors that dictate how women are "supposed" to relate to technology, must be challenged in significant and lasting ways.

Women do not stay away from these technologies because they are somehow inherently intimidated by the tools, but because they lack access to them, and even when they do have access to them, the spaces that exist within the technology, like the Internet and the World Wide Web, are most often actively and aggressively misogynistic. This first issue of *Brillo,* "Armed and Dangerous," takes as its task the challenge of these paradigms through the dissemination of information, tools and strategies. We hope to show that there are people out there changing these metaphors in significant and productive ways. And we're not just talking about the Internet and the WWW, but about how talented and brave people are challenging paradigms of all kinds—paradigms that actively exclude white women and people of color from a broad spectrum of cultural activities and pursuits—from religion to the media to business to electronic resources. And we hope that we can provide not only ideology, but practical examples and models of how these paradigms can be changed and how we can create useful alliances to effect substantial social change.

93

VIRGINIA EUBANKS

Hacking Barbie with the Barbie Liberation Organization (1998)

The Barbie Liberation Organization is an amorphous group of activists and media intervention superstars, whose most famous action involved switching the voice boxes in 300 Talking Barbie dolls and Talking G.I. Joe dolls during the Christmas season of 1989. The goal of the action was to reveal and correct the problem of gender-based stereotyping in children's toys. The "corrected" G.I. Joe doll said things like "I love school. Don't you?" and "Let's sing with the band tonight." The "liberated" Barbie said, and I particularly like this one, "Dead men tell no lies." The mainstream media, after some prodding, latched on and a legend was born which continues to be retold, recreated and augmented to this day. (You've all heard of Hacker Barbie, right?) Melinda, Igor and I talked about boy games, media and intervention, one-liners, fear, and some lessons and tactics they've learned that can be of help to other activists.

VE: With this first issue of *Brillo,* what we're tackling is the cultural paradigms that ex-

clude white women and people of color for the tools of cultural production: especially the media and especially new technology.

BLO: Amen!

VE: Yeah—about time . . . and we're taking a really broad view of that. From things as complex as how women's bodies fit into coming technology to things as simple and straight forward as, to use one of your examples, the "Math is Hard Barbie." We're also hoping to supply some kind of real, solid tools and strategies for challenging and changing these kinds of paradigms. Now, since you folks are old hands at challenging cultural myths and at actual intervention, we thought you would fit in really well for our first issue. Do you see some of the issues that you were attacking with the early BLO cropping up around newer technologies like the internet and the World Wide Web?

BLO: Yes and no. I feel like right now there's a real fetishization of new technologies, but I don't know about the kind of access people really have to them. There's the idea that this is space that is a democracy and everybody comes here onto an equal playing field . . . I don't really see it. I see the same kind of boy games going on. I'm an outsider here. I still make films and stay with that technology because it's not as intimidating. I don't know C or anything, and I feel like these are the things that exclude. You know, people start talking this language, and all the sudden, I missed out on the first issue of *Wired,* so I'm screwed.

VE: I think its not so much the programming, or the actual technology for a lot of women, that it's not the actual tools that women are uncomfortable with, but its the concept of it being so codified.

BLO: That's exactly what it is.

VE: The boys have the code, and that's the way it plays.

BLO: And it's updated every month! To the extent that if you don't buy all these magazines and you don't keep up, you really are subjugated to another realm. You're not a player. Because my livelihood doesn't depend on it, I

From *Brillo,* Number 1, http://www.virago-net.com/brillo/No1/blo.html (6/3/98). Reprinted by permission of the author.

don't have time to keep up with all that, therefore I'm dependent on somebody else. And that's where the frustration comes in. So I rely on older forms of distribution. We continue to go down to Kinko's late at night and send it off to our friends! Color Xeroxing is beautiful!

VE: How do you think the internet and the WWW *can* be used by people concerned with the media and intervention, like yourself?

BLO: I feel like it works as a networking tool, and to throw out ideas to an activist community. Like, here's this idea we're playing with—do you know anyone else who's doing this? It's very exciting to have live bodies from all over the world responding and giving addresses and phone numbers to other live bodies that share similar interests, as opposed to getting all your information from the stacks at the library. But I think there are limitations. I think its good for "one-liners," because people get so overwhelmed by the amount of JUNK out there. And there are other limitations. For example, I think the BLO missed out on a lot because we didn't have enough people to handle distribution. So in the middle of this distribution crisis, Igor decided, "What a great idea—I'll put something out on the internet and post it on a few of these boards like communications and technology feminist theory and media criticism." Somehow, it got back to the University of California and basically, the $%*# hit the fan. They told Igor, in no uncertain terms, you will *never* be able to advertise on the internet again. And it wasn't an advertisement. It was, "Look, if you're interested in what we're doing, you can call."

VE: And there's so much that goes on in the "college nodes" of the World Wide Web, that brings up some interesting questions about what's going to get censored, and by whom.

BLO: And I wonder how much longer it's going to be free. I mean, they don't let us park for free, I very much doubt they're going to continue to let us use this resource for free.

VE: We talked briefly about the reasons why you *don't* use the internet that much, and it sounds like it's pretty much a time issue for you. But even with people like myself, people with jobs in the "industry," I find a lot of the time that women get pigeonholed into jobs that are considered "soft technology," like on-line marketing and web page development. Because they're not considered "hard technology" jobs. And men in the industry are expected to learn the hard technology, so they are given the time to do so. So that issue of not having time to keep up is something that happens to women all across the spectrum. How do you think we can attack that paradigm? That concept that women just *won't* be able to handle anything too technical?

BLO: (laughter) Oh, if I had the answer to that . . . Umm, that's a really interesting question. All these things go through my mind . . . like what if we didn't think in those terms? But at this point, advocacy groups don't seem to work . . . you end up in this victim status. . . .

VE: Well, that's one of the reasons I wanted to talk to you folks—because you seem much more intervention oriented. So, say you had tons of time, the BLO was looking for a project, and you decided you were going to do something about the gender and racial imbalances on the WWW. What do you think might come out of a brainstorming session on that?

BLO: God. Um . . . now I'm brainstorming . . . what would happen? I don't know if you've heard about this one, but it fascinated me and it made me think, "Wow. There are interesting things you could do." This guy put a Dole campaign website up, and if you went to visit it, interested in how Dole's campaign was going, you would actually find out how many bananas, how many pineapples and how many Dole products Bob Dole had eaten each day. Very cutesy and fruit oriented metaphors. And I thought, that's really clever. And a lot of people had visited this site, there's a lot of people who are interested in these campaign sites, and the guy was saying, "I'm telling no more lies than the lies you're fed when you go onto the Bob Dole site." Again, that's a one-liner. You have to think on that level.

VE: It's a very low attention-span medium.

BLO: Exactly. So you'd have to come up with a one-liner about gender inequity. Something like Frederick's of Hollywood . . .

VE: Or "Babes on the Net?"

BLO: Yeah. Like "Come visit Frederick's of Hollywood and check out our new brassieres." And you could click on the bras to make them come off, and then there'd be GUNS or something! Because there is that sexy sort of appeal of the Internet. You're all alone in your house, nobody's supposed to be watching you, and you can do anything you want. And it's mostly men surfing the 'net, so how is it that you can entice them in this way? And then, get them with this surprise tactic. . . .

VE: You mentioned this new technology being "sexy." I think that it has been very highly sexualized, and that's one of the problems that women are going to have coming to terms with the technology. Even when women *do* have access, when they get passed being pigeonholed into jobs that aren't highly technical, or past not having the time, or past not having the resources, which is a whole other level of class imbalance and racial imbalance, just not having the tools, once you get past all of that, the atmosphere on the Web and on the interactive parts of the internet is most often straight up misogynistic! So it's not, again, that women are intimidated by the tools, but that once they get there, they just find the spaces so offensive that they don't want to deal with it.

BLO: Exactly. Here's this thing that's in the privacy of your own home and you're supposed to be able to enjoy it, but you log on and you're put in a position of reprimanding people and feeling like you *are* the police. Is that relaxation?? You don't necessarily want to create all-woman chat groups, but again, we're put in the exact same gendered spaces that we have in our everyday lives. So, its very frustrating.

VE: Speaking of policing . . . we talked briefly last time about the Telecommunication Act and how that besides the seven deadlies, the only topic of conversation that was actively excluded was abortion. Now, they've (oh, so magnanimously) said, "Oh. We guess that's not Constitutional," about that, but it's still on the books. What do you think that this kind of effort to censor any kind or real talk of issues, es-

pecially of women's issues, means for the future of this medium?

BLO: I think it's another strategy of fear. Even if it's not officially on the books, it might keep you from talking about these issues. For me, it's that simple. Already there's things that, as a teacher on the University campuses, there's certain things that just *aren't* talked about, and I think that's because there's such an element of fear. These things are taboo. Therefore, we do *not* talk about them. And this is one of those things. The terrain is definitely shifting. Yeah, freedom of speech is on the books, too. But that doesn't mean much anymore. I think people are afraid. Nobody's stopping us yet, but we're stopping ourselves. It's got to be fear. Someone instills this fear in us, and then we police ourselves.

VE: What other lessons and tactics have you learned in your experience with media intervention that you think can be applied to the new technology?

BLO: You have to really have control over your message at all times. And the way you do that is by playing out every possible scenario and answering those scenarios before those questions come back to you later on. Represent yourself in ways that are beneficial to your story. You're not actually lying, but you don't necessarily tell the whole story. Acknowledge your multiple positions in society and utilize those when its best suited to the fight that you're involved in. Don't be tied to one position, because that position could be the thing that topples you in the end. Also, really have control over your message. It's a pre-packaged society that we live in, that's what the nightly news is day after day after day. I think that's how the BLO made it as far as it did. It had these video press releases that kicked ass, with a very succinct story that was easy to follow, but there was this deeper message there as well. Document everything, from the beginning. What if this is a project that will help a lot of people in the end? You need to be able to give them that knowledge, and that knowledge starts from a point in time not just half-way through. It's important to know all the stuff along the way.

94

MELISSA KLEIN

Duality and Redefinition: Young Feminism and the Alternative Music Community (1997)

I am twenty-five years old. On my left upper arm I have a six-inch long tattoo of a voluptuous cowgirl. One of her hands rests jauntily on her jutting hip. The other is firing a gun. An earlier feminist might frown upon my cowgirl's fringed hot pants and halter top as promoting sexual exploitation, and might see her pistol as perpetuating male patterns of violence. Yet I see this image as distinctly feminist. Having a tattoo signifies a subculture that subverts traditional notions of feminine beauty. That this tattoo is a pinup girl with a gun represents the appropriation and redefinition of sexuality, power, and violence—ideas characteristic of third wave punk feminism.

I was born in 1971 and am part of a generation of young women who grew up during or after the feminist "second wave" and who, as a result, have mixed feelings about traditional feminism. Many young women hesitate to take on the mantle of feminism, either because they fear being branded as fanatical "feminazis" or because they see feminism not as a growing and changing movement but as a dialogue of the past that conjures up images of militantly bell-bottomed "women's libbers." The issues pertinent to older women do not necessarily resonate in our lives. We do not, for instance, experience the double burden of the proverbial "superwoman"—attempting to be both model

From Leslie Heywood and Jennifer Drake, eds., *Third Wave Agenda: Being Feminist and Doing Feminism* (Minneapolis: University of Minnesota Press, 1997), 207–25. Reprinted by permission of the author.

mother and ambitious professional—because we often have neither "real" jobs nor children.

A new social context means that within the alternative music community and elsewhere, girls have created a new form of feminism. Much in the same way that race relations in this country have moved from the ideal of the "color-blind society" toward the promotion of diversity and multiculturalism, feminism has moved away from a struggle for equality toward an engagement with difference, an assertion that girls can have the best of both worlds (that they, for example, can be both violently angry and vampily glamorous). This feminism owes much to the struggles of the second wave, yet it differs in many ways, especially in the way it is defined by contradiction.

Third wave feminism is certainly not confined to punk culture. For many women in my age range, because *sexism* is a word in our vocabulary, we have the means to recognize it in our lives, even if this recognition does not occur immediately and even if we have had to find new ways to analyze sexism and to take action. Though we grew up in the so-called aftermath of feminism and have taken some of its gains for granted, we experienced the backlash in areas such as reproductive rights as a rude jolt into action. Activism in the arena of AIDs drew renewed attention to gay and lesbian rights. The resurgence of interest in these and other issues began to shape a new feminism, a new kind of activism emphasizing our generation's cynical and disenfranchised temperament, born of distaste for the reactionary politics and rat-race economics of the 1980s. Our politics reflects a postmodern focus on contradiction and duality, on the reclamation of terms. S-M, pornography, the words *cunt* and *queer* and *pussy* and *girl*—are all things to be reexamined or reclaimed. In terms of gender, our rebellion is to make it camp. The underground music community has served as a particularly fertile breeding ground for redefining a feminism to fit our lives.

For many of us, our paradoxical identity with traditional feminism began in childhood.

Thanks to the gains of second wave feminists, we grew up in a comparatively less gender-segregated environment and with expanded expectations of ourselves. My parents made sure the idea that girls are equal to boys was strongly ingrained in me. My mother marched at pro-choice rallies and tried to teach the neighborhood boys how to sew. She subscribed to *Ms.*, and each month I would look over the "No Comment" section (which I liked because it had pictures) and read the stories for kids. My father taught me to read when I was four, ordered science projects by mail for me and my two younger sisters, and played softball and soccer with us in our overgrown backyard. I even had an early introduction to the subject of gay pride when, at my day camp, I kissed another girl on the cheek and a boy said, "Eeeewww! You're a lesbian!" That afternoon when my mom picked me up in our old Ford Falcon, I asked her to explain the word *lesbian,* and she told me it meant a woman who loved other women. Reasoning that I loved my mother and sisters, and not quite comprehending the difference between loving and being in love, I went back to camp the next day and fiercely told the boy, "So what if I'm a lesbian? I'm proud I'm a lesbian."

The remarks of my less-than-enlightened fellow camper demonstrate that despite substantial gains made by the second wave and the influence of these gains in my life, the world around me was not a totally radical place. Within my family I was encouraged to do whatever I wanted, yet in the outside world I was encouraged toward "female" pursuits. I could throw a ball, and I could do more chin-ups than anyone else in my class, yet I spent more time on gymnastics, ballet, and diving—"female" activities that emphasized aesthetics, individual achievement, and grace, rather than aggression, strength, and teamwork. Like many girls, my self-confidence dwindled in adolescence. As I approached an age when peer support became more important than family support, my alienation grew, because I did not fit into the ideal of the popular girl. Whereas before, my self-

confidence had come from my status as an academic achiever, I now suspected that my worth depended on my attractiveness to boys.

In the year I turned thirteen, I would smile whenever a female classmate came to school wearing a T-shirt that said, "A woman's place is in the House . . . and in the Senate." Yet that was the year I tried on high heels for the first time and started taking off my glasses at lunch when the boy I liked was nearby, even though it reduced my vision to such a blur that I could barely make him out. As I reached a crisis of confidence, my grades suffered. An often-praised A student in seventh-grade science class, by ninth grade I was getting D's in biology. Instead of doing my homework, I watched soaps, lounged in bed, or experimented in the mirror with makeup. In tenth grade at my new high school, I decided not to try out for the diving team and weaseled my way out of a semester of swimming, because I didn't want anyone looking at me in a bathing suit.

Around fourteen, I became interested in the punk scene. Here mainstream tastes in music and other things were scorned, and thrift-store clothes and outcast status worn with pride. Though my original style was more "traditionally" punk—I favored raccoon-style black eyeliner, combat boots, and the Sex Pistols—I soon gravitated toward the more politicized style prevalent at the time in Washington, D.C., where the close-knit punk community centered on Dischord, a record label started by Ian MacKaye and Jeff Nelson in 1981. The underground music scene provided an alternative to mainstream culture and politics in many ways. There were women within the punk scene who challenged gender ideals and who served as examples of strength and independence: they rode and fixed their own motorcycles, worked at clubs or booked shows, or documented their scene by taking photographs. Yet the punk scene was predominantly male. At this time in punk music (the mid-1980s), there were very few women in bands. When I saw the first show of Fire Party, a local band made up of all women—Kate Samworth, Natalie Avery,

Nicky Thomas, and Amy Pickering—I realized it had never occurred to me that this could even be possible.

In 1988, three women, Leslie Clague, Cynthia Connolly, and Sharon Cheslow, published *Banned in D.C.: Photos and Anecdotes from the D.C. Punk Underground, 1979–1985*. The photos and stories in this book document the presence of women early in the D.C. punk scene.[1] It is important to Cheslow, who currently both plays and distributes music, to credit the continuum of women in rock. To this end, she has been working on a project documenting women in early punk bands. In a *Village Voice* article about Cheslow's project, entitled "Punk's Matrilineage," Evelyn McDonnell comments dryly, "If you've labored at your art in relative obscurity for a decade and a half, only to suddenly find your milieu—in this case, 'angry women in rock'—touted as the Big New Thing, well you can either laugh or cry, or reeducate forgetful minds."[2]

As Cheslow's project points out, female-powered bands such as the Raincoats, the Slits, the Runaways, and X-Ray Spex played a pivotal part in the early history of punk as raucous waves of sound reverberated across the Atlantic from the United Kingdom to the big cities of the United States. Yet as punk seeped into the suburbs, it mutated into hard-core, fueled by the young male angst of the surfer-skater scene and characterized by pounding drums, frenzied guitar, and testosterone-laden lyrics. According to Cheslow, "As hard-core became more prevalent around 1981, a lot of the girls who had been involved in the mid to late seventies dropped out because of the increasingly macho and violent tendencies of the boys."[3]

Rock in this regard, has been a kind of last frontier for women. The rock image—being confrontational, lewd, angst-ridden, wild, and loud—has been a male domain met with a head-shaking but tolerant "boys will be boys" attitude. The "bad boy" has always had a sanctioned niche in the mainstream that the "bad girl" has not. The rebel, the James Dean character, wins the heart of the wholesome pretty girl next door. The rock star (even if supremely ugly) marries the supermodel, a scenario that has no parallel with the gender roles reversed. Though many girls in the alternative community held as fierce and well thought-out opinions as boys did, when it came to the all-important subject of music, they felt relegated to sideline roles such as fan or girlfriend.

The boys we associated with led "bohemian" lifestyles, questioned mainstream values, and held politically leftist viewpoints. They were unfailingly pro-choice, played benefit shows, believed in gay rights, and so on. And because they had been raised in a society that had assimilated feminist values, they, like us, held less fixed or negative assumptions about gender than any generation before them. Yet the music around which the scene revolved was generally played by boys. Boys occupied the public sphere. They were the ones onstage, the ones literally making the noise; girls occupied a supplementary place.

In a project for the June 1988 issue of the self-published fanzine *Maximum Rock'n'roll*, Cynthia Connolly, Sharon Cheslow, Amy Pickering, and Lydia Ely arranged three sessions in which groups of sixteen women and eight men answered questions about the issues of women in the D.C. punk scene. The introduction of their article states, "In our music community, most men and women treat each other first and foremost as human beings." Yet one of the questions posed by the women was this:

"Why has our 'alternative' society developed in the same way that 'mainstream' society has—where females do organizational, behind-the-scenes tasks, and men perform? When we developed the list of people to invite for this,

---

1. Leslie Clague, Cynthia Connolly, and Sharon Cheslow, *Banned in D.C.: Photos and Anecdotes from the D.C. Punk Underground, 1979–5* (Washington, D.C.: Sun Dog Propaganda, 1988).

2. Evelyn McDonnell, "Punk's Matrilineage," *Village Voice*, May 21, 1996, 57.

3. This and subsequent quotations from Sharon Cheslow are taken from a personal interview by the author in San Francisco in July 1996.

almost all the men were in bands. Most of the women were involved in some ways but not in bands—like working for Dischord, or working on fanzines, or doing booking at clubs. Promoting, encouraging, supporting."

I see punk, like the antiwar and civil rights movements before it, as a place where young women learned or solidified radical means of analyzing the world and then applied these powers of analysis to their own lives, only to realize that, as girls, they felt disenfranchised within their own supposedly "alternative" community.

In 1970, women's rights leader Robin Morgan wrote of the experience of women in the student movement, "Thinking we were involved in the struggle to build a new society, it was a slowly dawning and depressing realization that we were doing the same work and playing the same roles in the Movement as out of it: typing speeches that men delivered, making coffee but not policy. . . ."[4] Despite the similarities in coming to consciousness, the means and methods through which women in the alternative music community chose to express themselves differed from those of earlier feminists, because they stemmed from our experiences as girls in a subculture whose roots lay in disaffection, destruction, and nihilism rather than in peace and love; that is, we were punk rather than hippie. The 1960s counterculture represented a challenge to conformity and an optimism that society could change. Punk was also a reaction against conformity, but one tempered by a disillusionment with the 1960s. Punk feminism grew not out of girls wanting sensitive boys so much as girls wanting to be tough girls; instead of boys wearing their hair long and getting called pansies, girls cut their hair and were called dykes.

Yet the seeds of our feminism did grow out of our participation in structures established by the second wave: taking women's studies classes in college, volunteering at a battered women's shelter or at the rape crisis hotline, attending pro-choice events. For me, the foreshadowing of my punk feminism was the frustration I felt when I would go out with my boyfriend, who was in the band, and other boys would come over, sit down without saying hello to me, and start talking to him about music and "the revolution," which was mainly one of aesthetics rather than politics. I began to wonder what was so damned revolutionary about staying up all night and combing your hair a certain way, when I had gotten up at four o'clock on a freezing January morning to hold hands with other women defending a clinic, and had listened to a boy whose girlfriend was inside having an abortion as he confided that he had sold his stereo to pay for the procedure and asked me how he could help her when it was over. I began to wonder, as many other girls did before and after, why we did not get or give each other credit for the contributions we made, and why toughness, anger, and acts of rebellion were considered a male province.

As we began thinking individually about how we had experienced oppression on the basis of gender, we also started making connections with each other. We critiqued both popular culture and the underground culture in which we participated. We thought about school and the books we had read, about the way that despite the second wave, we had learned history with no idea how or whether women could be great or brave. We realized that early on in life we had learned a self-conscious sense of the male gaze, a constant awareness of the physical impression we make. Boys cannot appreciate this, unless perhaps they imagine as constant the feeling of walking alone at night through an unfamiliar neighborhood under hostile scrutiny. Upon examination, we saw that we shared with other girls experiences of being made uncomfortable, unsure of ourselves, or even abused because we were female. Girls began to draw parallels between different experiences; shame at being fat and bitterness at caring so much about our looks; secret

4. Robin Morgan, ed., *Sisterhood Is Powerful: An Anthology of Writings from the Women's Liberation Movement* (New York: Vintage, 1970), xxiii.

competitiveness with other girls, coupled with self-dislike for being jealous; the unsettling feeling that we could not communicate with a boy without flirting; the sudden, engulfing shock of remembering being molested by a father or stepfather when we were too small to form words for such a thing. Straight and bi girls talked about having to give anatomy lessons every time we had sex with a boy. Queer and questioning girls talked about isolation and about mothers bursting into tears when they learned their daughters were gay. Girls who wanted to play music talked about not knowing how to play a guitar because they had never gotten one for Christmas like the boys did. Girls who played music complained that they were treated like idiots by condescending male employees when they went to buy guitar strings or drum parts. We began to see the world around us with a new vision, a revelation that was both painful and filled with possibility.

Young women's anger and questioning fomented and smoldered until it became an all-out gathering of momentum toward action. In the summer of 1991, the bands Bratmobile and Bikini Kill, self-proclaimed "angry grrrl" bands, came to D.C. for an extended stay, on loan from Olympia, Washington. Bikini Kill promoted its ideas under the slogans "Revolution Girl Style Now" and "Stop the J-Word Jealousy from Killing Girl Love." While subletting a room in the house where I lived, Allison Wolfe worked with Bratmobile bandmate Molly Newman to produce Riot Grrrl's earliest manifestation, a pocket-sized fanzine by the same name. An initial experimental all-girl meeting evolved into a weekly forum for girls to discuss political, emotional, and sexual issues. That August also saw the International Pop Underground Convention (IPU), a brainchild of stalwart Olympia indie K ("No lackeys to the corporate ogre allowed"). IPU opened with Girl Day. As the idea of Riot Grrrl spread via band tours, fanzines, high school and college networks, and word of mouth, chapters sprang up around the country. A year later, in July 1992, the weekend-long Riot Grrrl Conven-

tion took place in D.C. Women gathered together for workshops on topics including sexuality, rape, unlearning racism, domestic violence, and self-defense, as well as attending two shows featuring female bands and spoken-word performers, and the "All-Girl All-Night Dance Party."

Riot Grrrl meetings owed much to the "personal as political" precedent set by second wave feminists. In *Civics for Democracy,* Katherine Isaac writes about women from the 1960s Student Nonviolent Coordinating Committee and the Students for a Democratic Society, who felt frustrated at the lack of seriousness with which the concerns of women's rights were taken:

"Many of these women began to meet with each other to form a separate movement. They used their organizing skills to set up small "consciousness-raising" discussion groups, which quickly multiplied across the country. As historian Sara Evans describes these groups, 'The early meetings were intense and exhilarating. In a style they had learned in the civil rights movement and the new left, women explored the political meaning of their personal experiences. Again and again, individuals were shocked to discover that their lives were not unique but part of a larger pattern. The warm support and understanding of other women empowered them as they reclaimed the lost legacy of sisterhood.'"[5]

Like earlier movements, Riot Grrrl also relied on the strength of numbers to question male territory, but for purposes specific to punk. In "Revolution Girl Style Now," a 1992 *L.A. Weekly* article later reprinted in *Rock She Wrote,* Emily White writes:

"One of the most engaging metaphors of the Riot Girls is their dramatic invasion of the mosh pit. In Olympia, bands often don't perform on risers, so only the people up front can really see, and, given the violent crush of the

5. Katherine Isaac, *Civics for Democracy* (Washington, D.C.: Essential, 1992), 106, quoting Sara M. Evans, *Born for Liberty: A History of Women in America* (New York: Free Press, 1989), 282.

pit, those people are almost always boys. The girls got tired of this. But most of them didn't want to dance in the pit—it hurts your boobs. And getting touched by a bunch of sweaty male strangers has all-too-familiar, nightmarish connotations for many girls. Perhaps moshing is just another one of what Barbara Kruger calls those 'elaborate rituals' men have invented 'in order to touch the skin of another man.' But the girls wanted a space to dance in, so they formed groups and made their way to the front, protecting each other the whole way. Any boy who shoved them had a whole angry pack to deal with."[6]

Early Riot Grrrl ideology was much like the "safe-space," women-only feminism that characterized the second wave. Riot Grrrl often used second wave activist techniques but applied them to third wave forms. The "safe space" Riot Grrrl created was more often the mosh pit than the consciousness-raising group, but lyrically the music often functions as a form of CR. And whereas some second wave feminists fought for equal access to the workplace, some third wave feminists fought for equal access to the punk stage.

One of the most obvious ways that girls strove collectively to end the disparities within punk music was to put women onstage. The phenomenon of girls playing music grew explosively and exponentially. Girls taught their friends how to play instruments and encouraged through words or example. Some chose to play with other girls to demonstrate unity, whereas others avoided the "girl band" stereotype and proved that they could "rock with the guys" by doing exactly that. There was encouragement to overcome intimidation, to just get up and play. Sometimes this resulted in debate about whether just playing, or "going for it," was the most important thing, or whether it undermined the status of women in rock to perform ill-played sets. I remember wincing at

certain overly cutesy, discordant performances. Yet there is something about the mere image of a woman playing guitar that is thrilling, that gives me the same impression as the painting of Rosie the Riveter on my kitchen wall—a strong woman with a power tool waiting to be bent to her will.

While reworking feminism, these girls were simultaneously reworking punk, getting back to its roots, to a time when raw honesty of expression counted for more than perfect playing. Interviewed by Andrea Juno in *Angry Women in Rock,* Lois Maffeo, who had an early-1980s all-girl radio show and has been performing music herself since the mid-1980s, discounted the idea of musical "virtuosity":

"Men think that if you can do a really flawless guitar solo, you're a great musician! To me that's bogus. My own career is based on the eradication of the guitar solo. I think that is just complete wanking, and I don't want anything to do with it! People talk about hooks and bridges within songs and I'm like, 'Call 'em whatever you want, I can only write a song as it comes out, and my songs don't have to have a structure that's already well-defined in male-dominated music.' . . . It's not virtuosity, it's mimicry in a lot of these people who are supposedly great musicians."[7]

Maffeo was an early supporter of punk feminism's do-it-yourself ethic, which functioned, as male punk had functioned in relation to the rock establishment before it, to challenge conventional notions of authenticity, greatness, and aesthetic value.

It is important to remember that not all music created by young women was the same, despite press coverage that made it sound that way. Nor did all feminists in the alternative scene identify themselves as Riot Grrrls, though journalistic overgeneralization sometimes made it seem so. Valerie Agnew of 7 Year Bitch complains that on her band's first European tour, they were labeled "Riot Grrrls from

6. Emily White, "Revolution Girl Style Now," *L.A. Weekly,* July 10–16, 1992; reprinted in *Rock She Wrote,* ed. Evelyn McDonnell and Ann Powers (New York: Dell, 1995), 398–9.

7. Lois Maffeo, interview by Andrea Juno, *Angry Women in Rock* (New York: Juno Books, 1996), 132–3.

Seattle," although "Riot Grrrl was always peripheral to us. . . . It was the new bratty young women's way of feminism—which I don't relate to."[8]

Rather than constituting a homogeneous mass, the different bands girls played in were characterized by the contradiction that distinguished other aspects of their lives. They reflected the full spectrum of personas among which young women felt pulled. The music and lyrics combined toughness and tenderness, vengefulness and vulnerability. A political message was often conveyed through graphic personal stories. The songs ranged from fierce exaltation in female anger, to anguish about the pain of relationships, to celebration of noncompetitive love between girls. Stage presence often reflected quality as well, for example, contrasting a physical emphasis on overt sexuality with lyrics about sexual abuse. Vocals swung back and forth between harsh, wrenching screams, sweet, soulful siren intonations, and childish singsong.

As women began to form and perform in more bands, they not only changed the face of punk but changed its fabric. They reclaimed punk as the legacy of the outsider, and previously marginalized issues became more prominent. Early influences on the new punk feminism were the self-published queer-girl fanzines *Sister Nobody,* by Laura Sister Nobody, and *Chainsaw,* by Donna Dresch, who was later to start a record label of the same name and playing the all-dyke band Team Dresch. In the introduction of *Chainsaw* number 2, Dresch writes:

"Right now, maybe CHAINSAW is about Frustration. Frustration in music. Frustration in living, in being a girl, in being a homo, in being a misfit of any sort. In being a dork, you know the last kid to get picked for the stupid kickball team in grade school. Which is where this whole punk rock thing came from in the first place. NOT from the Sex Pistols or L.A.

But from the GEEKS who decided or realized (or something) to 'turn the tables' so to speak, and take control of their (our) lives and form a Real underground. Which is ALSO where the wholeheart of CHAINSAW comes from."

Feeling in multiple ways like outsiders as feminism became more prevalent among younger women, these musicians demonstrated the punk method of bypassing the co-option of the mainstream through self-sufficiency by photocopying fanzines and distributing them by hand or by mail. These 'zines became a means of feverish expression and collaboration. They employed a format traditionally used to review records and conduct band interviews, not only to spotlight female musicians but also to share insights, ideas, and information (such as how to induce a late period through herbal teas), to rant and reflect, and to tell personal stories—some humorous, some horrifying, some uplifting. Like other means of expression, fanzines embodied an attempt to process a wide variety of past and present images of femininity. Illustrations ran the gamut from photography hyping girls currently involved in music, to cartoon sex kittens, to torrid lesbian pulp-fiction covers, to hilariously wholesome advertisements from the old *Life* magazines. Fanzines helped girls form a network with each other, not only between towns such as Olympia, D.C., and San Francisco, but also among other places, smaller places, suburbs. Hard-core enabled young suburban boys to vent their anger at the world; Riot Grrrl allowed young suburban girls to vent their anger at the world of suburban boys.

Like the women's bands, not all angry-girl fanzines will go down in history as brilliant masterpieces. Often they were crudely constructed and consisted entirely of free-form rants, fragmented diatribes, and uncensored accusation. I have picked up fanzines that I have found literally impossible to read. Yet because young women are so often made to feel invisible, it is vital for them to elevate their everyday lives outside the everyday. I liken this to Frida Kahlo painting herself over and over. It is the

8. Valerie Agnew, interview by Andrea Juno, in ibid., 107.

pounding of the fist on the table, claiming, "I exist, I exist." Maybe creating a fanzine is cathartic to one young girl alone in her bedroom. Maybe it helps another young girl, reading it alone in her bedroom, come out or speak out or just feel less alone. And if these things are true, then that fanzine has fulfilled its fundamental task of fostering creativity and communication.

For me, fanzines were and are important because I did not have a desire to play music—I express myself through writing. Moreover, Riot Grrrl itself felt less vitally necessary to me, because I had already taken women's studies courses and had already processed many of these issues. It was not a revelation to me that Barbie's blond tresses, wasp waist, and permanently high-heel-molded feet provided a less-than-wonderful role model. I understood the anger, because I felt it myself, particularly around issues such as street harassment. This anger and figuring out how to confront it were important in defining a feminism particular to young women. We tend to live in neighborhoods that are not homogeneous, and harassment often involves undertones of racial or socioeconomic friction. The lifestyles we lead and the fact that we can't always afford cars means that we are outside often and sometimes late at night, and because we are young we are considered prime sexual targets by men. They lounge on street corners and outside stores to hiss insolent comments at us. They drive by in cars and holler or honk heir horns, startling us out of daydreams or conversations. We feel as if we are entering a war zone every time we walk down a crowded sidewalk wearing shorts.

Constant sexual appraisal is exasperating and degrading. Yet we want to be able to feel good about our bodies, and we do not want to give up our freedom to walk anywhere or to wear what we like. We refuse to return to the days of masculine protection, asking boys to walk us home or to fight anyone who insults our honor. We are not damsels in distress who stand idly by, hysterical, high-pitched screams issuing from our mouths while the knight in shining armor slays the dragon. We want to be our own warriors.

Street harassment is something all girls have in common, and the discovery and discussion of this served as a catalyst for widespread feminist activism. Talking about it together made us view our experiences not as degradation by men but as a source of communal action among women. Girls who began bands sang raw, outraged anthems about the subject; girls who wrote fanzines banged out their aggression on battered Smith-Coronas. We pondered the mind-boggling possibility that our harassers considered their bruising words to be compliments. We found that sometimes if we stopped to engage one of them and told him he was hurting us, he would feel ashamed and apologize profusely.

Many girls discussed guerrilla tactics, and even if we never carried them out, we felt better for thinking about them. I remember laughing gleefully when a girl told me that a mutual friend had confronted a man who would not stop bothering her, by taking a used maxipad out of her bag and throwing it at him. My then-roommate Nikki Chapman and I contemplated a secret plan of assault with squirt guns filled with pee. Wanting to claim my looks as my own and to challenge the double standard of judgment, I learned to respond to someone yelling, "Hey baby, looking good!" by spitting back something like, "Yeah—that makes one of us."

Fanzines and punk shows created forums for young women to speak out as survivors of sexual abuse and to share success stories and painful secrets. As in any movement, it was and is important to rise from pure anger to action. The do-it-yourself ethic in towns such as Olympia and Washington, D.C., has long dictated that the answer to a problem lies not just in pointing fingers but also increasing solutions. No place for your band to play? Play in your friend's basement, in a church, in a community center. No record labels will put out your band's music? Start your own label (Dischord and K Records, started by Calvin Johnson, being the primary examples in D.C.

and Olympia, respectively). Thus, women looked not only at the problem of sexual assault, but also at innovative solutions. From this was born the idea of *Free to Fight! An Interactive Self-Defense Project,* a twenty-eight-song CD and thick booklet released on Portland-based label Candy-Ass, owned by Jody Blyle of Team Dresch. The CD intersperses self-defense instruction, anecdotes, and songs, including rap by African American and Latina women.[9]

As with some aspects of second wave feminism, issues of violence against women form a basis for biracial, cross-cultural coalition. But, perhaps because our scene has punk rather than hippie roots, because we grew up in a more violent society, and because we feel frustrated at the seeming lack of progress in preventing rape, we are more likely than some second wavers to see violence as a legitimate form of equalizing gender dynamics, of reclaiming power. Harassment of young women occurs not only on the street but also at work. We often have the types of low-paying jobs in which sexism is an undercurrent. I worked for six months as a cocktail waitress in a nightclub where the waitstaff were all female, every bartender and barback but one was male, and all the doorpeople were large, male, and black. I knew that my being hired and the amount of money I would make in a nightclub depended on my ability to look cute and to chat in a friendly, flirtatious manner with drunken men. To accomplish this, I had to endure guys trying to put tips down my shirt and asking if they could lick Jello shooters off my breasts. My favorite holiday present that year was a button that my little sister Alison gave me, which said, "That's not in my job description."

Because young women often feel exploited in the workplace, we see sex-trade work in less black-and-white terms than older feminists do. We reason that because our bodies are appro-

priated through looks or comments anyway, we might be better off at least profiting from it. Young women sometimes have a fascination with the idea of being a stripper or a dominatrix, because we see it as having a kind of subversive glamour, and as a means of "exploiting our exploitation." Yet this engenders debate about whether this fascination is healthy, whether it is empowering to utilize blatantly our sexuality, or whether it is simply falling prey to societal demands to objectify ourselves and make our looks the most important thing about us. An interview I conducted with Kathleen Hanna of Bikini Kill, which appeared in the February 1993 issue of *off our backs,* illustrates this debate:

Melissa: How do you feel about the whole idea of exploiting your exploitation? Working as a dancer, do you feel that since this attitude already exists of having your body appropriated—that every time you walk down the street, through looks or comments your body is being appropriated by this male audience— that if this male attitude already exists, you might as well make money from it? That you might as well use the system that already exists to your advantage?

Kathleen: Yeah, yeah. I mean, exactly. The guy on the bus jacks off under his coat and looks at me and he doesn't give me money, but the guy in the club does give me money. And in a way I don't think my work is any more fascinating than working at Burger King. I think that when I worked in a McDonald's as a pretty female, I was 15 years old and pregnant by the way, and working there to get an abortion, I was being exploited because they made me wear a uniform that was two sizes too tight in the middle of summertime in Richmond, Virginia, where it was over a hundred degrees. And they made me stand up in the front line and all the girls with acne or who were fat were put in the back cooking. It's totally ridiculous because they were exploiting my little sexual figure to sell burgers. And yet I was being paid $4.50 an hour, $4 an hour, whatever it was at the time. I don't see that huge of a difference

---

9. *Free to Fight! An Interactive Self-Defense Project* (Candy-Ass Records, 1996). See Jen Smith's "Doin' It for the Ladies—Youth Feminism: Cultural Productions/Cultural Activism" (this volume) for a fuller description of this project.

between what I'm doing except that I make a lot more an hour. And it's really, really disgusting to me how people discriminate against sex trade workers. . . . I might be pretty and I might be near the ideal and I am exploiting that to my own benefit. But I'm not exploiting, I'm NOT exploiting anyone else, you know? . . . And when people discriminate against me because of that, when people tell me I'm not a feminist because of that, they can go fuck themselves because that's bullshit. I fucking feed my friends. I take care of my friends when they're sick. I am one person in this community who gives girls rides places at night. People call me and come to my house when they're sexually abused and talk to me and I can do that because I don't have to go to work fucking five days a week for The Man and make shit money. I make enough money in two days a week that I can live off of that and support other people at certain times.

Melissa: Well, I don't know—sometimes I have a problem just in general with that idea because it sounds like ends justifying means. . . . It's like the whole idea of, OK, would I do a commercial for a product I don't believe in because it would give me a lot of money and I could do beneficial things with that, or do I not do a commercial and then just in my own life, I'm less capable financially but maybe I'm providing more of a . . . positive example?[10]

This debate, although ongoing, marks a difference from the social context of the second wave that is historically specific: the sheer number of women of all races and classes in the workplace.

Although reflections about rape, relationships, and reclaiming our sexuality constituted the burgeoning of our feminism, they also revealed important differences between our definition of it and that of the second wave. Though old stereotypes reverberate in modern gender dynamics, they do not exist in the same clear-cut form. In a society that takes premari-

tal sex for granted, the "virgin/whore" dichotomy that underpins much earlier feminist theory has mutated. Instead of experiencing strict sexual repression, we are taught through advertising that sexuality determines how we are rated; it is a potent form of power we must struggle to possess. Yet it is not a power we ask for or control. In the aftermath of 1970s feminism, we experience both the loss of chivalrous standards that require "respect for ladies," and the post-"free-love" backlash against women's prominent sexuality, which uses our sexuality to thwart us.

Unlike older, Dworkin-MacKinnon feminists, young punk feminists tended to be very pro-sex, more likely, for example, to celebrate female-centered pornography than to censor male-centered porn. This comes partially from a distaste for the censorship in creative circles that developed during the mid-1980s: the Parents' Music Resource Coalition's record-labeling efforts, the outcry over Robert Mapplethorpe's sexually explicit photographs, and the attempted anti-flag-burning amendment. We were also influenced by the publication of the RE/Search book *Angry Women* in 1991. An ad for the book asks, "How can you have a revolutionary feminism that encompasses wild sex, humor, beauty, spirituality *plus* radical politics? How can you have a powerful movement for social change that's inclusionary—not exclusionary?" The ad then goes on to tout the book as covering "a wide range of topics: menstruation, masturbation, vibrators, S/M and spanking, racism, failed Utopias, the death of the Sixties and much more."[11] The book contains in-depth interviews with ex activists Susie Bright and Annie Sprinkle, as well as cultural critic bell hooks. The influences of these women can be seen in the pro-sex attitudes and analyses of racism in later angry-girl music and writing.

Conflicting ideas about the meaning of sex and sexiness are often reflected in the way punk

---

10. Kathleen Hanna, "Revolution Girl Style Now!" interview by Melissa Klein, *off our backs,* February 1993, 11.

11. Andrea Juno and V. Vale, eds., *Angry Women* (San Francisco: RE/Search Publications, 1991). The advertisement quotation is from a promotional postcard for the book.

feminists look. Punk fashion has always reflected irony. Because clothes come from thrift stores, they reflect whatever era of clothing people are discarding at any given time. Wardrobes consist of the past, bought for pennies and reworked, reinvented. In this way, the idea of identity is turned on its head. This might mean wearing a gas station attendant's jacket with someone else's name on it. It might mean wearing army gear although you are antimilitary. It might mean mocking capitalism by wearing a T-shirt advertising a ridiculous product you would never buy. For women, punk fashion irony has often been reflected through gender parody.

During the heyday of hard-core and the early politicization of punk in D.C., girls felt compelled to dress and act like guys—black jeans and no makeup were de rigueur. But ultimately, as girls came into their own, the solution became not to demand equity but to celebrate difference, whether this meant strutting their butchness or being a vampy femme or combining both. Punk female fashion trends have paired 1950s dresses with combat boots, shaved hair with lipstick, studded belts with platform heels. We dyed our hair crazy colors or proudly exposed chubby tummies in a mockery of the masculine ideal of beauty. At the same time, we fiercely guard our right to be sexy and feminine. We might get harassed less if we dressed and acted exactly like boys, but we would see this as giving up. We are interested in creating not models of androgyny so much as models of contradiction. We wanted not to get rid of the trappings of traditional femininity or sexuality so much as to pair them with demonstrations of strength or power. We are much less likely to burn our bras communally than to run down the street together clad in nothing but our bras, yelling, "Fuck you!"

Another paradox of punk feminism is that it exists within what has traditionally been youth culture, yet no one stays young forever. So what do we do now? How do we grow up? And how do we negotiate the media representations of our efforts? Laura Sister Nobody self-

published a fanzine that contained a prophetic warning about the fickleness of media attention to the Riot Grrrl movement:

"Us, we are women who know that something is happening—something that seems like a secret right now, but wont stay like a secret for much longer. . . . why does usa today, abc, nbc, cbs and every other corporate media fuck want to get a hold of bikini kill and riot grrrl? because theyre not fools—they know somethings happening too—but theyre terrified of it and they want to take it and twist it and package it and spit it out to the masses as the next latest thing in order to kill it. we have to understand that they will try sneakily and unrelentingly to suck the life out of our fight and we have to be ready."

Early Riot Grrrl publications pointed out that the name was not copyrighted and encouraged other women to start their own groups. It was never a movement with membership rolls and dues; thus, the media pronouncements of its rise and fall are mostly hype. I am less interested in the EKG status of Riot Grrrl than in the idea that women's work is definitely thriving, though, for what it is worth, Riot Grrrl does currently exist on-line and as a fanzine-distribution press.

For me, looking at the past, present, and future of women in the alternative music community, I see a continuum of struggle, spiraling upward. This struggle does not depend on the name it takes. Punk has assimilated the demands of girl revolutionaries—there are women tour managers, engineers, and label owners, as well as a plethora of women musicians. But perhaps more important to me is not only that women make up a much more equal balance of those playing music, but also that as women occupy a more respected space, support grows for their work outside the traditional punk music arena. Initially we had to fight just to breathe, to keep ourselves alive. Now that we can stop and take a breath, we can go more in-depth, we are freer to branch off into our specific interests, to leave our own lasting landmarks combining creativity and social change. My friend Dara Greenwald, discussing the idea of starting an alternative school for at-risk girls using music as a focus, says, "We need to start creating our own institutions."[12] I am inspired as I see women mobilizing to hold on to creativity and the do-it-yourself ethic while stepping beyond the traditional guitar-bass-drums punk rock arena. A sampling of recent self-published fanzines illustrates this diversity. In issue 3 of *I'm So Fucking Beautiful,* Olympian Nomy Lamm's confrontation of fat oppression includes a comic of herself in a tight T-shirt, proclaiming, "No more mumus!" In *Bamboo Girl* number 4, from New York, Sabrina Sandata tackles bands, breast biopsies, and Tagalog tidbits from a take-no-prisoners queer Filipina perspective. In *Femme Flicke* number 5, editor Tina Spangler, from Cambridge, Massachusetts, interviews queer-core filmmaker G. B. Jones and lists resources throughout the country for girls to get their own films seen. In *Doris* number 5, from Berkeley, Cindy writes sad and beautiful personal stories wrapped in red duct tape. In my own recent San Francisco *Inkling* number 2, I document the often forgotten history of women outlaws in the Old West and humorous trips to places of historical interest to women.

I would like to see this branching out continue in other areas. For example, I have had to step outside the punk scene into social service work to confront race, aging, and poverty issues, because the punk scene remains predominantly young, white, and middle class. I would like to see us use punk feminist tactics to deal with these issues in an innovative way. I would like to see a feminism that does not grow lazy because of certain gains. I would like us to question the ways that major-label-MTV co-option of "alternative" music has impacted our scene even if we personally have steered away from it—for example, by asking ourselves how the recent punk trend toward superskinniness, supershort skirts, plucked eyebrows, and platform heels is influenced by a mainstream, media-friendly aesthetic.

12. Dara Greenwald, conversation with author, San Francisco, July 1996.

I am confident that we have the structures to continue questioning, collaborating, and creating, whether this takes the form of *Free to Fight,* Cha-Cha Cabaret, or Sharon Cheslow's Women in Punk project, and whether we call it making music, movies, comics, fanzines, or social change. The dueling images of femininity and feminism found in music and writing produced by young women may initially seem confused or confusing. Yet these fanzines, songs, and other forms of expression represent a mode of activism that is challenging rather than didactic and that leaves room for different and changing roles—for boys as well as for girls. I regard the willingness to experiment, to accept duality, and to have more questions than answers, as positive attributes—attributes that have given birth to a new brand of activism, a striving for social change unique to the young women of my community and my generation.

Acknowledgment: This essay is dedicated to Sharon Cheslow for her great encouragement, Jen Smith for her genius and friendship, and to my mother, Kim Florence Klein, for constant inspiration.

95

RACHEL ORVIRO

I Am a Girl (1998)

At 24 years old, I'm not afraid to call myself a girl. But if someone had called me a girl even a few months ago, you bet I would have given them hell. See, I spent a year at Mills, a women's college, and that was a place where one became extremely well-versed in correcting anyone who dared refer to females over the age of 16 as "girls." But something has changed.

Being called a girl just doesn't seem so bad anymore. In fact, the idea of reclaiming my

From *Sacramento News & Review,* May 11, 1995, as reprinted at http://www.voiceofwomen.com/girl. html (7/1/98). Reprinted by permission of the author.

girlhood in all its freshness and limitless potential is incredibly appealing. I'm not talking here about docile, timid, self-effacing girlhood. I'm talking about re-claiming the girl who swung with abandon from the monkey bars, who spent hours telling wild and creative stories into a tape recorder, who gloried in strange costumes, who danced in a skill-less frenzy, who wasn't afraid to cry when upset, nor yell insults when angry.

I see that girl captured repeatedly in the black and white images my mother caught with her Leica as she snapped hundreds of photos throughout my childhood. But frozen on film as well is the sulky adolescent who came after. The one who thought girls shouldn't speak their minds for fear of ridicule or play tennis with the speed of the boys. I study that sullen 13-year-old face, masked in makeup and a pout, and wonder where did the knowledge that "girls could do anything" go? Where did the enthusiasm go? Where did the girl go? I'm still wondering how to get her back.

This return to girlhood thing is not just about me; society has seen a resurgence of all things girlie in the past few years. In fact, girls have made an unmistakable comeback, starting with the riot grrrl movement growing out of Washington state in the early '90s, developing middle-market appeal for teens with *Sassy* magazine, and finally surfacing into the mainstreamed girl fashions of today. And rather than viewing it as yet another backlash-inspired retreat to femininity, women my age are starting to consider this resurgence as part of a grrrl revolution—one that precedes feminist credos and righteous indignation and returns our thoughts to youth in all her possibilities. To feel great about being the center of our own universe, to shout in the face of convention, to play dress-up without worrying about fashion or whether our mates like how we look, to enjoy the fun and not worry about the responsibility—these are some of the elements of girlhood we crave.

"For so long, girls have just been painted over," Lara Stemple, a 22-year-old legal assis-

tant, tells me. "The boys are shown to have all of the adventures. But anyone who has been a girl knows, it wasn't just a time where we sat around in lace dresses playing with dolls." Sacramento High junior Vanessa McLean puts it this way: "I feel like the range of things I can do are greater because I'm a girl. . . . The most important part of being female is fertility in all areas—a growing and expanding potential to do anything." Tapping into that possibility and re-establishing the power we had as girls isn't a vindictive thing against guys or a preemptive strike against a patriarchal society. It has little or nothing to do with the male gender. Rather, it's a way for us to take back the strength, the confidence, the opportunities lost to us before we even realized what we had.

There are stacks of studies—like those done at Harvard in 1992 by Carol Gilligan and Lyn Mikel Brown—which show that girls lose their sense of power and self-esteem as they approach adolescence. Young girls increasingly become quieter, less aggressive . . . and less adept in school, especially in math and science. They retreat into themselves and away from the classroom, the playing field, the adventure. If we're lucky enough to come out the other end of all this in our late teens and renew our confidence, we're usually already on the path to grown womanhood with all of its trials and responsibilities. The question is no longer who can scream the loudest or run the fastest, but how can I provide for my family? Where do I go in my career? We skipped the good stuff along the way to becoming an adult. How can we be Superwoman without having been Supergirl?

The whisperings of the girl movement started coming out of the underground a few years ago, bandied about on the Xeroxed pages of zines. There were simultaneous screams, too—howls from the punk stages through the mouths of Babes in Toyland, L7 and Bratmobile. Just take a look at the names: Bikini Kill, Hole, 7 Year Bitch—all fierce rockers who took the language used against women and co-opted it to work in their favor, twisting insults into strengths. These musicians put this anger into their music and drew hordes of young women—and men—to bathe in the shower of their wrath.

Resistant as many of these performers were to suddenly being the new messiahs of feminism, young women turn to them both for the power of the tunes and the teeth-gnashing rage of the players. They told us that anger is all right, that screaming for attention is a good thing (reminiscent of the leg-kicking temper tantrums of childhood), that we don't have to sacrifice our girlness to get what we want, 'cause grrrl is power, strength and intensity. As the riot grrrl music scene took off, its young audience found their voices in fanzines raving about the bands and what they had to say.

"It was liberation," said Jessica Hopper, the first time she saw Babes in Toyland screaming their guts out on stage in 1990. Hopper, the creator of a riot grrrl zine *Hit It or Quit It,* subsequently became a spokeswoman for the media-deluged riot grrrl movement, championing the rights of young women to play in bands and "scream like the boys." The riot grrrl messages soon became even more general, with publications springing up from Olympia, Washington, to Sussex, UK, growling "Girls Rule" and "Girls, Get Savage." The anger of the punk scene is there in stories about rape, incest, abuse by a loved one. But also present is the glory of girls—reminiscence about *Teen Beat* and Shaun Cassidy, arguments over which Duran Duran guy was the cutest, tales of Barbie's wild times with G.I. Joe and Ken in the pink dream house. These are girl memories, good and bad, validated in their importance and discussed in appropriate magnitude. The zines let us know that humor and self-expression aren't for boys only. The "No Girls Allowed" sign has been ripped off the Little Rascals clubhouse and crushed beneath moshing feet.

"Ever since riot grrrls put the growl back into girlhood and Cindy Brady grew up to become Courtney Love, the meaning of girl has changed," writes Celina Hex in a recent issue of *Bust,* a New York zine that dedicated its winter/spring issue to girls and girls alone. "Remember your own fierce inner-girl," Hex urges her readers. Meanwhile, we see girl icons such as Barbie winking from the cover of a New England zine called *Ooompa! Ooompa!* geared toward teenage grrrls worried about everything from sexism to breasts. Then there's the ravenous, wild-eyed cartoon chick. *Deep Girl* zine penned by San Franciscan Ariel Bordeaux—"Starring Me, Me, Me," screams the cover copy. "There's nothing wrong with a little self-obsession," 24-year-old Jennifer told me as she flipped through a gritty-looking zine at Tower Books on Broadway. "It's more interesting than some babes and muscle mag."

"I love reading about all the cool things these girls are doing and saying," agreed her friend Megan. "You can't find this shit anywhere else."

Going beyond the zines and the music, we've also seen a growth of girlness epitomized in high and low fashion. From the runways of Paris to urban thrift stores, baby doll T-shirts and dresses, little patent leather shoes, plastic barrettes in the shape of teddy bears and tiny bows have brought girl-style to the forefront of trendy fashion. It's a style, however, that carries with it a serious attitude. "It's fun," said Rasean Pennock, the owner of The Village Exchange Clothing Co., a thrift store in Sacramento, CA. "And there's definitely an attitude that goes with it—much more confident, not caring about what society or men think about it. "It's OK to dress like a little girl now, but the women are still making grown-up decisions," she added. Pennock's store is full of girl stuff, from the rack of summer shirts labeled "girlie tops" to the flowered baby doll dresses hung on the wall. A framed picture of the ultimate wild girl, Drew Barrymore, sits next to the cash register. Pennock has been in the fashion industry for 10 of her 27 years and admits to loving the girlie look and what she's seen come with it.

"It's a way of expressing yourself, of making feminism fun for this generation," Pennock said. "I feel sassy," one twentysomething summarized as she twirled around in her newly acquired girlie dress. Therein lies the key to our girldom and the importance of keeping that energy in our grown-up lives. We strive to be progressive thinking, to stand up for our rights as women, to take responsibility for our lives and communities, our families, our action . . . but sometimes it's all just overwhelming. Somehow, the girl revolution is making it OK for women to reach back and glory in a time before all that—to reclaim the girl we were without giving up the strides we've made as grown women. Maybe girls do just want to have fun—but we're still going to kick some serious ass along the way.

96

PUNKGRRRL

I Wanna Riot (1998)

(what i feel riot grrrl is)

riot grrrl originated in the punk movement. grrrls and wimyn in the movement didn't feel like there was enuff support within the movement for wimyn so they started groups and zines and bands and started to get together. they called their new faction of the punk movement RIOT GRRRL. riot grrrl is just grrrls getting together for a cause. Those grrrls are everywhere. in college, on the streets, in high school, middle school, preps, jocks, punks, folky people, hippies, sXe, vegans and lesbians. when a grrrl wants to fight for her rights she has a little piece of riot grrrl in her. if we can put all of these scattered pieces together we could have one REAL powerful grrrl. A grrrl that will stomp out sexism, unequal pay and jobs, domestic violence, rape and the idea that wimyn are just a "pretty decoration on a man's arm." This

From personal web page at http://members.tripod .com/~punkgrrrl/index-2.html (7/1/98). Reprinted by permission of the author.

grrrl really IS in all of us, guys 2. All we need is a little unity.

join some pro-wimyn group!!! start a group near you. put out flyers. have meetings. ANYWHERE!!! encourage grrrls to get involved!!! maybe not in riot grrrl, maybe a young feminists club or something. just get involved, its important for our future as wimyn. its not over yet. . . .

97

CYNTHIA

Join the Riot (1998)

Riot Grrrl is a movement in feminism. This is about wimmin sticking together (bois too), and fighting for equal rights and opportunities for everyone, regardless of gender, ethnicity, or sexual orientation. Many of us are vegetarians, many are punk, but these are not requirements—a riot grrrl can be anyone who is tired of this male-dominant sexist world. Music often known and labeled as "riot grrrl" is usually punk rock. "Revolution Grrrl Style Now!" We are strong, determined individuals: wimmin and men who are banning together for the most important campaign for equality since the 1920s. Riot Grrrl began in 1991, in Olympia Washington, and we are combatting oppression in all forms. Fellow girls should join together in this movement to fight for our rights! We fight with words not weapons— with poetry, music, literature, and art. Start a zine, a band, anything, get involved and help make change.

By the way, this is my perception of what riot grrrl is. I'm not speaking for every grrrl in the world, as it has many different associations with different people. Hope you learn something from this page.

From personal web page at http://members.aol. com/HoleGrrl1/index.html (7/1/98). Reprinted by permission of the author.

98

JOAN MORGAN

The Bad Girls of Hip-Hop
(1997)

It would have been easier if the honors had gone to Lyte, Latifah, Salt-N-Pepa or Yo Yo. Then we could have waxed eloquent about Afro-feminine regality, refined sensuality and womanist strengths. But it didn't go down like that. The history makers were DaBrat, the first female rapper to have her premier album go platinum, and Foxy Brown and Lil' Kim, both of whom debuted at the top of the Billboard chart—sistas with the lyrical personas of stay-high juvenile delinquents and hypersexed (albeit couture-clad) hoochie mamas. And while I hardly consider this a feminist victory, the success of these baby girls speaks volumes about the myths shrouding feminism, sex and Black female identity.

When it comes to hip-hop, I've always been a bit dismayed at how quickly even feminist women resort to tired victimization theories. But trying to pretend that these sistas were the prey of sexist record execs goes against all reason. Girlfriends stomped onto the scene more empowered than any female MCs in rap's history. They arrived at a time when female MCs ceased to be a novelty. They benefited from the musical miscegenation of hip-hop and R&B. (Guest spots on the tracks of R&B and rap heavyweights Toni Braxton, LL Cool J and The Notorius B.I.G. helped make Foxy Brown and Lil' Kim household names long before their debut releases.) Unlike their "bad girl" predecessors—Bitches With Problems and Hoez With Attitude—they are not the Svengali creations of male producers with dollar-bill signs in their eyes. Whether we like it or not, DaBrat, Lil' Kim and Foxy Brown are creatures of their own design who exercise the same creative rights as their male counter-

parts—coupling highly materialistic, violent and lewd personas with deliciously infectious rhythms and rhymes.

Their success drives home some difficult truths. The freedom earned from feminist struggle is often a double-edged sword. Now that women are no longer restricted to the boundaries of gender expectations, there will be those who choose to empower themselves by making less than womanist choices—and they are free to do so. Contrary to popular belief, absence of the Y chromosome does not guarantee women immunity from societal influences. As DaBrat observes on the single "Sittin' on Top of the World," "With 50 grand in my hand, steady puffin' on a blunt, sippin' Hennessy and Coke, give ya what ya want." It is obvious that the relentless pursuit of status, power and ducats is not gender-specific, as evidenced by the willing complicity of not only these rappers but also umpteen scantily clad "video hoes," back-stage skeezers and gold-digging groupies—sistas who are going to get theirs by any scandalous means necessary. Rather than granting them victim status, I suggest we start holding them accountable.

But before we break out the crucifixes, we as a community have to acknowledge our own culpability. DaBrat, Foxy and Kim are what has been happening to young Black women while the brothers (and some sistas) were busy rescuing The Endangered Black Man. Few were willing to believe that Black girls growing up in the same violent, materialistic, and economically and spiritually impoverished environments were likely to suffer their own pathologies. Black women are dying in disproportionate numbers of AIDS, cancer and drug abuse, and the exploding female prison population and teenage pregnancy rate have become damned near cultural norms. Is it really surprising that some female MCs (like their male counterparts) would decide to get paid by glamorizing that reality?

And the onus does not fall exclusively on African-American men. The punanny-for-sale materialism that dominates Lil' Kim's album, for example, is rampant among some young fe-

From *Essence*, March 1997. Reprinted by permission of the author.

males. Sex has become the bartering chip many women use to gain protection, wealth and power. In the Black community, where women are given little access to all of the above, "trickin'" can become a way of leveling the playing field. It's ironic that the same sistas who boogied through the 1980's singing Gwen Guthrie's "Ain't Nothing Going on But the Rent" are up in arms because their daughters are singing "No money, money; no licky, licky; f—k you dicky, dicky" along with Lil' Kim or "takin' it all from the stash to the keys" with Foxy Brown. Both reduce the value of a brother to what can be found in his wallet. Both delude Black women into thinking that punanny is their most valuable asset.

Ultimately Foxy Brown's and Lil' Kim's success shows how much we have yet to teach our little sistas about sex, feminism and power. Feminism is not simply about being able to do what the boys do—get high, talk endlessly about their wee-wees and what have you. At the end of the day, it's the power women attain by making choices that increase their range of possibilities. The girls possess undeniable talent, but longevity for rappers depends a lot on safe, commercial appeal. Diva hoes *don't* get called to star in sitcoms or play that all-American hero in mega-action films. And none of them own record companies.

Until we are in the throes of a total feminist revolution, marketing yourself as a I'm-a-nasty-little-freak-brave-enough-to-talk-about-it will be a very risky thing for Black women. Our power lies in what our grandmothers taught us. Whether it's the bedroom or the boardroom, the women who rise to the top are the sisters who selectively ration their erotic power. Men are notorious for greedily consuming the sexually available, then discarding them. Even Madonna—who is also White, blonde and a marketing genius—knew this. Girlfriend teased a good long time before giving up that sex book. Adina Howard of "Freak Like Me" fame didn't know, and where is she *now*?

As far as our rhyming bad girls go, as a feminist weaned on hip-hop, I'm not mad at

them. Truly significant hip-hop reflects the images of Blackness we refuse to see. If we take note of them, then maybe we'll get mad enough to do something about them.

99

Nancy Coulter

The Lilith Fair: A Celebration of Women in Music (1997)

This past week I had the joy of going to the first all women music festival—Lilith Fair.

The name of "Lilith" comes from an old Hebrew folk tale about Adam's first wife, Lilith. Apparently, she wasn't as inferior to Adam as he wanted. She wanted to be her own person, not Adam's wife-slave. Because of this, she was banished from Eden and became a spirit associated with the seductful side of a woman. Eve came in her place to stand behind Adam, not beside him.

Sarah McLachlan is the woman behind Lilith Fair. She has continually stated that the Fair isn't to exclude men, but to celebrate women. After spending a day with these women, I realize we have a lot to celebrate.

A few years ago, a concert bill of all women would have been unthinkable. Promoters would see it as a financial suicide and there would have been no backing for it. Even the thought of a woman opening up for another woman in a "regular" concert was unheard of. Well, thankfully we've broken through that barrier.

If you took a look at the Top 40 music charts in the US, you'll notice that most of the artists are women. Radio stations no longer have a policy of not playing women "back to back" in any of their sets. In fact, there is almost a reverse sexism going on now because it is hard for a man to break through on his own in

From Suite101.com, Women's Issues at http://www.suite101.com/articles/article.cfm/2588 (7/9/98). Reprinted by permission of the author.

the music business. However, for some reason, I doubt that will last as long as the sexism against women in music has lasted.

One of the most surprising things about the Fair was the amount of men there to enjoy the music. I'm not talking about the men who were dragged along by their girlfriends, but the ones who went just because they wanted to. I almost expected to have to search to find a man there enjoying himself. I was very wrong. A little bit less than half of the people there were men. Men who were enjoying the music. It wasn't some huge "feminazi festival" like some people have called it. It was people enjoying music that women have done.

Right now, I can't wait till next summer so that I can get to see the Lilith Fair again. It opened up my eyes to how far women have come and it boosted my spirits in believing that women can get what they want, no matter what men think they should have.

Oh, and to top the night off, I did end up meeting Sarah McLachlan and I got her autograph. She happens to be a woman who I admire greatly. Meeting her just made the concert that much better!

100

Andrea Dworkin

Dear Bill and Hillary (1998)

Monica Lewinsky is in a terrible, terrible mess. She's being threatened by a very mean special prosecutor who has unlimited powers. And he plays hard ball. She has my sympathy. Of everyone who is a player in this game, she is the one who is going to be destroyed by it.

We are talking about a man who, in a predatory way, is using women, particularly young women. In this case, a woman who was working as an intern, for no money, because of her devotion to the Democratic Party and to

From *The Guardian* (London), January 29, 1998. Reprinted by permission of the author.

him. In an alcove next to the Oval Office, he simply unzips his pants and she sexually services him.

Bill Clinton's fixation on oral sex—*nonreciprocal* oral sex—consistently puts women in states of submission to him. It's the most fetishistic, heartless, cold sexual exchange that one could imagine.

People are characterizing this as a sexual scandal, but it's an abuse-of-power scandal. It corroborates what both Paula Jones and Gennifer Flowers have said, and it's a disaster for this particular young woman, Monica. I think there probably are many more of them, but I don't know how many will come forward. Whoever steps into this is stepping not just into public spectacle, but onto a legal landmine. And it is a very hard thing for someone who is 20, 21, to find herself in the middle of all this, subpoenaed to talk about her sex life.

The second issue that concerns me is what Hillary Clinton is doing, which I think is appalling. She is covering up for a man who has a history of exploiting women. If there is one thing being a feminist has to mean it's that you don't do that. You don't use your intellect and your creativity to protect a man's exploitation of other women. She's done it before and she's doing it again.

Ever since she went to the White House as First Lady, her life has been going down the tubes. She had to give up her profession and she's been the staunch wife standing by her husband, no matter what vile things he does to humiliate her. It's pathetic. She should pack her bags and leave.

Women of Hillary's age—*my* age—have a responsibility not to let the men who are our peers exploit and destroy younger women. It breaks my heart to see Hillary on television. It's a performance and as such it's a lie. Whatever kind of deal they made in their marriage, I don't believe it included the public humiliation of her. And this has to be the most towering humiliation of all.

I had great hopes for her at the beginning. I thought: "How wonderful—a feminist in the

White House. She's so smart." But I have not understood the choices she's made and I have not been able to respect them. In protecting her husband, she is betraying younger women.

Maybe it was different 20 years ago. Maybe it looked different to her when Bill was fooling around in Arkansas. She had her job and her child, perhaps she didn't care. But now this is a man, her husband the president, being sexually serviced by a 21-year-old woman—in *her* house.

It's impossible to believe that she, and everyone who works in the White House, doesn't feel utterly betrayed by him. They really thought he had stopped all this. They thought he was a creep before—even Monica calls him a creep—but when he became president, they thought he knew he couldn't get away with it any more.

There is a strain of misogyny in him, though. People say it has nothing to do with the way he makes social policy, but I think it does. These things are connected. There are plenty of women who are simply expendable to him— clearly the White House interns are.

As for the conspiracy theory, I just don't believe it. Yes, there are right-wing people who hate the Clintons, but to think there's a conspiracy would mean somehow the rightwing planted the young woman in Clinton's office to entice him into sexual acts.

I have a modest proposal. It will probably bring the FBI to my door, but I think that Hillary should shoot Bill and then President Gore should pardon her.

The silence from other feminists in this country is deafening. There's no outcry against Clinton, there's no outcry against Hillary for fronting for him. I think a lot of feminists are very distressed and disappointed in him, but they don't want to say so publicly because many of them are connected to the Democratic Party. It's a problem. It was a problem when Bill Clinton threw poor women off welfare and used pregnant teenage girls as scapegoats as if they were causing the economic problems of our country. Clinton has good policies for middle-class women, but I don't think he has good policies for poor women.

Male politicians' policies in respect of women are important, but sexual harassment is an issue, too. You don't say it's OK for the leader of your country to be having his cock sucked, by someone half his age, while he is in the people's house. Yes, the law says that if both parties are consenting, it's not sexual harassment, and it's not illegal. As far as we know, Monica was consenting, but I believe Clinton is culpable because I think he's guilty of exploitation. I care about how men in public life treat women. Clinton shows a real callousness in what he was doing to someone who was just about his daughter's age.

He may not have to resign, but I think he should and I think he will. I don't want him as my president. I think he's toast, I think he's done, I think he's outta there. And I'm glad about that. Most of my feminist colleagues won't be. They feel he's a good president and the country's in good shape, they feel he's a good guy. Yeah, he just did this one little thing that was wrong, but he's really a nice guy. Au revoir, Slick Willy.

III. Toward a Third Wave

THE LATE 1980S AND EARLY 1990S BROUGHT retrenchment and backlash against feminism. A crucial book defining this period of feminist decline is Susan Faludi's *Backlash: The Undeclared War against American Women* (1991). What Faludi calls the "backlash" against feminism began somewhere in the mid-1980s (the height of the Republican Reagan-Bush years and of the "New Right") and lasted at least until the mid-1990s, dislodged by the so-called third wave of feminism. The ideas that constitute the "backlash" are, as Faludi describes them, nothing new; in fact, there have been periods of backlash against feminism before—after the resurgence of women's rights activism in the mid-nineteenth century (the inception of the woman's movement), after the early 1900s (the fight for suffrage), following the outbreak of World War II (as women went to work in the 1940s), and after the early 1970s (second-wave feminism). The mid-1980s recycled many of the same ideas as in earlier times—except the mass media of the late twentieth century ensured that virtually no woman would go unexposed. The charges were all variations on the same theme: women have equality now (something Faludi and *all* the writers in this section utterly refute), yet they are miserable—burned out, depressed, confused, infertile, and sexually frustrated. The women's movement of the 1970s may have given women many things, the argument goes, but it deprived them of the two things that really mattered—a man and a child. The view that a severe "man shortage" and an "infertility crisis" awaited any woman who postponed either marriage or childbearing to pursue a career was actively promoted in all the media, despite the downright shakiness of studies that showed such results and the prevalence of studies that refuted them. As an antidote to the backlash, Faludi argues instead that if women are unhappy, their biggest concern is not too much equality but *not enough*; in public opinion polls, women still rank their own inequality at work and at home among their most pressing concerns. In the mid-1980s, though, it seemed no one was listening. The backlash against feminism was in full tilt: women wanted a family and blamed feminism for depriving them of it.

Not surprisingly, women's notorious disengagement from feminism in this period may have stemmed in part from their being bombarded with news reports, magazine articles, television shows, and movies telling them how disenchanted they were with their newfound equality with men and the barrenness of their lives—all courtesy of the women's movement. Certainly this backlash caused some concerned introspection, as feminists asked themselves: how far have we come? Have we failed and, if so, how? What should be the movement's next agenda? As feminist thinkers attempted to address feminism's apparent stagnation and the growing disengagement of masses of women, they often did so within the long-standing rubric of equality vs. difference—and each side came up with very different diagnoses for the ills of the feminist movement. Some saw the problem as the women's movement's purposeful dedication to the single issue of women's equality with men; others saw the problem as a resurgence of difference feminism that seems to exalt women's victimization rather than celebrating their uniqueness.

In "What NOW? The Women's Movement Looks Beyond 'Equality'" (1986), published in *The New Republic*, Dorothy Wickenden blames the feminist movement's failure on its single-minded pursuit of absolute equality for women—a goal epitomized by the continual reappearance, and defeat, of the Equal Rights Amendment. Since its conception, the ERA, above all other issues, has most clearly and consistently elucidated the ideological divide between those who espouse equality feminism and those who espouse difference feminism. From the 1920s onward, the National Woman's Party, among other feminist organizations, fought for a federal amendment to the Constitution that would declare women's legal equality with men and forbid all discrimination on the grounds of sex. The ERA was challenged not only by antifeminists but also by women's groups (like the Women's

Trade Union League) who had themselves fought hard to pass protective labor legislation for women, guaranteeing women a minimum of equitable pay, safe conditions, and reasonable working hours. According to Wickenden, the women's movement failed to learn from history, as it continued in the 1970s and 1980s to ignore the majority of women who did not want complete equality with men and, more important, did not want the erasure of their unique feminine roles—what they believed to be the *significant* biological and cultural differences between men and women. All that feminists have done, Wickenden claims, in refusing to acknowledge women's attachment to their roles as wife and mother, is to hand over the support of the family to the conservatives, who experienced a surge in power in the 1980s precisely because they stepped into the vacuum left by feminists. Wickenden ends by insisting that a viable feminist movement for the late 1980s must take account of the realities of women's private lives as wives and mothers as well as their public lives under law and in the workplace. It must give women practical answers to the problems they face as working mothers, beginning with affordable and available day care.

Like Wickenden, Barbara Ehrenreich, in "Beyond Gender Equality: Toward the New Feminism" (1993), published in *Democratic Left*, argues that the feminist movement needs to revise its traditional approach to equality—that is, its insistence that women have the same opportunities as men and that they not be held back by "male supremacist beliefs and practices." Ehrenreich, however, does not oppose the fight for equality but is more concerned about the quality of the world *within which* women are seeking equality: "Equality is a fine goal, but it has to be equality for all in a society that's worth being equal in." Racism and capitalism still make U.S. society radically unequal along the lines of race and class as well as gender: during the 1980s the number of impoverished people in the United States rose, the wages of the poorest people fell, and Aid to Families with Dependent Children (AFDC) dramatically failed to keep up with inflation. Wickenden and Ehrenreich illustrate perfectly the historically persistent divide between reformist and revolutionary feminism: while Wickenden does want to address the economic problems of women, she wants to do so while keeping "essential sexual difference" intact, and without an analysis of the interlocking systems of gender, class, and race; Ehrenreich, on the other hand, recognizes that so-called essential sexual difference, along with racial and class differences, are *part of the problem* and ensure that women will remain second-class citizens, most of them permanently a part of the economic underclass.

In "Are Women Morally Superior to Men?" (1992), written for *The Nation*, Katha Pollitt shows the skewed focus, even outdatedness of Wickenden's critique of a feminism supposedly wholeheartedly committed to an androgynous equality that denies sexual difference. She points to the incredible enthusiasm, both popular and academic, that has greeted difference feminists in the 1980s. Nancy Chodorow's *The Reproduction of Mothering* (1978), Carol Gilligan's *In a Different Voice* (1982), Sarah Ruddick's *Maternal Thinking* (1989), and Deborah Tannen's *You Just Don't Understand* (1990) all elaborate theories of women's difference—notably women's emphasis on forming relations rather than asserting autonomy, on nurturance rather than competition and aggression, on mediation rather than argument. While some of the authors give a nod to the fact that these differences may be culturally created (women are more nurturing because they mother, because U.S. society assigns them that role), the overwhelming impression they give is that women are fundamentally and inherently different—and, moreover, fundamentally and inherently morally superior. Difference feminists of the 1980s have done exactly what "domestic" and "social" feminists of the mid- and late nineteenth century did; they have turned feminine traits that the culture devalues and converted them into positive virtues. Pollitt thoroughly debunks these thinkers, however, arguing that they find only the morally superior qualities in women which they seek: she claims that most mothers, for instance, hit their children as a means of controlling them, which makes Pollitt wonder why motherhood is seen as the font of those warm and tender principles that are antithetical to violence; also, in the face of the many women who fought enthusiastically in the Gulf War (1991), Pollitt asks how femininity can be described as inherently paci-fist. Pollitt sees difference feminism, finally, as demeaning to women, since it asks for women's full ac-ceptance into public life *not* because it is a right but because women have deserved it by being "good" and because women can help improve the world.

Whatever their divergent beliefs in the path feminism should take, the essays by Wickenden, Ehrenreich, and Pollitt are all compelled by a problem more specific than a general malaise in the feminist movement. They are driven by the *increasing* disinclination of women throughout the 1980s and 1990s to consider themselves feminists, even while polls consistently show that a majority of women support key feminist ideals (equal pay and opportunity in the workplace, reproductive choice, family leave). For instance, in a CBS News poll reported in the *New York Times* on December 14, 1997, 74 percent of women said that the status of women had improved in the last twenty-five years (a testament to the efficacy of feminism, one would think); however, the number of women who call themselves feminists has dropped by about 10 percent since 1989, and the number of women who think the term is an insult has jumped from 16 percent to 21 percent since 1992. In large part, the reluctance of women to self-identify as feminists, and their propensity to consider the term one of opprobrium, is a result of the widespread stereotype—created and fed by the main-stream media (concerned mainly with sensation and extremism) and neoconservatism—of a femi-nist as a puritanical, man-hating (often lesbian), family-destroying, strident bitch. Both Wickenden and Ehrenreich, to different ends, raise this stereotype: Wickenden argues that feminists have them-selves helped create this stereotype; they have failed women by focusing on a kind of solipsistic, an-drogynous equality and ignoring their attachment to their traditional roles and their family. Ehren-reich, on the other hand, does not have much sympathy for women who want to preserve traditional roles, whether of gender, sexuality, race, or class; she insists that feminists should be proud of being called a bitch or a lesbian as a sign of a reinvigorated movement that demands equality for everyone. The contradictions of women's responses in polls—their attachment to feminist goals but not to fem-inism—suggest that, despite the flourishing of difference feminism pointed out by Pollitt, somehow the stigma remains that feminism is synonymous with a single-minded push for complete sexual equality that most women read as sameness. And most American women, it seems, do not want to be the same as men; any woman who tries risks being distorted into the sexless, male-bashing, shrewish bitch that has become the archetypal feminist in the public's mind.

In her essay for *The Atlantic Monthly*, "Feminism's Identity Crisis" (1993), Wendy Kaminer di-rectly addresses how feminism has lost its momentum, has alienated the mass of women, precisely because it has been unable to conform itself to women's conflicted desires. Faced with the contra-dictory ways in which women construe their own identities, feminism, too, is in the throes of an iden-tity crisis. Framing the problem in the terms that Wickenden, Ehrenreich, and Pollitt all employ—equality and difference—Kaminer argues that as feminism embarks on a "third wave," it must address the fact that while most American women want equality with men in the workplace, they don't want it in the bedroom and are, in fact, generally unwilling to question their familial roles and the as-sumptions about femininity and sexuality on which they depend. "[M]any people," Kaminer claims, "manage to separate who they are in the workplace from who they are in bed, which is why femi-nism generates so much cognitive dissonance"—because the feminist movement—at least second-wave feminism—demanded a revolution of sex roles in *both* workplace and bedroom. So, to the ex-tent that feminism promotes change in the workplace, women tend to support it; to the extent that it advocates change in the bedroom, in women's most personal of lives, it would appear that many women tend to resist it vehemently. According to Kaminer, most women tend to agree with the in-famous remark of Marilyn Quayle (a lawyer and the wife of George Bush's vice president, Dan Quayle) that women don't want to be liberated from their "essential natures." The backlash against the feminist movement, Kaminer suggests, has come in part at least because feminists are perceived as having taken the ideal of equality too far—into those intimate spaces of women's lives that they do *not* want radicalized.

However, like Pollitt, Kaminer balances this pervasive yet skewed portrait of an ERA-dominated movement (not even true in the 1970s) with the actual resurgence of difference feminism in the 1980s. However, this renewed interest in what Quayle called women's "essential nature" has also, paradoxically, contributed to feminism's negative image. Like Pollitt, Kaminer shows how the celebration of women's "true" femininity shades disturbingly into an embrace of vulnerability and frailty and, finally, into the emerging orthodoxy, even "exaltation," of women's victimization. Feminists in the 1980s have been increasingly preoccupied, Kaminer argues, with issues such as child abuse, pornography, sexual harassment, rape, and other kinds of violence against women. They have made a feminist saint out of Anita Hill, who charged that Supreme Court nominee Clarence Thomas harassed her while she continued to work for him—a questionable choice for sainthood, Kaminer argues: "Was she too hapless to know better? Feminists are not supposed to ask." The glorification of women's victimization, Kaminer ends, runs at odds with any political resurgence of feminism and the fight for an equality still unattained. Kaminer's essay leaves the reader with the depressing sense that feminism cannot win—is caught between the Scylla of an absolute equality women don't want and the Charybdis of a difference that ends up telling women they are simply victims. Although Kaminer sees the principal cause of feminism's failure as coming from within the movement—the "most effective backlash against feminism almost always comes from within"—it is hard to see what, exactly, feminists could do to remedy an identity crisis that is based more on women's false perceptions than on reality. Kaminer underestimates the role of the media in popularizing only extreme versions of both equality and difference arguments, and the ways in which the backlash against feminism stems from the pervasiveness of such extreme images.

A forum in *Ms.* magazine, "Let's Get Real about Feminism—The Backlash, the Myths, the Movement" (1993), offers the differing views of bell hooks, Gloria Steinem, Urvashi Vaid, and Naomi Wolf on why women in the 1990s were alienated from the feminist movement and what could be done to reverse that estrangement. Inevitably, differences emerge among the participants themselves, but those differences produced a fascinating array of analyses of the backlash: that the media are controlling the imagery of feminism, shaping consistently negative views of feminists and vacating any meaningful debate on its issues; that women are shying away from the burden of becoming activists and of taking on the necessary job of taking on patriarchy (read—U.S. society), and they are instead retreating into an ambiguously effective "lifestyle" feminism involving personal habits and style that eschew collective action; that racism in the movement and homophobia in the society at large cause women to keep away; that feminists are perceived as (and often are) judgmental, especially when it comes to the politicization of sexuality; and that feminism has been directing its energies mostly toward the legislative and political arena, losing its relevance at a local, grassroots level and its centrality in real women's everyday lives. The consensus of all four participants is that the feminist movement needs to find a way to reach women, both through the media and in their home communities, and convince them that feminism is critical to their daily lives; feminism has to live close to where women live, not as an abstract stereotype created by interests indifferent or hostile to the continuing problems of sexism, racism, capitalism, and homophobia in the 1990s.

What all these writers of the late 1980s and early 1990s had in common was a posture of self-reflection, a sense that feminism was failing or plain irrelevant as far as those it wanted to serve were concerned, and a desire to revitalize the movement for the twenty-first century. To some extent, this introspection ended with what has come to be called "third-wave" feminism—a new brand of feminism that may be quite different from anything the older generation of feminists envisioned. The third wave of young feminists are those whose birth dates fall roughly after 1963, and who have felt most alienated from and misrepresented by what they see as second-wave feminism and its perceived 1980s legacy of women's sexless equality and victimized difference. Some of its most visible proponents are Katie Roiphe, Karen Lehrman, Cathy Young, Christine Hoff Sommers, and Rene Denfeld. In the most basic sense, third-wave feminism has emerged from an intergenerational conflict and as a resistance to the professed limitations of foremothers—as the titles of some of the most important books of young feminists suggest: for instance, Katie Roiphe's *The Morning After: Sex, Fear, and Feminism on Campus* (1993), Christine Hoff Sommers' *Who Stole Feminism? How Women Have Betrayed Women* (1994), and Rene Denfeld's *The New Victorians: A Young Woman's Challenge to the Old Feminist Order* (1995). This intergenerational conflict, moreover, does not only engage young women and the leaders of second-wave feminism—Gloria Steinem and Betty Friedan, for instance; rather, it is frequently fought between twenty-something women and women themselves only in their thirties—notably Susan Faludi and Naomi Wolf.

Interestingly, what is at stake in this intergenerational battle is in part the age-old divide between equality and difference. Put broadly, third-wave feminists eschew not only the idea that women as a group need protection because they are naturally weaker or more vulnerable than men, but also the idea that women as a group are the subject of wholesale gender oppression. They charge "older" feminists such as Susan Faludi (in *Backlash*) and Naomi Wolf (in *The Beauty Myth*) with exaggerating women's passivity and victimization and promoting a caricatured view of a vast conspiracy of powerful men out to block women's progress. In her book, *The New Victorians*, for instance, Rene Denfeld dismisses Faludi's notion of "backlash" as "paralyzing paranoia." In invoking the idea that older feminists are falsely demonizing all men, the younger feminists have certainly contributed to the old stereotype that feminists are male-bashing man haters—one of the notable pejorative connotations of feminism that drives women to decline being labeled as such.

Instead of focusing on women's subjugation by patriarchy, third-wave feminists tend to promote the idea of women's individuality, to focus on the number of bars to women's equality that have already been dismantled, to celebrate women's freedom in the workplace and the bedroom, and to find allies among men, not all of whom are co-opted by patriarchy. To demonstrate the predominance of the cult of victimization in the 1980s, Kaminer questioned the way in which feminists had turned the harassed Anita Hill into a saint. Illustrative, perhaps, of the third-wave feminism of a decade later is the way in which 1990s feminists positioned themselves in relation to the hot topic of 1998—President Bill Clinton's admitted "relationship" with twenty-something White House intern Monica Lewinsky. In an article in *The New Republic* in September 1998, Andrew Sullivan makes the following comment: "We have been instructed by third-wave feminists that, since the Lewinsky affair was obviously consensual, it was not exploitative." Interesting, it was left to a man to point out that there is no greater disproportion of power than that between an intern and the president of the United States.

The generational contentiousness between feminists has come visibly to the fore in debates over university women's studies programs, which some claim are simply intellectual extensions of an anachronistic and rigidly ideological feminist movement. In her essay published in *Mother Jones*, "Off Course—and Responses" (1993), one of the leaders of the new feminism and author of *The Lipstick Proviso: Women, Sex and Power in the Real World* (1997), Karen Lehrman, writes of her experience sitting in on classes in four women's studies programs—at the University of California, Berkeley; the University of Iowa; Smith; and Dartmouth. Lehrman identifies several problems with women's studies programs, which are, she claims, undermining the ideal of a liberal education: first, classrooms are no longer the place for rigorous intellectual analysis and debate but for consciousness-raising and a touchy-feely therapy; second, courses routinely proselytize a narrow and politicized agenda, smacking of the politically correct, and no dissent is allowed from the relentless feminist ideology which now masquerades as scholarship; third, women are studied only as the perennial victims of patriarchy, and students are primarily encouraged to discover their own victimization. In a fascinating string of letters written in response to Lehrman's article, she clashes with, among others, that bugbear of third-wave feminism, Susan Faludi. Faludi is incredulous that Lehrman faults feminism for being ideological ("feminism is an ideology," she writes) and for being in the process of writing a book on what Faludi sees an impossible contradiction in terms— "postideological feminism." As Lehrman responds to Faludi, she unveils some fundamental assumptions about her view of feminism, assumptions that have won great credence since the mid-1990s: she insists that her "postideological" feminism does not vacate politics from feminism but simply means "there's no one telling women what to think or what to value—no feminist leaders." As well as this distinctly individualized view of what has historically been considered of necessity a *collective* social movement, Lehrman also voices the third wave's distaste for the ideology of victimization: women "can also believe in feminism and not agree that they personally are oppressed victims of the patriarchy." In this last statement Lehrman seems to take an individualistic feminist ethos almost to the point of an "I'm OK, you're OK" view of the world, one that refuses to reach across difference and recognize women's shared experience.

Susan Faludi is, along with Naomi Wolf, one of the "elder stateswomen" of 1990s feminism— and as such has been one of the targets of younger thinkers (as her clash with Lehrman in the pages of *Mother Jones* demonstrates), charged with perpetuating a cult of victimization and rigid ideological thinking. In her essay in *Ms.* magazine, "I'm Not a Feminist but I Play One on TV" (1995), Faludi dismisses Roiphe, Young, Lehrman, and Denfeld, calling them media-made "pseudo-feminists" or "pod feminists" planted by the right and representing "the Invasion of the Feminist Snatchers." Faludi argues that these false feminists have been embraced by the media in large part because their message is positive and nonthreatening: they tend to think that women have made sufficient progress and that "now should be a time of back-patting and 'reconciliation' with men"; and thus they are not demanding a revolution in the social order—or even much change for that matter—so they scare neither women nor men. Faludi calls them the "'I am a feminist but . . .'" women, and her summary of what follows the "but," of what these young feminist thinkers believe, is worth quoting: "'I don't believe women face discrimination anymore; I don't see any reason for women to organize politically; I don't think the pay gap, sexual harassment, rape, domestic violence, or just about any other issue feminism has raised are real problems; I don't see why we even need to bother with gender analysis anymore; and, on the whole, I find feminists to be little more than victim-mongering conspiracy nuts.'" In the end, Faludi concludes that feminists who want to drop any gender analysis and talk only about "people" are basically self-serving—interested only in their own individual advancement, having already relinquished the notion of collective struggle for the rights of the many, and uninterested in any change beyond their own success.

In her criticism of the young women, whom Faludi clearly does not acknowledge as true feminists (they are faux, pseudo, and pod), she could be seen to embody the fixed political agenda that Lehrman and the others have so often accused feminism of imposing. For instance, Faludi questions their credentials as feminists by charging that they attend conservative conferences and publish in conservative magazines (like *National Review* and *Commentary*), that they have not been in "the feminist trenches of pro-choice demonstrations," and that they are hostile to certain "feminist issues" as sexual harassment, domestic violence, rape, pay equity, child care, and welfare rights. The question, of course, arises: Can one be a conservative feminist? a pro-life feminist? a feminist skeptical about the supposed pervasiveness of sexual harassment or rape? a feminist who thinks Lorena Bobbitt was wrong (the woman who cut off her abusive husband's penis when he was asleep, and whom Young has accused feminists of making Feminist of the Year)? a feminist who thinks the welfare system should be fixed and child care should remain privatized? Faludi implies that a feminist would not take such positions; the younger feminists disagree.

The mass of young women in their twenties over whose interests and future feminists such as Faludi and Lehrman so vehemently disagree did, of course, have their own opinions. Whereas Lehrman tends to present women's studies students as mindless drones intoning a preprogrammed ideological message, in reality the current skepticism of women toward feminism reflected in polls also pervaded college campuses—although reasons given for that skepticism by bell hooks and Lisa Maria Hogeland do not include the loudly proclaimed message of Faludi's "pod feminists" that women have got all the rights they need. bell hooks, in "Black Students Who Reject Feminism" (1994), published in *The Chronicle of Higher Education*, and Lisa Maria Hogeland, in "Fear of Feminism: Why Young Women Get the Willies" (1994), published in *Ms.*, both explore the complex reasons for college women's widespread disengagement from feminism. hooks, a Professor of English at the City College of the City University of New York, tells what to her is the stunning story of young African American women's continuing alienation from the women's movement because of racism—because feminism is "only about the needs of white women." hooks talks about a further "backlash" against feminism on the part of black college students because of increasingly prominent ideals of racial separatism, neonationalism, and Afrocentric thinking. hooks urges students that African Americans have always been part of feminism, and that feminism should be an integral part of the lives of all black people. Implicit in hooks' argument is that black students are politicized, but politicized only around race. Hogeland, on the other hand, makes the case that her students shy away from the political commitment necessary to feminism. Hogeland teaches English and women's studies at the University of Cincinnati, and she is very sympathetic to her students' fear of politics; they should be, she claims, for becoming a feminist can bring very dangerous consequences. Among other things, Hogeland points out how girls in our culture are often given no choice but to develop their sense of identity within the framework of their sexuality and their intimate relations with men. Feminism threatens this sense of identity: "When you live on Noah's ark," Hogeland writes, "anything that might make it more difficult to find a partner can seem to threaten your very survival." In the era of what has been called "lifestyle" feminism, where becoming political can be as easy as wearing certain clothes, listening to certain music, and making certain other individual choices that have little effect on other women, hooks and Hogeland both bring a refreshing sense of the difficulties and the costs of becoming a feminist.

Many of the documents in this section (notably Naomi Wolf's contribution to the forum on the feminist backlash in *Ms.* and Susan Faludi's article on the "pod feminists") insist on the central role the mass media have had in defining feminism (often in quite distorted ways) in the 1980s and 1990s. One of the most contemporary media, though, the Internet, has been a site ripe for the flourishing of a kind of grassroots cyberfeminism—a site where real women of all shades of feminism can exchange ideas on the "new" feminist movement and on what it means. Several essays from the Website www.neofeminism.com illustrate the diversity of young women's definitions of feminism. There are, however, some commonalities.

First, these "neofeminist" contributors are notably part of the third wave in that they characteristically tend not to see themselves as simply "women" in a battle against "men." They have learned from the wholesale critique of the overwhelmingly white, middle-class second-wave movement mounted by generations of women of color, working-class women, and lesbians. They know that the explanatory framework of a viable feminism is not dualistic; masculinity and femininity are not the only analytical categories. As Wendy Kaminer describes third-wave feminists, writing about a representative contributor to Findlen's *Listen Up* in her *New York Times Book Review* essay: "The children of identity politics, they routinely deconstruct themselves. 'As an educated, married, monogamous, feminist, Christian, African-American mother, I suffer from an acute case of multiplicity,' Sonja D. Curry-Johnson explains." In "Neofeminism?" by Robin McAndrews, she calls for a neofeminism that is basically equated with diversity, that will simply make room for everyone. Her own feminism consists in her insistence that people take her as she is: "hyper, nerdy, idealistic, blatantly queer, and hopelessly unable to eat spaghetti in a socially acceptable fashion." McAndrews' listing of the various aspects of her unique self, and thus the qualities of her feminism, is a common strategy in this Website. In "What Is Neofeminism?" by Celeste Hutchins and Christi Denton, neofeminism is described as meaning "women of color, working-class women, fat women, Jewish women, Pagan women, Hindu women, Moslem women, lesbians, bisexuals, male-to-female women, women who are now men, women who are both, old women, rural women, women with disabilities, women with AIDS, women with cancer, battered women, and men who are oppressed from the same sources and reasons as women." While these calls that feminism must shake its old reputation of exclusivity, its old association with only white, middle-class women are certainly admirable; sometimes its seems that a diverse movement becomes an end in itself rather than the *means* to an end. That is, "neofeminism" risks becoming simply about naming, acknowledging, and accepting all women rather than furthering their needs. Acceptance is a first step, however, and the needs of male-to-female women, for instance, cannot be furthered if they are not recognized as existing.

A second commonality of the contributions to the neofeminism Website is their resistance to what McAndrews calls a "one-page-or-so written down somewhere rigid ideology that never changes." In this, these neofeminists are like their more visible sisters (Lehrman, Roiphe, et al.) in insisting on their right to make their own choices, to call themselves feminist for those choices, and not be subject to any negative judgment from others. For McAndrews, neofeminism is defined by the identities, the lifestyle, and the choices of each of its individual followers. And, as Hutchins and Denton put it: "Neofeminism is about women making their own choices that don't limit the choices other women get to make. . . . It's about you being whoever you want to be." In "You Are a Feminist," Danica Nuccitelli writes about being sick of hearing the "I'm not a feminist but . . ." line and urges women to embrace feminism. In doing so, she gives a list of qualifications for neofeminism, which seems at first to counter the other writers on the site in being prescriptive. However, her characteristics of a neofeminist are purposefully designed to embrace even contradictory practices. For instance: "You are a neofeminist if you can put lipstick on without a mirror" is right above "You are a neofeminist if you think lipstick is only good for faking tribal markings or football smudges on your face." No one need be excluded from the all-inclusive "neofeminism."

Not all new feminists are to be found only on television and the Web, however, and not all third-wave feminists define themselves against their predecessors. "Shall We Dance" (1997), written for *Ms.* by Anastasia Higginbotham, represents the perspective of a young feminist who admires, respects, and is nurtured by her foremothers, who is part of what some might call the mainstream feminist establishment. Higginbotham does describe her differences with older feminists, but she roots those differences in the gains that "previous generations of the sisterhood" fought for and won; they enabled Higginbotham and her generation "to feel entitled to equal rights, opportunity, education, and justice." As a consequence, Higginbotham claims, her generation is able to inhabit a "*how-dare-you* approach to sexism and linking oppressions."

That "how-dare-you" outrage is also evident in the writing of another third-wave feminist associated with *Ms.*, and directly tied to the older generation of feminists through her mother, Alice Walker. Rebecca Walker, twenty-eight, is a contributor to *Ms.* magazine, editor of *To Be Real: Telling the Truth and Changing the Face of Feminism* (1995), and a leading spokesperson for a "third wave" of black feminism. Rebecca Walker's essay "Becoming the Third Wave" (1992) tells of her embrace of feminism, her realization that the backlash against women is real, in the aftermath of the Anita Hill–Clarence Thomas hearings. Walker describes two experiences with black men that made her realize women are "neglected, violated, devalued, ignored"—and that the race struggle alone will never improve their situation. Unlike the highly individualistic, often depoliticized third-wave feminism of white women, Walker recognizes that to be a feminist she must "integrate an ideology of equality and female empowerment into the very fiber of my life," and that she must join in sisterhood with other women. Also, unlike the generational conflict of white third-wave feminists, Walker's dramatization of her political conversion through personal experience draws a line connecting her version of the third wave to the second-wave ideal of the efficacy of consciousness raising within feminist politics.

Both bell hooks in "Feminism—It's a Black Thang!" (1992) and Kristal Brent Zook in "A Manifesto of Sorts for a Black Feminist Movement" (1995) begin, as did Walker, by portraying the sexism of black men and the desperate need for a feminism that will name this violence and seek to end it. While bell hooks talks about continued domestic and sexual violence, Zook notes the virtual apotheosis of violent black men by the media in the 1990s: wife abuser O. J. Simpson (acquitted in a criminal trial but convicted in a civil trial of killing his ex-wife and a friend); misogynist rap singer Tupac Shakur; convicted rapist Mike Tyson; and accused sexual harasser Clarence Thomas have all become dubious heroes for the black community—including for black women. They have become icons of the "Endangered Black Man," a continuation of Michele Wallace's identification of a myth of "Black Macho" in the 1970s. While in some ways the recognition that black men are endangered in a still virulently racist society is a legitimate point, Zook points out that it is done at the expense of black women, who are supposed to bear any abuse to protect their men no matter what they may have done. bell hooks agrees, for she, too, links the routine daily violence committed on black women by black men to the lionization of women-hating rap stars and "heroes" like Mike Tyson. In a sense, black feminism has suffered from its own media-produced backlash, as television, news, and the recording industry have focused the issue of race around men and rallied women's support for causes that are essentially against their own interests as women and as African Americans.

Despite the reiteration, in much 1990s feminist writing, that women have not gained equality with men yet—that the pay gap is real, the glass ceiling is real, escalating domestic violence and rape are real, sexual harassment is real—women have certainly made vast inroads into previously all-male bastions: politics, academia, medicine, the law, corporate America, and professional and collegiate athletics. This success raises the inevitable questions: What price success? Is an individually successful woman necessarily a role model for other women, a representative of other women, even a trail-blazing feminist? The answer must be—not necessarily. Unfortunately, in fact, oftentimes the success of an individual woman happens precisely at the cost of her cutting herself off from any sense of solidarity with other women. In the forum in *Ms.* magazine, Gloria Steinem, for instance, talks of her active (unsuccessful) campaigning in Texas to defeat Kay Bailey Hutchinson's attempt to win a seat in the U.S. Senate. As Steinem says, "she opposes nearly every feminist issue there is." To be successful in what is still primarily a "man's world," women typically have to employ what Audre Lorde famously called "the master's tools." Does that inherently compromise their ability to claim the title of feminist?

These questions and many others—including the still-pressing problem of why so few women make it to the top of corporate America—are addressed in an interview conducted by *Harper's* senior editor Barbara Jones with Anita Blair, Barbara Ehrenreich, Jeanne Lewis, Arlie Russell Hochschild, and Elizabeth Perle McKenna, entitled "Giving Women the Business: On Winning, Losing, and Leaving the Corporate Game" (1997). The six women, some of whom are or were in corporate America and some of whom study it, discuss why so many women hit the glass ceiling (the answers ranging from outright sexism, to lack of women role models, to women's failure to meet the standards of the "meritocracy" of the boardroom, to women's plain distaste for the kind of life corporate success entails); whether traditional feminine attractiveness is an asset or a liability; whether women can succeed in business and also raise children; and whether women who do succeed have a responsibility to look out for other women and to change the rules of a male-dominated culture. Unfortunately, the two women who are leaders in the corporate world, Blair and Lewis, both insist that a female executive does *not* have a responsibility either to have a gendered social policy or to specifically help along other women.

101

DOROTHY WICKENDEN

What NOW? The Women's Movement Looks Beyond "Equality" (1986)

Nobody seems to have a kind word for the women's movement these days. Its leaders are suffering from "post-feminist depression." It has reached a state of "profound paralysis." Its largest and strongest proponent, the National Organization for Women, has shown itself to be nothing more than a "colorless liberal organization." American women "have less economic security than their mothers did, and are considerably worse off than women in other advanced countries." Only the first of these assessments is from a conservative ideologue—Dinesh D'Souza, in an article called "The New Feminist Revolt: This Time It's Against Feminism." The second is from NOW's founder, Betty Friedan, whose advice on "How to Get the Women's Movement Moving Again" was prefaced by a stern critique of its current strategies; the third is from a radical feminist, Brett Harvey; and the fourth is from an economist, Sylvia Ann Hewlett, whose new book, *A Lesser Life: The Myth of Women's Liberation in America,* is a withering examination of the failures of contemporary feminism.

Meanwhile, there have been cries of betrayal within NOW. Last July the press relished a ruthless battle for NOW's presidency between the incumbent, Judy Goldsmith, and her predecessor, Eleanor Smeal. Behind the personal feud was a significant disagreement over tactics. The "moderate" Goldsmith charged Smeal with "character assassination" and "a ward boss mentality." She called Smeal's relentless pursuit of the Equal Rights Amendment "an exercise in futility." She pleaded for coalition-building and expanding NOW's agenda. The "militant" Smeal accused Gold-

From *The New Republic,* May 5, 1986. Reprinted by permission of *The New Republic,* copyright 1986, The New Republic, Inc.

smith of abandoning the ERA, losing NOW members, and becoming a mere "arm of the Democratic Party." She talked of revolution. "We don't take our right-wing fascist opponents seriously enough," she scolded the delegates at the convention in New Orleans. "We must recognize bigotry when it raises its ugly head. We must wrap it around the neck of the right wing." Smeal defeated Goldsmith. And as promised, she took women back to the streets with a rousing national march for abortion rights and birth control. Eighty thousand people showed up for the March 9 demonstration in Washington, representing groups ranging from Baby Boomers for Choice to Lesbian and Gay Quakers.

Fractiousness among feminists and our predictions of the movement's imminent collapse are nothing new. Ten years ago, when the radical revolt against liberal feminism was at its peak, Veronica Geng wrote off NOW in an article for *Harper's* called "Requiem for the Women's Movement." NOW, she said, "tried to refute a male fantasy with another male fantasy: see Betty's wholesome family, see Gloria's beauty, see Marlene's fulfilling job, see our docile masses, who all think the same reasonable thoughts. As it turned out, this strategy played a large part in creating the worst possible image; that of an unwelcoming movement, closed to dissent." Over half a century ago—when traditionalists were claiming that expanding women's lives beyond the domestic realm would lead to effeminacy among men and insanity among women—suffragists were divided among themselves over strategy. And while suffragists proclaimed that the women's vote would usher in an era of enlightened social reform, other feminists warned that it would do nothing to improve the lot of women who needed it most: the working class and poor. The current debate is only the latest expression of a century-old split among feminist forces about how to revolutionize the role of women in American society.

Much of this dissension has grown out of a flaw at the heart of mainstream feminist theory, which has both exaggerated the potential for political unity among women and slighted the significance of biological distinctions between the sexes. The premise of "equal rights" feminism is that social, legal, and economic equality must be pursued in defiance of gender differences. By contrast, social feminists, radical feminists, and others have always been dubious about the wisdom of aspiring to standards of public and private life established by and for men. At the turn of the century Charlotte Perkins Gilman argued not only that women had the right to employment, but that society would have to find a way to make it possible to balance the demands of child-rearing and work. Today even women who fought most vigorously for equal rights are finding the approach increasingly problematic. Yet the voices of dissent are not urging a recantation of feminism. They urge a new definition of equal opportunity—one that will be almost as unsettling to NOW as to Reaganites. As Betty Friedan put it in *The Second Stage* (1981): "The equality we fought for isn't livable, isn't workable, isn't comfortable in the terms that structured our battle."

That battle was largely shaped, of course, by Friedan herself and the National Organization for Women. She and a dozen or so other activists established NOW in 1966 after concluding that the 1964 Civil Rights Act, which banned job discrimination on the grounds of sex as well as race, religion, and national origin, would not be enough to prod government agencies to act on complaints of sex discrimination. NOW's intention never was to subvert male bastions of power, but to work through the legislatures, Congress, courts, and grassroots organizations to enable women to work alongside men in education, employment, and politics.

The successes of the egalitarian tradition of feminism—from the 19th Amendment in 1920 to *Roe v. Wade* in 1973—have been considerable. The women's movement has knocked down sex discrimination in higher education and Olympic sports, in credit applications and

the English language. It has shaped policy in the professions and politics, reconstituted relations between the sexes, and dramatically altered the terms of debate within the Catholic Church. Nevertheless, its limitations are clearer than ever. The issues that feminists historically have rallied around—the Equal Rights Amendment and reproductive freedom—arguably have helped to marshal reactionary forces as much as to mobilize women. The reason is obvious. Women bear children, a fact that cannot be transformed by legislation or swept away with rhetoric. A politics built upon the right to control childbearing and the denial of sexual differences is dangerously vulnerable when it comes to one of the most fiercely guarded institutions of American society: the family.

This weakness has been exposed in two critical political battles over the ERA. In 1923, when the ERA was first proposed by Alice Paul's National Women's Party, it aroused deep disagreement among women over promised public freedoms and existing private responsibilities. Many feminists, including Eleanor Roosevelt and groups such as the National League of Women Voters, the Women's Trade Union League, and the Council of Jewish Women, actively opposed the ERA, arguing that women's needs are different from men's, and that it would deprive women of the few social supports they had. Far from uniting women along the lines of gender, the ERA divided them along the lines of class. In *Women and Equality* (1977), William H. Chafe describes the strategy of the National Women's Party. He could almost be describing NOW's strategy in the 1970s:

". . . the NWP devoted its entire energies to the fight for an ERA, eschewing identification with other questions such as birth control or maternal and infant care. . . . in the process . . . the NWP, already a small elitist organization, alienated most working women (the ERA prior to 1941 would have brought invalidation of protective legislation for working women such as minimum-wage laws), spent an excessive amount of energy battling other women's organizations, and tended to ignore the extent to which the roots of sex inequality went beyond the reach of even the most powerful constitutional amendment."

In the 1970s the ERA became a cause not only for women demanding their full legal rights as American citizens, but also for the conservatives "pro-family" agenda. The final ratification drive gave Phyllis Schlafly and the burgeoning Moral Majority (not to mention the John Birch Society) a platform from which to blame feminism for robbing women of their livelihood, releasing dangerous male sexual urges, destroying the family, and murdering the unborn. This hysterical response caught feminists off guard. Schafly's STOP ERA campaign was largely a reaction to the counterculture, yet the ERA campaign was in part an effort by the moderate women's movement to shake off the vague revolutionism of radical feminism. Smeal and Goldsmith say that in the end it wasn't Schlafly that killed the ERA, but the obstructionist tactics of a handful of legislators and lobbyists in a few conservative states. There are, though, less visible lessons of the ERA's defeat, which NOW still refuses to recognize. The first is the political delicacy (and the unintended consequences) of any move to amend the Constitution. The second is that even many supporters of the ERA were skeptical about its potential for bringing about a more egalitarian society. The third is that investing too heavily in a single approach to women's rights can be foolhardy.

Today Eleanor Smeal stubbornly insists that the best way to revive the women's movement is to renew the ERA campaign and undercut the right on the issues of birth control, abortion, and pay equity. "There is no liberty for women," she told me, "if they can't control their own fertility." In a recent speech to Catholic University students, she took up this theme with fervor, stressing the urgency of retaining women's right to birth control in this country, and pressing for it in Africa. After her talk, when a Hispanic woman rose to ask why minorities had the impression that NOW

sometimes seems oblivious to their concerns, Smeal replied indignantly, "The opposition is primarily male. That's a fact. . . . You should be proud of the fight women have waged."

To be sure, it is thanks to the organized women's movement that a majority of American women now take for granted the right to control their own fertility. And professional women are reaping the rewards of the efforts of NOW, the Women's Equity Action League, the National Women's Political Caucus, and numerous other groups. College graduates are routinely postponing marriage and pursuing careers in fields that used to be virtually closed to women: law, medicine, engineering, banking. And women are getting elected to political office in unprecedented numbers. Fourteen years ago there were 362 female state legislators; today there are 1,103. So far 19 women have announced plans to run for governor in 1986. Yet NOW and its sister organizations have been unable to shake the charge of elitism. In particular, they are accused of benignly neglecting what has become the most intractable "women's issue": the worsening economic plight of millions of American women and their children.

Thus while Smeal continues to warn her audiences of creeping fundamentalism, women from outside the NOW camp are warning of the pitfalls of egalitarian feminism. Some (who emphasize that they fully support the prochoice cause) complain that in effect the most powerful groups have been pursuing a kind of trickle-down feminism: open up opportunities in mayoralties and state legislatures and the U.S. Congress, in higher education and the professions, and eventually all women will benefit. Julia Scott at the Children's Defense Fund says that in the long fight for the ERA, "the fight to help support the working class and poor was dropped." Eleanor Guggenheimer, at the Child Care Action Campaign, says that the ERA proved to be such a tremendous fund-raising success that NOW lost sight of the immediate worries of many women: how to care for their children while meeting the demands of their jobs. "You ask women how they feel about the family, and the floodgates open. They will tell you it's unbelievably difficult to find day care. Divorced women will tell you their fears of taking another day off when their child is sick—they're scared to death of being fired. They worry about keeping food on the table."

The fact is that millions of American women aren't doing well at all. There is still a large discrepancy between male and female wages. (According to the U.S. Census Bureau, women who work full-time still earn on average only 61 cents to every dollar paid to men.) Working women still cluster in low-paying, sex-segregated jobs in the "pink-collar ghetto." And female poverty gets worse all the time. Three out of five adults officially designated as below the poverty line are women, and close to half of the poor families in America are headed by women. Minority women and their children are the most disadvantaged group in America: two-thirds of the children in black and Hispanic female-headed households are poor. All of these trends have been exacerbated by the Reagan counter-revolution. While talking about the sanctity of family life, the right has whittled away social programs that serve primarily the families of poor and working women: AFDC, child nutrition, food stamps, day care.

The biggest challenge for women's organizations is no longer simply to expand equal opportunities, or even to fight the Reagan administration on affirmative action and social issues. The most critical and difficult work lies in finding ways to help women maintain a decent standard of living without neglecting their children. The traditional approach to equality has proved inadequate here. Women, like minority groups, have discovered that discrimination is not the only significant barrier to economic advancement and that equal rights and even ostensibly equal treatment does not necessarily lead to true equality.

In some cases the sex-blind pursuit of equal rights has even exacerbated social and economic injustices. The reforms in divorce law, for example, which set out to ensure equal treatment for men and women, have instead helped men at women's expense, as Lenore Weitzman shows in *The Divorce Revolution*. (See "Cruel Contracts" by Maggie Scarf, *The New Republic*, April 21.) Although Smeal says that she and other feminists had reservations about the equitable divorce laws all along, the principle behind them is precisely that principle of equality supported by NOW. "No-fault attempts to treat men and women equally—*or as if they were equal*—at the point of divorce," Weitzman says. "However, it ignores the *structural* inequality between men and women in the larger society." Under the new system, judges rarely acknowledge the economic vulnerability of women who have spent years raising their children. Instead, they assume that the real barrier to self-sufficiency is the woman's reluctance to go out and get a job. Permanent alimony—which was always rare (in 1968, for example, under 20 percent of divorced wives in California were awarded alimony)—is now virtually nonexistent, and by 1978 only 13 percent of mothers with children under six were awarded even temporary alimony. What's more, although the vast majority of divorced women continue to care for their children, child support is grossly inadequate, and between 60 and 80 percent of fathers refuse to comply with court-ordered payments. Not surprisingly, within the first year of divorce, women and their children experience a 73 percent drop in their standard of living, and men a 42 percent rise.

In the workplace, too, a doctrinaire adherence to the ideal of equality has proved troublesome. The women's movement, along with numerous civil rights and labor groups and the Democratic Party, believes that the way to correct the disparities between men's and women's work and wages is through comparable worth, or "pay equity," as it is now called. The proponents of pay equity have made Americans aware of the dismal facts about job segregation and its threat to women's economic well-being and by now most states either have introduced or are considering pay-equity plans. They have been less successful in analyzing and attacking the underlying sources of the wage gap.

Pay-equity enthusiasts assume that long-standing patterns of sexual discrimination are the principal reason that women continue to be underpaid and segregated in "women's work." They tend to downplay women's other handicaps, such as less education and job training and fewer years in the work force. They largely overlook sweeping socioeconomic changes of the last decade—such as deindustrialization and the rise of service industries—which also shape employment patterns. And they often fail to take account of women's continuing responsibilities at home.

The dangers of a single-minded focus on discrimination as the cause of women's low status and low pay on the job suddenly became evident when the long discrimination case against Sears Roebuck & Company was lost. In 1979 the Equal Employment Opportunities Commission filed suit, charging Sears with sex discrimination in hiring, promotion, and pay. But the court found that not only had Sears met reasonable standards for hiring women; its record on affirmative action was commendable. It was the first big retail chain in the country to adopt an affirmative action plan. Moreover, the EEOC never came forth with a witness who could convincingly testify to discrimination. The judge criticized the statistical evidence presented by the EEOC showing the paucity of women in commission sales jobs, and said that women had proved to be both less interested in and less qualified for those jobs. NOW and other women's groups, which had championed the case, greeted the decision with dismay. It is all the more difficult to argue for proportional representation if women don't clamor as eagerly as men to sell automotive parts and aluminum siding.

Barnard history professor Rosalind Rosenberg, who testified on behalf of Sears in the suit, points out that feminists' preoccupation with discrimination "threatens to cripple the cause of working women, not advance it." Per-petually worried about potential encroachment upon equal opportunities, NOW doesn't fully concede the more obvious restrictions on women's time and ambitions: the presence of small children, the absence of affordable day care, and the difficulty of taking on jobs that require extra training, overtime, and travel. Pay equity may result at last in higher wages for women in underpaid jobs. But it will not necessarily ensure an equal distribution of labor.

Another source of controversy among feminists is the issue of benefits for pregnant workers. NOW is currently airing the same debate that divided feminists in the 1920s. Does protective legislation, granting women different benefits from those of their male co-workers necessarily discriminate unfairly against women? Does an insistence on sex-neutral policies necessarily work in women's best interest? One of NOW's achievements, in Smeal's first term as president, was passage of the 1978 Pregnancy Discrimination Act, which prohibits employers from firing a woman solely because she is pregnant. Today NOW, the ACLU, and the League of Women Voters, along with conservative business groups and the Reagan Justice Department, are challenging a California law requiring employers to grant special benefits to pregnant employees (up to four months' leave, and a guarantee to reinstate them afterward). NOW believes that the disability benefits should be extended to all workers; the Justice Department wants to eliminate them. Both argue that the law discriminates against workers who are not pregnant. The case has gone to the Supreme Court.

Smeal says: "Our worry is protective labor legislation. In the past it was used not to hire women. . . . Our fear is that what appears to be a benefit will be used against us. If a person is disabled—male or female—she should be able to take a four-month leave without pay, and not be fired." This stand is clearly sensible, and NOW was an early supporter of Representative Pat Schroeder's Parental and Medical Leave Bill, currently before Congress, which would require employers to provide up to 26 weeks of unpaid leave for all employees with medical disabilities, including pregnancy, and would enable either parent to take up to 18 weeks of leave after the birth or adoption of a baby, or to care for a sick child. The worker would also be guaranteed the same or a similar job upon return.

Others, though, insist that women will never be able to compete fairly in public life if they aren't granted compensation for their work as mothers. Sylvia Hewlett charges in *A Lesser Life* that one result of the movement's reluctance to publicize women's continuing responsibilities at home is that the United States is the only industrial country in the world with no statutory maternity leave, and one of the few without subsidized day care. Hewlett argues that the social feminists in Western Europe have achieved more for working women by demanding special privileges than the equal-rights feminists in America have by taking an uncompromising stand on sex-blind laws and social policy. In France, Sweden, West Germany, Denmark, Italy, and England—all of which provide some form of subsidized day care, job protection, and paid maternity leave—the difference between male and female wages has been narrowing. The wage gap in America is the same as it was in 1939.

The tactics of mainstream feminists have been harshly scrutinized lately in politics as well. While saying that women in the workplace are driven by the same motivations as men, NOW has consistently argued that the sexes think and behave differently in politics. In 1984 Smeal wrote a book called *Why and How Women Will Elect the Next President,* which predicted that a woman would strengthen the presidential ticket and widen the gender gap, and that abortion and the ERA would be major election issues. Both Smeal and Goldsmith resent the labeling of NOW as a special-interest group. But NOW treats women as a critical voting bloc sharing distinctive concerns, and uses this presumption to wield its considerable

influence in pressuring politicians. This is the role of any lobbying group. The problem in the 1984 election was that NOW's highly publicized demand that Walter Mondale choose a female running mate was seen by Mondale supporters (and exploited by Reagan supporters) as conclusive evidence that he was indeed the malleable captive of special interests. Liberal columnists came down particularly hard on NOW. During its July convention in Miami, where Mondale was welcomed with the chant, "Win with a woman, run with a woman," Richard Cohen wrote that the Democratic candidate was being "henpecked." "It will seem to many Americans that the choice of a woman . . . will result not from Mondale's sincere commitment to feminism . . . or even the stellar qualifications of a particular woman, but from the hectoring and—yes—threats of the organized women's movement."

In the end, the gender gap proved to be far less decisive in the 1984 presidential campaign than the Democrats had hoped and the Republicans had feared. And the pressure to choose a female running mate caused Mondale to select a woman with liabilities and a lack of qualifications that would have ruled out a male candidate. The vanishing promise of the gender gap may be largely attributed to Mondale's overwhelming weaknesses and Reagan's unassailable strengths. But far from helping to overcome those failings, NOW helped to expose them.

Betty Friedan, for one, has long been imploring her followers to accept the limits of legal remedies and divisive political tactics. In *The Second Stage* she replaced her explosive talk of "the comfortable concentration camp" of the suburban housewife with heady visions of "the new frontier where the issues of the second stage will be joined": the family. But this change of tack has elicited mutters of annoyance from the movement's current leaders, one of whom calls her criticisms "cavalier and galling." It was *The Feminine Mystique,* after all, which first emboldened a generation of women to shake off the constraints of traditional motherhood and marriage.

Friedan self-righteously blames her radical sisters for the movement's vulnerability on the family issue. "For us, with our roots in the middle American mainstream and our own fifties' families," Friedan wrote in *The Second Stage,* "equality and the personhood of women never meant destruction of the family, repudiation of marriage and motherhood, or implacable sexual war against men." That "pseudo-radical cop-out" was perpetrated by young extremists, "scarred early by the feminine mystique, and without firm roots in family or career, [who] gave vent to their rage in a rhetoric of sexual politics based on a serious ideological mistake." Perhaps. The radical feminists were certainly more uncompromising in their desire to overthrow what Kate Millet described as "patriarchy's chief institution." Yet in the 1960s and 1970s the liberal feminists showed scant concern for that institution themselves, except where it impinged on their independence. It is only in recent years that the family has become politically fashionable again.

Today the weaknesses of the old tactics are clear, yet the solutions seem to be as elusive as ever. Like the civil rights movement it sprang from, the women's movement is having trouble reconciling the old politics of separatism with the new politics of accommodation. *The Second Stage* ends with a peroration on the need for "*human* liberation," and Friedan's recent article on resuscitating feminism talks lyrically of "international networking" with Third World women under a baobab tree in Nairobi at the U.N. Conference for Women. Her list of priorities includes: "a new round of consciousness-raising," "get off the pornography kick," "confront the illusion of equality in divorce," "affirm the differences between men and women," and so on. Nothing objectionable there, but not much to rally around either.

On the other hand, feminists won't get the better of fundamentalists in an overwrought debate over the rights of the unborn vs. the rights of women. Smeal has it wrong when she blames "the opposition" for all that ails feminism. This is just a more sophisticated strain of the paranoia that has long run through the rhetoric of the movement. Generic man is no longer the enemy (except in the eyes of antipornography fanatics like Andrea Dworkin). Today the oppressor that NOW denounces is embodied in "the male Catholic hierarchy," fundamentalists like Jerry Falwell, and ideologues like Ronald Reagan. In fact the women's movement has been remarkably successful in securing individual rights. What's needed is a new, generous, workable ideal of social justice. NOW, like the Democratic Party, hasn't yet convinced the public that it has more to offer than ineffectual reaction to Reaganism.

The sanctimony and hypocrisy behind the conservative talk about the family is obvious, and feminists should be the first to do something about it. As Goldsmith says, "We need to comfortably and affirmatively take back that ground that is legitimately ours. We are the people who really care about that family." This means vigorously endorsing progressive programs that work. The Child Care Action Campaign, working with other natural child-care agencies and an insurance agent, recently succeeded in obtaining liability insurance for day-care centers, family day-care homes, and Head Start programs across the country that had been on the verge of closing. The Children's Defense Fund, long before Bill Moyers, has discussed the crisis in teenage pregnancy and tirelessly reported the effects of Reagan budget cuts on children. The House Select Committee on Children, Youth, and Families has been a forceful advocate of Schroeder's parental leave policy, and of tax reforms that would aid families. And it has drafted a bill that would improve and expand day-care facilities through public-private partnerships, and would restore federal funding to programs serving poor families.

Kathy Wilson, the former head of the National Women's Political Caucus, rightly points out that NOW serves an invaluable function as "the two-by-four used to get the attention of the mule." Pat Reuss, the legal director at the Women's Equity Action League, says that the moderate women's movement "has to have a group on the cutting edge. We pray they won't embarrass us, but we're glad they're out there." NOW's energetic lobbying in recent months on behalf of the Civil Rights Restoration Act (which would overturn the Supreme Court's *Grove City* decision limiting the government's ability to enforce civil rights laws at federally funded institutions) has been commended by feminists from many camps.

Few would question that the victories won by the equal rights advocates have formed the foundations of contemporary feminism. But the time has come for a radical departure. Instead of simply fighting off the "pro-family" and anti-civil rights crusaders, NOW could use its political power to launch a major offensive for a series of concrete social reforms and changes in the workplace—beginning with affordable, widely available, licensed day care. That may sound more pragmatic than principled. But it could enable women, and men, to meet the demands of both their public and private lives. And it would address the fundamental family issue of the 1980s, which is the economic one.

Back in 1938, in an editorial in *The New Republic* expressing strong reservations about the ERA, Felix Frankfurter was quoted as saying: "The legal position of woman cannot be stated in a single, simple formula, because her life cannot be expressed in a single, simple relation. Woman's legal status necessarily involves complicated formulations, because a woman occupies many relations. The law must have regard for woman in her manifold relations as an individual, as a wage-earner, as a wife, as a mother, as a citizen." It is this expansive vision that feminists need to recapture. NOW's problem these days, for all Smeal's rhetoric, is that it isn't militant enough.

102

BARBARA EHRENREICH

Beyond Gender Equality: Toward the New Feminism (1993)

In reflecting on women's progress in the last couple of decades, it is important to ask: How far did we get and is there anything left over for anybody else to do? When we assess this progress, we have to remember that there were always at least two goals for the women's movement. The first goal is equality, which is a simple, though not necessarily easy, goal. It means simply that women's life chances must not be diminished by male supremacist beliefs and practices.

The second goal, which often gets lost or forgotten, involves challenging oppression based on race and class and all the other dimensions of potential inequality and injustice. A feminism oriented simply around gender equality would be empty and meaningless for most women in a society like ours, in which a woman earning $500,000 a year can hire another woman from the third world to care for her child and pay her only $5 an hour.

How far have we gotten on the first goal—equality? Not far enough. In the 1970s and 1980s we broke down barriers—women got into law schools and into medical schools. Doors that had been shut for centuries were knocked down.

This was important, but just a start compared to what lies ahead. I want to run through a few issues that reveal how we fall short of straightforward equality. In the area of power, for example, there was a lot of fuss about the "year of the woman" in 1992 and about women getting into the Senate and into the House. In reality, despite noteworthy gains, very *few* get

From *Democratic Left,* July/August 1993. Reprinted by permission of the author, *Democratic Left,* and Democratic Socialists of America.

into the Senate and House. We still have less than 10 percent representation in Congress. Two hundred years after the Boston Tea Party, women still endure taxation without representation.

And then there's another area of basic equality. Basic equality depends on reproductive rights. This struggle is far from over. The Supreme Court's *Casey* decision gives states the right to impose almost any restrictions they want on abortion. These can include a 24-hour waiting period, which is fine if you can afford to stay in a hotel overnight and hire a babysitter to take care of your kids at home. It's not fine if you're very young or if you don't have a lot of money. Feminist struggles have at least turned the climate of public opinion around on this issue. We must now work to make abortion a true right, and not simply an economic privilege.

Another aspect of equality involves relationships with men. Fifty percent of American fathers report that they have never changed a diaper and that they spend on the average only 38 seconds a day with their infant children. Even more disturbing is that the incidence of reported violence against women—rape and battering—has increased since the 1970s when the second wave of feminism began. Every 15 seconds a woman is battered; two to four million are battered every year. Violence against women in the home represents the most serious cause of injury to women, and results in more emergency room injuries than rape, muggings, illnesses, or car accidents all combined. In other words, for a woman, the most dangerous place she can be is at home.

Another area where we are far from equal is in the economy. Most of those gains made in the '70s and '80s in opening up new occupations for women involved the professions. It's wonderful to have women professionals in those roles. But most women aren't professionals. The great majority of working women are still in stereotypically female kinds of jobs— clerical work, sales, nursing, assembly line

work. Women in those jobs earn a little more than half of what men earn in comparable types of occupations.

A final dimension of inequality is self-esteem. We know a lot more about this issue than we did just a few years ago. We know that girls' self-esteem, measured in psychological tests, tends to go way down at ages 11 to 13. Boys' self-esteem also goes down somewhat at puberty, but their self-esteem tends to rebound as they get older. Girls' self-esteem goes down and stays low. This is very discouraging, because just as we get to the point where women have opportunities that weren't available before, suddenly a little voice goes off inside us saying, "Forget it, you can't do it, you're worthless, no point in even trying."

Another part of women's chronic low self-esteem comes from women's tendency to reject ourselves as physical beings. Studies show that women consistently overestimate their body size by about 25 percent. This self-rejection manifests itself in eating disorders, which can involve levels of starvation serious enough to affect body organs, such as the heart, or to affect and interrupt menstruation. Too many of us have accepted the cultural idea that there's only one way to look attractive, and if you're the wrong color, the wrong size, the wrong age, then you have to be sliced up and redone to resemble a "Barbie doll" model of beauty.

So if you define feminism simply as a struggle for equality, and if you define the goal as simply to do anything that men can do and feel good about yourself in the process, we are certainly not there yet.

Equality, however, was never the entire goal. In fact there's an old feminist slogan that goes: If you think equality with men is the goal, your standards are too low. We want equality, but we also want a world worth being equal in—a world in which repression and rigid forms of hierarchy would be seen as ugly relics. It's pointless even to imagine what equality for women would mean or could mean in the context of racial and class inequalities for both women and men. We reject, in fact, the idea of equality for women as a category, so long as there is inequality along these other lines, on the lines of color, ethnicity, and class. Women are also members of classes and races and ethnic groups—so it wouldn't make any sense to have one equality without the other. If feminism means anything it means a movement for all women, not just some women, not just white women, or corporate lawyer women, or wealthy women. We have to look to not just letting a few women onto the top, but also ask: How are we going to change that hierarchy that puts some women on top of others?

So equality is a fine goal, but it has to be equality for all in a society that's worth being equal in. We're a long way from that. Consider just a few depressing facts about the society in which women have been seeking equality. It's a society, as you know, marred by very deep economic inequality. Officially only 14 percent of the American people are poor, but that number rises to 20 percent if poverty is defined more realistically than it is by the official federal definition. We know that African Americans are three times more likely than whites to be poor, and that there are similar disparities for Latino families and communities. And we're talking about a society, too, that is becoming *more,* not less unequal in economic and class terms. Between 1977 and 1992, the wealthiest 1 percent of Americans saw their incomes rise by 136 percent. Meanwhile, the poorest 10 percent of Americans in the same time periods saw their incomes fall by over 20 percent.

Look at what has happened to Aid to Families with Dependent Children, which is a program almost entirely for single women and their children. Between 1970 and 1992, welfare benefits fell by 42 percent in inflation-corrected dollars. No other area of public policy is so obscured by right wing myths. There is the myth that welfare is draining the federal treasury. Actually, welfare is less than 1 percent of the federal budget. Then there's the

myth that welfare recipients are lazy or just aren't doing anything. Well, there's another old feminist slogan here: every mother is a working mother. These are women raising children on their own, which is a lot harder than raising children with a partner. Another myth is that people on welfare just need jobs. They need jobs, but they need good jobs, jobs that would actually pay enough to live on and support children on. Since nearly 20 percent of the workforce already works full time and is not getting out of poverty, where are we going to generate jobs for large numbers of women trying to enter the workforce from welfare?

The next wave of feminism will require a renewed vision of what it is we're trying to achieve, all of us who are working for social change in whatever way. We must outline how we believe that the community of human beings can live together more equitably and peacefully than it does now. The vision has to be a vison beyond capitalism, with its inevitable economic injustice. This is a time when people looking for change don't have some kind of precise model to inform that struggle for change. Everybody has some responsibility to start imagining, dreaming, inventing, and visualizing the kind of future we would like. In the movement I want to be a part of, everyone is a leader and everyone has responsibility to imagine the future.

There are times to be nice and accommodating and play by all the rules, but not all the time. If we're ever going to recapture our self-esteem, we're going to have to be proud to be strident, proud to be bitchy, and proud to be lesbians, and proud to be mistaken for lesbians. Remember the advice of the great early twentieth century labor organizer, Mother Jones, who would tell women that she was organizing: "Whatever you do, don't be ladylike." In fact, as I think about it, considering 100 years or so of feminist struggle behind us and many more still to come, it may even be that part of what Marilyn Quayle calls our "essential nature" is to get out there, year after year, decade after decade, and raise hell.

103

KATHA POLLITT

Are Women Morally Superior to Men? (1992)

Some years ago, I was invited by the wife of a well-known writer to sign a women's peace petition. It made the point such documents usually make: that women, as mothers, caregivers and nurturers, have a special awareness of the precariousness of human life, see through jingoism and cold war rhetoric and would prefer nations to work out their difficulties peacefully so that the military budget could be diverted to schools and hospitals and housing. It had the literary tone such documents usually have, as well—at once superior and plaintive, as if the authors didn't know whether they were bragging or begging. We are wiser than you poor deluded menfolk, was the subtext, so will you please-please-please listen to your moms?

To sign or not to sign? Of course, I was all for peace. But was I for peace *as a woman?* I wasn't a mother then—I wasn't even an aunt. Did my lack of nurturing credentials make my grasp of the horrors of war and the folly of the arms race only theoretical, like a white person's understanding of racism? Were mothers the natural leaders of the peace movement, to whose judgment nonmothers, male and female, must defer, because after all we couldn't *know,* couldn't *feel* that tenderness toward fragile human life that a woman who had borne and raised children had experienced? On the other hand, I was indeed a woman. Was motherhood with its special wisdom somehow deep inside me, to be called upon when needed, like my uterus?

Complicating matters in a way relevant to this essay was my response to the famous writer's wife herself. Here was a woman in her 50s, her child-raising long behind her. Was

From *The Nation,* December 28, 1992. Reprinted with permission from the December 28, 1992 issue of *The Nation* magazine.

motherhood the only banner under which she could gain a foothold on civic life? Perhaps so. Her only other public identity was that of a wife, and wifehood, even to a famous man, isn't much to claim credit for these days. ("To think I spent all those years ironing his underpants!" she once burst out to a mutual friend.) Motherhood was what she had in the work-and-accomplishment department, so it was understandable that she try to maximize its moral status. But I was not in her situation: I was a writer, a single woman, a jobholder. By sending me a petition from which I was excluded even as I was invited to add my name, perhaps she was telling me that, by leading a nondomestic life, I had abandoned the moral high ground, was "acting like a man," but could redeem myself by acknowledging the moral pre-eminence of the class of women I refused to join.

The ascription of particular virtues—compassion, patience, common sense, nonviolence—to mothers, and the tendency to conflate "mothers" with "women," has a long history in the peace movement but goes way beyond issues of war and peace. At present it permeates discussions of just about every field, from management training to theology. Indeed, although the media like to caricature feminism as denying the existence of sexual differences, for the women's movement and its opponents alike "difference" is where the action is. Thus, business writers wonder if women's nurturing, intuitive qualities will make them better executives. Educators suggest that female students suffer in classrooms that emphasize competition over cooperation. Women politicians tout their playground-honed negotiating skills, their egoless devotion to public service, their gender-based commitment to fairness and caring. A variety of political causes—environmentalism, animal rights, even vegetarianism—are promoted as logical extensions of women's putative peacefulness, closeness to nature, horror of aggression and concern for others' health. (Indeed, to some extent these causes are arenas in which women fight one another over definitions of femininity, which is why debates over disposable diapers and over the wearing of fur—both rather minor sources of harm, even if their opponents are right—loom so large and are so acrimonious.) In the arts, we hear a lot about what women's "real" subjects, methods and materials ought to be. Painting is male. Rhyme is male. Plot is male. Perhaps, say the Lacanian feminists, even logic and language are male. What is female? Nature. Blood. Milk. Communal gatherings. The moon. Quilts. . . .

"RELATIONAL" WOMEN, "AUTONOMOUS" MEN

In the 1950s, which we think of as the glory days of traditional sex roles, the anthropologist Ashley Montagu argued in "The Natural Superiority of Women" that females had it all over males in every way that counted, including the possession of two X chromosomes that made them stabler, saner and healthier than men, with their X and Y. Montagu's essay, published in *The Saturday Review* and later expanded to a book, is witty and high-spirited and, interestingly, anticipates the current feminist challenge to male-defined categories. (He notes, for example, that while men are stronger than women in the furniture-moving sense, women are stronger than men when faced with extreme physical hardship and tests of endurance; so when we say that men are stronger than women, we are equating strength with what men have.) But the fundamental thrust of Montagu's essay was to confirm traditional gender roles while revising the way we value them: Having proved to his own satisfaction that women could scale the artistic and intellectual heights, he argued that most would (that is, should) refrain, because women's true genius was "humanness," and their real mission was to "humanize" men before men blew up the world. And that, he left no doubt, was a full-time job.

Contemporary proponents of "difference feminism" advance a variation on the same argument, without Montagu's puckish humor. Instead of his whimsical chromosomal explana-

tion, we get the psychoanalytic one proposed by Nancy Chodorow in *The Reproduction of Mothering:* Daughters define themselves by relating to their mothers, the primary love object of all children, and are therefore empathic, relationship-oriented, nonhierarchical and interested in forging consensus; sons must separate from their mothers, and are therefore individualistic, competitive, resistant to connect with others and focused on abstract rules and rights. Chodorow's theory has become a kind of mantra of difference feminism, endlessly cited as if it explained phenomena we all agree are universal, though this is far from the case. The central question Chodorow poses—Why are women the primary caregivers of children?—could not even be asked before the advent of modern birth control, and can be answered without resorting to psychology. Historically, women have taken care of children because high fertility and lack of other options left most of them no choice. Those rich enough to avoid personally raising their children often did, as Rousseau observed to his horror.

Popularizers of Chodorow water down and sentimentalize her thesis. They embrace her proposition that traditional mothering produces "relational" women and "autonomous" men but forget her less congenial argument that it also results in sexual inequality, misogyny and hostility between mothers and daughters, who, like sons, desire independence but have a much harder time achieving it. Unlike her followers, Chodorow does not romanticize mothering: "Exclusive single parenting is bad for mother and child alike," she concludes; in a tragic paradox, female "caring," "intimacy" and "nurturance" do not soften but *produce* aggressive, competitive, hypermasculine men.

Thus, in her immensely influential book *In a Different Voice,* Carol Gilligan uses Chodorow to argue that the sexes make moral decisions according to separate criteria: women according to an "ethic of care," men according to an "ethic of rights." Deborah Tannen, in the best-selling *You Just Don't Understand,* claims that men and women grow up with "different cultural backgrounds"—the single-sex world of children's play in which girls cooperate and boys compete—"so talk between men and women is cross-cultural communication." While these two writers differ in important ways—Tannen, writing at a more popular level, is by far the clearer thinker and the one more interested in analyzing actual human interactions in daily life—they share important liabilities, too. Both largely confine their observations to the white middle class—especially Gilligan, much of whose elaborate theory of gender ethics rests on interviews with a handful of Harvard-Radcliffe undergraduates—and seem unaware that this limits the applicability of their data. (In her new book, *Meeting at the Crossroads,* Gilligan makes a similar mistake. Her whole theory of "loss of relationship" as the central trauma of female adolescence rests on interviews with students at one posh single-sex private school.) Both massage their findings to fit their theories: Gilligan's male and female responses are actually quite similar to each other, as experimenters have subsequently shown by removing the names and asking subjects to try to sort the test answers by gender; Tannen is quick to attribute blatant rudeness or sexism in male speech to anxiety, helplessness, fear of loss of face—anything, indeed, but rudeness and sexism. Both look only at what people say, to what they do. For Tannen this isn't a decisive objection because verbal behavior is her subject, although it limits the applicability of her findings to other areas of behavior; for Gilligan, it is a major obstacle, unless you believe as she apparently does, that the way people say they would resolve farfetched hypothetical dilemmas—Should a poor man steal drugs to save his dying wife?—tells us how they reason in real-life situations or, more important, what they do.

But the biggest problem with Chodorovian accounts of gender difference is that they credit the differences they find to essential, universal features of male and female psychosexual development rather than to the economic and so-

cial positions men and women hold, or the actual power differences between individual men and women. In *The Mismeasure of Woman,* her trenchant and witty attack on contemporary theories of gender differences, Carol Tavris points out that much of what can be said about women applies as well to poor people, who also tend to focus more on family and relationships and less on work and self-advancement; to behave deferentially with those more socially powerful; and to appear to others more emotional and "intuitive" than rational and logical in their thinking. Then, too, there is the question of whether the difference theorists are measuring anything beyond their own willingness to think in stereotypes. If Chodorow is right, relational women and autonomous men should be the norm, but are they? Or is it just that women and men use different language, have different social styles, different explanations for similar behavior? Certainly, it is easy to find in one's own acquaintance, as well as in the world at large, men and women who don't fit the models. Difference feminists like to attribute ruthlessness, coldness and hyperrationality in successful women—Margaret Thatcher is the standard example—to the fact that men control the networks of power and permit only women like themselves to rise. But I've met plenty of loudmouthed, insensitive, aggressive women who are stay-at-home mothers and secretaries and nurses. And I know plenty of sweet, unambitious men whose main satisfactions lie in their social, domestic and romantic lives, although not all of them would admit this to an inquiring social scientist. We tend to tell strangers what we think will make us sound good. I myself, to my utter amazement, informed a telephone pollster that I exercised regularly, a baldfaced lie. How much more difficult to describe truthfully one's moral and ethical values—even if one knew what they were, which, as Socrates demonstrated at length, almost no one does.

So why are Gilligan and Tannen the toasts of feminist social science, endlessly cited and discussed in academia and out of it too, in gender-sensitivity sessions in the business world and even, following the Anita Hill testimony, in Congress? The success of the difference theorists proves yet again that social science is one part science and nine parts social. They say what people want to hear: Women really are different in just the ways we always thought. Women embrace Gilligan and Tannen because they offer flattering accounts of traits for which they have historically been castigated. Men like them because, while they urge understanding and respect for "female" values and behaviors, they also let men off the hook: Men have power, wealth and control of social resources because women don't really want them. The pernicious tendencies of difference feminism are perfectly illustrated by the Sears sex discrimination case, in which Rosalind Rosenberg, a professor of women's history at Barnard College, testified for Sears that female employees held lower-paying salaried jobs while men worked selling big-ticket items on commission because women preferred low-risk, noncompetitive positions that did not interfere with family responsibilities [see Jon Wiener, "Women's History on Trial," September 7, 1985]. Sears won its case.

MOTHER KNOWS BEST

While Chodorow's analysis of psychosexual development is the point of departure for most of the difference feminists, it is possible to construct a theory of gender ethics on other grounds. The most interesting attempt I've seen is by the pacifist philosopher Sara Ruddick. Although not widely known outside academic circles, her *Maternal Thinking* makes an argument that can be found in such mainstream sources as the columns of Anna Quindlen in *The New York Times*. For Ruddick it is not psychosexual development that produces the Gilliganian virtues but intimate involvement in child-raising, the hands-on work of mothering. Men too can be mothers if they do the work that women do. (And women can be Fathers—a word Ruddick uses, complete with arrogant capital letter, for

distant, uninvolved authority-figure parents.) Mothers are patient, peace-loving, attentive to emotional context and so on, because those are the qualities you need to get the job done, the way accountants are precise, lawyers are argumentative, writers self-centered. Thus mothers constitute a logical constituency for pacifist and antiwar politics, and, by extension, a "caring" domestic agenda.

But what is the job of mothering? Ruddick defines "maternal practice" as meeting three demands: preservation, growth and social acceptability. She acknowledges the enormously varying manifestations of these demands, but she doesn't incorporate into her theory the qualifications, limits and contradictions she notes—perhaps because to do so would reveal these demands as so flexible as to be practically empty terms.

Almost anything mothers do can be explained under one of these rubrics, however cruel, dangerous, unfair or authoritarian—the genital mutilization of African and Arab girls, the foot-binding of pre-revolutionary Chinese ones, the sacrifice of some children to increase the resources available for others, as in the killing or malnourishing of female infants in India and China today. I had a Caribbean student whose mother beat all her children whenever one got into trouble, to teach them "responsibility" for one another. In this country, too, many mothers who commit what is legally child abuse *think* they are merely disciplining their kids in the good old-fashioned way. As long as the practices are culturally acceptable (and sometimes even when they're not), the mothers who perform them think of themselves as good parents. But if all these behaviors count as mothering, how can mothering have a necessary connection with any single belief about anything, let alone how to stop war, or any single set of personality traits, let alone nonviolent ones?

We should not be surprised that motherhood does not produce uniform beliefs and behaviors: It is, after all, not a job; it has no standard of admission, and almost nobody gets fired. Motherhood is open to any woman who can have a baby or adopt one. *Not* to be a mother is a decision; becoming one requires merely that a woman accede, perhaps only for as long as it takes to get pregnant, to thousands of years of cumulative social pressure. After that, she's on her own; she can soothe her child's nightmares or let him cry in the dark. Nothing intrinsic to child-raising will tell her what is the better choice for her child (each has been the favored practice at different times). Although Ruddick starts off by looking closely at maternal practice, when that practice contradicts her own ideas about good mothering it is filed away as an exception, a distortion imposed by Fathers or poverty or some other outside force. But if you add up all the exceptions, you are left with a rather small group of people—women like Ruddick herself, enlightened, up-to-date, educated, upper-middle-class liberals. . . .

As Gilligan does with all women, Ruddick scrutinizes mothers for what she expects to find, and sure enough, there it is. But why look to mothers for her peaceful constituency in the first place? Why not health professionals, who spend their lives saving lives? Or historians, who know how rarely war yields a benefit remotely commensurate with its cost in human misery? Or, I don't know, gardeners, blamelessly tending their innocent flowers? You can read almost any kind of work as affirming life and conferring wisdom. Ruddick chooses mothering because she's already decided that women possess the Gilliganian virtues and she wants a non-essentialist peg to hang them on, so that men can acquire them too. A disinterested observer scouring the world for labor that encourages humane values would never pick child-raising: It's too quirky, too embedded in repellent cultural norms, too hot.

MAN'S WORLD, WOMAN'S PLACE

Despite its intellectual flabbiness, difference feminism is deeply appealing to many women. Why? For one thing, it seems to explain some important phenomena: that women—and this is a cross-cultural truth—commit very little criminal violence compared with men; that women fill the ranks of the so-called caring professions; that women are much less likely than men to abandon their children. Difference feminists want to give women credit for these good behaviors by raising them from the level of instinct or passivity—the Camille Paglia vision of femininity—to the level of moral choice and principled decision. Who can blame women for embracing theories that tell them the sacrifices they make on behalf of domesticity and children are legitimate, moral, even noble? By stressing the mentality of nurturance—the *ethic* of caring, maternal *thinking*—Gilligan and Ruddick challenge the ancient division of humanity into rational males and irrational females. They offer women a way to argue that their views have equal status with those of men and to resist the customary marginalization of their voices in public debate. Doubtless many women have felt emboldened by Gilliganian accounts of moral difference: Speaking in a different voice is, after all, a big step up from silence.

The vision of women as sharers and carers is tempting in another way too. Despite much media blather about the popularity of the victim position, most people want to believe they act out of free will and choice. The uncomfortable truth that women have all too little of either is a difficult hurdle for feminists. Acknowledging the systematic oppression of women seems to deprive them of existential freedom, to turn them into puppets, slaves and Stepford wives. Deny it, and you can't make change. By arguing that the traditional qualities, tasks and ways of life of women are as important, valuable and serious as those of men (if not more so), Gilligan and others let women feel that nothing needs to change except the social valuation accorded to what they are already doing. It's a rationale of the status quo, which is why men like it, and a burst of grateful applause, which is why women like it. Men keep the power, but since power is bad, so much the worse for them.

Another rather curious appeal of difference feminism is that it offers a way for women to define themselves as independent of men. In a culture that sees women almost entirely in relation to men, this is no small achievement. Sex, for example—the enormous amount of female energy, money and time spent on beauty and fashion and romance, on attracting men and keeping them, in placating male power, strategizing ways around it or making it serve one's own ends—plays a minute role in these theories. You would never guess from Gilligan or Ruddick that men, individually and collectively, are signal beneficiaries of female nurturance, much less that this goes far to explain why society encourages nurturance in women. No, it is always children whom women are described as fostering and sacrificing for, or the community, or even other women—not husbands or lovers. It's as though wives cook dinner only for their kids, leaving the husband to raid the fridge on his own. And no doubt many women, quietly smoldering at their mate's refusal to share domestic labor, persuade themselves that they are serving only their children or their own preferences, rather than confront the inequality of their marriage.

The peaceful mother and the "relational" woman are a kinder, gentler, leftish version of "family values," and both are modern versions of the separate-spheres ideology of the Victorians. In the nineteenth century, too, some women tried to turn the ideology of sexual difference on its head and expand the moral claims of motherhood to include the public realm. Middle-class women became social reformers, abolitionists, temperance advocates, settlement workers and even took paying jobs in the "helping professions"—nursing, social work, teaching—which were perceived as extensions of women's domestic role although practiced mostly by single women. These women did not deny that their sex fitted them for the home, but argued that domesticity did not end at the front door of the house or confine itself to dusting (or telling the housemaid to dust). Even the vote could be cast as an extension of domesticity: Women, being more moral than men, would purify the government of vice and corruption, end war and make America safe for family life. (The persistence of this metaphor came home to me this summer when I attended a Women's Action Coalition demonstration during the Democratic National Convention. There—along with WAC's funny and ferocious all-in-black drum corps and contingents of hip downtown artists brandishing Barbara Kruger posters and shouting slogans like "We're Women! We're Angry! We're Not Going Shopping!"—was a trio of street performers with housecoats and kerchiefs over black catsuits and spiky hair, pushing brooms: Women will clean up government!)

Accepting the separate-spheres ideology had obvious advantages in an era when women were formally barred from higher education, political power and many jobs. But its defects are equally obvious. It defined all women by a single standard, and one developed by a sexist society. It offered women no way to enter professions that could not be defined as extensions of domestic roles—you could be a math teacher but not a mathematician, a secretary but not a sea captain—and no way to challenge any but the grossest abuses of male privilege. Difference feminists are making a similar bid for power on behalf of women today, and are caught in similar contradictions. Once again, women are defined by their family roles. Child-raising is seen as women's glory and joy and opportunity for self-transcendence, while Dad naps on the couch. Women who do not fit the stereotype are castigated as unfeminine—nurses nurture, doctors do not—and domestic labor is romanticized and sold to women as a badge of moral worth.

WHAT'S LOVE GOT TO DO WITH IT?

For all the many current explanations of perceived moral difference between the sexes, one hears remarkably little about the material basis of the family. Yet the motherhood and womanhood being valorized cannot be considered apart from questions of power, privilege and money. There is a reason a non-earning woman can proudly call herself a "wife and mother" and a non-earning man is just unemployed: the traditional female role, with its attendant real or imagined character traits, implies a male income. Middle-class women go to great lengths to separate themselves from this uncomfortable fact. One often hears women defend their decision to stay at home by heaping scorn on paid employment—caricatured as making widgets or pushing papers or dressing for success—and the difference feminists also like to distinguish between altruistic, poorly paid female jobs and the nasty, profitable ones performed by men. In *Prisoners of Men's Dreams*, Suzanne Gordon comes close to blaming the modest status of jobs like nursing and flight attending on women's entry into jobs like medicine and piloting, as if before the women's movement those female-dominated occupations were respected and rewarded. (Nurses should be glad the field no longer has a huge captive labor pool of women: The nursing shortage has led to dramatic improvements in pay, benefits and responsibility. Now nurses earn a man-sized income, and men are applying to nursing school in record numbers—exactly what Gordon wants.) It's all very well for some women to condemn others for "acting like men"—i.e., being ambitious, assertive, interested in money and power. But if their husbands did not "act like men," where would they be? Jean Bethke Elshtain, who strenuously resists the notion of gender ethics, nevertheless bemoans the loss to their communities when women leave volunteering and informal mutual support networks for paid employment. But money must come from somewhere; if women leave to men the job of earning the family income (an option fewer and fewer families can afford), they will be economically dependent on their husbands, a situation that, besides carrying obvious risks in an age of frequent divorce, weakens their bargaining position in the family and insures that men will largely control major decisions affecting family life.

Difference theorists would like to separate out the aspects of traditional womanhood that they approve of and speak only of those. But the part they like (caring, nurturing, intimacy) are inseparable from the parts they don't like (economic dependence and the subordination of women within the family). The difference theorists try to get around this by positing a world that contains two cultures—a female world of love and ritual and a male world of getting and spending and killing—which mysteriously share a single planet. That vison is expressed neatly in a recent pop-psychology title, *Men Are From Mars, Women Are From Venus*. It would be truer to say men are from Illinois and women are from Indiana—different, sure, but not in ways that have much ethical consequence.

The truth is, there is only one culture, and it shapes each sex in distinct but mutually dependent ways in order to reproduce itself. To the extent that the stereotypes are true, women have the "relational" domestic qualities *because* men have the "autonomous" qualities required to survive and prosper in modern capitalism. She needs a wage earner (even if she has a job, thanks to job discrimination), and he needs someone to mind his children, hold his hand and have his emotions for him. This—not, as Gordon imagines, some treason to her sex—explains why women who move into male sectors act very much like men: If they didn't, they'd find themselves back home in a jiffy. The same necessities and pressures affect them as affect the men who hold those jobs. Because we are in a transition period, in which many women were raised with modest expectations and much emphasis on the need to please others, social scientists who look for it can find traces of empathy, caring and so on in some women who have risen in the world of work and power, but when they tell us that women doctors will transform American medicine, or women executives will transform the corporate world, they are looking backward, not forward. If women really do enter the work force on equal terms with men—if they become 50 percent of all lawyers, politicians, car dealers and prison guards—they may be less sexist (although the example of Russian doctors, a majority of them female, is not inspiring to those who know about the brutal gynecological customs prevailing in the former U.S.S.R.). And they may bring with them a distinct set of manners, a separate social style. But they won't be, in some general way, more honest, kind, egalitarian, empathic or indifferent to profit. To argue otherwise is to believe that the reason factory owners bust unions, doctors refuse Medicaid patients and New York City school custodians don't mop the floors is because they are men.

The ultimate paradox of difference feminism is that it has come to the fore at a moment when the lives of the sexes are becoming less distinct than they ever have been in the West. Look at the decline of single-sex education (researchers may tout the benefits of all-female schools and colleges, but girls overwhelmingly choose coeducation); the growth of female athletics; the virtual abolition of virginity as a requirement for girls; the equalization of college-attendance rates of males and females; the explosion of employment for married women and mothers even of small children; the crossing of workplace gender lines by both females and males; the cultural pressure on men to be warm and nuturant fathers, to do at least some housework, to choose mates who are their equals in education and income potential.

It's fashionable these days to talk about the backlash against equality feminism—I talk this way myself when I'm feeling blue—but equality feminism has scored amazing successes. It has transformed women's expectations in every area of their lives. However, it has not yet transformed society to meet those expectations. The workplace still discriminates. On the home front few men practice egalitarianism, although many preach it; single mothers—and given the high divorce rate, every mother is potentially a single mother—lead incredibly difficult lives.

In this social context, difference feminism is essentially a way for women both to take advantage of equality feminism's success and to accommodate themselves to its limits. It appeals to particular kinds of women—those in the "helping professions" or the home, for example, rather than those who want to be bomber pilots or neurosurgeons or electricians. At the popular level, it encourages women who feel disadvantaged or demeaned by equality to direct their anger against women who have benefitted from it by thinking of them as gender traitors and of themselves as suffering for their virtue—thus the hostility of nurses toward female doctors, and of stay-at-home mothers toward employed mothers.

For its academic proponents, the appeal lies elsewhere: Difference feminism is a way to carve out a safe space in the face of academia's resistance to female advancement. It works much like multiculturalism, making an end-run around a static and discriminatory employment structure by creating an intellectual niche that can be filled only by members of the discriminated-against group. And like other forms of multiculturalism, it looks everywhere for its explanatory force—biology, psychology, sociology, cultural identity—*except* economics. The difference feminists cannot say that the differences between men and women are the result of their relative economic positions because to say that would be to move the whole discussion out of the realm of psychology and feel-good cultural pride and into the realm of a tough political struggle over the distribution of resources and justice and money.

Although it is couched in the language of praise, difference feminism is demeaning to women. It asks that women be admitted into public life and public discourse not because they have a right to be there but because they will improve them. Even if this were true, and not the wishful thinking I believe it to be, why should the task of moral and social transformation be laid on women's doorstep and not on everyone's—or, for that matter, on men's, by the you-broke-it-you-fix-it principle. Peace, the environment, a more humane workplace, economic justice, social support for children—these are issues that affect us all and are

everyone's responsibility. By promising to assume that responsibility, difference feminists
lay the groundwork for excluding women
again, as soon as it becomes clear that the
promise cannot be kept.

No one asks that other oppressed groups
win their freedom by claiming to be extra-
good. And no other oppressed group thinks it
must make such a claim in order to be accom-
modated fully and across the board by society.
For blacks and other racial minorities, it is
enough to want to earn a living, exercise one's
talents, get a fair hearing in the public forum.
Only for women is simple justice an insufficient argument. It is as though women don't
really believe they are entitled to full citizenship unless they can make a special claim to
virtue. Why isn't being human enough?

In the end, I didn't sign that peace petition,
although I was sorry to disappoint a woman I
like, and although I am very much for peace. I
decided to wait for a petition that welcomed my
signature as a person, an American, a citizen implicated, against my will, in war and the war
economy. I still think I did the right thing.

104

Wendy Kaminer

Feminism's Identity Crisis
(1993)

My favorite political moment of the 1960s was
a Black Panther rally in a quadrangle of Smith
College on a luxuriant spring day. Ramboesque
in berets and ammunition belts, several young
black males exhorted hundreds of young white
females to contribute money to Bobby Seale's
defense fund. I stood at the back of the crowd
watching yarn ties on blonde pony-tails bob-
bing up and down while the daughters of CEOs
nodded in agreement with the Panthers' attack
on the ruling class.

From *The Atlantic Monthly,* October 1993. Reprinted
by permission of the author.

It was all so girlish—or boyish, depending
on your point of view. Whatever revolution was
fomenting posed no apparent threat to gender
roles. Still, women who were not particularly
sensitive to chauvinism in the counterculture
or the typical fraternity planned to attend graduate or professional school and pursue careers
that would have been practically unthinkable
for them ten years earlier. Feminism was altering their lives as much as draft avoidance was
altering the lives of their male counterparts.

Today, three decades of feminism and one
Year of the Woman later, a majority of American women agree that feminism has altered
their lives for the better. In general, polls conducted over the past three years indicate strong
majority support for feminist ideals. But the
same polls suggest that a majority of women
hesitate to associate themselves with the movement. As Karlyn Keene, a resident fellow at the
American Enterprise Institute, has observed,
more than three quarters of American women
support efforts to "strengthen and change
women's status in society," yet only a minority,
a third at most, identify themselves as feminists.

Many feminists take comfort in these
polls, inferring substantial public support for
economic and political equality, and dismissing
women's wariness of the feminist label as a
mere image problem (attributed to unfair media portrayals of feminists as a strident minority of frustrated women). But the polls may
also adumbrate unarticulated ambivalence
about feminist ideals, particularly with respect
to private life. If widespread support for some
measure of equality reflects the way women
see, or wish to see, society, their unwillingness
to identify with feminism reflects the way they
see themselves, or wish to be seen by others.

To the extent that it challenges discrimination and the political exclusion of women, feminism is relatively easy for many women to embrace. It appeals to fundamental notions of
fairness; it suggests that social structures must
change but that individuals, particularly women,
may remain the same. For many women, femi-

nism is simply a matter of mommy-tracking, making sure that institutions accommodate women's familial roles, which are presumed to be essentially immutable. But to the extent that feminism questions those roles and the underlying assumptions about sexuality, it requires profound individual change as well, posing an unsettling challenge that well-adjusted people instinctively avoid. Why question norms of sex and character to which you've more or less successfully adapted?

Of course, the social and individual changes demanded by feminism are not exactly divisible. Of course, the expansion of women's professional roles and political power affects women's personality development. Still, many people manage to separate who they are in the workplace from who they are in bed, which is why feminism generates so much cognitive dissonance. As it addresses and internalizes this dissonance and women's anxiety about the label "feminism," as it embarks on a "third wave," the feminist movement today may suffer less from a mere image problem than from a major identity crisis.

It's difficult, of course, to generalize about how millions of American women imagine feminism and what role it plays in their lives. All one can say with certitude is that different women define and relate to feminism differently. The rest—much of this essay—is speculation, informed by conversations with editors of women's magazines (among the most reliable speculators about what women want), polling data, and ten years of experience studying feminist issues.

RESISTANCE TO THE LABEL

Robin Morgan, the editor in chief of *Ms.*, and Ellen Levine, the editor in chief of *Redbook,* two veterans of women's magazines and feminism, offer different views of feminism's appeal, each of which seem true, in the context of their different constituencies. Morgan sees a resurgent feminist movement and points to the formation of new feminist groups on campus

and intensified grass-roots activity by women addressing a range of issues, from domestic violence to economic revitalization. Ellen Levine, however, believes that for the middle-class family women who read *Redbook* (the average reader is a thirty-nine-year-old wage-earning mother), feminism is "a non-issue." She says, "They don't think about it; they don't talk about it." They may not even be familiar with the feminist term of art "glass ceiling," which feminists believe has passed into the vernacular. And they seem not to be particularly interested in politics. The surest way not to sell *Redbook* is to put a woman politician on the cover: the January, 1993, issue of *Good Housekeeping,* with Hillary Clinton on the cover, did poorly at the newsstands, according to Levine.

Editors at more upscale magazines—*Mirabella, Harper's Bazaar,* and *Glamour*—are more upbeat about their readers' interest in feminism, or at least their identification with feminist perspectives. Gay Bryant, *Mirabella*'s editor in chief, says, "We assume our readers are feminists with a small 'f.' We think of them as strong, independent, smart women; we think of them as pro-woman, although not all of them would define themselves as feminists politically." Betsy Carter, the executive editor of *Harper's Bazaar,* suggests that feminism has been assimilated into the culture of the magazine: "Feminism is a word that has been so absorbed in our consciousness that I don't isolate it. Asking me if I believe in feminism is like asking me if I believe in integration." Carter says, however, that women tend to be interested in the same stories that interest men: "Except for subjects like fly-fishing, it's hard to label something a man's story or a woman's story." In fact, she adds, "it seems almost obsolete to talk about women's magazines." Carter, a former editor at *Esquire,* recalls that *Esquire*'s readership was 40 percent female, which indicated to her that "women weren't getting what they needed from the women's magazines."

Ruth Whitney, the editor in chief of *Glamour,* might disagree. She points out that *Glamour* runs monthly editorials with a decidedly "feminist" voice that infuses the magazine. *Glamour* readers may or may not call themselves feminists, she says, but "I would call *Glamour* a mainstream feminist magazine, in its editorials, features, fashions, and consumerism." *Glamour* is also a pro-choice magazine; as Whitney stresses, it has long published pro-choice articles—more than any other mainstream women's magazine, according to her. And it is a magazine for which women seem to constitute the norm: "We use the pronoun 'she' when referring to a doctor, lawyer, whomever, and that does not go unnoticed by our readers."

Some women will dispute one underlying implication of Betsy Carter's remarks—that feminism involves assimilation, the merger of male and female spheres of interest. Some will dispute any claims to feminism by any magazine that features fashion. But whether *Ms.* readers would call *Harper's Bazaar, Mirabella,* and *Glamour* feminist magazines, or magazines with feminist perspectives, their readers apparently do, if Betsy Carter, Gay Bryant, and Ruth Whitney know their audiences.

Perhaps the confident feminist self-image of these up-scale magazines, as distinct from the cautious exploration of women's issues in the middle-class *Redbook,* confirms a canard about feminism—that it is the province of upper-income urban professional women. But *Ms.* is neither up-scale nor fashionable, and it's much too earnest to be sophisticated. Feminism—or, at least, support for feminist ideals—is not simply a matter of class, or even race.

Susan McHenry, a senior editor at *Working Woman* and the former executive editor of *Emerge,* a new magazine for middle-class African-Americans, senses in African-American women readers "universal embrace of women's rights and the notion that the women's movement has been helpful." Embrace of the women's movement, however, is equivocal. "If you start talking about the women's movement, you hear a lot about what we believe and what white women believe."

For many black women, devoting time and energy to feminist causes or feminist groups may simply not be a priority. Black women "feel both racism and sexism," McHenry believes, but they consider the fight for racial justice their primary responsibility and assume that white women will pay primary attention to gender issues. Leslie Adamson, the executive secretary to the president of Radcliffe College, offers a different explanation. She doesn't, in fact, "feel" sexism and racism equally: "Sex discrimination makes me indignant. Racial discrimination makes me enraged." Adamson is sympathetic to feminism and says that she has always "had a feminist mind." Still, she does not feel particularly oppressed as a woman. "I can remember only two instances of sex discrimination in my life," she says. "Once when I was in the sixth grade and wanted to take shop and they made me take home economics; once when I visited my husband's relatives in Trinidad and they wouldn't let me talk about politics. Racism has always affected me on a regular basis." Cynthia Bell, the communications director for Greater Southeast Healthcare System in Washington, D.C., offers a similar observation: "It wasn't until I graduated from college that I encountered sexual discrimination. I remember racial discrimination from the time I remember being myself."

Black women who share feminist ideals but associate feminism with white women sometimes prefer to talk about "womanism," a term endorsed by such diverse characters as Alice Walker (who is credited with coining it) and William Safire. Susan McHenry prefers to avoid using the term "women's movement" and talks instead about "women moving." She identifies with women "who are getting things done, regardless of what they call themselves." But unease with the term "feminism" has been a persistent concern in the feminist movement, whether the unease is attributed to racial divisions or to residual resistance to feminist ideals. It is, in fact, a complicated historical phenomenon that reflects feminism's successes as well as its failures.

"THE LESS TAINTED HALF"

That feminism has the power to expand women's aspirations and improve their lives without enlisting them as card-carrying feminists is a tribute to its strength as a social movement. Feminism is not dependent on ideological purity (indeed, it has always been a mixture of conflicting ideologies) or any formal organizational structure. In the nineteenth century feminism drew upon countless unaffiliated voluntary associations of women devoted to social reform or self-improvement. Late-twentieth-century feminism has similarly drawn upon consciousness-raising groups, professional associations, community-action groups, and the increased work-force participation of middle-class women, wrought partly by economic forces and a revolution in birth control. Throughout its 150-year history feminism has insinuated itself into the culture as women have sought to improve their status and increase their participation in the world outside the home. If women are moving in a generally feminist direction—toward greater rights and a fairer apportionment of social responsibilities—does it matter what they call themselves?

In the nineteenth century many, maybe most, women who took part in the feminist movement saw themselves as paragons of femininity. The great historic irony of feminism is that the supposed feminine virtues that justified keeping women at home—sexual purity, compassion, and a talent for nurturance—eventually justified their release from the home as well. Women were "the less tainted half of the race," Frances Willard, the president of the National Woman's Christian Temperance Union, declared, and thus were the moral guardians of society.

But in the long run, identifying feminism with femininity offered women limited liberation. The feminine weaknesses that were presumed to accompany feminine virtues justified the two-tier labor force that kept women out of executive positions and political office and out of arduous, high-paying manual-labor jobs (although women were never considered too weak to scrub floors). By using femininity as their passport to the public sphere, women came to be typecast in traditional feminine roles that they are still playing and arguing about today. Are women naturally better suited to parenting than men? Are men naturally better suited to waging war? Are women naturally more cooperative and compassionate, more emotive and less analytic, than men?

A great many American women (and men) still seem to answer these questions in the affirmative, as evidenced by public resistance to drafting women and the private reluctance of women to assign, and men to assume, equal responsibility for child care. Feminism, however, is popularly deemed to represent an opposing belief that men and women are equally capable of raising children and equally capable of waging war. Thus feminism represents, in the popular view, a rejection of femininity.

Feminists have long fought for day-care and family-leave programs, but they still tend to be blamed for the work-family conundrums. Thirty-nine percent of women recently surveyed by *Redbook* said that feminism had made it "harder" for women to balance work and family life. Thirty-two percent said that feminism made "no difference" to women's balancing act. This may reflect a failure of feminists to make child care an absolutely clear priority. It may also reflect the association of feminism with upper-income women like Zoë Baird, who can solve their child-care problems with relative ease. But, as Zoë Baird discovered, Americans are still ambivalent about women's roles within and outside the home.

Feminism and the careerism it entails are commonly regarded as a zero-sum game not just for women and men but for women and children as well, Ellen Levine believes: wage-earning mothers still tend to feel guilty about not being with their children and to worry that "the more women get ahead professionally, the more children will fall back." Their guilt does not seem to be assuaged by any number of studies showing that the children of wage-earning mothers fare as well as the children of full-time homemakers, Levine adds. It seems to dissipate only as children grow up and prosper.

Feminists who dismiss these worries as backlash risk trivializing the inevitable stresses confronting wage-earning mothers (even those with decent day care). Feminists who respond to these worries by suggesting that husbands should be more like wives and mothers are likely to be considered blind or hostile to presumptively natural sex differences that are still believed to underlie traditional gender roles.

To the extent that it advocates a revolution in gender roles, feminism also comes as a reproach to women who lived out the tradition, especially those who lived it out unhappily. Robin Morgan says, "A woman who's been unhappily married for forty years and complains constantly to her friends, saying 'I've got to get out of this,' might stand up on a talk show and say feminism is destroying the family."

THE WAGES OF EQUALITY

Ambivalence about equality sometimes seems to plague the feminist movement almost as much today as it did ten years ago, when it defeated the Equal Rights Amendment. Worth noting is that in the legal arena feminism has met with less success than the civil-rights movement. The power of the civil-rights movement in the 1960s was the power to demonstrate the gap between American ideals of racial equality and the American reality for African-Americans. We've never had the same professed belief in sexual equality: federal equal-employment law has always treated racial discrimination more severely than sex discrimination, and so has the Supreme Court. The Court has not extended to women the same constitutional protection it has extended to racial minorities, because a majority of justices have never rejected the notion that some degree of sex discrimination is only natural.

The widespread belief in equality demonstrated by polls is a belief in equality up to a point—the point where women are drafted and men change diapers. After thirty years of the contemporary women's movement, equal-rights feminism is still considered essentially abnormal. Ellen Levine notes that middle-class family women sometimes associate feminism with lesbianism, which has yet to gain middle-class respectability. Homophobia is not entirely respectable either, however, so it may not be expressed directly in polls or conversations; but it has always been a subtext of popular resistance to feminism. Feminists have alternately been accused of hating men and of wanting to be just like them.

There's some evidence that the fear of feminism as a threat to female sexuality may be lessening: 77 percent of women recently surveyed by *Redbook* answered "yes" to the question "Can a woman be both feminine and a feminist?" But they were answering a question in the abstract. When women talk about why they don't identify with feminists, they often talk about not wanting to lose their femininity. To the extent that an underlying belief in feminine virtues limits women to feminine roles, as it did a hundred years ago, this rejection of the feminist label is a rejection of full equality. In the long run, it matters what women call themselves.

Or does it? Ironically, many self-proclaimed feminists today express some of the same ambivalence about changing gender roles as the "I'm not a feminist, but . . ." women (". . . but I believe in equal opportunity or family leave or reproductive choice"). The popular image of feminism as a more or less unified quest for androgynous equality, promoted by the feminists' nemesis Camille Paglia, is at least ten years out of date.

THE COMFORTS OF GILLIGANISM

Central to the dominant strain of feminism today is the belief, articulated by the psychologist Carol Gilligan, that women share a different voice and different moral sensibilities. Gilligan's work—notably *In a Different Voice* (1982)—has been effectively attacked by other feminist scholars, but criticisms of it have not been widely disseminated, and it has passed with ease into the vernacular. In a modern-day version of Victorian True Womanhood, feminists and also some anti-feminists pay tribute to women's superior nurturing and relational skills and their "general ethic of caring." Sometimes feminists add parenthetically that differences between men and women may well be attributable to culture, not nature. But the qualification is moot. Believers in gender difference tend not to focus on changing the cultural environment to free men and women from stereotypes, as equal-rights feminists did twenty years ago; instead they celebrate the feminine virtues.

It was probably inevitable that the female solidarity at the base of the feminist movement would foster female chauvinism. All men are jerks, I might agree on occasion, over a bottle of wine. But that's an attitude, not an analysis, and only a small minority of separatist feminists turn it into an ideology. Gilliganism addresses the anxiety that is provoked by that attitude— the anxiety about compromising their sexuality which many feminists share with nonfeminists.

Much as they dislike admitting it, feminists generally harbor or have harbored categorical anger toward men. Some would say that such anger is simply an initial stage in the development of a feminist consciousness, but it is also an organizing tool and a fact of life for many women who believe they live in a sexist world. And whether or not it is laced with anger, feminism demands fundamental changes in relations between the sexes and the willingness of feminists to feel like unnatural women and be treated as such. For heterosexual women, feminism can come at a cost. Carol Gilligan's work valorizing women's separate emotional sphere helped make it possible for feminists to be angry at men and challenge their hegemony without feeling unwomanly. Nancy Rosenblum, a professor of political science at Brown Univer-

sity, says that Gilliganism resolved the conflict for women between feminism and femininity by "de-eroticizing it." Different-voice ideology locates female sexuality in maternity, as did Victorian visions of the angel in the house. In its simplest form, the idealization of motherhood reduces popular feminism to the notion that women are nicer than men.

Women are also widely presumed to be less warlike than men. "Women bring love; that's our role," one woman explained at a feminist rally against the Gulf War which I attended; it seemed less like a rally than a revival meeting. Women shared their need "to connect" and "do relational work." They recalled Jane Addams, the women's peace movement between the two world wars, and the Ban the Bomb marches of thirty years ago. They suggested that pacifism was as natural to women as childbirth, and were barely disconcerted by the presence of women soldiers in the Gulf. Military women were likely to be considered self-hating or male-identified or the hapless victims of a racist, classist economy, not self-determined women with minds and voices all their own. The war was generally regarded as an allegory of male supremacy; the patriarch Bush was the moral equivalent of the patriarch Saddam Hussein. If only men would listen to women, peace, like a chador, would enfold us.

In part, the trouble with True Womanhood is its tendency to substitute sentimentality for thought. Constance Buchanan, an associate dean of the Harvard Divinity School, observes that feminists who believe women will exercise authority differently often haven't done the hard work of figuring out how they will exercise authority at all. "Many feminists have an almost magical vison of institutional change," Buchanan says. "They've focused on gaining access but haven't considered the scale and complexity of modern institutions, which will not necessarily change simply by virtue of their presence."

Feminists who claim that women will "make a difference" do, in fact, often argue their case simply by pointing to the occasional female manager who works by consensus, paying little attention to hierarchy and much attention to her employees' feelings—assuming that such women more accurately represent their sex than women who favor unilateral decision-making and tend not to nurture employees. In other words, different-voice feminists often assume their conclusions: the many women whose characters and behavior contradict traditional models of gender difference (Margaret Thatcher is the most frequently cited example) are invariably dismissed as male-identified. . . .

FEMINISM SUCCUMBS TO FEMININITY

The feminist drive for equal rights was supposed to have been revitalized last year, and it's true that women were politically activated and made significant political gains. It's clear that women are moving, but in what direction? What is the women's movement all about?

Vying for power today are poststructural feminists (dominant in academia in recent years), political feminists (office-holders and lobbyists), different-voice feminists, separatist feminists (a small minority), pacifist feminists, lesbian feminists, careerist feminists, liberal feminists (who tend also to be political feminists), anti-porn feminists, eco-feminists, and womanists. These are not, of course, mutually exclusive categories, and this is hardly an exhaustive list. New Age feminists and goddess workshoppers widen the array of alternative truths. And the newest category of feminism, personal-development feminism, led nominally by Gloria Steinem, puts a popular feminist spin on deadeningly familiar messages about recovering from addiction and abuse, liberating one's inner child, and restoring one's self-esteem.

The marriage of feminism and the phenomenally popular recovery movement is arguably the most disturbing (and potentially influential) development in the feminist movement today. It's based partly on a shared concern about child abuse, nominally a left-wing analogue to right-wing anxiety about the family. There's an emerging alliance of anti-pornography and anti-violence feminists with therapists who diagnose and treat child abuse, including "ritual abuse" and "Satanism" (often said to be linked to pornography). Feminism is at risk of being implicated in the unsavory business of hypnotizing suspected victims of abuse to help them "retrieve" their buried childhood memories. Gloria Steinem has blithely praised the important work of therapists in this field without even a nod to the potential for, well, abuse when unhappy, suggestible people who are angry at their parents are exposed to suggestive hypnotic techniques designed to uncover their histories of victimization.

But the involvement of some feminists in the memory-retrieval industry is only one manifestation of a broader ideological threat posed to feminism by the recovery movement. Recovery, with its absurdly broad definitions of addiction and abuse, encourages people to feel fragile and helpless. Parental insensitivity is classed as child abuse, along with parental violence, because all suffering is said to be equal (meaning entirely subjective); but that's appropriate only if all people are so terribly weak that a cross word inevitably has the destructive force of a blow. Put very simply, women need a feminist movement that makes them feel strong.

Enlisting people in a struggle for liberation without exaggerating the ways in which they're oppressed is a challenge for any civil-rights movement. It's a particularly daunting one for feminists, who are still arguing among themselves about whether women are oppressed more by nature or by culture. For some feminists, strengthening women is a matter of alerting them to their natural vulnerabilities.

There has always been a strain of feminism that presents women as frail and naturally victimized. As it was a hundred years ago, feminist victimism is today most clearly expressed in sexuality debates—about pornography, prostitution, rape, and sexual harassment. Today sexual violence is a unifying focal point for women who do and women who do not call themselves feminists: 84 percent of women surveyed by *Redbook* considered "fighting violence against women" to be "very important." (Eighty-two percent rated workplace equality and 54 percent rated abortion rights as very important.) Given this pervasive, overriding concern about violence and our persistent failure to address it effectively, victimism is likely to become an important organizing tool for feminism in the 1990s.

Feminist discussions of sexual offenses often share with the recovery movement the notion that, again, there are no objective measures of suffering: all suffering is said to be equal, in the apparent belief that all women are weak. Wage-earning women testify to being "disabled" by sexist remarks in the workplace. College women testify to the trauma of being fondled by their dates. The term "date rape," like the term "addiction," no longer has much literal, objective meaning. It tends to be used figuratively, as a metaphor signifying that all heterosexual encounters are inherently abusive of women. The belief that in a male-dominated culture that has "normalized" rape, "yes" can never really mean "yes" has been popularized by the anti-pornography feminists Andrea Dworkin and Catharine MacKinnon. (Dworkin devoted an entire book to the contention that intercourse is essentially a euphemism for rape.) But only five years ago Dworkin and MacKinnon were leaders of a feminist fringe. Today, owning partly to the excesses of multiculturalism and the exaltation of victimization, they're leaders in the feminist mainstream.

Why is feminism helping to make women feel so vulnerable? Why do some young women on Ivy League campuses, among the most privileged people on the globe, feel oppressed? Why does feminist victimology seem so much more pervasive among middle- and upper-class whites than among lower-income women, and girls, of color? Questions like these need to be aired by feminists. But in some feminism circles it is heresy to suggest that there are degrees of suffering and oppression, which need to be kept in perspective. It is heresy to suggest that being raped by your date may not be as traumatic or terrify-

ing as being raped by a stranger who breaks into your bedroom in the middle of the night. It is heresy to suggest that a woman who has to listen to her colleagues tell stupid sexist jokes has a lesser grievance than a woman who is physically accosted by her supervisor. It is heresy, in general, to question the testimony of self-proclaimed victims of date rape or harassment, as it is heresy in a twelve-step group to question claims of abuse. All claims of suffering are sacred and presumed to be absolutely true. It is a primary article of faith among many feminists that women don't lie about rape, ever; they lack the dishonesty gene. Some may call this feminism, but it looks more like femininity to me.

Blind faith in women's pervasive victimization also looks a little like religion. "Contemporary feminism is a new kind of religion," Camille Paglia complains, overstating her case with panache. But if her metaphor begs to be qualified, it offers a nugget of truth. Feminists choose among competing denominations with varying degrees of passion, and belief; what is gospel to one feminist is a working hypothesis to another. Still, like every other ideology and "ism"—from feudalism to capitalism to communism to Freudianism—feminism is for some a revelation. Insights into the dynamics of sexual violence are turned into a metaphysic. Like people in recovery who see addiction lurking in all our desires, innumerable feminists see men's oppression of women in all our personal and social relations. Sometimes the pristine earnestness of this theology is unrelenting. Feminism lacks a sense of black humor.

Of course, the emerging orthodoxy about victimization does not infect all or even most feminist sexuality debates. Of course, many feminists harbor heretical thoughts about lesser forms of sexual misconduct. But few want to be vilified for trivializing sexual violence and collaborating in the abuse of women.

THE ENEMY WITHIN

The example of Camille Paglia is instructive. She is generally considered by feminists to be practically pro-rape, because she has offered this advice to young women: don't get drunk at fraternity parties, don't accompany boys to their rooms, realize that sexual freedom entails sexual risks, and take some responsibility for your behavior. As Paglia says, this might once have been called common sense (it's what some of our mothers told us); today it's called blaming the victim.

Paglia is right: it ought to be possible to condemn date rape without glorifying the notion that women are helpless to avoid it. But not everyone can risk dissent. A prominent feminist journalist who expressed misgivings to me about the iconization of Anita Hill chooses not to be identified. Yet Anita Hill is a questionable candidate for feminist sainthood, because she was, after all, working for Clarence Thomas voluntarily, apparently assisting him in what feminists and other civil-rights activists have condemned as the deliberate nonenforcement of federal equal-employment laws. Was she too helpless to know better? Feminists are not supposed to ask.

It is, however, not simply undue caution or peer pressure that squelches dissent among feminists. Many are genuinely ambivalent about choosing sides in sexuality debates. It is facile, in the context of the AIDS epidemic, to dismiss concern about date rape as "hysteria." And it takes hubris (not an unmitigated fault) to suggest that some claims of victimization are exaggerated, when many are true. The victimization of women as a class by discriminatory laws and customs, and a collective failure to take sexual violence seriously, are historical reality. Even today women are being assaulted and killed by their husbands and boyfriends with terrifying regularity. When some feminists overdramatize minor acts of sexual misconduct or dogmatically insist that we must always believe the woman, it is sometimes hard to blame them, given the historical presumption that women lie about rape routinely, that wife abuse is a marital squabble, that date rape and marital rape are not real rape, and that sexual harassment is cute.

Feminists need critics like Paglia who are not afraid to be injudicious. Paglia's critiques of feminism are, however, flawed by her limited knowledge of feminist theory. She doesn't even realize what she has in common with feminists she disdains—notably Carol Gilligan and the attorney and anti-pornography activist Catharine MacKinnon. Both Paglia and MacKinnon suggest that sexual relations are inextricably bound up with power relations; both promote a vison of male sexuality as naturally violent and cruel. But while Paglia celebrates sexual danger, MacKinnon wants to legislate even the thought of it away. Both Paglia and Gilligan offer idealized notions of femininity. But Gilligan celebrates gender stereotypes while Paglia celebrates sex archetypes. Paglia also offers a refreshingly tough, erotic vison of female sexuality to counteract the pious maternalism of In a Different Voice.

To the extent that there's a debate between Paglia and the feminist movement, it's not a particularly thoughtful one, partly because it's occurring at second hand, in the media. There are thoughtful feminist debates being conducted in academia, but they're not widely heard. Paglia is highly critical of feminist academics who don't publish in the mainstream; but people have a right to choose their venues, and besides, access to the mainstream press is not easily won. Still, their relative isolation is a problem for feminist scholars who want to influence public policy. To reach a general audience they have to depend on journalists to draw upon and sometimes appropriate their work.

In the end feminism, like other social movements, is dependent on the vagaries of the marketplace. It's not that women perceive feminism just the way Time and Newsweek present it to them. They have direct access only to the kind and quantity of feminist speech deemed marketable. Today the concept of a feminist movement is considered to have commercial viability once again. The challenge now is to make public debates about feminist issues as informed as they are intense.

It's not surprising that we haven't achieved equality; we haven't even defined it. Nearly thirty years after the onset of the modern feminist movement, we still have no consensus on what nature dictates to men and women and demands of law. Does equality mean extending special employment rights to pregnant women, or limiting the Sixth Amendment rights of men standing trial for rape, or suspending the First Amendment rights of men who read pornography? Nearly thirty years after the passage of landmark federal civil-rights laws, we still have no consensus on the relationship of individual rights to social justice. But, feminists might wonder, why did rights fall out of favor with progressives just as women were in danger of acquiring them?

The most effective backlash against feminism almost always comes from within, as women either despair of achieving equality or retreat from its demands. The confident political resurgence of women today will have to withstand a resurgent belief in women's vulnerabilities. Listening to the sexuality debates, I worry that women feel so wounded. Looking at feminism, I wonder at the public face of femininity.

105

BELL HOOKS, GLORIA STEINEM, URVASHI VAID, AND NAOMI WOLF

Let's Get Real about Feminism—The Backlash, the Myths, the Movement (1993)

[Panel Discussion]

Naomi Wolf: I wanted to know why younger women often do not identify with the word "feminism," so I began asking on college campuses, "What is your problem with this word?"

What I found is confirmed by research that feminist organizations have been working on:

From *Ms.*, September/October 1993. Reprinted by permission of *Ms.* Magazine, copyright 1993.

more women support the women's rights agenda than are willing to identify themselves as feminists.

So what has alienated so many women? The alienation that I encountered was influenced by the media and the backlash, but not entirely. There are some things that we could be doing better.

bell hooks: There is also denial. To me, the essence of feminism is opposition to patriarchy and to sexist oppression. A lot of women who go for the notion of equal rights cannot go for the notion of opposing patriarchy, because that means a fundamental opposition to the culture as a whole. That's more scary to people. When young women say to me that they don't want to identify with feminism because of all the negative things it stands for, I think there's a real fear of opposing men when men are sexists.

Gloria Steinem: The real opposition comes when you say, "I'm a feminist, I'm for equal power for all women," which is a revolution, instead of "I'm for equal rights for me," which is a reform.

Urvashi Vaid: One other reason people resist calling themselves feminists is because of the association of feminism with lesbianism. Most people are homophobic. No poll is going to show that people love gays and lesbians—yet.

N.W.: A lot of the women I speak to actually aren't homophobic. But they are resistant to feminism because the word is synonymous with lesbianism in many parts of the country. We are asking them not to be afraid of the stigma attached to feminism by homophobia, to identify themselves in a way that even gay people in those regions have trouble doing because it can mean loss of their jobs. I am by no means justifying this, I'm just saying that it's not enough to say, "They are simply homophobic."

U.V.: Our feminist leaders do make the connection that the media and the backlash against women labeled every strong woman a dyke. But we need more heterosexual women to come out and talk about this and say, "Look, to be a feminist does not necessarily mean that you're a lesbian, although there's nothing

wrong with being a lesbian and a feminist."
What if instead of running away from it, we
took it head-on and created the space for those
women that Naomi is talking about to feel a little more safe and comfortable?

b.h.: But there are also lots of lesbians who
don't identify as feminists, and there are lots of
young lesbians who are just as turned off to the
idea of feminism as are young heterosexual
women. There are a lot of women who feel they
can't identify with feminism. If you go house to
house and ask people, "Do you think women
should be beaten by men?" most will say no. But
when you say to them, "In order to change that,
we have to challenge patriarchy and male domination," then the resistance comes in. Because
there's a tremendous gap between the values
people hold around gender and the actual struggle that people have to go through in order to
make those values a part of daily life.

G.S.: One of the ways to make change is to
look at the reality of the alternative: If you
don't call yourself a feminist, how much easier
does that actually make your life? I think the alternative to being a feminist is, in some sense,
being a masochist. Either we're whole human
beings or we're not.

And on the question of lesbianism: we have
to make lesbianism an honorable choice, because until it is, all women who don't conform
will be held back by this word.

But there's something much deeper—the
politicization of sexuality—which says that all
sex that doesn't take place inside patriarchal
marriage and isn't directed toward having children is wrong. That's what the right wing is saying. They're very clear and we have to get clarity on our side.

Our common cause comes from our mu-
tual need to depoliticize sexuality, to free it.

N.W.: I do think it's my job as a straight
woman to talk about homophobia. I'm constantly on the receiving end of the heterosexual
benefit-of-the-doubt. I continually experience
how much more credibility one automatically
gets by fucking men. There are things that I'm
allowed to say because I have a boyfriend.

But I also have heard straight women say, "I
am intimidated to go to feminist meetings because I feel like there's this judgment against me
because I sleep with the enemy." It is very clear
to me that I haven't slept with my enemies.
Straight women are not facing the kind of entrenched, gutter discrimination that lesbians are,
but there's too much sexual judgment going on.

b.h.: I think that this is really racialized,
Naomi. I don't hear women of color saying "I
can't go to feminist things because of lesbianism." I hear them saying, "I cannot go to feminist things because of the racism of white
women and because the movements don't meet
my needs."

I see a fundamental questioning of feminism growing among women of color that
doesn't have to do with sexuality. And a lot of
lesbian women of color are at the forefront of
that questioning.

N.W.: Let me make it clear, I didn't say that
these women weren't getting involved because
of lesbianism. I said they were scared to get involved because they were afraid that their own
sexuality would be judged.

U.V.: bell, I think you have a point when
you bring in the race dynamic. And I wonder,
Naomi, who are the women you are talking to?

N.W.: Overwhelmingly white women in
some communities but not in others. Obviously,
I'm not a social scientist. I'm just listening, and I
listen particularly acutely to women of color, to
gauge what the differences are, but the dissatisfaction that I've heard cuts across demographic
lines; it is really not class or race specific.

b.h.: But you don't acknowledge that there
are some of us whose constituencies are much
more people of color.

N.W.: Can I just follow-up? Among the
women I heard from, what they don't like
about feminism is the sense that it is inaccessible. Their feminism isn't coming from the
movement: they're getting their feminism from
mainstream culture.

b.h.: The real question is one of literacy. As
long as we have a feminist movement in which
the bulk of our ideas is shared only through

books, we will never have a mass-based movement. We have got to have other kinds of strategies. I would like us to name what some of those strategies might be, because it's not enough just to make a critique.

For example, I know that a disproportionate number of black people in the U.S. are not in colleges. If I go somewhere to talk, I will call a restaurant or club where black people hang out and say to them: "This is who I am and this is what I do. I'd like to come and sit in your restaurant for a couple of hours, and anybody who wants to, can come and talk with me about what feminism is."

They don't have to pay anything. They don't have to be in a large hall of people using words they don't understand. They can argue, because, let's face it, it takes more than just hearing a lecture and asking your one question. I'm for a door-to-door movement to educate people about feminism.

G.S.: I always wanted to radicalize all the Avon ladies, send them out door-to-door selling feminism.

U.V.: I always wanted the violence against women movement not to be so focused on image and representation, but to focus on community and neighborhood organizing, dealing with violence block by block.

G.S.: This is the single most crucial thing: a geographically based women's movement.

We're facing an ultra-right-wing movement that has thousands of fundamentalist churches, with voting operations in the basement of every one. The women's movement needs grass-roots, local structures that don't depend totally on national groups. Although we also need lots more organizers crisscrossing the country helping to create local groups.

b.h.: I have to say that I don't use the term "women's movement"—I believe that men must be part of the feminist movement, and they must feel that they have a major role to play in the eradication of sexism. The term "women's movement" reproduces the notion that somehow feminism is this plantation that only women should labor on.

The major advocacy I do in black communities these days is convincing folks that feminism as a critique of masculinity can be life-affirming for black men. I can quote the statistics about black male homicide and say, "Patriarchy is part of this, and if you really care about black men, as an endangered species—a word I don't like to use but one that resonates for people—then feminism has something to offer black men in the struggle for their lives." As long as feminism gets identified as "It's about women," people think: "I don't have to listen. I don't have to read. I don't have to engage."

U.V.: I wanted to return to that question about the arenas in which we do feminist work. I think that one of the critiques that I would make of the gay movement and of the women's movement is that we've become very collapsed into a legislative and political arena. Neighborhood organizing is exactly what we need. It's almost like a return to consciousness-raising, but with more of an action component. An organizing activity that brings people together.

N.W.: A lot of women don't want to spend their lives being activists and resent the idea that feminism has to tell them how to run their lives. They would like to have a feminism that has a line-item veto, so they don't feel they have to buy the whole package. They would like to contribute toward raising the status of women in a way that they can control. Take, for instance, the Ms. Foundation's idea of having a bank card or a credit card, and every time you use it, money goes to women's organizations. A lot of the women I hear from say: "Yes, give me something that's under my control, that doesn't have to run my life. Make it easy. I've got a lot of other demands in my life." I think there's room for that as well as grass-roots activism.

G.S.: Well, what you're talking about *is* grass-roots activism, because it empowers the individual. But I would argue for small collective groups in addition to individual acts. I think the common theme here is that feminism has been made to seem hard, and women's lives are already incredibly hard.

U.V.: I think the problem is that we're not framing the issues that women care about in ways that they can hear. For example, if I say, "I want you to be an activist," most people are going to say, "Get out of my life." But if I say, "You know, the school board is talking about this curriculum that is going to affect your three kids," a lot of women are going to care about that. Or, if I say, "The cost of health care premiums disproportionately affects you, because as a woman you are being charged more." If we break it down in a different way, then we can reach women. That's what the right wing does. It successfully creates a way for women to feel they can affect the things they care about.

b.h.: But one thing that the Right does not do is talk just about women. We also have to talk about women and men and families, and as long as we identify feminism solely with women, we lose those women who already believe that we really are anti-male, anti-family.

To change the nature of feminism, we've got to change how we talk about it. I never say, "Feminism is about women." I say, "Feminism is about everybody in this room. It's about children and their right to be cared for." Automatically, that makes people say, "Oh, I thought feminism was just about women and abortion." So I say, "Well it is about those things, but it's also about 'How do you raise your son?'" These are the big issues among working-class people and among black people specifically. And that's where I see feminism losing ground.

G.S.: Well, we spent the first 20 years demonstrating that women can do what men can do, and most of the country believes that now. But we have not demonstrated that men can do the reverse—what women can do.

Until children are raised by men as well as by women, until men aren't burdened by this compulsion to be in control or even violent, we won't have change. My last book ended up being for men, too. And there are more men in my audiences now than ever before. But the responses that are most moving to me still come from women who are saying, in various ways,

"Oh, I didn't think I was strong enough to be a feminist." It's as if it's a burden.

b.h.: I want people to advocate feminism as a politics. Feminism is perceived as a lifestyle, as something you become rather than something you *do*. I'm concerned about getting people to think of it as a movement to change something. It's not just a movement about women getting equal pay, which I believe masses of people are more willing to deal with. And that's why, Naomi, I get scared when I hear you say that people tell you, "I don't want to be an activist."

N.W.: Let me make a distinction. What they want is a way to stick up for women's rights that is not dictated to them and that comes organically out of their own experience. The backlash years drove us, or certainly drove me, into feeling embattled and needing to huddle together against the inhospitable forces out there. And this created a subculture within feminism. We have to end that.

b.h.: I don't think the backlash created a subculture. Bourgeois feminism started out creating that subculture by not choosing issues that embraced a mass-based group of people; it automatically became a subculture based on who decided which concerns—

N.W.: What issues are you talking about?

b.h.: Issues like abortion. To most women of color that I talk with, abortion is not considered the major reproductive rights issue—

G.S.: But the issue was not only abortion. It was also forced sterilization.

b.h.: But it quickly became abortion. Why?

G.S.: Because of the informed consent guidelines about sterilization in California, thanks mostly to Chicana activism. The abortion issue—the canceling out of men's sperm—became much more politicized.

b.h.: It didn't just become more politicized. A lot more privileged white women were interested in abortion than in sterilization. If you look at who wrote the books, who wrote the articles, people wrote about their own issues.

G.S.: I don't dispute that, but abortion that is illegal or unfunded does punish poor women more than middle-class women. Also the sterilization issue did come first, but the racist right wing focused on eliminating abortion because white women were using both it and contraception more. As they put it, "The white race is committing suicide," and abortion moved forward much more quickly.

U.V.: bell, if you say bourgeois feminist values have steered the movement in a certain direction for the last 20 years, my question is: How do we then steer it in a different direction?

b.h.: It's not just bourgeois white feminism. It's also those strands of feminism that the mass media pick up on. Let's face it, working-class lesbians of all ethnicities create a lot of feminist theory, but the mass media didn't focus on it. In order to change feminism, we also have to change who mass media talk to and what they say about us. Most people learn about feminism from the mass media, not from reading books by feminist thinkers.

N.W.: So, how do we fix that? Women have to realize their own power as consumers of media and have to force a readers' uprising in order to get decent representation and coverage in the mainstream press.

G.S.: It will never work with women's magazines. Readers don't control them, advertisers do.

b.h.: Okay, why don't we have commercials? Yes, I know, commercials are about money. That's why we need a feminist party, because that's the only way that we're going to amass the funding to make those interventions in mass media.

U.V.: Perhaps it's time for the separate single-issue feminist organizations to come together into the broader feminist vision that we're talking about—and buy that 30-minute infomercial.

N.W.: It has to happen now in order to open up the imagery of feminism. We often miss the fact that a lot of feminism has moved out into the world, where it's not labeled but

it's happening: in women's magazines, on television, in movies. There's a huge, strong, thriving feminist current in these things waiting for us to tap. Within all of these giant conglomerates, there are dozens and dozens of very powerful sympathizers who would be willing to put their clout on the line to redeem the image of feminism, if we worked on this together.

G.S.: I'd like to step back a minute and say that the right wing didn't trust the mainstream media. It didn't sit around waiting for mainstream media to interpret it correctly. It created its own media, its own "lay your hands on the television set and commune with God" show. It had its own newsletters. It has its own "800" and "900" numbers. And meanwhile, we goody-two-shoes here have been trying to influence the mainstream media. We have to construct our own. Do it house by house, knocking on the doors, just like they do. We have to be both inside and outside the system—

b.h.: But we have to be wary. As a fanatical reader of fashion magazines, I see a lot of ads and a lot of articles that bring up feminist issues. But it's also clear that they individualize and privatize these issues.

G.S.: They put the burden right back on the individual again.

U.V.: I'm a little overwhelmed by the different levels on which we're talking. I don't even know which one to leap into. On the media, I think it's problematic for us to rely on the goodwill of essentially capitalist organizations. But I want to support Naomi on the fact that there are more receptive people in the mainstream media now.

N.W.: We don't realize our own power. What frustrates me is that the girls who most need and deserve these ideas don't read *The Village Voice*. They don't read *Ms.* magazine. They read *Seventeen* and *Glamour*. And yet, very often I am criticized by women who are very committed to feminism for going into the mainstream press.

b.h.: Who here doesn't believe that we should use all the vehicles available to us? But I think we also have to be honest about who those vehicles are available to. I have written eight feminist books. None of the magazines that have talked about your book, Naomi, have ever talked about my books at all. Now, that's not because there aren't ideas in my books that have universal appeal. It's because the issue that you raised in *The Beauty Myth* is still about beauty. We have to acknowledge that all of us do not have equal access. We should use these things, but at the same time we have to talk about alternatives, particularly since there are masses of people who don't even have access to magazines and books.

G.S.: I think we had some tactics in the beginning that we should rethink and reconstitute. One is that we went around in rather intimidating groups to see the editorial boards of major newspapers, of local television stations, and we did this regularly. We also monitored these folks. We refused to lecture one at a time. We refused to lecture without racial diversity. We just wouldn't go.

U.V.: I feel that two things happened. One was that each front became particularized into its own organization. Reproductive rights became abortion rights organizations, rape crisis centers came into existence, feminist theory went into the academy. The second was that the broad movement got more and more focused on electoral political work: electing women, organizing the vote. The direction that needs to come back into the movement is the coming together of the separated.

When I look at the national organizations that are feminist, the one that comes the closest to being the broadest based in terms of issues and strategies is the National Organization for Women. And because of its reputation for being a predominantly white middle-class organization, it's still problematic.

b.h.: Where feminism has the most potential to convert and inspire people is in its effort to speak to the needs of everyday life. This became a big issue for me when one of my sisters said: "This is what my husband does to me in front of the kids. He tells me to shut up. He

puts me down. You're the feminist. Tell me what I can do to change this." That made me realize how rarely feminist theory provides any actual strategies for altering everyday lives.

G.S.: But we actually did: that's where we started out.

b.h.: But where are our manuals that tell how to do it?

G.S.: A lot of them were written in the wind.

b.h.: It's linked with what Urv was saying. The two central issues—a national strategy and a local strategy. I see people converted when they take some feminist idea and are able to utilize it in their daily lives. That goes back to Naomi's group of people saying, "We don't want something forced on us. We want something that we can use and that we can shape and redefine according to our needs."

G.S.: But that's where feminism came from. And that's exactly what we lost.

N.W.: Just take the idea of dissent. This is a huge issue. The media space given to us has been so limited and so full of caricature, there's been a real dearth of public debate.

U.V.: We need public debate because our issues get so polarized.

b.h.: We need debate because one of the perceptions of feminism is—

N.W.: We all think alike?

b.h.: Not only that, but a lot of women left feminism because they felt that if you dissented from what was seen as the dominant viewpoint, you could have no voice, you could have no presence. So, people didn't want to come to feminist gatherings anymore.

G.S.: We are so conscious of the fact that every time we disagree on something, somebody comes along and says, "Look, those two women can't agree."

I just had a relevant experience. I went to Texas and campaigned against Kay Bailey Hutchinson, the new senator. I campaigned against her because she's supported by Rush Limbaugh, and she opposes nearly every feminism issue there is. I'm happy she's got a job, but if the job is representing other women, then she ought to at least represent issues that women care about. So, I got lots of editorials against me because I was campaigning against a woman.

N.W.: It was because you called her a "man in drag."

G.S.: No, I called her a "female impersonator." She is.

I am too—in my manners because I'm a 1950s person.

But I got a lot of shit for that, and I was feeling very misunderstood until it dawned on me that if I had supported her, I would have been criticized for supporting her only because she is a woman. There is nothing we can do that the establishment is going to say is right, so we might as well do what we believe in.

b.h.: If we had a discussion or a public framework where we said, "part of the feminist movement is to encourage intellectual dissent among women of all classes and men of all classes. . . ." That hasn't been the image of feminism. The image has been that there's a party line.

G.S.: But that was not the reality of feminism. We came out of small groups where the whole point was that you listened with respect to other people who spoke from the "I." You didn't try to tell somebody else what to do. You didn't try to judge them. You just each spoke the truth—

b.h.: I don't think that's dissent, Gloria. I think that is something that turns me off.

G.S.: It's respect for individual experience.

b.h.: That's exactly the model that nauseates me. I hate being in a room where we're made to feel like everybody has an equal voice. Because I've seen that model close down dissent, make it appear that all opinions are equal. It's like you've got your opinion, I've got mine—

G.S.: Part of the ethic of these groups was "experience." It wasn't about opinion.

b.h.: But I think that we were very good at hearing each other's experience. Dissent is when we can argue a point in a dialectical way.

U.V.: That raises the issue of strategies, because one of the things we've talked about is

the fear of airing our dirty linen. How do we strategize to have that discussion in public, so that enough women feel part of it, but that it isn't picked up and used against us?

N.W.: If we do have a public debate, the opposition will have a minute and a half to say women can't get along. Then they'll be drowned out because there's such a hunger among women to see principled debate about these things that they'll create more and more debate. Then the narrative of feminism will get going again. Because, frankly, the narrative stopped. The story stopped.

G.S.: I don't think the story has stopped. I think we've got a movement that's created everything from new jobs to new ideas.

N.W.: I'm not saying that the historical events, or the story of the historical events, stopped at all. I'm talking about a symbolic level, on the level of sound bites, if you like, on the level of people thinking they know what feminism is if their only contact with it is the mass media.

U.V.: I'm intrigued by how many times the conversation returns to the representation of feminism or the image of feminism, as opposed to the reality of the feminist movement. We keep getting into how we are represented and what people think of us.

N.W.: My concern is that all over the country I meet women whose only contact with these ideas, even though they're wrestling with them every day, is from degraded, ridiculous sound bites.

b.h.: Okay, but I raised the issue of everyday life. I think we skip over things like that because it's a lot easier to critique the media.

U.V.: What I hear Naomi saying is that in everyday life people's only experience of feminism is coming at them through television, film, and news media.

b.h.: I don't think that mass media influence a feminist practice in everyday life. I think mass media give a false impression of feminism in everyday life.

I'm interested in how we create a politics of everyday life. That means not only challenging mass media. It means coming up with some very different strategies: one, for sharing what feminist thinking and practice are, and two, for talking about how you utilize them in your life.

N.W.: What I see going on in America is that women of all backgrounds, most of whom don't call themselves feminists, are very busy engaged in feminist practice in their everyday lives and don't need us to show them how to do it.

b.h.: But that's bullshit. If that were true, we wouldn't even need a feminist movement. If people don't have a sense of what feminism is as a political movement, it does not produce a feminist movement.

What produces a feminist movement is first and foremost a commitment on the part of individuals to feminist politics.

N.W.: What I'm trying to say is that a lot of women are really alienated by the concept that there is a feminist politics that someone owns.

b.h.: Hey, let's face it. There are a lot of women in this country who are alienated from politics. I think that we have to fight the idea that somehow we have to refashion feminism so that it appears not to be revolutionary—so that it appears not to be about struggle. There is no way to change sexism and sexist oppression that does not involve resistance and struggle. So if people are saying, "I never want to struggle, I never want to resist," they're saying they don't want a feminist movement.

U.V.: We're taking on too much. We need to put into this conversation why those women have a problem going to the women's center. Forget about the media. Let's talk about religion. Let's talk about the state. These institutions don't validate women's experience in the same way that they legalize and validate men's experience, and that's what we're up against.

We're forgetting that it's not just ours to correct. The feminist movement isn't the only reason those women aren't coming to, and may never come to, a feminist institution.

b.h.: It's about women's role in politics in this society. A lot of women are much more comfortable with the idea of feminism as a lifestyle movement.

U.V.: Sure, but bell, we're not going to convert everybody into political activists. We're not going to convince every woman to be a warrior.

G.S.: You cannot just say to women, "Oppose male dominance and oppose the patriarchy," when they know they're going to get hit in the head if they do this, unless there's also some support.

N.W.: This is probably going to annoy a lot of you, but I think that there's a perception that there is a "club feminism" and certain people decide who's in and who's out on the basis of what they believe. I would say women struggle and make feminism decisions, whether they call it that or not, in a million ways every single day. These women that we would not recognize as part of our particular belief system have a sense of their own outrage. They just go about it differently. There's a sense that feminism is one big No.

b.h.: Naomi, I don't feel like I even understand where you're coming from, implying that somehow there's this "club feminism"—I don't see myself as a part of that. I see myself as a part of a movement that has tried to go out and meet with people and say to them, "What do you want to know about feminism?" I think that Naomi has to own that when she uses "club feminism" she is responding to the type of bourgeois feminism that has gotten the most attention.

N.W.: Gloria, what do you say to the idea that feminism should be a bipartisan movement?

G.S.: Feminism has always been bipartisan, and most women are independents. We didn't change, the ultra-right infiltrated the Republican party.

b.h.: I say that the minute you begin to oppose patriarchy, you're progressive. If our real agenda is altering patriarchy and sexist oppression, we are talking about a left, revolutionary movement.

G.S.: But we're redefining revolutionary, because the Left was talking about [men] taking over from their fathers—

b.h.: You two think "white men" when you use the word "Left." I think George Jackson. I think Angela Davis. I have hope for revolutionary feminism because I see more women and men deeply troubled about gender, and I see that pain and trouble as a place of intervention.

U.V.: I think it's going to be a revolutionary theory *and* a reformist practice. You are extremely eloquent in defining the kind of feminism that I believe in, bell, but we're going to be at it for the next 30 years or more, and we have to be very practical—

G.S.: If you're talking about pace, I agree with the idea of reform, but when it comes to content, radicalism works better than liberalism because it's more true. We don't just want to have a piece of the pie. We want to make a whole new pie.

b.h.: I do think we need a deeper discussion on whether there are possibilities for solidarity between the revolutionary, radical feminist practice that I would argue for, and what Naomi might argue for.

N.W.: Please don't assume that because I'm talking about using mainstream media, because I believe there is a culture of unlabeled feminism, that therefore it means that I'm nervously drawing into the center. My politics are probably your politics, but I'm saying that something's not translating, and what is not translating has to do with the way in which feminism has been defined too narrowly.

I think we also need safehouses right now, where women and men can come together to have real conversations across gender lines, ask stupid questions and make mistakes. We need safehouses where women and men can talk across racial divisions as well.

b.h.: It's beginning. This year the focus of the Black Gay and Lesbian Leadership forum was "coalition-building," and they wanted speakers of diverse sexual practices to broaden the discussion. There are models. The issue is,

"How do we make it happen more often? How do we make it happen on lots of different levels?" Most early civil rights and feminist organizing was done in living rooms. We have to go back to that model. It's cheap, it's easy, and people can bring their kids.

U.V.: We need cable TV shows.

G.S.: I'm hooked on the idea of a "900" number. Women and men who are too busy can call up and get a smart, funny message that says, "You want the political joke of the week? The demonstration of the month? You want to know what your senator is doing?" It's a combination of the group in your living room and the way that individuals can be activists without going to meetings.

U.V.: We need to talk about our vision of women as opposed to the Right's vision. You can't stress that enough, because in each of our lives, no matter what age we are, we have seen the role of women change in the world. And it's because of the feminist movement. There's nobody else. You have to keep talking about what that has opened up for so many women, although it hasn't been equal for women of all classes.

It would be very exciting if, as an organizing strategy, this issue of *Ms.* could launch a wave of conversations like this with different groups of people in communities around the nation.

N.W.: There are ways the feminist movement can structure pleasure and fun and triumph talk as well as what's been called troubles talk into women's and men's discussions around these issues. For example, a lot of feminist meetings I've gone to are set up to ensure the maximum amount of discomfort, anxiety, and boredom. Why aren't we incorporating food, drink, and music—

b.h.: And humor. But I'd also like to see *Ms.* have some space where we focus on how women who have empowered themselves use that power for other women.

G.S.: And, I think we need to talk about the joy. I get such joy out of feminism. It is the greatest joy of my life, and somehow we don't translate that.

106

KAREN LEHRMAN AND OTHERS

Off Course—and Responses (1993)

It's eight o'clock on a balmy Wednesday morning at the University of California at Berkeley, and Women's Studies, 39, "Literature and the Question of Pornography," is about to begin. The atmosphere of the small class is relaxed. The students call the youngish professor by her first name: the banter focuses on finding a man for her to date. She puts on the board "Write 'grade' or 'no grade' on your paper before turning it in." Students—nine women and one man—amble in sporadically for the first twenty minutes.

Today's discussion involves a previous guest speaker: feminist-socialist porn star Nina Hartley. The professor asks what insights the students gained from Hartley's talk. They respond: "She's free with her sexuality. . . . I liked when she said, 'I like to fuck my friends.' . . . No body-image problems. . . . She's dependent in that relationship. . . ." The professor tries to move the discussion onto a more serious question: have traditional feminists, in their antiporn stance, defined women out of their sexuality? After a few minutes, though, the discussion fixes on orgasms—how they're not the be-all and end-all of sexual activity, how easy it is to fake one. The lone male stares intently at a spot on the floor; occasionally he squirms.

I never took a porn class when I went to college ten years ago. In fact, I never took a women's studies class and don't even know if the universities I attended offered any. Women's studies was about a decade old at the time, but it hadn't yet become institutionalized (there are now more than six hundred programs), nor gained notoriety through debates

From *Mother Jones*, September/October 1993. Reprinted with permission from *Mother Jones* magazine, copyright 1993, Foundation for National Progress.

over the canon and multiculturalism. But even if I had been aware of a program, I'm certain I would have stayed far away from it. It's not that I wasn't a feminist: I fully supported equal rights and equal opportunities for women. But I was feminist like I was Jewish—it was a part of my identity that didn't depend on external affirmation.

Perhaps more important, as a first-generation career-woman, I felt a constant need to prove my equality. I took as many "male" courses—economics, political science, intellectual history—as I could; I wanted to be seen as a good student who happened to be a woman. There were a couple of problems, though: I didn't learn much about women or the history of feminism, and like most of my female peers, I rarely spoke in class.

Last spring I toured the world of women's studies, visiting Berkeley, the University of Iowa, Smith College, and Dartmouth College. I sat in on about twenty classes, talked to students and professors at these and other schools, amassed syllabi, and waded through the more popular reading materials. I admit to having begun with a nagging skepticism. But I was also intrigued; rumor had it that in these classes, women talked.

And they do. The problem, as I see it, is what they're often talking about. In many classes discussions alternate between the personal and the political, with mere pit stops at the academic. Sometimes they are filled with unintelligible post-structuralist jargon; sometimes they consist of consciousness-raising psychobabble, with the students' feelings and experiences valued as much as anything the professor or texts have to offer. Regardless, the guiding principle of most of the classes is oppression, and problems are almost inevitably reduced to relationships of power. "Diversity" is the mantra of both students and professors, but it doesn't apply to political opinions.

Not every women's studies course suffers from these flaws. In fact, the rigor and perspective of individual programs and classes vary widely, and feminist academics have debated nearly every aspect of the field. But it seems that the vast majority of women's studies professors rely, to a greater or lesser extent, on a common set of feminist theories. Put into practice, these theories have the potential to undermine the goals not only of a liberal education, but of feminism itself.

This doesn't mean, as some critics have suggested, that these programs should simply be abolished. Women's studies has played a valuable role in forcing universities to include in the curriculum women other than "witches or Ethel Rosenberg," as Iowa's Linda K. Kerber puts it. The field has generated a considerable amount of first-rate scholarship on women, breaking the age-old practice of viewing male subjects and experience as the norm and the ideal. And it has produced interdisciplinary courses that creatively tied together research from several fields.

Whether all this could have been accomplished without the creation of women's studies programs separate from the traditional departments is a moot question, especially since these programs have become so well entrenched in the academy. The present challenge is to make women's studies as good as it can be. Although the problems are significant, they're not insurmountable. And perhaps more than anything else, women's studies prides itself on its capacity for self-examination and renewal.

Berkeley was the only stop on the tour with an actual women's studies department. It is one of the largest, most established and respected programs in the country. Overall, it impressed me the least. At the other extreme was Smith, where the classes tended to be more rigorous and substantive and there was a greater awareness of the pitfalls of the field. (The students were also far more articulate, though that may have little to do with women's studies.) I found the most thoughtful professors in Iowa's program, which doesn't even offer a major. The program at Dartmouth, perhaps compensating for the school's macho image, seemed the most prone to succumbing to the latest ideological fads.

CLASSROOM THERAPY

"Women's studies" is something of a misnomer. Most of the courses are designed not merely to study women, but also to improve the lives of women, both the individual students (the vast majority of whom are female) and women in general. Since professors believe that women have been effectively silenced throughout history, they often consider a pedagogy that "nurtures voice" just as, if not more, important than the curriculum.

Women's studies professors tend to be overtly warm, encouraging, maternal. You want to tell these women your problems—and many students do. To foster a "safe environment" where women feel comfortable talking many teachers try to divest the classroom of power relations. They abandon their role as experts, lecturing very little and sometimes allowing decisions to be made by the group and papers to be graded by other students. An overriding value is placed on student participation and collaboration: students make joint presentations, cowrite papers, and use group journals for "exploring ideas they can't say in class" and "fostering a sense of community." Because chairs are usually arranged in a circle, in a couple of classes taught by graduate students I couldn't figure out who the teacher was until the end.

To give women voice, many professors encourage all discourse—no matter how personal or trivial. Indeed, since it is wisely believed that knowledge is constructed and most texts have been influenced by "the patriarchy," many in women's studies consider personal experience the only real source of truth. Some professors and texts even claim that women have a way of thinking that is different from the abstract rationality of men, one based on context, emotion, and intuition. Fully "validating" women, therefore, means celebrating subjectivity over objectivity, feelings over facts, instinct over logic.

The day I sat in on Berkeley's "Contemporary Global Issues for Women" (all women except for one "occasional" male), we watched a film about women organizing in Ahmadabad, India. The film was tedious, but it seemed like grist for a good political/economic/sociological discussion about the problems of women in underdeveloped countries. After the film ended, though, the professor promptly asked the class: "How do you *feel* about the film? Do you find it more sad or courageous?" Students responded to her question until the end of class, at which point she suggested, "You might think about the film in terms of your own life and the life of your mother. Women are not totally free in this culture. It just might come in more subtle ways."

[. . .]

Of course, self-discovery and female bonding are important for young women, and so, one might argue, are group therapy and consciousness-raising. Indeed, I wish I had had some when I was that age; it might have given me the courage to talk in classes and to deal with abusive bosses late in life. But does it belong in a university classroom?

Many of the professors I talked with (including the chair of Berkeley's women's studies department) viewed the more touchy-feely classes as just as problematic as I did. I saw a couple of teachers who were able to use personal experience, either of historical figures or students, to buttress the discussion, not as an end in itself. But even these classes were always on the verge of slipping into confession mode.

[. . .]

But the problem with a therapeutic pedagogy is more than just allowing students to discuss their periods or sex lives in class. Using the emotional and subjective to "validate" women risks validating precisely the stereotypes that feminism was supposed to eviscerate: women are irrational, women must ground all knowledge in their own experiences, etc. A hundred years ago, women were fighting for the right to learn math, science, Latin—to be educated like men; today, many women are content to get their feelings heard, their personal problems aired, their instincts and intuition respected.

POLITICS, AS USUAL

"Don't worry. We've done nothing here since she forgot her notes a couple of weeks ago," Michael Williams reassures another male student. "We'll probably talk about Anita Hill again." We're waiting for Berkeley's "Gender Politics: Theory and Comparative Study" to begin. When the professor finally arrives and indicates that, yes, we'll be talking about Anita Hill again, the second male student packs up and bolts. Williams tells me that during the first week or two, whenever a male student would comment on something, the professor would say, "What you really mean is . . ." Most men stopped speaking and then dropped out. "Other classes I walk out with eight pages of notes," says Williams. "Here, everybody just says the same thing in a different way." (He stays, though, for the "easy credits.")

Most women's studies professors seem to adhere to the following principles in formulating classes: women were and are oppressed; oppression is endemic to our patriarchal social system; men, capitalism, and Western values are responsible for women's problems. The reading material is similarly bounded in political scope (Andrea Dworkin, Catharine MacKinnon, bell hooks, Adrienne Rich, and Audre Lorde turn up a lot), and opposing viewpoints are usually presented only through a feminist critique of them. *Feminist Frontiers III,* a book widely used in intro courses, purports to show readers "how gender has shaped your life," and invites them to join in the struggle "to reform the structure and culture of male dominance."

Although most of the classes I attended stopped short of outright advocacy of specific political positions, virtually all carried strong political undercurrents. Jill Harvey, a women's studies senior at Smith, recalls a feminist anthropology course in which she "quickly discovered that the way to get A's was to write papers full of guilt and angst about how I'd bought into society's definition of womanhood and now I'm enlightened and free."

[. . .]

Many women's studies professors acknowledge their field's bias, but point out that all disciplines are biased. Still, there's a huge difference between conceding that education has political elements and intentionally politicizing, between, as Women's Studies Professor Daphne Patai puts it, "recognizing and minimizing deep biases and proclaiming and endorsing them." Patai, whose unorthodox views got her in hot water at the University of Massachusetts, is now coauthoring a book on the contradictions of women's studies. "Do they really want fundamentalist studies, in which teachers are not just studying fundamentalism but supporting it?"

A still larger problem is the degree to which politics has infected women's studies scholarship. "Feminist theory guarantees that researchers will discover male bias and oppression in every civilization and time," says Mary Lefkowitz, a classics professor at Wellesley. "A distinction has to be made between historical interpretation of the past and political reinterpretation." And, I would add, between reading novels with an awareness of racism and sexism, and reducing them entirely to constructs of race and gender.

Apparently there has always been a tug of war within the women's studies community between those who most value scholarship and those who most value ideology. Some professors feel obligated to present the work of all women scholars who call themselves feminists, no matter how questionable their methodology or conclusions.

Unfortunately, women's studies students may not be as well equipped to see through shoddy feminist scholarship as they are through patriarchal myths and constructs. One reason may be the interdisciplinary nature of the programs, which offers students minimal grounding in any of the traditional disciplines. According to Mary Lefkowitz, women's studies majors who take her class exhibit an inability to amass factual material or remember details; instead of using evidence to support an argument, they use it as a remedy for their personal problems.

But teaching students how to "think critically" is one of the primary goals of women's studies, and both students and professors say that women's studies courses are more challenging than those in other departments. "Women's studies give us tools to analyze," says Torrey Shanks, senior women's studies and political science major at Berkeley. "We learn theories abut how to look at women and men; we don't just come away with facts."

Most of the women's studies students I met were quite bright, and many argued certain points very articulately. But they seemed to have learned to think critically through only one lens. When I asked some of the sharpest students about the most basic criticisms of women's studies, they appeared not to have thought about them or gave me some of the stock women's studies rap. It seemed that they couldn't fit these questions into their way of viewing the world.

For instance, when I expressed the view that an at-times explicit anticapitalist and anti-Western bias pervades the field, a couple of majors told me they thought that being anticapitalist was part of being a feminist. When I asked whether, in the final analysis, women weren't still most free in Western capitalist societies, the seemingly programmed responses ran from "I wouldn't feel free under a glass ceiling" to "Pressures on Iranian women to wear the veil are no different from pressures on women in this country to wear heels and miniskirts."

THE STUDENT PARTY LINE

Despite the womb-like atmosphere of the classrooms, I didn't see much student questioning of the professors or the texts. Although I rarely saw teachers present or solicit divergent points of view, the students' reluctance to voice alternative opinions seemed to stem more from political intolerance and conformity on the part of fellow students.

In Smith's "Gender and Politics" class, several students spoke against the ban on gays in the military before Erin O'Connor, her voice shaking, ventured: "I think there is something to the argument of keeping gays out of the military because of how people feel about it."

After several students said things like, "The military should reflect society," O'Connor rebounded: "I'm sick and tired of feeling that if I have a moral problem with something, all of a sudden it's: 'You're homophobic, you're wrong, you're behind the times, go home.' There must be someone else in this classroom who believes as I do."

Professor: "No one is saying that support of the ban is homophobic."

"I would make that assertion," offered a student.

Professor: "But you can argue against the ban from a nonhomophobic perspective."

Another student: "It's homophobic."

When class ended, another woman approached O'Connor and said: "You're absolutely right, and I'm sure there are others who felt the same way but just didn't say anything. You went out on a limb."

No one used the word homophobic until O'Connor did. Still, students, especially in this ostensible "safe environment," shouldn't have to overcome a pounding heart to voice a dissident opinion. "Women's studies creates a safe space for p.c. individuals, but doesn't maintain any space for white Christians," says O'Connor, an English and government major and member of the College Republican Club.

In a study by the Association of American Colleges, 30 percent of students taking women's studies courses at Wellesley said they felt uneasy expressing unpopular opinions; only 14 percent of non-women's studies students felt that way.

[. . .]

POST-STRUCTURALISM
AND MULTICULTURALISM

Perhaps the most troubling influence on women's studies in the past decade has been the collection of theories known as post-structuralism, which essentially implies that all texts are arbitrary, all knowledge is biased, all standards are illegitimate, all mortality is subjective. I talked to numerous women's studies professors who don't buy any of this (it's typically more popular in the humanities than in the social sciences), but nevertheless it has permeated women's studies to a significant extent, albeit in the most reductive, simplistic way.

According to Delo Mook, a Dartmouth physics professor who is part of a team teaching "Ways of Knowing: Physics, Literature, Feminism," "You can't filter other cultures through our stencil. Nothing is right or wrong."

What about cannibalism? Clitorectomies? "Nope. I can only say, 'I believe it's wrong.'"

But post-structuralism is applied inconsistently in women's studies. I've yet to come across a feminist tract that "contextualizes" sexism in this country as it does in others, or acknowledges that feminism is itself a product of Western culture based on moral reasoning and the premise that some things are objectively wrong. Do feminist theorists really want the few young men who take these classes to formulate personal rationales for rape? There's a huge difference between questioning authority, truth, and knowledge and saying none of these exist, a difference between rejecting male standards and rejecting the whole concept of standards.

Like post-structuralism, the concept of multiculturalism has had a deep influence on women's studies. Professors seem under a constant burden to prove that they are presenting the requisite number of books or articles by women of color or lesbians. Issues of race came up in nearly every class I sat through. I wasn't allowed to sit in on a seminar at Dartmouth on "Racism and Feminism" because of a contract made with the students that barred outside visitors.

Terms like sexism, racism, and homophobic have bloated beyond all recognition, and the more politicized the campus, the more frequently they're thrown around. I heard both professors and students call Berkeley's women's studies department homophobic and racist, despite the fact that courses dealing with homosexuality and multiculturalism fill the catalog and quite a number of women of color and lesbians are affiliated with the department.

Although many professors try to work against it, in the prevailing ethos of women's studies, historical figures, writers, and the students themselves are viewed foremost as women, as lesbians, as white or black or Hispanic, and those with the most "oppressed" identities are the most respected. Feminist theorists now generally admit that they can't speak for all women, but some still presume to speak for all black women or all Jewish women or all lesbians. There's still little acknowledgment not only of the individuality of each woman, but of the universal, gender-blind bond shared by all human beings.

THE ROAD NOT TAKEN

Women's studies programs have clearly succeeded with at least one of their goals: whether because of the mostly female classes, the nurturing professors, or the subject matter, they have gotten women students talking.

But getting women to speak doesn't help much if they're all saying the same thing. Women's studies students may make good polemicists, but do they really learn to think independently and critically?

Elizabeth Fox-Genovese says she had envisioned Emory's women's studies program as a mini-women's college: "I thought it should be a special environment that took women seriously and asked them to be the best that they could be by the standards of a good, liberal arts education." Young women—and men—would be steeped in sound scholarship on women, but they would also be offered a variety of theories and viewpoints, feminist and otherwise.

Unfortunately, this hasn't been the perspective of most women's studies professors. Women's studies was conceived with a political purpose—to be the intellectual arm of the women's movement—and its sense of purpose has only gotten stronger through the years. The

result is that the field's narrow politics have constricted the audience for nonideological feminism instead of widening it, and have reinforced the sexist notion that there is a women's viewpoint. There's a legitimate reason why two-thirds of college women don't call themselves feminists. "When I got here I thought I was a feminist," Erin O'Connor from Smith told me. "I don't want to call myself that now."

Clearly the first step is for women's studies to reopen itself to internal and external criticism. The intimidation in the field is so great that I had trouble finding dissident voices willing to talk to me on the record. The women's movement has come a long way in the past twenty-five years—feminists should feel secure enough now to take any and all lumps.

Young women should also no longer feel it necessary to shun classes devoted to women, as my friends and I did. Women today still have to work for their equality, but they don't have to prove it every second. And as the status of women in this country evolves, so should the goals of women's studies. It's for its own sake that women's studies should stop treating women as an ensemble of victimized identities. Only when the mind of each woman is considered on its own unique terms will the minds of all women be respected.

[RESPONSES TO "OFF COURSE"]

Faludi Lashes Back

Maybe it should have been a tip-off that we are about to enter an Orwellian doublespeak universe when the bio under writer Karen Lehrman's name advised us that she is "writing a book on postideological feminism." What next? A call for postpolitical government? A new era of posteconomic capitalism? Reality check time: feminism is an ideology; always has been, always will be. That's the whole point. Imagining that a politics-free feminism will advance women's cause is about as realistic as trying to rouse the masses with six-packs of caffeine-free Coke.

In her critique of academic feminist studies programs ("Off Course," Sept/Oct), Lehrman seems to want to indict women's studies for the mortal sin of harboring a political perspective. Women's studies courses are downright "infected," as she puts it, by ideology. Like other academic disciplines are devoid of political content? Like the many professorial gentlemen who have been relentlessly promoting a womanless history-and-literature curriculum all these years have no ideological point of view? And when did political consciousness become an "infection" that must be stamped out, anyway? The capacity to analyze the world in political terms is not a disease; it's a healthy and fundamental prerequisite for moral engagement in the world. It should probably be a requirement for college graduation.

Lehrman complains that she saw too much "consciousness-raising" in feminist studies class and not enough hard-nosed rational scholarship. She says: "A hundred years ago, women were fighting for the right to learn math, science, Latin—to be educated like men; today many women are content to get their feelings heard, their personal problems aired, their instincts and intuition respected." Maybe, just maybe, having one's intuition respected is a bit more crucial to the average young woman's educational growth than mastery of a dead language. Feminism in the academy is about more than women getting the right to absorb the male-defined curriculum; it's about challenging the foundations of that curriculum. What Lehrman dismisses as "therapeutic pedagogy," others may characterize as the basis of learning. Paulo Freire, the pioneering Brazilian philosopher and educator of the poor, writes in his classic work, *Pedagogy of the Oppressed,* of the paralysis and passivity bred by the traditional "'banking' concept of education," in which students are treated like deposit boxes to be crammed with facts and figures. "Knowledge emerges only through invention and re-invention," he writes, "through the restless, impatient, continuing, hopeful inquiry human beings pursue in the world, with the world, and with each other." This restless and impatient process may look "emotional" or irrational to an onlooker, especially an onlooker who fears the questioning of authority, but it is the essential starting point of a genuine education.

Susan Faludi
Palo Alto, California

Lehrman showed up one day in my course on the history of U.S. women's political activism, the focus of which contradicts her assertion that women's studies ignores "women who have achieved anything of note." Perhaps that's why she made no mention of it.

Lehrman did not tape our interview and only occasionally took notes. Clearly she knew what she wanted to say before she had even begun reporting this story, and she certainly wasn't going to let facts get in the way of her desire to do a hatchet job on women's studies

Annelise Orleck
Assistant Professor of History
Dartmouth College

Lehrman Responds

I was disappointed in Susan Faludi's response, and especially in its condescending tone. Maybe she feels that, as a newly ordained "feminist leader," she stands above all debate on these issues. Or perhaps she has learned too well one of the orthodoxies of women's studies and the women's movement in general: dismiss all criticism.

This probably explains why she hasn't bothered to grasp the distinction between ideological and nonideological feminism. What Faludi and many in women's studies don't seem to get is that women (and men) can believe in the essential theory of feminism—equal rights and equal opportunities for women—and disagree on how to achieve that. They can also believe in feminism and not agree that they personally are oppressed victims of the patriarchy, that their entire lives are open to political interpretation. Postideological feminism means there's no one telling women what to think or what to value—no feminist leaders. Maybe that's why Faludi has chosen to mock rather than address the concept.

As I wrote in the piece, of course all academic courses are politicized to some degree. But other disciplines (except perhaps for African-American studies or gay and lesbian studies) don't have a political litmus test for all of the professors or the curriculum. It's interesting that Faludi believes that the "capacity to analyze the world in political terms . . . should probably be a requirement for college graduation." Whose "political terms"? Are Rush Limbaugh's OK, too?

The whole idea of a liberal education is to encourage independent and critical thinking— and that's certainly the alleged goal of women's studies. Should we really want universities to replace one set of dogma with another? Does Faludi believe that it doesn't matter if scholarship on women is substandard, so long as it advances the cause of women?

I fully agree with Faludi that women's studies should challenge the male-defined curriculum and pedagogy, and that it has produced a wealth of first-rate scholarship on women. What I don't accept is that a female-defined curriculum needs to be so heavily politicized, and that a female-defined pedagogy should be based on women's feelings, "contexual" thinking, or special sense of intuition. In *Backlash,* Faludi attacked "relational" feminist theorists as soldiers in the war *against* women: "Special may sound like superior, but it is also a euphemism for handicapped." Has she changed her mind?

[. . .]

I took three pages of notes during my interview with Orleck. On one of those pages I wrote that Orleck decided to offer more balanced readings after she received some negative course evaluations. "I had been accused of going down the p.c. checklist of what bad things the U.S. government has done," she told me, and I appreciated her honesty.

[. . .]

107

Susan Faludi

I'm Not a Feminist but I Play One on TV (1995)

According to the latest lifestyle headlines and talk-show sound bites, from *USA Today* to *Good Morning America,* we are witnessing the birth of a new wave of feminism. It's "like a second revolution in the women's movement," the Washington *Times* enthused, referring us to one of the nouveau revolution's adherents, who "compares her position with the 1970s feminists who burned their bras." The neo-rebel tells the *Times,* "I feel the same as I did when I was 19 years old during the women's liberation movement"; she confides she even had a 1970s-style "'click' moment" of feminist revelation.

The evidence of what the *Washington Times* calls "a nationwide trend"? New "feminist" organizations called the Women's Freedom Network, the Independent Women's Forum (IWF), and the Network for Empowering Women (or NEW, which, to hear its organizers tell it, will soon be displacing NOW). New inspirational "feminist" tracts like *Who Stole Feminism?* and *Feminism Without Illusions.* New "feminist" voices from a younger generation, like Katie Roiphe, author of *The Morning After: Sex, Fear, and Feminism,* and Rene Denfeld, author of *The New Victorians: A Young Woman's Challenge to the Old Feminist Order.* And members of a new "feminist" intelligentsia like philosophy professor Christina Hoff Sommers, hailed in the *Boston Globe*'s headlines as A REBEL IN THE SISTERHOOD who WANTS TO RESCUE FEMINISM FROM ITS "HIJACKERS."

That feminist leaders don't seem to be embracing these new reinforcements does give the trend's reporters pause—but only momentarily. Feminist standoffishness must just be jealousy— or, as the *Chicago Tribune* put it, "sibling rivalry."

From *Ms.,* March/April 1995. Reprinted by permission of *Ms.* Magazine, copyright 1995.

But big-sister envy is not the problem here.

Perhaps the nature of the "click" experienced by the *Washington Times*'s "feminist" heroine should have been a clue: she says she sprang into action after she became outraged . . . by a feminist colleague's joke about Dan Quayle. Or perhaps the fact that the *Washington Times* was tickled pink over this new feminist birth in the first place should have been the tip-off; this conservative and Moonie-funded paper is not known for its enthusiasm over the women's movement. Cheap broadsides against Anita Hill are more in its line of work.

What is being celebrated is no natural birth of a movement—and the press that originated the celebration is no benign midwife. It would be more accurate to describe this drama as a media-assisted invasion of the body of the women's movement: the Invasion of the Feminist Snatchers, intent on repopulating the ranks with Pod Feminists. In this artificially engineered reproduction effort, the press has figured twice; the right-wing media have played the part of mad-scientist obstetrician-cum-spin doctor, bankrolling, publishing, and grooming their pod women for delivery to a wider world of media consumption. And the mainstream media have played the role of trend-hungry pack-journalism suckers; in their eagerness to jump on the latest bandwagon, they have gladly accepted the faux feminists' credentials without inspection.

If journalists were to investigate, they would find the "new" feminist movement to possess few adherents but much armament in the way of smoke and mirrors. The memberships of such groups as NEW are each in the low to mid three-digits, compared with NOW's 250,000. And they wouldn't find these women out on the hustings, in the streets, guarding a family planning clinic from anti-abortionist attacks, or lending a hand at a battered women's shelter. Instead, if the media were to take a closer look, they would find a handful of "feminist" writers and public speakers who do no writing, speaking, organizing, or activism on behalf of women's equality at all. A review of their published writings unearths not one example of a profeminist article or book.

They define themselves as "dissenters" within the feminist ranks, but they never joined feminism in the first place; they have met each other mingling at conservative academic gatherings (like the "anti-P.C." National Association of Scholars) and conservative Washington networking circuits, not the feminist trenches of pro-choice demonstrations and clerical unionizing meetings. They define themselves as politically diverse, but the leadership of the Women's Freedom Network, the IWF, and NEW is overwhelmingly rightward leaning. And when one looks back at where these women were launched as writers, it is, over and over, conservative antifeminist journals like *National Review* and *Commentary,* or the, of late, feminist-bashing pages of *The New Republic.* They define themselves as representing "the average woman," but they are privileged women who rarely stray from their ivory-tower or inside-the-Beltway circles; they are in touch with "the average woman" only to the extent that such a phrase is a code word or signal that they themselves are white and middle- or upperclass. And their opposition to government assistance for women who need help with child care, education, basic shelter, and nutrition betrays a lack of concern, and a buried well of racially charged and class-biased ill will toward women who don't fit the narrow confines of their "average woman." They define themselves as feminists, but their dismissive-to-outright-hostile attitudes toward feminist issues—from sexual harassment to domestic violence to rape to pay equity to child care to welfare rights—locate them firmly on the antifeminist side of the ledger.

Yet their rallying cry—or more precisely, their resting cry, their call to disarm—appeals to some women for its comforting message of female victory and success. Christina Hoff Sommers, author of *Who Stole Feminism?* and her pod sisters—columnist Cathy Young; history professor and *Feminism Without Illusions* author

Elizabeth Fox-Genovese; former *New Republic* writer Karen Lehrman; and writer Katie Roiphe, who, as a graduate student at Princeton, brought us *The Morning After,* to name the prime anointed media stars—maintain that sufficient progress has been made and that now should be a time of back-patting and "reconciliation" with men. Their conferences aren't planning sessions to advance women's rights; they are well-heeled business-card-swapping events where conservative luminaries speak from the podium about how feminism has gone too far—and how women should quit pressing for their rights and start defending men's. Women shouldn't try to spark social change; rather, as the Women's Freedom Network's mission statement asserts, "male and female roles should be allowed to evolve naturally"— that is, without a political shove in a feminist direction. Of course, as the most casual student of women's history could tell you, allowing gender roles to evolve "naturally," without the aid of political agitation, means allowing gender roles to evolve not at all.

Theirs is a beguiling line of argument because it is (a) positive, in a rah-rah "Year of the Woman" way, and (b) nonthreatening. NEW, et al., aren't encouraging women to pursue social change, and they certainly aren't asking men to change. It is no-risk feminism for a fearful age: just post your achievements, make nice with men, and call it a day. The Power of Positive Thinking will take care of the rest.

[. . .]

The podding-of-feminism phenomenon is most publicly demonstrated on the talk-show sets and lifestyle pages. In the past, when the media broached the topic of feminism, they often rigged the outcome by throwing their support to the antifeminist camp, but at least they clearly labeled the two sides. But over the past decade, the rigging has been obscured by a blurring of the lines.

First, around about the mid-eighties, the media began replacing the curmudgeonly feminist baiters like Norman Mailer and George Gilder (who actually seem rather endearing

now, with their frank grumblings about independent women) with either a younger male model of the slickly earnest, collegiate variety— typically a Dinesh D'souza-type editor of the *Dartmouth Review* or some other "anti-P.C." college paper kept afloat by right-wing foundation largesse—or with an older female model of the pursed-lipped Phyllis Schlafly variety, who claimed to be the real spokeswoman for the "average" middle-American female. By the late eighties, both of these representatives of the far right were displaced on our talk-show sets by the young college woman eager to say, "I'm not a feminist, but . . ."—as in "I'm not a feminist, but . . . I sure expect to get equal pay, equal opportunity, and reproductive rights." She seems an ideal decrier of the women's movement because she had nonpolitical allegiances; she was just a neutral party, representing Everywoman— or rather, Every White Middle-Class College-Educated Woman. But having her eschew the women's rights struggle still wasn't as delicious as the ultimate in feminist denouncers: a woman who would actually call herself a feminist. Now, there would be a coup.

Come the nineties, a handful of women came forward to volunteer for such a part— and soon found themselves inundated with media casting calls. These women take the opposite tack of the young women who preceded them. Their slogan is "I am a feminist, but . . ."— as in "I am a feminist, but . . . I don't believe women face discrimination anymore; I don't see any reason for women to organize politically; I don't think the pay gap, sexual harassment, rape, domestic violence, or just about any other issue feminism has raised are real problems; I don't see why we even need to bother with gender analysis anymore; and, on the whole, I find feminists to be little more than victim-mongering conspiracy nuts." These are "feminists" who weigh in to the debate only to speak out against feminism's "excesses." None has yet to appear on a talk show to take any profeminist position—although they have devoted considerable energy to promoting their "pro-men" platform. NEW, for instance, holds that women's most "urgent" need now isn't economic or political progress but making amends with those poor feminist-bashed men. (It's even the slogan printed on NEW's business cards.) IWF is producing a video and a helpful media guide listing several hundred women who are ready and willing to hit the talk shows to dispute the "old" feminists. Their branch of feminism doesn't appear to run deeper than a surface gimmick to get airtime. Maybe their slogan should be "I'm not a feminist, but I play one on TV."

The precursor to the pods, the mother of all "I'm a feminist, but . . ." declaimers, is that made-for-TV antifeminist feminist Camille Paglia, whose latest "book," *Vamps and Tramps,* is an exhaustive, and exhausting, gaze into the mirror of her many media moments. She differs from the antifeminist feminists who came in her wake in that she is more of an attention-seeking generator of outrageous one-liners than a conservative in feminist costume. She dons and discards so many masks—from drag-queen celebrator to bondage 'n' leather poster girl—that it's hard to say whether under her many veils a person with a coherent set of political beliefs really exists at all.

Paglia's tactic of labeling herself a "feminist, but . . ." has been followed, without the wit, by a small cast of media stars who emerged in the early nineties. Most prominent is Sommers, who says she's a feminist, but . . . has mass-marketed her belief that feminists should just shut up now because women have pretty much attained equal opportunity and anyone who claims otherwise is a liar and a whiner. Joining her in deputy status is Roiphe, who calls herself a feminist, but . . . has peddled the idea that acquaintance rape is really a minor problem that feminists have exaggerated all out of proportion. Then there's Cathy Young, who says she's a feminist, but . . . has convicted feminist leaders on the false charge of having crowned Lorena Bobbitt as Feminist of the Year. And there's Elizabeth Fox-Genovese, who says she is a feminist, but . . . was most eager last

year to testify in court (and later, at greater length, in the conservative *National Review*) against women's admission to the Citadel, the state-supported all-male military academy in South Carolina. There's Karen Lehrman, a journalist and author of a forthcoming book on what she calls "postideological feminism" (whuh?), who says she's a feminist, but . . . has tarred all of feminist scholarship with her sneering accounts of a few instances of excessive touchy-feeliness and self-involvement in the women's studies classroom.

The cherry-picking of "feminist excesses" is a favored strategy—and an effective one, because there *are* some feminists (particularly on campus, where many of the pod feminists reside) who say "all men" are creeps, or who jump down your throat for less than perfectly P.C. terminology, or who get mortally offended over minor slights, or who want to "share" tedious personal revelations in the classroom. Surely one can always find psychobabble and navel-gazing in an undergraduate population . . . or even in gatherings like, ahem, the pod feminists' "International Gender Reconciliation Conference" last September, which offered such sessions as "Looking at Yourself," "Women's Wounds," "Emotional Support," and even a "Healing Break." Every movement with a membership larger than ten will have such folks, but the women's movement has consistently been tarred in the press for the overzealous or dippy remarks of a very few. The media have exploited these "excesses," distorting them into an emblematic portrait of the movement. And so, when the pod feminists come along and decry such behavior, it rings true for many readers and viewers who get their portrait of the women's movement from the media—and hence have come to believe that feminism is, in fact, overpopulated by shrieking ninnies.

If the pod feminists have adopted the strategy of co-option pioneered by conservative advisers to George Bush, they also have echoed another behavioral pattern of recent vintage among right-wing pols: projection of their sins onto their opponents. Just as family-man-from-hell

Newt Gingrich charged Democrats with home wrecking, just as illegal-immigrant-employing senatorial candidate Michael Huffington accused Democrats of illegal-alien coddling, so have the pseudofeminists laid at feminism's doorstep an indictment that could more properly be served on them. The main charges on their citation sheet: (1) feminists stifle the view of dissenting women; (2) feminists are paranoid whiners who like to imagine all women as helpless victims; (3) feminists spread falsehoods and myths about women's condition.

Take point one: feminists stifle diversity of thought. The "statement of principles" issued by the Women's Freedom Network asserts its intent to combat this number one crime: "We do not expect uniformity of opinion among women. Our commitment to genuine diversity is reflected in our advisory board, where libertarians, liberals, communitarians, and conservatives are all active participants." But the "diverse" leadership of the network, like that of its sister organizations such as NEW, is solidly conservative, typified by such luminaries as Jeane Kirkpatrick of the American Enterprise Institute; Ricky Silberman, Equal Employment Opportunity Commission vice chairwoman under Bush and a vocal booster of Supreme Court Justice Clarence Thomas; and Mona Charen, feminist-bashing columnist. As one member of the IWF told the press, "This group represents an opportunity for folks who don't fall into a particular camp to get involved in an intellectual way in policy issues." But this member most definitely did fall into a camp: he was Tom Boyd, an assistant attorney general in the Reagan and Bush administrations. And IW forums are notably feminist-free: they showcase such conservative litmus-test passers as Diane Ravitch, Bush's former undersecretary of education, and Mary Ellen Bork, antifeminist activist and wife of you-know-who. This spectrum of views on the subject of feminism is about as diverse as eighties Republicanism was a "big tent" (to quote the late Lee Atwater) for opinions on abortion. What Lehrman wants to label "postideological feminism" is just right-wing thought un-

dercover. It's enough to make you yearn for the unvarnished antifeminist tirades of Jerry Falwell—at least he was honest.

While the pods don't seem to tolerate much dissent in their own ranks, they still succeed in exploiting the claim that feminists stifle contrary views. There are indeed feminist activists who think only their opinions are the right ones and get hot under the collar when questioned. This phenomenon is typically portrayed in the media as the hip-booted feministo crushing her sisters under her iron-tipped heel. What this portrayal misses is that for every feminist trying to dictate policy in one direction, there's another challenging her. Heated exchanges, not censorship, characterize feminists' approaches to difficult subjects like pornography, surrogate motherhood, or RU 486. These differences of opinion—and the willingness to argue passionately over them—are precisely what strengthen the vitality of the women's movement, or any movement. But these points are quickly lost in the pods' endless loop of logic, which goes something like this: the antifeminist feminists say feminists stifle disagreement. A feminist disagrees with this statement. She must be trying to stifle dissent. And so on.

O.K., take point two: feminists are paranoid whiners who like to imagine women as helpless victims. The pseudofeminists maintain that feminist books like Naomi Wolf's *The Beauty Myth* and, well, my own *Backlash,* bellyache about a fantastical conspiracy plot hatched behind the scenes by mustache-twirling misogynists who have succeeded in brainwashing a mass female population. But both of these works took pains to spell out how this cultural counterreaction to feminism is "not a conspiracy." Moreover, the pseudofeminist critics missed a recurring theme, underscored rather obviously, I thought, in the conclusion of *Backlash:* women have resisted efforts to discourage them from pursuing their rights and independence; far from embracing victimhood, they have fought challenges to their freedoms tooth and nail. I would go one step farther here and argue that women's unladylike, un-victim-minded response to a backlash is, in fact, the enduring legacy of feminism. If feminism stands for anything, it is the belief that women can and must stand up and speak out. Feminism identifies victimization not so we can wallow in it, but so we can wallop it. Indeed, once feminist voices were able to force their way through the 1980s' right-wing wall of sound and make themselves heard in the bookstores, the cinema, and, most important, on live television (Anita Hill before the Senate Judiciary Committee), masses of women responded not with sniffling victim whimpers but with roaring outrage that found its outlet in historic-sized pro-choice rallies and historic gender gaps at the voting booths.

On the other hand, let us look at the pod feminists' own paranoia about—and now *this* is fantastical—the machinations of a "feminist-dominated" establishment. (Would it were true!) Christina Hoff Sommers writes that "clever and powerful feminists," backed by "well-funded, prestigious organizations as well as individuals," are pulling the wool over women's eyes and tricking them into believing that such a thing as the patriarchy still exists. She presents herself as a brave lone crusader (well, not that lone: she did receive the generous monetary backing of the well-endowed, right-wing Olin and Bradley foundations) going up against the reigning feminist matriarchy, venturing into, as she puts it histrionically, "the very dens of the lionesses." These lionesses, to hear Sommers tell it, have U.S. women under their intimidating thrall. To hear the pseudofeminists tell it, feminists are the ultimate string-pullers and women their victimized puppets: women are so defenselessly stupid, these writers suggest, that they'll swallow any mind-clouding swill that feminism dishes out. Women easily fall prey to feminists' trickery, and once under their spell, Sommers writes, women are "primed to be alarmed, angry, and resentful of men" and

even "ready to fabricate atrocities." Now who's talking victimology?

The pod feminists themselves are not above whining, not to mention complaining to the press that they are victims—of that big, bad feminist establishment, of course. Roiphe has reportedly griped to journalists that she is the victim of feminist threats; she's even "heard," she reports with high melodrama, that "they" wish a rape on her. When you cross the feminist cabal, she whimpered to the Cleveland *Plain Dealer,* "all the guns are taken out."

This brings us to point three: feminists spread falsehoods and myths about women's condition. The pod feminists argue that the feminist "establishment" exaggerates women's inferior social and economic status to generate attention and support for its cause. From sexual harassment to eating disorders to rape to adolescent girls' low self-esteem—you name it, the pods say, it's all hot air and hype. Furthermore, they say that feminists manage to pass off this malarkey as truth because the feminist-blinded media just buy what the women's movement has to sell without examining it.

But if the media have failed to challenge anyone, it's pseudofeminists like Roiphe and Sommers, whose books are packed with misleading and false information. When this is pointed out to the members of the media, they tend to show a remarkable lack of interest. I learned this for myself when, several months back, I made the mistake of agreeing to go on *Good Morning America* with Roiphe, in hopes I'd get the chance to explain how her book misrepresented rape statistics. But the moment I began to discuss the flaws in her statistical model, the host, Charlie Gibson, cut me off, saying he wanted "to nip in the bud" any tiresome foray into facts and figures. I had a similar encounter with a *Newsweek* researcher reporting a story about Roiphe's "findings": a few sentences into the interview, she ended it, explaining forthrightly that she needed to quote feminists who agreed with Roiphe. (So far, she noted, she only had one: Camille Paglia, who, in spite of her utter lack of knowledge on rape research, was the first person the *Newsweek* researcher called.)

Actually, there are many in the media who do agree. While the Roiphes and the Sommerses claim to be going against the cultural grain, they are really auditioning for the most commonly available, easiest parts to get in the pop culture drama: the roles of the good girls whose opinions are dutiful in line with prevailing prejudice. The problem is not their contrariness—feminism is lucky to be full of contention, and there are feminists I admire whose opinions differ vehemently from my own. The problem is reductionist, erroneous, easy opinions parading as serious and daring ideas. A case in point is Roiphe's claim that date rape is rare and that feminist rape researchers exaggerate the numbers. That is, simply, wrong. Her book cites one so-called expert, who has never actually done any research on rape and is notably biased; he has a record of crusading against feminist legislation. Roiphe ignores a dozen studies, conducted by feminist and nonfeminist social scientists alike, that find that between one in four and one in 12 women will experience an attempted rape or a rape in the course of their lifetimes. But Roiphe never reviews the statistics on rape, never interviews any rape researchers, never talks to a single woman who has been raped. The only "evidence" she marshals to disprove the statistic that one in four college women experience a rape or an attempted rape is her astonishing remark that, as far as she knows, none of her college girlfriends has ever been raped. Yet, none of this low-rent logic seems to faze the media—and why should it? They, after all, haven't bothered to do any serious reporting on the prevalence of rape either.

Sommers, likewise, claims to be a debunker. But if you look closely at her sources, you find she is not doing original research; she is drawing her "facts" from the claims of the same antifeminist men who, a few years ago, would have been the ones sitting in her seat on the talk shows. She claims, for example, that the feminists are foisting upon the U.S. a massive $360 million bureaucracy that will place gender equity and sex harassment police in every high school and college. In fact, the program, the Gender Equity in Education Act, is slated to cost $5 million, features a bureaucracy of one, and has no provisions for such gender police. Where did she get this idea? Not from reading the legislation, but from reading an opinion column by a conservative male pundit.

For the sake of full disclosure, I should say that I'm one of the many feminists to land on the Sommers hit list, and so I have some experience with her technique, which amounts to a full-blown denunciation based on nit-picks. One of her most blazing broadsides against my book, in fact, involves a few words that appear in parentheses. But that seems to characterize the tactics of the antifeminist feminists, who are forever combing the footnotes of feminist works till they find a typo and declaring, "Aha! The whole thesis must be bunk!" The point isn't who's right and who's wrong in the error department. Surely all books have mistakes. The point is: Do the errors undermine the central thesis of the author? And are the media, in promoting the antifeminist feminists' gleeful announcements that they found another boo-boo in a feminist work, trading in real ideas—or simply playing a game of gotcha journalism?

[. . .]

Like the seedless pods of that B-grade horror film, the pod feminists are incapable of bringing new life to the women's movement. Theirs will always be a stillborn form of feminism, because it is an ideology that will not and does not want to generate political, social, or economic change. The pods do not look forward to creating a better future, only inward to the further adulation of self as this year's "most talked-about" model. No matter how many times they replicate themselves on the television screen, they will never produce a world that is wider or fairer for their sex.

108

BELL HOOKS

Black Students Who Reject Feminism (1994)

Recently I stood in a crowded auditorium talking about the ways feminist thinking had changed my life, naming the joy I experience in the feminist movement. When I finished, the only black female student who rose to speak gave an impassioned diatribe against feminism, insisting that it could not meet "our" needs because it was only about the needs of white women, with whom black women had nothing in common. I was stunned. My presence as a black woman academic celebrating the power of feminist thought and practice had in no way challenged her to rethink her ideas about feminism. Indeed, her gaze was not on me but on some imagined group of white women who were making a feminist movement that had nothing to do with her. Nothing I had said had shifted that gaze.

This experience troubled me greatly. Even though feminist scholars like me have worked to create an inclusive feminist movement, one that acknowledges the importance of race and embraces black perspectives, many of today's black students seem to reject the entire idea of feminism.

Most young black females learn to be suspicious and critical of feminist thinking long before they have any clear understanding of its theory and politics. From the mass media and such unlikely sources as black male rap stars, they learn that feminism only serves white women and that "dissin'" it will win them points with just about anybody, particularly sexist black men. Just as some black males hold on to macho stereotypes about maleness as a way of one-upping white men, whom they characterize as wimpy, some young black females feel that they finally can one-up white

From *The Chronicle of Higher Education*, July 13, 1994.

girls by insisting that they are already "real" women, taking care of business, with no need of feminism. These young women are more likely to have read what the rapper Ice T has to say about feminism, in his collection of essays *The Ice Opinion*, than they are to have read a feminist book. Without saying where his understanding of feminism comes from, Ice T asserts: "I don't believe the conflict with feminists is between feminists and men. I think the real controversy is between feminists and other feminists." His attitude conveys the message that there is a problem with feminism itself.

Given that such attitudes reflect a broad suspicion of feminism in our culture, it is not surprising that when black female college students challenge sexism, many want to do so outside the framework of feminist politics. Many of these students call themselves "womanists," as opposed to feminists (even though the writer Alice Walker defined "womanism" as synonymous with feminism). Without rigorously engaging feminist thought, they insist that racial separatism works best. This attitude is dangerous. It not only erases the reality of common female experience as a basis for academic study; it also constructs a framework in which differences cannot be examined comparatively.

Some of the students who reject feminism have taken women's-studies classes in which the professor and most of the students have been white. The black students have been disappointed to find little discussion of how sexism affects male and female roles in black culture. In such classrooms, black students often feel that their perspectives are devalued and their voices silenced, until the rare moment when they may be asked to speak as the "expert" on race.

Furthermore, they encounter a substantial body of work that is racially biased, often written from a standpoint that ignores black women's experiences and thus reinforces white supremacist thinking by viewing white women's experiences as the universal standard for evaluating gender status and identity.

Although I and other progressive feminist

thinkers, both women of color and white women, acknowledge the biases in some feminist work, we nevertheless still urge all women and men to study feminist thought. We believe that it is especially crucial for black females to be active in producing and analyzing feminist theory and feminist politics. When black students refuse to engage feminist thinking, they deny themselves full understanding of a broad base of knowledge that is needed for their intellectual growth and development. Women and men cannot create unbiased scholarship—or even challenge sexism in the workplace and in other aspects of their daily lives—without an understanding of feminist thought grounded in historical knowledge of gender relations and in theoretical arguments.

The notion that black folks have nothing to learn from scholarship that may reflect racial or racist biases is dangerous. It promotes closed-mindedness and a narrow understanding of knowledge to hold that "race" is such an overwhelming concept that it negates the validity of *any* insights contained in a work that may have some racist or sexist aspects. Students may believe that rejecting, without serious critical inquiry, any body of knowledge that emerges from a "racist" source is a form of political resistance, a challenge to mainstream ways of knowing. This may be especially true of black students who embrace neonationalist conceptions of black identity. Actually, such actions promote a cultural narcissism that mirrors the narcissism in Eurocentric thinking that ignores black perspectives in the first place.

Separatism of any kind promotes marginalization of those unwilling to grapple with the whole body of knowledge and creative works available to others. This is true of black students who do not want to read works by white writers, of female students of any race who do not want to read books written by men, and of white students who only want to read works by white thinkers. When the issue is learning, racial separatism of any kind reinforces the dangerous notion that it is acceptable for one group to distort ideas to perpetuate its own

specific interests and biases. The dangers are apparent when we remember that it has taken years to undo the racist and sexist scientific scholarship that once held that women were biologically inferior to men and blacks were inferior to whites.

The hostility to feminism that we see among many black college students today is part of a backlash that includes a strand of Afrocentric thinking that incorporates rigid gender roles supposedly drawn from ancient Africa. Dismissing feminism in this way allows students to ignore the ways that feminist thinking enriches and expands our understanding of black experience. Black female thinkers have continually-challenged biases within mainstream feminist scholarship, insisting that race be recognized as a crucial factor shaping identity.

In the last five years, our work, along with that of other women of color, has pushed feminist thinking to grow and change. For example, feminism began with the premise that women were not part of the work force and would be liberated when they joined it. But when we saw that black women have always worked—without necessarily breaking away from male domination or altering their own ideas of appropriate female behavior—we realized that work was not the only key to improving women's lives. The tremendous revolution in feminist theory generated by collective recognition of the significance of race shows that white supremacist thinking and the racist biases it stems from are not absolute but can be documented and then changed in the face of persuasive evidence.

Although the struggle of progressive feminists to challenge biases continues, our students need to understand that many feminist thinkers have broadened their perspectives. Such openness to learning and to critical inquiry is essential to academic study and to the promotion and preservation of intellectual life.

We must continually remind students in the classroom that expression of different opinions and dissenting ideas affirms the intellectual process. We should forcefully explain that our role is not to teach them to think as we do but rather to teach them, by example, the importance of taking a stance that is rooted in rigorous engagement with the full range of ideas about a topic.

In learning communities from grade school to college, everyone, especially those of us from marginalized groups, must critically resist any thinking that encourages us to close our minds and hearts. We must constructively confront our differences. Through interaction, questioning, and rigorous exchange of ideas, we learn to be more responsive to the actual world of diversity that we encounter, in one way or another, every day of our lives.

We are rarely able to interact only with folks like ourselves, who think as we do. No matter how much some of us deny this reality and long for the safety and familiarity of sameness, inclusive ways of knowing and living offer us the only true way to emancipate ourselves from the divisions that limit our minds and imaginations.

109

Lisa Maria Hogeland

Fear of Feminism: Why Young Women Get the Willies (1994)

I began thinking about young women's fear of feminism, as I always do in the fall, while I prepared to begin another year of teaching courses in English and women's studies. I was further prodded when former students of mine, now graduate students elsewhere and teaching for the first time, phoned in to complain about their young women students' resistance to feminism. It occurred to me that my response—"Of course young women are afraid of feminism"—was not especially helpful. This essay is an attempt to trace out what that "of course" really means; much of it is

From *Ms.*, November/December 1994. Reprinted by permission of *Ms.* Magazine, copyright 1994.

based on my experience with college students, but many of the observations apply to other young women as well.

Some people may argue that young women have far less to lose by becoming feminists than do older women: they have a smaller stake in the system and fewer ties to it. At the same time, though, young women today have been profoundly affected by the demonization of feminism during the 12 years of Reagan and Bush—the time when they formed their understanding of political possibility and public life. Older women may see the backlash as temporary and changeable; younger women may see it as how things are. The economic situation for college students worsened over those 12 years as well, with less student aid available, so that young women may experience their situation as extremely precarious—too precarious to risk feminism.

My young women students often interpret critiques of marriage—a staple of feminist analysis for centuries—as evidence of their authors' dysfunctional families. This demonstrates another reality they have grown up with: the increased tendency to pathologize any kind of oppositional politics. Twelve years of the rhetoric of "special interests versus family values" have created a climate in which passionate political commitments seem crazy. In this climate, the logical reasons why all women fear feminism take on particular meaning and importance for young women.

To understand what women fear when they fear feminism—and what they don't—it is helpful to draw a distinction between gender consciousness and feminist consciousness. One measure of feminism's success over the past three decades is that women's gender consciousness—our self-awareness as women—is extremely high. Gender consciousness takes two forms: awareness of women's vulnerability and celebration of women's difference. Fear of crime is at an all-time high in the United States; one of the driving forces behind this fear may well be women's sense of special vulnerability to the epidemic of men's violence.

Feminists have fostered this awareness of violence against women, and it is to our credit that we have made our analysis so powerful; at the same time, however, we must attend to ways this awareness can be deployed for nonfeminist and even antifeminist purposes, and most especially to ways it can be used to serve a racist agenda. Feminists have also fostered an awareness of women's difference from men and made it possible for women (including nonfeminists) to have an appreciation of things pertaining to women—perhaps most visibly the kinds of "women's culture" commodified in the mass media (soap operas and romance, self-help books, talk shows, and the like). Our public culture in the U.S. presents myriad opportunities for women to take pleasure in being women—most often, however, that pleasure is used as an advertising or marketing strategy.

Gender consciousness is a necessary precondition for feminist consciousness, but they are not the same. The difference lies in the link between gender and politics. Feminism politicizes gender consciousness, inserts it into a systematic analysis of histories and structures of domination and privilege. Feminism asks questions—difficult and complicated questions, often with contradictory and confusing answers—about how gender consciousness can be used both for and against women, how vulnerability and difference help and hinder women's self-determination and freedom. Fear of feminism, then, is not a fear of gender, but rather a fear of politics. Fear of politics can be understood as a fear of living in consequences, a fear of reprisals.

The fear of political reprisals is very realistic. There are powerful interests opposed to feminism—let's be clear about that. It is not in the interests of white supremacy that white women insist on abortion rights, that women of color insist on an end to involuntary sterilization, that all women insist on reproductive self-determination. It is not in the interests of capitalism that women demand economic rights or comparable worth. It is not in the interests of many individual men or many institutions that women demand a nonexploitative sexual autonomy—the right to say and mean both no and yes on our own terms. What would our mass culture look like if it didn't sell women's bodies—even aside from pornography? It is not in the interests of heterosexist patriarchy that women challenge our understandings of events headlined MAN KILLED FAMILY BECAUSE HE LOVED THEM, that women challenge the notion of men's violence against women and children as deriving from "love" rather than power. It is not in the interests of any of the systems of domination in which we are enmeshed that we see how these systems work—that we understand men's violence, male domination, race and class supremacy, as systems of permission for both individual and institutional exercises of power, rather than merely as individual pathologies. It is not in the interests of white supremacist capitalist patriarchy that women ally across differences.

Allying across differences is difficult work, and is often thwarted by homophobia—by fears both of lesbians and of being named a lesbian by association. Feminism requires that we confront that homophobia constantly. I want to suggest another and perhaps more subtle and insidious way that fear of feminism is shaped by the institution of heterosexuality. Think about the lives of young women—think about your own. What are the arenas for selfhood for young women in this culture? How do they discover and construct their identities? What teaches them who they are, who they want to be, who they might be? Our culture allows women so little scope for development, for exploration, for testing the boundaries of what they can do and who they can be, that romantic and sexual relationships become the primary, too often the only, arena for selfhood.

Young women who have not yet begun careers or community involvements too often have no public life, and the smallness of private life, of romance as an arena for selfhood, is particularly acute for them. Intimate relationships become the testing ground for identity, a reality that has enormously damaging consequences for teenage girls in particular (the pressures both toward and on sex and romance, together with the culturally induced destruction of girls' self-esteem at puberty, have everything to do with teenage pregnancy). The feminist insistence that the personal is political may seem to threaten rather than empower a girl's fragile, emergent self as she develops into a sexual and relational being.

Young women may believe that a feminist identity puts them out of the pool for many men, limits the options of who they might become with a partner, how they might decide to live. They may not be wrong either: how many young men feminists or feminist sympathizers do you know? A politics that may require making demands on a partner, or that may motivate particular choices in partners, can appear to foreclose rather than to open up options for identity, especially for women who haven't yet discovered that all relationships require negotiation and struggle. When you live on Noah's ark, anything that might make it more difficult to find a partner can seem to threaten your very survival. To make our case, feminists have to combat not just homophobia, but also the rule of the couple, the politics of Noah's ark in the age of "family values." This does not mean that heterosexual feminist women must give up their intimate relationships, but it does mean that feminists must continually analyze those pressures, be clear about how they operate in our lives, and try to find ways around and through them for ourselves, each other, and other women.

For women who are survivors of men's violence—perhaps most notably for incest and rape survivors—the shift feminism enables, from individual pathology to systematic analysis, is empowering rather than threatening. For women who have not experienced men's violence in these ways, the shift to a systematic analysis requires them to ally themselves with survivors—itself a recognition that *it could hap-*

pen to me. Young women who have not been victims of men's violence hate being asked to identify with it; they see the threat to their emergent sense of autonomy and freedom not in the fact of men's violence, but in feminist analyses that make them identify with it. This can also be true for older women, but it may be lessened by the simple statistics of women's life experience: the longer you live, the more likely you are to have experienced men's violence or to know women who are survivors of it, and thus to have a sense of the range and scope of that violence.

My women students, feminist and nonfeminist alike, are perfectly aware of the risks of going unescorted to the library at night. At the same time, they are appalled by my suggesting that such gender-based restrictions on their access to university facilities deny them an equal education. It's not that men's violence isn't real to them—but that they are unwilling to trace out its consequences and to understand its complexities. College women, however precarious their economic situation, and even despite the extent of sexual harassment and date rape on campuses all over the country, still insist on believing that women's equality has been achieved. And, in fact, to the extent that colleges and universities are doing their jobs—giving women students something like an equal education—young women may experience relatively little overt or firsthand discrimination. Sexism may come to seem more the exception than the rule in some academic settings—and thus more attributable to individual sickness than to systems of domination.

Women of all ages fear the existential situation of feminism, what we learned from Simone de Beauvoir, what we learned from radical feminists in the 1970s, what we learned from feminist women of color in the 1980s: feminism has consequences. Once you have your "click!" moment, the world shifts, and it shifts in some terrifying ways. Not just heterosexism drives this fear of political commitment—it's not just fear of limiting one's partner-pool. It's also about limiting oneself—about the fear of commitment to something larger than the self that asks us to examine the consequences of our actions. Women fear anger, and change, and challenge—who doesn't? Women fear taking a public stand, entering public discourse, demanding—and perhaps getting—attention. And for what? To be called a "feminazi"? To be denounced as traitors to women's "essential nature"?

The challenge to the public-private division that feminism represents is profoundly threatening to young women who just want to be left alone, to all women who believe they can hide from feminist issues by not being feminists. The central feminist tenet that the personal is political is profoundly threatening to young women who don't want to be called to account. It is far easier to rest in silence, as if silence were neutrality, and as if neutrality were safety. Neither wholly cynical nor wholly apathetic, women who fear feminism fear living in consequences. Think harder, act more carefully; feminism requires that you enter a world supersaturated with meaning, with implications. And for privileged women in particular, the notion that one's own privilege comes at someone else's expense—that my privilege *is* your oppression—is profoundly threatening.

Fear of feminism is also fear of complexity, fear of thinking, fear of ideas—we live, after all, in a profoundly anti-intellectual culture. Feminism is one of the few movements in the U.S. that produce nonacademic intellectuals—readers, writers, thinkers, and theorists outside the academy, who combine and refine their knowledge with their practice. What other movement is housed so substantially in bookstores? All radical movements for change struggle against the anti-intellectualism of U.S. culture, the same anti-intellectualism, fatalism, and disengagement that make even voting too much work for most U.S. citizens. Feminism is work—intellectual work as surely as it is activist work—and it can be very easy for women who have been feminists for a long time to for-

get how hard-won their insights are, how much reading and talking and thinking and work produced them. In this political climate, such insights may be even more hard-won.

Feminism requires an expansion of the self—an expansion of empathy, interest, intelligence, and responsibility across differences, histories, cultures, ethnicities, sexual identities, othernesses. The differences between women, as Audre Lorde pointed out over and over again, are our most precious resources in thinking and acting toward change. Fear of difference is itself a fear of consequences: it is less other women's difference that we fear than our own implication in the hierarchy of differences, our own accountability to other women's oppression. It is easier to rest in gender consciousness, in one's own difference, than to undertake the personal and political analysis required to trace out one's own position in multiple and overlapping systems of domination.

Women have real reasons to fear feminism, and we do young women no service if we suggest to them that feminism itself is safe. It is not. To stand opposed to your culture, to be critical of institutions, behaviors, discourses—when it is so clearly *not* in your immediate interest to do so—asks a lot of a young person, of any person. At its best, the feminist challenging of individualism, of narrow notions of freedom, is transformative, exhilarating, empowering. When we do our best work in selling feminism to the unconverted, we make clear not only its necessity, but also its pleasures: the joys of intellectual and political work, the moral power of living in consequences, the surprises of coalition, the rewards of doing what is difficult. Feminism offers an arena for selfhood beyond personal relationships but not disconnected from them. It offers—and requires—courage, intelligence, boldness, sensitivity, relationality, complexity, a sense of purpose, and, lest we forget, a sense of humor as well. Of course young women are afraid of feminism—shouldn't they be?

110
CELESTE HUTCHINS, CHRISTI DENTON,
TAMERA FERRO, AND DANICA
NUCCITELLI
Neofeminism (1998)

WHAT IS NEOFEMINISM?
BY CELESTE HUTCHINS AND
CHRISTI DENTON

Why "neo-feminism?" It's the semantics game. Lately, we've been hearing about this new movement, the "post-feminist" movement. Feminism is passe, an outdated movement, they say. Feminism sucked, because feminism was about not doing your hair, and not doing your makeup.

Well, yeah, if it was really all about hair and makeup, it would suck. But what's the point in arguing about it, when with the wave of the magic prefix wand, post-feminism becomes past tense, and a new movement (re)emerges. Neofeminism. Because post-feminism sucked.

Neofeminism isn't about hair or makeup. But it's not about not doing your hair or makeup. Neofeminism is about women making their own choices that don't limit the choices other women get to make. It's about equal rights, equal pay, equal respect and equal opportunity. It's about you being whoever you want to be.

Antifeminists say feminism is about hating men—and so we give you the right to choose whether you want to hate men. It's not about hating men, 'cause it's not about men. Our self worth is not about how men feel about us. Have you ever noticed how any discussion of feminism almost invariable comes around to men? Someone suggests that it's a reaction against men, or they begin listing statistics that

From http://www.neofeminism.com (6/3/98).

compare women and men, or they relate stories about being a feminist which all center around sexist oppression by men. It's not about men. If it were about men, men couldn't be feminists or neofeminists and we know plenty of feminist, even radical, men. It's about much more than that.

As Rebecca West said back in 1913, "I myself have never been able to find out precisely what feminism is; I only know that people call me a feminist whenever I express sentiments that differentiate me from a doormat." Charlotte Bunch said that "feminism is a transformational force, an individual and social force. It is a way of looking at the world—a questioning of power/domination issues, an affirmation of women's energy." If this is true, then, neofeminism goes even further. Just as neo-Marxism weaves race, gender, sexuality, and other caste systems into the economic class-based analyses of Marxism, neofeminism brings an awareness of these issues into feminism. For example, the campaigns around an anti-affirmative action proposition here in California said that it would hurt "minorities and women," as if the two never crossed and there were no women of color in the world. This is where many people feel that feminism fails; its mainstream face, at least, is white and middle-class.

Neofeminism must do better, and fight to mean women of color, working-class women, fat women, Jewish women, Pagan women, Hindu women, Moslem women, lesbians, bisexuals, male-to-female women, women who are now men, women who are both, old women, rural women, women with disabilities, women with AIDS, women with cancer, battered women, and men who are oppressed from the same sources and reasons as women. We cannot change the world unless we understand that everyone and everything in it is connected in this way. And that's how you can explain it to your friends: neofeminism is the force that is going to change the world.

UTILITARIANISM = NEOFEMINISM
BY TAMERA FERRO

. . . I was one of the lucky ones . . . my parents never expected me to wear a dress or act like a lady. They taught my brother and I the same lessons . . . gardening, working in the tool shop, sewing. I never equated sewing with being "femmy," most likely because my brother was far better at it than I. I was required to fix the brakes on my mom's car before being allowed to use it for my driving test. I'm sick of being told I want to be a man because I know how to fix cars and use power tools. Because I hold the door for you, because I can DO IT MYSELF thank you very much? Utilitarianism is neofeminism. Self-reliance is power. Just because we don't want to be helpless coddled things doesn't mean we don't want to be females. Power is female. Women are not inherently weak, we have a higher pain tolerance, we are built to survive. The backlash against feminism is that women have everything men have, the same opportunities, quit your whining and shut up. Would that it were true! But, it's not. There's still a glass ceiling. There's still a salary difference. I've been asked in job interviews for a date. If these things bother me, I must want to be a man. Yeah, that's it. I am told by society that "boys will be boys." And little girls are still told to act like a lady and play with their pink bake-and-go oven.

So who are your idols? Are they women? Shouldn't they be?

YOU ARE A FEMINIST . . .
BY DANICA NUCCITELLI

I'm sick of hearing women say, "I'm not a FEMINIST, BUT . . ." I'm not a feminist, but I think my daughter should be able to play Little League if she wants to. I'm not a feminist, but I believe Anita. I'm not a feminist, but I think they should stop bashing Hillary all the time. What the hell do you mean you're not a feminist? Do you mean, "I'm not one of those

ugly hairy undesirable women who seems so 'angry' all the time"? Or, "I agree with feminists but I don't identify as one because you might think I'm a lesbian"? Or what? Cause if you can't get comfortable with your own sexuality, if you need to worry all the time about what people might think of you, then maybe you should get ON the feminist train and start being open about your beliefs. Maybe you should study feminism past the twisted images we get from the media about it. You might find out that you really DO support feminist, women's, issues. You might find that listening to the opinions of people who hate feminists doesn't really give you a good overview of what feminists say and think. And you might just find that feminism has done a lot of good in the past twenty years and it's far from being over yet!

You are a neofeminist if you believe that women are equal to men.

You are a neofeminist if you believe that women and men are not treated equally.

You are a neofeminist if you are sick of only seeing super-thin, femme women in TV or movies or ads.

You are a neofeminist if you're sick of going online with a "feminine" name and being approached by guy after guy for cyber-sex.

You are a neofeminist if Hothead Paisan is your idol.

You are a neofeminist if you know that you don't have to be fat or hairy or a lesbian or burn your bra to be a feminist.

You are a neofeminist if you're fine with being fat or hairy or a lesbian or burning your bra anyway.

You are a neofeminist if you want more from a "women's" magazine or "women's" cable channel than just shopping, crafts, family, and fashion.

You are a neofeminist if you can put lipstick on without a mirror.

You are a neofeminist if you think lipstick is only good for faking tribal markings or football smudges on your face.

You are a neofeminist if you're proud of your anger.

You are a neofeminist if you're not afraid to say what you feel.

111

Anastasia Higginbotham

Shall We Dance? (1997)

I think most young feminists planned to dance at the revolution. For whatever hardship or revelation opened our eyes, brains, and hearts to injustice, the moment we linked arms with the women standing next to us was a joyful one. And maybe for the first time in our lives we felt like we had chosen something rather than absorbed it. We were investing in our own future and in those of our someday daughters and sons, we were joining the ranks and enjoying the legacy of our foremothers—in some cases our actual mothers—who were sticking it to the patriarchy long before we were even a sparkle.

But we are more than a sparkle now. We are ablaze and we've begun to dance. For now, the party that is this movement belongs mostly to the foremothers. They've rented the space, provided food and drink, music and ambience. For now, young feminists are mostly stacking cups and refilling the chip bowls, tending to the seating charts and working coat check. For now, we are watching the scene and every once in a while taking a spin on the dance floor, playing with the big girls. For now, the party is mostly theirs, and someday it will be mostly ours.

Of course, not all of us are standing on the sidelines. I could rattle off a list of women under 30 who are already heading their own organizations, pumping out prizewinning fiction, and purging the world of evil, while others of us think about whether we should maybe con-

sider going to grad school or try something other than typing envelopes for the revolution. But I am more interested in what the majority of women of my generation are bringing to the movement now, in terms of vision, energy, and expectations, as everything from worker bees to divas in our own right, and in how we are being received, mentored, and embraced (or rejected) by the women whose work and dedication brought us here.

I'm one of the lucky ones, privileged to be asked to fill a few pages in the twenty-fifth anniversary issue of *Ms.* I am currently being mothered and mentored by some truly exceptional women. Women who appreciate and reward my ability to organize files as much as they value my ability to write a good fund-raising letter. Women who encourage and expect one to think, act, rebel, and strive for every little thing I want in my life. Women who have already been through most of what I'm just now experiencing for the first time, but who never make me feel like an idiot for not knowing better how to navigate a difficult situation.

But my luck was absolutely intentional. I came to the party straight out of college because my experiences there had turned me into an angry little beast, and all I wanted to do afterward was dive headfirst into the movement, history in the making. So I moved to New York and signed myself up. As an intern/worker bee, I cheerfully went out for coffee and M&M's, opened mail, took messages, and sucked in information like a sponge. As a fly on the wall at the party, I discovered that some prominent feminists who are highly respected for their work are known on the inside for being downright mean to other women. I also met veterans of this movement so cool and kind and full of earthly goodness, I felt like I could ask to sleep over and tell stories in bed.

My life, like the lives of a lot of young feminists, makes sense at this party. We share a common language, stories that overlap and bleed into one another, sometimes literally. We got fucked over somewhere along the way by a system and a set of beliefs that say we're not worthy. A handful of us were raised to recognize the signs immediately by mothers and fathers who were down with the cause in the sixties and seventies. Others of us never heard the word "feminism," certainly not in any positive context, until a few years ago, and still feel pressured to silence that part of ourselves when we go back home to where it just isn't O.K. to say or be such a thing. Being and belonging among other activists and freedom fighters solidifies our commitment to mend, change, or overthrow the very things that hurt us.

Previous generations of the sisterhood raised the standards and secured the laws that enable youngsters like myself to feel entitled to equal rights, opportunity, education, and justice. We are still committed to fighting for the basics: safe and legal abortion on demand; affordable child care and health insurance; safety from violence in our homes, in our workplaces, and in the streets; jobs that pay a living wage; and to be taken seriously by folks who hold great gobs of power. All the same things our predecessors wanted, just further along toward actually getting it. If and when we do get screwed, we can take our abusers to court.

That's impressive. Women's lives today do not resemble the lives of women past. We have inherited and absorbed a *how-dare-you* approach to sexism and linking oppressions. And we wear our entitlement on our sleeves, along with the painful awareness that we are far from fully liberated. In terms of violence against women, the violence of poverty, and a culture that all but endorses rape and battery, this is still a pretty scary time to be female.

Generally, young women are no more ungrateful for the radical improvements in our quality of life than any other crop of brassy feminist upstarts in history. In fact, I think we are more attuned to our privileged place in the world as a result of the women's studies, ethnic and cultural studies, and comprehensive history classes many of us took in college. Somebody sat our butts down and showed us the *Eyes on the Prize* documentary series, films about worker rebellion, Rosie the Riveter, the centuries-long struggle for suffrage. They made us read *The Woman Warrior, Incidents in the Life of a Slave Girl, The Yellow Wallpaper,* poetry by Ntozake Shange and Audre Lorde. Things couldn't help but click, click, click, click, click like a rollercoaster on its way up that first big incline.

Most of us know where we came from and are smart enough to bring that knowledge and reverence to the party with us. We know that at some point in history, someone we strongly identify with, someone we knew or are descended from, was burned, detained, gassed, lynched, whipped, relocated, imprisoned, exploited, and/or maligned in service to the status quo, and that this is still happening all over the globe in new and improved ways. It tends to make a person cranky at least, enraged and empowered to do something about it at best.

So what do we plan to do about it? Well, how about much of what's been done before, only more, in less time and with even better results? We're already working like hell, getting law degrees and Ph.D.s, teaching the children, and learning (or pretending) to be businesslike. We're borrowing the master's tools to start our own companies, invade the Internet, and publish and produce our own writing, music, and art as rebellion. We want to change the world and we want our efforts to be noticed—by our enemies whom we hope to get through to, by each other, and by the women who inspired us.

But some of those women who inspired us are not so happy to have us at this party. And sometimes we wish those women would just get off the dance floor and go home. While I suppose this illustrates a tension that is both natural and ancient, our ageist assumptions about one another are no less disappointing, and must be acknowledged and addressed now.

I had a conversation with a woman recently at a conference where the group discussed intergenerational connections and chasms. She was many years my senior in age and experience—and adamant about my generation's disregard for the tireless efforts, sacrifices, and accomplishments bestowed upon us by the women of her generation. I readily admitted that there are those of us who don't get it, but told her there are more who do and who want nothing more than a chance to be part of the history and legacy, to infuse our own spirits into the body and soul of this movement. She was unconvinced. She implied that what she and her sister activists had done was beyond my capacity to even understand, let alone match in this lifetime. Now, that's annoying.

Excuse me for being bon in 1971, but wasn't the whole point of this movement to clear a path so that future generations of women could travel more freely, safely, and courageously than our past-life sisters and be rewarded rather than punished for our bravery and intellect? If our lives look easy, that's precisely because earlier efforts paid off. If our lives look easy, she's not looking closely enough.

Like most women, too many young women are stuck in dead-end jobs, unable to afford an education, let alone health insurance. We are still shamed, blamed, and reviled as much for speaking out against an exploitative situation as we are for being the victims of it.

And no, I will never experience the full impact of growing up in the fifties. I should hope no one would ever wish it upon me. But what I can do—what young women can do—is show an interest in and listen to the stories of those who did survive, who turned survival into defiance, outrage into action. That's really what led us here in the first place. I don't think any of us joined the party so that we could wrestle the torch from the white-knuckled grip of the matriarchs of this movement; we'd be killing off our own army. But don't let us stand against the wall feeling like we don't deserve to be here. We were invited.

And since we're here, we may as well do more than stack cups. A lot of us are earning our livelihoods as assistants—a euphemized version of the secretary and a perfect entry into this movement. Having worked as an assistant for four years, my pride in this job, in my ability to do it well, is the direct result of a feminist education, having learned to value and appreciate the work of the domestic, women's work. But while it's important to me and to the people who pay me that it be done accurately and consistently, I often feel like the only one who still believes in the revolutionary idea that the person who provides clerical support is (1) not stupid and (2) not lowering herself to do it.

Working as an assistant—ideally the updated version of the apprentice—is the best way to absorb the process and details of a workplace, and in this case, a movement. Assistants cannot afford to be stupid; but, on the other hand, the fact that we may have a college degree as well as many aspirations, doesn't mean we're too good to make copies and take messages.

As employers and employees at so-called feminist organizations, we have got to get beyond this idea that only leaders have value. And that until we become the leaders, young women are invisible. We are expected to climb, climb, climb, underpaid and underappreciated, until the big day when we're suddenly older and the boss says, "Hooray, you've reached the top! You'll be paid $100,000 a year from now on. Feel free to go home early and write that novel you've been whining about." This is someone else's model and it's glaring with errors.

When we are cultivated as apprentices, assistants, and decently paid worker bees, young women can have a much greater impact on this movement than if we are made to feel we are paying our dues, biding our time until we can quit these lousy jobs and do something really impressive. A little mentoring goes a long way and doesn't require that a person take great big chunks out of her day to coddle young egos. What young women need are role models who are competent and, for the most part, happy in their work, clear in their instructions, and respectful of our time and talent. The woman I work for ten hours a week refers to her vision of mentoring as putting Post-it notes on whomever is in her charge—gentle reminders to bring a lot to this life; value what you bring; work, play, and expect a lot in return.

None of this should imply that we want all the foremothers to love us—or that we must love them. "That's not the goal here," says Lisa Bowleg, a young feminist and social psychologist at Georgetown University, pointing out that if we're not careful, we end up getting trapped in "appropriate" roles for women where we're failures as females if we don't make nice all the time. "There's work to be done. So rather than sit here nursing this relationship, let's just keep moving forward," adds Bowleg.

Young feminists are already doing really impressive things and most of us are thrilled to be on the arm of the older woman who's taken it upon herself to make sure we develop the right skills and feel welcome anywhere we choose to plant ourselves in the movement. The best part is, we twenty- and early thirty-somethings are not even the littlest sisters at this party. There are a bunch of girls and young women from the single digits on up who are looking in our direction with those big, starry eyes we have surely worn on our own eager faces. Bringing them along is our responsibility, and their contributions, with any luck, will far surpass our own.

And do we all have our work cut out for us or what? A lot of doors have been thrown wide open and are banging on their hinges as more and more women flood through to academia, law, politics, medicine, science, sports, finance, and every other institution that has excluded women with varying degrees of misogyny and blockheadedness throughout history. But the women who reached those doors first are un-coincidentally mostly white and/or middle- to upper-class. That's Agenda Item Number 1. Number 2: other doors have been opened for just a second and then slammed back in our faces by someone shouting "Bitch!" from the other side of the wall. And yes, I do mean The Citadel.

But we are getting there, and we're as deliberate and unified as feminists have ever been. Thanks to the women who got the party following, we'll be dancing this revolution into the dawn.

112

Rebecca Walker

Becoming the Third Wave (1992)

I am not one of the people who sat transfixed before the television, watching the Senate hearings. I had classes to go to, papers to write, and frankly, the whole thing was too painful. A black man grilled by a panel of white men about his sexual deviance. A black woman claiming harassment and being discredited by other women. . . . I could not bring myself to watch that sensationalized assault of the human spirit.

To me, the hearings were not about determining whether or not Clarence Thomas did in fact harass Anita Hill. They were about checking and redefining the extent of women's credibility and power.

Can a woman's experience undermine a man's career? Can a woman's voice, a woman's sense of self-worth and injustice, challenge a structure predicated upon the subjugation of our gender? Anita Hill's testimony threatened to do that and more. If Thomas had not been confirmed, every man in the United States would be at risk. For how many senators never told a sexist joke? How many men have not used their protected male privilege to thwart in some way the influence or ideas of a woman colleague, friend, or relative?

For those whose sense of power is so obviously connected to the health and vigor of the penis, it would have been a metaphoric castration. Of course this is too great a threat.

While some may laud the whole spectacle for the consciousness it raised around sexual harassment, its very real outcome is more informative. He was promoted. She was repudiated. Men were assured of the inviolability of their penis/power. Women were admonished to keep their experiences to themselves.

From *Ms.*, January/February 1992. Reprinted by permission of *Ms.* Magazine, copyright 1992.

The backlash against U.S. women is real. As the misconception of equality between the sexes becomes more ubiquitous, so does the attempt to restrict the boundaries of women's personal and political power. Thomas' confirmation, the ultimate rally of support for the male paradigm of harassment, sends a clear message to women: "Shut up! Even if you speak, we will not listen."

I will not be silenced.

I acknowledge the fact that we live under siege. I intend to fight back. I have uncovered and unleashed more repressed anger than I thought possible. For the umpteenth time in my 22 years, I have been radicalized, politicized, shaken awake. I have come to voice again, and this time my voice is not conciliatory.

The night after Thomas' confirmation I ask the man I am intimate with what he thinks of the whole mess. His concern is primarily with Thomas' propensity to demolish civil rights and opportunities for people of color. I launch into a tirade. "When will progressive black men prioritize my rights and well-being? When will they stop talking so damn much about 'the race' as if it revolved exclusively around them?" He tells me I wear my emotions on my sleeve. I scream "I need to know, are you with me or are you going to help them try to destroy me?"

A week later I am on a train to New York. A beautiful mother and daughter, both wearing green outfits, sit across the aisle from me. The little girl has tightly plaited braids. Her brown skin is glowing and smooth, her eyes bright as she chatters happily while looking out the window. Two men get on the train and sit directly behind me, shaking my seat as they thud into place. I bury myself in *The Sound and the Fury*. Loudly they begin to talk about women. "Man, I fucked that bitch all night and then I never called her again." "Man, there's lots of girlies over there—you know that ho, live over there by Tyrone? Well, I snatched that shit up."

The mother moves closer to her now quiet daughter. Looking at her small back I can see that she is listening to the men. I am thinking of how I can transform the situation, of all the people in the car whose silence makes us complicit.

Another large man gets on the train. After exchanging loud greetings with the two men, he sits next to me. He tells them he is going to Philadelphia to visit his wife and child. I am suckered into thinking that he is different. Then, "Man, there's a ton of females in Philly, just waitin' for you to give 'em some." I turn my head and allow the fire in my eyes to burn into him. He takes up two seats and has hands with huge swollen knuckles. I imagine the gold rings on his fingers slamming into my face. He senses something, "What's your name, sweetheart?" The other men lean forward over the seat.

A torrent explodes: "I ain't your sweetheart, I ain't your bitch, I ain't your baby. How dare you have the nerve to sit up here and talk about women that way, and then try to speak to me." The woman/mother chimes in to the beat with claps of sisterhood. The men are momentarily stunned. Then the comeback: "Aw, bitch, don't play that woman shit over here 'cause that's bullshit." He slaps the back of one hand against the palm of the other. I refuse to back down. Words fly.

My instinct kicks in, telling me to get out. "Since I see you all are not going to move, I will." I move to the first car. I am so angry that thoughts of murder, of physically retaliating against them, of separatism, engulf me. I am almost out of body, just shy of being pure force. I am sick of the way women are negated, violated, devalued, ignored. I am livid, unrelenting in my anger at those who invade my space, who wish to take away my rights, who refuse to hear my voice. As the days pass, I push myself to figure out what it means to be a part of the Third Wave of feminism. I begin to realize that I owe it to myself, to my little sister on the train, to all of the daughters yet to be born, to push beyond my rage and articulate an agenda. After battling with ideas of separatism and militancy, I connect with my own feelings of powerlessness. I realize that I must undergo a transformation if I am truly committed to women's empowerment. My involvement must reach beyond my own voice in discussion, beyond voting, beyond reading feminist theory. My anger and awareness must translate into tangible action.

I am ready to decide, as my mother decided before me, to devote much of my energy to the history, health, and healing of women. Each of my choices will have to hold to my feminist standard of justice.

To be a feminist is to integrate an ideology of equality and female empowerment into the very fiber of my life. It is to search for personal clarity in the midst of systemic destruction, to join in sisterhood with women when often we are divided, to understand power structures with the intention of challenging them.

While this may sound simple, it is exactly the kind of stand that many of my peers are unwilling to take. So I write this as a plea to all women, especially the women of my generation: Let Thomas' confirmation serve to remind you, as it did me, that the fight is far from over. Let this dismissal of a woman's experience move you to anger. Turn that outrage into political power. Do not vote for them unless they work for us. Do not have sex with them, do not break bread with them, do not nurture them if they don't prioritize our freedom to control our bodies and our lives.

I am not a postfeminism feminist. I am the Third Wave.

113

BELL HOOKS

"Feminism—It's a Black Thang!" (1992)

It is obvious that most Black men are not in positions that allow them to exert the kind of institutionalized patriarchal power and control over Black women's lives that privileged white men do in this society. But it is undeniable that

From *Essence,* July 1992. Reprinted by permission of the author.

they do exert a lot of power over Black women and children in everyday life. Most of us are, however, reluctant to admit that male domination causes much of the gender conflict and pain experienced in Black women's lives.

Whether a man demands that "his" woman turn her signed paycheck over to him or forces his female companion to do the "wild thing" without a condom (because "the condom hurts" him), such assertions of power are sexist and abusive. And even if Black women do not have to face the sexist threats of male domination in the home, all too often when we walk down the streets, it is the brothers, not white men, who address us with sexual taunts. And if we do not respond, they become hostile and scream epithets at us like "Bitch, you think you too good to speak to me?" And when sexist incidents like this occur, Black women feel afraid—afraid that we may be hit, raped, robbed or some combination of the above.

Yet in spite of the fact that thousands of Black women are assaulted by Black males on the street or in the home every day, in most of these cases our male offenders do not believe that they've done anything wrong. Note recent conversations among Black folks about the Tyson case, where, by and large, men and women tend to see the woman as guilty, even though Tyson's own public history reveals him to be a man who has consistently abused women.

It is also no comfort to any of us that so much Black popular music—especially the growing subgenre of women-hating rap—encourages Black males and every other listener to think there is nothing wrong with abusing women in general, and Black women in particular. That a Black male rap group like N. W. A. can become richer and even more famous than they already are by pushing woman-bashing lyrics is a sign of how dangerous these times are for women. And if any of us should think the boys are just having a little fun at our expense, we should take note of the fact that one of the group members is being sued for assaulting Black female televison host Dee Barnes in an L.A. club. He has responded by bragging in *Rolling Stone:* "It ain't no big thing—I just threw her through a door." Let's face it, abusive Black male domination of Black women and children is so much a regular part of everyday Black life that most Black folks do not take it seriously.

Every Black person concerned about our collective survival must acknowledge that sexism is a destructive force in Black life that cannot be effectively addressed without an organized political movement to change consciousness, behavior and institutions. What we need is a feminist revolution in Black life. But to have such a revolution, we must first have a feminist movement.

Many Black folks do not know what the word *feminism* means. They may think of it only as something having to do with white women's desire to share equal rights with white men. In reality, feminism is a movement to end *all* sexism and sexist oppression. The strategies necessary to achieve that end are many. We need to find ways to address the specific forms that sexism takes in our diverse communities. We must start by educating our communities—at the grass-roots level—as to what sexism is, how it is expressed in daily life and why it creates problems.

Today many Black women and men are afraid that if we say that we support feminist movements, we will either be seen as traitors to the race or be privately or publicly humiliated by other Black people. In the past few months I have talked at colleges around the country where young Black men are physically threatening and even assaulting Black female students for criticizing and resisting Black male sexism, for starting Black female consciousness-raising support groups and even for taking women's studies classes.

A feminist movement that addresses the needs of Black women, men and children can strengthen our bonds with one another, deepen our sense of community and further Black liberation. We must not be afraid to create such a movement.

114

KRISTAL BRENT ZOOK

A Manifesto of Sorts for a Black Feminist Movement (1995)

When Mike Tyson's a hero, Louis Farrakhan's a leader and the old guard of women stands silent, it's left to a new generation to change the rules.

Wedged into a string of small black-owned art galleries in Los Angeles's Afrocentric cultural district of Degnan Avenue sat the Western-region headquarters for the Million Man March. "Let's start this off with a prayer, sisters, 'cause I got the devil in me tonight." The meeting of 20-odd "sisters in support" of the march has only just begun and their commando was already squaring off with Satan. Most of the women present were members of the Nation of Islam. A few, like the speaker, were community activists and church leaders. To my left, a woman from US (United Slaves), a black nationalist organization founded in the 1960's, took notes on a yellow legal pad. As if lifted from the set of Mario van Peebles's "Panther," her ensemble was classic Black Power, complete with a medium-length Afro, embroidered dashiki and oversize black-rimmed glasses. I turned to her and asked if the issue of women's marching had been addressed yet. She shook her head no and then said, "Maybe we should do that now."

But the speaker wasn't having it. The group had already agreed to raise bus fare for low-income teen-age boys who wanted to make the trip, and a great deal of work had yet to be done. "That question needs to be answered and should be answered," she announced, "but it'll have to be at another time, in another place."

If that time isn't now, then when should it be? More than 23 years have gone by since Shirley Chisolm's failed Presidential campaign,

From *The New York Times Magazine,* November 12, 1995. Reprinted by permission of the author.

but today, black feminism is not only a shunned political platform: it has become the great unspoken. When I talked to Constance Rice, the Western regional counsel of the NAACP Legal Defense and Educational Fund, she chided me by speaker phone. Writing about black feminism only "contributes to the Willie Hortonization of black men," she said, and warned me to "think hard" before embarking on such an "injurious" path. And Rice is not alone. According to a widely cited University of Chicago survey released earlier this year, 29 percent of African-Americans believe that black feminists do little more than "divide the black community."

But it's already divided: black women's voices don't move through public arenas in the same way that black men's do. We live in an era in which the narrative of the Endangered Black Man resonates with increasing force among both women and men because, as Cornel West put it, "the vilification of the black male is a crucial component in the way in which white supremacy is being used in our society." But by exalting the persecutions of black men, the narrative elevates their particular truths to the mythical status of universal black reality.

It was this myth that former Representative Mel Reynolds of Illinois invoked (as did Clarence Thomas and Marion Barry before him) after being sentenced to five years in prison for having sex with an underage campaign worker. Reynolds's comparison of his own predicament to the shackling of his slave ancestors would have been laughable if it hadn't been so pathetic. A few weeks later, Brenda Moran, a juror in the O. J. Simpson trial, said that the prosecution's discussion of domestic violence was "a waste of time" given that the case was about murder. The news reports on the day of the verdict were full of shots of battered black women cheering the verdict in a shelter. But nowhere was there mention of the 54 percent of black women who suffer abuse at the hands of men who say they love them.

And then came Oct. 16, the day Louis Farrakhan declared that black men would finally stand up and seize their rightful place as leaders of their communities. The march was, as Kimberle Crenshaw, a law professor at Columbia University, put it, the political incarnation of Shahrazad Ali's "Blackman's Guide to Understanding the Black Woman," her incendiary treatise that advocated, among other things, a good backhand slap to keep one's woman in line.

It wasn't banishment from the march that was so offensive—after all, black women have certainly convened our share of closed-door assemblies. It was being told to stay home with the children, to be quiet and prepare food for our warrior kings. What infuriated progressive black women was that the rhetoric of protection and atonement was just a seductive mask for old-fashioned sexism. And no wonder: the march, planned by Louis Farrakhan, the Nation of Islam leader, and the Rev. Ben Chavis, the former executive director of the N.A.A.C.P., was entrenched in the hierarchies of church and mosque, institutions that have historically cast women as helpmates rather than equals.

Behind the banner of the Endangered Black Man, former gang leaders and members of the hip-hop community were able to forge common ground with Bible-quoting Baptists and Koran-quoting Muslims. Even traditional female-dominated organizations like the National Association of Black Social Workers, the National Council of Negro Women and the National Political Congress of Black Women, founded by C. DeLores Tucker, offered their endorsements despite the march's dangerous nationalistic call for a romanticized black masculinity. In Tucker's view, the world needed "to see that black mothers and grandmothers did not give birth to gangsters, robbers, thieves and rapists."

And she had a point. The Endangered Black Man narrative speaks to very real assaults on the material and spiritual well-being of black men. But it is also part of the larger myth of racial authenticity that has been so successfully cultivated in ghettocentric culture, a myth that renders invisible the specific contours of living in female, working-class, gay and lesbian black bodies. The notion of black authenticity tricks us into equating support of the Million Man March, or O. J. Simpson for that matter, with support for black people, because anything else is considered race treason.

Well, many of us have grown tired of such backwoodsman reasoning. When the names Rodney King, O. J. Simpson, Mike Tyson, Marion Barry and even Clarence Thomas become symbolic, like "Scottsboro," black women are left without a way to talk about how some of the Scottsboro "boys" (accused of raping two white women) actually did commit acts of violence and murder against their girlfriends and wives. Black women are left without a way to address Rodney King as anything other than victim, even after his second arrest for domestic violence. And we have no response to Tupac Shakur's nameless accuser, whose lonely plea—"I did not deserve to be gang-raped"— paled in comparison to *Vibe* magazine's five-page cover story on Shakur as the "misunderstood" thug.

The choice between "keeping it real" (whatever that means) and not being "black enough" has become an increasingly pressing one for my generation. Growing up after civil rights, women's lib and the sexual revolution, my generation of black women is not necessarily obsessed with the Man in the same ways that the old guard was. Many of us live among, and even love, white people. Some of us are biracial. And some are bisexual. We are more conscious than ever about the ways in which our lives both intersect with and differ from those of white women, other women of color and third-world peoples. We do not easily side with "good race women" who sacrifice their own complexities in the interest of blind race unity. And our politics are about more than awkward adjustments of protocol, or having a woman as the head of the N.A.A.C.P. They're about the fact that although we remember the same racist violations as black men, we also remember some that are very different.

Like the time that a Guatemalan immigrant neighbor pushed my flannel nightgown over 8-year-old hips and rammed thick, brown fingers where they had no place. Or a couple of years later, when a white stranger conned me into lifting my calico sun dress for him by promising to make me a Sears bikini model. These intrusions have something, though not everything, to do with race. Such memories make for a world view that looks nothing like those of leather-clad heroes fighting police brutality in the streets of Oakland; nothing like the nightmares of Mississippi brothers and sisters who last saw their grandparents swinging from trees. My memories more closely resemble those of a Manhattan Beach, Calif., white woman who, upon opening her door to me one chilly December evening as I canvassed for National Action Against Rape, saw not the brown skin of the Other, but herself.

At the same time, she could never fully appreciate the specific ways in which I've learned to confuse love with kinship. Or what it means to grow up knowing only two black men. Only two. One, an uncle who overdosed on heroin long before I hit puberty, and the other, his brother who sometimes hopes for a similar fate, even today.

[. . .]

There is a gaping divide between traditional black leaders and those of us they should be passing the torch to, but what else is new? After all, even Ida B. Wells, who was the voice of the anti-lynching movement, was denied a place on the N.A.A.C.P.'s board—and by none other than W.E.B. DuBois. Still, for all our "double jeopardy" consciousness about being both black and female, progressive black women have yet to galvanize a mass following or to spark a concrete movement for social change.

Deborah Gray White, a historian at Rutgers University, argues that the blueprint for such a movement did in fact exist in the late 19th century. The National Association of Colored Women, a federation of 200 black women's clubs founded in 1896, was particularly militant under the leadership of Mary Church Terrell, White says, adopting "a feminism that was unprecedented" for its time. But as White also acknowledges, the club women's declaration of equality with (and even superiority to) black men was deeply tied to 19th-century bourgeois norms that regarded women as the moral sex. For all of the club movement's good works, including employment agencies and self-improvement programs for women, it never abandoned its need to play it safe and be polite.

The legacy of the club movement persists within black women's organizations today. The National Political Congress of Black Women, for example, was founded by C. DeLores Tucker in 1984 to increase the number of African-American women in both elective and appointive offices. The group's mandate, Tucker says, is to "serve as a collective voice on issues pertaining to the economic and social empowerment of black women." When I spoke with Tucker about the march, her work and feminism, she graciously invited me to her organization's annual awards brunch at the Congressional Black Caucus Legislative Conference in Washington. Clearly, she was excited about this year's program, in which, as she put it, "our three queens" would be honored: Coretta Scott King, Betty Shabazz and Myrlie Evers-Williams, all widows of black martyrs. I couldn't bring myself to say so at the time, but to venerate women solely on the basis of the men they married is just inexcusably retro.

In the words of Prof. Lisa A. Crooms at Howard University Law School, it is precisely "our institutional history of club- and church-based movements" that forces black women into restrictive molds of middle-class femininity. Even Jewell Jackson McCabe's National Coalition of 100 Black Women, one of the first traditional black women's organizations to publicly support Anita Hill and by far the most progressive, looks a lot like Tucker's group. Both organizations are more conducive to professional networking than to radical social change.

It struck me at one point that black women like Alice Walker, Toni Morrison and Maya Angelou have been more successful using literary rather than political forums to articulate the specific realities of our lives. In fact, one could regard Oprah Winfrey's ownership of the film rights to novels like Morrison's "Beloved" and Zora Neale Hurston's "Their Eyes Were Watching God," coupled with her roles in "The Women of Brewster Place" and "The Color Purple," as something of a one-woman crusade to bring black feminist thought to popular culture. Of course, part of the reason she, the ultimate club woman, can do this is that she makes millions more than most, black or white. Then too, the consciousness raised by these productions doesn't necessarily translate into things like prenatal health care, jobs or scholarships.

There are those black women, of course, who reject club movement groups and try to create their own coalitions, women who could be seen as the bridge between conventional leadership and a new guard. A gathering of such women took place six days before the Million Man March. Several dismayed activists and scholars met to draft a statement of protest and plan a teach-in at Columbia University for the day of the march. Among those in attendance were the group's core organizers—including Kimberle Crenshaw, Angela Davis, Jewell Jackson McCabe, Marcia Ann Gillespie and Paula Giddings—and participants like Michele Wallace, Rebecca Walker and Derrick Bell. But such formations are rare.

Among my generation, a few women are creating mobile, multicultural and coed groups of diverse sexual orientations and class backgrounds. Kimberly Weaver, the 21-year-old chairwoman of the N.A.A.C.P.'s National Youth Work Committee, is one of them. Currently in her last year at Emory University, Weaver has begun to turn from the N.A.A.C.P. to conduct feminist workshops for members of black and white sororities. "I try to hook it up to literature to explain how movements have gone, things that people have written and thoughts that other women have had," she says. "For Sisterhood Week, we talked about bell hooks's 'Ain't I a Woman?' and our problems with the term feminism, and then you give them something like Barbara Smith's black feminist criticism."

Rebecca Walker founded Third Wave in 1992, a multi-issue activist group whose membership's average age is 25, in response to both the Clarence Thomas hearings and the Rodney King beating. That summer 150 young people (mostly women) participated in their own version of Freedom Summer, traveling through 23 cities and registering 20,000 voters. "There were people who had just come out of drug rehab, people who had been living on the streets, people who had just graduated from Ivy League colleges, people who had been organizers all their lives," said Walker, a writer whose mother is Alice Walker. In 1996, the group, now numbering between 500 and 600, plans to do another Freedom Summer, this time riding through rural areas of the Middle West to address health care and reproductive freedom in places where "pro-choice is really at risk."

But while pockets of activists like Walker can be found outside traditional black organizations or, like Weaver, barely hanging on from the inside, rank and file black feminists remain essentially leaderless. We have no "Great Heroes" T-shirts like those with the faces of Malcolm X, Martin Luther King Jr., Marcus Garvey, Nelson Mandela and Bob Marley clustered across them. Mike Tyson, O. J. Simpson and Tupac Shakur have already been added to the iconography, but it's unlikely that we'll ever see the brothers on the corner peddling righteous images of Anita Hill or Joycelyn Elders.

The other night as I was thinking about such things, I heard a black woman's voice steadily rise outside my window. As she castigated her lover for some act that I had yet to make out, he remained oddly silent. The woman was Shahrazad Ali's perfect prototype of the Emasculating Black Bitch. You know, the same one that so many marching men had hoped to exorcise once and for all. Anything but submissive, she was the reason, we're told,

black men date white women—sisters are too hard, too mean, too damn loud.

So how do we practice the art of vulnerability without losing ourselves in antiquated notions of queenliness and the good wife? How do we survive in a world that abhors us? The source of our power is larger than beauty contests and star chasing (which may or may not have been what Desiree Washington had in mind), just as black men are far more noble than the twisted norms of athlete culture have made Mike Tyson believe.

Why, then, do we remain stuck in the past? The answer has something to do with not just white racism but also our own fear of the possible, our own inability to imagine divinity within ourselves. There are so many of us yearning to fight the good fight. In our hearts we know, as Cornel West put it to me, that our struggle lies in that space between black suffering and "the degree to which that focus is obscured by patriarchal, homophobic and other xenophobic sensibilities." We know this. But instead of picking up where Ida B. Wells left off, black women too often allow our struggle to be reduced to the anti-lynching campaigns of the Tupac Shakurs, the Mike Tysons, the O. J. Simpsons and the Clarence Thomases of the world. Instead of struggling with, and against, those who sanction injustice, too often we stoop beneath them, our backs becoming their bridges. In our homes, we continue to make love despite a continuum of sexual aggression both behind and beyond our doors, and we find ways to stow away our memories. But most of us do not act. And we are not public with our pain.

Now, more than ever, is the time for a complex unity between black women and men, not a habitual one. If that means that we are rejected by black men—or the straight or the rich or the nationalistic among us—then so be it. Many in my generation intuitively understand that black women don't always think or feel or even look black in the "authentic," stereotypical sense of the word. We don't always think or feel or look like "women." But we are black. We are women. And we are human.

More than 76 years ago, the historian Carter G. Woodson wrote that the race needs workers, not leaders. My generation of black women must begin to lead one another, more vigilantly, to the work that our hearts demand we do. And we must create public spaces along the way in which we can use our hardness, our meanness, our loudness, to challenge the models we've inherited. Only then will we have constructed a path worth following. Only then will we have entered that other time, that other place.

115

Barbara Jones, Anita Blair, Barbara Ehrenreich, Jeanne Lewis, Arlie Russell Hochschild, and Elizabeth Perle McKenna

Giving Women the Business: On Winning, Losing, and Leaving the Corporate Game (1997)

When Brenda Barnes, one of the highest-ranking female executives in the United States, announced last September that she had resigned as president and CEO of Pepsi-Cola North America to spend more time with her children, the media promptly cast her as a representative casualty of the anxiety and ambivalence forced on women by the terms of corporate success. Although Barnes asked that her choice not serve as a basis for generalization, some observers could not do otherwise. "This has set the rest of us back a long time," a female marketing consultant told the *Wall Street Journal,* warning that Barnes "was *too* honest. . . . [T]he workplace isn't the place for frankness."

Wishing to offer an opportunity for such forbidden frankness, *Harper's Magazine* invited five interested parties to discuss women and their ongoing troubles inside corporations.

From *Harper's Magazine,* December 1997. Reprinted with the permission of *Harper's Magazine.*

The following forum is based on a discussion held over lunch in the Summit room on the sixtieth floor of the John Hancock Mutual Life Insurance Company building in Boston. Barbara Jones served as moderator.

Barbara Jones is a senior editor of *Harper's Magazine.*

Anita Blair is CEO of the Independent Women's Forum, a Washington, D.C., think tank devoted to women's business issues, and a founding partner of Welty & Blair, a business-law practice in Arlington, Virginia. As a member of the Virginia Military Institute's Board of Visitors, she led the unsuccessful campaign to go private rather than admit women.

Barbara Ehrenreich is a political essayist, columnist, and social critic, and the author, most recently, of *Blood Rites: Origins and History of the Passions of War.* Her report "Spinning the Poor into Gold: How Corporations Seek to Profit from Welfare Reform" appears in the August issue of *Harper's Magazine.*

Arlie Russell Hochschild is a professor of sociology at the University of California at Berkeley. She is the author of *The Time Bind: When Work Becomes Home & Home Becomes Work* and, with Anne Machung, of *The Second Shift: Working Parents and the Revolution at Home,* among other books.

Jeanne Lewis is the senior vice president, Retail and Small Business Marketing, of Staples, Inc., a national office-supply chain with annual sales of approximately $4 billion, where she has strategic, operational, and financial responsibility for retail marketing.

Elizabeth Perle McKenna is a former associate publisher of Bantam Books and the former publisher of Prentice-Hall, Addison-Wesley, William Morrow, and Avon Books. She is the author of *When Work Doesn't Work Anymore: Women, Work, and Identity.*

THE SITUATION

Barbara Jones: You are a vice president, on your way to becoming a senior vice president, at a Fortune 500 company where you've worked for twelve years. As it happens, your husband has recently lost his job as a college professor and is seeking adjunct work. But whether or not he finds a job, you are the family breadwinner. You also bring home the health insurance and retirement benefits. You've been working since you got out of college, and you love your job. You have a big appetite for corporate life. You want to climb as far up the ladder as you can. But there are forces in play at your company that are not about the work itself. You watch the men play golf and call it business, which you can understand, but after some female colleagues have been in your office discussing work, you overhear a senior male colleague disparage this meeting as a coffee klatch. A young female associate tells you that at her review her boss complained that she spent too much time in the bathroom; he added that women employees often spend too much time in the bathroom. Another woman learns that she's making significantly less than a new male employee with precisely her background and responsibilities; when she asks for a raise, she's given a small increase that does not make her salary comparable to his; she's also given the big chill. You learn that another woman at your office has been criticized by a senior man for not dressing femininely enough. You hear a joke—or a rumor, you're not really sure which—that a female senior vice president has became a parent by surrogate pregnancy, because there's no time at this company for a real pregnancy and—as everyone knows—clients don't like to meet with pregnant women. When a male senior manager calls a 7:00 P.M. meeting and a male associate says he needs to be home with his children and asks how the senior manger can stay so late when he has children too, the manager jokes, "I've got a wife. Why don't you get a wife?" Your mentor, who is very competitive and very successful at what she does, gives birth to a third child and quits her job to be with her children; a man gets her position. Your mentor was insightful, if, perhaps, too feminist for you, about what she thought was

happening at the office. She talked about the corporate culture as a male culture, created by and for white men, and not a good culture for human life or commerce. She talked about a clash between the values she wants to have as a parent versus the values of the office. She told you once, bitterly, that her boss said of her first pregnancy, "That's wonderful, just don't tell anyone about it." This first-rate woman's departure discourages you, because you *do* want to be part of corporate life. You *do* want to stay in and climb the ladder.

This scenario is a compilation of some of the real situations I've heard about in the past few months. It seems, on an anecdotal level, that women are having a hard time in corporate America. The statistics are sketchy but seem to support the anecdotal evidence. For the first time in nearly twenty years, the wage gap between men and women is widening (full-time working women make just under 75 percent of men's median income, down from 77 percent four years ago). Although 46 percent of the U.S. workforce is female, nearly 98 percent of the senior-level management of Fortune 500 companies are males. Less than 2 percent of Fortune 500 top wage earners are women. Under .5 percent of Fortune 500 CEOs are women. In a 1995 Yankelovich poll, only 2 percent of professional and executive women said they were ever satisfied with their jobs. What is really going on?

Arlie Russell Hochschild: Women haven't cracked into the corporate elite for a lot of reasons. They don't have powerful sponsors at work. And they don't have "wifes" at home, so they are strapped for time. Junior male executives who are, in a way, defectors from the senior male culture have told me, in whispers, "What senior men say to us is, 'These family-friendly places are nothing. I don't want to hear another word about work-family balance.'" In the top circles family-friendly policies are a fig leaf over a highly workaholic culture. The enormous time demands are a way of shunting women out, women being the ones who often feel more responsibility for kids.

Elizabeth Perle McKenna: Except that I have one child and three stepchildren instead of three children, the mentor who quit her job muttering about values could have been me, although I didn't leave to be at home with my son but to find work that was sane, which is a very important point. Yes, I define myself by my job. Is it all of me? No. But is it the cornerstone of my identity? Absolutely.

Let's face it, the rules for success, which are unwritten, are really a value system. The first thing I learned when I went to work was that it was more important to act right than be right. I had to look as if work was everything. Long hours are a requirement. Nothing, absolutely nothing, can appear to be more important than what you do. Now, these rules *may* have made sense in the 1950s, in an affluent culture during an aberrant hiccup of history when Americans had enough money that someone could stay home and do all the work of child rearing and taking care of sick relatives for free and someone could go to the office and be sacrificed to the pillar of success. But these rules don't make sense now, and not just for women. They don't make sense for a whole generation of people who need two incomes to pay the bills.

Jones: Aren't time demands necessary for a corporation to produce?

Hochschild: Most people believe that. But that statement is overly simple, bordering on false. What matters most is not how long you work but how you work. Lotte Bailyn, an MIT sociologist who studied a team of long-hours engineers at Xerox, found that they could never meet their project deadlines. But when, at her suggestion, the company established midday "library hours" during which no one (not even nervous managers) was allowed to interrupt the engineers, they met their deadline for the first time. They didn't work longer to produce more.

Jeanne Lewis: I disagree with the picture you're painting of the workplace. Well, I half disagree. Whenever I read articles or hear things about corporate America, a homoge-

neous notion doesn't spring to mind. I think of individual places I've worked. I worked in the banking industry before going to business school, and I've been fortunate enough to be with Staples since business school. Culturally, the banking industry sounds like what you're talking about, but the retail industry, and in particular where I work, could not be more different. Even within a corporation, different departments are subcultures within a culture. I don't think a homogeneous corporate culture exists.

Hochschild: Well, take it subculture by subculture.

Anita Blair: That doesn't work either. It's not even industry specific. Probably Staples and your competitor Office Depot are quite different.

Lewis: I can speak from experience on that, because we almost merged with Office Depot. We had the opportunity to see what their culture is like and they are very different from us.

Blair: Men and women both gravitate to companies where they can feel culturally at home. And if you don't feel at home in a particular industry, that doesn't mean you're never going to find a home in so-called corporate America. It means that you're not compatible with a particular company or a particular department.

Lewis: I've got to believe, though, that Staples is not unique. I have friends participating in other corporate environments who are having experiences similar to mine: they're producing and being rewarded.

Barbara Ehrenreich: But you're inside. You see individual companies. I'm outside. To me, from the outside, the phrase "corporate culture" means something. It's a very hierarchical culture and, compared with one of the few other kinds of organizations I've worked in, which is academic, the corporate culture demands a lot of conformity. You are kept in line. In fact, even as you talk, Jeanne, I'm wondering, "How free is she to talk here, knowing that this is going to be published?" You can say, "Oh, that's insulting. I can say what I want." But I can say anything and I can't be fired. And Arlie can say pretty much anything, because the sociology department at UC Berkeley is not going to say, "We heard you said such and such at a *Harper's Magazine* forum" and toss her out.

Jones: We did speak with a number of women executives, many of whom gave me an earful about their personal experiences, but it was very difficult to find anyone who could speak on the record and feel safe about her job.

McKenna: Of the 200 women I spoke to for my book, nobody spoke on the record. Everyone said, "I'll give you the truth, but you've got to give me a new name." And I can understand their position. In corporate life, I was told to not rock the boat. Shut up. Toe the line. Support the agenda.

Lewis: I actually have a problem even with—this is not a Staples-specific issue, but—I have a problem when people talk about child care and work-family balance and men are not part of that discussion. It should matter to them as well.

Jones: A man is not going to be fired because his wife is going to have a baby. His family's pregnancy is not going to enter into his job equation.

Blair: But it's illegal to fire somebody for pregnancy.

Jones: It's still happening.

Blair: As a lawyer, what I find often happens is that somebody is pregnant, and she's having a terrible time of it and missing a lot of work. That person may be fired for missing work. That's not the same as getting fired for being pregnant.

Jones: But if we want a next generation, and if women are working, working women are going to have to have babies, right?

Blair: You've still got a job that needs to be done. The deal between the employer and the employee was not: "I'm going to pay you regardless of how many hours you came to work." The deal is: "You work, you get paid."

McKenna: My private name for what's going on is "Ophelia goes to the office." We're all aware that young women now face very real,

difficult decisions about how they're gong to fit in to the culture—they've got to be quiet and popular, or speak out and maybe not be accepted—and I think a similar set of pressing decisions follows women into the office environment: What am I trading to stay at this job? What am I pushing down inside of me?

Hochschild: What is also happening is that the workplace itself, the thing women are moving into, is shifting. We have to keep our eye on two balls; what women are doing, and what the workplace is doing. What the workplace is doing is dividing the workforce into two tiers. One tier is a kind of workaholic cult at the top; the other tier is made up of contingency workers, part-time workers, temporary workers, contract workers, who often don't have benefits. The top tier is getting smaller, and the bottom tier is getting bigger. From the point of view of capitalism and shareholders, the system can have more flexibility this way. There are always oscillations in demand for goods and services, and now you don't have to hold onto workers and pay their benefits while demand is low. You can forget about them. You can store them and just call on them when you want to. This makes bottom-line sense. But it exacerbates competition in the top tier, so fewer and fewer of the women who are hanging on at the top can also have a—

McKenna: A life.

Hochschild:—a personal life. Women should be equal to men, but in what kind of system? You could have a company that rewarded productivity but didn't push family life so far into the margin.

Blair: I attribute the problems you describe almost entirely to regulation. The reason there's this bottom tier is that government has imposed a lot of demands and requirements on business that business simply can't handle. When government says pay people X amount of money and give everybody health insurance, it severely restricts the ability of business to negotiate with workers. When businesses have to treat everybody the same, they have to shrink the number of their everybodies. Businesses didn't wake up one day and say, "We're going to have part-timers and independent contractors, and we're going to try to do our best to get rid of people." Instead, they woke up and said, "We're subject to all these taxes and labor rules, and if we're going to exist and make money, then we have to do different things with our personnel than we used to do."

Jones: Are you saying that if the government were not leaning on corporations, there would be more women at the top?

Blair: No, I disagree with the whole premise of your question. The problems you describe of getting to the top of a big corporation are not unique to women. It's a false dichotomy to say that somehow men have it easy and just swim to the top whereas women have all these problems. News flash: men have problems, too. It's very, very competitive to get to the top of any hierarchical organization such as business is, and business is that way because historically it's worked. People can not easily achieve their ambitions as a result of a lot of these things we're talking about, but the obstacles are not exclusive to women. Incidentally, I reject the notion of a level playing field. Only God can make a level playing field. Fate intervenes, no matter what. There's no way that we can create a level playing field, and it doesn't seem to exist in nature either.

Hochschild: You're saying that it's impossible to have equal terms for people?

Blair: Sure, you can have equal terms for people, but that's not a level playing field. You still can break your leg. Things that are beyond anyone's control will affect the outcome.

Jones: Well, why should women even try to compete in these bad corporate environments?

Blair: Indeed why, when they have choices? Corporate America, and particularly the large corporations, is really only one of the choices a person has. There is government, which employs 15 percent of all workers in the United States; there are nonprofits, educational institutions, hospitals, and so forth. There is small business, and there's religion and the military— old classical occupations. So I have no sense that

women are somehow being herded into corporate America and there made to suffer.

Hochschild: Quite the opposite. [Laughter]

STAYING IN THE GAME

McKenna: A company I know, which is a small unit of a big company and predominantly women, found that—there must have been something in the water—seven of the forty-eight women were pregnant at the same time. It was a highly sophisticated company, technologically, and the manager went in to her boss, who was a man whose wife had stopped working to raise their children, and said, "Okay, here's the deal. It's going to be very empty around here. What I would like to do is create some alternative work arrangements to make sure that all the work is covered. The kind of work we do and the kind of work some of these people do can be done from home with computers. Let's plan this now—we have nine months to figure it out—so that we can keep these people who have a long history with the company." And the boss said, "Absolutely not. Our company has never allowed that." The manager then went to the business manager, who was a woman who had had a child of her own and had negotiated these hurdles herself. She said, "Come on, help me. This is crazy. These are great, talented people. And some of them would rather forgo the meager salaries they're getting not to have to pay the day care. You're going to force people out of the company." And this colleague said, "We can't rock the boat. We haven't had a good enough year." Of those seven women, you know how many are left in that unit? One. What did the company lose? Talented, experienced people. We all know how much time and productivity are lost by retraining people and getting them up to speed.

Blair: The end of the story is what happened to the company.

McKenna: The company's been downsized so much at this point that it is now a tiny unit, and its revenue is substantially reduced from what it was at the time.

Blair: I'm sure that lesson is appreciated by people looking at the company.

McKenna: Not by the women who had to leave.

Jones: How many women are being cut out this way because they've taken time off to care for their children?

Blair: There are women who choose not to have children and who go at it just as hard as any man. There are other women who have children and still, you know, get the nanny and do the whole full-time-worker-who's-also-a-mother thing. And there are many, many women who have a child and then say, "I want to be with this child." These are personal decisions.

Hochschild: You're focusing on choice, but let's examine what an American woman's *options* are. In Norway, with its thirty-seven-hour workweek and generous parental-leave policies, a woman's choice to be with her child would allow her to continue more easily in the corporate world.

Blair: Is she going to get to be CEO, say, even after she hasn't spent the same amount of consecutive time and gathered the same experiences as people who put in more hours and acquired more expertise? Do they just draw lots out of a box for their CEOs in Norway?

Hochschild: No. But in Norway what counts as "full time" or "long hours" is very different. The playing field—I know you don't like that term, Anita—is more advantageous to those who also spend time caring for people. The point isn't choices; it's what a culture holds out as options.

Lewis: Choice is less of a burden in Norway.

Blair: Look, I would be more concerned if American women didn't have choices, if somebody were saying to me here that people are stuck in terrible jobs because the economy is so stagnant that no new jobs are being created and there are no other opportunities. If people couldn't get capital to start business, that would concern me, but merely to hear the story of somebody who worked for a bunch of jerks, my answer is, "Find another job or make peace with what you have." Those are the only alternatives that make sense. What else should we do? Regulate jerks out of existence?

Ehrenreich: There's a thought. But seriously, there's something else going on. I read management books now and then to get a glimpse of corporate culture, and I remember a book in which a woman at business school was assigned the problem of figuring out whether people are irritated by how slowly ketchup comes out of bottles and if a faster-flowing ketchup should be developed or if we really like the struggle with ketchup. She finally determined that we really like our ketchup slow. My thought was, "For *this* we left the kitchen?" What else could this obviously very bright, creative person have been doing with her time? If I had been in her position I would have said, "I'm going home to be with my kids. I may have no master of business degree, but at least we'll squeeze the ketchup bottles together. . . ."

Blair: The squeeze bottle *was* a great step forward.

McKenna: When I surveyed women, meaning was up there on the list of what was most important in their lives; time for themselves, time for their family, and meaning. They look at this glass ceiling and say, "I'm gettin' old here. And what do I want to do with the rest of my life?"

Blair: It's a luxury to be able to have that complaint. I'm thinking back to my father and men of his generation. My father, who worked at IBM, could look up the ladder and see that there weren't very many men like him up there. Yet he had a wife and four kids, so he plugged along and did his duty.

McKenna: I hate to see progress tossed off as luxury.

Blair: I'm pointing out that limited success is not unique to women. I'm sure there are a lot of men who can realistically say, "There's not a great future for me in this joint—I don't play golf with the big boys—but either I'm going to quit or I'm going to make a rational decision to stick with this and do what I have to do."

McKenna: It's no secret that men have less of a culturally acceptable alternative in this world.

Ehrenreich: But I'm not interested in seeing women spend their time on the ketchup problem. It's not an immoral thing to do, but we should be able to bring some personal sense of meaning into any situation, including a corporate situation. Women historically don't compartmentalize as well as men to use a stereotype. So *good*. Let's act on that. Don't check your desire for meaningful work in the cloakroom when you go to the office.

Jones: Does women's inability to compartmentalize have something to do with why they're bailing out of the corporate world? Are women saying, "I have gotten close enough to the top to see the big piece of cheese, to see what it means to be CEO, say, and I do not want that"?

McKenna: Women are bailing because they're looking up and saying, "Hey, there's nobody who looks like me up there. Am I going to knock myself out for the next twenty years only to be passed over for a man?" My last job was with the Hearst Corporation, which, as we know, makes its money off the backs, literally, of women, off what women are wearing, and I looked upstairs and didn't see any women up there. Women are bailing not just because of the massive organizational skills you need to be a woman and a worker at the same time if you have a family but because they look up and realize, "You know what? I could knock myself out for the rest of my life and end up three offices closer to the corner. Let me out. I want to do something in my life that matters."

BABES AT THE OFFICE

Jones: Fortune magazine has been trying to highlight women in business on its cover for the past year or so, and more than one of those articles has hinged on the "babe-ness" of women. A recent cover story, about Darla Moore, CEO of Rainwater, Inc., was titled "The Toughest Babe in Business."

Ehrenreich: She didn't really look like a babe to me. [Laughter]

Jones: And *Fortune* had a previous cover story about seven women who got to the top doing it

their own way—which, in each case, had something to do with using sexual power, being very feminine. This is also related to one of the few gender-discrimination-in-the-workplace cases that has been litigated and won, a case in which a woman at Price Waterhouse was not made a partner because, she was told, she didn't wear lipstick. When the case got to court, the judge said, "This is a gender-discrimination case. They have to make you a partner." And the woman became a partner and got more than $370,000 in back pay.

Blair: There was more to it than just lipstick. There were complaints that she was nonfeminine.

Jones: Exactly.

Blair: She had a loud voice or something like that—

Jones: It's possible that the wage gap starts to widen when women are in their late thirties and older because women are bailing. But is age also a factor? Is it possible that women have to be feminine young things for men at work, and is this a factor in women's job potential?

McKenna: What a wild question.

Blair: In my experience as a corporate lawyer, being a babe in the classic sense does get you in the door. But longevity is based purely on performance. At a certain point it might even be detrimental to be a babe, because you give the appearance of not performing, of spending more time on your hair than worrying about the company.

Hochschild: In the company I studied, sex appeal backfired. The norms are that you dress in a very conservative way and don't accent your sexuality. There are feelings against being overly sexual as well as against being undersexual. You should sort of be moderately sexual. [Laughter] If there is discrimination, it might be against a careening sexuality, which would distract men from their work.

McKenna: Studies show that it's an advantage to be tall and handsome for men, too. But good pecs are a lot less intimidating than great tits.

Ehrenreich: I've heard men use the expression "D cups" to mean "dumb women." The implication is that, to fit in, you can't have ex-aggerated secondary sex characteristics. You can't be "too female."

McKenna: This is all about making women disappear and not be women. Men sometimes don't want to be reminded that they're dealing with women, because women come with a bunch of sloppy concerns that have to be ad-dressed. We have ovaries and uteruses that eventually produce something that interrupts the work flow. Or, God forbid, we're ugly; America hates ugly. As women, our power base has traditionally been our beauty. That's how we found men to support us so that we could have the children. That's the traditional model, let's face it. It's all part of a very real gender in-doctrination that still exists in the minds even of people who don't want it to be there.

Blair: Can it be eradicated? We do, after all, come in two sexes and reproduce by virtue of attraction between men and women. I don't think that if you wanted to you could simply eliminate that aspect of humanhood.

GETTING TO THE TOP

Jones: Jeanne, why are all the top officers at Staples men?

Lewis: When you say top officers, you mean the group of seven? How do you define top? Yes, the CEO and the president are men, but there are an increasing number of women who are executive vice presidents and senior vice presidents. The women are part of the pool of talent from which promotions are made.

Jones: At Staples, there's one executive vice president, out of five, who is a woman; she's in human resources. Staples actually has pretty progressive numbers compared with other companies. I mean, here's enlightened Staples and still . . . What are the numbers on the sen-ior vice presidents?

Lewis: Five of seventeen are women.

Jones: People on the inside tend to talk about office politics on a case-by-case basis. They say, "It depends not on whether it's a woman or a man but on who the woman or the man is." But if you're really making decisions on a case-by-case basis and not basing them on dis-criminatory prejudices, why are men in more positions of power and making more money than women?

Lewis: Women exit the workforce—to have a family or whatever—prior to reaching the upper levels. If you need to accumulate some experience in business as a prerequisite for running a Fortune 500 company, and I think we'd all agree that you do, then to the extent that women exit before they accumulate that experience, it should not be a surprise that the numbers are lopsided.

Jones: But if women started entering the U.S. workforce in large numbers in the 1970s, shouldn't they have enough years of experience by now?

Blair: In the early 1970s, the percentage of women getting MBAs was under 5 percent, so it's a minuscule number of women who are coming along at this point who are hitting their stride, ready with the MBA and the years of ex-perience.

Lewis: And this assumes that those who en-tered the workforce *stayed,* which the statistics say is not the case.

Blair: People outside corporate America underestimate the degree to which it is a real meritocracy.

Jones: Is it a meritocracy? The Glass Ceiling Commission, which was started under the Bush Administration and oversaw a number of inde-pendent studies on women in business, found that the reason women are not at the top has less to do with seniority than with mentoring: it's a bias problem. All of the studies showed that business is not a meritocracy.

Blair: Then what is it?

Jones: It's a schmoozocracy: you advance because of who you get along with at the office. So if there's a difference in culture between men and women, gender enters this equation.

Ehrenreich: That corporate America is not a meritocracy, that there has been some sort of systematic bias against women in addition to whatever choices women make, is old, old news.

Jones: The majority of women managers are in departments where the people they manage are predominantly women. Those fields are health care, personnel, labor relations, public relations. If there's an executive vice president who's a woman she's in human resources, and she will not become president of the company. Are women so different from men, biologically or sociologically, that they're self-selecting out of engineering, self-selecting out of operations—present company excepted, Jeanne—self-selecting out of the positions that would put them in line for the top?

Blair: Well, to be in engineering, for example, you need to have an engineering degree, and you start moving toward an engineering degree probably in junior high or high school. So that's a track that requires a decision way back in your career. A better question would be, Are companies irrationally overlooking human resources and P.R. and marketing and so forth when they seek a CEO?

Hochschild: That's a good question.

Blair: That depends on the nature of the company's business. For example, when you describe Staples, it seems to me that Staples is not going to go off into a division other than merchandising, saying, "Let's get our CEO from over here." Whatever kind of people populate the heart of the business, whether they are men or women, they're going to have a better chance at becoming the company's president. There *is* some self-selection that goes on in women's choice of work, because a lot of women appear to prefer—when they have children or plan to have children—to have jobs that allow them to exit and enter the workforce.

Lewis: When I was at Harvard Business School, I was shocked to find women who were probably twenty-seven years old, women who had accumulated about five years of work experience, stating as one of their goals for going to Harvard Business School that they were planning to exit the workforce and felt it would be easier to exit and reenter if they had a Harvard MBA. Women were paying $70,000 over

two years so that they could *not* work for a while.

McKenna: That shows the extreme lengths to which people will go to try to strike a balance between their work and their home life.

MAKING CHANGE

Jones: Would it be good for society in general if women stayed in the corporation and tried to bust through to the top?

McKenna: It's easier to make social change at the top, because people have to do what you say, but you can make social change from varying levels. As the companies I worked for merged with other companies, and I got farther and farther away from the top while sitting in the same place, it actually freed me to speak out a little more.

Ehrenreich: How much change that will affect other women has been made by women who've gotten near the top in corporations? In medicine, women coming in as doctors have made a bit of change; women doctors are supposedly more personable, more holistic, et cetera. But if a woman gets higher and higher in a corporation, is she going to be in a position to do things that will affect the women who are keeping the shelves stocked in the average Staples store? I haven't seen a lot of that. What I see is a woman getting dragged onto televison whenever a corporation dumps some hazardous chemicals: she's the P.R. person. Denny's, for Christ's sake, put a black woman on TV to explain why Asian Americans get beaten up in their parking lot. That's tragic. Before I can get behind you getting to the top, I want to know what it's going to mean for the rest of us.

Lewis: You've just made two assumptions. The first is that when women rise to top positions they will then be able to make the changes that you're talking about, if they even subscribe to those changes. And second, you're assuming that change can be made only at the CEO level. That's obviously not the case. One of the toughest problems in a very large company is that the bigger you get, the faster you grow, the higher up you go within an organization, the more stuff happens down below that you feel you have no control over. There are women who are making changes who may not be CEOs or senior vice presidents.

Ehrenreich: Let me put this to you personally, Jeanne. Is change for women part of your agenda? As you rise, do you want to make changes that will improve the life of the seven-dollar-an-hour woman in a Staples outlet?

Lewis: Even though I'm in retail, I don't run or operate the stores.

Ehrenreich: All right, if not change for the store clerks then change for somebody else in the corporate hierarchy. Do you have a larger social goal for yourself as an executive?

Blair: That's a stereotype of women that I think has to be objected to. The women I know in so-called corporate America are an unbelievably diverse group.

Ehrenreich: I'm just asking this one.

Blair: Yes, but it assumes—

Ehrenreich: We'll get to YOU.

Blair:—that a woman has to have a social policy, and she *doesn't* have to.

Ehrenreich: Okay, she can tell me she doesn't give a damn, and that'll be my answer. She can say that she shouldn't be burdened with that concern.

Lewis: Let me just make sure I understand the question.

Ehrenreich: What are you, Jeanne, going to do for women? Suppose my sister is working in a Staples outlet? I just want to know.

Lewis: That's a bad example. Within the area I currently run, we have women and we have men, and what you're asking me is: Do I have an agenda to improve the work environment for just women? The answer is no. Do I have an agenda to improve the working environment of the men and women who work there and to attract the best talent? The answer is yes.

McKenna: Does that agenda include quality-of-life issues?

Lewis: Absolutely. I'll give you a specific example. Our executive vice president, who is a woman, who does run human resources but within a retail environment—and human resources in a company that is built on store labor is a very important position; we have thirty to forty employees per store, and we have 600 stores and are opening two of them a week—she's looking into providing on-site day care. For me, I look at the talented group of people in my area—I don't even know how many people; fifty, sixty, seventy—and if people are excited about what they're doing, if they're able to concentrate when they're at work, and if they feel fulfilled, not project by project but over the long haul, if they feel that they're being developed and invested in, then that's good for the company.

McKenna: These are human values, not just women's values, is what you're saying.

Lewis: Yes

Hochschild: To me the issue is double. On the one hand, how can we create equal opportunity so that women are at the helm and get the rewards and, we hope, are able to change things, to humanize the culture, to make more Staples-type cultures, which are better for the workers and their families. On the other hand, what about the downsized refugees? That second tier. This is speaking sociologically, not personally but from a God's-eye view.

Jones: Of sociologists. [Laughter]

Hochschild: Of *all* of us, as we sit here on the sixtieth floor. How can we redistribute *respect*? To me, that's the key. It's through windows like these, here on the sixtieth floor, that corporations see the world. From here you can't easily see the bottom, but it's important to see the bottom. I don't like the hard edge of the corporate culture women are trying to get equal in; it's a culture that doesn't have empathy for the people who are at the bottom. In addition to trying to get equal consideration in the corporation, women need to fight to change that culture. Why I am more worried about the capitalist system than you are, Anita, is that capitalism gets us hooked on respect for productivity and cuts out respect for care. We've got to be wired into a high-paying job in order to feel good about ourselves. Local civic organizations—the League of Women Voters, the Lions Clubs—are losing members because they don't command much respect anymore. We would do better to redistribute respect to the folks who are caring for others—men and women, on and off the job.

Blair: People are already protesting the high price of a high paycheck. They say, "I want more control over my life. And I will trade money for it." They're coming away from the notion that I am how much money I have.

Ehrenreich: I wouldn't want to go to the boss for a raise and have him say, "Hey, money shouldn't mean that much to you." I absolutely agree with you that money is not how we should measure ourselves or assign respect to others. But, boy, I would fight if I got that kind of line from the boss.

Blair: People *are* voting with their feet. They are leaving big corporations and starting their own businesses. Particularly women. It was a historical aberration in this century when women were just home keeping house. Before the industrial revolution, women and men worked together on the family farm or whatever the family's trade was. And it was only that little blip of history that somebody referred to earlier that put women at home. It was an unsuccessful experiment [laughter], and what I see now is a great trend toward self-empowerment. The exodus from big companies is very positive. Large corporations are a vestige of a past industrial age, and in my mind the sooner we can get rid of them the better—for women and families and everybody else—because people will be able to achieve what they want individually much more readily. They will be able to define it and to go after it rather than having to fit themselves into an excessively large organization that is no longer operating at a human scale.

Hochschild: Why wouldn't companies be perfectly happy to have all their women leave and then just fill the slots with men?

Lewis: Because of talent. Not all talent sits with your male candidates. I face it every day when I'm hiring: it's tough to get good talent, regardless of gender.

McKenna: The accounting firm Deloitte & Touche found that 90 percent of their women

were gone by partnership time—not a very nice statistic. Ninety percent of these women went to other jobs, where they could get more respect and where they might get more money or a better quality of life. Poor old Deloitte & Touche said, "Oh my goodness, we've spent millions of dollars training these women, and they're leaving with our connections!" So the company organized a big task force and spent a lot of time and money analyzing why these women were leaving and what could have made them stay, and the company *changed.*

Blair: Decisions about whether or not we're gong to use teams or innovate in some way should relate to the mission of creating value for the shareholders; otherwise, the company's going to fail. America is a capitalist country ultimately. Short term, many times, there is a dislocation as people seek new ways. You find that you can't sell buggy whips anymore, so no matter how good a buggy-whip maker you are, no matter how nice you are to the mothers who make buggy whips, you just can't sell enough anymore. There's going to be dislocation. But the idea of competition, which is inherent in capitalism, impels us all toward something better. Under a competitive system, you have to be better than the next company. We try things; sometimes we make mistakes. If we don't try things, that's a mistake. But that is the only way I can see to have rational progress in the world. I don't think that you can define in advance what's going to work and expect it to work through the millennia.

McKenna: You *can* look at the needs and values of your present working constituency and make the work fit into their lives so the company can continue to grow and be profitable and the employees can have working environments where they aren't tearing themselves apart. Unfortunately, we've gotten very complacent, because we're afraid. We're afraid of losing our jobs, so we've shut up. We've stopped talking about values. It's only the numbers of upper-management women who are voting with their feet that is forcing the values discussion back on the agenda. Most people can't vote with their feet, because they have to pay the bills and have health insurance. We need to continue an unfinished revolution and broaden it so that it's a human revolution and not just a feminist revolution. I'm not saying, "Don't have capitalism, don't be profitable." I'm saying, "If your car is broken, don't go back and get a horse and buggy. Go get the car fixed." We're not talking about going back to a time when women didn't work; we're talking about fixing the work environment to reflect basic human realities.

Ehrenreich: Women have not yet lived up to their responsibility as outsiders in corporations. I think they've been beaten back, beaten down, and when they're beaten out, the explanation is always framed in reproductive, physical sorts of terms. But it is right and human to want to raise your children and live with your family, and the corporation should adjust. We're not making that case clearly enough. And in an era of downsizing, people tend, in general, to drop their criticisms of the world of employment, saying, "I'll take whatever I can get." Women in corporate America, so far, have been silenced, especially those women at the relative top. But they should allow themselves to ask the challenging, subversive questions—not just how do we work but what are we working for? What are we making? What are we producing?

McKenna: But I think you see a change as women get older. The silence—the years of silence, which are an absolute requirement for advancement for 90 percent of the corporate culture—catch up to you. You've seen the toll it takes, and you start to get a little more courageous. Older women are more willing to say, "I have to stop trying to cram my foot into a slipper that doesn't fit me and waltz around saying, 'Isn't this great?' I have to say, 'Can I get some new shoes, please? I still want to dance the dance, but I want some new shoes.'"

Jones: Why should corporate America let you wear those new shoes?

McKenna: Because I have twenty years of great experience. Because I have a proven track record of producing bestsellers. And it's not just me. Every woman I know who faces this, you know, doesn't face it in the third year of work. She doesn't have enough experience accumulated. She faces it closer to her fifteenth year of work, when she's got a lot of experience, a lot of perspective, and probably some influence too.

Jones: Then why isn't the structure changing? Or is it?

McKenna: The structure *is* changing, but not a lot and not quickly. We got very spoiled by the women's revolution, which happened over thirty years. This corporate revolution is a much slower one, because numbers matter: there needs to be critical mass first, a pipeline full of people with whom these issues resonate, before you can have meaningful social change. Also, this is a movement without leaders. We have to stop being such good girls. And we better start doing things within communities again, *not* as individuals. Because you cannot change the values of a community or a business or an office or a corporation or a society by yourself. All you can do is go home and feel that you've failed, alone, and blame yourself.

Jones: Public-opinion research has shown that although women are eager to work together on issues of shared concern, they are strongly resistant to describing themselves as feminist or to joining a "women's movement."

Blair: In the public mind, a *woman* is someone who acknowledges that men are part of the human race, and a *feminist* is somebody who puts women and women's interests ahead of men, and frequently ahead of children.

Ehrenreich: But the corporate world is a perfect case where that view of feminism could be refuted in practice. Women, as the relative outsiders, can say, "No one should have to live like this." We cannot have corporate America destroying American families, and that transcends gender. In fact, if we are militant enough about the need for livable family-friendly jobs, the guys will thank us.

Suggestions for Further Reading

Carabillo, Toni, Judith Meuli, and June Bundy Csida. *Feminist Chronicles: 1953–1993*. Los Angeles: Women's Graphics, 1993.

Chodorow, Nancy. *The Reproduction of Mothering: Psychoanalysis and the Sociology of Gender*. Berkeley: Univ. of California Press, 1978.

Davis, Flora. *Moving the Mountain: The Women's Movement in America Since 1960*. New York: Simon and Schuster, 1991.

Denfeld, Rene. *The New Victorians: A Young Woman's Challenge to the Old Feminist Order*. New York: Warner, 1995.

DuBois, Ellen Carol, and Vicki L. Ruiz, eds. *Unequal Sisters: A Multicultural Reader in U.S. Women's History*. New York: Routledge, 1990.

Faludi, Susan. *Backlash: The Undeclared War against American Women*. New York: Anchor Books, 1991.

Ferree, Myra Marx, and Beth B. Hess. *Controversy and Coalition: The New Feminist Movement across Three Decades of Change*. New York: Twayne, 1994.

Findlen, Barbara, ed. *Listen Up: Voices from the Next Feminist Generation*. Seattle: Seal, 1995.

Friedman, Susan Stanford. "'Beyond' Gynocriticism and Gynesis: The Geographics of Identity and the Future of Feminist Criticism." *Tulsa Studies in Women's Literature* 15 (1996): 13–40.

Gatlin, Rochelle. *American Women Since 1945*. Jackson: Univ. Press of Mississippi, 1987.

Garcia, Alma M. "The Development of Chicana Feminist Discourse, 1970–1980." In DuBois and Ruiz, *Unequal Sisters*, 418–31.

Gilligan, Carol. *In a Different Voice: Psychological Theory and Women's Development*. Cambridge, Mass.: Harvard Univ. Press, 1982.

Heywood, Leslie, and Jennifer Drake, eds. *Third Wave Agenda: Being Feminist, Doing Feminism*. Minneapolis: Univ. of Minnesota Press, 1997.

hooks, bell. *Ain't I a Woman: Black Women and Feminism*. Boston: South End Press, 1981.

———. *Feminist Theory from Margin to Center*. Boston: South End Press, 1984.

———. *Outlaw Culture: Resisting Representations*. New York: Routledge, 1994.

———. *Talking Back: Thinking Feminist, Thinking Black*. Boston: South End Press, 1989.

———. *Yearning: Race, Gender and Cultural Politics*. Boston: South End Press, 1990.

Kaminer, Wendy. "Feminism's Third Wave: What Do Young Women Want?" *The New York Times Book Review*. June 4, 1995, 3, 22–23.

Kaminsky, Amy. "Gender, Race, Raza." *Feminist Studies* 20 (1994): 7–31.

Lehrman, Karen. *The Lipstick Proviso: Women, Sex and Power in the Real World*. New York: Doubleday, 1997.

Maglin, Nan Bauer, and Donna Perry, eds. *"Bad Girls"/"Good Girls": Women, Sex and Power in the Nineties*. New Brunswick: Rutgers Univ. Press, 1996.

Paglia, Camille. *Sex, Art, and American Culture: Essays*. New York: Vintage, 1991.

Roiphe, Katie. *The Morning After: Sex, Fear, and Feminism on Campus*. New York: Little, Brown, 1993.

Ruddick, Sarah. *Maternal Thinking: Toward a Politics of Peace*. New York: Ballantine, 1989.

Ryan, Barbara. *Feminism and the Women's Movement: Dynamics of Change in Social Movement, Ideology and Activism*. New York: Routledge, 1992.

Sommers, Christina Hoff. *Who Stole Feminism? How Women Have Betrayed Women*. New York: Simon and Schuster, 1994.

Tannen, Deborah. *Talking from 9 to 5: Women and Men in the Workplace*. New York: Avon, 1994.

———. *You Just Don't Understand: Women and Men in Conversation*. New York: Morrow, 1990.

Taylor, Charles. "The Politics of Recognition." In Amy Gutman, ed., *Multiculturalism: Examining the Politics of Recognition*. Princeton: Princeton Univ. Press, 1994, 25–73.

Tobias, Sheila. *Faces of Feminism: An Activist's Reflections on the Women's Movement*. Boulder, Colo.: Westview Press, 1997.

Walker, Rebecca, ed. *To Be Real: Telling the Truth and Changing the Face of Feminism*. New York: Doubleday, 1995.

Wolf, Naomi. *The Beauty Myth: How Images of Beauty Are Used Against Women*. New York: Morrow, 1991.

———. *Fire with Fire: The New Female Power and How It Will Change the 21st Century*. New York: Random House, 1993.

———. *Promiscuities: The Secret Struggle for Womanhood*. New York: Ballantine, 1997.

Index

About the Editors

Dawn Keetley is assistant professor of English at Lehigh University and teaches nineteenth-century and twentieth-century U.S. literature, women's studies, and American studies. She is currently working on a book-length project entitled *The Othello Complex: The Invention of Men's Homicidal Jealousy in Nineteenth-Century America* and has published articles on antebellum literature and culture in numerous journals, including *American Quarterly, Emerson Society Quarterly,* and *Legacy: A Journal of Women Writers*.

John Pettegrew teaches modern U.S. history and directs the American studies program at Lehigh University. He is currently completing a book entitled *Brutes in Suits: The De-Evolutionary Origins of American Masculinity*. He also edited and wrote the introduction and a chapter for *A Pragmatist's Progress? Richard Rorty and American Intellectual History*.